THE GREAT E C T HOAX
L O H
E N E
C V R
T U A
R L P
O S Y
I
V
E

(Manufacturer Fraud and Deception)

VOLUME II of II

Douglas G Cameron

The Great Electro Convulsive Therapy Hoax Volume II

(Manufacturer Fraud and Deception)

Douglas G Cameron

Cover art
By Donna Zoe Grabow

ISBN: 979-8-9881280-1-4

Brave New World Publishing LLC
17350 State Hwy 249
Ste 220 # 15783
Houston TX 77064

DEDICATION

To all my fellow human beings who have suffered at the cruel hands of the mental health system
and
To my three children Doug, Scott, and Chris
who grew up watching me write this book for over thirty years of their lives.

Table of Contents

Abstract v

Introduction vii

Part VII

SECTION VIII: Third, Fourth, and Fifth Generation--Fraud and Deception 1

CHAPTER 49: Initiates Call For "First" Major Power Increase in BP Devices 1

CHAPTER 50: Manufacturers Oppose Official Adoption of the 1989 IEC Standard Cont'd 5

CHAPTER 51: Manufacturers Oppose Adoption of the 1989 IEC Standard—Cont'd. 11

CHAPTER 52: Summary--Manufacturers Oppose Adoption of 1989 IEC Standard--Back to 100J 13

CHAPTER 53: The Best Defense is a Strong Offense: Somatics opts for More Power with 3rd Gen. BP Devices 17

SECTION IX: Conspiracy 23

CHAPTER 54: Somatics' Richard Abrams Calls for a "First Time" Power Enhancement 23

CHAPTER 55: MECTA - Co-conspirator: Sackeim's Call for Increased Power 33

CHAPTER 56: 1997 IEC Proposal "Allowing" Third, Fourth, and Fifth Generation BP Devices 45

SECTION X: Weiner's De Facto Standard: 3rd, 4th, and 5th Gen. BP Devices 55

CHAPTER 57: Third Generation Brief Pulse Devices 55

CHAPTER 58: Weiner's 1997 "Standard" in Greater Detail: What Happened to ER/RRC? 67

CHAPTER 59: Fourth Generation Brief Pulse Devices 75

CHAPTER 60: Fifth Generation BP Devices 87

CHAPTER 61: Conclusion for Extant 3rd, Probable 4th, and Hypothetical 5th Generation BP Devices 91

CHAPTER 62: Power and Invisibility: 1000% Increase in Power 93

SECTION XI: Conformity to Weiner's 1997 de facto Standard 107

CHAPTER 63: MECTA Second to Third Generation BP Devices: UL vs. BL Outputs 107

CHAPTER 64: Somatics Third Generation BP Devices: UL vs. BL Outputs 111

CHAPTER 65: Confirmation of Charge Thresholds for 2nd Gen. BP Devices via Conversion to Joules 113

CHAPTER 66: Minimum Charge Thresholds for Third Generation MECTA BP Devices 115

CHAPTER 67: Confirmation of Charge Thresholds for Fourth Generation BP Devices 119

CHAPTER 68: Confirmation of Charge Thresholds for Fifth Generation BP Devices 125

SECTION XII: Summaries and Charts Pertaining to Weiner's 1997 de facto "Standard" 127

CHAPTER 69: Summary and Charts 3rd, 4th, and 5th Gen. BP Devices under 1997 de Facto Standard 127

CHAPTER 70: Summation 3rd, 4th, and 5th Gen. BP Devices under Weiner's De Facto Standard Cont'd 131

SECTION XIII: Weiner's "Dose Sensitive," "Threshold Doubling" Contentions 133

CHAPTER 71: Questioning Weiner's 1997 Contentions 133

SECTION XIV: Winding Up Weiner 145

CHAPTER 72: More Proof Machines Already Met 1997 Call for More Power for 2 and 4 x Threshold 145
CHAPTER 73: All Ages 149
CHAPTER 74: The How and the Why of Weiner's 1997 Proviso 151
CHAPTER 75: The Easy Way: Back to Joules 153
CHAPTER 76: Tables Delineating Charge vs. EO in Joules 161
CHAPTER 77: Manufacturer Secret Revealed--Doubling MTTLOI Per Each New BP Generation 167
CHAPTER 78: The Dropping of ER/RRC 171
SECTION XV: To Compare SW with Early and Later BP Devices 173
CHAPTER 79: J/Ω Ratios 173
Part VIII
SECTION XVI: Comparing Sine Wave to Brief Pulse 189
CHAPTER 80: The Medcraft B-24 SW vs MECTA "C" vs Later BP Devices 189
CHAPTER 81: The Cameron Paradigm 193
CHAPTER 82: Facts about Medcraft's B-24 SW Compared to BP and the Basis of "the Cameron Paradigm" 199
CHAPTER 83: Maximum and "Minimum" SW Settings for All Age Categories 203
CHAPTER 84: Summation of Max/Min SW Settings in Terms of Dangerousness vs Current BP Devices 229
CHAPTER 85: SW Charts of True Min., Probable Min. and Max. Outputs for All Age Categories 251
CHAPTER 86: Weiner's 1982 APA Criteria Charts for Writing the 1982 APA Standard 283
CHAPTER 87: Early BP 287
CHAPTER 88: Inversion Exploitation of Brief Pulse 293
CHAPTER 89: Conclusion 301
Appendix A: Limitation of SW amperage to 1.0A 307
Appendix B: More Details of B-24 in Chart Form Limited and Not Limited to 1.0A Compared to BP 315
Appendix C: Summarizing the Cameron Paradigm 319
Appendix D: J/Ω Limited to 1.0A 321
Appendix E: "ECT" Compared to Tasers and Defibrillators 325
Works Cited 327

Those who suppress history doom humankind to repeat it.

Abstract

In spite of an article the author published in Journal of Mind and Behavior (Cameron 1994), delineating the preponderant power of modern day Brief Pulse (BP) devices compared to Sine Wave (SW) in most age categories, there yet lingers the misconception that modern day BP-"ECT" devices are lower in Energy Output (EO) or power than SW devices. This manuscript explains why this misperception persists, how and why BP advocates have covered up the preponderant power of BP devices misleading the American Public and the FDA for more than forty years, why the "ECT" of today is not the ECT grandfathered in, in 1976, but something else entirely, and how and why the entire concept of convulsion as therapy is based upon sixty years of fraud. This manuscript explains in detail how the so-called new and improved BP machines, in lieu of diminishing in power, first doubled and then quadrupled in power without public awareness, how manufacturers have disparately and fraudulently interpreted never before examined national and international standards, and how modern machines' have invisibly quintupled electrical titration per individual age category with the latest Brief Pulse generation. In sum, this manuscript examines fraudulent safety studies, misleading MRI studies, why "ECT" is no longer "ECT," but ENR (Electro Neurotransmission Reduction), the true goal of so-called "ECT," why it is no surprise that the most revealing MRI study ever performed reveals gross reduction in neuro-connections following "ECT," and finally what the correlation is between neurotransmission reduction and the increase in device power with each new Brief Pulse device generation.

Introduction

In spite of a 1994 article (Cameron 1994) published in the Canadian *Journal of Mind and Behavior* clearly showing the preponderant power of modern day Brief Pulse (BP) devices compared to the older Sine Wave (SW) devices, research and media articles, and even Surgeon General reports continue to assume that modern day BP is a lower Energy device and thus safer than the previous SW models. (Fink 1997; Fodero, 1993; Food and Drug Administration, 1986B, p.13; Food and Drug Administration, 1990, September 5, p.36581; Kellner, 1994, February 2; National Institute of Mental Health and Center for Mental Health Services, 1994; Sackeim, 1991, p.234; Satcher, August 16,1999; Stone, 1994; Weiner, 1979, 1980; Welch, 1982). This manuscript explains why this longstanding misperception persists, why it is totally incorrect, how manufacturers have deliberately cultivated this falsehood, and the consequences to the world at large. This book clearly exposes how and why for decades manufacturers have deceived the American Public, the FDA, the ERA (European Regulatory Agency), the IEC (International Electrotechnical Commission), and even practicing physicians via manufacturer cover-ups regarding the true power of their devices, devices delivering suprathreshold dosages under the false guise of minimal stimulus output. In short, this manuscript patently, and for the first time, depicts the historical evolution of the initial minimal stimulus, lower Energy Output (EO) Brief Pulse devices (as opposed to SW) devices—compared to the much more powerful Brief Pulse devices in use today, BP devices surreptitiously and conspiratorially manufactured not only to equal but to surpass the well-known damaging outputs of Sine Wave in almost every age category. These "modern-day" Brief Pulse devices are designed to deliver, deliberately and premeditatedly, excessive, damaging, suprathreshold dosages of electricity all in order to make the procedure "work." In brief, Volume I discloses for the first time how modern day BP devices more than double in power immediately following the close of the first FDA investigation of ECT in 1982 while Volume II discloses how a third generation of souped-up BP devices subsequently quadruples in power about 1995--all without public awareness. Indeed, manufacturers go to great lengths to convince the public of the exact opposite. In addition, Volume I and II explain how the quadrupling of power is concomitant with quadrupled threshold output per individual recipient--again sans public awareness and again while manufacturers simultaneously disseminate misleading information regarding the "minimal stimulus" power of modern day Brief Pulse devices. Revealed in Volume I is the history of how manufacturers on a world-wide basis have furtively misinterpreted standards in order to make damaging outputs "legal," and in Volume II how manufacturers have dispensed with regulations altogether. Too, Volume I reveals how almost all "safety studies" for "the newer 'ECT'" BP devices have been performed at minimal stimulus output far below the clinically applied pre-set doses utilized by all modern day manufacturers and why none of these studies have detected the patently identifiable damage which occurs following "ECT. " Indeed, the actual manufacturer goal of so-called "ECT" substantiated by the actual power of these devices is set forth here for the first time ever. In sum, all manufacturer secrets regarding the composition, and so the true power and purpose of these devices is revealed in Volume I and II for first time in the long history of this sordidly deceptive process, most specifically, the increasing power of each new device generation with the express goal of destroying a greater and greater percentage of neuronal connections.

But let me be even clearer regarding the books' thesis of fraud. Once Congress granted the FDA power to condone or condemn medical devices in 1976, "ECT" became scrutinized for the first time since the machine's invention in 1938. As a result, manufacturers introduced the Brief Pulse device as a safer alternative to Sine Wave utilized from 1938 to 1976 (and beyond as we shall observe). In short, Brief Pulse was introduced as an improvement over SW by virtue of its capacity to administer "convulsive therapy" with half the electrical energy of SW while still inducing the same so-called "adequate" seizures. In this way, cognitive dissonance, namely, long term memory complaints would be addressed, the chief objection to the SW device. Once the investigation was over, however, and as we shall witness, manufacturers furtively began increasing the power of Brief Pulse, first equaling and then surpassing SW in power. Manufacturers cover up the true power of these devices, but also attempt to justify "moderate" increases first by claiming UL (Unilateral) "ECT" "dose-sensitive," requiring twice the electricity needed to induce an adequate seizure to be effective. Manufacturers then claim both BL (Bilateral) and UL "ECT" require twice the electricity needed to induce an adequate seizure to be effective in that both BL and UL "ECT" double in resistance (Impedance) over a course of "treatments." In this way, UL ECT requires four times threshold while BL ECT requires twice threshold to remain effective at the end of a "treatment course." So powerful did Brief Pulse devices become, however, that manufacturers have been forced to hide the actual power increases which soared well over the so-called "justification increases" as we shall see. However, in that it has always been excessive electricity, electricity well over that required to induce an adequate seizure that has been associated with cognitive dissonance reflective of brain damage, manufacturers have been forced to cover up the true power of these devices. The truth is, these devices do not work with adequate seizure at all. Instead, they work as they have always worked, past and present, as a result of adequate amounts of electricity. In brief, manufacturers have been forced to cover up the power of their devices in that excessive electricity damages the brain resulting in long term memory dysfunction. In sum, these machines must damage the brain in order to "work," a fact of which manufacturers are only too well aware.

Volume I and II of *The Great Electroconvulsive Therapy Hoax* exposes for the first time ever, in detail, the true power emissions of these machines. Finally, I wish to apologize for the necessity of mathematical proofs throughout the texts. However, long experience has taught me that without these irrefutable proofs, advocates of these devices will simply label these findings --"anecdotal." Feel free, if you are not mathematically inclined, therefore, to skim over these proofs and go directly to the facts found in the narration and the various charts and graphs revealing detailed power. For those who need these proofs such as regulatory experts, attorneys, and physicians, on the other hand, that is, who must verify my results, I welcome your perusal.

PART VI

SECTION VIII: Third, Fourth, and Fifth Generation--Fraud and Deception

CHAPTER 49

Initiates Call For "First" Major Power Increase in BP Devices

Between 1982 and 1989, manufacturers deliberately created the impression of circa 100J standards and circa 100J Brief Pulse devices for what were actually much more powerful second generation Brief Pulse devices. Nevertheless, these already powerful second generation BP devices were enhanced even further with third generation BP devices in the latter part of the last decade of the twentieth century (1995) beginning with the false contentions and plaintiff cries of manufacturer-affiliated "experts" demanding what they deceptively claimed to be a "first time" increase in machine power. The justification behind the cries to increase the power of what regulators and media supposed to be first generation BP devices (but which were actually second generation BP devices) was the same old assertion that UL "ECT" is "dose-sensitive" and so needs twice threshold to succeed in that minimal stimulus output (to induce the adequate seizure with UL "ECT") is simply not as effective as previously thought, and finally that seizure threshold sometimes doubles over a treatment series with both UL and BL "ECT." Most damningly to the manufacturer-affiliated "experts" calling for this increase in machine power, however, is that the called for increase in power about 1986 is falsely represented as a ***first*** major enhancement of Brief Pulse apparatuses since the re-introduction of Brief Pulse by MECTA circa 1978 (Sackeim, 1991, p. 233-234).[1] Indeed, manufacturer generated demands for a first time increase in power about 1986, are blatantly belied by the facts that not only had very early manufacturers of both Brief Pulse and Sine Wave devices known of the ***inefficacy*** of adequate seizure since the late 1940s (Cameron, 1994), but that the first great power increase of the modern Brief Pulse era (beginning in 1976), had already taken place circa 1982 via the spuriously invisible "Mectan Transmutation." In short, what continued after 1982 to be touted as first generation American BP devices were actually second generation American BP devices, which by 1985, were already administering (in the case of MECTA and Somatics) two and one half times minimal stimulus with BL "ECT" (Beale et al., 1994), about two and half times the power of the first generation MECTA "C" in every age category. Indeed, as we shall see in this section, the appearance of what are actually third generation Brief Pulse, devices allegedly created to satisfy a "first time" major power increase, in fact

---

[1] Regulatory agencies, academics not associated with manufacturers, psychiatrists in general, the lay public, and perhaps, especially the media, appear to lack any awareness of the fact that beginning in 1982, American BP machines dramatically increased in power (from circa 100J devices). In fact, all these entities appear to assume that BP remains a reduced EO device compared to SW. As late as 1999, the Surgeon General of the United States publicly announced that newer machines incorporated reduced electricity compared to SW (Satcher, August 16, 1999) in accordance with NIMH (National Institute of Mental Health) which has published several brochures also describing BP as reduced in electricity. With respect to rampant media blurbs of improved electroshock devices by virtue of reduced electricity, none, not the FDA, the NIMH, manufacturers, academics generally, and even the Surgeon General have ever made any attempt to correct this false assumption. The most generous assumption regarding this silence is that these entities simply do not know. In any case, such false information is a serious breach of public trust in that based upon the notion of a "kinder, gentler" in short, much more "innocuous" treatment," tens of thousands of individuals continually make the decision to receive electroshock or permit the procedure to be administered to loved ones. Based on this same erroneous information, psychiatrists continue to administer it.

represent not the first, but the second major power enhancement of modern day BP devices, doubling the power and so the MTTLOI not for the first, but for the *second* time since 1978. In short, this supposed "first call" for a major power increase beginning around 1986, is not a doubling, but a quadrupling of Brief Pulse power and so a quadrupling of Multifold Threshold Titration Level Output Intensity (MTTLOI) in every age category, as we shall now observe. We shall now witness through the "legalization" and production of what are actually third generation Brief Pulse apparatuses, the invisible evolution of the most powerful devices in "ECT" history.

Manufacturers Oppose Adoption of 1989 IEC (International Electrotechnical Commission) Standard

By 1989, the international or IEC standard officially depicted Brief Pulse devices as limited to "100J at 300Ω." Thus, on the surface, the 1989 IEC Standard appeared, more or less, to conform to the 1982 APA Standard which depicted a "70J at 220Ω" conditional-ER/RRC with a 110J maximum ceiling (70J/220Ω = 95J/300Ω). The 100J figure within the IEC Standard, like the 1982 APA Standard, once again seemed to be based on Weiner's original 1982 assertion to the FDA, that no more than 100J is required to induce a grand mal seizure in even the most seizure recalcitrant recipient.[2]

> Using a pulse device, the [1978 APA] Task Force has determined that only 0.6% of seizure thresholds were greater than 70 [actual] Joules and that none were greater than 100 [actual] Joules. (Weiner, Department of Health and Human Services, 1982a, p. A53)

Consequently, as exemplified by the MECTA "C," the 1989 IEC Standard seemed to assure minimal stimulus output just as the 1982 APA Standard had. Perhaps, based on very recondite reporting and because American manufacturers seemed to be voluntarily complying with the 1982 APA Standard and thus what appeared to be a similar 1989 IEC (International Electrotechnical Commission, 601-2-14) Standard for ECT devices, the FDA had never officially mandated adoption of either. In short, every American BP manufacturer (falsely) implied compliance with both.[3] [4] In brief, FDA may have never overtly enforced either standard due to the appearance of American (and European) voluntary compliance to about 100 maximum joules. Thus, manufacturers only

---

[2] The 1989 IEC standard also seemed to conform to the APA Standard's "70J at 220Ω" conditional-ER/RRC in that the 1989 IEC Standard featured a "100J at 300Ω" phrase erroneously interpretable as a circa "70J at 220Ω" conditional-ER/RRC with 100J ceiling (100J/300Ω = 73J/220Ω), in essence, the 1982 APA standard.

[3] After NIMH spent millions of taxpayer dollars on what could be called safety and efficacy studies as we have seen, and FDA many more thousands over a period of twenty years investigating "ECT" (Grahn et al., 1977), based upon this information and information supplied by the manufacturers and the APA, FDA had determined and maintained for more than twenty years that a Standard could be written (Grahn et al., 1977)—in spite of which there is yet no mandatory American standard. Now, just as FDA had begun to act independently of APA--moving to adopt the then prevailing (1989) IEC Standard for "ECT" Devices (International Electrotechnical Commission, 1989), manufacturers via a Weiner led panel of "experts," as we shall see, suddenly called for a complete withdrawal of the IEC Standard for ECT (International Electrotechnical Commission, 1997, Dec 26). Apparently, neither manufacturers nor manufacturer affiliated "experts" desired the standard recommended by Utah so that their deceptiveness, refusal to regulate and report honestly, and be held to a mandatory safety standard for all new pre-market approval applications--would ultimately prove their undoing.

[4] While Medcraft, Elcot, Somatics, and MECTA through creative interpretation were technically in compliance with parts of the 1989 IEC Standard, they had not been in compliance with the 1982 APA standard since 1982; neither did they report actual EO at various impedances or absolute EO ceilings required by the 1989 IEC Standard (International Electrotechnical Commission, 1989, pp. 11, 23). In a sense, because the APA standard was never made mandatory and the 1989 IEC Standard on ECT never adopted as a mandatory national Standard, American BP Manufacturers were not technically in violation of any mandatory standard (there being none). Nevertheless, this does not relieve American (or European) manufacturers from illegal deception regarding the 1982 APA standard, covering up the actual and increasing power of their devices, or falsely and deceptively reporting to the FDA and consequently American public that BP devices are minimal stimulus devices, allegedly emitting far less energy than SW devices. The lack of a mandatory standard does not condone misreporting and mislabeling of BP devices as minimal stimulus "ECT" devices as all manufacturers have implied since 1940. Finally, the lack of a mandatory standard is no excuse for manufacturers claiming IEC compliance to the 1989 IEC Standard while failing to report actual EO ceilings required by that standard.

seemed (through mathematical manipulation as we have seen) to be self-regulating both nationally and internationally.

In fact, as already noted above, American manufacturers MECTA and Somatics were utilizing the covert Mectan Transmutation to emit about 250 unreported joules for their second generation made-for-America BP devices while surreptitiously interpreting the IEC standard to allow an unreported 216.6 maximum joules which they then breached to accommodate between 230 and 240 maximum joules, in short, circa 2.3 to 2.5 x 100 joules. Through the illusion of self-regulation, and by continually implying to the FDA that an official adoptable standard was just around the corner, American BP "ECT" device manufacturers via their national and international spokesperson Richard Weiner, had, by 1997, managed to forestall FDA adoption of any official ECT standard whatsoever for almost twenty years. When, in 1997, then, the FDA unexpectedly--though quite logically and long overdue--suddenly proposed universal adoption of international (IEC) Standards for all medical devices, which included the 1989, 601-2-14 section of the IEC (International Electrotechnical Commission) Standard for ECT devices, Brief Pulse ECT device manufacturers panicked. A Weiner-led IEC subcommittee composed of manufacturer affiliates from around the world deemed "Subcommittee 62D Working Group 2" or "WG2" at once petitioned the IEC to replace the 1989 IEC Standard for ECT devices with a new standard, a standard dramatically expanding device parameters and thus overall power (International Electrotechnical Commission, 1997, Dec 26, p. 4).[5] When the IEC immediately rejected the proposal, the same WG2 Weiner-led committee just as quickly followed with an alternative proposal. Desperate to alter or block the ECT portion of the IEC Standard before it could be codified into national and international law, the Weiner-led WG2 committee now submitted a unanimous WG2 petition to entirely withdraw the then current 1989 IEC Standard for ECT devices--with no replacement whatsoever. The proposal was allegedly based on the purported supposition that the 1989 IEC Standard for ECT devices had become "obsolete" (International Electrotechnical Commission, 1997, Dec 26, p. 2).[6] Wishing to chronicle its own refusal to adopt Weiner's 1997 replacement proposal as well as the WG2 follow-up motion to then withdraw the 1989 IEC standard for ECT altogether, the IEC responded with the following:

> As agreed by subcommittee 62D meeting in Denmark [composed of IEC electrical engineers generally], the [Weiner-led] project to revise 60601-2-14 [that is, replace the 1989 IEC standard specific to ECT devices with one of their own recommendation] . . . has been removed [withdrawn] from the subcommittee 62D program . . . on a recommendation from . . . Working Group 2 [following its rejection].[7] The [general] subcommittee [non-ECT electrical engineers] . . . agreed to conduct this . . . report of IEC 60601-2-14 [for ECT devices] [8] . . ., noting the WG2 recommendation that the . . . [the 1989 IEC standard specific to ECT devices] should be

---

[5] Theresa Zuraski was the U.S. contact for IEC, U.S. technical advisor to the U.S. working committee for ECT devices, Assistant Secretary for AAMI, and Assistant Secretary for the IEC sub-committee 62D composed of world-wide manufacturer affiliated experts, including Richard Weiner, main U.S. spokesperson for ECT. Zuraski informed me in a personal phone interview, that she coordinated the U.S. working group committee which met periodically, but which was also composed of members concerned with electrical medical devices other than ECT devices. Apparently, the general committee came to the conclusion in a September 15, 1997 meeting that they could not continue working on a revision of 601-2-14 (601-2-14R) because the draft, mainly authored by Richard Weiner was too confusing and there was not enough interest from different parts of the world. She also indicated that the draft made the working committee uncomfortable and that the working committee would not approve it. In that light, Weiner's committee recommended that Weiner's proposed replacement Standard (601-2-14R) which would have supplanted the 1989 standard in 1998, be withdrawn, but that the then current (1989) Standard 601-2-14, also be withdrawn so that no specific Standard for ECT devices would exist whatsoever. This occurred. To this day, this is still the case—no IEC standard whatsoever exists for ECT.

[6] The withdrawal is disconcerting in that the 1989 IEC Standard at least limited the devices to around 250-300 Joules (International Electrotechnical Commission, 1989, p. 23). Moreover, the 1989 Standard technically forced manufacturers to report actual EO at particular impedances up to the 500Ω maximum (Ibid p. 11).

[7] Subcommittee 62D (SC62D) was a general group of experts on various electrical devices but with no particular expertise on ECT devices. Subcommittee 62D Working Group 2 (SC62D/WG2) was composed of a smaller group of experts within subcommittee SC62D--mostly manufacturer affiliated advocates of the device whose specialty and vested interest was the ECT device. Of interest was the additional title of the 62D/WG2 Committee - "Electroconvulsive equipment WG AAMI (Association for the Advancement of Medical Instrumentation) Neurosurgery Committee" (Association for the Advancement of Medical Instrumentation, 1998, February 4).

[8] 60601-2-14 also known as 601-2-14 was the 1989 IEC Standard specifically for "ECT" devices.

> [entirely] withdrawn for . . . [the] reason [provided by the WG2 committee] that . . . [the IEC Standard] . . . is [allegedly] no longer clinically relevant since it is based on treatment parameters which have [purportedly] been obsolete both in clinical practice and in commercial products. (International Electrotechnical Commission, 1997, Dec 26, p. 2)

In other words, the IEC refused Weiner's replacement recommendation (very likely because the electrical parameters seemed excessive) but accepted Weiner's follow-up proposal to entirely remove the 1989 IEC standard for ECT devices from the IEC Standard generally. In short, there would be no IEC Standard for the ECT device at all. But if manufacturers were circuitously interpreting the then current 1989 IEC Standard for ECT devices to secretly accommodate up to 216.6 Joules, and in fact, when slightly breached, to accommodate between 230 to 240 Joules as previously noted, why indeed did ECT device manufacturers oppose FDA adoption of the 1989 IEC Standard for so-called "ECT" devices, preferring instead to entirely delete the standard? Why, in short, when manufacturers had already modified or interpreted (albeit covertly) the 1989 IEC Standard to accommodate their already enhanced second generation BP devices both in America and abroad, didn't manufacturers zealously aspire to have this 1989 IEC standard for ECT devices adopted? Why in fact, why ***didn't*** manufacturers ardently espouse FDA approval of a 1989 IEC Standard which would have more or less "legalized" their unreported second generation BP devices?

In that Weiner and associates had for some twenty years carefully avoided official adoption of the 1982 APA Standard due to its minimal stimulus mandate of 110J maximum joules, and so the implied 1.1 MTTLOI ceiling for BP devices for all age categories (110J ÷ 100J = 1.1), one might assume American manufacturers would support FDA adoption of the much more liberally construed 1989 IEC Standard for ECT devices, "allowing" more than twice the power. After all, it was only the formal espousal of an official standard that stood in the way of the higher more desirable Class II and perhaps even Class III FDA re-classification of ECT devices generally, an aspiration which BP device manufacturers had been striving arduously to achieve since the reintroduction of Brief Pulse to the United States in 1976. (Even today, all "ECT devices" continue to remain in FDA's lowest and thus least desirable Class I categorization for medical devices for which no official standard either can be or has been written.)

There are, in fact, several reasons why manufacturers objected to official FDA adoption of their own 1989 IEC Standard for ECT. One reason may have been a statute within the 1989 IEC Standard for ECT (601-2-14) mandating full disclosure of EO (Energy Output), that is, "full details . . . when connected . . . to resistive loads of 100Ω, 200Ω, 300Ω and 500Ω," as well as a mandate requiring the reporting of "maximum output energy" at maximum Impedance:

> 6.8.3 Technical description
> Additional term:
> aa) The technical description shall additionally give:
> -full details of the OUTPUT WAVEFORM when the EQUIPMENT is connected in turn to resistive loads of 100Ω, 200Ω, 300Ω and 500Ω.
> - the maximum output energy and the relevant load resistance.
> [International Electrotechnical Commission,1989, p. 11]

CHAPTER 50

Manufacturers Oppose Official Adoption of the 1989 IEC Standard Cont'd

While American BP manufacturers had reported "100 Joules at 220Ω" in the U.S. (via the Mectan Transmutation) and "100 Joules at 300Ω" internationally (via the 1989 IEC Standard), American and European manufacturers had, in fact, neglected to report actual *maximum* output (in joules) since about 1982, this, in spite of the fact that the 1989 IEC statute clearly required manufacturers to do so. In fact, 100J reports at 220Ω and 300Ω nationally and internationally, as well as circa 100J maximum machine readouts, continued to create the distinct impression that BP devices remained limited to the circa 100 Joule maximum output identified by both the 1977 Utah Biomedical test laboratory report (Grahn et al. 1977) and the 1982 APA Standard (110J) as "safe" (as the devices can be) and thus written into a standard which guaranteed "minimal stimulus" output. [9] Indeed, through numerous circuitous techniques such as the reporting of Charge in place of EO, underreporting Voltage, underreporting Impedance, underreporting and/or failing to report maximum EO in joules etc., both European and American "ECT" device manufacturers had proactively prolonged dispelling the false impression of circa 100J maximums both in Brief Pulse machines and Brief Pulse standards for as long as humanly possible (Royal College of Psychiatry, 1995, p. 124-125; see English Devices in *How Manufacturers Figure Output* in the previous section). [10] [11] Conveniently, in fact, no standard and certainly not

---

[9] Manufacturers gave regulators every reason to believe that "100J at 220Ω" and "100 at 300Ω" phrases, like the 1982 APA Standard which preceded them, were *conditional* ER/RRCs, limiting BP devices to 100 maximum Joules and thus minimal stimulus outputs. For example, MECTA and Somatics depicted circa 100J maximums for their second generation machine readouts both in the U.S. and abroad.

[10] Early European manufacturers, like the Americans, initially developed devices far less powerful than SW, also touted to be "new and improved" (Ottoson, 1960; Delmat-Marselet. 1942; Grahn et al., 1976, 1977). Like American manufacturers, however, modern day European BP devices now emit energy outputs far surpassing that of the older SW devices originally criticized by both American and European device manufacturers as being too powerful (Ottoson, 1960; Delmat-Marselet, 1942; Weiner, 1979; 1980). Like the Americans, the European practice of reporting EO in joules is eventually discarded. ECT committees affiliated with the Royal College of Psychiatrists just as ECT committees affiliated with the American Psychiatric Association abandoned the practice for third generation BO devices. As such, comparison of mega powerful European BP devices to previously manufactured Half SW/Half BP, chopped SW, and even pure SW devices do not make clear that modern day BP has become more powerful than ECT devices both of the more immediate and distant past. In fact, committees associated with European, American, Canadian, and British Psychiatric Associations have now called for even more souped up devices no longer measured in joules, but in Charge (International Electrotechnical Commission, 1997, Dec 26, p. 5).

[11] The previously prevailing 1989 IEC Standard (International Electrotechnical Commission, 1989), which was, of course, international in scope, may have been created by European (albeit led by American) manufacturers in league with their respective Psychiatric Associations (through ECT committees replete with manufacturer affiliates), resulting in what might be described as an international conspiracy to hide the power of third generation BP devices, suppressing the fact that BP has surpassed SW in raw power (Cameron, 1994). In spite of euphemistic concepts such as "the therapeutic window" in current academia suggesting both safe and efficacious dosing, the suprathreshold output emitted by modern day BP devices has totally eliminated the initial safety improvement of BP over SW (Robin and De Tissera, 1982; Squire and Zouzounis, 1982). In fact, all evidence points toward damaging dosages of electricity as the agent involved in ECT efficacy (Breggin, 1979, pp. 114, 122; Krystal, Weiner, and Gassert, 1996; Malitz, Sackeim, and Decina, 1979; Perrin et al. 2012; Squire and Zouzounis, 1982), not minimally stimulated adequate seizures (Robin and De Tissera,

an IEC Standard had ever up to this point--1997--been officially adopted by any official U.S. agency, including ANSI, AAMI, HIMA, APA and the FDA (Sackeim, 1991, p. 235).[12] Not since 1982 then, had U.S. manufacturers been so imminently confronted with a legal mandate to confine or even report actual maximum EO in accordance with a mandatory standard. Official FDA adoption of the 1989 IEC Standard, therefore, might have created grave difficulties for American manufacturers who by 1997 had for several decades, been quietly producing much more powerful devices than that inferred by their obscure reporting paradigms (International Electrotechnical Commission, 1989, p. 11).

Official adoption and so careful scrutiny of the 1989 IEC Standard, in short, might have meant exposing Brief Pulse as having surpassed SW in raw power, including the detail that the modern BP device was no longer a minimal stimulus device at all, but an ENR (Electro Neurotransmission Reduction) device and had been so since at least 1982. Close examination of the IEC standard, in fact, might have drawn attention to the point that the difficult to derive 1989 IEC output ceiling as interpreted by manufacturers, in no way conformed to the 1982 APA Standard of 110 maximum joules. Indeed, as interpreted by manufacturers, the true albeit unreported IEC ceiling standard of 216.6 Joules (with slight breaching), actually facilitated more than twice the output of the (110J) APA ceiling standard. Adoption of the 1989 IEC standard for ECT, compelling manufacturers to report true EO maximums, therefore, might have exposed to the FDA. the IEC, as well as the public, the devastating fact that American (and European) BP devices no longer emitted half the EO of SW devices at all, but had become even more powerful than SW, and so more dangerous.[13] Certainly, since 1982, American manufacturers had been utilizing their own outrageously manipulative math paradigms to hide the increasing power of American BP devices--now well out of compliance with criteria developed by the FDA through Grahn et al., criteria concretely reflected within the 1982 APA Standard itself (Grahn, 1976; Grahn et al., 1977). News that so-called "improved" (by virtue of reduced output) Brief Pulse machines actually emitted more power than the SW devices of the past might very well have damaged years of PR touting the Brief Pulse device as the "new and improved" and thus "safer" minimal stimulus apparatus of the future. Such PR damage might not only have affected the marketing of Brief Pulse generally, but--even worse-- triggered yet another FDA investigation (Cameron, 1994; Department of Health and Human Services, 1982a, E20). FDA adoption of the 1989 IEC Standard for "ECT" then, would have placed a spotlight on manufacturers' novel interpretation of the IEC standard for "ECT," possibly exposing actual machine outputs, re-initiating FDA scrutiny not only of Brief Pulse "ECT" devices generally, but of "convulsion theory" specifically.[14]

But American manufacturers might have resisted official adoption and thus close scrutiny of the 1989 IEC Standard for ECT devices for an additional, even more subtle reason. Because the 500Ω IEC Impedance ceiling within the 1989 IEC standard applied internationally, thereby officially supplanting the 600Ω APA ceiling, the 600Ω international ceiling could have forced recalls of the slightly more powerful, still in use MECTA and Somatics second generation made-for-America BP devices manufactured between 1982 and 1994 still in use in America. For example, MECTA's second generation *made-for-Europe* JR 1 and 2 IEC models emit (a

---

1982). The association of efficacy with damaging doses of electrical output remains an international constant, and, in fact, the secret application of this principle has not altered since the inception po ECT in 1938 (Cameron, 1994).

[12] By avoiding any mandated standard, American (and European) manufacturers, by default, continue to grant themselves license to produce and hide the true power of their devices through math manipulation. On an international basis, the practice of discarding EO reporting altogether and reporting only in terms of Charge, hides the fact that BP machines on a world-wide basis are no longer minimal stimulus devices and are, in fact, much more powerful generally than the SW devices of the past. Strong evidence identified in this manuscript, suggests an international conspiracy between manufacturers and ECT committees under the auspices of various Psychiatric Associations to secret this revealing data. With withdrawal of the 1989 IEC Standard on ECT, manufacturers began making more and more powerful devices as we shall see.

[13] If these facts had become known, the public relations image of BP as a "new and improved 'ECT' device" could have been irreparably damaged, affecting the illusion of safety and thus marketability. Importantly, psychiatrists themselves have been misinformed by both manufacturers and the APA (influenced by and even composed of manufacturers) in that practitioners are instructed merely to set the dial to the age of the recipient before applying electricity. Many psychiatrists continue to believe, as do many consumers, that BP emits far less EO than SW. Manufacturers have even rationalized away the suspicious practice of ending "treatment" only after pathological brain wave activity appears on the EEG as an alleged indication of therapeutic response (MECTA Corporation, 1987) through the claim that dysfunctional brain wave activity is "reversible." Perrin eventually showed a gross reduction in frontal lobe connectivity following modern day ECT with second generation devices (Perrin et al. 2012).

[14] One of manufacturers' greatest concerns may have been the underground consumer/survivor movement composed of tens of thousands of angry, injured, and outraged citizens whose lives have been decimated as a result of these lies. Not only could such an uprising have resulted in the demise of the industry, but as a result of fraudulent claims, huge lawsuits might have emerged.

probable) 230 and 240 unreported joules respectively; whereas MECTA's JR and SR 1 and 2 *made-for-America* devices could emit almost 260 unreported joules; Somatics' American made-for-Europe (IEC) DGx device emits 227 maximum joules; whereas, its' made-for-America Thymatron DG can emit 252 maximum joules.[15] While none of these outputs has ever been reported, the slightly reduced power output of second generation made-for-Europe models had, in fact, been modified by MECTA and Somatics solely due to the mandatory application of the IEC Standard in European countries. Official American adoption of the IEC standard, therefore, might well have led to mandatory recalls of MECTA's and Somatics' slightly more powerful second generation made-for-America BP versions already prolific in the U.S.

Manufacturers Oppose Adoption of the 1989 IEC (International Electrotechnical Commission) Standard Continued--the 100J Ceiling

Even more dramatically, American adoption of the international standard might have opened up manufacturers to an even more extreme possibility. Upon official FDA adoption of the 1989 IEC standard for ECT devices, FDA regulators and American advocacy groups could have argued for a strict interpretation of the IEC Standard's overt "100J at 300Ω" phrase as well as the implicit "130J at 300Ω" phrase concealed deeper within the IEC standard for all so-called "ECT" devices. In short, calls for a strict interpretation could have limited Brief Pulse devices to an actual 100 joules (just as the standard superficially appeared to do) or at most, to the less obvious 130 maximum Joules indirectly derivable from a subtler aspect of the standard incorporated into the standard's subsequent wording. Either way, the possibility could have endangered the continuation of thousands of Brief Pulse machines already in use, in fact, exposing the actual hidden power of Brief Pulse "ECT" devices manufactured after 1982 and thus the secret of their efficacy. Not only might future marketability of Brief Pulse devices have been compromised, but the scrupulousness of manufacturers themselves. That made-for-America second generation BP devices were based upon the illicit Mectan Transmutation was completely unknown. Indeed, close scrutiny of a newly adopted IEC standard for ECT devices might have exposed the 1989 IEC standard for ECT devices as but a facsimile of the illicit Mectan Transmutation upon which both MECTA and Somatics had based all their made-for-America second generation BP devices. Such a revelation not only threatened to call attention to the actual power of second generation BP devices both in America and internationally, but as mentioned above, may have raised questions regarding the legitimacy of "convulsion theory" itself.[16] [17] Because manufacturers' Pure-ER/RRC interpretation of the 1989 IEC Standard had enabled much higher electrical dosages than the 1982 APA Standard allowed, possible exposure of specific outputs must have left manufacturers feeling insecure. In short, the deceptive construction of the 1989 IEC standard, itself patterned on a clear corruption of the 1982 APA Standard (via the Mectan Transmutation), might not have born close analysis. Certainly, manufacturers must have been restive at the prospect of having to explain to the FDA, the ERA, the IEC, and watch-dog groups both in the U.S. and abroad, a never before reported interpretation of the IEC Standard for ECT devices allowing never before reported outputs two and a half times minimal stimulus and two and a half times that allowed by the 1982 APA Standard, surpassing SW in cumulative output.

---

[15] Somatics eventually did abandon the 252J made-for-America Thymatron DG for the more ubiquitous use of the 227J DGx, but were never forced to recall the DG. Even so, Somatics soon began manufacturing a third generation BP device as we shall soon see.

[16] The Mectan Transmutation has never been exposed as the corruption of the APA Standard it actually is.

[17] A very cogent argument can be made for interpreting the 1989 IEC Standard (of "100J at 300Ω") as limiting devices to 100 actual Joules, an interpretation which would have forced BP manufacturers to honor the promise pledged (1976-1982) to FDA and the American people of a circa 100J minimal stimulus device supplanting SW. Not only have manufacturer affiliated academics representing psychiatric associations as well as BP manufacturers themselves actively misled the public into believing that modern BP devices are less powerful and therefore superior devices safety-wise to SW, but BP manufacturers and psychiatric associations have passively watched a misinformed media, in turn, misinform the world public at large.

Manufacturers Oppose Adoption of the 1989 IEC (International Electrotechnical Commission) Standard Continued

In addition, even accepting the most liberal interpretation of the 1989 IEC Standard--a pure-ER/RRC--allowing a rather difficult to derive and never before reported 216.66J maximum, made-for-Europe Somatics and MECTA devices, albeit minimally, nevertheless breached even this most liberal 217J construal. For instance, although Somatics brochures claimed the second generation made-for-Europe Thymatron DGx (and even the second generation made-for-America Thymatron DG[18]) to be in compliance with the 1989 IEC Standard, in actuality, the 226J DGx was in violation of even the liberally construed 216.66J IEC Standard and had been since the standard's inception.

Similarly, MECTA claimed in its U.S. brochures, a maximum machine resistance of 400 ohms (mimicking the MECTA "C") for its made-for-Europe second generation BP devices falsely indicating circa 100J ceilings.[19] Certainly, this was untrue (International Electrotechnical Commission, 1989, p. 11). Neither of MECTA's second generation IEC BP devices limited Impedance to 400Ω; both utilized the IEC standard's 500Ω maximum Impedance, greatly surpassing the 100 Joule mark implicitly suggested not only by MECTA's false reporting of a 400Ω maximum Impedance, but more definitively, via its misleading machine readouts.[20] [21] In sum then, all MECTA IEC BP devices surpassed even the most liberally construed Pure-ER/RRC interpretation of even the implicit "130J at 300Ω" phrase subsumed and so cached within the IEC Standard for ECT devices, itself permitting a questionable never before reported 216.66 maximum joules, surpassing that of SW.[22] In fact, MECTA's second generation IEC versions emitted between 230-240 maximum joules,[23] outputs unknown to anyone but the Brief Pulse manufacturers themselves. Clearly, through underreporting and misreporting, MECTA, by 1989, had been implying 100J ceilings for both its second generation US and IEC BP devices since about 1982, never revealing that both had been emitting well over 200 Joules for at least seven years and by 1997, for some fifteen years. [24] Moreover, even though manufacturers might have been able to argue that the 1989 IEC Standard had legally enhanced the ceiling for BP devices from the 110J APA ceiling to a 216.66J IEC ceiling, no manufacturer had ever reported the 216.66J figure; in fact, no manufacturer (with the exception of Medcraft) had ever reported actual maximum output (in joules) for any of their second generation BP apparatuses. As such, second generation BP devices themselves, in effect, had never been reported at all. Even with impending FDA adoption of the 1989 IEC Standard, therefore, a major obstacle stood in the way of manufacturers. Both through the 1989 IEC standard's featured "100J at 300Ω" phrase and through MECTA's and Somatics' deceptive machine readouts plainly depicting 100 maximum joules, American Brief Pulse manufacturers both at home and abroad, as noted, had continued to maintain their circa 100J ceiling charade

---

[18] All American BP manufacturers have been out of compliance with the APA Standard since about 1983 and decidedly since 1985.

[19] The false 400Ω Impedance ceiling falsely indicated a 100J ceiling.

[20] There is good reason to suspect that MECTA underreports impedance (as well as Voltage) both in their brochures and on international devices (Royal College of Psychiatry, 1995, p. 124). MECTA may have switched from reporting dynamic to static impedance, that is, impedance measured in advance of applying the stimulus. Indeed in a 1997 IEC revision proposal, Weiner makes the switch (International Electrotechnical Commission, 1997, Dec 26, p. 6). Thus, the 400Ω reported by MECTA may be a report of maximum static-- not dynamic--impedance, a violation of the 1989 IEC Standard (International Electrotechnical Commission, 1989, p. 11). Thus, International versions of MECTA devices may have, like U.S. versions, have been underreported in Impedance and Voltage, giving the appearance of 100 Joule devices.

[21] Both the second generation made-for-America Thymatron DG and second generation made-for-America JR/SR 1 and 2 utilized close to 555 ohms resistance, 55.5 ohms greater than the 500 ohm ceiling regulation stipulated within the 1989 IEC standard.

[22] 130J/300Ω = 216.66J/500Ω.

[23] MECTA's second generation made-for-America BP devices emitted approximately 256 Joules while both MECTA and Somatics third generation versions emit approximately 500 Joules as we shall soon see.

[24] Parameters given in the Royal College of Psychiatry's (1995) *ECT handbook,* list MECTA devices as having a maximum of 400Ω and maximum 240V. The author rejects these figures, in that 320V-- not 240V is required to attain a reported 400Ω resistance (Ohm's Law: Voltage = Resistance x Amperage; 400Ω x .8A = <u>320V</u>). RCP may have mistaken the 240V power source (wall current listed in the MECTA manual) for maximum Voltage emitted by the device itself. However, MECTA has a history of reporting most commonly used, rather than actual or maximum Impedances from which Voltage can be derived (Department of Health and Human Services, 1982a). In fact, Voltage is hidden by MECTA and must be conjectured. In that 500 ohms is allowed by the IEC Standard (1989), we can very reasonably assume MECTA utilizes this maximum from which we then derive a likely actual 400V maximum (500 ohms x .8 Amperage = 400V). Interestingly, if we utilize the exact figures spuriously provided by RCP for the IEC versions probably provided by MECTA, we misleadingly obtain approximately 100 maximum Joules.

for what were actually second generation BP devices of more than twice the power. Right up to FDA's proposal to adopt the IEC Standard for ECT devices in 1997, in fact, manufacturers like MECTA and Somatics had continued to imply the 100J ceiling stipulation both via the 1989 IEC standard and via the devices themselves. In spite of a possible FDA adoption of the 1989 IEC standard for ECT devices possibly legitimizing a circa 217J ceiling, therefore, a difficult quandary persisted for device makers--how would American and European manufacturers explain their continuous intimations of circa 100 Joule maximums since 1976? Why, with the original passage of the 1989 IEC Standard, had manufacturers not simply reported actual machine maximums, under which these maximums could now be argued as legal (or almost so) via the most liberal IEC interpretation? Indeed, if the 1989 IEC standard for ECT devices could be interpreted as broadly as American manufacturers had actually been doing, why, even with their slight breaches, hadn't they reported to FDA or ERA a new IEC ceiling standard of 217J? By 1997, eight years after the fact, if manufacturers were suddenly to report and argue for the broadest IEC interpretation, the question would invariably arise--"Why had manufacturers never until now published the actual 217J ceiling 'newly allowed' by the 1989 IEC Standard for ECT devices?" Why, indeed, had manufacturers never revealed the power of what were actually second generation Brief Pulse machines readily exceeding 200 maximum joules? Why, in fact, hadn't manufacturers told the truth about their Brief Pulse machines instead of continually implying maximum emissions of circa 100 maximum joules? Looked at in this light, Brief Pulse manufacturers may have felt compelled to remain reticent. Suddenly reporting actual machine outputs, in conjunction with defending a never before reported 217J IEC ceiling might have precipitously exposed the fact that both American and European BP devices had not only surpassed SW in raw power, but had been doing so since at least 1982. Indeed, as noted, BP manufacturers had been producing second generation BP devices more than twice the output of the first generation MECTA "C" since at least 1982 and had never up to this point reported it. In truth, by 1997, the resurgent Brief Pulse device originally limited to circa 100 maximum joules, the purportedly new and improved BP apparatus, safer than SW by virtue of drastically reduced output, already belonged to the distant past.

CHAPTER 51

Manufacturers Oppose Adoption of the 1989 IEC Standard—Cont'd.

Adoption of the IEC standard for ECT devices inviting close scrutiny then, would have revealed actual maximum outputs of both the IEC standard and what were actually second generation Brief Pulse machines. Even if manufacturers had defended the 217 joule maximum output allowed by a 1989 IEC standard via Pure-ER/RRC interpretation, and even had this argument been accepted by the FDA, official adoption of the IEC standard for ECT devices might yet have forced American manufacturers to strictly adhere to the 217J standard, forcing a recall of second generation made-for America BP devices and perhaps even second generation IEC BP devices, both of which breached the 217J standard. For instance, as previously mentioned, Somatics might have been forced to recall all made-for-America Thymatron DG devices capable of emitting 252J maximums and to modify the 227J DGx to 217 maximum joules.[25] Likewise, MECTA might have been forced to recall its second generation made-for-America BP devices capable of 259J as well as modify its 230 to 240J MECTA IEC BP devices to the strict 217J maximum. In a word, adoption of the 1989 IEC standard leading to close scrutiny of machines could have led to mandatory conformity to at least the broadest interpretation of the standard, still problematic even for second generation made-for-America and made-for-Europe Brief Pulse devices. Remember too, that while the most generous interpretation might have meant device modification, the strictest interpretation might have spelled disaster for the Brief Pulse industry as a whole. The most stringent interpretation of the adopted 1989 IEC standard, a conditional-ER/RRC interpretation, could have forced both MECTA and Somatics to adhere to between 100 and 130J maximums, that is, the minimal stimulus devices that BP apparatuses were originally purported to be and that the 1982 APA Standard plainly required. After all, the 1989 IEC Standard, with its "100J at 300Ω" phraseology might have been logically interpreted to limit devices to the same circa 100J maximum stipulated by the 1982 APA Standard, about the power of the original 108J MECTA "C" or at most, the implicit 130J maximum covertly incorporated within the same 1989 IEC standard, as noted. American manufacturers, via the Mectan Transmutation and via Machine Readouts, as mentioned, had been reporting the same circa 100J ceiling for their BP devices since 1976, the year FDA first began regulating medical instrumentation generally, while, in fact, as we have seen, MECTA and Somatics had been marketing BP devices two and a half times 100 joules since about 1982.

Getting wind of FDA's deliberations to adopt the IEC Standard generally, Harold Sackeim, a long-time spokesperson for MECTA and author of numerous articles extoling "ECT," made this telling 1991 statement:

> At present, there are no legally binding national Standards in the U.S. that constrain the maximal output of ECT devices. However, international bodies, like the International

---

[25] While allegedly conforming to the 1989 IEC Standard still in effect in 1997, the Thymatron DGx made for Europe device, yet appears to have been out of compliance with even the broadest possible interpretation. Though the DGx conformed to the 500 ohm ceiling, nevertheless, the "100J at 300Ω" phrase limits output to 166.6 Joules (100J/300Ω = 166.6J/500Ω). Even adding the 30% addendum aspect of the standard, the maximum output under the 1989 IEC standard would still have been 216..66 Joules (30% of 166.66J = 50J. 166.66J + 50J = 216.66J). The Thymatron DGx, emitting 227J, is thus off by 10 Joules, perhaps not a serious breach, but indicatory of how manufacturers, left up to their own devices, push and stretch ceilings beyond regulatory limits.

> Electrotechnical Commission (IEC) have developed Standards that limit the output characteristics of ECT devices and these Standards are applied in other countries . . . Consequently, it may be necessary for the output characteristics of devices used in the U.S. to be different from those used elsewhere. (Sackeim, 1991, p. 235)

In short, manufacturers recognized that official adoption of the IEC standard would be problematic for machines marketed in the United States. Indeed, in creating the illusion of 100J maximum BP devices and thus the illusion of self-conformity to the 1982 APA Standard, by the official year the U.S. adoption of IEC standards would have taken place--1997--American manufacturers had already managed to stave off official adoption of APA and IEC standards for some fifteen years (since 1982). In fact, it was by misrepresenting the power of their BP devices to the FDA that by 1997, American manufacturers had managed to remain virtually unregulated in the U.S. Thus, while the 1989 IEC Standard might have cemented a circa 217J output for what were actually second generation BP devices, and even though compliance with the broadest interpretation of the 1989 IEC Standard might have meant relatively few changes for second generation BP devices generally, any FDA adoption of the 1989 IEC Standard for ECT devices would have meant permanent technical confinement to 217 maximum joules, something Brief Pulse manufacturers sought to avoid, as we shall see. Too, the worst case scenario continued to exist--that a strict conditional-ER/RRC interpretation of the 1989 IEC standard for ECT devices might actually have forced American manufacturers to limit the power of their devices to between 100 and 130 maximum Joules, a devastating 50 to 60% power reduction of the second generation BP devices they had by that point been marketing and using for well over a decade.[26] [27] In any case, as noted, adoption of the IEC Standard would almost certainly have led to closer scrutiny of the standard and its various interpretations as well as the machines themselves, almost positively exposing actual device outputs which at this juncture (1997) had been hidden for some fifteen years. Adoption of the IEC standard for ECT, in sum, might have placed American manufacturers in a financially, technically, and politically precarious posture. Any defense of even the broadest interpretation of the IEC Standard for so-called ECT devices, as noted, would have entailed acknowledging and thus defending that BP devices had surpassed the overall power of SW some years previously, a fact still unknown to the public, the FDA, the ERA, and even the IEC. Manufacturers, consequently, even though this meant their devices would remain in Class I indefinitely, the least desirable FDA classification for medical devices, preferred total withdrawal of the then current IEC standard to a possible power reduction of their devices which official adoption of the 1989 IEC Standard for ECT devices might have meant, an action which threatened to bring unwanted scrutiny upon both manufacturer interpretation of the IEC standard and the true unreported power of Brief Pulse machines, generally.

---

[26] 256J/100J = 100%/X% = 39%. 100% - 39% = 61%. 256J/130J = 100%/X% = 50.8%. 256J/238J = 100%/X% = 93%. 100% - 93% = 7%.

[27] Elcot, the fourth U.S. Manufacturer is defunct. The Medcraft B-24 SW, although emitting 200 Joules only in rare circumstances, might have failed the 1989 IEC Standard anyway in that IEC appears to disallow peak currents greater than 1 ampere, whereas the strictest interpretation of 100 Joules would certainly have eliminated SW completely.

CHAPTER 52

Summary--Manufacturers Oppose Adoption of 1989 IEC Standard--Back to 100J

As discussed, perhaps the most disconcerting possibility for manufacturers and the ECT industry at large as a result of adopting the 1989 IEC Standard for ECT devices was the very strong counterargument that the proper interpretation of the 1989 IEC Standard should limit all ECT devices to between 100 and 130 maximum Joules (similar to the 1982 APA Standard), a common sense regulatory stipulation reasonably cutting in half via Brief Pulse, the identifiably problematic and all too powerful 200J SW device of old.[28] In other words, the key phrase, "100J at 300Ω" within the 1989 IEC Standard, like the "100J at 220Ω" phrase within the 1982 APA Standard,[29] could, and perhaps should have been interpreted as a conditional-ER/RRC, meaning that machines were not only to adhere to gradational outputs with respect to age, but, as noted, to a conditional overall ceiling of between 100 and 130 maximum Joules. Such a ceiling would have guaranteed a 1.0 to 1.3 MTTLOI for all age levels, in short, the expected minimal stimulus output in all age categories which Brief Pulse manufacturers initially appeared to promise. Thus, while Impedance under the 1989 IEC Standard could reach up to 500Ω under the IEC Standard, a strict stipulation of a 1.0 to 1.3 MTTLOI (based on a 100 to 130J overall ceiling) would have required correspondent reductions of electrical parameters at various age-related Impedances.[30] Public exposure of the far higher outputs emitted under a much broader Pure-ER/RRC (in lieu of a Conditional-ER/RRC) interpretation of both the 1989 IEC standard and the "modified" 1982 APA Standard via the Mectan Transmutation, might plausibly have led to both FDA and IEC (International Electrotechnical Commission) insistence that, in fact, both standards should limit Brief Pulse devices to between 100 and 130 absolute Joules. Certainly, arguments for a circa 100J ceiling interpretation are both cogent and plenteous including: (1) Brief Pulse can induce adequate seizures for all age groups in all circumstances with 100 Joules or less (Department of Health and Human Services, 1982a, pp. A53, E20), (2) BP is only superior to SW (with respect to memory damage) when BP is administered at just above threshold output (Squire and Zouzounis, 1986), (3) the APA Standard clearly stipulates a 110 Joule ceiling precedent, an output implicitly stipulating a 1.1 MTTLOI maximum stimulus emission at every resistance or age level (Department of Health and Human Services, 1982a, pp. A53, E20), and (4) 100 joules is the single EO mentioned within the 1989 IEC Standard with 130 joules only indirectly derivable deeper within the standard. In short, the absence of any specific EO depiction other than the key 100J phrase and an indirectly derivable 130J output within the 1989 IEC Standard for ECT was strongly suggestive of a maximum output of between 100 and 130J (International Electrotechnical Commission, 1989, p. 23). In addition, (5) it is only with a circa 100J ceiling that BP manufacturers could legitimately lay claim to a reduced output apparatus using half the EO of SW (Department of Health and Human Services, 1982a, pp. G3-G4), (6) the EO output emitted by SW has been shown as detrimental due to inconsistent, but mostly unnecessarily excessive electrical outputs (Grahn et al., 1976), (7) studies have established that an inversely proportional relationship exists between electrical output and safety; that is, safety

---

[28] A conditional-ER/RRC interpretation of "100J at 300Ω" or "100J at 300Ω" could be an ER/RRC mandating gradient outputs ultimately limited to a 100 or 130J ceiling meaning a 1.0 or 1.3 MTTLOI for all age categories.

[29] The 1982 APA Standard stipulated "70J at 220" with a conditional 110J overall ceiling.

[30] This is the principle upon which the APA standard's "70J at 220Ω" conditional ER/RRC was based and upon which the "100J at 220Ω" ER/RRC (of the Mectan Transmutation) was thought to be based. The 110J ceiling implicitly stipulated reduced electrical parameters to limit output to a 1.1 MTTLOI or minimal stimulus for all age categories.

diminishes as electrical output increases and vice-versa (Squire and Zouzounis, 1986), (8) manufacturer promises made to the FDA, the American people, and the world wide public at large for a safer new BP device compared to SW are entirely contingent upon the circa 100J ceiling of Brief Pulse (Grahn et al., 1976; Department of Health and Human Services, 1982a, pp. A53, E20), (9) convulsion theory is based on the efficacy of the adequate seizure alone--not adequate amounts of electricity--and has been the alleged scientific principle underlying "ECT" since the procedure's inception in 1938 (Grahn, 1976; Grahn et al., 1977), (10, 11) arguments for improvement made between 1976-1982 to the FDA for continuation of ECT are specifically based upon the validity of convulsion theory and thus the promise of a new and improved reduced output Brief Pulse device inducing the same "adequate" seizures as SW but at half the output, specifically--100 joules or less, (12) and finally, both European and American Brief Pulse manufacturers continued to engender the overall impression that modern day "ECT" is safer specifically by virtue of the reduced output Brief Pulse device. (Indeed, the actual hidden outputs of current day "ECT" devices appear to constitute fraud.)

Manufacturers Oppose Official Adoption of the 1989 IEC Standard--Back to 100J Continued

Indeed, if manufacturers suddenly began defending the broader pure-ER/RRC interpretation of the IEC Standard, permitting a never before reported 217J ceiling, necessarily arguing against a 100 and even 130J ceiling interpretation of the IEC Standard, how could manufacturers account for the false impression they had been creating for regulatory agencies (i.e. FDA, ERA, and IEC) and for the general public since 1976 that their Brief Pulse apparatuses were reduced output devices compared to the 200J SW devices of the past. How could they account for circumventing the contention that Brief Pulse was an improved apparatus equally effective (to SW) but at half the output, i.e. via the 110J maximum stipulated within the 1982 APA Standard? How, in fact, could manufacturers have rationalized the subtle unreported transitions from a circa 100 Joule absolute ceiling to a misleading 100 Joule average and finally to a 100J pure-ER/RRC (permitting between 217 and 259 Joule outputs)? How, moreover, could manufacturers have justified an IEC Standard based on a never before reported Mectan Transmutation of the 1982 APA standard, a clear corruption of the original 1982 APA Standard, the transmutation of which surreptitiously allowed BP devices to readily surpass 200J, while at the same time creating the impression that modern day BP devices continued to sustain the same circa 100J ceiling as the MECTA "C"? In short, how could a legitimate IEC Standard be based on an illicit Mectan Transmutation surreptitiously allowing BP devices to become more powerful than the SW devices they were supposed to replace? How indeed could this occur even as BP manufacturers on a world-wide basis continued to mislead regulators and the international public that their "new and improved" Brief Pulse devices emitted much less output than the SW devices of the past?

In adopting the IEC Standard, in sum, how could manufacturers have accounted for the detail that both the illicit transmutation of the APA standard (the Mectan Transmutation) and the subtle construct of the 1989 IEC standard--directly emulative of the Mectan Transmutation--permitted BP devices to surpass the identifiably dangerous 200J output emitted by the unacceptably powerful SW devices of old--a turn entirely unbeknownst to federal regulatory bodies both nationally and internationally? Indeed, the APA Standard, as well as the deceptive constructs of both the Mectan Transmutation and the IEC Standard seemed to reassure regulatory bodies and advocacy groups that the "new and improved ECT" delivered with the "new and improved Brief Pulse device" continued to utilize minimal stimulus output--the least amount of electricity possible to induce so-called adequate seizures. In sum, the misleading nature of both the Mectan Transmutation and the IEC Standard in conjunction with devious manufacturer reporting strategies seemingly corroborative of minimal stimulus outputs, particularly via spurious machine readouts, appeared to have ensured the replacement of SW with the Brief Pulse device alone for the specific and inherent purpose of dramatically reducing EO and so dramatically enhancing safety (Department of Health and Human Services, 1982a, pp. A44-A45).

Additional Problems for "ECT" Manufacturers in Adopting the IEC Standard

In addition to closer scrutiny of machine power, adoption of the 1989 IEC standard (in 1997) would have meant closer scrutiny of accompanying claims to justify increased power, for example, the spurious assertion that UL

"ECT" alone is "dose-sensitive" (that is, the claim that UL "ECT" anomalously requires twice threshold to be effective) as opposed to "non-dose-sensitive" BL ECT (the most common form) allegedly administered at just above threshold, both declarations of which are untrue. Indeed, FDA adoption of the IEC standard might first have meant exposing deceptive readout maximums on all American made second generation BP devices. Astoundingly, these machines falsely depict circa 100J ceilings--a manufacturer stratagem which has long misled even administering physicians. Certainly, exposure of this deception threatened to shine a bright light on the world-wide cover-up of the increasingly powerful Brief Pulse device, increases designed to steadily enhance Brief Pulse's MTTLOI (Multifold Threshold Titration Level Output Intensity), in spite of Brief Pulse's promise to reduce all output to the least amount of electricity possible. Can it be mere coincidence that both the introductory American MECTA "C" Brief Pulse device and the introductory British Brief Pulse Series 2/3 devices, both of which initially conformed to the 1982 APA 110 Joule ceiling, were originally featured to their respective regulatory bodies during sensitive periods of FDA and ERA scrutiny as "the future of ECT," impressing each continent's agency with the newer, "safer" reduced output Brief Pulse? Indeed, these were claims by which approval was gained for the ongoing utilization of the procedure in both America and Europe. Why, if not a cover-up, as Brief Pulse machines became increasingly more powerful on both continents, did manufacturers suddenly avoid reporting maximum EO ceilings clearly mandated by the 1989 IEC Standard itself? Moreover, why, according to configurations provided directly by manufacturers to the RCP (Royal College of Psychiatry, 1995, pp. 124-125) did MECTA IEC BP devices utilized in the United Kingdom and thus designed to conform to the 1989 IEC Standard, falsely appear limited to 100 maximum Joules? [31] Clearly, as we have seen, the FDA's plan to officially adopt the 1989 IEC Standard in 1997, risked exposing the 200J plus outputs of second generation Brief Pulse machines, generally.

Even as late as 1997, the year of FDA's proposed IEC adoption, no journal article or agency had yet identified, commented on, or challenged American manufacturers' corruption of the APA Standard (here deemed "the Mectan Transmutation"); neither had any European agency questioned European and American manufacturers' dubious interpretation of the 1989 IEC Standard, both "standards" of which manufacturers had extraordinarily stretched to permit unreported outputs of between 236-260 Joules--outputs never revealed by any American or European BP manufacturer. Indeed, few, if any regulatory bodies, could have fathomed the creative methodologies by which manufacturers were interpreting and reporting under the two "standards." Neither were regulatory bodies aware that by 1997, BP devices had been delivering EO more than twice the 100 Joule mark (the moniker of minimal stimulus) for the past twenty years, easily surpassing the raw EO maximum of SW, as noted, with which advocates of Brief Pulse had originally seemed so concerned. But how could these regulatory agencies have been aware of such inconsistencies when these same regulatory agencies had themselves deferred all responsibility to the device makers themselves. How could these regulatory agencies have been made aware of these falsehoods when they had come to rely upon information provided by the very manufacturers they were allegedly regulating? [32] [33] By depending upon the specialized

---

[31] This was done by MECTA's false reporting of 400Ω maximums as well as spurious machine readouts. Indeed, utilizing multifold threshold outputs while reporting minimal stimulus is reminiscent of safety testing, including MRI studies, at minimal stimulus while testing for efficacy at suprathreshold outputs (Beale et al., 1994), conflicting details never reported to any regulatory body.

[32] One very interesting phenomenon is the reliance of regulatory agencies on information emanating from psychiatric associations. In that psychiatric associations are not the actual manufacturers, the semblance of an objective third party is created, the more so in that psychiatric association committees are often made up of MDs or "scientists." Upon closer scrutiny, however, psychiatric association committees are not independent of the manufacturers, but, in fact, in a very authentic sense, are the manufacturers themselves. Numerous members of these committees appear to have close financial ties to manufacturers (Cameron, 1994) and no care is taken by agencies to insure independence. Psychiatric Associations themselves, notedly more and more dependent upon the donations and endorsements of powerful drug companies, are plainly vulnerable to scientific compromise (Breggin, 1991). Finally, the demand for an incarceratory mental health system in general, similar to the prison system, comes not from consumers--or rather inmates--but from family members and society. As such, the main impetus and thus the most saleable commodity, becomes "control." Perhaps the most powerful tool ever devised for management and control--other than psychosurgery--is ECT, accounting for the desperate lengths both manufacturers and psychiatry have gone in order to retain it, not to mention the blind eye society, in turn, has turned toward the practice.

[33] The common practice of permitting manufacturers often via psychiatric association committees, to test and report their own findings, is plainly a conflict of interests, defeating the very raison d'etre of the regulation itself. Manufacturers, as seen in a previous section, in proving "safety," had performed studies by administering the more benign albeit ineffective threshold dosages of ECT as opposed to the more effective, but dangerous suprathreshold dosages administered in actual clinical practice. But while consumer complaints in the ordinary medical arena often spell the demise of harmful drugs which occasionally reach the marketplace, consumer complaints

committees (both nationally and internationally) of various psychiatric association committees in lieu of independent research institutions and independent laboratories, i.e. Utah Biomedical Test Laboratories (Grahn et al., 1977), by 1997, regulatory bodies had come to totally depend upon cleverly suppressed and misleading reporting for almost two decades. This spurious reporting included 100J averages and 100J ERs disguised as 100J ceilings, safety studies performed at minimal stimulus in lieu of clinically applied outputs, and efficacy studies performed at actual suprathreshold outputs. How could regulatory agencies have been aware of never reported MTTLOIs the very term of which had to be invented by the author of this manuscript to even describe the totally unreported concept. Indeed, regulatory agencies had long been under the false impression that only "dose sensitive" UL ECT was being administered at suprathreshold outputs, and finally, that modern day BP devices were much less powerful than SW devices, generally. What chance had regulatory agencies to become aware of these matters with false 100J/500mC (EO/Charge) equivalencies in place, and spurious machine readouts suggestive of 100J maximums seemingly corroborated by misleading standards also suggestive of circa 100J maximums (and so, minimal stimulus). Who or what agency, for instance, could possibly have imagined that standards emphasizing 100 or 110 Joules respectively had actually expanded into 230 to 260J maximums--almost two and a half times the output referred to by either the APA or IEC Standard?[34]

have not acted as a safeguard against malignant psychiatric products wherein tens of thousands of "patient" grievances continue to be ignored under the rationale of "mental illness." Recipients of non-mental health related drug and other types of therapy are not coerced into "consuming" (until recently) whereas, to various degrees, coercion is still permitted with respect to ECT (and psychiatric drugs) in at least 48 of the United States. In that behaviorism is often the central issue in mental health related issues, a practitioner often relies upon second or third party satisfaction, i.e. family member or "society." Unlike ordinary medical issues, psychiatric practitioners may not rely upon direct recipient or direct consumer satisfaction. This scenario provides a natural mindset for ignoring the noxious effects of treatments experienced by the mental patient himself. In that it is not the second or third party who must bear the ill effects, the litmus of successful mental health treatment—efficacy--becomes commonly albeit subtly defined as control or manageability of the patient, all from other party perspectives; individual satisfaction, individual comfort, and even individual safety is either relegated to minor considerations or completely ignored. The result is a system which primarily caters to other party satisfaction---not direct consumer satisfaction often at odds with other parties. As such, the mental health system is much more akin to the criminal justice system than the medical paradigm with which mental health "therapies" are often misleadingly associated. As second and third party satisfaction becomes a priority over first person satisfaction, effects which are harmful to the recipient himself suddenly become forgivable both to doctor and second parties, whereby, patient complaints can be "safely" disregarded. Lack of efficacy in terms of behaviorism, that is, lack of "patient control" on the other hand is not forgivable by the second or third party (i.e. society) who demands it of the practitioner. In turn, society does not forgive the practitioner who fails to achieve "control." Indeed, the "other"--not the patient--becomes the "consumer;" so that consumer satisfaction becomes second or third party (societal) satisfaction, and product marketability and practitioner demands become entirely tied to second and third party demands alone—not the consumer himself. Consequently, where safety and efficacy regarding "treatment" do not exist simultaneously, and where safety is a first person priority and efficacy, an "other" priority--manufacturers of somatic mental health "therapies" often find themselves in the acquitable, often compelling position--of having to overlook safety altogether to focus on "efficacy" alone. Indeed, the sole emphasis is typically on the "other" party satisfaction so that efficacy is solely defined as managing the patient, and so demanded of the practitioner even at the price of harming the direct consumer.

[34] Not only are these actual EOs not alluded to within the IEC or APA standards, but the featured "100J" figure within the 1989 IEC Standard, as well as what turns out to be 100J averages and 100J ERs utilized under the transmuted APA Standard (used by manufacturers after 1982), created the advertently false impression that "ECT" devices were limited to approximately 100 actual Joules and thus minimal stimulus.

CHAPTER 53

The Best Defense is a Strong Offense: Somatics opts for More Power with 3rd Gen. BP Devices

But American manufacturers in 1997, objected to the American adoption of the 1989 IEC Standard for "ECT" for yet another, even more powerful and more disconcerting reason--one which not only aimed at covering up and maintaining what were already dangerously enhanced second generation BP devices, but one which sought to cover up the enhancement of BP devices even further. Under no official mandate to regulate their BP devices in America, American manufacturers beginning about 1995, had already begun producing new third generation BP devices, indeed, doubling the power of second generation BP devices. Unbeknownst to consumers and regulatory bodies, even while second generation BP devices were eliciting an unreported circa 2.5 MTTLOI with BL ECT and a circa 5.0 MTTLOI with UL ECT, new third generation BP devices were by now emitting a circa 5.0 MTTLOI with BL ECT and a circa 10.0 MTTLOI with UL ECT. Trapped, manufacturers, who were by that time marketing third generation BP devices more than twice as powerful as even the broadest interpretation the 1989 IEC Standard allowed and roughly five times the power of the original MECTA "C" (in all age categories), knew that FDA adoption of the 1989 IEC standard in 1997, though surreptitiously sanctioning the enhanced power of second generation IEC BP devices, was nowhere near high enough to sanction their later third generation BP devices, which by 1997 had already been marketed and distributed for some two years. To make matters worse, FDA had no idea that these Brief Pulse devices had become any more powerful (in all age categories) than the first generation minimal stimulus Brief Pulse MECTA "C" device presented to the FDA around 1978. In short, based on the undisclosed knowledge that increasing efficacy is directly correspondent to increasing electrical power and increasing MTTLOI, manufacturers were unnerved by possible adoption of the 1989 IEC standard in 1997 which not only threatened to expose the power of second generation BP devices, but threatened to altogether expose and curtail never before reported third generation BP devices! To avoid admitting to even more powerful third generation BP devices and in order to maintain their reduced output marketing viability then, manufacturers moved in the only direction they could--an even newer standard more than doubling the power allowed by even the broadest interpretation of the then current 1989 IEC standard. Indeed, manufacturers not only wanted to protect the power and thus the marketability of already extant third generation BP devices, the power of which had never been reported to any regulatory body, but manufacturers wanted to insure the possibility of even more enhanced Brief Pulse machines for the future. Not only did manufacturers need to fight FDA adoption of the IEC standard, therefore, but in order to accommodate already marketed third generation and the probability of even more powerful fourth and even fifth generation BP devices, manufacturers found themselves in a position of having to lobby for total replacement the 1989 IEC standard for ECT devices with an even newer more wide-ranging standard. This newest standard at minimum, had to allow more than twice the unreported output than even the broadest interpretation of the 1989 IEC standard had surreptitiously permitted. In short, if the FDA was going to officially adopt all IEC standards for medical devices, a completely new IEC standard for "ECT" devices incorporating the power of already extant third (and possibly even fourth and fifth) generation BP devices had to be implemented.

Daunting Problem

Thus, even though the broadest possible interpretation of the 1989 IEC Standard for ECT devices surreptitiously "legalized" souped-up second generation BP devices capable of emitting a circa 2.5 MTTLOI for BL ECT and a circa 5.0 MTTLOI for UL ECT worldwide, an opaque tactic manufacturers themselves had invented and successfully lobbied into the 1989 IEC Standard, American manufacturers were now forced to vehemently oppose FDA adoption of their own 1989 IEC Standard. They did so to vie for an even newer standard authorizing at least twice the power of the 1989 IEC Standard. In brief, they had to take this stand in order to protect third generation BP devices which by 1997, had already been marketed and utilized the previous two years. The daunting problem manufacturers faced, in effect, was not only the supplanting of the 1989 IEC standard with a newer standard sanctioning the power of their most recent third generation BP devices (and to make room for even more powerful future BP devices), but to do so without revealing the degree of enhancement they were seeking and thus the embarrassing fact that manufacturers had already covered up the first and second major amplifications more than doubling and now more than quadrupling the power of first generation BP devices. Such outputs far surpassed SW in raw power. In short, manufacturers needed a way to subtly introduce the necessity of much greater electrical power while at the same time once again hiding the degree of enhancement from both the public and regulatory agencies. Certainly, they had to find a way of "legalizing" already extant third generation BP devices. Thus, in 1997, a newer IEC Standard for ECT devices was needed which not only covered up the first doubling of power which had occurred about 1982, but the second doubling in power comprised of third generation BP devices manufactured about 1995, BP devices which had an even greater surpassing power over SW than the yet unreported power of second generation BP devices. Impossibly, moreover, manufacturers had to accomplish this change while continuing to suggest Brief Pulse less powerful than SW in order to maintain the critical reputation of Brief Pulse as a "new and improved 'ECT' apparatus" (compared to SW) via "reduced electrical output"!

Tall Order

Afraid of being locked into second generation machine maximums, of even being forced to cut in half the power of second generation BP devices, and worse yet, afraid of libel, both American and European manufacturers concomitantly demanded the right to boost the power of their BP devices for what they brazenly asserted a first time power augmentation of what appeared to be circa "100J maximum first generation BP devices." Boldly declaring the 1989 IEC Standard obsolete, a standard which seemed to limit devices to between 100 and 130 maximum Joules (but which actually allowed up to circa 217J and more with slight breaching), manufacturers, led by Weiner, suddenly demanded a complete revision of the 1989 IEC Standard for ECT devices. In fact, the proposed revision would not maintain, reduce, or regulate power as standards are wont to do, but would surreptitiously sanction even more powerful already extant third generation BP devices which had been on the marketplace since at least 1995. To rationalize and underplay the "new" power boost, manufacturers resurrected the bygone argument that a new IEC standard for enhancing output on ECT devices was needed for "dose sensitive" UL "ECT." In fact, unknown to all but the manufacturers, the new Weiner revised IEC replacement, would double the power of Brief Pulse machines not for the first, but for the second time and not merely for UL ECT, but for BL ECT as well. Moreover, this newest "standard," sanctioning the tripling (and more than tripling) of Brief Pulse power generally, would no longer apply to Europe only, but this time, to the world as a whole. In short, the new machine specifications would become the official standard on a worldwide basis.[35] [36] Finally, however, manufacturers had to write the standard in such a way that not only the new

---

[35] UL ECT, which requires half the output of BL ECT to induce seizure, has been administered at the same output as BL ECT since the beginning. In short, UL ECT was administered at twice threshold even with the MECTA "C" so that the first doubling of power (via second generation BP devices) meant four to five times threshold with UL "ECT" and the second doubling of power (via third generation BP devices) meant about ten times threshold with UL "ECT." (Second generation BP devices use about 2.5 times threshold for BL ECT and about 5.0 times threshold for third generation BP devices.)

[36] FDA's trust in the APA is entirely misplaced in that APA, Royal College of Psychiatry, and other psychiatric fraternities whose specialty groups are endowed with the authority of "science," are by no means independent entities serving the people, but private

degree of enhancement, but comparison to previous (BP and SW) devices would become all but impossible to discern.

The Then Current 1989 IEC Standard

It is important to understand that the 1989 IEC Standard for ECT devices which would have become law via the proposed 1997 FDA adoption of IEC Standards generally, and which albeit furtively, had already doubled the output of first generation BP devices from 110 to circa 217 Joules (and with slight breaching, even higher), had only been officially adopted by the IEC (for European devices) eight years earlier, in 1989. In short, BP manufacturers, who under the auspices of Richard Weiner had lobbied the IEC for a number of years to adopt what was to become the European standard for ECT devices, had only succeeded as late as 1989, thereby in a manner of speaking, "legalizing" second generation BP devices, devices which had actually been in use internationally since about 1982. In brief, the 1989 adoption of the IEC standard for "ECT" devices had taken place more than six years following the actual manufacturing and marketing of the 200J plus second generation BP devices in use both in America and in Europe since about 1982. Despite these newer 200J plus outputs, moreover, the illusion of the 100J ceiling had remained implicit in both machine and standard, an appearance partly engendered though the featured "100J at 300Ω" phrase within the 1989 IEC Standard for ECT devices, partly through the featured "100J at 220Ω" phrase within the Mectan Transmutation of the 1982 APA Standard, and partly through deceptive reporting strategies of manufacturers themselves, not the least of which included circa 100J maximum machine readouts depicted on all second generation MECTA and Somatics BP devices. In fact, American made MECTA and Somatics second generation Brief Pulse devices were actually capable of 259 and 252 maximum joules respectively in America and between 226-240 maximum joules respectively in Europe. Manufacturers, in brief, had effectively maintained an illusory 100 Joule ceiling continuum from 1976 through to about 1995 (the inception date of 3rd generation BP devices as we shall soon see in detail). Manufacturers, therefore, had maintained the appearance of the circa 100J ceiling even while utilizing second generation BP devices from 1982 to 1995 with unreported ceilings of between 226 and 260 joules both nationally and internationally (Cameron, 1994). To be clear, the circa 100J ceiling (specifically 110J) reported for first generation U.S. BP devices made from 1976-1981 was actual, whereas the circa 100J ceiling reported or implied after 1982 (for what were actually second generation BP devices) was illusory. Both the "100J at 220Ω" Mectan Transmutation and the "100J at 300Ω" 1989 IEC Standard were newly (and surreptitiously) interpreted by manufacturers, as already noted, as unexplicated pure-ER/RRCs (based on maximum Impedance in lieu of a specific 100 or 110J ceiling), "permitting" much higher unreported outputs, in fact, circa 2.5 times first generation (i.e. the MECTA "C") outputs. The 1989 IEC Standard, then, while arguably "legalizing" second generation BP devices, nevertheless perpetuated a 100 Joule ceiling illusion in order to carry on the appearance of minimal stimulus outputs (at which almost all MRI "safety" studies had been performed). So successful was this ruse, that neither the unreported 216.6J maximum that manufacturer interpretation of the 1989 IEC standard actually "allowed," nor the unreported 260J ceiling American manufacturers administered in America through the Mectan Transmutation, nor the 226J maximum output made-in-America second generation IEC Brief Pulse devices actually emitted, have ever been identified by or revealed to any regulatory body on any continent in any corner of the world (Cameron, 1994). Manufacturers' conflation of the original 1982 APA Standard with the Mectan Transmutation and then with the later 1989 IEC Standard yet suggesting a continuous circa 100J ceiling, together with misleading reporting stratagems such as 100J machine readout maximums support the notion that both the Mectan Transmutation and the 1989 IEC Standard were designedly engineered by manufacturer-affiliated academics to project an illusory 100 Joule ceiling continuum from 1976 to about 1997 both in the United States and Eurasia. At the same time, manufacturers were able to covertly "legalize" second generation BP devices two and one half times more powerful than the 100J chimera both the American (1982 APA Standard) and the European (1989 IEC Standard) "standards" appeared to project. Typical of manufacturers and professional ECT proponents then, as late as 1992, Abrams, as can be seen in his statement below, along with several other manufacturer

---

non-profit associations whose main concern is the protection of its' membership. Such organizations rather than motivated in main to safeguard the public interest, are primarily committed to the de-regulation of medicine, in this instance, the avoidance of any regulation whatsoever.

affiliates, as noted, now began calling for what they were suggesting to be a "first time" doubling in power of Brief Pulse devices, falsely signifying that BP devices had up to that point remained limited to circa 100J ceilings, in short, falsely indicating that from 1976 to 1997, so-called Brief Pulse devices had, in effect, never increased in power.

"ECT" History--First, Second, and Third Tidal Waves of Fraud

Going back in time, the first tidal wave of fraud began in the late 1940s amidst the Sine Wave era with the rejection of the first Brief Pulse machines, the adoption of more powerful SW devices, and the false claim that Sine Wave devices used minimal stimulus when, in fact, such SW devices were not convulsive therapy devices at all, but rather Electro Neurotransmitter Reduction devices--apparatuses actually dependent upon adequate amounts of electricity rather than adequate convulsion.[37] Beginning about 1982, as noted earlier, the second great tidal wave of fraud [38] began within the "ECT" industry, this time amidst the resurgent Brief Pulse Era originating circa 1976. This second wave, commencing with the souping up of secret second generation Brief Pulse devices circa 1982, similarly, albeit secretly, turned convulsion oriented Brief Pulse apparatuses into electro-dependent Brief Pulse mechanisms. Finally, with manufacturers' 1997 opposition to and rejection of the 1989 IEC standard for ECT devices, a third major tidal wave began, covering up even more souped-up, more powerful, unreported third generation Brief Pulse devices, in fact, doubling the output of never reported second generation Brief Pulse devices which had already doubled first generation BP devices. The power of both second and third generation BP devices had to be hidden in that these are clearly electro-dependent and so clearly no longer "ECT" devices at all. Allegedly a first time enhancement to accommodate the purported need for a 4.0 fold suprathreshold dosage requirement for so-called "dose-sensitive" UL "ECT" in order that UL ECT would continue to be administered at a "requisite" 2.0 fold threshold output even at the end of a treatment series led, in 1997, to what are actually third generation BP devices introduced as second generation BP devices to "newly" address a "problem" already addressed circa 1982. Indeed, as noted above, the alleged enhancement for UL "ECT" (and the alleged doubling of Impedance over a “treatment” series) had already been accommodated by the first major enhancement in 1982 of which, unfortunately, none but manufacturers were aware. Because the first major enhancement had been secreted, the same call for the same reasons began to be repeated between 1991 and 1996, again to "accommodate" UL "ECT," but also to accommodate the alleged 2.0 fold initial threshold output "required" for BL ECT due to the an alleged twofold threshold increase over a "treatment" series. In this way, "dose-sensitive" UL "ECT" could remain at least two fold threshold even at the end of treatment series while BL "ECT" could remain just above threshold even at the end of a "treatment" course. Unbeknownst to regulators, of course, the hypothetical UL anomaly allegedly "requiring" two fold threshold even at the end of a treatment course, and the initial two-fold threshold "requirement" for BL "ECT" in order to remain just above threshold even at the end of a "treatment" course had already been utilized by the unreported 1982 enhancement facilitating never properly reported second generation Brief Pulse devices. Because Brief Pulse, as late as 1997, was yet thought to be administered at about 100 maximum joules, or just above threshold with BL "ECT" and so twice threshold with UL "ECT" (which required only half the output of BL to overcome seizure threshold), the UL "dose-sensitive" anomaly in conjunction with the alleged doubling of threshold over a “treatment” course theory, continued to serve as the 1991-1997 rationale for what was yet touted to be a "first time call" for Brief Pulse power enhancement. In fact, as we shall eventually see, much more powerful third generation BP devices marketed since at least 1995, emitting twice the power of second generation BP devices, were already emitting an unreported initial circa 5.0 MTTLOI with BL "ECT" and an initial circa 10.0 MTTLOI with UL "ECT" in all age categories. In short, by 1995, the second major power enhancement of extant third generation Brief Pulse devices had already doubled the power and so doubled the MTTLOI of never properly reported second generation Brief Pulse devices manufactured circa 1982. Third generation machines secretly marketed in 1995, in sum, had already more

[37] There is reason to believe that SW devices cannot be set even at minimal stimulus for SW. The evidence is in the B-25 Brief Pulse device which cannot be set for minimal stimulus in the younger age categories. Indeed, the B-25 may have been made in the image of the B-24 SW device.

[38] The first great wave occurred when SW manufacturers such as Medcraft rejected early BP devices for more powerful SW devices while still claiming to administer “ECT” at minimal stimulus.

than quadrupled first generation BP devices both in power and MTTLOI for each individual recipient with both UL and BL "ECT." [39] Simply put, Brief Pulse manufacturers MECTA and Somatics were desperate to "legalize" already extant, albeit unreported third generation Brief Pulse devices manufactured and in use since about 1995. Moreover, they needed to hide the power of these devices in that the machines were clearly based on adequate amounts of electricity, indeed, doubling the output required for both the so-called UL "dose-sensitive" anomaly as well as doubling that required for the purported doubling of Impedance over a "treatment" course. Ultimately then, both MECTA and Somatics together had successfully concealed the initial 1982 doubling of Brief Pulse power through publications by their manufacturer-affiliated academics in conjunction with misleading and spurious reporting, including blatantly spurious machine readouts on both MECTA and Somatics second generation BP devices. In short, MECTA and Somatics worked together to conceal the 1982 power enhancement facilitating initial circa 2.5 and 5.0 fold threshold outputs with both BL and UL "ECT" respectively in a first attempt to make the treatment "effective." The cover-up, of course, was motivated by the simple desire to conceal what manufactures had known or should have known for at least sixty years at that time, the detail that convulsion by and of itself has little to no therapeutic value and that in order for the devices to be effectual, Brief Pulse manufacturers both in 1982 (and again in 1995) had been forced to enhance their Brief Pulse devices electrically, surpassing the raw power of SW in almost every age category. Clearly recognizing the need for suprathreshold electrical dosing at least as powerful as the B-24 SW for both BL and UL "ECT" in order to make the procedure "work," manufacturers had been compelled to conceal this critical information in order to circumvent FDA scrutiny and to retain Brief Pulse's critically important reputation as a reduced output device. Moreover, they hid the power in order to protect convulsion theory, generally.

Having successfully survived the FDA investigation between 1976 and 1982 by introducing the 108J MECTA "C" BP device in accordance with the 1982 APA Standard stipulating 110 maximum joules, manufacturers had become anxious to avoid the threat of further inquiry with respect to second and the even greater increase in electrical output with third generation BP devices. Specifically, manufacturers wanted to avoid the benefit-risk analysis of the grossly enhanced output required for “efficacy”; in short, manufacturers sought to circumvent FDA criteria for approval of the later "ECT" devices by hiding the need for unacceptably high electrical outputs which manufacturers knew full well to be brain damaging. To this end, as stated above, both MECTA and Somatics simply covered up the increased power of what were actually second generation Brief Pulse devices as if the original doubling in power had never occurred. As noted earlier, they did this through both the misleading Mectan Transmutation and a similarly corrupt interpretation of the 1989 IEC Standard. As such, manufacturers were able to continue marketing their Brief Pulse devices as a major improvement over SW just as FDA expected. Indeed, based on the 1982 APA Standard condoned by both the FDA and the Utah Biomedical Test Laboratory, the FDA had stipulated "ECT" devices be not only as "effective" as SW, but "safer" than SW by virtue of greatly reduced output. [40] Simply put, the benefit of "ECT" had to outweigh the risk of electrical morbidity, a feat supposedly accomplished with the reintroduction of Brief Pulse in accordance with the 1982 APA Standard. In spite of later claims of what would be "dose sensitivity" and alleged "doubling of Impedance over a ‘treatment’ series,” therefore, during the first and foremost investigation of the "ECT device" itself from 1976 to 1982, Weiner, clearly asserted to the FDA within the 1982 APA Standard which he himself had composed:

---

[39] Manufacturers hid the power of souped up second generation BP devices in order to maintain the illusion that BP was far less powerful and, therefore, safer than SW. Souped up third generation BP devices which made their appearance about 1995, emerged far enough away time-wise from the original BP comparisons to SW that these initial comparisons had been forgotten along with the original intent of Brief Pulse. Moreover, the transition from EO in Joules (by which Weiner had compared the original Medcraft B-24 SW with the MECTA “C” Brief Pulse in 1982) to Charge in Millicoulombs (also by Weiner) now veiled comparative efforts insuring public amnesia of those original critical comparisons.

[40] With Abrams and Sackeim's statements regarding the suggested equivalence of 100 Joules with 500mC and the false intimation of continued minimal stimulus with BL ECT, we glean what may have been a conspiratorial arrangement between MECTA and Somatics to cover up the 1982-3 doubling in power of BP devices facilitated by both companies. Both surpassed the B-24 SW in power and both violated the original APA standard resulting in a corruption of the standard which the author deems the “Mectan Transmutation.” Both manufacturers continued to deceive the American people into believing that the newer (second generation) BP “ECT” machines were “safer and gentler” than SW.

> Using a pulse device, the [1978 APA] Task Force has determined that only 0.6% of seizure thresholds were greater than 70 [actual] Joules and that none were greater than 100 [41] Joules. (Department of Health and Human Services, 1982a, p. A53) [42]

In short, Weiner clearly asserted to the FDA that 100 joules would be the maximum electrical "dosage" ever needed for even the most seizure recalcitrant recipient even at the end of a treatment course, a promise which contained the heart of the 1982 APA Standard itself, the only standard approved by both Utah and the FDA, ensuring that no Brief Pulse device would ever surpass 110 maximum joules, circa half the maximum output of SW. Moreover, it was this pledge incorporated into the heart of the 1982 APA Standard which at the close of the investigation in 1982, convinced FDA to allow the continuation of the procedure into the future in spite of tens of thousands of long term memory complaints. Not surprisingly then, manufacturers covered up the first power enhancement via second generation BP devices leading to the second cover up of third generation BP devices in that manufacturers knew these devices violated all three precepts--minimal stimulus induced seizures, reduced power compared to SW, and the 1982 APA Standard. Moreover, while one power enhancement could be justified with the alleged requirement of just above seizure threshold with BL "ECT" at the end of a "treatment" course and double the threshold with UL "ECT" at the end of a "treatment" course, a second power enhancement, quadrupling the power of the MECTA "C" could not. Indeed, quadrupling the output meant two times threshold with BL "ECT" at the end of a "treatment" course and quadruple the threshold with UL "ECT" at the end of a "treatment" course, destroying the "dose-sensitive" anomaly with UL alone compared to BL "ECT" which was supposed to effective at just above seizure threshold. The quadrupling of output clearly threatened to reveal an electro-dependent as opposed to a seizure dependent procedure. SW, of course, had run its course, having at last been acknowledged as heavily contributing to memory dysfunction and even brain disablement by virtue of its "twice-fold" output compared to Brief Pulse. Indeed, though SW was never officially banned, the preferred device via the 1982 APA Standard condoned by the FDA, had clearly been the "new and improved" Brief Pulse device by virtue of "reduced output" compared to SW. Indeed, successful marketing of Brief Pulse depended upon "reduced output" or at least the Illusion of it.

---

[41] The MECTA "C" clearly emitted an actual 108 maximum Joules. When manufacturers souped up BP devices, they began transitioning from actual EO reporting to the reporting of average outputs and then ER outputs based upon ER Impedance. The result was gross underreporting of actual EO ceilings and the false impression that no power enhancement had taken place from 1976 to at least 1997 (see Cameron, 1994). To further discourage comparison, manufacturers finally transition to Charge reporting alone, dropping EO altogether as we shall see.

[42] The author believes this statement, asserted by Weiner to the FDA during the investigative period, and fully the heart of the 1982 APA Standard, is true. In short, no more than 100 joules is ever needed to adequately seize even the oldest, most seizure recalcitrant recipient, even at the end of a treatment series. Indeed, the author is convinced that 100 joules is liberally construed and in most cases, much less output in required.

SECTION IX: Conspiracy

CHAPTER 54

Somatics' Richard Abrams Calls for a "First Time" Power Enhancement

Following a 1991 MECTA based experiment, in 1992, psychiatrist Richard Abrams, founder of Somatics Incorporated, [43] warned:

> Our results (Abrams, Swartz, and Vedak 1991) clearly do not support the call for higher-powered ECT devices that are capable of administering several times the maximum stimulus dose for ECT now permitted by the International Electrotechnical Commission (Sackeim, 1991a, b; Sackeim et al, 1991). Dissatisfied with the limited therapeutic effects they [44] achieved with what is essentially a 1-second stimulus duration, these authors [Sackeim et al., 1991, pp. 233-234] administered a 1792 mC[45] bilateral ECT stimulus to an elderly man who had a seizure threshold of 672 mC . . . , and further asserted their conviction that to achieve a comparable clinical efficacy with bilateral ECT, right unilateral ECT will have to be given at a stimulus dose that is 5.5 times seizure threshold.

---

[43] Abrams is one of a handful of American psychiatrists closely affiliated with manufacturers who have influenced the public's image of "ECT," falsely intimating that such devices are less powerful than SW. Before exposure that Abrams owned Somatics Incorporated, the company responsible for manufacturing the Thymatron DG and Thymatron DGx, Abram's articles were the most heavily quoted of the 1990 APA Task Force Report on ECT. A USA Today article exposed the fact that Oxford University Press, publisher of his book, *Electroconvulsive therapy* (Abrams, 1982; 1988) were unaware he owned the company. His book was and may be yet prolifically utilized in medical schools within the U.S. and abroad.

[44] Harold Sackeim has close ties to MECTA (Cameron, 1994; MECTA Corporation, 1987). Thus, Abram's statements criticizing Sackeim's study might be seen as one competing manufacturer (Somatics) criticizing another (MECTA). In a moment we shall see how these two warring entities ultimately appear to agree.

[45] Only an experimental device could have delivered a 1792mC charge at this point, i.e. the ElCot MF-1000, the Neurotronics 068-100/200, or an experimental version of then currently manufactured BP devices (Sackeim, 1991, p. 234). Note that the purported Charge is approximately two and one half times Charge threshold for BL "ECT" (1792 mC ÷ 672 mC = 2.667) and that 5.5 times threshold is reserved for UL ECT. The Energy Output for these procedures might be estimated on the Elcot device at more than 800 Joules (1 Ampere x 200 pulses x .002 pulse width x 4 seconds = 1600 mC x 500 Volts = 800 Joules). EO on the 068-100/200 cannot be estimated in that the Designers refused to divulge Voltage (Ibid).

> [. . .] [46] [47] [48] The clinical justification for such mega-stimuli is obscure, considering that excellent clinical responses to right unilateral ECT can routinely be obtained well within accepted dosage safety limits simply by administering fixed-high-dose stimuli of longer duration. (Abrams, 1992, p. 115)

Four years later, in 1996, however, just before the proposed FDA adoption of all IEC standards for medical devices, but shortly after Somatics had begun marketing a new third generation BP device of its own, Abrams changed his tune. Somatics, via its founder Richard Abrams, now joined MECTA in calling for a revised IEC standard with increased electrical parameters. Abrams now complained:

> [A]n energy limitation is imposed on modern ECT devices by the International Electrotechnical Commission (IEC) [49] and the Food and Drug Administration (FDA) [50] of 100 Joules at 220 Ohms impedance, or about 500mC of charge, which simply does not permit giving the doses of 2.5 to 5 times threshold that are required to treat many patients when administering unilateral ECT. (Abrams, 1996, p. 703)

Richard Abrams, owner of Somatics Incorporated, is not only carping here about the so-called 1989 IEC constraints with respect to "ECT," [51] but has clearly identified the 1982 APA Standard with the 1989 IEC Standard, implying that both standards limited output to the same circa 100 maximum joules. Indeed, the 1982 APA Standard, which manufacturers had clearly ignored, did indeed limit output to 110 maximum joules, whereas, the 1989 IEC Standard, had surreptitiously increased output to 217 joules, twice that of the APA Standard. Moreover, both MECTA and Somatics breached the standard, secretly utilizing up to 240 joules. Like Weiner, who has represented all American manufacturers before the FDA and Sackeim who is an affiliate of MECTA, Abrams appears to be participating in what had now become a common manufacturer stratagem. First, as noted, Abrams identifies both (the 1982 APA and the 1989 IEC) standards as similar in scope, thereby implying both limit output to circa "100 Joules," [52] so that the phrase "100J at 220Ω" used in the Mectan Transmutation and the "100J at 300Ω" used in the 1989 IEC Standard appear, like the original 1982 APA Standard, to contain conditional-ER/RRCs. That is, the latter two, like the 1982 APA Standard, falsely appear to be limited to a circa 100J overall ceiling which Abrams then equates with a circa 500mC Charge. The

---

[46] Abrams goes on to say: "This would have required administering a 3696 mC stimulus charge to their elderly high-threshold patient, or more than 7 times the maximum output of any U.S. or foreign ECT device. 3697 ÷ 7 = 528mC, about that of second generation BP devices. However, Abrams' 3697mC configuration regarding UL ECT is incorrect. UL threshold output is about one half that of BL ECT. As such, the 1792mC Charge would remain the same for both BL and UL ECT regardless of the disparity in multifold threshold. [2.667 fold threshold for BL ECT x 2 = 5.334 fold threshold for UL ECT; 5.334 x 336mC (half the threshold of BL ECT) = the same 1792mC.] The practice of doubling titration for UL ECT which requires half the output of BL ECT to reach threshold, is convenient for manufacturers in that they have no need to reset their devices to accommodate so-called "dose-sensitive" UL ECT.

[47] The call for more machine power to accommodate an atypically high individual threshold is typical of the "exceptional case" scenario, one of the rationale's used by manufacturers to justify universal enhancement of machines. In fact, the enhanced power is actually used to deliver multifold threshold dosages for every individual recipient.

[48] The 1792mC mentioned in the Sackeim study--more than three times the Charge maximum of second generation BP devices manufactured between 1983-1994 (500mC), is not too far removed from the maximum Charge delivered by current third generation BP machines capable of emitting 1200mC of Charge as we shall see (International Electrotechnical Commission, 1997, Dec 26; Royal College of Psychiatry, 1995, pp. 124-125).

[49] This refers to the 1989 IEC Standard 601-2-14 (International Electrotechnical Commission, 1989, p. 23).

[50] This refers to the 1982 APA STANDARD within Weiner's Petition to Reclassify (Department of Health and Human Services, 1982a, p. E20).

[51] It should be pointed out that the "100 Joules at 220 Ohms" mentioned by Abrams is interpreted as a pure-ER from which both the 1989 IEC Standard and the transmuted 1982 APA Standard were surreptitiously interpreted by manufacturers to permit between circa 230 and circa 260 Joules respectively. In short, Abrams and others who parrot each other, are here calling for third generation BP devices, devices not merely greater than 100J, or even the double of 100J, but devices doubling second generation outputs already emitting between 230 and 260 Joules. Third generation BP devices, as we shall see are capable of emitting up to circa 500 Joules of energy output.

[52] We must remember that the second generation BP devices Abrams' company manufacturers and to which he is referring display machine readouts of 99.4 maximum joules.

implication of a circa 100J ceiling is further strengthened by the fact that only a circa 100J ceiling could disallow the 2.5 to 5.0 MTTLOI with UL "ECT" Abrams claims manufacturers need. Indeed, the 110J ceiling of the original 1982 APA Standard limits output to an initial 1.1 MTTLOI with BL "ECT" or just above threshold output, and, by implication, an initial 2.2 MTTLOI with UL ECT, exactly as the 1982 APA Standard intended. Indeed, only the "MECTA C" conformed to the 1982 APA Standard, a machine which, by 1996, had long ago been replaced by never clearly reported second generation BP devices. Plainly, Abrams' 1996 call for an enhancement to boost output to between 2.5 and 5.0 fold threshold output with UL "ECT" is disingenuous, in that we now know that extant second generation BP devices (including Abram's own Thymatron DGx and Thymatron DG manufactured beginning about 1983) had already been emitting between 230 to 260J respectively for some 13 years before Abram's call. Indeed, Somatics' second generation machines already facilitated a 4.6 to 5.2 initial MTTLOI with UL "ECT" and so a 2.3 to 2.6 MTTLOI with the same UL "ECT" even assuming doubling of Impedance at the end of a "treatment" course.

Not only could Abrams' own second generation BP devices already emit the circa 2.5 to 5.0 MTTLOI Abrams is calling for in 1996 then, but first generation BP devices are not associated with a 500mC Charge maximum. Instead, it is Abram's own second generation BP devices which emit 500mC of Charge. Both Abram's Thymatron DG and his Thymatron DGx, already in existence at the time of Abram's comment, utilized a .001 second pulse width, .9A, 140 maximum pulses, and a 4.0 second maximum Duration from which can be derived the circa 500mC Charge maximum to which Abrams refers. (Charge = Current x (Hz x 2) x Wave Length or Pulse Width x Duration: .9A x 140 pulses x .001Sec. x 4.0 Seconds = .504C.) In short, 500mC does not correspond to the 100 or 110 joules stipulated by the 1982 APA Standard; neither does 500mC reflect first generation BP devices such as the MECTA "C" which emitted a maximum Charge of about 320mC. Rather circa 500mC is reflective of the much higher energy outputs (circa 252 and 227J respectively) of Abrams' own second generation Thymatron DG and DGx BP devices. Clearly, Abrams, like Sackeim and Weiner, is pretending second generation BP devices had never been manufactured, machines his own company had been making since circa 1983.

Indeed, Abrams' call for new Brief Pulse machines which can elicit between a 2.5 and a 5.0 MTTLOI with UL "ECT" is based on two half-truths also exploited by MECTA. The first half-truth is that UL "ECT" is "dose-sensitive" so that it must always be administered at twice threshold to be effective; the second half-truth is that Impedance may double over a treatment series. In short, Abrams is suggesting that UL "ECT" must be administered at an initial 5.0 MTTLOI so that at the end of a treatment series (after Impedance has allegedly doubled), UL is still effective at more than twice threshold, both assertions of which appear doubtful upon close examination. But even if we accept Abrams half-truths, Abrams call for increased Brief Pulse power to accomplish that which had already been accomplished with second generation BP devices is simply disingenuous.

The simplest way of exposing the duplicity of Abrams' quest to double the power of Brief Pulse machines in order to accommodate UL "ECT" (sensitivity), is simple extrapolation. Since an "adequate" seizure can be induced with UL "ECT" with only half the output needed to induce an "adequate seizure" with BL "ECT," the same electrical dosage which elicits an initial 5.0 MTTLOI with UL "ECT" must elicit an initial (5.0 ÷ 2 =) 2.5 MTTLOI with BL "ECT." Moreover, if Impedance really doubles over a treatment series, the same electrical dosage used to elicit a 2.5 MTTLOI at the end of a "treatment series with UL "ECT" must elicit a (2.5 ÷ 2 =) 1.25 MTTLOI with BL "ECT" at the end of a treatment series. BL "ECT," remember, unlike UL "ECT", is allegedly effective at just above threshold, that is, it is allegedly not "dose-sensitive." Thus, using the same electrical dosage for both UL and BL "ECT" (as manufacturers do) we can see that Abrams is actually calling for a standard allowing enough power for a Brief Pulse device to administer an initial 2.5 MTTLOI with BL "ECT" and so at least a 1.25 MTTLOI with BL "ECT" at the end of a "treatment" course.

Abrams' own second generation made-for-America Thymatron DG elicits 252 maximum joules. Thus, in 1996, the year Abrams calls for more powerful Brief Pulse machines to accommodate UL "ECT" dose "sensitivity," Abram's Thymatron DG had already been administering an initial default (252J ÷ 100J =) 2.52 MTTLOI output for all age categories with BL "ECT" since 1983, and so a default 1.25 MTTLOI for all age categories with the same BL "ECT" even at the end of a treatment series. This means the then thirteen year old Thymatron DG was already emitting an initial (252J ÷ 50J =) 5.04 MTTLOI default output for all age categories with UL "ECT" and at least a 2.5 MTTLOI default output for all age categories with the same UL "ECT" even at the end of a “treatment” series. Moreover, Abrams' second generation Thymatron DGx IEC BP device used in Europe since about 1983, already "legal" under the 1989 IEC Standard (a facsimile of the corrupt

Mectan Transmutation), was eliciting an initial default (226J ÷ 100J =) 2.26 MTTLOI for all age categories with BL "ECT" and so at least a 1.13 MTTLOI even at the end of "treatment" series. This means that Abram's DGx was already emitting an initial default (226J ÷ 50J =) 4.52 MTTLOI in all age categories with UL "ECT" and so a (4.52 ÷ 2 =) 2.26 MTTLOI in all age categories even at the end of a "treatment" series. In brief, even if UL "ECT" is "dose-sensitive" as is the claim, and even if Impedance allegedly does double over a "treatment" series, Abram's own second generation BP devices would have already fulfilled this criteria. In short, there would be no need to enhance the 1989 IEC Standard interpreted as a Pure-ER/RRC (as manufacturers did) with a new standard in order to compensate for "dose sensitive" UL "ECT." In turn, there would be no need to enhance the power of Abrams' own (second generation) Brief Pulse devices in that these devices would have already fulfilled Abrams,' Sackeim's, and Weiner's alleged justifications for enhanced power.

Abrams' statement that:

> [A]n energy limitation is imposed on modern ECT devices by the International Electrotechnical Commission (IEC)[53] and the Food and Drug Administration (FDA) [APA Standard][54] of 100 Joules at 220 Ohms impedance, or about 500mC of charge, which simply does not permit giving the doses of 2.5 to 5 times threshold that are required to treat many patients when administering unilateral ECT. (Abrams, 1996, p. 703)

is true only if we interpret the "100J at 220Ω" phrase within the Mectan Transmutation as a conditional ER/RRC, that is, if we interpret the phrase as limiting maximum output to 100 or even 110J according to the original 1982 APA Standard to which only the first generation MECTA "C" conformed. With respect to the MECTA "C," however, the Charge maximum is much less than 500mC as noted--indeed about 320mC. What Abrams and others are not disclosing is that manufacturers such as Somatics and MECTA, around 1982, corrupted the newer "100J at 220Ω" phrase by re-interpreting it as a pure-ER/RRC (the Mectan Transmutation) in lieu of the conditional-ER/RRC (within the 1982 APA Standard), thereby theoretically permitting up to a never before reported (100J/220Ω = X̲J/600Ω; X =) 273J maximum in the U.S. In short, by suggesting that machines need to increase in power to deliver a 5.0 to a 2.5 MTTLOI with UL "ECT," tantamount to a 2.5 to 1.25 MTTLOI with BL "ECT," Abrams is falsely suggesting that either all Brief Pulse devices up to that point were yet confined to 100 or 110 maximum joules emissive of an initial 1.1 MTTLOI maximum with BL ECT and an initial 2.2 MTTLOI maximum with UL ECT or that second generation BP devices which more than doubled that power (under the Mectan Transmutation) had never been invented. Like Weiner and Sackeim, Abrams is clearly suggesting that by 1996, all extant Brief Pulse devices emitted minimal stimulus outputs only.

In reality, at the time of his statement, Abram's second generation made-for-America Thymatron DG and made-for-Europe DGx, each based on the Mectan Transmutation, already emitted a default maximum Charge of 504mC and unreported 252 and 227 joule maximums respectively. Similarly, MECTA second generation made-for America and made-for Europe BP devices, also already in existence at this time, emitted about 576mC Charge maximums while emitting unreported 256 and 230 joule maximums respectively. What the Abrams statement does not clarify then, along with numerous other manufacturer related reports equating "100J at 220Ω" with a circa 500mC Charge maximum (for what are actually second generation BP devices) is that, the circa 500mC maximum Charge (of second generation BP devices) is not equivalent to the 110 Joule maximum depicted within the original 1982 APA Standard, but to new transmutational never reported maximums of between 227 and 259 unreported joules. This is in spite of the fact that all four American made second generation Brief Pulse machines (the Somatics' DG and DGx, the MECTA JR/SR 1 and 2) continued to depict circa 100J maximum machine readouts on the devices themselves. In sum, at the moment of Abrams 1996 call for a more liberal IEC standard allowing for more powerful devices, what were actually second generation BP devices, were already emitting more than twice the power of first generation BP devices and had been doing so since about 1982 or 1983. The MECTA "C," which indeed, was in compliance with the 110J ceiling of the 1982 APA Standard, had by Abrams' announcement, as noted, long been abandoned. In other words, at the point in time of Abrams 1996 call for doubling the power of first generation BP devices, second

---

53 This refers to the 1989 IEC Standard 601-2-14 (International Electrotechnical Commission, 1989, p. 23).

54 This refers to the 1982 APA STANDARD within Weiner's Petition to Reclassify (Department of Health and Human Services, 1982a, p. E20).

generation BP devices, though not reported as such, had already been surpassing 200J SW machines in raw power for some 14 or 15 years. In total, extant second generation BP devices were already emitting the 2.5 to 5.0 MTTLOIs with UL "ECT" that Abrams was now calling for. Indeed, manufacturer interpretation of the 1989 IEC Standard as a Pure-ER/RRC, had already "permitted" these "called for" outputs. What Abrams and other manufacturers were actually calling for in 1996, then, was a new IEC standard which would encompass the much greater power of what were, in fact, already extant third generation BP devices, as we will eventually observe, machines not allowed even under the corrupted 1989 IEC Standard.

Thus, while Abram's statement gives the impression that, like the original 1982 APA Standard, both the Mectan Transmutation and the 1989 IEC Standard contain a "100J at 220Ω" conditional-ER/RRC, confining output to a 110J or 100J ceiling, manufacturers never interpreted them as such. In fact, it was with the introduction of Abrams' second generation souped-up Somatics' Thymatron DG in 1983, capable of an unreported 252 maximum Joules (Cameron, 1994) in conjunction with the other major American manufacturer--MECTA Corporation, that Somatics Incorporated and MECTA began conspiratorially reinterpreting the 1982 APA standard as a "100 at 220Ω" pure-ER/RRC, altogether dropping the original 110J ceiling.[55]

In summation, second generation BP devices, including Abrams' Thymatron DG, had already been eliciting initial (circa) 2.5 fold threshold outputs with BL "ECT" and initial (circa) 5.0 fold threshold outputs with UL "ECT" since about 1983. Thus. manufacturers' (i.e. Abrams' Somatics' Incorporated) demand for a "first time" enhancement was really a call for a second enhancement more than quadrupling EO as we shall soon see in detail. In essence, the doubling of power around 1982 (in America) and 1989 (in Europe) had not only gone unreported but had been thoroughly covered up.

Somatics'--A Few More Specifics of Abrams' Call for more Powerful Brief Pulse Machines

First, note Abrams' "100J at 220Ω" depiction of both the 1982 APA and 1989 IEC Standards:

> [A]n energy limitation is imposed on modern ECT devices by the International Electrotechnical Commission (IEC) [56] and the Food and Drug Administration (FDA) [APA Standard] [57] of 100 Joules at 220 Ohms impedance . . .." (Abrams, 1996, p. 703)

As such, Abrams co-mingles the "100J at 220Ω" transmutational depiction of the 1982 APA Standard (re-interpreted by American manufacturers via the Mectan Transmutation) with the "100J at 300Ω" phrase found within the 1989 IEC Standard to depict the power of second generation BP devices from 1982 to 1994.[58] This conflation of the "100J at 220Ω" phrase reported via the Mectan Transmutation with the "100J at 300Ω" phrase reported via the 1989 IEC Standard is suggestive of the original 110 Joule ceiling clearly depicted within the original 1982 APA Standard, implying the 1982 APA Standard and 1989 IEC standards synonymous. In other words, both standards appeared to limit Brief Pulse devices to the same circa 110 Joule ceiling depicted within 1982 APA Standard. In fact, neither the Mectan Transmutation nor the 1989 IEC Standard limited outputs to 100 or even 110J. Consequently, while Abram's statement gives the impression that, like the original 1982 APA Standard, both the Mectan Transmutation and the 1989 IEC Standard contain a "100J at 220Ω" conditional-ER/RRC, confining output to a circa 100J ceiling, neither, of course, do. Indeed, as noted earlier, it was with the introduction of Abrams' second generation souped-up Somatics' Thymatron DG in 1983, capable of a never reported 252 maximum Joules (Cameron, 1994), that Somatics Incorporated, in conjunction with the other major American manufacturer, MECTA Corporation, began conspiratorially reinterpreting the 1982 APA

---

[55] The suggestion is a Conditional ER/RRC, meaning a 100 or 110J maximum like the 1982 APA Standard or the EO can be based upon an "average" 220 Ohms resistance in all cases, regardless of much higher actual resistances, the result of which is yet a 100 Joule <u>average</u>. In fact, the actual maximum output, 252 Joules, has never been reported (Cameron, 1994).

[56] This refers to the 1989 IEC Standard 601-2-14 (International Electrotechnical Commission, 1989, p. 23).

[57] This refers to the 1982 APA Standard within Weiner's Petition to Reclassify (Department of Health and Human Services, 1982a, p. E20).

[58] The APA Standard actually reads "70J at 220Ω" with 110J ceiling.

standard as a "100 at 220Ω" pure-ER/RRC (the Mectan Transmutation), altogether dropping the original 110J ceiling. [59]

Moreover, it was with this transmutation, that both Somatics and MECTA totally stopped reporting actual EO ceilings (in joules), reporting instead, only the phrase, "100J at 220Ω" (in America). The third extant American BP manufacturer, Medcraft, also reported a simple "100J at 220" phrase (though interpreting it much differently as has been heretofore explained). Certainly, as noted elsewhere, "100J at 220Ω" is the APA transmutational equivalent of the hidden "130J at 300Ω" phrase [60] derivatively subsumed within the 1989 IEC standard, both phrases of which manufacturers furtively and illicitly interpreted as Pure-ER/RRCs. This interpretation, of course facilitated new, but never reported 273J (Mectan transmutation) and 217J (1989 IEC Standard) maximums respectively. Thus, it was the "100J at 220Ω" Mectan Transmutation, a corruption of the original 1982 APA Standard which was used to more than double the output of first generation made-for-America machines in America resulting in second generation BP devices manufactured between 1982 and 1994. Specifically, these second generation BP machines were manufactured by Somatics Incorporated (Abrams' company), and MECTA Corporation, as well as a third, now defunct American BP manufacturer, Elcot. Indeed, it was the "Mectan Transmutation" which was used to "justify" and cover up what were actually made-for-America second generation BP devices newly eliciting up to 260 unreported joules.[61]

At the same time, the phrase "100J at 220Ω" (as noted elsewhere) continued to suggest the circa 100J ceiling (specifically 110J) depicted within the original 1982 APA Standard generally adhered to in America between 1976 and 1982 for first generation Brief Pulse machines (Cameron, 1994), machines presented to the FDA during its investigation of "ECT" between 1976 and 1982.[62] Moreover, it was the 1989 IEC Standard (for ECT devices) featuring the "100J at 300Ω" facsimile of the 1982 American transmutation ("100J at 220Ω") also interpreted as a pure-ER/RRC which was used and, in fact, stretched to justify the use of American made, second generation BP devices in Europe newly eliciting up to 240 unreported joules. In spite of this increase in power both in Europe and America, however, the "100J at 300Ω" IEC Standard, like the "100J at 220Ω" Mectan Transmutation, continued to intimate the 110J ceiling stipulation found within the original 1982 APA Standard, thereby, keeping alive the illusion of circa 100J Brief Pulse devices. That this illusion was deliberate, is supported by American made second generation BP devices both in Europe and America falsely depicting machine readout maximums of circa 100 maximum joules. Succinctly, the first doubling of machine power around 1982 and 1983 remained clandestine. Indeed, as previously noted, second generation BP devices, including Abrams' Thymatron DG, had already been eliciting 2.5 fold threshold outputs or a 2.5 MTTLOI with BL "ECT" and 5.0 fold threshold outputs or a 5.0 MTTLOI with UL "ECT" for all age categories since at least 1983. The point is, manufacturers' call for a "first time" enhancement (i.e. Somatics' in 1996), was really a call for a second-time enhancement, more than quadrupling EO (compared to the 1982 APA Standard of a 110J ceiling) purely in order to "legalize" third generation BP devices as we shall see in a moment.

Somatics'--A Few More Specifics of Abrams' Call for more Powerful Brief Pulse Machines Continued

Now let us examine only once more, Abram's 1996 implication (typical of manufacturers) that the newly reported "100J at 220Ω" phrase circa 1982 was a conditional ER/RRC limiting output to between 100 and 110 Joules "equivalent" to a circa 500mC Charge. Abrams states:

---

[59] The "average" EO is based upon an "average" 220 Ohms resistance in all cases, regardless of much higher actual resistances. The result is a 100 Joule <u>average</u>. The actual maximum, 252 Joules, has never been reported (Cameron, 1994).

[60] The inconspicuous "130J at 300Ω" IEC Standard was actually breached and stretched into a 136J at 300Ω pure-ER/RRC equivalent to the "100J at 220Ω" Mectan transmutation (100J/220Ω = XJ/300Ω. X = 136J).

[61] The transmutation allowed up to 273J, from which the machines used up to 260J.

[62] Beginning in 1982, American manufacturers switched from reporting an absolute 110 Joule ceiling to 100J based upon an "average" 220 ohms, thus reporting a 100 Joule "average" allowing up to 200J. A little later, based on a pure-ER/RRC interpretation of "100J at 220Ω" (100J/220Ω = 273J/600Ω), American made devices manufactured between 1983 and 1994 could deliver up to 260 Joules of EO (Cameron, 1994).

> [A]n energy limitation is imposed on modern ECT devices by the International Electrotechnical Commission (IEC)[63] and the Food and Drug Administration (FDA) [APA Standard] [64] of 100 Joules at 220 Ohms impedance or about 500mC of charge. (Abrams, 1996, p. 703)

Note how Abrams' has switched the conditional-ER/RRC of " '70J at 220Ω' with 110J ceiling" comprising the original 1982 APA Standard (Department of Health and Human Services, 1982a, E20) to "100J at 220Ω" with no mention of a 110J ceiling. Indeed, Abrams never mentions that the 110J ceiling has been dropped in the newer (at that time) Mectan Transmutation description of simply "100 Joules at 220Ω." Briefly, Abrams' Somatics Inc., like MECTA, is utilizing the corrupt Mectan Transmutation which via a Pure-ER/RRC (as opposed to a Conditional-ER/RRC) interpretation, secretly "allowed" his Somatics' Thymatron DG to deliver up to a never reported (100J/220Ω = XJ/555.5Ω; X =) 252J ceiling. Abrams then equates "100 Joules at 220" (implying a 100J ceiling, but which is actually an unreported 252J ceiling) with ". . . about 500mC of charge" (Abrams, 1996, p. 703).

In order to fully appreciate this misleading equivalency, we must reiterate that by 1983, the seemingly familiar, but newly interpreted transmutational phrase "100 Joules at 220 Ohms" was no longer construed by American manufacturers as the anticipated conditional-ER/RRC based on a 100 or 110J ceiling (like that utilized in the 1982 APA standard), but had been transmuted by manufacturers to a Pure-ER/RRC based on no adjunctive EO ceiling at all (i.e. 110J), but rather on each machine's maximum Impedance (i.e. 555.5Ω), an interpretation referred to in this manuscript as "the Mectan Transmutation." In short, the misleading "100J at 220Ω" phrase no longer limited output to a 100 or 110J ceiling as did the original "70J at 220Ω" phrase. Instead the general ceiling became limited only by the APA's 600Ω maximum Impedance, tantamount to a new and never before reported 273J ceiling for American made, made-for-America second generation BP devices (100J/220Ω = XJ/600Ω =) 273. Specifically, the ceiling depended on whatever the maximum machine Impedance happened to be up to 600Ω for any particular BP device. The "100J at 220Ω" phrase, recall, is also tantamount to the "136J at 300Ω" [65] pure-ER/RRC (100J/220Ω = 136J/300Ω) derivable from slight breaching of the implicitly derivable "130J at 300Ω" phrase discoverable within the corrupted 1989 IEC Standard also surreptitiously interpreted by manufacturers as a Pure-ER/RRC. For example, the "136J at 300Ω" phrase based on the 500Ω maximum Impedance allowed by the IEC Standard became factually tantamount to a never before reported 227J [66] ceiling for Abrams' European Thymatron DGx device (100J/220Ω = 136J/300Ω = **227**J/500Ω = 252J/555.5Ω = 273J/600Ω), which is, in fact, the maximum albeit never reported output for that particular BP device. In a nutshell, manufacturers no longer interpreted either the "100J at 220Ω" phrase or its IEC (European) equivalent, "136J at 300," as a conditional-ER/RRC with stipulated 100, 110, or even 136J ceiling, limiting outputs to an initial 1.0, 1.1, or 1.36 MTTLOI with BL ECT and thus initial 2.2 MTTLOI with UL ECT. Instead, manufacturers had secretly transitioned both phrases ("100J at 220Ω" and "136J at 300") into Pure-ER/RRCs based on maximum machine Impedances (i.e. DG-555.5Ω and DGx-500Ω respectively), enhancing Abrams' devices from minimal stimulus MTTLOIs for all ages (or a 1.1 MTTLOI with BL ECT) to a 2.52 MTTLOI with BL "ECT" for all ages (via Abrams' Thymatron DG in America). Abram's European device, the Thymatron DGx, emitted an initial 2.27 MTTLOI with BL "ECT" for all ages. In short, the made-for-America DG delivered an initial default 5.04 MTTLOI to all age categories with UL "ECT" while the made-for-Europe DGx delivered a default 4.54 MTTLOI to all age categories, about two and a half times the output per recipient allowed by the original 1982 APA Standard in America. At the time of Abrams' 1996 call for machines eliciting 2.5 to 5 times threshold, Abrams' own devices were no longer minimal stimulus ECT devices confined to adequate seizures at all, but were already ENR devices dependent upon adequate Multifold Threshold Titration Level Output Intensities of electricity to work. In sum, Abrams, like his colleagues Weiner and Sackeim, was surreptitiously and conspiratorially calling for a new standard to "legalize" already extant third generation BP devices (including his own) capable of emitting at least twice what manufacturers appeared to be calling for.

---

[63] This refers to the 1989 IEC Standard 60601-2-14 (International Electrotechnical Commission, 1989, p. 23).

[64] This refers to the 1982 APA Standard within Weiner's Petition to Reclassify (Department of Health and Human Services, 1982a, p. E20).

[65] The actual 1989 IEC ER/RRC is 130J at 300Ω, but American manufacturers breached this slightly (136J at 300Ω) to make it synonymous with the 100J at 220Ω ER/RRC (100J/220Ω = 136J/300Ω). Both were then interpreted as pure-ER/RRCs.

[66] Again, the actual derivation is 217 Joules (130J/300Ω = 216.6J/500Ω), but both Somatics and MECTA breached this figure to attain a 227J and 230J maximum respectively (136J/300Ω = 227J/500Ω; 138J/300Ω = 230J/500Ω).

Once again, to discover the actual unreported maximum output in joules which these devices administer, we simply set up these newly interpreted pure-ER/RRC phrases against their maximum machine Impedances, as seen above. For example, Abrams' DGx machine designed for IEC usage in Europe had a maximum 500Ω machine Impedance from which we can indirectly derive the machine's unreported 227J maximum thusly: 100J/220Ω = 136J/300Ω = XJ/500Ω; X = 227J.[67] The circa "500mC of Charge" which Abrams equates in his statement with the "100J at 220Ω" phrase (also equivalent to "136J at 300Ω") is misleading in that manufacturers had newly begun interpreting the "100 at 220Ω" and "136J at 300Ω" phrases as pure-ERRRC phrases--no longer conditional-ER/RRCs (with conditional maximum outputs of 100, 110, 130, or 136J ceilings), while the 500mC Charge maximum, albeit approximate, was actual. That is, the Energy outputs (in joules) emitted by the circa 500mC Charge cited by Abrams are not equivalent to 100 or 110J ceiling stipulations as in the 1982 APA Standard, but rather the 252 and 227 unreported joules emitted by his second generation DG and DGx respectively (100J/220Ω = 252J/555.5Ω = 136J/300Ω = 227J/500Ω), already more than twice the 110J conditional ceiling stipulated by the original 1982 APA Standard.

Specifically then, Abram's second generation made-for-America Thymatron DG and made-for-Europe DGx each emit a maximum Charge of 504mC while also emitting unreported 252 and 227 joule maximums respectively. As noted above, both the DG and the DGx utilize .9A, 140 maximum pulses, a .001 second pulse width, and a 4.0 second maximum Duration from which manufacturers derive the circa 500mC Charge to which Abrams refers. (Charge = Current x (Hz x 2) x Wave Length or Pulse Width x Duration: .9A x 140 pulses x .001Sec. x 4.0 Seconds = **.504C**.) Similarly, it is not the first generation 108J MECTA "C" which is associated with circa 500mC of Charge. Rather, it is MECTA's second generation made-for America and made-for Europe BP devices depicted as "101J at 220Ω" (tantamount to "138J at 300Ω") that are equated with circa 576mC of actual maximum Charge. Moreover, their "101J at 220Ω" ER/RRCs do not emit 101 maximum joules based on a conditional-ER/RRC interpretation as might be expected (based on the APA Standard). Instead, based on pure-ER/RRC, they emit unreported 259J and 230J maximums respectively (101J/220Ω = **259J**/562Ω = 138J/300Ω = **230J**/500Ω). What the Abrams statement does not reveal then, along with numerous other manufacturer-related reports equating circa "100J at 220Ω" with a circa 500mC Charge maximum (for what are actually second generation BP devices) is that the circa 500mC maximum Charge is not equivalent to the 110 Joule ceiling depicted in the original 1982 APA Standard as both Somatics and MECTA suggest, but to new transmutational never reported maximums of between 227 and 259 unreported joules respectively, this, in spite of both MECTA and Somatics second generation BP devices continuing to depict circa 100J maximum machine readouts.

At the time of Abrams 1996 call for a more liberal IEC standard allowing for more powerful devices then, what were actually second generation BP devices were already emitting circa two and half fold the power of first generation BP devices and had been doing so since about 1982. Indeed, first generation BP devices, in general compliance with the 110J ceiling of the 1982 APA Standard, by 1996, had already been abandoned for well over a decade. In fact, by Abrams 1996 announcement calling for a "first time enhancement" of Brief Pulse devices, second generation BP devices, though not reported as such, had already been surpassing 200J SW machines in raw power for some 14 or 15 years. What Abrams, Sackeim, Weiner, and others were actually calling for in 1996 then, as noted, was a new IEC standard which would encompass the much greater power not of second generation BP devices, but already extant third generation BP devices.

Specifically, the misleading, but common manufacturer practice of equating what appeared to be a "100J at 220Ω" conditional-ER/RRC with a 500mC Charge maximum for what appeared to be first generation BP devices, camouflaged the actual EO or power of the second generation Brief Pulse device and, in fact, promoted the continuing impression of a circa 100 Joule ceiling continuum from 1976 forward. In essence, the "100J at 220" phrase mistakenly interpreted as a conditional-ER/RRC successfully veiled the dropping of the 110J EO ceiling. Because the "70J at 220Ω" phrase within the original 1982 APA Standard was not a Pure-ER/RRC, but rather a Conditional-ER/RRC, that is, contingent upon a 110J ceiling in lieu of maximum machine Impedance, uninformed onlookers simply assumed the same interpretation true for the newer slightly higher "100J at 220Ω" phrase. In short, onlookers assumed that the phrase was yet contingent upon a 100 or 110J ceiling. In fact, with no mention of the dropping of the 110J ceiling, the newer "100J at 220" phrase (initiating the Mectan Transmutation) somehow seemed to incorporate a circa 100J ceiling within the phrase itself,

[67] Abrams' DG machine designed for usage in America has a maximum 555.5Ω machine Impedance from which we can indirectly derive the machine's unreported 252J maximum: 100J/220Ω = 136J/300Ω = XJ/555.5Ω; X = 252J.

suggesting either a newer, stricter 100J ceiling stipulation or (because there was no mention of its removal) that the same 110J ceiling stipulation continued to apply, an assumption undeniably supported, as already observed, by the circa 100J machine readout maximums emitted by all second generation MECTA and Somatics BP devices, readouts read and believed by administering physicians themselves. In sum, Abrams, Sackeim's, and Weiner's call for more powerful Brief Pulse devices seemed to be based on first, not second generation BP devices, still emitting around 100 maximum joules.

Brief Summary

Abrams' seemingly innocuous phrase:

> 100 Joules at 220 Ohms impedance or about 500mC of charge (Abrams, 1996, p. 703)

actually equates an unexplained "100J at 220Ω" pure-ER/RRC (that is, a phrase absent the APA 110J ceiling stipulation) with an actual Charge maximum of about 500mC, one of the methods by which manufacturers were able to maintain the suggestion of a 100 Joule ceiling continuum while simultaneously more than doubling the power of first generation BP devices. This method birthed what were actually second generation BP devices. Specifically, the only visible change from the original 1982 APA Standard appeared to be a very minor, rather innocuous transition from "70J at 220Ω" to circa "100J at 220Ω." The hidden transmutation to a "100J at 220Ω" pure-ER/RRC (as opposed to a "70J at 220Ω" conditional-ER/RRC restricted to a 110J ceiling), however, and its juxtaposition to actual Charge ceilings of about 500mC had actually facilitated new MTTLOIs 2.5 times 100J. Insidiously, what appeared to be conditional-ER/RRC phrases of "100J at 220Ω" and "100J at 300Ω" (or about 100J maximums) then equated to actual maximum Charges of about 500mC, completely covered up the enhancement! [68] The 1996 call for replacing the "old" (1989) IEC standard with a new one and which appeared to call for a first time doubling from 100J, then, was, really a push to more than quadruple the power allowed by the 1982 APA Standard in order to "legalize" third generation BP devices which, though unreported, were already, at that time, being marketed throughout the world.

Abrams and Somatics Second Generation BP devices Concluded

By now, we should no longer be surprised to learn that Abrams' 1996 call for enhanced devices and Weiner's 1997 proposal to replace the 1989 IEC Standard for "ECT" devices was actually designed to incorporate third generation BP devices with default settings eliciting an initial circa 5.0 MTTLOI with BL ECT and an initial circa 10.0 MTTLOI with UL ECT for all age categories. By 1996, the year Abrams (as well as others) made his above demands and unabashed assertions of a first time enhancement in 1996, Abrams' company, Somatics Incorporated, as well as MECTA Incorporated, had already been manufacturing and marketing new third generation BP devices in abject violation of the 1989 IEC Standard for ECT devices for several years. Because manufacturer-affiliated experts seemed to suggest that (the transmuted 1982 APA and 1989 IEC) standards (of "100J at 220Ω" and 100J at 300Ω respectively) were conditional ER/RRCs limited to circa 100J maximum outputs seemingly corroborated by circa 100J machine readout maximums on all MECTA and Somatics second

---

[68] 100 Joules is not equivalent to 500mC Charge. Based on the original 1982 APA ceiling standard of 110J, we might assume that "100 Joules at 220 Ohms" or "100 Joules at 300 Ohms" incorporates a conditional 100J ceiling. On the other hand, if we do interpret the phrases as pure-ERs, we may be lulled into assuming that the pure-ER interpretation is based on the APA standard which it is not. The original APA Standard is based a "70J at 220Ω" conditional-ER/RRC in that the standard calls for a 110J overall ceiling. The pure-ER interpretation of both the Mectan Transmutation and the 1989 IEC Standard for ECT devices "allow" up to 273 and 217 Joules respectively. In short, the implied equivalency of 100J with 500mC Charge is false. The newer pure-ER interpretation of the 100J figure within the "100J at 220Ω" Mectan Transmutation actually "permitted" circa 2.5 fold the circa 100J power of first generation BP devices manufactured between 1976 and 1982, a fact never fully unreported. The MECTA "C" for instance, had an actual 108J ceiling. Conversely, the reported 500mC Charge for what were actually second generation BP devices was not an ER (like the 100J indicated under the Mectan Transmutation) but actual output. Juxtaposing an ER figure in joules with an actual output figure in millicoulombs, and particularly the 100J figure, is wholly misleading.

generation BP machines, Abrams actually seems to be equating the implied 100J maximum with a circa 500mC Charge. In fact, circa 500mC, as noted above, is tantamount to between 227 and 259J or an initial 2.27 to 2.59 MTTLOI with BL ECT and between a 4.5 and 5.18 initial MTTLOI with UL ECT--in short, second generation BP devices. By falsely associating 100J with 500mC, moreover, a doubling of 100J to 200J would logically correspond to the new 1000mC called for (as we shall see) whereas, in fact, 1000mC is more or less equivalent to a circa 500J ceiling indicative of third generation BP devices. (See the Somatics System IV and METCA third generation BP devices later in this section). Consequently, Abrams is mendaciously calling for an enhancement of what appears to be a just above threshold output with BL ECT (1.1 MTTLOI) and about a 2.2 MTTLOI with UL ECT to a "new" initial ceiling" of circa 2.5 MTTLOI with BL ECT and a "new" initial ceiling of circa 5.0 MTTLOI with UL ECT [69] whereas, in fact, Abrams and other manufacturer affiliate experts are actually calling for a new IEC standard incorporative of between 4.5 to 5.2 MTTLOI with BL ECT and between a 9 and 10 MTTLOI with UL ECT, MTTLOIs which had been emitted by illegal third generation BP devices since at least 1995. In short, as previously noted, Abrams, just as Weiner, is attempting to sanction not the doubling of first generation BP devices, but the doubling of second generation BP devices in order to "legalize" what are actually extant third generation BP devices already being manufactured and marketed throughout the world at the time of Abrams' call for increased power.

[69] Abrams seems to imply that outputs should begin with a 5.0 MTTLOI with UL "ECT" so that at the end of a treatment series, the MTTLOI could maintain a minimum MTTLOI of 2.5 with UL ECT. This would mean that BL "ECT" was being enhanced from initial threshold output to a 2.5 MTTLOI so that BL "ECT" could remain at threshold following a treatment series. In fact, as noted, this was already true for extant second generation BP devices which the broadest interpretation of the 1989 IEC Standard already "allowed."

CHAPTER 55

MECTA - Co-conspirator: Sackeim's Call for Increased Power

In another editorial comment, as early as 1991, entitled, "Are ECT Devices Underpowered" (Sackeim, 1991, p. 233-234), Harold Sackeim, another "ECT expert," but this time closely associated with manufacturer MECTA Corporation (Cameron, 1994, p. 180; MECTA Corporation, 1987) also called for doubling the power of BP devices. Like Somatics, Sackeim's call occurs nine years following MECTA's production and marketing of its own second generation BP devices. Once again, this is not a call to double first generation BP devices as Sackeim implies, but a call to double never properly reported second generation Brief Pulse devices. Thus, in spite of MECTA's and Somatics' furtive manufacturing of second generation BP devices with a pre-set circa 2.5 MTTLOI and 5.0 MTTLOI with BL and UL "ECT' respectively for all age recipients since about 1982, Sackeim, in typical manufacturer fashion, seems to generally suggest the following. Sackeim indicates (1) that although all current BP devices elicit just above threshold seizures for all age groups, "minimal stimulus" is no longer considered effective, (2) that more power is needed for the "newly discovered" need for the 5.0 fold threshold dosing required of "dose-sensitive" UL "ECT" (so that it will still be effective with at least a 2.0 fold threshold output at the end of a "treatment" series), (3) that suprathreshold dosing is required not only to make UL "ECT" effective, but also (he concedes) in order to make BL "ECT" effective, and finally that (4) difficult cases, that is, individuals with extremely high thresholds--cannot be administered the necessary suprathreshold dosing required to achieve efficacy with the circa 500mC Charge "limitation" [of what were actually second generation BP devices] [70] (Sackeim, 1991, p. 233-234). For these reasons (according to Sackeim) more powerful devices were necessary and so implicitly, a new standard allowing for these more powerful Brief Pulse devices. (Sackeim wanted to increase the power allowed by the 1989 IEC Standard secretly allowing up to 217J and even the Mectan Transmutation secretly allowing up to 273J, both corruptions of the 1982 APA Standard, but which yet did not "allow" the degree of power manufacturers actually sought).

Sackeim's 1991 piece is an illuminating editorial for several reasons. While Sackeim falsely suggests that what are actually second generation BP devices only administer minimal stimulus for both BL and UL ECT, that is, administer a 1.1 and 2.2 MTTLOI respectively (since UL ECT is supposedly "dose-sensitive"), quite exceptionally, Sackeim pointedly informs us that just above threshold (or minimal stimulus induced) seizures, are often ineffective not only for UL electrode placement, but for BL electrode placement as well. He instructs:

> It is now known that . . . generalized seizures of adequate duration can be reliably produced and yet such treatments lack antidepressant effects . . . . The findings from our work indicate

---

[70] The "higher power for difficult cases" scenario often appears to imply that the "excess" power in more powerful devices, that is, power beyond that required for minimal stimulus, is only used only for "exceptional" cases wherein threshold cannot be reached with typical outputs. This rationale can easily be defeated simply by observing the back of the Somatics manual depicting a detailed chart for the second generation BP device, the Thymatron DG, (Swartz and Abrams, 1996, back cover; Abrams and Swartz, 1988, back cover). All 504mC of Charge and consequently, all 252-256 Joules are evenly distributed amongst recipients 5-100 years of age, showing that all the power is utilized for default outputs and no reserve of unused power is withheld. Distribution of all available power is distributed in an unreported, but circa 2.5 MTTLOI for BL ECT and circa 5.0 MTTLOI for UL ECT for all aged recipients (Beale et al., 1994). Third generation devices, as we shall see, circa double this MTTLOI for every individual recipient.

that the stimulus dose [that is, the amount of power used] may influence . . . whether or not patients respond at all. (Sackeim, 1991, p. 233-234)

While Sackeim's implicit acknowledgement that electrical "dosage" and "efficacy" are directly related, which is, in fact, true, his implicatory introduction, “it is now known,” suggesting that the need for suprathreshold dosing to achieve efficacy (even with BL placement) is a newly discovered principle, is bogus. Manufacturers have known of the direct relationship between electrical dosing and efficacy with both BL and UL ECT (albeit publicly suppressed) since the 1950s (Cameron 1994; Rice 1982). Indeed, the suggestion that more powerful Brief Pulse devices are needed to accommodate this “freshly discovered principle,” signifies that all BP devices manufactured between 1976 and 1991 induced seizures at just above threshold. Sackeim’s indication that Brief Pulse devices had remained minimal stimulus from 1976, the year Brief Pulse was first re-introduced amidst the first FDA investigation of "ECT," to the year of Sackeim's published commentary above in 1991 (Sackeim, 1991, p. 233-234) is, of course, entirely false. The first doubling in power and thus doubling of MTTLOI for both BL and UL "ECT" in modern BP history (that is, since 1976) as Sackeim had to have been aware, occurred between 1982 and 1983. Thus, (like Abrams' 1996 article) Sackeim's 1991 assertion that more powerful machines are needed in order to induce a circa 5.0 MTTLOI for "dose-sensitive" UL ECT, a phenomenon which had already been incorporated into second generation BP devices introduced in 1982, is wholly ingenuous. In fact, it was just three years following Sackeim's above statement that Beale et al. proved that both MECTA and Somatics made-for-America second generation BP devices had been pre-set to a circa 2.5 fold MTTLOI with BL "ECT" and thus a circa 5.0 MTTLOI with UL "ECT" for all age recipients since at least 1982 (Beale et al., 1994).[71]

For Harold Sackeim, who has published several hundred articles on electrical dosing and who is closely affiliated with MECTA, the ubiquitous need for suprathreshold outputs with both UL and BL "ECT" cannot have been new; neither can he have been ignorant of the fact that MECTA BP devices manufactured after 1982 were no longer set to induce seizures at just above threshold outputs with either BL or UL "ECT." Indeed, Sackeim must have been aware well before his 1991 announcement, that adequate seizures induced at just above threshold outputs are ineffective with both UL and BL placement. Indeed, this principle was first discovered as long ago as the late 1940s and early 1950s by both Liberson and Wilcox (Cameron, 1994; Impastato, 1957). In fact, inefficacy at just above threshold appears to be the chief reason these very early Brief Pulse devices failed to sell and so were subsequently discarded bringing the first BP era to a close (Ibid).[72] In fact, some of the first SW manufacturers, i.e., Medcraft, which, as early as 1940 had claimed that its SW machine could administer seizures at electrical "dosages" close to threshold, had by 1950, clearly acted upon the realization that suprathreshold dosing was requisite for both BL and UL efficacy. Rather than opting to adopt or even imitate the newly available very low dosage Brief Pulse devices (fully capable of inducing adequate seizures at much lower outputs than SW), Medcraft not only chose to continue with Sine Wave in

---

[71] For years, manufacturers suggested that age-related pre-set dosages for both the second generation Thymatron DG and second generation MECTA devices were being delivered at minimal stimulus for BL ECT and thus about 2.5 times threshold for UL ECT. Not until Beale at el. (1994) discovered that initial dosages were actually administered at 2.5 times threshold for BL--not UL ECT--and thus 5.0 times threshold for UL ECT, was there any reason to suspect that BL ECT had been administered at a consistent 2.5 MTTLOI since at least 1983. Even after the Beale publication, however, manufacturers appear to have ignored Beale’s findings so that by 1997, in order to “legalize” third generation BP devices, manufacturers disingenuously call for “a first time power enhancement” to accommodate “dose sensitive UL ECT,” “newly discovered dose sensitive BL ECT,” or to accommodate the hyperbolic notion that threshold doubles over a “treatment” course. In short, manufacturers were forced to justify the creation of a standard incorporating extant third generation BP devices, but fail to specify the detail that this meant legalizing already extant machines eliciting a circa 10.0 MTTLOI for UL ECT and 5.0 MTTLOI for BL ECT for every age category.

[72] Due to their failure to sell, Liberson, originator of BP in the 1940s, was forced to make his devices more and more powerful in an effort to make BP effective, including progressing from unidirectional to bi-directional current and broadening pulse widths (Cameron, 1994). Wilcox too, eventually abandoned low dosage unidirectional devices for the more powerful AC devices (Impastato et al., 1957). Thus, the knowledge that much higher dosing than that required to induce adequate seizures alone is necessary to make BP effective has been known since at least the fifties, and is one of the chief reasons that resurgent BP manufacturers in 1976 began with bi-directional current (AC) rather unidirectional current (DC) as well as fairly broad pulse widths. This was built into the resurgent BP devices in spite of the known phenomena that unidirectional current and briefer pulses can induce adequate seizures with even lower electrical dosing than those re-introduced in 1976. The superficial concern over unidirectional currents causing polarization of cells resulting in greater amnesic effects (American Psychiatric Association, July 9, 1979) has never been substantiated. In fact, it is probable that due to the lower dosing required to induce adequate seizures with unidirectional currents, just the opposite is true.

lieu of Brief Pulse, but chose to enhance the power of its then contemporary SW device by producing the newer more powerful B-24 SW device (Cameron, 1994) still in use today. (Indeed, there is ample evidence to suggest that even "minimum" settings for the B-24 SW are set for multifold threshold outputs. See later comments on the B-24). Such facts could hardly have been foreign to Sackeim. But even if they were, as an affiliate of MECTA, he could not have been ignorant of the detail that modern day second generation BP machines then used on an almost daily basis by Sackeim himself, already emitted pre-determined default outputs informed by age related or "dial-to-age" charts based on circa 2.5 MTTLOI with BL "ECT" and circa 5.0 MTTLOI with UL ECT and had been doing so since at least 1982 (Beale, 1994; Cameron, 1994). Indeed, MECTA's made-for-America second generation JR/SR 1 and 2 BP devices are invisibly pre-set at circa 2.6 times threshold with BL ECT and circa 5.2 times threshold with UL ECT in every age category (Ibid).

Strategy to Reveal without Revealing

MECTA's made-for-America second generation JR/SR 1 and 2 BP devices, as noted above, are invisibly pre-set at circa 2.6 times threshold with BL ECT and circa 5.2 times threshold with UL ECT in every age category (Ibid) while Somatics' second generation Thymatron DG is invisibly pre-set at circa 2.52 times threshold with BL ECT and circa 5.04 times threshold with UL ECT in every age category--BP machines all manufactured in the early 1980s. Plainly, manufacturers MECTA and Somatics withheld this information from both the FDA and the American public. Stated differently, at the time of Sackeim's 1991 comments above, the actual power and thus MTTLOI of both MECTA and Somatics second generation BP devices was and still remains suppressed (Beale et al., 1994; Cameron, 1994). Quite simply, manufacturers' clear pretense of the "newly discovered need" for ubiquitous suprathreshold dosing not only with UL, but with BL electrode placement in order to achieve efficacy, had by 1997, been understood and acted upon by these same manufacturers and their academic affiliates (i.e. Harold Sackeim for MECTA, Richard Abrams for Somatics, and Richard Weiner for both) for almost twenty-five years. Indeed, by 1991, these facts had been knowingly concealed from both the public and regulatory bodies at least fifteen years into the modern BP era, principles understood even from the earliest inception of Brief Pulse itself. The principle behind adequate electricity theory--the inverse of adequate seizure theory--is that rather than avoiding excessive electrical dosing, the procedure actually depends upon excessive electrical dosing, a fact inextricably suggestive of neurotransmitter impairment or "brain disablement" in order to achieve "efficacy" (Perrin et al., 2012; see also Breggin, Peter, Toxic Psychiatry). With regulatory and public memory fading regarding why the Brief Pulse device had been re-introduced in the first place, still feeling somewhat protected by MRI and EEG "safety" studies almost all of which had been misleadingly performed at minimal stimulus, and in that damage as a result of "ECT" occurs on a nano-level, invisible even to MRI and so must chiefly be identified via prospective signal data with respect to neurotransmissions, a factor not discovered until 2012 (Perrin et al., 2012), Sackeim, Abrams, and Weiner appear to have decided that public revelation of the "newly discovered 'need' for ubiquitous suprathreshold dosing" with both BL and UL "ECT" was in manufacturers' best interests. Fearful of possible exposure that their alleged minimal stimulus second generation BP devices had actually been administering suprathreshold dosages of electricity for almost a decade and by 1995, with even more powerful third generation BP devices already on the marketplace, announcing the "newly discovered" need for electricity well above seizure threshold in order to achieve efficacy with both UL and BL ECT seemed prudent. Publishing the need for increased electricity due to rising seizure threshold over a "treatment" course to account for BL suprathreshold dosing seemed the safest alternative. In any case, having completely withdrawn the 1989 IEC Standard for ECT from the general IEC standards for all other medical devices, and knowing they had introduced extant third generation BP devices to the marketplace in 1995, Brief Pulse manufacturers felt compelled to declare present standards antiquated and consequently demand more powerful Brief Pulse machines, generally. Indeed, Brief Pulse manufacturers were abruptly saddled with the task of both "legitimizing" and "legalizing" exceedingly powerful Brief Pulse devices far in excess of seizure threshold. In short, manufacturers and manufacturer-affiliated experts began vociferously calling for a new IEC standard to encompass the degree of suprathreshold dosing already utilized by extant albeit never before reported third generation BP devices and even more powerful BP devices to come.

To accomplish this, as noted earlier, American Brief Pulse manufacturers' now adopted the strategy of calling for a "new" standard to supplant the 1989 IEC Standard. Ingenuously, they called for a standard "sanctioning" outputs of up to 5.0 fold threshold for UL ECT and by implication up to 2.5 fold threshold for BL ECT, outputs which second generation BP devices had been delivering by default since at least 1982 and which manufacturers had already been "allowing" through interpreting the 1989 IEC Standard for ECT devices as a pure-ER/RRC. In any case, manufacturers were now forced to exploit the "newly discovered" necessity of suprathreshold dosing in order to achieve efficacy with both UL and BL ECT, further bolstered by "dose-sensitive" UL "ECT" and by the "newly discovered" concern--"the doubling of Impedance over a treatment course." Such was the redundantly familiar rationale used to "defend" Somatics' and MECTA's consensual petition for what would supposedly be a "first time" doubling of Brief Pulse power seemingly unchanged in output since 1976. In short, manufacturers used these "first time" justifications to explain their unlikely opposition to the 1989 IEC Standard for ECT devices, which according to Somatics and MECTA, seemed to allow only minimal stimulus outputs in accordance with the 1982 APA Standard. It was a rationale that effectively covered up MECTA's and Somatics' deceiving both the FDA and the American Public with respect to the increased and increasing power of their Brief Pulse devices since at least 1982 at which point the first power doubling of Brief Pulse had actually occurred. Supported by APA Task Forces on ECT comprised, in large, by manufacturer-affiliated "experts," manufacturers vocalized what appeared to be a first time demand for more Brief Pulse power. Unsurprisingly, the demand was spearheaded via their one time spokesperson Richard Weiner, who from 1976 to 1982, had promoted Brief Pulse to the FDA as a newly discovered, reduced electrical output device compared to SW, a claim which had ushered in the modern BP era and even the continuation of "ECT" generally into the last quarter of the twentieth and the first quarter of the twenty-first centuries (American Psychiatric Association, 1979, July 9; Grahn et al., 1977; Department of Health and Human Services, 1982c). By intimating as late as 1997 that the call for more powerful devices was a first time demand, and that this increased power was needed not only for UL ECT, but quite possibly for BL ECT together with the "newly" emphasized rationale that threshold or Impedance can double over a treatment course, Weiner and his manufacturers were not only able to cover up the first doubling in power of what were actually extremely potent second generation BP devices, but now hoped to gain acceptance of what were actually third generation Brief Pulse devices already on the marketplace, twice as powerful as second generation BP devices. Following the complete withdrawal of the 1989 IEC Standard for "ECT" devices, Weiner hoped to do this through an entirely new, albeit equally obfuscated standard.[73] In sum, manufacturers wanted to achieve normalization of super powerful Brief Pulse devices at least four times as powerful as the MECTA "C" through the "introduction" of an even newer and even more enhanced standard which, in actuality, would allow not a first, as noted, but a second major escalation of Brief Pulse power. In fact, such a standard would not only "legalize" even more powerful already extant third generation BP devices, as we have seen, but would make room for even more powerful devices for future device generations. To achieve this goal, moreover, Weiner's newly proposed standard would have to artfully cover up the extent of the increases which he would accomplish through the cryptic supplanting of EO (measured in joules) with a newer more "up-to-date" emphasis on Charge alone (measured in millicoulombs). Indeed, Weiner's new standard would have to be cleverly enough designed to effectively prevent comparison to previous BP devices, thereby burying manufacturers' earlier indiscretions by cutting off any comparative links to recently discarded Brief Pulse devices. With such a standard In place, manufacturers would not only be able to hide that the power of their BP devices had initially doubled in circa 1982, emitting more raw power than SW, but manufacturers could secretly and conspiratorially sanction what was actually a second major enhancement, without revealing to regulators the degree of the enhancement. If such a standard could be written, that is, a standard which could pass under the guise of a first time enhancement of Brief Pulse power needed for both "dose-sensitive" UL "ECT" and the supposed "doubling of threshold with BL "ECT" over a treatment course," manufacturers might even be able to get away with maintaining the reputation of Brief Pulse as a "reduced output" device, even as they enhanced the power of Brief Pulse for a second consecutive time.[74] In point of fact, as we shall see, the new standard concocted by

---

[73] Weiner would soon introduce new arguments explaining the need for suprathreshold dosing for so-called "non-dose-sensitive" BL ECT.

[74] As we shall see, in manufacturers calling for the doubling of Charge from the then present circa 500mC to more than 1000mC, manufacturers were actually vying for third generation BP devices. Due to the transition from absolute output reporting to average and ER-output reporting as well as the false equivalence of 100 Joules with circa 500mC, the initial power doubling of machines around 1983 was covered up. In addition, until about 2012 (Perrin 2012), almost all MRI studies were performed at minimal stimulus (circa 100 maximum joules) and second generation BP devices all contained false readouts limited to circa 100 maximum joules. In

Weiner would permit outputs up to circa 5.0 fold threshold for BL ECT and up to circa 10.0 fold threshold for UL ECT (and even more). Indeed, by 1991, manufacturers had already planned out the unreported production and marketing of third generation BP devices so that by 1995, even before the existence of Weiner's new "standard," manufacturers were already producing and marketing them, doubling the unreported power of already doubled second generation BP devices. On the other hand, in spite of Sackeim's singular concession that both BL and UL "ECT" require suprathreshold dosing to be effective, manufacturers yet needed to safeguard "convulsion theory" even while increasing the power of their Brief Pulse devices once again. In spite of Sackeim's propensity to be truthful regarding BL "ECT," then, others appear to have realized the self-defeating consequences of such a concession. Manufacturers' rationale for more power would generally have to emphasize the "dose-sensitivity" UL ECT alone. While manufacturers wanted and did include justifying increased power due to the alleged doubling of threshold at the end of a series with BL "ECT," then, manufacturers were forced to underscore UL "dose-sensitivity" requiring double the threshold output to be effective argument. BL "ECT," in sum, needed to remain effective at just above threshold. In short, manufacturers could not justify making Brief Pulse devices any more powerful than the second generation BP devices already in existence without conceding that both BL and UL “ECT” required suprathreshold dosing to be effective. This is because second generation BP devices, though not published as such, already at least doubled the output necessary for adequate seizure with BL "ECT" at the beginning of a series so that, BL outputs still surpassed threshold even at the end of a series. Indeed, though not reported, such machines, as noted, already surpassed SW in cumulative power. In fact, even "dose sensitive" UL "ECT was already quadrupled at the beginning of a series with second generation BP devices , thereby doubling threshold output with UL “ECT” even at the end of a series. Justifying increased power by arguing "dose-sensitivity" for both UL and BL "ECT" was simply not possible, as this called into question the effectiveness of convulsion theory, generally. The new standard, in effect, would somehow have to cover up the first increase in power so that third generation BP devices appeared to be second generation BP devices. The third justification for a "first time" increase and thus the need for a "new standard" included the well-worn "exceptional case for individuals with 'extremely high thresholds," argument, all three developed, in main, by mastermind and manufacturer-spokesperson, Richard Weiner. Of course, this too, had already been addressed by the unreported power of second generation BP devices.

MECTA co-conspirator: MECTA's Sackeim Calls for Increased Power, Continued

Now let us examine more of Sackeim’s 1991 rationale to increase the power of BP devices. Sackeim comments:

> One of the implications of these findings [that adequate seizures alone may not produce an anti-depressant effect and that instead, adequate dosage is critical to achieve efficacy] is [that] the current generation of ECT devices may be significantly underpowered. The devices presently manufactured in the United States for the most part adhere to a[n] upper output limit of approximately 100J (energy) or approximately 500-600mC (charge). The range of stimulus intensity of Standard devices is sufficient to produce seizures of adequate duration in the vast majority of patients. For a small minority, the upper limits are insufficient and clinicians resort to techniques such as quickly giving two stimulations in a row (“double stimulation”), the use of caffeine to lower the seizure threshold, or reverting to use of older generations of sine wave ECT devices that have higher output capabilities. In addition to this problem, the upper limits on stimulus intensity mean that many patients with relatively high seizure thresholds can only be treated with stimulus intensities very near threshold. (Sackeim, 1991, p. 234)

Let us first examine the portion of Sackeim's assertion which claims that:

---

short, manufacturers and their associates were falsely suggesting to onlookers that the 1991-1996 call to double the power of Brief Pulse was a first. Certainly BP devices had been emitting pre-set suprathreshold dosages for both BL and UL ECT since at least 1983.

> . . . devices presently manufactured in the United States for the most part adhere to a[n] upper output limit of approximately 100J (energy) or approximately 500-600 mC (charge). The range of stimulus intensity of Standard devices is sufficient to produce seizures of adequate duration in the vast majority of patients. (Sackeim, 1991, p. 234)

Sackeim, typical of the handful of manufacturer-affiliated experts [75] responsible for flooding the academic literature with these kinds of misrepresentations, wishes the reader to believe, as does Somatics' owner Richard Abrams above, that as late as 1991, the upper limit of BP devices in the United States remained an actual circa 100 Joules, comparable to the minimal stimulus MECTA "C" Brief Pulse device. By 1991, as already noted, manufacturers such as MECTA (and Somatics) had long since moved from the circa 100 Joule upper limit reported to the FDA between 1976-1982 depicted in the original 1982 APA Standard, to--via the Mectan transmutation--an unexplicated "100J at 220Ω" Pure-ER/RRC resulting in unreported ceilings typically two and one half times 100 Joules (Cameron, 1994; see second generation devices in Volume I).

Sackeim's phrase,

> . . . approximately 100J . . . or approximately 500-600 mC . . . (Sackeim, 1991, p. 234)

is, once again, blatantly deceptive. Once more, we witness the adroit sleight of hand in equating what appears to be 100J, but which is actually a 100J-ER, to an actual 500-600 millicoulomb Charge. As per Abrams assertion above, the 500-600 millicoulombs charge mentioned by Sackeim corresponds ***not*** to 100 Joules, but, for instance, on the (second generation made-for-America) Thymatron DG, 252 (unreported) joules, and on the (second generation made-for-America) MECTA SR1 and SR2 devices, 259 (unreported) joules.[76] In point of fact then, the 560mC maximums emitted from both second generation made-for-America MECTA devices equate not to 100J, but to 259J. Like Abrams' correlation above, Sackeim's direct correlation of "100J" with the circa "500-600mC" [77] Charge output of second generation BP devices is false, skipping over the circa 150J increase (100J + 150J = 250J) in what were actually second generation BP devices capable of outputs two and a half fold 100J. This stratagem is typical of manufacturers in conjunction with their blatantly spurious "first-time" calls for doubling the power of what seem to be circa 100J maximum Brief Pulse devices. Like Abrams' call, Sackeim's call for doubling power is actually a second call for the doubling of power not of 100J first generation BP devices, but of circa 250J second generation BP devices. Both American Brief Pulse manufacturers appear to conspire in this ploy. Let us not forget that both Somatics and MECTA second generation BP devices contain misleading machine readouts of circa 100 maximum joules.

Next Sackeim states:

> The range of stimulus intensity of Standard devices is sufficient to produce seizures of adequate duration in the vast majority of patients. (Sackeim, 1991, p. 234)

Here again, Sackeim lulls us into accepting the notion that what are actually suprathreshold second generation BP devices (manufactured between 1982-1994) remain comparable to the 108J minimal stimulus MECTA "C" device presented to the FDA circa 1978. In short, Sackeim is suggesting that the original 1982 power enhancement more than doubling the power of the MECTA "C," never took place. Designed to

---

[75] Sackeim has a longstanding association with MECTA Corporation.

[76] MECTA parameters are more difficult to calculate than the Thymatron DG for which Somatics reports 500 maximum Volts. It is the author's opinion, expressed elsewhere in this document, that although MECTA withholds Voltage (and other) information, that the second generation MECTA SR 1 and 2 devices are comparable to the Thymatron DG.

[77] It should be pointed out that while circa 500mC is typically equivalent to about 250 maximum joules, there is no 500mC upper limit within either the original APA Standard or the 1989 IEC Standard for ECT devices. Reporting of actual Charge in mC is simply a manufacturers' preference at this point, ignoring, in fact, mandatory requirements under the 1989 IEC Standard to report actual EO in Joules (International Electrotechnical Commission, 1989, p. 11). If 500-600mC had been an absolute ceiling, Medcraft's B-25, capable of emitting up to 840mC Charge would have been blatantly illegal under the 1989 IEC Standard.

administer just above threshold dosages with BL ECT (and thus twice threshold for UL ECT), it was the 108J MECTA "C" alone--not second generation BP devices--which conformed to the 1982 APA Standard located within Weiner's *"Petition to Reclassify . . . "* and which Weiner promised to the FDA (Department of Health and Human Services, 1982a, E20). Indeed, it is within the 1982 APA Standard that Weiner's revealing criterial assertion is made, underpinning the association of the circa 100J ceiling with minimal stimulus output via Brief Pulse:

> Using a pulse device, the [1978 APA] Task Force has determined that only 0.6% of seizure thresholds were greater than 70 [actual] Joules and that none were greater than 100 [actual] [78] Joules. (Department of Health and Human Services, 1982a, p. A53)

Totally ignoring the original APA standard then, manufacturers of second generation BP devices, in use all over America and Europe at the time of Sackeim's 1991 assertions above, had, as noted, already more than doubled the output and MTTLOI of the original MECTA "C" Brief Pulse Device in every age category. What must be emphasized here anew, is that immediately following the 1982 FDA hearings, not only were BP devices peremptorily souped-up relative to the MECTA "C," and made to emit between 227 and 259 unreported joules or a 2.27 to 2.59 MTTLOI for all age categories in Europe and the U.S. respectively (Cameron, 1994), but that manufacturers and their affiliate "experts" concealed the initial 1982 enhancement. By 1991 then, the year Sackeim announced the need for power greater than "100 joules," MECTA and Somatics BP devices had not been limited to the 110 Joule upper limit depicted in the 1982 APA Standard exemplified by the MECTA "C," the device introduced during the 1976-1982 FDA hearings as the Brief Pulse prototype, for some nine years. Brief Pulse devices manufactured after 1982, as has been pointed out, no longer conformed to the 1982 APA standard, but to the misleading Mectan Transmutation. It was under this tainted "standard" that both MECTA's and Somatics' post 1982 Brief Pulse devices had been covertly souped-up to more than double the MTTLOI and electrical power of the MECTA "C" not only with UL "ECT," but also BL"ECT" (Beale, 1994; Cameron, 1994).[79] [80] Indeed, because both manufacturers and their academic affiliates hid the enhancement from regulators, more than a decade would pass (from circa 1982) before researcher Mark D. Beale and researcher D. G. Cameron would discover this first major enhancement (Beale at al. 1994; Cameron, 1994). Indeed, it was Beale who first discovered that both MECTA and Somatics Brief Pulse devices were by 1994 pre-set to a circa 2.5 MTTLOI with BL ECT and thus a circa 5.0 MTTLOI with UL ECT in every age category (ibid) and had been so since circa 1982. Unfortunately, due to a flood of smoke-filled journal articles to the contrary and the fact that Beale reported his findings in Charge rather than EO (in joules) as we shall see, the full significance of this revelation was never fully appreciated. [81] Only now, perhaps with the publication of this manuscript, which puts Beale's and Cameron's discovery in context, can the hidden significance of the first major power enhancement of Brief Pulse devices in the modern Brief Pulse era be fully realized. Sackeim, Weiner, Abrams, and other manufacturer-affiliated experts, a number of whom resided on the several APA Task Forces on ECT active throughout the modern Brief Pulse era (from 1976 forward), clearly participated together in covering up the first major power enhancement of MECTA and Somatics Brief Pulse devices manufactured after 1982. Professional affiliates of both MECTA and Somatics, and even Medcraft, contributed in keeping alive the false notion that what were actually second generation Brief Pulse machines appeared to correspond in power to the first generation MECTA "C," thereby engendering the ongoing illusion that the Brief Pulse apparatus continued to

---

[78] The MECTA "C" clearly emitted an actual 108 maximum Joules. When manufacturers souped up BP devices, they began transitioning from actual EO reporting to the reporting of average outputs and then ER outputs based upon ER Impedance. The result was gross underreporting of actual EO ceilings and the false impression that no power enhancement had taken place from 1976 to at least 1997 (see Cameron, 1994). To further discourage comparison, manufacturers finally transition to Charge reporting alone, dropping EO altogether as we shall see.

[79] The fact that ten years later, Cameron (Cameron, 1994) discovered that what were actually second generation BP machines had doubled in power (compared to the MECTA "C") while Beale et al. (1994) discovered that BL ECT was no longer administered at just above threshold, but rather circa 2.5 times threshold--is not coincidental.

[80] This contradicted manufacturers' assertion of BL ECT efficacy at threshold, and consequently the public promise of minimal stimulus BP and thus outputs much lower than SW, all unreported (Abrams, 1996, p. 703; American Psychiatric Association, 1979, July 9, p. 2; Department of Health and Human Services, 1982a, pp. A44-A45; G2-G3).

[81] Cameron is not an M.D. and so his work, published in *The Journal of Mind and Behavior*, was, for the most part, ignored.

induce just above threshold seizures for the most commonly administered form of the procedure--"BL ECT." [82] In short, both manufacturer-affiliated academics and Brief Pulse manufacturers themselves participated in reporting or implying continuous circa 100 Joule ceilings and thus minimal stimulus output with Brief Pulse machines manufactured from 1976 to 1995. Both MECTA and Somatics pushed the spurious equivalency between what appeared to be circa 100J MECTA C-like BP devices and 500-600mC maximum Charges, charges, in fact, emitted by second generation BP devices capable of eliciting unreported outputs of between 227 and 259 joules. Abrams, Sackeim, and Weiner's continuous claims and implications that BL "ECT" continued to be administered at minimal stimulus output seemingly corroborated by 100J readouts on all American-made second generation BP devices as late as 1991 and even 1996 are clearly conspiratorial attempts to make what were actually second generation BP devices appear comparable to the first generation 108J MECTA C. This implication, along with the bogus assertion that what were actually second generation BP devices continued to emit only half the power of SW devices, can only have occurred with manufacturers' participatory pretense that the 1982 increase in the power of both MECTA and Somatics Brief Pulse devices, resulting in circa 2.5 and 5.0 MTTLOI with BL and UL "ECT" respectively--had never taken place.

MECTA co-conspirator: MECTA's Sackeim Calls for Increased Power, Continued 2

As noted then, manufacturers began by doubling the power of the MECTA "C" in order to try to make the procedure effective through electrical enhancement. Because manufacturers could not reveal increased efficacy as the chief reason for increasing electrical power, in that such a concession would undermine adequate convulsion theory generally, manufacturers created exceptions, anomalies, Impedance escalation, and "dose sensitivity" to justify the call for increased Brief Pulse power. Neither could manufacturers reveal that the 1991 to 1996 call for more power was the second major enhancement for which no explanation could be made, but the need for efficacy solely based upon enhanced electrical output. The need of a second enhancement following a first which accommodated all possible “anomalies” would have been to acknowledge that adequate convulsion simply does not work--that convulsion theory is myth. A second enhancement would be admitting that for the procedure to work, adequate amounts of electricity were needed, the very element positively identified with long term memory morbidity strongly associated with brain injury. Thus, from about 1991 to 1996, manufacturers began calling for what appeared to be a "first time" power enhancement of Brief Pulse based on "dose-sensitive" UL ECT, the doubling of threshold over a treatment course, and "atypically high thresholds." Since these had already been accommodated with the unreported power of second generation BP devices, the true goal, of course, was increased efficacy due to increased electrical output. Certainly, manufacturers could not reveal actual maximum outputs of what were, in fact, third generation BP

---

[82] It has long been established that UL electrode placement can induce an adequate seizure at half the output of BL ECT (Alexander, 1953, p. 62; Liberson, 1948, p. 32). Thus, if the MECTA “C” administered about 1.08 fold threshold or just above threshold dosages for BL ECT and these same electrical dosages were administered to the same age groups for UL “ECT,” UL was being administered at about 2.16 fold threshold even with the MECTA “C.” It was due to the multifold threshold dosing of UL “ECT” relative to BL “ECT” that UL “ECT” was initially reported as more effective than BL ECT (Malitz et al., 1986; Welch et al. 1982). Eventually - around 1982, UL “ECT” was deemed “dose sensitive” allegedly requiring twice threshold to be effective compared to BL which was allegedly ***“not”*** dose sensitive (Abrams, 1996, p. 703). Thus, in spite of machine enhancement, souped up BP machines manufactured after 1982 continued to be reported as administering BL at threshold while UL “ECT” was allegedly administered at 2.16 to 2.5 times threshold (Abrams, and Swartz, 1988, pp. 28-29). After Beale et al. (1994) and Cameron (1994) revealed that BP machines manufactured after 1982 administered BL “ECT” not at threshold, but 2.5 times threshold and thus UL ECT--not at 2.5 times threshold--but circa 5.0 times threshold, it should have become clear that the newer second generation BP devices had been falsely reported as equal to the MECTA “C” both in power and titration settings. Manufacturers had plainly hidden the fact that BP apparatuses had undergone a secret power enhancement beginning about 1982. The cover-up included: (1) an initial transition from an absolute 100J to an unreported 100J average (2) followed by an unreported transition to pure-ER (the Mectan transmutation) wherein “100J” could continue to be featured (3) the false equivalency of 100 Joules to the 500-600mC Charge emitted by second generation BP devices (4) the continuous false reporting of BL ECT at threshold and UL ECT at circa 2.5 times threshold, suggesting that no significant change had taken place since the MECTA “C,” (5) false machine readouts of circa 100 maximum Joules for second generation BP devices, (6) MRI studies performed at 100 joules or less during this period and finally, the motive for the cover-up (7) the continually false implication that BP produced less EO than SW widely reported in the media (Fodero, 1993, July 19; Kellner, 1994, February 2. Finally there was the false rationale that SW was sometimes necessary in difficult cases misleadingly suggesting the greater power of SW in all age categories (Food and Drug Administration, 1990, September 5).

devices or that what was actually a second enhancement represented a more than quadrupling of first generation Brief Pulse devices which had been fully capable of inducing adequate seizures in all age categories throughout a "treatment" series. In short, then, manufacturers could not afford to reveal that efficacy depended not on adequate convulsion, but adequate amounts of electricity. Not only does the requirement of adequate electricity undermine convulsion theory upon which "ECT" theory is wholly and irretrievably based then, but it is high electrical dosing that has long been associated with long term cognitive dysfunction. Indeed, reduced electrical dosing was the very reason Brief Pulse had been reintroduced under FDA auspices between 1976 and 1982, as it was reduced electrical dosing, as noted, which promised reduced cognitive dysfunction and thus increased safety compared to SW. The following Sackeim statement already noted above, attempts to justify the need for higher output for those with exceptionally high Impedances:

> For a small minority, the upper limits are insufficient and clinicians resort to techniques such as quickly giving two stimulations in a row ("double stimulation"), the use of caffeine to lower the seizure threshold, or reverting to use of older generations of sine wave ECT devices that have higher output capabilities. In addition to this problem, the upper limits on stimulus intensity mean that many patients with relatively high seizure thresholds can only be treated with stimulus intensities very near threshold. (Sackeim, 1991, p.234)

Sackeim is using "the exceptional case" scenario to justify what is supposed to be a "first time" doubling of Brief Pulse power, devices which had already more than doubled circa 1982. Of special significance here is the phrase: "reverting to use of older generations of sine wave--ECT devices that have higher output capabilities." Sackeim is, of course, clearly claiming that what are actually second generation BP devices are much less powerful than SW--patently untrue at the time of his statement and a fact of which Sackeim cannot possibly have been ignorant. Only by his falsely claiming that made-for-America (second generation) Brief Pulse devices at this time emitted an actual maximum output of circa 100 Joules (above)--an absolute falsehood--can Sackeim make such an assertion. In short, Sackeim is denying the existence of second generation BP devices. Note too, the statement, " . . . many patients with relatively high seizure thresholds can [now] only be treated with stimulus intensities very near threshold" again suggesting that (what are actually second generation) BP machines continued to emit minimal stimulus outputs similar to the 108J MECTA "C," a clear denial of the first major enhancement. [83] By this time, of course, manufacturers had clearly realized that what was being referred to as "ECT" worked not through adequate seizure, but rather through adequate amounts of electricity. Second generation BP machines had already transitioned into adequate electricity or Electro Neurotransmitter Reduction devices as noted above, and so, in calling for what is actually a second major power enhancement, Sackeim is actually calling for the "legalization" of third generation Brief Pulse machines which MECTA would begin marketing in 1995, departing even further from the "adequate seizure" devices the Brief Pulse apparatus was initially purported to be. In short, instead of more refined adequate seizure devices by virtue of even more reduced electricity, third generation Brief Pulse devices would double the MTTLOI of second generation BP devices, quadrupling MTTLOI, to become even more extreme ENR devices, devices less and less embracive of so-called "convulsive therapy," indeed, the antithesis of "convulsive therapy." Not only would third generation BP devices no longer guarantee safer treatment by virtue of reduced output then, but the "treatment" administered from such devices now clearly depended upon suprathreshold dosages of electricity in lieu of adequate convulsion for both BL and UL "ECT." In sum, by 1991, manufacturers were already planning third generation BP devices which burgeoned on the marketplace about 1995. What none, but manufacturers realized, is that even the 1989 IEC Standard for ECT devices which more or less accommodated the unreported power of second generation BP devices was by 1991, no longer adequate for forthcoming third generation BP devices already in the making. Certainly, by 1997, with third generation BP devices actually manufactured, marketed, and utilized in clinical practice, manufacturers could no longer allow the 1989 IEC standard for ECT devices to become the official FDA standard.

---

[83] Second generation made-for-America BP devices were pre-set to deliver 2.5 fold threshold BL-ECT outputs at constant current for every individual recipient in every age category. While SW devices may have delivered inordinately high multifold threshold outputs to the very young, much older patients, those with high thresholds, even set on maximum output, received close to threshold with SW in that that SW machines simply do not have the power to induce multifold threshold titration level output intensities in the older age categories (see the section on SW devices).

MECTA co-conspirator: MECTA's Sackeim Calls for Increased Power, Concluded

Sackeim, as noted above, thus concludes within the same 1991 document:

> In my view, a strong argument can be made that the next generation of ECT devices have significantly higher upper output limits, perhaps at least double what is available with the current generation [of devices]. At present, there are no legally binding national Standards in the U.S. that constrain the maximal output of ECT devices. However, international bodies, like the International Electrotechnical Commission (IEC) have developed Standards that limit the output characteristics of ECT devices and these Standards are applied in other countries . . ..
>
> (Sackeim, 1991, p. 235)

Clearly, by 1991, manufacturers had already planned to double the unreported power of second generation BP devices, all without acknowledging the first doubling of power which had taken place around 1982. Thus, unbeknownst to all but manufacturers, the doubling of what were actually second generation BP devices to form third generation BP devices would now more than quadruple the power of the MECTA "C," more than quadruple the 110J ceiling depicted in the 1982 APA Standard, and so more than quadruple the MTTLOI for each individual recipient administered BL ECT compared to the previous MECTA "C." Indeed, third generation BP devices would approach a ten-fold MTTLOI with UL ECT for all age categories. Thus, although manufacturers' Pure-ER/RRC interpretation of the 1989 IEC Standard had deceptively facilitated devices more than twice as powerful as that permitted by the never officially adopted 1982 APA Standard (alluded to by Sackeim above), potential American adoption of the 1989 International Standard (IEC) in 1996 now stood in the way of the even more powerful third generation BP devices which would begin being manufactured circa 1995.[84] Moving toward increased output in lieu of more reduced output devices, that is, moving toward adequate electricity devices as opposed to adequate seizure (and so minimal stimulus) mechanisms, manufacturers and particularly American manufacturers, naturally and vehemently opposed national and international adoption of the 1989 IEC Standard for ECT devices.

From Joules to Millicoulombs

To add to the evidence of a conscious cover-up of the power of second generation BP devices, from about 1983, in spite of the fact that both the 1982 APA and 1989 IEC standards for ECT devices called for EO reporting in joules,[85] manufacturers completely stopped reporting actual maximum output in joules, supplanting actual outputs for ER outputs (i.e. "100J at 220Ω) required by neither standard, in turn juxtaposed to maximum Charge reporting. The overall impression, as we have now seen, was that devices appeared to be confined to 100 or 110 maximum joules (minimal stimulus) and that this "maximum" output of 100 or 110J corresponded to the circa 500 plus millicoulomb Charges actually emitted by second generation BP devices. Succinctly then, manufacturers never informed regulators or the public that the circa "100 Joules at 220 Ohms" phrase reported by all three American manufacturers (MECTA, Somatics, and Medcraft) for their second generation BP devices no longer restricted Brief Pulse devices to a 100 or 110J ceiling as did the 1982 APA Standard. Neither did manufacturers reveal that newly figured albeit never reported maximum outputs in joules were newly based upon maximum machine Impedances, meaning new unreported ceilings of between 226 to 259 Joules (depending on the machine's maximum Impedance). In short, neither regulators nor the public were ever informed that the later Brief Pulse machines were no longer first, but second generation Brief Pulse devices.

---

[84] No device manufacturer adheres to the original APA Standard.

[85] The 1989 IEC Standard for ECT devices required reporting of maximum EO (Joules) at various impedances including maximum impedance. Manufacturers ignored this fact and instead chose to report ER-outputs in conjunction with actual Charge maximums.

In sum, regulators, the public, and even practicing professionals were never advised that the actual (circa) 500mC Charge maximums cited by manufacturer affiliated academics like Abrams were the equivalent--not of the familiar 100 or rather 110 joules indicated by the APA Standard seemingly confirmed by circa 100J maximum machine readouts depicted on all American made second generation BP devices. Rather, as noted above, the reported 500 plus millicoulomb Charge maximums were actually equivalent to the 227 to 259J second generation BP devices. The unexplicated reporting of a pure-ER/RRC phrase in conjunction with actual maximum Charge (of circa 500mC) designedly camouflaged the critical detail that BP machines had more than doubled in power between 1982 and 1983. Regulators could not know that the 1996 call for a new standard to enhance power, then, was really a call to double the power not of first generation Brief Pulse devices, but of second generation BP devices in order to encompass, as already noted above, the power of then already extant third generation BP devices, as we shall very quickly see. In brief, the 1996 demand for more power was really a call to more than quadruple the power of first generation BP devices and to more than quadruple the power of the 1982 APA Standard. We shall now see how Weiner, the godfather of manufacturer deceit, included this same ploy within his 1997 de facto standard, officially eliminating all vestiges of EO in joules and creating the impression of a first time power enhancement for Brief Pulse devices, generally.

CHAPTER 56

1997 IEC Proposal "Allowing" Third, Fourth, and Fifth Generation BP Devices

Fearful of imminent FDA adoption of the 1989 IEC Standard for ECT devices, which threatened to both expose the power of second generation BP devices and make obsolete already marketed third generation BP devices, device manufacturers in 1997, quietly assembled to discuss strategy. Meeting internationally in Denmark, August of 1997, a committee of "ECT experts" designated the "IEC Subcommittee 62D--Working Group 2," quietly proposed a revision of the 1989 IEC Standard for ECT devices, a revision designated "601-2-14R." Quite simply, their proposal entailed the total supplanting of the "601-2-14" section of the 1989 IEC Standard for ECT devices, with a completely new standard allowing for much more powerful devices. Led by American psychiatrist-engineer Richard Weiner, manufacturer spokesperson (to the FDA and now IEC), the newly assembled working group designed the replacement standard, "601-2-14R" to furtively legalize third (and possibly fourth and fifth) generation BP devices by invisibly, but grossly increasing the 1989 IEC power parameters for ECT (International Electrotechnical Commission, 1997, Dec 26). Proposed by Weiner and so, in main, by the United States component of the international "IEC Subcommittee 62D--Working Group 2" (composed mostly of U.S. manufacturer-affiliate "experts"), the revision contained only a few minor comments from "ECT" representatives of other countries.

Not surprisingly then, every major change--the purpose of which was to invisibly more than double the existing power of what were actually second generation Brief Pulse devices--originated from the United States National Committee component alone, for whom the main spokesperson, as already noted, was American Psychiatric Association ECT chair, electrical engineer, and manufacturer spokesperson, Richard Weiner. Submitted principally by the United States, therefore, containing but a few relatively insignificant comments by German, Japanese, and Swedish committee members, a detailed perusal of the 1997 revision proposal--"601-2-14R"--is critical in understanding and revealing the new power parameters of third, and potentially forth and even fifth generation Brief Pulse devices in use today. [86]

It is important to note that Weiner's proposed replacement standard met with immediate resistance from the main body of the IEC. Uncomfortable with Weiner's replacement proposal to more than double the power of then current (second generation) BP devices, an IEC appellate committee composed of IEC electrical experts not specifically affiliated with ECT, patently rejected Weiner's "international" revision proposal. As a result, the Weiner-led subcommittee was forced to withdraw the "601-2-14R" revision proposal. Even as Weiner's subcommittee withdrew the proposal, however, an alternative proposal by the same Weiner-led subcommittee (IEC Subcommittee 62D--Working Group 2) was quickly submitted to the same appellate committee, this time a proposition to simply remove the then current 1989 IEC Standard for ECT devices altogether on the basis that the standard had become "obsolete." If approved, then, there would be no IEC standard for ECT devices at all, in that the 1989 IEC standard for ECT devices would simply disappear. For manufacturers, elimination of the 1989 IEC Standard for ECT devices would serve almost the same purpose as their initially proposed

[86] A typical example of the minor proposals proffered by the additional three countries is Japan's proposal to "Replace the misspelled word 'beeing' with 'being'" (International Electrotechnical Commission, 1997, Dec 26, p. 2) or Germany's proposal to "Replace 'must' by 'shall' and 'USER' by 'OPERATOR'" (Ibid, p. 6).

revision deemed "601-2-14R". Indeed, with no international standard whatsoever, manufacturers would no longer be hampered by FDA's plan to wholly adopt the 1989 IEC standard for [all] medical devices in that the general IEC Standard for medical devices would no longer contain a specific standard for "ECT" devices. In short, manufacturers would be free to create their own de facto "regulations." Tentatively agreed to by the "appellate" committee,[87] the IEC's final decision to withdraw the 1989 IEC standard for ECT devices remained for a time on hold (International Electrotechnical Commission 1997, Dec 26).[88] While there were disadvantages to manufacturers having no official standard whatsoever, the total absence of a specific standard for "ECT," was, nevertheless, much more beneficial to "ECT" device manufacturers than retaining the then current (1989) IEC standard. After all, complete withdrawal of the 1989 IEC standard for ECT devices would prevent official FDA adoption of the general IEC standard from putting any limitations on ECT apparatuses, including prohibiting third generation BP devices which by 1997, had already been on the market for about two years. A complete withdrawal of the "ECT" standard from the IEC Standard generally, then, would not only eliminate prohibition of third generation BP devices, permitting manufacturers to maintain already marketed electrically enhanced machines in accordance with Weiner's initial revision proposal, but manufacturers would now be technically free to enhance the power of their devices almost limitlessly. With no IEC standard for ECT devices at all, FDA adoption of the general IEC Standard (which included numerous other medical devices) would now have no effect on American or European "ECT" manufacturers whatsoever. Like the U.S., moreover, European "ECT" device manufacturers (and perhaps even Asian "ECT" device manufacturers) could escape any official mandatory regulation.[89] Indeed, this is exactly what occurred. The 1989 IEC Standard for ECT devices was withdrawn from the general IEC Standard with no successive replacement. On the other hand, though never approved by the IEC, perusal of Weiner's 1997 replacement proposal for the 1989 IEC Standard for "ECT" devices spearheaded by Weiner and the United States, but also supported by British (and other) "ECT" manufacturers, provides us with an accurate blueprint of manufacturers' paradigm world-wide; that is, it is a blueprint of what, in effect, is the current unofficial standard for "ECT" Brief Pulse devices, a "standard" no longer sanctioning only second, but now third (and even fourth and fifth) generation BP devices, as we shall now see. Weiner's [90] 1997 revision proposal by which third generation Brief Pulse devices would have been "legalized" begins with the telltale excerpt below.

Weiner's "601-2-14R" IEC Replacement Proposal--Transitioning from Energy (Output in Joules) to Charge (in Coulombs and Millicoulombs)

As noted above, Weiner's [91] 1997 revision proposal by which third generation Brief Pulse devices were to be "legalized" begins with this telltale excerpt below.

> "Change the word "energy" to 'charge balance.' "
> (International Electrotechnical Commission, 1997, Dec 26, p. 2)

---

[87] Apparently, the general committee felt less liability in withdrawing the then present (1989) IEC Standard than in an active approbation of Weiner's revision. Nevertheless, the consequences of their passive rather than active agreement would have the same end result—open the door to even more enhanced devices.

[88] A somewhat moot option to form a new working group committee to continue working on the revision pended. Barring another revision attempt; however, the total withdrawal of the IEC Standard for ECT devices appeared inevitable.

[89] While FDA regulators and even advocacy groups assumed manufacturer conformity to the original 1982 APA Standard, the standard was never officially adopted all because manufacturers had been allowed to "regulate" themselves. Indeed, with the total withdrawal of the 1989 IEC Standard, there would now be no official standard for ECT devices either in the U.S. or Europe.

[90] Weiner represents a typical FDA practice, in this instance, entrustment to the privately formed American Psychiatric Association, in effect, the manufacturers themselves, to protect psychiatric "consumers." Through the dangerous naivety of entrusting the brains of "patients" to APA committees comprised of manufacturer-affiliated "experts," FDA has failed miserably in its duty to protect the American consumer.

[91] Weiner represents a typical FDA practice, in this instance, entrustment to the privately formed American Psychiatric Association, in effect, the manufacturers themselves, to protect psychiatric "consumers." Through the dangerous naivety of entrusting the brains of "patients" to APA committees comprised of manufacturer-affiliated "experts," FDA has failed miserably in its duty to protect the American consumer.

Thus, the first order of business within Weiner's proposed revision was to dispense with the mandatory reporting of "Energy Output" depicted in joules, supplanting all EO reporting (in terms of joules) with cumulative electricity or "Charge" reporting. In short, Joules were to be exchanged for Coulombs (or millicoulombs). In that the make-over to Charge is total, Weiner's revision document is replete with amendments similar to the one above, wherein Weiner supplants the word "energy" with "charge" (International Electrotechnical Commission, 1997, Dec 26, p. 1, 2, 3, 4, 5, 7, 8). In that the power of both SW and first generation Brief Pulse devices were originally measured in joules, so that if the power of second generation Brief Pulse devices, though never accurately reported, had been correctly depicted in joules, one could easily have seen that second generation Brief Pulse devices deliver greater overall EO than SW, as well as more than twice the power of first generation Brief Pulse devices such as the MECTA "C" (Cameron, 1994). Indeed, unlike SW devices, modern day second generation made-for America BP devices have the capacity to overcome any resistance up to circa 600Ω and circa 500Ω for made-for-America and made-for-Europe BP devices respectively all while maintaining constant currents. Unlike SW, Brief Pulse devices achieve this constant current (in spite of increasing impedances) through incrementally increasing voltage (Cameron, 1994). In short, Brief Pulse devices are much more efficient, but also much more powerful than SW devices. Via the 1982 APA Standard, American BP manufacturers (all of which were represented by Weiner during the 1976-1982 FDA investigation) portrayed Brief Pulse as needing only half the power of Sine Wave. Proof of Brief Pulse as a reduced output device lay in the manifest disparity between the 100J required to induce adequate seizure in all recipients with Brief Pulse (Department of Health and Human Services, 1982a, p. A53) reflected by the 108J MECTA "C" Brief Pulse and the alleged 200J Medcraft B-24 (Sine Wave) portrayed in the 1982 APA Standard by Weiner himself. The Brief Pulse "C," as already noted, was much touted as having the power to induce seizures one hundred per cent of the time with never more than 100 Joules—with its just above threshold 108J capacity (Department of Health and Human Services, 1982a). Indeed, in accordance with the reduced output representation of Brief Pulse, Weiner testified to the FDA in 1982 the importance of reporting in joules:

> Since most ECT devices are either constant voltage or constant current, leaving the respective current or voltage to vary with the impedance across the patient's scalp, the most accurate and consistent manner to measure overall stimulus intensity is by energy [joules], as this parameter intrinsically takes electrode impedance into account.
> (Department of Health and Human Services, 1982a, p. E19)

In addition, Weiner stated:

> The energy output [that is, measurement in joules] takes into account all stimulus intensity parameters (including duration) along with variations in load impedance, and is therefore a useful means of setting requirements upon stimulus output. In addition, energy output [joules] is a potential factor in the production of adverse effects.
> (Department of Health and Human Services, 1982a, p. A46)

Certainly, because Brief Pulse is more efficient than Sine Wave, BP can induce seizures with half the output of SW. Measuring both SW and BP in joules was thus beneficial to BP manufacturers so long as BP devices were set for minimal stimulus, that is, emitted the least amount of EO necessary to induce adequate seizures and so less than half the EO of SW. As the power of Brief Pulse began to be exploited, however, that is, as BP devices began surpassing SW in power (Cameron, 1994), manufacturers not too surprisingly, stopped reporting maximum output in joules.[92] They stopped in spite of EO (in joules) being "the most accurate and consistent manner of measuring overall stimulus intensity" as well as an indicator or "potential factor in the production of adverse effects" (see Weiner above). With the advent of second generation BP devices, however, manufacturers abruptly shifted reporting maximum machine output from Joules to Charge (cumulative

---

[92] Energy Output may be translated into watts and so long as one divides that number by duration in seconds, any lay person can understand the wattage per second or the cumulative wattage through Joules or EO. For example, a output of 250 Joules over four seconds is approximately 63 watts per second, and 250 cumulative watts, equivalent to the electrical transmission of a 60 watt bulb for four seconds. Newer devices would double this wattage.

electricity), concealing not only maximum EO in joules relative to SW, but concealing the maximum EO of (what were actually) second generation BP devices compared to the maximum EO of first generation BP devices such as the MECTA "C." Moreover, although EO continued to be reported at "100 Joules" or "100 Joules" relative to "typical" Impedances of 220Ω (U.S.) and "100J at 300Ω" (Europe) for second generation BP devices, these misleading figures, as explained earlier, had, in fact, transitioned into pure-ER outputs as opposed to conditional-ER outputs with 110J ceiling. In addition, manufacturers often stopped reporting Voltage from which true EO maximums in Joules might actually be derived. MECTA, for instance, has failed to report accurate Impedances as well as Voltage for their Brief Pulse devices since at least 1982 (Cameron, 1994), the year Brief Pulse devices first equaled (then surpassed) SW devices in cumulative power. On the other hand, neither maximum Voltage nor maximum Impedance is necessary to determine maximum Charge, the later manufacturer-preferred measure of electrical output reporting. [93] Conversely, while maximum EO in joules can be determined via maximum Charge, maximum EO can only be determined if maximum Impedance is also known.[94] In short, by withholding the reporting of both maximum Impedance and maximum Voltage, determination of maximum EO for any specific Brief Pulse device becomes impossible.[95] Indeed, Charge reporting in the absence of accurate Voltage and accurate Impedance, both of which MECTA neglects to report, is not only incomplete, but very often misleading.[96] In short, actual EO of Brief Pulse devices was now being suppressed. To complete the cover-up, all made-in-America second generation BP machine readouts, as noted numerous times above, depict circa 100J maximums (patently false in the case of second generation MECTA and Somatics devices). Complementing these spurious 100J machine readout maximums for second generation BP devices, as also heretofore noted, manufacturers now utilized unexplained and unidentified 100J ER (Equivalent Ratio) outputs to "allow" much greater albeit unreported outputs, often impossible to identify as ERs. The reporting of actual Charge maximums in conjunction with what were actually circa 100J ERs, as previously described, illusorily suggest that what are actually second generation BP devices are limited to circa 100 maximum joules and thus in conformity with the APA standard.[97] In short, by transitioning from the reporting of actual EO maximums (in joules) to the reporting of actual Charge maximums in conjunction with unexplained ER maximums (in joules), BP manufacturers had discovered a clever way of avoiding the reporting of actual maximum EO (in Joules) for second generation Brief Pulse devices, indeed, creating a false impression of circa 100J devices. By 1997, moreover, what had been a partial transition to Charge reporting for second generation BP devices in conjunction with manufacturers' use of unexplicated and misleading 100J ER outputs via both the Mectan Transmutation in the United States and the 1989 IEC standard in Europe, had now, under Weiner's unofficial IEC revision, evolved into total Charge reporting for third generation BP devices, wherein Energy Output (in joules) was altogether abandoned. The result was total discarding of EO in Joules for both second and third generation Brief Pulse devices and thus the suppression of any meaningful comparisons.[98] In fact, under Weiner's new 1997 de facto IEC revision standard, EO in joules for what are actually third, fourth, and fifth generation BP devices are both grossly enhanced and grossly hidden from view--both of which became possible through the total supplanting of EO reporting in Joules with Charge reporting in Coulombs and Millicoulombs, as we shall now see.

Weiner's 1997 "601-2-14R" IEC Replacement Proposal Continued

Given that by 1995, manufacturers had doubled the power of already enhanced second generation BP devices both within the U.S. and abroad, thus more than quadrupling the power and more importantly, more than

[93] Charge = Current x (hz x 2) x WL x Duration.

[94] EO = Charge x Current x Impedance.

[95] (EO = (Current squared) x Impedance x (hz x 2) x WL x Duration; EO = Voltage x Current x (hz x 2) x WL x Duration)

[96] Voltage is often difficult to obtain and is commonly misrepresented by manufacturers. For instance, MECTA does not accurately report voltage in their brochures and the author has not been able to obtain this information from MECTA. A figure of 240 volts for the MECTA JR/SR 1 and 2 cited in a publication by the Royal College of Medicine (Royal College of Psychiatry, 1995, p. 139) is almost certainly incorrect. Moreover, a Somatics figure of 450 volts (Royal College of Psychiatry, 1995, p. 124) does not conform to Somatics own reporting of 500 volts (Abrams and Swartz, 1988; Swartz and Abrams, 1996). Neurotronics, an English producer of an extremely powerful "ECT" device, flatly refuses to report maximum voltage (Royal College of Psychiatry, 1995, p. 133).

[97] The original APA standard was inclusive of an actual—not Equivalent Ratio—110J ceiling.

[98] MECTA has avoided accurate reporting of Impedance, Voltage, and consequently specific EO since at least 1985. All BP manufacturers avoid accurate reporting of Impedance, perhaps the most important means of calculating EO (Cameron, 1994).

quadrupling the Multifold Threshold Titration Level Output Intensity (MTTLOI) of the original MECTA "C," manufacturers, should have been made to report actual EO for these devices, particularly *maximum* EO in actual Joules. Of course, the consistent reporting of accurate, actual EO for each succeeding generation of Brief Pulse devices would have made clear to regulators that--as a result of applying Weiner's de facto enhancements under his *1997 "601-2-14R" IEC Replacement* Proposal--modern day Brief Pulse devices are not only far more powerful and thus at least as dangerous as the SW devices of the past, but each succeeding generation has become progressively more powerful and thus more and more, not less and less dangerous. Continually fluctuating from Voltage to Joules to Charge as manufacturers have practiced throughout the history of the "ECT" device since its inception (Cerletti and Bini, 1938), has effectively undermined consistency and clarity in the reporting of power and output, thereby obfuscating comparative analysis. Indeed, inconsistent reporting with variant measuring mechanisms unique to succeeding generations of Brief Pulse devices have engendered a kind of encryption, allowing for a kind of doublespeak, abetting confusion and uncertainty of actual parameters--veiling not only actual device power, but exponential rises in MTTLOI accompanying each of these power increases (Beale, 1994; Cameron, 1994). Certainly, while actual maximum Charge reporting is essential, regulators must compel manufacturers to report actual Energy Output (in joules), especially maximum EO (in joules) in order to clearly reveal the devolution (increase in power) of the so-called "ECT" device, generally.

Another example of the complete transition from EO to Charge excerpted from Weiner's 1997 IEC revision proposal, can be seen below in Weiner's initial proposition to replace the 1989 "IEC Section 6.8.3 for 'ECT' devices" with his proposed 1997 "601-2-14R." The ***1989*** IEC standard reads:

> 6.8.3 aa) The technical description shall additionally give
> -the maximum output energy and the relevant load resistance.
> (International Electrotechnical Commission, 1989)

Weiner's ***1997*** replacement proposal reads:

> 6.8.3 aa) The technical description shall additionally give
> -the maximum charge delivered and the relevant load resistance.
> (International Electrotechnical Commission, 1997, Dec 26)

In short, what has become Weiner's (and thus manufacturers') 1997 de facto standard ("601-2-14R"), as noted, includes a total transition from Output Energy (in Joules) to Charge (in Coulombs) for what are actually third, and possibly fourth and fifth generation Brief Pulse devices as has been mentioned. As we might expect, the switch effectively camouflages the fact that manufacturers of third generation Brief Pulse devices have doubled the power of their apparatuses for a second time. In brief, manufacturers, just as they had with second generation BP devices, continued to avoid reporting actual EO in joules, but this time with complete and irretrievable thoroughness. As EO is entirely deleted, the total switch to Charge reporting conceals the fact that third generation Brief Pulse devices actually exceed the most extreme raw power potential (200J) of the most powerful B-24 SW device marketed by Medcraft by circa 2.5 fold, compared to which, in 1982, Brief Pulse was purportedly half as powerful as SW and by implication, half as dangerous regarding "adverse effects" (Department of Health and Human Services, 1982a, G2).

Let us examine some more of Weiner's proposed ("601-2-14R") changes to the 1989 IEC Standard. Under:

> SECTION EIGHT of the (1989) IEC Standard - ACCURACY OF THE OPERATING DATA AND PROTECTION AGAINST INCORRECT OUTPUT, 51.2, Limitation of Output Values

the 1989 IEC standard reads:

> The output energy shall be limited to a maximum of 100 J at 300 Ω for each treatment initiation. Within this energy limit the output voltage shall be limited to a peak level of 1kV and the current to a peak level of 2A at any load resistance . . .
> (International Electrotechnical Commission, 1989, pp. 21-22)

Weiner's 1997 replacement recommendation alters the above excerpt to read:

> The stimulus output shall consist of a constant current pulse train, with pulse width no greater than 2 milliseconds. The stimulus output charge shall be limited to 1200 mC for each treatment initiation for a load resistance of 100-500 Ohms, with a rate of delivery of no more than 2 mC/phase and 300 mC/second. Within this output charge limit, the output voltage shall be limited to a peak level of 1kV and the current to a peak level of 2A at any load resistance . . .
> (International Electrotechnical Commission, 1997, Dec 26, p. 4)

Succinctly, Output charge supplants Output energy; measurements in terms of EO (joules) are thus totally eliminated, once again making meaningful comparisons to previous Brief Pulse devices and even to Sine Wave, impossible. Note too, how the limiting adjunct, the ER/RRC expressed in the 1989 Standard as "100 Joules at 300 ohms" (which, with an adjunctive provision within the 1989 IEC Standard is actually a "130J at 300Ω" Pure-ER/RRC) and which limited most Brief Pulse devices to a circa 500 to 600 mC Charge (as noted earlier),[99] is to be replaced by a new specific maximum ceiling of 1200 mC Charge for all treatments between 100 and 500 ohms resistance, more than doubling the actual Charge allowed. (Recall that second generation Brief Pulse devices emitted between 500 to 600 mC of Charge.) Note too, the new "2 mC/phase and 300 mC/second" 'regulatory' phrases as well as the phrase carried over from the 1989 standard, "Within this output charge limit, the output voltage shall be limited to a peak level of 1kV and the current to a peak level of 2A at any load resistance." Note particularly the maximum 2A current which with Weiner's increased parameters, now comes into play. What were actually second generation Brief Pulse devices, more potent than the powerful SW devices of old, as we have noted earlier, already emitted unreported maximum outputs of between 230-260 unreported Joules (compared to SW's 200J maximum).[100] Unbelievably, based on Weiner's new parameters, the EO ceiling for Brief Pulse devices now soared from an unreported potential 600 maximum Joules (but limited to 217J by the "130J at 300Ω" pure-ER/RRC), to an unreported potential 1200 maximum Joules as can be verified with the formula: EO = Charge x Impedance x Amperage; 1.2C x 500Ω x 2.0A = 1200 Joules. The new standard has no limiting ER/RRC. (Previously, the maximum allowed under the 1989 IEC Standard was (EO = .6C x 500Ω x 2.0A =) 600 Joules further limited to 217J by the 130J at 300Ω pure-ER/RRC interpretation (130J/300Ω = ***217J***/500Ω) and illusorily limited (via the expected conditional-ER/RRC interpretation) to circa 130 maximum Joules. Previously, though present, the 2.0A never came into play due to the presence of the "130J at 300Ω" ER/RRC interpreted as a pure-ER/RRC so that the maximum EO allowed was actually (EO = .6C x 500Ω x 1.0A =) 300 Joules further limited to **217J** by the 130J at 300Ω pure-ER/RRC (130J/300Ω = 217J/500Ω), an undepicted ceiling then breached by American manufacturers to emit between 226-240J. Tellingly, no ER/RRC limiter is present in Weiner's 1997 de facto standard.

Should a mandatory reporting of actual EO have been required of Weiner's 1997 revision configurations instead of the new phrase:

> The stimulus output charge shall be limited to 1200mC for each treatment initiation for a load resistance of 100-500 Ohms.

Weiner's new IEC Standard proposal (as we shall ultimately substantiate), would have been forced to state:

---

[99] Charge = EO/Current x Impedance; Using ER and MECTA and Somatics parameters respectively, 130J/.8A x 300Ω = .542C; 130J/.9A x 300Ω = .481C. In fact, the companies, through illegal breaching of the "Pure-ER/RRC" of 130J at 300Ω, used closer to .600C Charge.

[100] Though breached somewhat, the 1989 IEC ceiling, due to the Pure-ER/RRC of 130J at 300Ω, was technically limited to 216.66 Joules (130J/300Ω = 216.66J/500Ω).

> The output energy shall be limited to approximately 1200 Joules for each treatment initiation for a load resistance of 100-500 Ohms.

Had ER/RRC phrases continued to be reported--the reporting of which is totally dropped in Weiner's new revision proposal--what in 1989 was a 100J at 300Ω Pure-ER/RRC which read:

> The output energy shall be limited to a maximum of 100 J at 300 Ω for each treatment initiation,

and which, due to a cushion adjunct within the 1989 IEC Standard, could be stretched to an unreported 130J at 300Ω Pure ER/RRC, allowing (130J/300Ω = XJ/500Ω; X =) 217J, Weiner's new 1997 provision would have had to read:

> The output energy shall be limited to a maximum of 720 J at 300 Ω for each treatment initiation (720J/300Ω= 1200J/500Ω).[101]

Thus, at a 1200J maximum output (which shall be examined in detail shortly), if ER/RRC phrases had been retained under Weiner's proposed 1997 IEC Standard, the new 1997 IEC Standard would have been forced to read not a "100J at 300Ω" or even "130J at 300Ω" pure-ER/RRC permitting 217 unreported Joules (130J/300Ω = ***217J***/500Ω), but rather a whopping "720J at 300Ω" pure-ER/RRC permitting up to an incomprehensible 1200 maximum Joules (720J/300Ω = ***1200J***/500Ω). Under Weiner's proposal, in made-for-America terms, that is, under the Mectan transmutation based on a 100J at 220Ω pure-ER/RRC, manufacturers would no longer have been able to report even an unexplained **"100J at 220Ω"** pure-ER/RRC (with a potential 600Ω maximum Impedance): 100J/220Ω = **273J**/600Ω), but would have been forced to report a **"440J at 220Ω"** pure-ER/RRC (with a potential 600Ω maximum Impedance: 440J/220 = **1200J/*600Ω***). Based on a maximum 500Ω instead of 600Ω maximum Impedance and a 220Ω ER, even an unexplicated made-for-Europe pure-ER/RRC phrase would have to have been reported at **"528J at 220Ω,"** in order to allow (528J/220Ω = ***XJ/500Ω; X =***) **1200J**. Recall that the ER/RRC used in the 1982 APA Standard was a conditional-ER/RRC of "70J at 220Ω" confined to a specified **110J maximum**.

In sum, new (pure) ER/RRCs based on Weiner's 1997 revised standard would have to read:

XJ/300Ω = 1200J/500Ω; X = **720J at *300Ω***. (made for Europe)

XJ/220Ω = 1200J/600Ω; X = **440J at 220Ω**. (made for America)

XJ/220Ω = 1200J/500Ω; X = **528J at 220Ω** (made for Europe interpreted for America)

To be certain, the 720J at 300Ω pure-ER/RRC (IEC), 440J at 220Ω pure-ER/RRC (made-for-America), and 528J at 220Ω pure-ER/RRC (made-for-Europe translated to American terminology) phrases are but pure-ER/RRCs, all permitting Weiner's newly revised actual (but hidden) maximum machine output potential of **1200 Joules**. Again, compare this to the 1982 APA Standard of "70J at 220" with a **110J ceiling**, an astounding 990% increase in the potential power of the Brief Pulse device (1200 - 110 = 1090 ÷ 110J = 990%) over the original 1982 FDA approved APA Standard. Is it any wonder why ER/RRC reporting and every other form of EO reporting (in Joules) are completely expunged under Weiner's new de facto standard?

From these new unreported ER/RRC phrases, we can now derive the new maximum output potential for Brief Pulse devices under Weiner's new de facto standard, an output which under the de facto standard, can now be "legally" applied to the oldest and most seizure recalcitrant recipient, the 100 year old male. Moreover, we can derive Weiner's new (albeit unreported as such) consistently applied Multifold Threshold Titration Level Output Intensity (MTTLOI) which under his standard, can now be "legally" applied to every individual recipient

[101] 100J/300Ω = 166.66/500Ω;130J/300Ω = 216.66J/500Ω 720J/300Ω = 1200J/500Ω

in every age category. To the point then, Weiner's 1997 revision proposal allowing an unreported 720J at 300Ω pure-ER/RRC, now "permits" a 1200J output maximum both in the U.S. and abroad, in turn eliciting a 12.0 MTTLOI potential maximum for all age categories or twelve times threshold.

To arrive at this 1200J maximum output, we simply use the IEC's 500Ω maximum Impedance under both the IEC and Weiner's revision proposal and cross multiply with the new, though, unreported 720J at 300Ω Pure-ER/RRC that Weiner's proposal indirectly allows (720J/300Ω = **1200J**/500Ω). To derive the allowable MTTLOI under Weiner's new revision proposal, we merely divide the new 1200J maximum by 100J, the maximum output required to seize a 100 year old recipient: 1200J ÷ 100J = 12 MTTLOI (Department of Health and Human Services, 1982a, p. A53). Thus, under Weiner's replacement proposal, a Brief Pulse device based on Weiner's 720J at 300Ω Pure-ER/RRC derived from Weiner's new maximum 1200mC Charge maximum, now allows up to a 12.0 MTTLOI potential for every recipient in every age category with BL "ECT." Compare this to the 1.1 MTTLOI potential for every recipient in every age category with BL "ECT" allowed under the FDA approved 1982 APA Standard.

Hidden

Of course, regulators have never been made aware of the potential power of Brief Pulse devices under Weiner's new 1997 revision proposal in that what has become Weiner's de facto standard no longer provides even a pure-ER/RRC phrase from which we can determine both maximum output and the new maximum MTTLOI for all age groups. Indeed, there is no limiting ER/RRC. In brief, both the maximum output ceiling in joules and the ER/RRC limiters are absent or rather they are so high, they provide almost no safeguards whatsoever. The EO ceiling in joules is eliminated because if it were reported, Weiner's 1997 replacement standard would have been forced to reveal the 1200J ceiling upon which the Weiner de facto standard is actually based. Moreover, the pure-ER/RRC phrase is eliminated because had it been reported, Weiner's 1997 replacement standard would have been forced to reveal the "720J at 300Ω" pure-ER/RRC principle upon which the Weiner de facto standard is also based. In fact, with the reporting of the "720J at 300Ω" Pure-ER/RRC phrase, it would have been possible to deduce Weiner's new 1200J maximum output potential for all Brief Pulse devices both in Europe and America (720J/300Ω = **1200J**/500Ω) and thus the 12.0 MTTLOI "allowed" with BL "ECT" for every age recipient (1200J ÷ 100J = 12.0 MTTLOI) which Weiner's new de facto standard now makes possible. Tangentially, under this same new standard, a new 24.0 MTTLOI is "allowed" with UL "ECT."

If Revealed

If the Mectan Transmutation were to be actually exposed, regulators might first realize that the illicit Mectan Transmutation of "100J at 220Ω" at a 600Ω maximum Impedance actually "allowed" a never before reported (100J/220Ω = **XJ**/600Ω; X =) 273 joule maximum for second generation made-for-America BP devices and thus a 2.73 MTTLOI. Moreover, if Weiner's unofficial 1997 de facto standard which allows 1200 maximum joules were to be revealed, regulators might realize that the 1997 de facto standard represents not only a potential (12 - 2.73 =) 9.27 MTTLOI increase over the Mectan Transmutation for each individual recipient but a 4.4 fold increase in overall power (12 ÷ 2.73 = 4.4; 1200J/600Ω = 440J/220Ω; 440J at 220Ω vs 100J at 220Ω; 440J ÷ 100J = 4.4; 1200 ÷ 273 = 4.4) compared to second generation BP devices. In other words, the Weiner proposal more than quadruples the MTTLOI potential allowed for every individual recipient compared to that technically "allowed" for what are actually second generation made-for-America BP devices under the covert and quite illicit Mectan Transmutation.[102] Percentage-wise, in short, the newest 1997 Weiner standard represents a (1200 - 273 = 927J; 927J ÷ 273J = 3.40 =) 340% increase in Brief Pulse power and MTTLOI even compared to that illicitly allowed under the Mectan Transmutation. Compared to that allowed by the 1989 IEC Standard for second generation IEC BP devices (in Europe) which permitted a covert 217J ceiling, Weiner's new de facto standard represents a potential (12 - 2.17 =) 9.83 MTTLOI increase for each individual recipient and thus a 5.53 fold increase in overall power (12 ÷ 2.17 = 5.53; 1200J/500Ω = 720J/300Ω; 720J at 300Ω vs

[102] Also 1200J maximum ÷ 273J maximum = 4.4.

130J at 300Ω; 720J ÷ 130J = 5.53; 1200J ÷ 217J = 5.53). Percentage-wise, the Weiner de facto standard represents a (1200J - 217J = 983J; 983J ÷ 217J =) 453% increase in power even from that actually allowed by the corrupt 1989 IEC Standard.

Compared to first generation BP devices adhering to the original 110J ceiling stipulated under the 1982 APA Standard, Weiner's proposal provides for a (1200J - 110J =) 1090J increase in the original ceiling), a (12 - 1.1 =) 10.9 MTTLOI enhancement for each individual recipient[103] and a 10.9 fold increase in overall power (12 ÷ 1.1 = 10.9; 1200J ÷ 110J = 10.9). Percentage-wise, the Weiner de facto standard represents a (1200J - 110J = 1090J ÷ 110J = 9.90 =) 990% power increase compared to the 1982 APA Standard presented to and approved by the FDA for BP devices in 1982, a nearly 1000% increase in MTTLOI for all age recipients (12 - 1.1 = 10.9 ÷ 1.1 = 9.9 = 990%). Unfortunately, regulators have never been privy to such comparisons in that Weiner not only drops EO and ER/RRC reporting under his 1997 de facto standard, but excises any form of Joule reporting whatsoever, newly and totally supplanting maximum output in Joules with maximum output in Charge or millicoulombs. Due to the complete transition from EO (in terms of joules) to Charge (in terms of Coulombs), meaningful comparative analysis with previous Brief Pulse devices as well as with SW all but disappears. In brief, as a result of this metric transition and numerous other reporting strategies, the enhancement potential under Weiner's new de facto standard is invisible. Not surprisingly then, the increases in power with respect to extant third, potential fourth, and hypothetical fifth generation Brief Pulse devices compared to previous devices, including SW, have never been reported until now and so, the significance of the increase, never fully appreciated.

The 100J Figure and the Third Generation Brief Pulse Device

It bears emphasizing that because of the dramatically enhanced outputs of third generation BP devices allowed under Weiner's new de facto standard, manufacturers could no longer use the 100J figure even to report unexplicated ER/RRCs (in lieu of actual output in joules), without blatantly revealing jaw-dropping power and inconceivable MTTLOI enhancements. Maintaining the illusory 100J figure under Weiner's 1997 proposal standard would have meant replacing the "100J at 300Ω" pure-ER/RRC phrase depicted in the 1989 IEC standard with either an unwieldy and suspicious "100J at 41.6J" pure-ER/RRC phrase or replacing an already difficult to derive "130J at 300Ω" pure-ER/RRC with a very unwieldy 130J at 54.2Ω" pure-ER/RRC phrase, this or the astonishing "720J at 300Ω" or "528J at 220Ω" pure-ER/RRC phrases upon which the Weiner replacement standard is actually based (1200J/500Ω = 720J/300Ω = 100J/41.6Ω; 1200J/500Ω = 720J/300Ω = 130J/54.2Ω; 720J/300Ω = 528J/220Ω).[104] Clearly then, manufacturers chose to no longer report in Joules, opting instead not only to totally remove EO in joules, including unexplicated pure-ER/RRC reporting in terms of Joules/Impedance, but opting to report maximum output in terms of Charge alone, thus Weiner's new somewhat innocuous seeming 1200mC Charge maximum.

A General Preview of Third Generation Brief Pulse Devices

But while Weiner's new default standard potentially permits 1200J Brief Pulse devices, the actual third generation BP devices which began to emerge onto the marketplace about 1995 and which were to become "legal" under Weiner's new 1997 revision proposal, do not elicit 1200J. They do, however, elicit nearly 500J maximums, yet twice the power of second generation BP devices. This means third generation BP devices emit circa 5.0 MTTLOIs with BL "ECT" and circa 10 MTTLOIs with UL "ECT," doubling not only the output, but

---

[103] If we take the 70J at 220Ω ER/RRC allowed under the 1982 APA Standard and divide into 440J at 220Ω, we derive 6.3 fold (440J ÷ 70J = 6.3). However, this does not take into consideration the 110J ceiling in which case titration under Weiner's provision approaches eleven fold the dosing allowed under the 1982 APA Standard (1200J ÷ 110J = 10.9).

[104] Reporting the configuration "100J at 41.6Ω" would have revealed that 100J could be emitted circa seven times as fast relative to Impedance, delivering seven fold the electrical dosing delivered under the previously reported "100J at 300Ω" Pure-ER/RRC (100J/XΩ = 1200J/500Ω; X = 41.6Ω; 300/41.6 = 7.21 fold). Reporting "130J at 54.2Ω" would have revealed that 130J could be emitted roughly 5.5 times as fast relative to Impedance, delivering 5.5 fold the electrical dosing delivered under the previously allowed "130J at 300Ω" Pure-ER/RRC (130J/54.2Ω = 1200J/500Ω; 300/54.2 = 5.54 fold)

the MTTLOI of American-made second generation made-for-Europe MECTA and Somatics BP devices, and so almost quintupling the power of first generation made-for-America Brief Pulse devices. Certainly, the circa 500 Joules associated with third generation devices is an awesome figure in light of the original 110 Joule ceiling exemplified by the 108J MECTA "C" which when reported to the FDA in 1982, made Brief Pulse devices seem far superior to the high output emission and thus highly dangerous 200J B-24 Sine Wave device manufactured by Medcraft. Because the MECTA "C" was able to induce grand mal seizures at about half the power of SW, the reduced power of the prototypical MECTA "C" presented to the FDA between 1976 and 1982 seemed remarkably progressive (Department of Health and Human Services, 1982a, G2-G3). In that manufacturers were not able to make the same reduced output claims for second and third generation Brief Pulse devices, manufacturers quickly resorted to clever reporting tactics. Consequently, it is only by understanding that circa 100J machine readouts on second generation BP devices are actually reverse-ERs based on a false 220Ω Impedance constant, and it is only by converting newly reported Charge maximums to Joules for the newer third generation Brief Pulse devices, that the actual power of third generation Brief Pulse machines becomes apparent. Indeed, without conversion, the doubling of the unreported power and unreported MTTLOI of second generation IEC Brief Pulse devices (as opposed to first generation Brief Pulse devices), emitting a maximum output of about 230 unreported Joules (Cameron, 1994) remains invisible. In that neither the actual 273J ceiling for made-for-America second generation BP devices nor the 217J ceiling for made-for-Europe second generation BP devices has ever been reported until now, (but only false intimations of 100J maximums), the sudden revelation of circa 500J maximum third generation Brief Pulse devices, approximately five times the EO and MTTLOI of the 108J MECTA "C," circa 2.5 fold the maximum raw power potential of the (200J) B-24 SW by Medcraft, would have spelled disaster for Brief Pulse manufacturers, generally.[105] For Brief Pulse manufacturers, then, the only way forward seemed to be the passage of Weiner's then new 1997 IEC Standard for ECT devices greatly expanding the power restrictions of Brief Pulse, but couched in obfuscating terms, inconsistent with all previous Brief Pulse devices. Unfortunately for Brief Pulse manufacturers marketing third generation BP devices, the IEC wisely rejected the 1997 Weiner revision proposal. But while Weiner and associates were not able to convince the IEC that the Weiner 1997, 1200mC revision proposal for "ECT devices" should supplant the 1989 IEC standard for "ECT devices," thanks to the lobbying effort of the Weiner IEC sub-committee, as noted above, manufacturers did finally succeed in pressuring the IEC to withdraw the then current 1989 IEC standard for ECT devices altogether--the result of which was almost as good as the passage of Weiner's 1997 proposed revision itself! As noted above, by no longer having any official regulation to hinder them, manufacturers now became free to utilize Weiner's provision by default, thereby unofficially sanctioning already extant third generation Brief Pulse devices, moreover, quite possibly making even greater enhancements for even newer more powerful fourth and fifth generation Brief Pulse devices, as we shall soon examine.

To be sure, as already noted, third generation Brief Pulse devices do not reach 1200 joules, but they do double the output of second generation Brief Pulse devices as we shall now examine in detail. Indeed, the fact that under Weiner's new de facto standard, Brief Pulse machines could now emit 2.0 Amperes of current with an unreported 1200J ceiling with no reasonable ER/RRC limiter, in effect, meant that "ECT" devices were now deregulated, even allowing, as already noted, more powerful fourth and fifth generation Brief Pulse devices to come. Thus, while IEC electrical engineers out and out rejected Weiner's IEC replacement proposal for Brief Pulse "ECT" devices, this rejection failed to prevent the Weiner follow-up request for total withdrawal of the then current 1989 IEC Standard for "ECT" devices, so that Weiner's replacement proposal, though never officially adopted, has now become the world's de facto "standard." By preventing official adoption of both the 1982 APA Standard and the 1989 IEC Standard for "ECT" devices, and, indeed, by completely eradicating any official standard for "ECT" devices, no authorized regulation for "ECT" devices remains. Indeed, none exists today either in America or abroad. Not only is there no longer any regulation prohibiting third generation BP devices from being marketed and utilized in modern day clinical practice, then, but there is no longer any existing standard or regulation currently preventing or limiting the Weiner 1200J, 12.0 MTTLOI Brief Pulse device of the future. Indeed, such a monstrous device may already be in use.

---

[105] In that the B-24 was touted to elicit a 200J maximum and third generation BP devices are between 460 and 480J maximum, third generation BP devices are from (460J ÷ 200J = 2.3; 480J ÷ 200J =) 2.3 to 2.4 times the maximum power of the B-24. On the other hand, these maximums occur in disparate age categories.

SECTION X: Weiner's De Facto Standard: 3rd, 4th, and 5th Gen. BP Devices

CHAPTER 57

Third Generation Brief Pulse Devices

Though never reported as such, by using actual parameters reported to the Royal College of Psychiatry (correcting MECTA's flawed reporting), and then by simply substituting the remaining reported machine parameters into EO formulas: EO = Volts x Current x (hz x 2) x Wave Length x Duration, or EO = Current squared x Max Impedance x (hz x 2) x Wave Length x Duration, we can obtain the never before reported maximum outputs in Joules [106] of various American-made third generation Brief Pulse machines on the market today, devices which first appeared about 1995. We can then juxtapose the power of third generation BP devices with the power of equally unreported second generation BP devices, and finally with SW for meaningful contrasts. Somatics' third generation device is deemed the System IV [also known as the Somatics Thymatron DGx (FD x 2)]; while MECTA's two, third generation BP devices are deemed the JR/SR 1 "British" and JR/SR 2 "British." Simply by converting somewhat useless Charge figures back into Joules, therefore, we can, for the first time, see that extant third generation BP machines "allowed" under Weiner's new 1997 de facto revision proposal, emit 452, 460, and 480 maximum Joules respectively, twice as powerful as Somatics and MECTA made-for-Europe second generation BP devices.

(1) Third Generation System IV by Somatics Inc.

Under Weiner's default standard, as previously noted, third generation BP devices are no longer reported in terms of EO or Joules, but in terms of Charge or millicoulombs making comparison with previous devices much less telling, if not useless. Ignoring reports in terms of Charge, therefore, we can use the fact that Somatics Incorporated, unlike MECTA Corporation, provides enough information to convert and so determine the output ceiling of its third generation BP device in terms of Joules. By using the maximum Pulse Width (i.e. Wave Length) and maximum Duration reported by Somatics (for its third generation BP device)--as well as the 500Ω maximum Impedance ceiling (also reported by Somatics) used for international devices in general, [107] we can obtain the exact albeit never before reported EO ceiling in Joules for the 1995 third generation Somatics Thymatron DGx (FD x 2)--also known in America as the System IV (Royal College of Psychiatry, 1995, p. 125; Somatics Incorporated, 1999):

---

[106] The author's 1994 article published in *Journal of Mind and Behavior* (Cameron, 1994) pointed out that Brief Pulse devices had more than doubled in power to about 250 Joules since their 1976 resurgence. Weiner's new revision has allowed these same already enhanced second generation BP devices to double once again, this time to around 500 Joules.

[107] The 500Ω ceiling is contained within the both 1989 IEC standard and Weiner's 1997 de fact standard.

450 volts x .9 amps x 140 pulses x .0015 sec. pulse width x 5.32 seconds= **452.5J**.

or

.9 amps x .9 amps x 500Ω x 140 pulses x .0015 sec. pulse width x 5.32 seconds = **452.5J**.

As we can see, the Somatics third generation BP device emits an unreported 452J maximum output. Skipping (for now) details as to how the author derived various specifics, the chart below depicts the exact output of the third generation System IV in every age group (as well as numerous other detailed parameters).

ACTUAL CONSTANT CURRENT (**3rd Generation**)
SYSTEM IV BRIEF PULSE (IEC) DEVICE
by **SOMATICS** Inc. 1995
BASED ON UNREPORTED PURE-ER/RRC INTERPRETATION OF
"199J at 220Ω" or "272J at 300Ω"

VOLTAGE	POWER % @ Age	AGE Yrs	Ω Ohms	FREQUENCY (Hz)	DURATION (Secs)	CURRENT mAmps	ENERGY Joules	CHARGE mC
45	10	10	50	30	1.244	900	4.54	100.8
90	20	20	100	30	2.47	900	18.14	200.16
135	30	30	150	50	2.24	900	40.78	302
180	40	40	200	50	2.99	900	72.58	403.2
225	50	50	250	50	3.73	900	113.4	504
270	60	60	300	70	3.2	900	163.3	604.8
292.5	65	65	325	70	3.47	900	191.6	655.2
315	70	70	350	70	3.73	900	222.26	705.6
360	80	80	400	70	4.27	900	290.4	806.4
405	90	90	450	70	4.8	900	367.4	907.2
450	100	100	**500**	70	5.32	900	**452**	**1005**

(.0015 Sec. WL)

(2) 3rd Generation "JR/SR 1 British" by MECTA Incorporated

Though never reported in terms of EO (Joules) but only in terms of Charge, we can similarly and for the first time depict useful EO charts below (in terms of Joules) for both of MECTA's third generation BP devices.

Correcting a false 400Ω maximum Impedance and false 240V maximum Voltage provided by MECTA (to the RCP), the **3rd Generation MECTA "JR/SR 1 British"** device contains the following maximum output (Royal College of Psychiatry, 1995, p. 124):

400 volts x .8 amps x 180 pulses x .002 sec. pulse width x 4.0 seconds = **460J**[108]

or using another formula:

.8 amps x .8 amps x 500Ω x 180 pulses x .002 sec. pulse width x 4.0 seconds = **460J**.[109]

---

[108] Note that at the 240V maximum spuriously reported to the RCP by MECTA, the output equals the maximum allowed under the Mectan Transmutation of the 1982 APA Standard of 276J, falsely indicating a first time enhancement. (240 volts x .8 amps x 180 pulses x .002 sec. pulse width x 4 seconds = 276J).

[109] The author's 1994 (Cameron, 1994) publication on U.S. devices reported MECTA second generation devices capable of 256 Joules. This was based upon the author's conclusion that increments on the MECTA dial--256--represent Joules, concomitant with the fact that Voltage based upon 256J (444.4 volts), results in a precise 555.5Ω maximum, the exact Impedance provided by Somatics for its comparable second generation Thymatron DG, known to emit 500 maximum Volts. MECTA has long avoided reporting both Voltage and actual Impedance making true EO a speculative proposition. In 1995, as noted above, the Royal College of Psychiatry reported the MECTA devices utilizing 240 volts maximum. The author maintains this to be incorrect and stands by the approximate 444.4 volts reported in 1994 (Cameron, 1994) for the American versions of MECTA SR/JR 1 and 2. RCP's report of 240 volts may have been erroneously based on maximum Voltage reported in the MECTA manual for required power sources (wall voltage), but which does not reflect maximum Voltage of the device itself. Or more likely, MECTA reported not an actual but an unexplicated ER Voltage.

Saving derivation details for later, the chart below depicts approximate outputs at every age level for the third generation JR/SR 1 British Brief Pulse IEC device.

Approximate Actual CONSTANT CURRENT (**3rd GENERATION**)
"JR/SR 1 BRITISH" BRIEF PULSE **IEC** DEVICE
by **MECTA** Corp. 1995
BASED ON UNREPORTED PURE-ER/RRC OF
"202.4J at 220Ω" or "276J AT 300Ω"

VOLTAGE	POWER % @ Age	AGE Yrs	Ω Ohms	FREQUENCY (Hz)	DURATION (Secs)	CURRENT mAmps	ENERGY Joules	CHARGE mC
40	10	10	50	90	0.5	800	5.76	144
80	20	20	100	90	0.8	800	18.43	230
120	30	30	150	90	1.2	800	41.47	345.6
160	40	40	200	90	1.6	800	73.73	460.8
200	50	50	250	90	2.0	800	115.2	576
240	60	60	300	90	2.4	800	165.88	691.2
260	65	65	325	90	2.6	800	194.68	748.8
280	70	70	350	90	2.8	800	225.8	806.4
320	80	80	400	90	3.2	800	295	921.6
360	90	90	450	90	3.6	800	373	1036.8
400	100	100	500	90	4.0	800	460J	1152

(.002 WL)

(3) 3rd Generation "JR/SR 2 British" by MECTA Incorporated

Again, correcting a misleading 400Ω maximum Impedance and 240V maximum Voltage provided by MECTA (to the RCP), the 1995 **3rd Generation MECTA JR/SR 2** device deemed the "British" JR/SR 2 contains the following maximum output in Joules (Royal College of Psychiatry, 1995, p. 124):

400 volts x .8 x 180 pulses x .0014 sec. pulse width x 5.96 seconds = **480J.**

or

.8 amps x .8 amps x 500Ω x 180 pulses x .0014 sec. pulse width x 5.96 seconds = **480J.**[110]

Again, saving derivation details for later, the chart below depicts approximate outputs at every age level for the third generation JR/SR 2 British Brief Pulse IEC device.

(See second generation BP devices.) Beale et al. (1994) found MECTA and Somatics' devices comparable in terms of suprathreshold dosing, which the reported maximum 240 Volts (over a 4 second Duration) simply would not accommodate. Moreover, by Ohm's Law, 240 volts does not coincide with the 400Ω maximum reported for MECTA devices by RCP, which would require at least 320 Volts. The author has attempted both through freedom of information requests and personal interviews to obtain the actual Voltage and/or actual Impedance from MECTA, without which actual EO is impossible to determine. The reluctance to report and the tendency to manipulate the truth is typical of manufacturers and particularly of MECTA. Until manufacturers are forced to report the true parameters for their devices, therefore, the author is compelled to speculate, standing by his very plausible conclusions until proven otherwise.

[110] Though MECTA again claims an upper impedance of 400 ohms, no rule prevents MECTA from using a higher Impedance of 500Ω, and thus 500Ω is presumed here. But even if the MECTA device is only capable of 400Ω, a notion which the author patently rejects, the EO is still an awesome 384 Joules [.8 x .8 x 400Ω x 180 pulses x .0014 x 5.96 = 384 Joules].

Approximate Actual CONSTANT CURRENT **3rd GENERATION**
"JR/SR 2 BRITISH" BRIEF PULSE IEC DEVICE
by **MECTA** Corp. 1995
BASED ON UNREPORTED PURE-ER/RRC OF
"211.2J at 220Ω" or "288J at 300Ω"

VOLTAGE	POWER % @ Age	AGE Yrs	Ω Ohms	FREQUENCY (Hz)	DURATION (Secs)	CURRENT mAmps	ENERGY Joules	CHARGE mC
40	8.33	10	50	40	1.0	800	3.58	89.6
80	16.66	20	100	40	2.57	800	18.44	230.4
120	25	30	150	60	2.57	800	41.48	345.6
160	33.3	40	200	60	3.42	800	73.72	460.8
200	41.65	50	250	60	4.28	800	115.2	576
240	50	60	300	90	3.42	800	165.88	691.2
260	58.3	65	325	90	3.714	800	194.68	748.8
280	66.64	70	350	90	4.0	800	225.8	806.4
320	75	80	400	90	4.57	800	295	921.6
360	83.3	90	450	90	5.14	800	373	1036.8
400	91.6	100	500	90	5.7	800	460J	1152
400	100	100	500	90	5.96	800	480J	1200

(.001--.0014sec Pulse Width; only 0014 used in chart below)

Newly "allowed" by the withdrawal of the 1989 IEC Standard for ECT devices and thus the application of Weiner's new 1997 de facto standard (which calls for Charge outputs in millicoulombs in lieu of EO in Joules), the above 1995 third generation Somatics and MECTA BP devices are capable of outputs up to 453J, 460J, and 480J respectively. Marketed internationally, and yet limited to .9 and .8 Amperes of Current respectively as are 252 and 259J second generation made-for-America Somatics and MECTA BP devices based on the illicit, never before reported Mectan Transmutation, third generation BP devices, based on the newer 1997 Weiner revision proposal, have ***approximately*** doubled (compared to second generation IEC BP devices) both in output and MTTLOI. Compared to Somatics and MECTA second generation IEC BP devices which elicit unreported maximum outputs of 226J, 230J, and 240J, in turn based on the broadest possible interpretation of the 1989 IEC Standard, Somatics and MECTA third generation IEC BP devices ***exactly*** double the power and thus the MTTLOI of second generation IEC BP devices. While Charge reporting alone (sans joule reporting) hints that these devices have doubled in power compared to the previous generation of BP devices, that is from about 500-600mC up to a circa 1200mC maximum, Weiner's de facto standard makes it impossible to compare what are actually third generation BP devices to what are actually second generation BP devices in terms of EO or Joules; nor can we compare third generation BP devices to first generation BP devices for the same reason. Moreover, we cannot compare third generation BP devices to SW devices also previously measured in Joules. This is critical in that what seem like first generation BP devices (with circa 100J ceilings emitting 5-600mC Charge maximums) are actually second generation BP devices with circa 250J ceilings emitting 5-600mC Charge maximums. The absence of meaningful comparisons due to the absence of a single consistent measurement, in this case "Joules," blinds us to the truth--that these machines are becoming increasingly more, not less powerful over time. In lieu of merely doubling the output emitted by the 108 Joule MECTA "C" which indeed conformed to the original 1982, 110J APA ceiling standard, Weiner's transition to Charge absent EO (in joules), veils that what are actually third generation BP devices have more than quadrupled in power and MTTLOI compared to first generation BP devices, in some cases emitting almost five fold the output and MTTLOI of the original MECTA "C." Based on Charge reporting alone then, what appear to be second generation BP devices representing the first major power enhancement, are actually third generation BP devices representing the second major power enhancement within the modern BP era, enhancements which cannot be clearly viewed due to Weiner's obfuscation and elimination of consistent EO parameters, specifically--joules.

Charge Ceilings for Third generation BP Devices

Second generation made-for-America as well as made-for-Europe (IEC) BP devices manufactured by Somatics and MECTA between 1983-1994 emit maximum Charges of 504 and 576mC respectively (Cameron, 1994).
Weiner's 1997 revision proposal, now the default standard, reads:

> Output charge shall be limited to 1200mC.
> (International Electrotechnical Commission, 1997, Dec 26, p. 4)

Under Weiner's 1997 default standard containing a new 1200mC Charge ceiling, we can see that Charge more than doubles. In sum, the Charge elicited by what are actually third generation BP devices doubles the Charge elicited by what are actually second (not first) generation BP devices.

(1) ***The Somatics' System IV*: Charge for the Third Generation Somatics BP Device**

Third generation BP devices entail a simple doubling in power of second generation IEC BP devices. If, for instance we simply double the Pulse Width of the second generation Somatics' Thymatron DGx IEC BP device from .001 to .002 Seconds leaving all other parameters unchanged, the newly derived Charge output transitions from a second generation 504mC maximum Charge to a third generation 1008mC maximum Charge, exactly doubling the Charge of the second generation DGx:

Charge = .9A x (70hz x 2) x .002PW x 4.0 Secs. = 1008mC,

Indeed, 1008mC is the actual Charge reported by Royal College of Psychiatry for what is actually Somatics' third generation "System IV" (Royal College of Psychiatry, 1995, p. 124).
While the actual maximum Pulse Width of the third generation Somatics System IV [see Somatics and Royal College of Psychiatry (Royal College of Psychiatry, 1995, p. 124)] does **not** transition from the .001 Second Pulse Width (of the second generation Somatics device) to a simple .002 Second Pulse Width, the actual transition from a .001 Second Pulse Width to a .0015 Pulse Width, and from a 4.0 Second maximum Duration to a compensatory 5.33 Second maximum Duration achieves the same doubling effect. By plugging in the increases in both Pulse Width and Duration which Somatics actually employs for the Third Generation "System IV" then, we observe the perfect doubling of Charge, that is the 504mC maximum emitted by the second generation DGx transitions to a perfect 1008mC maximum emitted by the Somatics third generation "System IV:"

Charge = .9 x (70hz x 2) x .0015PW x 5.33 Secs. = 1008mC.

Thus, as noted, maximum power for the Somatics' third generation IEC BP device, the System IV, is a simple doubling of the power of Somatics' second generation IEC BP device, the Thymatron DGx, and this perfect doubling in power, as we shall see, occurs in all age categories with respect to MTTLOI (Multifold Threshold Titration Level Output Intensity) or X times threshold output.

Alternative formulas confirm the System IV's maximum EO of about 454 Joules:

Charge = EO/Impedance x Amperage; **EO** = Impedance x Amperage x Charge.
Charge = 454J/500Ω x .9 Amperes = 1008mC; 500Ω x .9A x 1.006C = **454J**.

Using the new (albeit unreported) pure-ER/RRC both at 220Ω and 300Ω (which has exactly doubled from "136J at 300Ω" or "99.4/7J at 220Ω" (for the DGx) to "272J at 300Ω" or "199.5J at 220Ω" [111] (for the Somatics' System IV), and which reflects the simultaneous doubling of MTTLOI from second to third generation BP devices, we can again derive the reported maximum Charge for the Somatics' System IV of 1008mC.

Charge (from ER/RRC) = 199.5J/220Ω x .9 Amperes = 1008mC.
Charge (from ER/RRC) = 272J/300Ω x .9 Amperes = 1008mC

The consistent 2.26 MTTLOI of the DGx (IEC Brief Pulse device) for all age groups now doubles to become a circa 4.52 MTTLOI, that is, 4.52 x Threshold Output for every age category. The third generation Somatics' System IV below, in short, exactly doubles the power of the second generation Somatics' DGx not only in Charge, but in unreported Joules, reflected by the perfect (albeit unreported) doubling of the pure-ER/RRC principle, the reporting of which, like joules generally, has been entirely dropped under the 1997 Weiner default standard. Below, in sum, are the second and third generation Somatics' BP devices in terms of both Charge and Joules for meaningful comparative analysis.

ACTUAL CONSTANT CURRENT THYMATRON DGx BRIEF PULSE DEVICE
(**2nd Generation**) by Somatics Inc. 1994[112]
BASED ON PURE-ER/RRC INTERPRETATION OF 136J AT 300Ω or 99.4/7J AT 220Ω

VOLTAGE	POWER % @ Age	AGE Yrs	Ω Ohms	FREQUENCY (Hz)	DURATION (SECs)	CURRENT mAmps	ENERGY Joules	CHARGE mC
45	10	10	50	30	.93	900	2.27	50.4
90	20	20	100	30	1.87	900	9.072	100.8
135	30	30	150	50	1.68	900	20.39	151
180	40	40	200	50	2.24	900	36.29	201.6
225	50	50	250	50	2.8	900	56.7	252
270	60	60	300	70	2.4	900	81.65	302.4
292.5	65	65	325	70	2.6	900	95.8	327.6
315	70	70	350	70	2.8	900	111.13	352.8
360	80	80	400	70	3.2	900	145.2	403.20
405	90	90	450	70	3.6	900	183.7	453.6
450	100	100	**500**	70	4.0	900	**226.8**	**504**

(.001 WL) (see also DGx FD)

ACTUAL CONSTANT CURRENT SYSTEM IV BRIEF PULSE DEVICE
(**3rd Generation**) By SOMATICS Inc. 1994
BASED ON PURE-ER/RRC INTERPRETATION OF 271.5J AT 300Ω or 199J AT 220Ω

VOLTAGE	POWER % @ Age	AGE Yrs	Ω Ohms	FREQUENCY (Hz)	DURATION (SECs)	CURRENT mAmps	ENERGY Joules	CHARGE mC
45	10	10	50	30	1.244	900	4.54	100.8
90	20	20	100	30	2.47	900	18.14	200.16
135	30	30	150	50	2.24	900	40.78	302
180	40	40	200	50	2.99	900	72.58	403.2
225	50	50	250	50	3.73	900	113.4	504
270	60	60	300	70	3.2	900	163.3	604.8
292.5	65	65	325	70	3.47	900	191.6	655.2
315	70	70	350	70	3.73	900	222.26	705.6
360	80	80	400	70	4.27	900	290.4	806.4
405	90	90	450	70	4.8	900	367.4	907.2
450	100	100	**500**	70	5.32	900	**452**	**1005**

(.0015 WL)

[111] ER derivation: XJ/220Ω = 452J/500Ω = 199.5J; XJ/300Ω = 452.5J/500Ω = 272J

[112] Maximum Voltage of 450 is provided by Somatics for the DGx. Charge, Duration, Frequency, Pulse Width (.001), Age correlation and Percentages of power are provided by Somatics for all categories (Swartz and Abrams, 1996, back cover). Percentages of Power can be translated into correlating Voltages. For instance, 90% of the maximum 450V = 405Volts. EO and Impedance at 90% can then be derived. Impedance = Voltage/Current. Impedance = 405/.9 = 450Ω at 90%. EO = Charge x Current x Impedance. EO = 183.7J at 90% of DGx's power.

The Somatics' System IV table directly above exactly doubles the power of the DGx IEC table (above that). The Somatics' System IV table is based upon known parameters of maximum Voltage, Impedance, Charge, Wave Length (.0015), Frequency, and Duration. Other figures are based upon the ratio of actual maximum charge to maximum threshold charge and actual maximum EO to threshold EO on the Thymatron DGx which is 2.268 fold threshold with BL "ECT" both in Charge and EO. Simply by dividing the known maximum Charge for the third generation System IV by the known maximum Charge for the second generation DGx (1005/504 = circa 2.0) a ratio can be deduced of 1:2; this translates into the third generation System IV having 2.0 fold the Charge outputs of Somatics' second generation IEC BP device (the DGx) for all age groups. This further translates into the System IV delivering a 4.52 MTTLOI for all age groups compared to the DGx delivering a 2.26 MTTLOI for all age groups.[113] The same method can be applied to EO in Joules (452J/226.8J = 2.0) resulting in the same 1:2 ratio between Somatics' second generation DGx and Somatics' third generation System IV. EOs translate into the System IV delivering a (2 x 2.26) = <u>4.52</u> MTTLOI with BL ECT in every age category compared to the DGx delivering a 2.26 MTTLOI with BL ECT in every age category. EO and Charge figures can be corroborated through the Charge formula for BP devices: (Charge = EO/Current x Impedance). Durations are adjusted accordingly: (Duration = Charge/Current x (hz x 2) x WL). With respect to the made-for-America Thymatron DG (as opposed to the made-for-Europe DGx) the entire last row of the DG is simply deleted, the remaining rows then doubled to form the System IV. This is because the DGx is limited to a 500 ohm Impedance maximum and thus 450V (in lieu of the DG's 500V) due to IEC regulations. The System IV is thus based on the second generation made-for-Europe DGx (the parameters of which are simply doubled) in lieu of the second generation made-for-America DG. The System IV third generation BP device thus delivers a <u>4.52</u> MTTLOI with BL ECT and a <u>9.04</u> MTTLOI with UL ECT in every age category compared to the DGx which delivers a <u>2.26</u> MTTLOI with BL ECT and a <u>4.52</u> MTTLOI with UL ECT in every age category. In short, with all parameters visible via conversion of millicoulombs to joules, it is easy to see that outputs and MTTLOIs for all recipients have exactly doubled from 2nd to 3rd generation Somatics BP devices. Additionally, we can now see that maximum raw power of the Somatics' System IV (circa 452J) is more than twice the maximum raw power of the B-24 SW even hyperbolically depicted as delivering a 200J maximum (452J/200J = <u>2.26 fold SW</u>).

In sum, Somatics' third generation Thymatron BP device known as "System IV" above is actually the 226.8J Thymatron DGx (which more or less "conforms" to the 1989 IEC Standard) doubled in power, newly "allowed" by Weiner's newer 1997 de facto standard. To accomplish this doubling, as already noted, the third generation System IV uses a combination enhanced Pulse Width and enhanced Duration compared to Somatics' second generation DGx. Succinctly, the power of Somatics second generation IEC BP device, the Thymatron DGx, doubles in power to form the Somatics third generation IEC device, the System IV, now "legal" under Weiner's 1997 IEC revision proposal. The 1997 IEC revision proposal has become the new general "standard" by default (due to the deletion of the 1989 IEC Standard for "ECT" Devices) as noted above, and which we shall further investigate.

(2) *Third Generation <u>MECTA JR/SR 1 (British) IEC Brief Pulse Device</u>:* Charge for Third *Generation MECTA JR/SR 1 Device*

One of the two MECTA third generation BP devices is known as the MECTA JR/SR 1 (British) IEC device. Actual parameters, including its maximum Charge of 1152mC used in the Charge formula below, are provided by MECTA and the Royal College of Psychiatry (Royal College of Psychiatry, 1995, p. 124)].

Charge = .8A x (90hz x 2) x .002PW x 4.0 = <u>1152mC</u>

Simply by observing the juxtaposed second and third generation MECTA BP charts (provided by the author--never by MECTA), we can see for the first time that the third generation MECTA IEC JR/SR ***1*** (British) Brief Pulse device is merely the second generation MECTA IEC JR/SR ***1*** Brief Pulse device with doubled Duration (from 2.0 to 4.0 Seconds). Both the unreported EO and the reported Charge thus doubles from the

[113] The second generation DGx delivers 2.26 times threshold for all age categories; whereas, the third generation System IV delivers 4.52 times threshold for all age categories.

second to the third generation BP device, in turn doubling its new (never before reported) pure-ER/RRC as well as doubling the equally unreported MTTLOI for every age recipient. Compare the second generation JR/SR 1 IEC Brief Pulse and the third generation JR/SR 1 (British) IEC Brief Pulse devices below:

Approximate Actual CONSTANT CURRENT **JR/SR 1** BRIEF PULSE **IEC** BP DEVICE
(2nd GENERATION) by MECTA Corp. 1985
BASED ON PURE-ER/RRC OF **"138J AT 300Ω"** or **"101.2J at 220Ω"**

VOLTAGE	POWER % @ Age	AGE Yrs	Ω Ohms	FREQUENCY (Hz)	DURATION (SECs)	CURRENT mAmps	ENERGY Joules	CHARGE mC
40	10	10	50	40	0 .45	800	2.30	57.6
80	20	20	100	40	0 .90	800	9.22	115.2
120	30	30	150	60	0 .864	800	20.74	172.8
160	40	40	200	60	1.20	800	36.86	230.4
200	50	50	250	60	1.50	800	57.6	288
240	60	60	300	90	1.20	800	82.94	345.6
260	65	65	325	90	1.30	800	97.34	374.4
280	70	70	350	90	1.40	800	112.9	403.2
320	80	80	400	90	1.60	800	147.5	460.8
360	90	90	450	90	1.80	800	186.48	518.4
400	100	100	500	90	2.0	800	230J	576

(.001--.**002 sec** Pulse Width; only .**002** used in chart above)

Figures for the second generation JR/SR 2 IEC device above are approximate, but probable. Charges are based upon the maximum Charge for second generation made-for-America BP devices.[114] EO is derived from the formula: EO (BP) = Charge x Current x Impedance.[115] Durations are derived from: Duration (BP) = Charge/Current x (hz x 2) x WL.; Voltage = Ohm's Law: Voltage = Current x Ω. Charge = Current x (hz x 2) x PW x Duration.

Approximate Actual CONSTANT CURRENT **JR/SR 1** BRIEF PULSE **IEC** BP DEVICE
(3rd GENERATION) "BRITISH" by MECTA Corp. 1995
BASED ON PURE-ER/RRC OF **"276J AT 300Ω"** or **"202.4J at 220Ω"**

VOLTAGE	POWER % @ Age	AGE Yrs	Ω Ohms	FREQUENCY (Hz)	DURATION (SECs)	CURRENT mAmps	ENERGY Joules	CHARGE mC
40	10	10	50	40	0.9	800	4.60	115
80	20	20	100	40	1.8	800	18.43	230
120	30	30	150	60	1.8	800	41.47	345.6
160	40	40	200	60	2.4	800	73.73	460.8
200	50	50	250	60	3.0	800	115.2	576
240	60	60	300	90	2.4	800	165.88	691.2
260	65	65	325	90	2.6	800	194.68	748.8
280	70	70	350	90	2.8	800	225.8	806.4
320	80	80	400	90	3.2	800	295	921.6
360	90	90	450	90	3.6	800	373	1036.8
400	100	100	500	90	4.0	800	**460J**	**1152**

(.001--.**002 sec** Pulse Width; only .**002** used in chart above)

EO is based upon: EO (BP) = Charge x Current x Impedance. Duration is based upon: Duration (BP) = Charge/Current x (hz x 2) x WL; Voltage = Ohm's Law: Voltage = Current x Ω. Also, Charge = EO/Current x Impedance. EO = Voltage x Current x (hz x 2) x WL x Duration. Charge = Current x (hz x 2) x PW x Duration.

Alternative formulas for MECTA JR/SR 1 (British) Third Generation IEC JR/SR 1 confirm 460J maximum EO in Joules (Charge = EO/Impedance x Amperage; EO = Impedance x Amperage x Charge), an output not legal under the 1989 IEC Standard for "ECT," but newly "legal" under Weiner's 1997 replacement provision.

[114] 576mC is reported for the MECTA second generation made-for-America devices but MECTA underreports maximum Charge for its second generation IEC devices (proved in the previous section) and this has been corrected by the author (Royal College of Psychiatry, 1995, p. 124).

[115] The second generation JR/SR 1--IEC BP device had an alleged minimal stimulus Duration of .5 Seconds. On the chart, a .45 Second minimal stimulus Duration is used to represent a 2.3 multifold threshold titration level output intensity of 2.3 Joules. The discrepancy is negligible and may be due to a slightly lower than 50Ω Impedance depicted for the ten year old child.

Charge = **460J**/500Ω x .8A = 1152mC; EO = 500Ω x .8A x 1.152C = **460J**

If we compare the unreported "138J at 300Ω" or reported "101.2J at 220Ω" second generation JR/SR 1 (two charts above) to the newly unreported "276J at 300Ω" or "202.4J at 220Ω" third generation JR/SR 1 British (directly above), the critical doubling of MTTLOI delivered to every age recipient is revealed. Using these new third generation pure-ER/RRC phrases, we can derive the reported maximum Charge for MECTA's third generation JR/SR 1 above, confirming the new albeit unreported pure-ER/RRCs.

Charge (from ER/RRC) = 202.4J/220Ω[116] x .8A = 1152mC
Charge (from ER/RRC) = 276J/300Ω x .8A = 1152mC

(3) *Third Generation MECTA JR/SR 2 (British) IEC Brief Pulse Device*: *Charge for Third Generation MECTA JR/SR 2 Device*

The second of MECTA's third generation Brief Pulse devices is known as the MECTA JR/SR 2 (British) IEC device. Some actual parameters (current, hertz, pulse width, and maximum duration) including the new maximum Charge of 1200mC used in the Charge formula below are again provided by MECTA via the Royal College of Psychiatry (Royal College of Psychiatry, 1995, p. 124)].

Charge = .8 x (90hz x 2) x .0014 x 5.96 = 1200mC

Observing the juxtaposed second and third generation Brief Pulse charts generated by the author below--never by MECTA, we can see for the first time anywhere that the third generation MECTA IEC JR/SR **2** (British) BP device is merely the second generation MECTA IEC JR/SR **2** with doubled Duration (2.98 maximum Seconds becomes 5.96 maximum Seconds). The (unreported) maximum EO (of 240 Joules) and maximum Charge (of 600mC) for the second generation JR/SR 2 IEC device below, clearly doubles to form the newer third generation JR/SR 2 IEC, in turn doubling the previous pure-ER/RRC, in turn doubling the critical MTTLOI for every individual recipient.

Approximate Actual CONSTANT CURRENT **JR/SR 2** BRIEF PULSE **IEC** BP DEVICE
(2nd GENERATION) by MECTA Corp. 1985
BASED ON PURE-ER/RRC OF **"144J at 300Ω"** or **"105.6J at 220Ω"**

VOLTAGE	POWER % @ Age	AGE Yrs	Ω Ohms	FREQUENCY (Hz)	DURATION (SECs)	CURRENT mAmps	ENERGY Joules	CHARGE mC
40	10	10	50	90	0.298	800	2.40	60
80	20	20	100	90	0.595	800	9.60	120
120	30	30	150	90	0.893	800	21.6	180
160	40	40	200	90	1.19	800	38.4	240
200	50	50	250	90	1.49	800	60.0	300
240	60	60	300	90	1.79	800	86.4	360
260	65	65	325	90	1.94	800	101.4	390
280	70	70	350	90	2.08	800	117.5	420
320	80	80	400	90	2.38	800	153.6	480
360	90	90	450	90	2.67	800	194.4	540
400	100	100	500	90	2.98	800	240J	600

(Modified to .001--.0014 Sec. Pulse Width; only .0014 used in chart above)

The probable 240J JR/SR 2 IEC device above is exactly half as powerful as the 3rd generation JR/SR 2 below, illegal under the 1989 IEC Standard. Except for the doubling of Duration and more flexible Frequency parameters, the dynamics of the (second generation) JR/SR 2 IEC device (based on the 1989 IEC standard)

---

[116] ER for Third Generation JR/SR 1: (To obtain ER/RRC: XJ/220Ω = 460J/500Ω. X = 202.4J at 220Ω); 202.4J/220Ω = 276J/300Ω = 460J/500Ω.

and the (third generation) JR/SR 2 IEC device (based on Weiner's newer 1997 revision provision) are identical.[117] In short, the third generation device has exactly doubled the second generation device in power and thus MTTLOI for every age recipient.

Approximate Actual CONSTANT CURRENT **JR/SR 2** BRIEF PULSE **IEC** DEVICE
(3rd GENERATION) "BRITISH" by MECTA Corp. 1995
BASED ON PURE-ER/RRC OF **"288J at 300Ω"** or **"211.2J at 220Ω"**

VOLTAGE	POWER % @ Age	AGE Yrs	Ω Ohms	FREQUENCY (Hz)	DURATION (SECs)	CURRENT mAmps	ENERGY Joules	CHARGE mC
40	10	10	50	40	1.34	800	4.8	120
80	20	20	100	40	2.68	800	19.2	240
120	30	30	150	60	2.68	800	43.2	360
160	40	40	200	60	3.57	800	76.8	480
200	50	50	250	60	4.46	800	120	600
240	60	60	300	90	2.58	800	172.8	720
260	65	65	325	90	3.88	800	202.8	780
280	70	70	350	90	4.16	800	235	840
320	80	80	400	90	4.76	800	307.2	960
360	90	90	450	90	5.34	800	388.8	1080
400	100	100	500	90	5.96	800	480J	1200

(.001--.0014 Sec. Pulse Width; only .0014 used in chart above)[118]

Alternative Charge formula for MECTA JR/SR 2 (British) Third Generation IEC JR/SR 1 confirms new 480J EO maximum twice as powerful as second generation: (Charge = EO/Impedance x Amperage; EO = Impedance x Amperage x Charge).

Charge (from non-speculative maximums) = **480J**/500Ω x .8A = 1200mC;
EO = 500Ω x .8A x 1.200C = **480J**.

Using the probable but unreported pure-ER/RRC of "144J at 300Ω" or "105.6J at 220Ω" for the second generation JR/SR 2 IEC Brief Pulse device two charts above, we can see that the third generation JR/SR 2 IEC (British) Brief Pulse device doubles to a never before reported "288J at 300Ω" or "211.2J at 220Ω" pure-ER/RRC (one chart above), doubling the MTTLOI in every age category. From the new ER/RRCs, we can derive the reported maximum Charge for MECTA's third generation JR/SR 2, newly expanded via the 1997 Weiner default standard. Not surprisingly, the reporting of the new third generation pure-ER/RRC phrase is discarded under Weiner's new 1997 de facto standard.

Charge (from ER/RRC) = 211.2J/220Ω[119] x .8A = 1200mC
Charge (from ER/RRC) = 288J/300Ω x .8A = 1200mC

In sum, under Weiner's new 1997 revision provision, the second generation JR/SR **1** IEC BP device doubles in power to become the third generation JR/SR **1** BP IEC BP device; whereas, the second generation JR/SR **2** IEC BP device doubles in power to become the third generation JR/SR **2** BP IEC device. The aim is to double the MTTLOI for every age recipient from 2.3 to 4.6 and from 2.4 to 4.8 respectively with BL "ECT" for all age categories. Accordingly, the MTTLOI with UL "ECT" doubles from 4.6 to 9.2 and from 4.8 to 9.6 respectively.

---

[117] The 240J second generation MECTA JR/SR 1 IEC above may have emitted only 230J (thus with the bottom row missing in the table above) but was more likely a 240J device in that the third generation is more likely an exact doubling of the second generation model.

[118] EO is based upon: EO (BP) = Charge x Current x Impedance. Duration is based upon: Duration (BP) = Charge/Current x (hz x 2) x WL; Voltage = Ohm's Law: Voltage = Current x Ω. Also, Charge = EO/Current x Impedance. EO = Voltage x Current x (hz x 2) x WL x Duration.

[119] ER/RRC for Third Generation JR/SR 2: (To obtain ER/RRC for 3rd generation JR/SR2: XJ/220Ω = 480J/500Ω. X = 211.2J at 220Ω). 211.2J/220Ω = 288J/300Ω = 480J/500Ω. 211.2J/220Ω = 288J/300Ω.

Conclusion:

Third generation Somatics and MECTA BP devices, based on Weiner's 1997 default standard, have been extant since at least 1995. These devices utilize never before reported output maximums of between 452 and 480J respectively, a never before reported circa "200J at 220Ω" Pure-ER/RRC (as opposed to a circa "100J at 220Ω" Pure-ER/RRC), and emit maximum reported Charges of between 1000 and 1200mC. In short, both Somatics and MECTA third generation Brief Pulse devices illegally produced and marketed in 1995, are newly "allowed" under Weiner's 1997 IEC de facto standard, a "standard" which eliminates both EO and pure-ER/RRC reporting (both of which are depicted in Joules). The new 1997 "standard" furtively permits up to 1200 Joules of output. In that in 1997, the 1989 IEC Standard for "ECT" devices was altogether withdrawn from the general IEC Standard for Medical Devices without replacement, beginning in 1998, international manufacturers of BP devices began utilizing Weiner's rejected 1997 revision proposal as a default "standard." In essence, "ECT" device manufacturers became and presently continue to remain unregulated.[120] Illegal under the 1982 APA Standard, illegal under the 1989 IEC Standard, and even illegal under the illicit "100J at 220Ω" Pure-ER/RRC Mectan Transmutation of the 1982 APA Standard, awesomely powerful third generation Brief Pulse devices manufactured since 1995, are presently "permitted" under Weiner's new 1997 de facto standard. In effect, unregulated, manufacturers utilize Weiner's 1997 revision proposal as a default standard to produce and market third generation supra-powerful Brief Pulse devices world-wide, more than quadrupling Multifold Threshold Titration Level Output Intensities with BL ECT and more than octupling MTTLOIs with UL ECT for every age recipient. The simple idea, though hidden, is to increase the effect through increased electrical output. We should remember that the most revealing of the MRI prospective studies, Perrin's 2012 MRI study entitled "Electroconvulsive therapy reduces frontal cortical connectivity in severe depressive disorder" (Perrin et al.) concludes that ". . . the average global functional connectivity was considerably decreased after eight ECT treatments" set at but a 2.0 MTTLOI with BL ECT (Ibid 5466). Indeed, several recipients showed almost complete connective eradication of the left prefrontal lobe and so complete eradication of connectivity of the left prefrontal lobe with the rest of the brain. Disconcertingly, now legal third generation Somatics and MECTA Brief Pulse devices, emit default outputs of 4.52, 4.6 and 4.8 MTTLOIs for all age categories with BL ECT, circa two and a half times more powerful than that used in the 2012 Perrin study.

[120] Before the period between 1976 and 1982, the years of the FDA investigation into ECT devices and so before medical devices were placed under the auspices of an FDA, the ECT industry was totally unregulated. After 1976, the industry remains unregulated via dubious reporting stratagems.

CHAPTER 58

Weiner's 1997 "Standard" in Greater Detail: What Happened to ER/RRC?

Examining Weiner's 1997 revision proposal in greater detail, we immediately note the conspicuous absence of ER/RRC (pure or conditional), i.e. "100J at 220Ω" or any other reference to Joules; although, the author of this manuscript has converted figures to Joules in the above section, without which, there are no meaningful contrasts. In short, not even a Pure-ER/RRC phrase remains within Weiner's 1997 revision provision with which to contrast third generation Brief Pulse devices with first or even second generation Brief Pulse devices. Once again, the heart of the 1997 Weiner Standard reads as follows:

> The stimulus output shall consist of a constant current pulse train, with pulse width no greater than 2 milliseconds. The stimulus output charge shall be limited to 1200 mC for each treatment initiation for a load resistance of 100-500 Ohms, with a rate of delivery of no more than 2 mC/phase and 300 mC/second. Within this output charge limit, the output voltage shall be limited to a peak level of 1kV and the current to a peak level of 2A at any load resistance . . ..
> (International Electrotechnical Commission, 1997, Dec 26, p. 4)

So where is the ER/RRC phrase which stipulates electrical dosage limits relative to age or Impedance? Moreover, where is overall maximum output in Joules? Finally, where is the revealing MTTLOI applicable to all age categories, characterizing the specific Brief Pulse machine? [121] Other than the conspicuous 1200mC Charge ceiling (new), Weiner's "regulations" include: "Pulse width no greater than 2 milliseconds" (not new), a 500 ohm Impedance ceiling (not new), and finally the sentence, "with a rate of delivery no more than 2 mC/phase and 300 mC/second" (new). Alas, it is this latter sentence along with the 1200 mC maximum, which seems to have replaced the no longer utilized "Joule" including the no longer mentioned ER/RRC phraseologies such as "70J at 220Ω" or "100J at 220Ω" and we shall discuss this seemingly innocuous aspect of Weiner's de facto standard in a moment.

A Word on the Transition of Conditional-ER/RRC to Pure-ER/RRC

To be clear, pure-ER/RRC phrases in the above charts which covertly transitioned from the original 1982 APA Standard's Conditional-ER/RRC of "70J at 220Ω" conditioned by a 110J ceiling, have been revealed not by manufacturers, but by the author alone. It is not that third generation Brief Pulse devices no longer have pure-ER/RRCs as do second generation BP devices; it is simply that, influenced by Weiner's new provision, manufacturers no longer reveal them. The original function of the ER/RRC, in brief, was to insure gradient outputs with respect to age. Later, with the dropping of the stipulated ceiling and so the manufacturer transition to Pure-ER/RRC, ER/RRC began to play a part in the ceiling output as well. Thus, a Pure-ER/RRC along with

---

[121] In fact, the MTTLOI has never been reported. Indeed, it is a concept invented by the author in order to accurately describe the true nature of these machines.

maximum Impedance, infers the machine's overall maximum output in Joules, and thus (albeit indirectly) the machine's consistent MTTLOI or multifold threshold output at which a particular machine is set (which no manufacturer reports). In other words, a Pure (not Conditional) ER/RRC of "70J at 220" reveals that a machine with a 600Ω maximum Impedance has a ceiling of (70J/220Ω = **XJ/**600Ω =) **191J** from which we derive the MTTLOI of (191J ÷ 100J =) **1.91** (fold threshold) for all age categories. Thus, a pure-ER/RRC interpretation in conjunction with maximum machine Impedance reveals the actual maximum output in joules (i.e. 191J) which the machine administers in the oldest age category as well as the MTTLOI for all age categories. But while a pure-ER/RRC with maximum machine Impedance assures that output will be administered gradationally relative to age and reveals the consistent MTTLOI administered to all age categories, a pure-ER/RRC even with maximum Impedance does not reveal specific default outputs for any but the oldest age category. For example, the JR/SR 2 second generation IEC BP device is based on an unreported pure-ER/RRC of "**105.6J at 220Ω"** with a 500Ω maximum, so that we can derive its (105.6J/220Ω = XJ/500Ω; X =) **240J** maximum output emitted at its 500Ω maximum Impedance. Too, we can derive its (240J ÷ 100J =) **2.4** default MTTLOI (or multifold threshold output) for all age categories. While this information is critically important, this does not mean we can simply plug in various Impedances to discover, for example, a 144J output delivered at 300Ω of resistance (105.6J/220Ω = **144J**/300Ω) for the sixty year old recipient as one might expect. (According to the above second generation JR/SR 2 IEC BP chart, 300Ω is the resistance for a 60 year old recipient who receives not 144J, but 86.4J [122]). Indeed, the default 2.4 MTTLOI in this age category is much less than 144J. Rather, we must determine outputs relative to age through pre-determined threshold outputs. In other words, the specific output delivered to each age category (with the exception of the oldest) must be determined by the relative threshold output constant with respect to age (see below) multiplied by the MTTLOI for that particular machine (in this case, a 2.4 MTTLOI). Relative constants or threshold outputs with respect to age in joules, as noted, are as follows:

10 year old male =	**1.00J**
20 year old male =	**4.004J**
30 year old male =	**9.00J**
40 year old male =	**16.00J**
50 year old male =	**25.00J**
60 year old male =	**36.00J**
65 year old male =	**42.25J**
70 year old male =	**48.97J**
80 year old male =	**64.00J**
90 year old male =	**81.00J**
100 year old male =	**100.00J**

The author discovered these threshold output figures after many years through trial and error, figures never before revealed. For example, Somatics provides the following parameters delivered to a 90 year old recipient by its early Thymatron device. The: Percent Energy delivered to the 90 year old is (90% which we multiply by maximum Voltage of 400V to derive 360V Voltage used in the 90 year old age category). The Number of Pulses delivered to the 90 year old is (hz x Duration or 140 x 3.6 Seconds =) 504 Pulses (see Abrams and Swartz, *Thymatron instruction manual*, 1985). Using the formula: EO = Voltage x Amperage x Pulses x Pulse Width, all provided by Somatics, we see that (360V x .9Amps x 140 Pulses x .001 PW x 3.6 Sec. =) **163** is delivered to the 90 year old on this machine. Since the Early Thymatron delivered a 201J maximum output, we simply divide the 163J delivered by the 2.01 MTTLOI to derive the (163J ÷ 2.01 =) 81J Threshold output used by manufacturers for a 90 year old recipient. All relative threshold constants were derived by the author in this manner and can be verified with any BP device of any BP generation so long as enough information is provided. In any case, the above perfect squares bear out as threshold outputs used by Brief Pulse manufacturers for each specific age category for all modern BP devices. Deductively then, since the constant threshold output for, for example, a sixty year old recipient is 36J (see above) and the MTTLOI is 2.4 for the JR/SR 2 second generation IEC BP device, the specific default output delivered to a 60 year old recipient by the JR/SR 2 second generation IEC BP device is about (36J x 2.4 =) 86.4J, whereas, an 80 year old, who

[122] This is discovered simply by dividing maximum Impedance (500Ω) by 10 and assigning increasing Impedance to every age category. For example, 50Ω = 10yrs, 100Ω = 20yrs, 150Ω = 30yrs, etc.

generally has a 64J threshold output is administered about (64J x 2.4 =) 153.6J on this same device. (See the JR/SR 2 second generation IEC BP device above.) Note then, so long as we have maximum machine Impedance, the pure-ER/RRC phrase can tell us true maximum output (based on maximum machine Impedance) and thus the MTTLOI for the device, (i.e. 105.6J/220Ω = XJ/500Ω; X = 240J. 240J ÷ 100J = 2.4 MTTLOI). But while we deduce the specific default output for the oldest age category of 240J and thus a 2.4 MTTLOI, to derive specific default outputs for all other age categories, we must multiply the pre-determined threshold outputs by the machine's MTTLOI for each specific age category. To Illustrate, the 60 year old has a pre-determined 36J constant threshold output which must be multiplied by the machine's 2.4 MTTLOI to discover the (36J x 2.4 =) 86.4J default output delivered to that specific age category on that specific device. To illustrate further: the 90 year old has an 81J threshold output (see above). Thus, (81J x 2.4 =) 194.4J is delivered to the 90 year old by default by the same device. In short, the 90 year old on the JR/SR 2 second generation IEC BP device receives a 194.4J default output emission from which we can derive the machine's consistent (194.4J ÷ 81J =) 2.4 MTTLOI.

Thus, the 1982 APA Standard output ceiling of 110 maximum joules was furtively dropped so that the reporting for what were actually second generation BP devices was surreptitiously interpreted as a "100J at 220Ω" pure-ER/RRC secretly increasing the ceiling to (100J/220Ω = XJ/600ΩJ =) 273J in the U.S. and (130J/300Ω = XJ/500Ω =) 217J in Europe, more than doubling the MTTLOI of Brief Pulse machines from 1.1 to between 2.73 and 2.17 respectively. But while the output for each age recipient increased dramatically, the corrupt "100J at 220Ω" and "100J at 300Ω" pure-ER/RRC interpretations nevertheless continued to at least somewhat regulate output, albeit much less stringently. Thus, while maximum output for second generation, made-for America BP devices soared from 110J to (100J/220Ω = **XJ**/600Ω; X =) 273J, made-for-America machines were at least limited to an unreported a 273 Joule maximum while European devices were at least limited to a (130J/300Ω = **XJ**/600Ω; X =) 217J with some breaching added. The maximum MTTLOI utilized for all age categories by second generation BP devices, though greatly expanded, in short, was nevertheless limited to a 2.73 MTTLOI in the U.S. and about a 2.4 MTTLOI in Europe. [123]

Weiner's 1200mC phrase

As already noted, manufacturers never reported the actual outputs of second generation BP devices. Instead, there was a conspiratorial effort to conflate their 5-600mC Charges with first generation BP devices emitting circa 100 maximum joules. In fact, the first generation MECTA "C" emits 108 maximum Joules and 336mC maximum Charge so that 5-600mC, as noted previously, was already twice circa twice that of first generation BP devices. As a result of the false association of circa 100J devices with 5-600mC then, Weiner's new "limit" of 1200mC, appeared to be a first time doubling of power, suggesting new outputs of between 230 to 260 maximum joules; whereas, in fact, the newer Brief Pulse devices beginning with what were actually third generation BP devices emitted between 460 and 480 unreported Joules. The illusion of going from 5-600mC falsely associated with circa 100J maximum devices to 1200mC clearly gave the impression of a first time doubling in power. Conveniently, Weiner had altogether dropped Joule reporting so that older Brief Pulse devices could no longer be meaningfully compared to the newer Brief Pulse devices.

[123] An easy way to derive the MTTLOI for any device is simply to take maximum output (designated for the 100 year old recipient) and divide it by the 100J threshold output for the same 100 year old recipient (273J ÷ 100J = 2.73). Thus the MTTLOI applied to all individual recipients here is a maximum 2.73 fold threshold. Second generation BP devices actually emitted closer to a 2.5 MTTLOI. For instance, the Thymatron DG emitted 252 Joules, thus a 2.52 MTTLOI for every individual recipient proved by Beale in terms of Charge (1994). (Though not always the case, as we shall see, the Charge MTTLOI, in essence used by Beale, is directly translatable into an EO MTTLOI, as has been noted elsewhere.)

A Glimpse at Weiner's New 2mC/phase and 300mC/second Phrases "Legalizing" Third Generation BP Devices

What then, do Weiner's replacement phrases, "limited to 1200mC" in conjunction with the phrase "no more than 2mC/phase and 300mC/second" (all of which replaced ER/RRC reporting) actually mean in terms of regulation?

Weiner's phrase: "with a rate of delivery no more than 2mC/phase," simply means that no more than two millicoulombs of Charge can be emitted for each single pulse or "phase" of electricity. Additionally, there cannot be a total of more than "300mC" per every second that passes (which includes the time between pulses) and the entire or cumulative Charge cannot surpass 1200mC total. (Note that Weiner's new "regulatory" language is depicted totally in terms of Charge.)

The third generation JR/SR 1 MECTA ("British") device, for example, utilizes a maximum of 180 pulses per second (90 Hz) and a maximum .002 second pulse width (PW). At its 180 pulses per second, .002 Second Pulse Width, and .8A current, MECTA's third generation JR/SR 1 machine emits 288mC of Charge per second.

Charge = Duration x Current x (Hz x 2) x PW

1.0 Seconds x .8A x 180 Pulses x .002 Pulse Width = **288mC/Second**.

If we multiply this by the machine's maximum Duration of 4.0 Seconds, we obtain the machine's total Charge of 1152mC.

4.0 Seconds x 288mC/Second = **1152mC**.

Thus the machine passes two of Weiner's new criteria--remaining within 300mC/sec and 1200mC total Charge. Finally, at 180 pulses per second and 288mC/Second, the machine elicits 1.6mC per pulse (or phase) conforming to the maximum 2mC per pulse criterion, all newly adhering to Weiner's new 1997 IEC default "standard."

288mC/sec. ÷ 180 pulses/sec. = 1.6mC/phase

The Somatics System IV third generation BP device and the third generation MECTA JR/SR 2, though slightly varied, also conform to Weiner's new 1997 default "standard," to insure (according to Weiner) "limited output." [124]

But what do these Charge "limitations" mean in terms of Joules? Without converting Coulombs to Joules and identifying a pure-ER/RRC in terms of Joules/Impedance (with which we have now become familiar with respect to previous Brief Pulse devices), meaningful contrast is no longer possible. We must, therefore, do what Weiner fails to do--convert.

Theoretically, a 1200mC ceiling can be reached with much lower outputs in Joules than the respective 452, 460, and 480 Joule third generation Somatics and MECTA BP devices.[125] On the other hand, as we have seen from the charts above, Weiner's, "2mC/phase, 300mC/Second, 1200mC total maximum Charge" regulation does not prevent new third generation BP devices from emitting their unreported circa 450-480 Joules of maximum output, doubling the Multifold Threshold Titration Level Output Intensity (compared to second generation IEC BP devices) for every individual recipient, more than quadrupling the first generation 108J maximum output in accordance with the 110J ceiling stipulation of the 1982 APA Standard. (The 450-480J figures we have already observed for third generation BP devices are not provided by any manufacturer.) By converting to joules then, though invisible under Weiner's 1997 revision "standard," we can see that third generation Brief Pulse devices have exactly doubled in power and MTTLOI at every age level compared to

---

124 System IV: 1.0 Seconds x .9A x 140 Pulses x .0015 Pulse Width = 189mC/Second; 5.32 Seconds x 189mC/Second = 1005mC; 189/140 = 1.35mC/phase. 3rd Generation JR/SR 2: 1.0 Seconds x .8A x 180 Pulses x .0014 Pulse Width = 201.6mC/Second; 5.96 Seconds x 201.6mC/Second = 1200mC; 201.6/180 = 1.12mC/phase.

125 The Medcraft B-25 emits an 840mC maximum Charge but is limited to 100 maximum Joules.

second generation IEC BP devices and more than quadrupled the power and MTTLOI of the MECTA "C." [126] Weiner's cloaking device consists solely of supplanting EO reporting (in Joules) with Charge reporting (in Coulombs). In general, then, Weiner's 1997 de facto Standard "legalized" the already extant third generation BP devices marketed since 1995. But is the unreported 450-480 Joule maximum output we have determined for third generation BP devices the maximum output allowed under Weiner's new 1200mC, 2mC/phase, 300mC/second provisions? In short, do the Weiner criteria accommodate even higher output devices?

Testing for Highest Outputs Under the Weiner's 1997 de facto Revision Standard

To test for the maximum energy output possible under Weiner's "new" 1997 Charge standard, we must, as noted, convert Weiner's 1997 Charge ceiling to EO in Joules. When we use the formula: EO = Charge x Impedance x Amperage, and plug in Weiner's maximum 1200mC total along with Weiner's 500Ω and 2.0 Ampere maximums (which now come into play), we obtain the following frightening result:

EO = 1.2C x 500Ω x 2.0A = **1200 Joules**.

Theoretically, then, Weiner's provision seems to permit a 1200J ceiling maximum, more than twice as powerful as extant third generation BP devices. But can this be accurate? Let us test a few combinations against Weiner's criteria. For example, if we use the maximum 2.0 Ampere ceiling and the maximum .002 Second Pulse width allowed under Weiner's "Standard," and, for instance, the 180 pulses per second used for second and third generation MECTA devices, and if we then test the results of this possible parameter combination against Weiner's 2mC/phase, 300mC/Second, 1200mC ceiling criteria, we discover that we have breached Weiner's criteria. For example, plugging the test parameters into the formula: Charge = Duration x Current x Hz x 2 x PW, we derive for a one second Duration, an unacceptable 720mC/Second, grossly violating Weiner's 300mC/Second Charge ceiling.

1.0 Seconds x 2.0A x 180 Pulses x .002PW = **720mC/Second**.

But let us test other more plausible combinations. For instance, we can reduce the number of pulses to 75 in order to meet the 300mC/Second criteria.

1.0 Seconds x 2.0A x **75 Pulses** x .002PW = **300mC/Second**

Moreover, if we limit the Duration to 4.0 Seconds, the cumulative Charge ceiling for this combination also becomes acceptable under Weiner's 1997 provision.

4.0 Seconds x 300mC/Second = **1200mC Charge**.

Let us once more convert to Joules. Using the two main EO formulas for BP devices, we discover that in order to derive 1200 Joules, we must utilize exactly 1000V, the maximum allowable under Weiner's default standard.

1000V x 2.0A x 75 Pulses x .002PW x 4.0 Seconds = **1200 Joules**

or

2.0A x 2.0A x 500Ω x 75 pulses x .002PW x 4.0 Seconds = **1200 Joules**

---

[126] While cumulative Charge does double compared to second generation BP devices, this does not necessarily affect EO (Joules) as seen with the Medcraft B-25 in the footnote above. Regarding the other two Charge parameters (mC/phase or mC/second), neither first nor second generation BP devices were previously measured in these terms.

Finally, let us test for Weiner's 2.0mC/phase criterion.

300mC ÷ 75 pulses = **4mC/phase**

Again, we fail to meet all of Weiner's criteria. The combination yields twice the allowable charge per pulse; therefore, a device using the above combination to elicit 1200 Joules is not allowable under the 1997 Weiner provision. In that fewer pulses mean wider pulses, and thus more Charge per phase, and in that 2.0mC/pulse is the maximum Charge per pulse permitted, we can now see that to utilize the maximum 300mC/Second under Weiner's criteria, 150 pulses is the least number of pulses allowed.

150 pulses ÷ 300mC/Second = **2.0mC/pulse**.

Let us continue testing for the maximum EO possible under Weiner's provisions, this time, however, increasing the number of pulses from the previous 75 to 150. In using 150 pulses in the combination above, however, we must reduce some other parameter in order to maintain the 1200J maximum output. Let us therefore, theorize some maximum "legal" combinations of Amperage, number of Pulses, and Pulse width combinations resulting in, but not surpassing maximum Charge per second (300mC/second) and maximum Charge per pulse (2mC/pulse) under the Weiner proviso. We can, for instance, reduce Amperage from 2.0A to 1.0 A. Subsequently, one possible legal combination we can utilize is 1.0 Ampere, 150 Pulses, and a .002 Second maximum Pulse Width from which we derive a legal maximum Charge of 300mC/second Charge.

1.0 Seconds x **1.0A** x 150 Pulses x **.002PW** = 300mC/Second.

Alternatively, we can derive a legal combination by reducing Pulse Width. Maintaining the maximum Amperage of 2.0A as well as the maximum 150 Pulses, but using a .001 Pulse Width instead of .002 second PW, we can obtain the same legal maximum Charge of 300mC/second Charge.

1.0 Seconds x **2.0A** x 150 Pulses x **.001PW** = 300mC/Second.

Of course, to conform to Weiner's 1200mC total Charge maximum, maximum Duration cannot exceed 4.0 Seconds in either combination. (4.0 Seconds x 300mC/Second = 1200mC.) Limited to 4.0 Seconds, then, neither combination surpasses Weiner's "2mC/phase" maximum (300mC/Second ÷ 150 pulses = 2.0mC/phase).

Thus, by plugging these acceptable parameters (under Weiner's provision) into the Charge oriented formula for Brief Pulse devices (EO = Charge x Ω x Amp), we can now identity the maximum Joules elicited. For the first combination, we obtain a disconcertingly "acceptable" maximum output of 600 Joules and for the second, a frighteningly "acceptable" maximum output of 1200 Joules.

1.2C x 500Ω x .1.0A = **600 Joules**.

1.2C x 500Ω x .2.0A = **1200 Joules**.

Is the maximum output in Joules under Weiner's regulation then, 600J or 1200J? Results seem conflicting. But are they? Does the math not tell us that we can legally build a 600J device using a 1.0A constant current, but also a 1200J device using a 2.0 Ampere constant current, both conforming to Weiner's provision? If correct, we should be able to build a theoretical 1200J device without surpassing either the 2.0A maximum current or the 1200mC Charge maximum (or any of the other Charge criteria) stipulated under the Weiner proviso. Apparently, then, an incredibly powerful 1200J device conforming to Weiner's provisions can be built, simply by using the legal 2.0 Ampere maximum current.

But can we build a 1200J Brief Pulse machine using Weiner's 2.0A maximum current and yet conform to Weiner's Charge regulations of 300mC/Second, 2mC/phase, and 1200mC total Charge?

Let's experiment. Let us construct our theoretical 1200J device using the 1000V maximum allowed under Weiner's provision, the 2.0A maximum, but this time, as we have learned, limited to 150 pulses per second (75 Hertz) and limited to a .001 Second PW (Pulse Width). Too, the Duration shall be limited to 4.0 maximum seconds.

Using the Voltage-oriented formula for deriving EO (EO = Voltage x Current x (Hz x 2) x PW x Duration), we indeed derive a 1200 Joule output.

1000V x 2.0A x 150Pulses x .001PW x 4.0 Seconds = **1200 Joules**.

Using a different formula for confirmation, the Impedance-oriented formula for finding EO [EO = Current squared x Impedance (Hz x 2) x PW x Duration], we obtain the same 1200J output.

2.0A x 2.0A x 500Ω x 150 pulses x .001PW x 4.0 Seconds = **1200 Joules**.

But can this theoretically fearsome device yet conform to Weiner's Charge regulations of 300mC/Second, 2mC/phase and 1200mC total?

Using the Charge formula: Charge = Duration x Current x (Hz x 2) x PW for one second of Duration, we indeed obtain an "acceptable" 300mC/Second:

1.0 Seconds x 2.0A x 150 pulses x .001PW = **300mC/Second**.

Over the maximum 4.0 Second Duration which we have incorporated into the machine, we also derive an "acceptable" 1200mC Charge maximum.

4.0 Seconds x 300mC/Second = **1200mC total**

Thus far, all criteria are met. But can the device meet the final 2.0mC/phase test?

300mC ÷ 150 pulses = **2mC/phase**

The answer is "yes." The 150 pulses/second indeed meets the "acceptable" 2mC/phase criterion. Amazingly then, all criteria are met.

In short, under Weiner's 1997 provisions, a 1200 Joule (or what might be deemed) a fifth generation Brief Pulse device, is both feasible and allowable under the Weiner criteria.[127] Under Weiner's 1997 de facto standard currently used by Brief Pulse manufacturers in general, then, not only do extant third generation Brief Pulse devices "legally" double the power of second generation Brief Pulse devices, but the new 1997 "standard" allows for even further enhancements, permitting potential fourth and even fifth generation BP devices. Under the Weiner "standard," fourth generation BP devices can "legally" double the output and MTTLOI of third generation Brief Pulse devices, while fifth generation BP devices can "legally" increase the output and MTTLOI even further.

Other legal combinations (emitting more than 150 pulses) deriving the same 1200J maximum are also possible under Weiner's 1997 provision. For example, still using a 2.0A current, we can utilize a Pulse Width of .00083 seconds while increasing the number of pulses per second to 180. Using 1000V and the same 4.0 Second maximum Duration, we can again obtain the same 1200 maximum Joules.

1000V x 2.0A x 180Pulses x .000833PW x 4.0 Seconds = **1200J**

or

[127] Fourth generation devices might double third generation BP devices to deliver about 900J while fifth generation devices might actually reach 1200J.

2.0A x 2.0A x 500Ω x 180 pulses x .000833PW x 4.0 Seconds = **1200J**

Testing for mC/Second, we obtain the same "acceptable" **300mC/Second**.

(Charge = Duration x Current x (Hz x 2) x PW)

1.0 Seconds x 2.0A x 180 Pulses x .000833PW = **300mC/Second**

Using a 4.0 Second maximum Duration, Charge is again an "acceptable" 1200mC maximum.

4.0 Seconds x 300mC/Second = **1200mC total**.

Finally, using 180 pulses, we obtain an "acceptable" 1.66mC/phase.

300mC ÷ 180 pulses = **1.66mC/phase**

Thus, under Weiner's 1997 IEC de facto standard, conforming to the new Charge configurations which allegedly "regulate" and "limit" so called "reduced output" Brief Pulse devices, we can legally build Brief Pulse devices emitting 1200 unreported Joules of output, emitting almost (1200J ÷ 110J = 10.9) eleven times the output of the MECTA "C", indeed (1200J - 110J = 1090J ÷ 110J = 9.91 =) 991% greater output than that allowed by the original 1982 APA ceiling Standard of 110 maximum Joules condoned by the FDA. This is (1200J ÷ 100J =) 12 fold the maximum dosage necessary to induce so-called "adequate seizures" for every individual recipient administered BL "ECT" and (1200J ÷ 150J =) 24 fold the maximum dosage necessary to induce so-called "adequate seizures" with UL "ECT." Weiner's new provision, far from regulatory in nature, then, is actually a de-regulatory "standard," facilitating the devolution (increase in power) of Brief Pulse machines in the direction of more and more powerful and more and more electro-centric pieces of equipment, machines no longer remotely based on adequate seizures at all, but rather, adequate amounts of electricity

CHAPTER 59

Fourth Generation Brief Pulse Devices

The Fourth Generation MECTA JR/SR 1 "British."

Third generation BP devices emitting 452, 460, and 480J outputs emitting circa 5.0 fold threshold outputs (that is, a circa 5.0 MTTLOI) for every individual recipient using BL "ECT," legal under Weiner's 1997 de facto standard, have been produced and marketed in both the U.S. and Europe since at least 1995. Fourth generation Brief Pulse devices capable of about 1000 Joules, also legal under Weiner's standard, as we have just seen above, may or may not exist. As an experiment, however, let us investigate the ease of transitioning from already extant third generation Brief Pulse devices to possible fourth generation Brief Pulse devices, emitting twice the power and MTTLOI of extant third generation Brief Pulse devices. The extant third generation MECTA JR/SR 1 utilizes a .8A constant current (in lieu of the possible 2.0A maximum available under Weiner's "standard"), a 400V maximum, 180 pulses, and a .002 second Pulse Width.

(Charge = Duration x Current x (Hz x 2) x PW)
1.0 Seconds x .8A x 180 Pulses x .002PW = **288mC/Second.**

We have already seen from charts above that the third generation MECTA JR/SR 1 emits approximately 460 Joules or a 4.6 Multifold Threshold Titration Level Output intensity (MTTLOI) for all age recipients with BL "ECT," easily permittable under Weiner's new 1997 "standard."

400V x .8A x 180Pulses x .002PW x 4.0 Seconds = **460 Joules**.

or

1.152C x 500Ω x .8A = **460 Joules**.

The Charge per pulse for the third generation MECTA JR/SR 1 is also well under Weiner's 2mC/phase "regulation."

288mC ÷ 180 pulses = **1.6mC/phase**

Simply by doubling Amperage and Voltage of the third generation JR/SR 1 from its present .8A and 400V maximums, to 1.6A and 800V maximums, but also reducing its pulse width from .002 to .001 seconds, we derive a "legal" **922J** fourth generation MECTA JR/SR 1 "British" device, not only doubling the 460J maximum output of the third generation JR/SR 1, but doubling the MTTLOI for every age category. The conformity of a theoretical fourth generation MECTA JR/SR 1 "British" BP device--with doubled Amperage and Voltage and halved Pulse Width--to Weiner's 1997 replacement provision, a machine capable of 922 Joules approaching a consistent 10.0 MTTLOI for each individual recipient receiving BL "ECT," can now be seen below:

Impedance-oriented formula for deriving EO:

EO = 1.6A x **1.6A** x **500Ω** x 180 pulses x .001PW x 4.0 Seconds = **922 Joules**

Voltage-oriented formula for deriving EO:

800V x **1.6A** x 180Pulses x .001PW x 4.0 Seconds = **922 Joules**.

Charge-oriented formula for deriving EO:

1.152C x 500Ω x **1.6A** = **922 Joules**

Checking against Weiner's 300mC/second criterion, we find this fourth generation device conforms at 288mC/Second.

1.0 Seconds x .1.6A x 180 Pulses and .001PW = **288mC/Second.**

Checking against Weiner's 1200mC (or 1.2C) total Charge criterion, we find the fourth generation device at 1152mC, again conforms.

Charge = 921J/1.6A x 500Ω = **1.152C** = **1152mC**

Checking against Weiner's 2.0mC/phase criterion, we find the fourth generation device again conforms at 1.6mC/phase.

288mC ÷ 180 pulses = **1.6mC/phase**

In conclusion, a fourth generation BP device wherein the EO emission of the extant third generation BP device doubles in every age category is perfectly "legal" under Weiner's "new" default standard. Extant Third and hypothetical but "legal" fourth generation BP devices, both "allowed" under the Weiner proviso, appear below:

Approximate Actual CONSTANT CURRENT **JR/SR 1** BRIEF PULSE IEC BP DEVICE
(3rd GENERATION) "BRITISH" by MECTA Corp. 1995
BASED ON PURE-ER/RRC OF **"276J AT 300Ω" or "202.4J at 220Ω"**

VOLTAGE	POWER % @ Age	AGE Yrs	Ω Ohms	FREQUENCY (Hz)	DURATION (SECs)	CURRENT mAmps	ENERGY Joules	CHARGE mC
40	10	10	50	90	0.5	800	5.76	144
80	20	20	100	90	0.8	800	18.43	230
120	30	30	150	90	1.2	800	41.47	345.6
160	40	40	200	90	1.6	800	73.73	460.8
200	50	50	250	90	2.0	800	115.2	576
240	60	60	300	90	2.4	800	165.88	691.2
260	65	65	325	90	2.6	800	194.68	748.8
280	70	70	350	90	2.8	800	225.8	806.4
320	80	80	400	90	3.2	800	295	921.6
360	90	90	450	90	3.6	800	373	1036.8
400	100	100	500	90	4.0	800	**460J**	**1152**

(**.002** Sec. Pulse Width)

PROBABLE CONSTANT CURRENT **JR/SR 1** BRIEF PULSE <u>**IEC**</u> BP DEVICE
(4th GENERATION) "BRITISH" by MECTA Corp. 2000?
BASED ON PURE-ER/RRC OF **"553J AT 300Ω" or "405J at 220Ω"**

VOLTAGE	POWER % @ Age	AGE Yrs	Ω Ohms	FREQUENCY (Hz)	DURATION (SECs)	CURRENT mAmps	ENERGY Joules	CHARGE mC
80	10	10	50	90	0.5	1600	11.52	144
160	20	20	100	90	0.8	1600	36.86	230
240	30	30	150	90	1.2	1600	82.94	345.6
320	40	40	200	90	1.6	1600	147.46	460.8
400	50	50	250	90	2.0	1600	230.4	576
480	60	60	300	90	2.4	1600	331.76	691.2
520	65	65	325	90	2.6	1600	389.36	748.8
560	70	70	350	90	2.8	1600	451.6	806.4
640	80	80	400	90	3.2	1600	590	921.6
720	90	90	450	90	3.6	1600	746	1036.8
800	100	100	500	90	4.0	1600	**922J**	**1152**

(**.001** Sec. Pulse Width)

Alarmingly, the reportable Charge emissions of 288mC/Second, 1.152C total Charge, and 1.6mC/phase for the fourth generation Brief Pulse machine above remain unchanged (from the third generation JR/SR 1 BP device above), making the doubling of power manifest only in Joules (which are no longer reportable under the "new" 1997 Weiner standard) and so no longer visible. In short, because there is no change in Charge from one device to the other, without conversion to EO in joules, the increase in power is totally invisible. (See the identical Charge columns in the right hand column of each device above.)

Briefly then, under Weiner's 1997 provision, all criteria for invisibly transitioning the already unreported 460J third generation JR/SR 1 BP device to a 922J fourth generation JR/SR 1 "British" BP device are fully met. Disturbingly, Charge remains the same while EO is doubled. Under Weiner's 1997 de facto standard, which totally supplants EO reporting (Joules) with Charge reporting (Coulombs), therefore, the new doubling in power and thus the doubling of MTTLOI for all age recipients, as noted above, is hidden.

In spite of the exact same Charge maximums (with respect to age) from the third generation BP device to the fourth generation BP device, the fourth generation JR/SR 1 now emits a 9.2 MTTLOI (in terms of Joules) with BL "ECT" for all recipients as opposed to the third generation JR/SR 1 which emits a 4.6 MTTLOI in terms of Joules with BL "ECT" in every age category. To illustrate this in another way, we can take the maximum Charge output from both devices--1.152 Coulombs--and divide by 4.6 (the MTTLOI) from which we obtain (1.152 ÷ 4.6 =) .2504C, the just above threshold Charge for a 100 year old recipient using the third generation JR/SR 1.[128] To convert this Charge parameter to Joules, we plug the threshold Charge figure into the EO formula, <u>EO = Charge x Current x Impedance</u>, to obtain the familiar minimum or just above threshold EO (100 Joules) for all recipients.

EO = .2504C x .8A x 500Ω = <u>***100.16 Joules***</u>

Multiplying the 100J figure by 4.6 (the MTTLOI), we then obtain the default 460 Joules of EO administered to the 100 year old recipient on the third generation JR/SR 1 above (see third generation JR/SR 1 chart above) or the 4.6 MTTLOI applicable to every age category.

100.16 Joules x <u>***4.6***</u> = <u>***460.7J***</u>

If we now take the same maximum Charge--1.152 Coulombs--used for the fourth generation device, but this time divide by 9.2 (the MTTLOI), we obtain <u>***.1252C,***</u> the just above (seizure) threshold output in terms of Charge for the 100 year old recipient on the fourth generation JR/SR 1. Plugging this (seizure) threshold Charge

---

[128] This is also based on Beale's 1994 study which identified 2.5 fold threshold Charge for second generation made-for-America BP devices (which is also 2.5 EO in terms of Joules). Third generation is a simple doubling of Charge and output and thus based on a circa 5.0 fold threshold titration dosage in terms of Charge and EO. Due to reduced maximum Impedance, from 600 to 500Ω for made-for-European devices, the 2.5 fold drops to about 2.3 fold and the 5.0 fold to about 4.6 fold.

figure into the same EO formula: EO = Charge x Current x Impedance, we obtain the same looked for constant just above threshold EO of 100.16 Joules for all 100 year old recipients.

EO = .1252C x 1.6 A x 500Ω = ***100.16 Joules***

This time, however, we must multiply the 100J EO figure by ***9.2*** to obtain the 922 Joules of EO administered to the 100 year old recipient on the fourth generation JR/SR 1 (see fourth generation JR/SR 1 chart above) or the 9.2 MTTLOI administered to every age recipient, invisible, as already noted, in terms of Charge alone (in that there is no increase in Charge).

100.16 Joules x 9.2 = ***922J***

Using the same 1152mC maximum Charge output, the same 100 year old receives a 4.6 MTTLOI from the third generation device while receiving a 9.2 MTTLOI from the fourth generation device. The hidden difference between just above threshold outputs in terms of Charge, that is, the difference in Charge thresholds with respect to the third versus the fourth generation Brief Pulse device (.2504C vs. 1252C) for the 100 year old recipient is actually due to the difference in Amperage. In spite of the wave length being reduced by half on the fourth generation Brief Pulse device resulting in the same Charge maximums on both devices, the doubling of Amperage (and Voltage) on the fourth generation BP device more than compensates for equal Charge outputs. In brief, only half the Charge output is required to seize individuals on the fourth generation device meaning that the same Charge outputs on the fourth generation BP device render two times the MTTLOI of the third generation device for each individual recipient. This critical difference only manifests itself via twice the output in terms of Joules relative to Impedance (or age) emitted by the fourth generation device (as opposed to the third generation device). Thus, there is a doubling of output in terms of Joules from third to fourth generation as opposed to Charge which does not change, due to an increase in Amperage. Succinctly, doubling the Amperage and thus the (unreported) EO, reduces Charge thresholds by half on the fourth generation BP device. That is, threshold in terms of Charge for the 100 year old recipient transitions from .2504C for the third generation BP device to .1252C for the fourth generation BP device (.2504C ÷ .1252C = 2.0). This means that the same 1152mC creates a (1.152C ÷ .2504C =) 4.6 MTTLOI for the 100 year old on the third generation device, but a (1.152C ÷ .1252 =) 9.22 MTTLOI for the same 100 year old on the fourth generation device. In that the 100 joule threshold figure for the 100 year old recipient is consistent as opposed to Charge threshold which is inconsistent, EO administered to the 100 year old manifestly doubles from 460J to 922J from third to fourth generation; 460J ÷ 100J = 4.6; 922J ÷ 100J = 9.22; whereas, Charge doubles by virtue of a halved threshold. This means that under Weiner's de facto standard which eliminates reporting in terms of joules, the overall doubling of output (from 460J to 922J) is not reported in that the maximum Charge administered of 1.152C remains the same for both third and fourth generation BP devices. In short, increasing the amperage from .8A to 1.6A halves the threshold output in terms of Charge while threshold output in terms of Joules remains the same. In that the threshold output in terms of Charge decreases with increased Amperage, without EO reporting in terms of Joules, the doubled MTTLOI becomes invisible, and so the Charge figures, deceptive. Meaningful contrast between third and fourth generation BP devices, in brief, is lost. Conversely, machine enhancement becomes immediately manifest in terms of Joules, but which are wholly purged under Weiner's 1997 de facto standard. In comparing third to potential fourth generation Brief Pulse devices, therefore, we can deduce that threshold output in terms of Charge is subject to change, whereas, threshold output in terms Joules remains relatively constant. In any case, despite unchanging Charge outputs from third to fourth generation Brief Pulse devices, the fourth generation BP device doubles in power, amplifying the 4.6 MTTLOI with BL ECT delivered by the third generation BP device in all age categories to a 9.22 MTTLOI with BL ECT delivered by the fourth generation BP device in all age categories, a fact only visible in terms of Joules. Thus, in spite of the same Charge parameters depicted for both third and fourth generation BP devices at every age level, there is a respective 4.6 to 9.22 MTTLOI augmentation from the third to the fourth generation JR/SR 1 BP "British" device in every age category, a phenomenon, as noted previously, only observable in terms of Joules. [129] [130] Charge parameters alone then, upon which the Weiner standard depends, are an unreliable and inconsistent means of reporting output in that MTTLOIs are, in fact, deceptive. EO alone (in terms of Joules) is the only reliably consistent means of transparently reporting power, power amplification, and finally the MTTLOI for all age categories, without which the true intent of the device is concealed.[131] Put another way, under Weiner's de facto standard, the third and fourth generation JR/SR 1 cannot be differentiated.

The Fourth Generation MECTA JR/SR 2 "British"

The paradigm of doubling Amperage and Voltage and reducing Pulse Width by half in order to easily transition from 3rd to 4th generation BP devices above is fully applicable to all MECTA and Somatics third generation BP devices.

For instance, the third generation MECTA JR/SR 2 "British" Brief Pulse device utilizes a .8A constant current, a 400V maximum Voltage, a .0014 second pulse width, and a 5.96 second maximum Duration. As already noted, the third generation MECTA JR/SR 2 emitting (an unreported) 480 maximum Joules is easily allowable under Weiner's new 1997 default "standard."

400V x .8A x 180Pulses x .0014PW x 5.96 Seconds = **480.6 Joules**.
or
1.200C x 500Ω x .8A = **480 Joules**.

The Charge per second is well under Weiner's 300mC/second "regulatory" statute.

[Charge = Duration x Current x (Hz x 2) x PW]
1.0 Seconds x .8A x 180 Pulses and .0014PW = **201.6mC/Second.**

The Charge per pulse is also well under Weiner's 2mC/phase "regulatory" statute.

201.6mC ÷ 180 pulses = **1.12mC/phase**

The paradigm to legally double third generation output under Weiner's provisions can now be applied. By doubling Voltage and Amperage of the third generation JR/SR 2 "British" Brief Pulse device from 400V and

---

[129] MTTLOI is only visible in terms of Joules unless, of course, we are informed that threshold output in terms of Charge has been reduced by half.

[130] Let us, for instance, take a 60 year old man. On both third and fourth generation BP devices, the Charge output delivered to the 60 year old man is the same .6912C (see charts above). If we divide this by 4.6, we obtain a .15026C threshold Charge for the third generation MECTA JR/SR 1. If we convert to Joules by multiplying .15026C x .8A x 300Ω, we obtain 36.06 Joules, the threshold output in Joules for the 60 year old man. Multiplying 36.06J by 4.6, we then obtain 165.88 Joules, or 4.6 fold threshold on the third generation JR/SR 1 BP device. If we now take the same .6912C Charge delivered to the same 60 year old man and divide by 9.22, we obtain .074976., the threshold Charge of a 60 year old man on the fourth generation JR/SR 1 BP device (half that of the third generation BP device). Converting to Joules: .074976C x 1.6A x 300Ω = 36J, we obtain the same threshold output of 36 Joules. Multiplying 36J by 9.22, we derive 331 Joules, the unreported output delivered to the 60 year old man on the fourth generation JR/SR 1, now a 9.22 MTTLOI for the 60 year old man (with 300Ω Impedance; see charts above). In short, the .6912C delivered to the 60 year old man by the third generation BP device is a 4.6 MTTLOI whereas the same .6912C delivered to the 60 year old man by the fourth generation BP device is 9.22 MTTLOI.

[131] We can exemplify the doubling of EO while maintaining the same maximum Charge with a simple experiment. Let us use the Amperage-oriented formula for deriving EO: EO = Current x Current x Impedance x (Hz x 2) x PW x Duration together with the EO-oriented formula for deriving Charge: Charge = EO ÷ Current x Impedance. Let us use some random figures: .5A x .5A x 100Ω x 120 Pulses x .001Sec PW x 5 Seconds = **15J**. 15J ÷ .5A x 100Ω = **.3C**. Now let us repeat the experiment after doubling the Amperage and reducing the PW by half. 1.0A x 1.0A x 100Ω x 120 Pulses x .0005 Sec PW x 5 Seconds = **30J**. 30J ÷ 1.0A x 100Ω = **.3C**. Note that while EO has doubled, Charge remains unchanged. This can only mean that the threshold output for Charge has been reduced by half, thereby doubling the Multifold Threshold Titration Level Output Intensity as manifested by the doubling of EO from 15 to 30J. Using Charge alone, however, the doubling of MTTLOI remains invisible.

.8A, to 800V and 1.6A respectively, and by similarly reducing pulse width by half from the third generation .0014 Sec. to .0007 Sec., we derive a circa **960J fourth** generation JR/SR 2 "British" BP device, “legally” doubling (under Weiner's default standard) the unreported 480J maximum output of the third generation JR/SR 2 "British." Duration, Impedance, and Hertz (90 Hz or 180 pulses) remain unchanged. The resulting "legal" configurations (under Weiner's de facto standard) for the fourth generation BP device, twice the power and MTTLOI of the third generation JR/SR 2 BP device, can be seen below:

Impedance-oriented formula for deriving EO:

EO = 1.6A x **1.6A** x **500Ω** x 180 pulses x .0007PW x 5.96 Seconds = **961J**.

Voltage-oriented formula for deriving EO:

800V x **1.6A** x 180Pulses x .0007PW x 5.96 Seconds = **961 Joules**.

Charge-oriented formula for deriving EO:

1.200C x 500Ω x **1.6A** = **960 Joules**

Let us check for adherence to Weiner's 300mC/second criterion.

1.0 Seconds x .1.6A x 180 Pulses x .0007 PW = **201.6mC/Second.**

Let us check for adherence to the 1200mC (or 1.2C) total Charge criterion.

Charge = 961J/1.6A x 500Ω = **1.200C** = **1200mC**

Charge = 5.96 Sec. x 1.6A x 180 pulses x .0007PW = **1.200C** = **1200mC**

Finally, let us check for adherence to Weiner's 2.0mC/phase criterion.

201.6mC ÷ 180 pulses = **1.12mC/phase**

Once again, in spite of doubling the Amperage and Voltage, by halving the Pulse Width, the reportable Charge emissions of 201.6mC/Second, 1200mC total Charge, and 1.12mC/phase remain unchanged from the third to the fourth generation JR/SR 2 BP device, while once again, the doubling of power and MTTLOI, manifest themselves only in Joules, and are thereby rendered invisible under Weiner's de facto standard.

(See tables below.)

Approximate Actual CONSTANT CURRENT **JR/SR 2** BRIEF PULSE **IEC** DEVICE
(3rd GENERATION) "BRITISH" by MECTA Corp. 1995
BASED ON PURE-ER/RRC OF **"288J at 300Ω"** or **"211.2J at 220Ω"**

VOLTAGE	POWER % @ Age	AGE Yrs	Ω Ohms	FREQUENCY (Hz)	DURATION (SECs)	CURRENT mAmps	ENERGY Joules	CHARGE mC
40	10	10	50	40	1.34	800	4.8	120
80	20	20	100	40	2.68	800	19.2	240
120	30	30	150	60	2.68	800	43.2	360
160	40	40	200	60	3.57	800	76.8	480
200	50	50	250	60	4.46	800	120	600
240	60	60	300	90	2.58	800	172.8	720
260	65	65	325	90	3.88	800	202.8	780
280	70	70	350	90	4.16	800	235	840
320	80	80	400	90	4.76	800	307.2	960
360	90	90	450	90	5.36	800	388.8	1080
400	100	100	500	90	5.96	800	480J	1200

(.001--.0014 Sec. Pulse Width; only .0014 used in chart above) [132]

HYPOTHETICAL CONSTANT CURRENT **JR/SR 2** BRIEF PULSE **IEC** DEVICE
(4th GENERATION) "BRITISH" by MECTA Corp. 1995
BASED ON PURE-ER/RRC OF **"576J at 300Ω"** or **"422.4J at 220Ω"**

VOLTAGE	POWER % @ Age	AGE Yrs	Ω Ohms	FREQUENCY (Hz)	DURATION (SECs)	CURRENT mAmps	ENERGY Joules	CHARGE mC
80	10	10	50	40	1.34	1600	9.6	120
160	20	20	100	40	2.68	1600	38.4	240
240	30	30	150	60	2.68	1600	86.	360
320	40	40	200	60	3.57	1600	153.6	480
400	50	50	250	60	4.46	1600	240	600
480	60	60	300	90	2.58	1600	345.6	720
520	65	65	325	90	3.88	1600	405.6	780
560	70	70	350	90	4.16	1600	470	840
640	80	80	400	90	4.76	1600	614.4	960
720	90	90	450	90	5.36	1600	777.6	1080
800	100	100	500	90	5.96	1600	960J	1200

(only .0007msec Pulse Width used in above chart)

Under Weiner's 1997 default standard, all criteria for invisibly transitioning the unreported 480J third generation JR/SR 2 "British" BP device to an unreported 960J fourth generation JR/SR 2 "British" BP device are fully met. Again, EO doubles while Charge remains unchanged. (Note the last columns of both tables above.)

Once again, in spite of exactly the same Charge outputs for each device, the fourth generation JR/SR 2 now emits a 9.6 MTTLOI with BL ECT as opposed to the third generation JR/SR 2 which elicits a 4.8 MTTLOI with BL ECT for all age groups. In spite of the halving of Pulse Width, due to the doubling of Amperage (in turn due to the doubling of Voltage), seizure threshold in terms of Charge is reduced by half, thereby, doubling not the actual Charge (which remains the same) but the MTTLOI, now only manifest in terms of joules. To illustrate this phenomenon, we take the maximum Charge on both 3rd and 4th generation JR/SR 2 devices--1.200 Coulombs and divide by 4.8 (MTTLOI) to obtain .2500C, the just above threshold Charge for a 100 year old recipient using the *third* generation JR/SR 2 "British" BP device. By plugging the threshold Charge figure (.2500C) for the third generation device into the EO formula: EO = Charge x Current x Impedance to convert to joules, we next obtain the consistent just above seizure threshold in terms of Joules for the 100 Year old recipient (which, as we know, is 100 Joules).

EO = **.2500C** x .8A x 500Ω = **100 Joules**

---

[132] EO is based upon: EO (BP) = Charge x Current x Impedance. Duration is based upon: Duration (BP) = Charge/Current x (hz x 2) x WL; Voltage = Ohm's Law: Voltage = Current x Ω. Also, Charge = EO/Current x Impedance. EO = Voltage x Current x (hz x 2) x WL x Duration.

Multiplying the 100J figure by the 4.8 MTTLOI, we then obtain the 480 Joules of EO utilized with the 100 year old recipient on the third generation JR/SR 2 above (see third generation JR/SR 2 chart above). We can also multiply the .2500C figure by 4.8 (the MTTLOI) to again obtain the maximum Charge administered to the same 100 year old on the third generation BP device.

100 Joules x 4.8 = **480J**
.2500C x 4.8 = 1.200C = **1200mC**

If we now take the same maximum Charge, 1.200 Coulombs, but this time divide by the 9.6 (MTTLOI), we obtain a .1250C, just above seizure threshold in terms of Charge for a 100 year old recipient using the *fourth* generation JR/SR 2 "British" BP device--half the .2500C just above seizure threshold Charge of the *third* generation JR/SR 2 "British" BP device. To prove this, we simply plug the .1250C threshold Charge figure into the EO formula: EO = Charge x Current x Impedance to obtain the same consistent just above threshold EO of 100 Joules. The derivation of the same 100J figure shows that a .2500C Charge is just above seizure threshold for the 100 year old on the third generation BP device and a .1250C Charge is just above seizure threshold for the 100 year old on the fourth generation BP device.

EO = **.1250C** x 1.6 A x 500Ω = **100 Joules**

Multiplying the consistent 100J EO figure by the 9.6 MTTLOI, we now obtain the 960 Joules of EO utilized for the 100 year old on the fourth generation JR/SR 2 "British" BP device (see fourth generation JR/SR 2 chart above), in short, a 9.6 MTTLOI for each individual recipient. We can also multiply the .1250C just above seizure threshold figure (in terms of Charge) for the 4th generation device by 9.6 (MTTLOI) to obtain the same 1200mC Charge (as the 3rd generation device) administered to the same 100 year old recipient on the fourth generation BP device (but with an entirely different MTTLOI).

100 Joules x 9.6 = **960J**
.1250C x 9.6 = 1.200C = **1200mC**

Thus, if one is aware that the seizure threshold output in terms of Charge has decreased by half on the fourth generation BP device from .2500C to .1250C, one can simply multiply the .1250C Charge threshold for the 100 year old recipient on the fourth generation BP device by 9.6 to obtain the same (1.2C ÷ .1250 = 9.6; 9.6 x 1.2C =) 1.2C or 1200mC total Charge. The fact that under Weiner's proviso standard, manufacturers are not required to inform us of the seizure threshold halving in terms of Charge, the fact that EO reporting has been expunged under Weiner's de facto "standard," and the fact that manufacturers are not required to, and, in fact, do not report MTTLOIs at all, much less EO in joules, all render the doubling in power of the fourth generation BP device effectively invisible. Insidiously, because Weiner's 1997 standard only requires that manufacturers report maximum Charge outputs (as opposed to joules), third and fourth generation BP machines under the Weiner default standard appear identical. **No enhancement can be detected.**

The inconsistency in Charge thresholds from third to fourth generation BP devices as has been noted, is once again due to the doubling of Amperage (and Voltage) on the fourth generation BP device (despite the halving of Pulse Width). While Charge maximums remain deceptively the same, therefore, the fourth generation BP device emits twice the output (as the third generation device) in terms of Joules relative to Impedance (or age) and twice the output in terms of overall Joules relative to overall Charge. The fact that overall EO doubles relative to overall Charge can only mean that seizure thresholds in terms of Charge have been reduced by half, in turn meaning that the same Charge on the fourth generation device now results in twice the MTTLOI (as the third generation BP device). Because actual Charge outputs are identical in both third and fourth generation machines, however, and because EO doubles from the third to the fourth generation device only in terms of Joules no longer reported under Weiner's de facto standard, the doubling in both power and MTTLOI for all age levels from third to fourth generation BP device is, as previously noted above, totally suppressed.

We can conclude that while doubling the Amperage reduces Charge thresholds by half (in spite of reduced Pulse Width), threshold outputs in terms of Joules remain constant. It is only through EO reporting alone, therefore, that the enhancement from third to fourth generation BP devices becomes visible. Similarly, MTTLOI, the most critical of all machine measurements, only becomes visible if we report in or convert to EO in Joules. In that seizure thresholds in terms of Charge are mutable, as we have seen, and seizure thresholds in terms of EO (Joules) relatively immutable, Charge reporting alone, as previously noted, is not only unreliable, but deceptive. In brief, in spite of what appears to be no change at all (under the Weiner de facto standard), the fourth generation BP device amplifies output to an almost ten MTTLOI for BL ECT as opposed to the circa five MTTLOI of the third generation BP device. In other words, despite equal Charge emissions from third and fourth generation BP devices at every age level, the critical enhancement from circa 5.0 to circa 10.0 MTTLOI from the third to the fourth generation BP device for every age grouping cannot be perceived. Charge parameters alone are not only an unreliable and inconsistent means of reporting power in that they may fail to identify enhancements in MTTLOI, but the lone reporting of Charge parameters (without EO), sets the stage for gross duplicity and deception. EO (in Joules) is the only consistent and thus reliable means of accurately reporting power, power amplification, and the critically important MTTLOI delivered by any particular BP device. In conclusion, under Weiner's 1997 standard, neither the doubling of power nor the doubling of MTTLOI from third to fourth generation BP devices can be detected.

The Fourth Generation Somatics "System V"

Finally, the third generation Somatics System IV utilizes a .9A constant current (in lieu of the maximum 2.0A), a **450V** maximum, a .0015 second Pulse Width, and a 5.32 second maximum Duration. Hertz is 70 (140 pulses per second). We have already seen that the third generation Somatics System IV emits an unreported 452 Joules, again, easily allowable under Weiner's new 1997 de facto "standard."

450V x .9A x 140Pulses x .0015PW x 5.32 Seconds = **452 Joules**.

or

1.005C x 500Ω x .9A = **452 Joules**.

The Charge per second is well under Weiner's 300mC/second "regulation."

1.0 Seconds x .9A x 140 Pulses and .0015PW = **189mC/Second.**

The Charge per pulse, of course, is also well under Weiner's 2mC/phase "regulation."

189mC ÷ 140 pulses = **1.35mC/phase**

Under Weiner's same provisions, the above mentioned paradigm for "legally" doubling third generation output can also be successfully applied to the third generation Somatics "System IV." By doubling Voltage from 450V to 900V and Amperage from .9A to 1.8A, and by similarly reducing pulse width by half from .0015 to .00075 Seconds, we derive a "legal" circa **904J** fourth generation "System V" device, doubling the 452J output of the third generation "System IV." Duration, Impedance, and Hertz once again remain unchanged as does Charge. Fourth generation adherence to Weiner's 1997 "standard" of (what the author has deemed) the Somatics "System V" can be seen below:

Impedance-oriented formula for deriving EO:

EO = 1.8A x **1.8A** x **500Ω** x 140 pulses x .00075PW x 5.32 Seconds = **904.9J**.

Voltage-oriented formula for deriving EO:

900V x **1.8A** x 140Pulses x .00075PW x 5.32 Seconds = **904.9 Joules**.

Charge-oriented formula for deriving EO:

1.005C x 500Ω x **1.8A** = **904.5 Joules**

Let us check "legal" outputs against Weiner's 300mC/second criterion.

1.0 Seconds x .1.8A x 140 Pulses x .00075 PW = **189 mC/Second.**

Let us check against Weiner's 1200mC (or 1.2C) total Charge criterion.

Charge = 904.9J/1.8A x 500Ω = **1.005C**

Charge = 5.32 Sec. x 1.8A x 140 pulses x .00075PW = **1.005C**

Finally, let us check against Weiner's 2.0 mC/phase criterion.

189mC/sec ÷ 180 pulses/sec = **1.05mC/phase**

Once again, the fourth generation Somatics "System V" device is "legal" under the Weiner proviso and once again reportable Charge emissions from third to fourth generation remain unchanged, making the doubling of power and MTTLOI invisible under Weiner's 1997 de facto standard (due to unreported joules).

ACTUAL CONSTANT CURRENT SYSTEM IV BRIEF PULSE DEVICE
(**3rd Generation**) By SOMATICS Inc. 1994
BASED ON PURE-ER/RRC INTERPRETATION OF 271.5J AT 300Ω or 199J AT 220Ω

VOLTAGE	POWER % @ Age	AGE Yrs	Ω Ohms	FREQUENCY (Hz)	DURATION (SECs)	CURRENT mAmps	ENERGY Joules	CHARGE mC
45	10	10	50	30	1.244	900	4.54	100.8
90	20	20	100	30	2.47	900	18.14	200.16
135	30	30	150	50	2.24	900	40.78	302
180	40	40	200	50	2.99	900	72.58	403.2
225	50	50	250	50	3.73	900	113.4	504
270	60	60	300	70	3.2	900	163.3	604.8
292.5	65	65	325	70	3.47	900	191.6	655.2
315	70	70	350	70	3.73	900	222.26	705.6
360	80	80	400	70	4.27	900	290.4	806.4
405	90	90	450	70	4.8	900	367.4	907.2
450	100	100	**500**	70	5.32	900	**452**	**1005**

(.0015 WL)

HYPOTHETICAL CONSTANT CURRENT SYSTEM V BRIEF PULSE DEVICE
(**4th Generation**) By SOMATICS Inc. 2000?
BASED ON PURE-ER/RRC INTERPRETATION OF 543J AT 300Ω or 398J AT 220Ω

VOLTAGE	POWER % @ Age	AGE Yrs	Ω Ohms	FREQUENCY (Hz)	DURATION (SECs)	CURRENT mAmps	ENERGY Joules	CHARGE mC
90	10	10	50	30	1.244	1800	9.08	100.8
180	20	20	100	30	2.47	1800	36.28	200.16
270	30	30	150	50	2.24	1800	81.56	302
360	40	40	200	50	2.99	1800	145.16	403.2
450	50	50	250	50	3.73	1800	226.8	504
540	60	60	300	70	3.2	1800	326.6	604.8
585	65	65	325	70	3.47	1800	383.2	655.2
630	70	70	350	70	3.73	1800	444.52	705.6
720	80	80	400	70	4.27	1800	580.8	806.4
810	90	90	450	70	4.8	1800	734.8	907.2

900	100	100	**500**	70 (.00075 WL)	5.32	1800	**904**	**1005**

Note how the doubling of output (in Joules) has no effect on Charge outputs including maximum overall Charge, all of which remain unchanged from 3rd to 4th generation BP devices. Thus, under Weiner's system of "Charge only" reporting, the doubling in power and MTTLOI from 3rd to 4th generation devices is undetectable.

Once again, in spite of exactly the same Charge emissions from third to fourth generation BP devices, the fourth generation "System V" now elicits a 9.04 MTTLOI with BL ECT as opposed to the third generation Somatics' "System IV" which elicits an unreported 4.52 MTTLOI in every age category. To illustrate this, we can take the maximum Charge for both devices, 1.005 Coulombs, and dividing first by 4.52, obtain .222C, to obtain the just above threshold Charge for a 100 year old recipient using the third generation "System IV." We can then convert this to Joules by plugging the threshold Charge (.222C) figure into the EO formula: EO = Charge x Current x Impedance, to obtain just above threshold EO in terms of Joules, which, not surprisingly, is 100 Joules.

EO = .222C x .9A x 500Ω = <u>100 Joules</u>

Multiplying the 100J figure by 4.52 (the MTTLOI), we obtain the maximum 452 Joules of EO administered to the 100 year old recipient on the third generation "System IV" above (see third generation JR/SR 2 chart above).

100 Joules x 4.52 = <u>452J</u>

We can now take the same maximum Charge, 1.005 Coulombs and divide by 9.04 (the MTTLOI) to obtain .111C, the just above threshold Charge for a 100 year old recipient on the fourth generation "System V." To convert this Charge figure into EO, we again plug the .111C Charge figure into the EO formula: EO = Charge x Current x Impedance, from which we obtain the same consistent just above threshold EO of 100 Joules for the same 100 year old recipient.[133]

EO = .111C x 1.8A x 500Ω = <u>100 Joules</u>

Multiplying the 100J EO figure by 9.04 (the MTTLOI), we obtain the 904J EO maximum utilized for the 100 year old recipient on the fourth generation "System V," a 9.04 MTTLOI administered to the 100 year old recipient, the same MTTLOI administered to all other recipients on this device; (see fourth generation "System V" table above).

100 Joules x 9.04 = <u>904J</u>

Of course, (if we had been informed of the change in Charge threshold from .222C to .111C), we could also multiply the new .111C Charge threshold for the 100 year old recipient by 9.04 to obtain the known circa 1.005C maximum Charge emitted by the fourth generation "System V." Conversely, we could have divided the 1.005C maximum Charge by the new .111C Charge threshold to obtain the new (9.04 x .111C = circa 1.005; 1.005 ÷ .111C =) circa 9.04 MTTLOI. To do so, of course, we would have to be aware of the reduced Charge threshold of the fourth as opposed to the third generation Somatics Brief Pulse device due to the doubling of Voltage and thus Amperage in spite of halving the Pulse Width on the fourth generation Brief Pulse device compared to the third generation BP device. This phenomenon, as already noted, doubles the output emitted in terms of Joules per age-related Impedance on the fourth generation BP device while Charge output, because Charge threshold has decreased by half, does not change at all. As noted above, doubling the EO (in joules)

---

[133] To obtain threshold dosing for all age groups on Somatics devices, we need only divide EO emitted at any particular age by 9.04 for the fourth generation BP device, 4.52 for the third generation BP device, and 2.26 for the second generation BP device, the DGx. 9.04, 4.52, and 2.26 are all derived by dividing maximum machine outputs by 100J (904J ÷ 100J = 9.04; 452J ÷ 100J = 4.52; 226J ÷ 100J = 2.26).

on the hypothetical fourth generation Brief Pulse device can only mean that doubling the Amperage and halving the Pulse Width has reduced threshold outputs by half in terms of Charge. Unfortunately, we can only come to this conclusion by observing that the EO (Joules) emitted in all age categories has doubled. Unfortunately, in that actual Charge outputs remain identical on third and probable fourth generation BP devices, observers remain unaware of the doubling of EO relative to the unchanged Charge outputs under Weiner's de facto "standard," and so unaware of the reduced Charge thresholds. In short, observers fail to see any enhancement. In sum then, doubling Amperage and halving Pulse Width, reduce Charge thresholds by half, while EO thresholds (Joules) remain unchanged. Thus, in that actual Charge outputs are identical on third and fourth generation BP devices, without EO reporting in joules, the halved Charge thresholds become invisible. In conclusion, the doubling in power from third to fourth generation BP devices, discernable only in terms of Joules, becomes completely imperceptible under Weiner's new 1997 de facto "standard."

Power, therefore, is not actually dependent upon cumulative Charge in that threshold outputs in terms of Charge can change. Conversely, age-related threshold outputs in terms of EO (Joules), remain relatively constant. In spite of appearances, then, the theoretical fourth generation BP device doubles the 4.52 MTTLOI elicited by the third generation BP device to a 9.04 MTTLOI (with BL "ECT"). In spite of the equal Charge maximums elicited by both third and fourth generation Somatics BP devices, then, under Weiner's proviso, the 4.52 MTTLOI doubling to a 9.04 MTTLOI in every age category remains invisible. Under Weiner's 1997 proviso, unless we realize that Charge threshold has been reduced by half, the doubling in power from third to fourth generation can only be seen in terms of EO (Joules). Once again then, we see that Charge reporting alone is not only an unreliable and inconsistent means of reporting power and MTTLOI, but can serve as a means of gross deceit and deception. Once again, moreover, we discover that EO in joules is the only reliable means of accurately reporting power, power amplification, and MTTLOI, the key characteristics of any Brief Pulse device.

Though imperceptible, all criteria for transitioning the unreported 452J third generation "System IV" device to a 904J fourth generation "System V" BP device are fully met under Weiner's 1997 default standard. In short, fourth generation BP devices are "legal" under Weiner's 1997 de facto standard currently used by most, if not all Brief Pulse manufacturers. Disconcertingly, in that Charge remains unchanged except in terms of threshold output, the doubling of power and MTTLOI from third to fourth generation BP devices is cloaked. Indeed, under the 1997 Weiner standard, third and fourth generation BP devices appear identical. From the 1995 emergence of unreported third generation BP devices in both Europe and America, then, have manufacturers been producing and marketing fourth generation Brief Pulse devices, legal under Weiner's proviso, devices administering an unreported circa ten MTTLOI to every age individual receiving BL "ECT" and a circa twenty MTTLOI to every age individual receiving UL "ECT"? Astonishingly, under the current de facto standard, while probable, the question cannot be answered.

CHAPTER 60

Fifth Generation BP Devices

Potential fifth generation device conformity (to Weiner's 1997 provision) has been illustrated above and is shown here again via the Voltage-oriented formula for deriving EO.

1000V x 2.0A x 150Pulses x .001PW x 4.0 Seconds = **1200 Joules**.

Using the Current-oriented formula for confirmation:

2.0A x 2.0A x 500Ω x 150 pulses x .001PW x 4.0 Seconds = **1200 Joules**.

Using the Charge formula: Charge = Duration x Current x (Hz x 2) x WL, we derive Weiner's "acceptable" 300mC/Second maximum:

1.0 Seconds x 2.0A x 150 pulses x .001PW = **300mC/Second**.

Using the maximum 4.0 Second Duration which we have incorporated into the fifth generation machine, we derive Weiner's "acceptable" 1200mC total Charge.

4.0 Seconds x 300mC/Second = **1200mC total**

Finally, by dividing millicoulombs per second by pulses per second, we obtain Weiner's "acceptable" 2.0mC/phase or 2.0mC/pulse.

300mC/sec. ÷ 150 pulses/sec. = **2mC/phase**

Thus the maximum 300mC/Second, 2mC/phase and 1200mC total Charge criteria for Weiner's 1200J maximum fifth generation Brief Pulse device all fall within the "legal" purview of Weiner's 1997 "standard" for Brief Pulse devices, generally.

But how difficult would it be to transition from fourth generation Brief Pulse devices to fifth generation Brief Pulse devices capable of the full unreported 1200J output under Weiner's 1997 de facto "standard"?

Simply doubling Amperage and Voltage of the third generation JR/SR 1 from .8A and 400V, to 1.6A and 800V respectively, but also reducing pulse width from .002 to .001 seconds, we derived the probable **922J** fourth generation JR/SR 1 "British" BP device, easily doubling the 460J output of the third generation JR/SR 1 "British BP device," in turn doubling the MTTLOI administered to all age categories. If we now take the theoretical, but probable fourth generation JR/SR 1 "British" BP device as our model and simply boost the Amperage from 1.6 to the legal maximum of 2.0 Amperes by enhancing maximum Voltage from 800 to the legal 1000V maximum, and finally if we reduce the number of pulses per second from 180 to 150 (75 Hertz), leaving all other parameters intact (including the .001 Second Pulse Width), we can construct a perfectly "legal" (albeit totally unreported) 1200J maximum BP device under the new 1997 Weiner standard, a fifth generation device capable of a "legal" 12.0 MTTLOI for each individual recipient administered BL "ECT" and a twenty-four MTTLOI for each individual recipient administered UL "ECT."

PROBABLE CONSTANT CURRENT **JR/SR 1** BRIEF PULSE **IEC** BP DEVICE
(4th GENERATION) "BRITISH" by MECTA Corp. 2000?
BASED ON PURE-ER/RRC OF **"553J AT 300Ω" or "405J at 220Ω"**

VOLTAGE	POWER % @ Age	AGE Yrs	Ω Ohms	FREQUENCY (Hz)	DURATION (SECs)	CURRENT mAmps	ENERGY Joules	CHARGE mC
80	10	10	50	90	0.5	1600	11.52	144
160	20	20	100	90	0.8	1600	36.86	230
240	30	30	150	90	1.2	1600	82.94	345.6
320	40	40	200	90	1.6	1600	147.46	460.8
400	50	50	250	90	2.0	1600	230.4	576
480	60	60	300	90	2.4	1600	331.76	691.2
520	65	65	325	90	2.6	1600	389.36	748.8
560	70	70	350	90	2.8	1600	451.6	806.4
640	80	80	400	90	3.2	1600	590	921.6
720	90	90	450	90	3.6	1600	746	1036.8
800	100	100	500	90	4.0	1600	**922J**	**1152**

(**.001** Sec Pulse Width)

HYPOTHETICAL CONSTANT CURRENT **JR/SR 1** BRIEF PULSE **IEC** BP DEVICE
(5th GENERATION) "BRITISH" by MECTA Corp. 2000?
BASED ON PURE-ER/RRC OF **"720J AT 300Ω" or "528J at 220Ω"**

VOLTAGE	POWER % @ Age	AGE Yrs	Ω Ohms	FREQUENCY (Hz)	DURATION (SECs)	CURRENT mAmps	ENERGY Joules	CHARGE mC
100	10	10	50	75	0.5	2000	15	150
200	20	20	100	75	0.8	2000	48	240
300	30	30	150	75	1.2	2000	108	360
400	40	40	200	75	1.6	2000	192	480
500	50	50	250	75	2.0	2000	300	600
600	60	60	300	75	2.4	2000	432	720
650	65	65	325	75	2.6	2000	507	780
700	70	70	350	75	2.8	2000	588	840
800	80	80	400	75	3.2	2000	768	960
900	90	90	450	75	3.6	2000	972	1080
1000	100	100	500	75	4.0	2000	**1200J**	**1200**

(**.001** Sec Pulse Width)

Let us test for Weiner conformity at any given age level via the potential 5th generation BP device above. Let us take, for example, the twenty year old receiving 240 millicoulombs over a .8 second Duration (see above chart). The Charge output per second is an "acceptable" 300mC/second.

240mC ÷ .8 Sec. = 300mC/second

150 Pulses per second leads to an "acceptable" 2mC/phase.

300mC ÷ 150 pulses = 2mC/phase

For the 50 year old receiving 600mC over a 2.0 second Duration, the output is again an "acceptable" 300mC/second which is again an "acceptable" 2mC/phase under Weiner's de facto "standard."

600mC ÷ 2.0 seconds = 300mC/phase
300mC ÷ 150 pulses = 2mC/phase

The 100 year old receiving 1200mC over a 4.0 second Duration also receives the consistent 300mC/second, once again (at 150 Pulses per Second) an "acceptable" 2mC/phase under Weiner's 1997 "standard."

1200mC ÷ 4.0 seconds = 300mC/phase
300mC ÷ 150 pulses = 2mC/phase

Thus at every age level, the potential fifth generation 1200J machine conforms in all respects to Weiner's 1997 de facto "standard," the unofficial "Standard" currently used by manufacturers today.

Note that the Charge parameters advance only minimally from a 1152 millicoulomb maximum on the fourth generation BP device to a 1200 millicoulomb maximum on the fifth generation BP device, while EO, still invisible under Weiner's "standard" advances dramatically. To illustrate, EO is enhanced from 922 Joules maximum via the probable fourth generation JR/SR 1 "British" BP device to 1200 Joules maximum on the hypothetical fifth generation JR/SR 1 "British" BP device, which means another major enhancement in MTTLOI (from 9.22 to 12 fold threshold) for each individual recipient administered BL "ECT." We can confirm this by equivalent ratio: 922J/9.22 = 1200J/X = 12.0. We can also simply divide maximum output in Joules by 100J--the consistent BL threshold output for the 100 year old recipient--to see the transition from fourth to fifth generation: 922 ÷ 100J = **9.22 fold** to 1200J ÷ 100J = **12 fold**. MTTLOI on all MECTA and Somatics BP devices is consistently applied to every age category, i.e. a 9.22 fold threshold for the fourth generation JR/SR 1 "British" BP device and a 12.0 fold threshold for the hypothetical fifth generation JR/SR 1 "British" BP device with BL placement. A 40 year old recipient, for example, who seizes at 16J receives circa 147.26 Joules or a 9.22 MTTLOI on the probable fourth generation BP device, whereas the same forty year old receives 192 Joules on the hypothetical fifth generation device, now a 12 MTTLOI. Note confirmation through ER.

$$147.52J/\underline{9.22} = 192J/\underline{X} = \underline{12}$$

Once again, however, the enhancement is visible only in terms of Joules: **9.22** x 16J (the constant threshold output for 40 yr. old) = **147.52J**; **12** x 16J (the constant relative threshold output for 40 yr. old) = **192J**. (Although EO increases dramatically, from 147.52J to 192J, note that Charge enhancement is minimal, from 460mC to 480mC.)

Regarding Somatics, the probable Somatics fourth generation "System V" emits a maximum 904 Joules or a 9.04 MTTLOI for every age category. Setting up an equivalent ratio with the maximum output (1200J) emitted by the hypothetical Somatics fifth generation BP device above, the same 12.0 MTTLOI can be derived.

$$904J/9.04 = 1200J/\underline{X} = \underline{12}$$

The fourth generation JR/SR 2 "British" BP device emits a maximum 960 Joules or a 9.6 MTTLOI. Setting up an equivalent ratio with the maximum output emitted by the hypothetical fifth generation BP device above (1200J), the same 12.0 MTTLOI is derived.

$$960J/9.6 = 1200J/\underline{X} = \underline{12}$$

Finally, note how with increased Amperage on the hypothetical fifth generation BP device, the Charge threshold on the fifth generation device has again decreased, this time to 100mC for the 100 year old recipient (1200mC ÷ 12 = 100mC), once again revealing the inconsistency of Charge thresholds and Charge reporting. Converting Charge to Joules, conversely, we once again see the consistent threshold output in terms of joules (100J) for the 100 year old recipient.

EO = .100C x 2.0 A x 500Ω = **100 Joules**.

Once again, under Weiner's system of reporting Charge only, the overall output amplifications and MTTLOI enhancements not only go unreported, but become imperceptible and thus misleading. Third and fourth generation BP devices emitting circa 500J, and circa 1000J maximums cannot be differentiated under the Weiner de facto "standard" while the fifth generation device emitting 1200J can be only nominally differentiated.

CHAPTER 61

Conclusion for Extant 3rd, Probable 4th, and Hypothetical 5th Generation BP Devices

The doubling of extant third generation Brief Pulse devices to devise probable fourth generation Brief Pulse devices (under Weiner's de facto provisions) is a simple matter of doubling Amperage and Voltage of third generation BP devices and reducing Wave Length by half. For probable fourth generation devices, i.e. the fourth generation JR/SR 1, the fourth generation JR/SR 2 MECTA "British", and what might be deemed the fourth generation "System V" Somatics' BP device, the pure-ER/RRC upon which they are based, though not reported under Weiner's 1997 default standard, soars to unconscionable figures of (XJ/220Ω = 921J/500Ω; **X =)** **405J at 220Ω** for the JR/SR 1, (XJ/220Ω = 960J/500Ω; **X =)** **422J at 220Ω** for the JR/SR 2 and (XJ/220Ω = 904J/500Ω; **X =)** **398J at 220Ω** for the System V respectively, doubling the already unlikely but equally unreported circa **200J at 220Ω** pure-ER/RRC of already extant third generation BP devices, more than quintupling the **70J at 220Ω** conditional-ER/RRC of the 1982 APA Standard**.** In transitioning from a conditional-ER/RRC (conforming to the 1982 APA Standard) to a pure-ER/RRC, second generation BP devices more than double the output and MTTLOI of first generation BP devices. Third generation BP devices double the output and MTTLOI of second generation BP devices, quadrupling the power of first generation BP devices. Probable fourth generation BP devices double the output and MTTLOI of third generation BP devices, circa quadrupling the power of second generation BP devices, and emitting approximately ten fold the output and MTTLOI of the MECTA "C" which alone conforms to the 1982 APA Standard. In short, probable fourth generation BP devices quadruple the reported but unexplicated circa **100J at 220Ω** pure-ER/RRC and MTTLOI of second generation BP devices. Compared to the MECTA "C" which emitted a 1.08 MTTLOI of the 1.1 MTTLOI allowed under the 1982 APA Standard, probable fourth generation BP devices emit a circa 10.0 MTTLOI in every age category.

Relative to SW, the circa 450J output maximum emitted by extant third generation BP devices delivers more than twice that of the most excessive SW output possible (450J ÷ 200J = 2.25) while the circa 900J maximum output of fourth generation BP devices, more than quadruples the most excessive SW output possible (900J ÷ 200J = 4.5)—albeit in divergent age categories. Finally, the 1200J output maximum of what under Weiner's de facto standard, is a hypothetical, but "lawful" fifth generation BP device, is more than six times the output of the most excessive SW emission possible (1200J ÷ 200J = 6.0), though, once again, in disparate age categories.[134]

Thus, while the maximum MTTLOI emitted by SW might yet surpass even the most powerful Brief Pulse device in the youngest age category, the raw power of the most extreme Brief Pulse devices allowed under the Weiner de facto standard have the capacity to deliver MTTLOIs far surpassing that of SW in the majority of age categories. Plainly, the newer enhanced BP machines, invented for the sole purpose of enhancing the MTTLOI applicable to all age categories, gradationally diminish in safety as they gradationally increase in power from the 1.1 MTTLOI emitted by first generation BP devices, to a circa 2.5 MTTLOI emitted by second generation BP devices, a circa 5.0 MTTLOI emitted by third generation BP devices, a circa 10.0 MTTLOI emitted by probable fourth generation BP devices, and finally a potential 12 MTTLOI emitted by hypothetical fifth generation BP devices with BL "ECT," all legal under the 1997 Weiner de facto standard. Astoundingly, compared to the APA Standard approved by the FDA in 1982, Weiner's de facto standard represents an

---

[134] Maximum output for SW occurs in the youngest age category; maximum output for BP occurs in the oldest age category.

unreported increase in power and MTTLOI of almost (1200J - 110J = 1090J ÷ 110J = 990%; 12 - 1.1 = 10.9 ÷ 1.1 = 990%) 1000%. Of equally critical concern, moreover, is that under Weiner's 1997 de facto standard, third, fourth, and fifth generation BP devices appear almost identical with respect to Charge; consequently, under Weiner's proviso, which totally expunges EO reporting in joules, ER/RRC, and MTTLOI increases in power from third to fifth generation BP devices are invisible; while comparison to the elusive second and even first generation BP devices both of which are depicted in joules, becomes obscure.

More Specifics of Actual and Potential Brief Pulse Devices "Allowed" Under Weiner's New 1997 De Facto Standard Compared to Brief Pulse Devices Allowed Under the 1982 APA Standard

Specifically, Somatics extant third generation BP device, the System IV, emits an unreported maximum of <u>453 Joules</u> and a reported maximum of <u>1008mC</u> (of Charge), while MECTA's third generation SR 1 and 2 "British" IEC BP devices emit unreported maximums of <u>460 and 480 Joules</u> and reported maximums of <u>1152 and 1200mCs</u> (of Charge) respectively. Modern extant third generation Somatics and MECTA BP devices more than quadruple the EO, MTTLOI, and Charge of the 108J, 1.08 MTTLOI, and 336mC MECTA "C" BP device originally submitted to the FDA as emblematic of Brief Pulse, generally. Condoned by both Utah and the FDA, only the MECTA "C" conformed to the 1982 APA Standard written and submitted to the American public and the FDA by Weiner himself. Touted as a safer apparatus by virtue of reduced output compared to SW, at 108 maximum joules, the "C" was hailed as emitting the least amount of electricity possible with BL ECT, half that of the 200J SW device, while inducing the same adequate seizures in all age categories. Conversely, under the current 1997 Weiner de facto standard, a probable fourth generation Somatics BP device can legally emit invisible maximums of 905 Joules or a 9.05 MTTLOI (with BL "ECT") at the same 1008mC Charge maximum as the third generation Somatics BP device. Probable fourth generation MECTA BP devices can legally emit unreported maximums of 920 and 960 Joules or a 9.2 and 9.6 MTTLOI respectively (with BL "ECT") at the same 1152 and 1200mC Charge maximums as third generation MECTA BP devices. In short, under Weiner's proviso, fourth generation BP devices are "allowed" to emit about nine times the power and MTTLOI of the MECTA "C" without clearly reporting the enhancement.

Finally, a potential fifth generation BP device under the same Weiner proviso can hypothetically, but "legally" emit an unreported 1200J or 12.0 MTTLOI maximum output (with BL "ECT") at almost the same circa 1200mC maximum Charge as third and fourth generation Somatics and MECTA BP devices. In brief, an unreported fifth generation BP device can legally emit more than (1200J ÷ 108J =) 11.11 fold the power and MTTLOI of the original MECTA "C" with BL "ECT" with no clear reporting of the increase. Thus, Weiner's 1997 "Standard," depicting maximum Impedance as 500 maximum ohms and Charge as 1200mC, in lieu of regulating or restricting the output of Brief Pulse devices so that they deliver less EO than SW, actually enables third generation BP devices to double the power of second generation BP devices, probable fourth generation BP devices to double the power of third generation devices, and hypothetical, but "allowable" fifth generation BP devices to dramatically enhance the power of probable fourth generation BP devices. Under the 1997 Weiner de facto "standard," fifth generation BP devices can emit six times the power of SW devices (1200J ÷ 200J = 6) all while claiming to be "kinder and gentler" reduced EO devices compared to SW. In sum, while Weiner's 1997 "standard" actually "legalizes" extant third generation BP devices and allows for even more powerful fourth and fifth generation BP devices, these increases go undetected due to the expungement of EO reporting in joules so that they cannot be meaningfully compared either to previous BP or SW devices and because Charge outputs are virtually the same for all three latter BP generations. Indeed, with what appears to be a single increase in Charge from circa 5-600mC to 1200mC, manufacturers have created the illusion of circa 200J maximum Brief Pulse devices, about that of maximum SW, while actually producing and applying the most powerful devices in "ECT" history. (See Appendix E: "ECT" Compared to Tasers and Defibrillators.)

CHAPTER 62

Power and Invisibility: 1000% Increase in Power

As a result of Brief Pulse architypes presented to the FDA amidst the first FDA investigation of the "ECT Medical Device" between 1976-1982, MECTA's presentation of the first generation MECTA "C" BP device emitting a maximum output of 108J followed by a Weiner penned (1982 APA) Standard promising to keep all future ECT devices at minimal stimulus, the FDA approved the continuation of ECT, generally. Soon following the close of the investigation, however, the second generation JR/SR 2 IEC BP device was manufactured, capable of emitting an unreported maximum output of circa 240J. By 1995, the third generation JR/SR 2 IEC BP device was manufactured in secret, capable of emitting an unreported circa 480J, and by 1997, a probable fourth generation MECTA device became "legal," capable of emitting an unreported circa 960J, as well as a potential fifth generation MECTA device, capable of emitting an unreported and unprecedented circa 1200J. In short, there have been ***four*** (major) ***sequential increases*** in BP power from first to fifth generation following the 1976-1982 FDA investigation. Beginning with the 1982 APA Standard which allowed 110 maximum Joules and a "70J at 220Ω" conditional-ER/RRC, these increases occurred as a result of the Mectan Transmutation in America which utilized a "100J at 220Ω" pure-ER/RRC in lieu of a "70J at 220Ω" conditional ER/RRC. This was followed by the 1989 IEC Standard in Europe which utilized slight breaching of a "130J at 300Ω" pure-ER/RRC, finally followed by Weiner's 1997 de facto standard. Weiner's standard, in effect today, uses unreported pure-ER/RRCs of **"288J at 300Ω"** or **"211.2J at 220Ω"** for the extant third generation JR/SR 2 IEC BP device, an unreported **"576J at 300Ω"** or **"422.4J at 220Ω"** for the probable fourth generation JR/SR 2 IEC BP device, and an unreported **"720J AT 300Ω" or "528J at 220Ω"** for the hypothetical 5th generation JR/SR device. These increases include a first to second generation enhancement (240J - 108J = 132J ÷ 108J = 122%) representing a **122%** increase; a second to third generation enhancement (480J - 240J = 240J ÷ 240J = 100%) representing another **100%** increase, a third to probable fourth generation enhancement (960J - 480J = 480J ÷ 480J = 100%) representing another **100%** increase, and a hypothetical, but "allowable" fourth to fifth generation enhancement (1200J - 960J = 240J ÷ 960J = 25%) representing an additional **25%** increase in power. Altogether, these maximum enhancements encompass a circa 1000% increase in power, specifically a (1200J - 108J = 1092J ÷ 108J =) **1011%** increase in power from the MECTA "C" which alone conformed to the 1982 APA Standard promised to and condoned by the FDA and Utah Biomedical Test Laboratory in 1982.

The first generation MECTA "C" BP device emitted a maximum 340mC of Charge. The most powerful second generation BP device emitted a maximum 600mC of Charge. The third, fourth, and fifth generation BP devices emit a circa 1200mC maximum Charge. Relative to EO, **Charge** reporting alone abstrusely reflects only ***two major increases*** in power, that is, an increase from the first to an elusive second generation BP device and an increase from an elusive second to what are actually third, fourth, and fifth generation BP devices (the latter three of which have the same virtual maximum Charge). Specifically, first to second (600mC - 340mC = 260mC ÷ 340mC =) represents a **76%** increase in Charge, while second to third, fourth, and fifth generation BP devices (1200mC - 600mC = 600mC ÷ 600mC =) represent another **100%** increase. Altogether, there is more than a 250% increase in Charge from first to fifth generation BP devices (1200mC - 340mC = 860mC ÷ 340mC = 253%). Even this number is misleading in that much greater power enhancements have actually taken place, enhancements only visible via the reporting of EO in Joules. In short, while the probable fourth generation BP device doubles in power relative to the third generation BP device, and the hypothetical but "allowable" fifth generation BP device is 25% more powerful than the fourth generation BP device, these two power increases are not perceptible via Charge reporting alone, only becoming manifest via EO (in joules) reporting, which has been entirely expunged via Weiner's 1997 de facto standard. Finally, manufacturers covered up the first Charge enhancement from 340mC to 600mC as we have seen, so that only one Charge enhancement from circa 600mC to 1200mC appears to have occurred.

Thus while sequential enhancements of third, fourth and fifth generation BP devices are "permissible" under the 1997 Weiner de facto standard, all we see reported (and only if we look very carefully) is a somewhat meaningless doubling in Charge from the circa 600mC maximum Charge of what seems to be first generation BP devices (but which are actually second) to the circa 1200mC maximum Charge of what seems to be second generation BP devices, but which are actually third, fourth, and fifth generation BP devices. The latter three, of course, are virtually indistinguishable via Charge reporting alone. In short, as we have seen, the transition to what are actually third generation BP devices appears to be a first time enhancement so that extant third generation BP devices appear to be second generation BP devices, an illusion further corroborated by second generation BP devices posing as first generation BP devices via the false depiction of circa 100J machine readouts evinced by the devices themselves. (We shall examine this in specific detail a little later.) Indeed, as heretofore noted, because third, fourth, and fifth generation BP devices are not reported in joules, what are actually extant third, probable fourth, and hypothetical but "permissible" fifth generation BP devices all appear to be second generation BP devices, suggestive of a single doubling in power of first generation BP devices. Though never reported as such, this illusion indicates outputs of circa 200 maximum joules, no greater than SW, a totally false assumption. As noted, because Charge maximums replace EO maximums under Weiner's 1997 de facto standard, and because 230-260J second generation BP devices are depicted as having circa 100J maximums, power and MTTLOI enhancements from second to third, fourth, and fifth generation BP devices appear to be first time enhancements. Indeed, as we have seen, enhancements from third to probable fourth, and fourth to possible fifth generation devices become entirely invisible under Weiner's 1997 de facto standard. This means that the manufacturing and marketing of third, fourth and even fifth generation BP machines emitting anywhere from 460 to 1200 maximum Joules, that is, from a 4.6 to a 12.0 MTTLOI for all age recipients (with BL "ECT"), may have all already taken place without ever being reported.[135] Under Weiner's 1997 Charge proviso wherein neither "EO in joules" nor even "pure-ER/RRCs" are any longer reported, there is simply no way of differentiating between third, fourth, and fifth generation BP devices as we have observed. Amazingly then, because EO in Joules has been dropped under the 1997 Weiner proviso, neither the actual power (EO), comparative output with preceding devices, nor the MTTLOI of third, probable forth, and possible fifth generation BP devices can be identified. In brief, while the first to second generation enhancement was never accurately reported, but, in fact, hidden, and because EO reporting in Joules has been totally supplanted by Charge reporting under Weiner's 1997 replacement proviso, most evidence of first to second, and second to third generation enhancement has been eradicated, and no evidence of third to fourth, and fourth to fifth generation enhancements has ever been recounted until now. In fact, under the Weiner proviso in which EO reporting has been replaced with Charge reporting, following what appear to be second, but which are actually third generation BP devices, there appear to be no other enhancements at all. In sum, the overall impression conveyed is that only one major enhancement has ever taken place since 1976, suggestive, as noted, of Brief Pulse machines around 200 maximum joules, but never actually reported as such. In fact, manufacturers continue to suggest and the myth remains firmly in place, that Brief Pulse devices emit half the EO of SW.

In sum then, compared to what are actually second generation made-for America BP devices secretly enhanced under the illicit 1982 Mectan Transmutation, Weiner's 1997 de facto standard permits a (1200J ÷ 273J =) 4.4 MTTLOI increase or a (1200J - 273J = 927J ÷ 273J =) 340% rise in power and MTTLOI with BL "ECT." Compared to the 1989 IEC standard or made-for-Europe second generation BP devices, Weiner's de facto standard represents more than a (1200J ÷ 217J =) 5.5 MTTLOI increase or a (1200J - 217J = 983J ÷ 217J =) 453% rise in power and MTTLOI with BL "ECT." Finally, compared to the 1982 APA Standard which Weiner himself presented to the FDA, Weiner's 1997 de facto standard permits an almost (1200J ÷ 110J = 10.9; 12 ÷ 1.1 =) 11.0 MTTLOI increase with BL "ECT," or an increase in power and MTTLOI of almost (1200J

[135] To appreciate this, as has already been pointed out, we must remember that under the Perrin study which discovered a large reduction in prefrontal neuronal connectivity following "ECT," recipients received a multifold threshold titration level output intensity of only 2.0 to 2.5 fold, and this with a second generation BP device (Perrin et al. 2012).

– 110J = 1090J ÷ 110J = 990%; 12 – 1.1 = 10.9 ÷ 1.1 = 990%) 1000%. This is worth repeating. The "allowable" power and MTTLOI of Brief Pulse devices has increased virtually 1000% compared to the 1982 APA Standard, the promise upon which the FDA based its approval for the continuation of "ECT," generally. The one fact that may be even more astounding than the increases themselves, is that due to an unbroken continuum of cleverly deceptive manufacturer reporting stratagems, Weiner's 1997 de facto standard ensures that almost all these enhancements have remained invisible—until now.

Deception

Between 1982 and 1985, as noted, American BP devices more than doubled in power from approximately 110 actual Joules to approximately 250 actual Joules (Cameron, 1994). Due to clever mathematical manipulation by American BP manufacturers who supplanted the original circa 100J ceiling, first with an unexplicated 100J average and then with an unexplained 100J pure-ER, the dropping of the circa 100J ceiling together with the first major Brief Pulse power enhancement (more than doubling output) was revealed neither to the FDA, nor to the IEC, nor to the American and European public. Following the 1997 withdrawal of the 1989 IEC Standard, BP manufacturers once more managed to hide what was now a more than quadrupling of output via third generation BP devices through the elusive transformation within Weiner's 1997 de facto standard--namely the total supplanting of EO reporting with Charge reporting. While an enhancement had been called for and even acknowledged with Weiner's 1997 proposal, it was due to the total disappearance of EO reporting in Weiner's revision proposal making comparison to previous BP devices almost impossible, that the degree of third generation enhancement--almost five fold the maximum output of first generation BP devices--remained obfuscated, indeed, never actually published (until now). While the 1997 Weiner de facto standard, as noted, did overtly double the Charge maximum from circa 600mC to circa 1200mC, the doubling of Charge, as we have observed, appeared to be a first time enhancement. This illusion was due firstly to the fact that there had never before 1997 been an official Charge ceiling, and secondly, that manufacturers had falsely associated first generation 100J Brief Pulse devices with 600mC Charge emissions. Indeed, the 600mC ceiling should have been associated with second generation BP devices emitting between 227 and 260 unreported Joules. Instead, 600mC second generation BP devices were misleadingly depicted as having circa 100J ceilings (corroborated by 100J machine readouts), which via the Mectan Transmutation, were actually 100J Equivalent Ratios. That Weiner's 1997 de facto standard actually "permitted" not only third generation BP device enhancements, but fourth and even fifth generation enhancements became a well-kept manufacturers' secret. Moreover, it was a secret which continued to be maintained by Weiner's emphasis on a much less significant 1200mC Charge ceiling in conjunction with the total expungement of EO reporting, as we have seen. Indeed, due to the false association of a circa 600mC Charge ceiling with what appeared to be first generation BP devices, the doubling of Charge (to 1200mC) as noted, seemed to reflect a first time doubling of the circa 100J ceiling. What was actually being doubled, of course, were not first--but 5-600mC second generation BP devices falsely associated with 100J ceilings. For example, the MECTA second generation SR 1 and 2 made-for Europe and made-for-America BP devices which emitted 576mC and 600mC Charges respectively, actually emitted never before reported Energy Outputs of 227 and 259J respectively. Thanks to Weiner's 1997 de facto standard, however, it was not MECTA's second, but MECTA's third generation BP devices which were being "legalized" under the 1997 Weinerian "standard, devices which indeed emitted between 1152mC and 1200mC of Charge. Third generation BP devices in use since 1995, actually emitted never before reported Energy Output maximums of circa 500J. Similarly, it was not Somatics' second generation DG and DGx BP devices emitting maximum Charges of 504mC with unreported maximums of 252J and 226J maximums respectively which became "legal" under Weiner's 1997 de facto standard—but Somatics' already extant third generation System IV Brief Pulse device which emitted a 1005mC maximum Charge and a never before reported 452J maximum. It was the false association of the 5-600mC second generation BP devices with the circa 110J first generation MECTA "C" BP machine and second generation devices falsely associated with 100J ceilings then, that falsely suggested a first time output doubling under Weiner's 1997 de facto standard, newly permitting a 1200mC Charge. The totally false impression of what were actually second generation BP devices seeming to be first generation BP devices was based on at least four factors: 1) the 110J ceiling reflected in the 1982 APA Standard, 2) the confusing "100J at 220Ω" pure-ER/RRC phrase the Mectan Transmutation used to supplant the 110J ceiling within the 1982 APA Standard, 3) the similarly reported unexplained "100J at 300Ω" pure-

ER/RRC phrase featured in the 1989 IEC standard, and finally 4) circa 100J machine readout maximums on all MECTA and Somatics second generation BP devices as we shall examine in detail at the end of the next section.

Thus, as we have seen, only by very close examination of the original 1982 APA standard, very close examination of the 1982 Mectan Transmutation requiring conversion of what are actually ER outputs, very close examination the 1989 IEC standard, an extension of the Mectan Transmutation, and finally very close examination of Weiner's 1997 default Standard (depicted only in terms of Charge), can we begin to see how what are actually third generation BP devices doubled in output not for the first, but for the second consecutive time. Indeed, unbeknownst to regulators, the "legalization" of third generation BP devices more than quadrupled the power of first generation BP devices. In fact, because manufacturers never reported and, in fact, secreted the doubling in power from first to second generation BP devices, what were actually third generation BP devices were able to mushroom under Weiner's 1997 de facto standard, to almost five fold the power of first generation BP devices without being noticed. Never completely comprehended then, third generation Brief Pulse devices increased almost five fold the power of the first generation 108J MECTA "C" originally represented to the FDA circa 1980 as the archetypal "new and improved "Brief Pulse" mechanism touted to replace the much criticized 200J SW device. Because the original APA ceiling Standard of 110 actual Joules presented to the FDA in 1982 was denoted in Energy Output (or Joules), and the 1997 default standard, upon which third (as well as fourth and fifth) generation BP devices are now depicted only in terms of Charge, meaningful comparisons to first and even elusive second generation BP devices, as well as the B-24 SW, became unachievable. Only by converting to joules can we meaningful compare modern day BP devices to the 108J MECTA "C," or comprehend that third generation BP devices represent a power enhancement up to (480J ÷ 108J =) 4.44 fold the first generation MECTA "C" and (480 ÷ 200J =) 2.4 fold the power of the B-24 SW. Indeed, without this conversion, Weiner's 1997 standard based on Charge reporting alone (in lieu of EO reporting), seems to suggest, as we have so carefully recorded, a first time doubling in power of BP devices and so an increase from about 100 to about 200 maximum Joules, even as the true circa 500J output maximum of third generation BP devices disappears from sight. In fact, until now, the true power of what are actually third generation BP devices has never been reported at all.

But just as deceiving, as we have observed, in spite of probable dramatic EO enhancements from third to fourth and possibly fourth to fifth generation BP devices, maximum Charge outputs for all three Brief Pulse devices remain misleadingly similar. Consequently, under Weiner's 1997 de facto standard, the probable third doubling of power--from third to fourth generation--and even hypothetical fourth enhancement--from fourth to fifth generation BP devices—-completely disappear from sight. Because all three Brief Pulse generations—extant third, probable fourth, and hypothetical fifth generation BP devices emit about 1200mC of Charge, what are actually three sequentially enhancing Brief Pulse generations completely vanish from view. In brief, the power increases from the circa 500J maximum third generation BP devices compared to the circa 1000J and 1200J output potentials of probable fourth, and hypothetical fifth generation BP devices, all "allowable" under Weiner's 1997 de facto standard, become indistinguishable under his proviso. Indeed, due to the transition from EO in Joules to Output in Charge alone, the enhancement from second to third is very difficult to detect. Finally, because of machine readouts depicting 100 maximum joules on what are actually second generation BP devices as we have seen, even the transition from first to second generation BP devices is difficult to perceive. Succinctly then, because Charge remains almost unchanged from extant third to probable fourth to hypothetical fifth generation BP devices, the sequential enhancements in power and consequently, the sequential enhancements in MTTLOI of these newly "allowed" devices under Weiner's de facto "standard," are almost wholly imperceptible while due to false readouts, sequential enhancements from first to second to third generation BP devices are also very well camouflaged.

Put a third way, partially due to false readouts on second generation BP devices and partially due to Weiner's switch to Charge reporting alone and thus the extirpation of EO reporting altogether under the 1997 Weiner "Standard," the dramatically enhanced 1200J potential "permitted" under the 1997 Weiner proviso, the nearly (1200J ÷ 110J = 10.9) eleven fold, 1000% increase from the original 110J ceiling stipulation stipulated in the 1982 APA Standard more than eleven fold the power of the first generation MECTA "C" (1200J ÷ 108J = 11.11) [136] disappears from view. Indeed, the stupendous increase in power from the 110 joules under the 1982 APA Standard characterized by the MECTA "C" presented to the FDA around 1980 as the archetypal

[136] 1200J ÷ 110J = 10.9

"new and improved reduced output" modern day Brief Pulse device to the 1200 joules “allowed” under the 1997 Weiner-generated, manufacturer-approved, international “standard” has never heretofore been revealed. Certainly, modern day Brief Pulse devices allowed under the 1997 Weiner proviso can emit 6.0 times as much raw power [137] as the maximum output emitted by the Medcraft B-24 SW device reported to the FDA in 1982 as twice the power of Brief Pulse. This is telling in that it was by comparison to the alleged 200J B-24 SW device by Medcraft that reportedly circa 100J maximum output BP devices were initially presented to the FDA as having the vitally important safety facility of inducing "adequate" seizures at half the EO of SW. [138] Most critically, however, are the unreported circa five, ten, and twelve MTTLOIs allowed with BL "ECT" in every age category delivered by extant third, probable forth, and potential fifth generation BP devices respectively, more than 4.0, 9.0, and 11.0 fold the output of the original MECTA “C respectively. These extremely high MTTLOIs administered by default to all age categories are alarming in that it was but a second generation Thymatron DGx, titrated to a circa 2.3 fold maximum which was used to administer circa eight BL "ECT" treatments to nine "ECT" recipients in the 2012 Perrin MRI prospective study found by very advanced mathematical data signaling to have prospectively reduced left prefrontal neuronal connectivity from 35% to, in some cases, 100% annihilation (Perrin et al. 2012). Given these facts, is it any wonder modern day Brief Pulse manufacturers seek to hide the awesome power of their modern day Brief Pulse devices?

Speaking "Charge"--More on Weiner's Deceptive Call for "Doubling" the Power of What Appears to be First Generation BP Devices in Collusion with Somatics' Owner, Abrams and MECTA's “Expert,” Sackeim

Although not reported as such, by 1982, the MTTLOI of made-for-America second generation BP devices [139] had already risen to pre-set outputs of about two and one half fold threshold in terms of Charge and EO with bilateral electrode placement, and thus five times threshold in terms of Charge and EO with unilateral electrode placement (Beale et al., 1994). Given this fact, the question arises--if a suprathreshold dosing of 2.5 times threshold with BL ECT and 5.0 fold threshold with UL ECT in every age category was already being universally applied in clinical settings via what were actually second generation BP devices, why the manufacturer call for enhancement? Richard Abrams (founder of Somatics Incorporated) and Harold Sackeim (closely associated with MECTA Corporation), both of whom we have examined, claimed the need for enhancement was due to dose sensitive UL ECT, but this makes little sense, as noted above, in that UL ECT was already being administered at a circa 5.0 MTTLOI with second generation BP devices and so circa 2.5 fold threshold even if it is true that Impedance can double at the end of a treatment series. What does make sense is that neither the public nor regulatory agencies were aware of the second generation enhancement in that manufacturers successfully suppressed this information, specifically with the spurious machine readouts on both MECTA and Somatics second generation BP devices of circa 100 maximum joules (see previous sections). Indeed, statements made by both Abrams and Sackeim above would have us believe that the first doubling in power around 1982, that is, the doubling in power of first generation BP devices to comprise second generation BP devices never took place. As noted previously, but now in more detail, based on excerpts taken from his 1997 IEC revision proposal, we see Weiner himself justifying his call for enhancement to 1200mC Charge in just this same manner with just this same assumption. Weiner states:

---

[137] Typically, third, fourth, and hypothetically fifth generation BP devices emit 2.4, 4.8, and 6.0 fold the maximum power of SW (480J ÷ 200J = 2.4; 960J ÷ 200J = 4.8; 1200J ÷ 200J = 6.0) though in disparate age categories compared to SW.

[138] The B-24 cannot be made to deliver these higher EOs automatically; rather, such dosages depend arbitrarily upon exceptionally low recipient thresholds due, for instance, to an exceptionally thin and/or young skull; moreover; the SW settings must be placed at maximum. In that the newest (third generation) American BP devices are pre-set to emit up to approximately 450-480 Joules, third generation BP devices emit around 2.4 fold the maximum EO of the B-24 SW—more than four times the EO of the 108J MECTA “C” (480J ÷ 108J = 4.44) introduced to the FDA between 1976 and 1982. Probable fourth generation BP devices emit close to 1000J, about 5.0 times the raw EO of SW (1000J ÷ 200J = 5.0) and more than 9.0 times the power of the MECTA “C” (1000J ÷ 108J = 9.26) while possible fifth generation BP devices emit close to six times the power of SW (1200J ÷ 200J = 6) and more than eleven times the power of the MECTA “C” (1200J ÷ 108J = 11.11).

[139] Second generation made-for-America BP devices emitted maximum outputs of between 250 and 260J.

In terms of the upper limit on stimulus output, recent data have indicated that higher levels of stimulus intensity than previously believed are essential to assure treatment adequacy. In this regard, the extent to which the stimulus exceeds seizure threshold, not absolute stimulus intensity [threshold or barely above threshold], appears to be the key factor. Present data suggest that with unilateral non-dominant electrode placement, stimulus intensity must be 2-4 times seizure threshold to be optimum from an efficacy standpoint. While initial seizure thresholds with unilateral ECT are nearly always below 300mC, they often rise as much as 100% or more over the course of treatments, so that a limit of at least 1200mC is clearly necessary. In this regard, multiple ECT devices with maximum outcharge levels of 1000-1500mC have recently been marketed in many countries, and recent clinical guidelines of the Royal College of Psychiatrists in Great Britain have called for an upper limit of at least 1000mC. American Psychiatric Association recommendations presently under development are anticipated to be at least as high. Results of animal investigations have demonstrated that these output levels are safe. Still, the requirements that the rate of charge delivery be no more than 2mC/phase nor 300mC/second provide an additional safety margin.
(International Electrotechnical Commission, 1997, Dec 26, p. 5)

Before we examine in detail Weiner's above claims in sequential order, it might be beneficial to once again identify the particular Charge ceiling Weiner is calling for under his 1997 IEC proposal for what are actually, already extant at this time, never reported third generation BP devices. Weiner states above:

[A] limit of at least <u>1200mC</u> is clearly necessary. [Ibid]

Here it is again useful to understand that the earliest 108J MECTA "C" presented to the FDA between 1976 and 1982 had a Charge ceiling of approximately 336mC and this only in the oldest age category, while the MECTA "D" may have emitted even less maximum Charge at about 270mC, figures which, because of the emphasis on Joules during the first generation Brief Pulse period of the new BP era have all but been forgotten. MECTA and Somatics second generation BP devices manufactured immediately following the 1976-1982 FDA investigation--machines made between 1982-1995, emitted maximum ceiling charges, as we have noted, of 576 and 504mC [140] respectively (Cameron, 1994),[141] and it was these (second generation) devices which were simultaneously reported in terms of "100J at 220Ω" and "100J at 300Ω," phrases. Such phrases, as we have learned were actually pure-ER/RRCs as opposed to conditional ER/RRCs.[142] As we have seen, maximum outputs of these devices were newly based upon maximum Impedances (in lieu of a stipulated EO ceiling), that is, equivalent ratio phrases based upon the American Standard's 600Ω maximum Impedance and the European Standard's 500Ω maximum Impedance. In both cases, moreover, and as already noted above, machine readouts depicted circa 100J ceilings for these same second generation BP devices. Consequently, a circa 100J ceiling became falsely equated with 500-600mC Charge maximums. [143] Conversely, 500-600m ceilings became falsely associated with first generation BP devices such as the MECTA "C." Weiner's 1997 de facto

[140] To underpin how Weiner's emphasis on Charge alone is inadequate, Medcraft's BP device, the B-25, could emit up to 840mC without surpassing 100 Joules.

[141] While both Charge and EO doubled from first to second generation BP devices and doubled again from second to third generation BP devices, the emphasis in reporting the MECTA "C" had been in EO or Joules and even second generation BP devices, following the Mectan Transmutation, though reported in the form of unexplicated ER/RRC also emphasized Joules. By transitioning completely away from Joules, and reporting only in Charge, comparison of previous BP devices and SW devices to what were actually third generation BP devices became obfuscated at best. Too, because second generation BP devices were reported as circa 100J devices, second generation BP devices, in essence, were never reported at all.

[142] Based on letters from regulators to manufacturers, regulators appeared to take the "100J at 220Ω" phrase as incorporating a 100J ceiling. While the "100 Joule" phrases do lend themselves to the possibility of ER, the emphasis on 100 Joules in both instances yet engendered confusion. Even when taken as ER phrases, the distinct impression remained that the original 1982 APA standard depicted the same "100J" ER phrase, which it did not. In fact, while the original APA standard depicted a "70J at 220Ω" ER/RRC, it also denoted a clear 110J ceiling or conditional ER/RRC. Second generation BP devices, recall, all contained circa 100J maximum machine readouts.

[143] MECTA's second generation BP devices specifically depicted 100J readout maximums.

Standard, doubling Charge to a ceiling of 1200mC, as noted, thus appears to but double the 100J output associated with what appeared to be first generation BP devices. As previously observed, however, the 5-600mC MECTA and Somatics second generation BP devices were actually emitting unreported outputs of up to 260J.

Weiner's 1997 IEC proposal, as we now know, was actually an attempt to make not second, but third generation BP devices "legal," devices which by 1997, were already reaching approximately 1200mC maximum Charge and which emitted not 200 plus Joules of EO, but up to (an unreported) 480 Joules of EO, doubling the unreported output (in Joules) not of first, but, as we have seen, of second generation BP devices (manufactured between 1982 and 1995). In brief, the reporting of Charge output alone under the 1997 Weiner proviso, without the accompanying EO (in Joules) which seems to facilitate a transition from a circa 100J, 5-600mC device to a circa 200J, 1200mC device, just as Abrams and Sackeim's statements suggest, falsely indicates a first time doubling in power of the archetypal MECTA "C," a false impression which, in corroboration with Abrams and Sackeim, appears to have been calculated.

Speaking "Charge" Continued--More on Weiner's Deceptive Call for "Doubling" the Power of What Appear to be First Generation BP Devices--Continued

Now let us carefully examine Weiner's whole passage sequentially. The first part of Weiner's 1997 justification for what appears to be "a first time" doubling of power asserts:

> In terms of the upper limit on stimulus output, recent data have indicated that higher levels of stimulus intensity than previously believed are essential to assure treatment adequacy. In this regard, the extent to which the stimulus exceeds seizure threshold, not absolute stimulus intensity, appears to be the key factor.
>
> (International Electrotechnical Commission, 1997, Dec 26, p. 5)

Here again, Weiner, as does Sackeim, makes what appears to be a clear concession that adequate seizure alone--that is--seizures induced at just above seizure threshold, though adequate in terms of full blown grand mal seizures of at least twenty-five seconds in length--are inadequate in terms of efficacy. Weiner appears to be acknowledging that the so-called "adequate seizure" is, in itself, insufficient--even with BL "ECT." Rather, what is actually necessary to make the procedure "work" is adequate "doses" of electricity. Here, then, electricity seems to be acknowledged not as a mere catalyst, but as an essential part of the treatment itself. In short, Weiner seems to be acknowledging that electrical output well over that required to induce a so-called "adequate seizure" is necessary to make the procedure "effective." The statement, in fact, appears to be an unclouded concession for the need of universal suprathreshold electrical dosing--not in order to compensate for rising threshold over the course of a procedure or to compensate for "dose-sensitive UL "ECT,"--but for efficacy purposes alone. Indeed, Weiner's initial statement does not differentiate between bilateral and unilateral electrode placement. This is a critical admission in that convulsion theory itself is decidedly undermined by the acknowledgement that both BL and UL "ECT" require not merely enough electricity to induce the adequate seizure, but suprathreshold dosages of electricity well above threshold for both BL and UL "ECT" to be effective (Cameron, 1994). It is in direct accordance with this concession, as we have now seen, that power and, consequently, MTTLOI for each individual recipient dramatically rises with each succeeding Brief Pulse generation for every age category and with both BL and UL "ECT." Clearly, the necessity of suprathreshold dosing in order to achieve efficacy for both forms of "ECT" casts misgivings on seizure theory generally; indeed, the necessity of suprathreshold electrical outputs for both forms of "ECT suggests that convulsion theory itself is unsound. In sum, if adequate seizures alone have little or no "therapeutic benefit" with either form of "ECT," but rather the procedure requires a specific MTTLOI with both forms in order to work, that is, if outputs multiple times the electrical dosage required to induce adequate seizures are required, then it must be the electricity either in part or in whole, certainly not the seizure alone and perhaps not the seizure at all that is responsible for the procedure's "efficacy." This is crucial in that the direct relationship between increasing electrical output and memory dysfunction is well known; in short, the higher the electrical dosage, the higher the MTTLOI, the greater the long term memory dysfunction, or more to the point, the greater the risk of brain injury, or even, the greater the actual injury.

The second part of Weiner's rationale for what appears to be "a first time" enhancement asserts:

> Present data suggest that with unilateral nondominant electrode placement, stimulus intensity must be 2-4 times seizure threshold to be optimum from an efficacy standpoint. (International Electrotechnical Commission, 1997, Dec 26, p. 5)

In referring to UL "ECT" specifically, Weiner, as does Sackeim, suddenly clouds what seems at first to be a clear concession that efficacy is directly associated with electricity with all forms of ECT (that is, with both BL and UL "ECT"). Here again, however, Weiner calls upon manufacturers' familiar reserve rationale for justifying any increase in power and titration--so-called "dose-sensitive UL 'ECT'"—suddenly obscuring his previous assertion that "the extent to which the stimulus exceeds seizure threshold, not absolute stimulus intensity, appears to be the key factor" for what initially seems to apply to both UL and BL "ECT." Suddenly, the idea that electricity is an essential part of the treatment itself, seems once again, to pertain to UL "ECT" only. The concept that both UL and BL electrode placement require multifold threshold electrical dosing in order to be effective is thus abruptly mitigated by the all too familiar claim that unlike BL "ECT," which we are now to assume effective at threshold, it is but "dose-sensitive" UL "ECT" alone which requires multifold threshold dosing. In short, Weiner's new 1997 call for power enhancement, and the association of electricity with efficacy that he makes above only applies to UL "ECT" after all, that is, suprathreshold dosing is only required of "dose-sensitive" UL "ECT" alone (Beale et al., 1994; Sackeim et al.,1987b; Swartz, and Abrams,1996, pp. 15, 48). So which is it? Does electricity play a part in efficacy for both forms of "ECT" then, or is Weiner now completely denying the role of electricity for the most common form of "ECT"--"BL 'ECT.'" Perhaps we can unravel this doublespeak by continuing to examine Weiner's assertion. Weiner next claims:

> [. . .] seizure thresholds with UL ECT [. . .] often rise as much as 100% or more over the course of treatments [. . .]. (International Electrotechnical Commission, 1997, Dec 26, p. 5)

If we assume that Weiner's 1997 default standard from which these assertions are excerpted, addresses the 100% rise in UL ECT thresholds over the treatment course and that for "unilateral non-dominant electrode placement, stimulus intensity must be 2-4 times seizure threshold to be optimum from an efficacy standpoint," we can logically assume that the 1997 standard permits an increase of about 4.0 fold threshold at the beginning of a series of UL "ECT" in order to emit a 2.0 fold threshold output at the end of treatment course to insure UL efficacy. In short, Weiner's new maximum output ceiling of 1200mC of Charge, should logically incorporate enough Charge to be able to pre-set newer more enhanced devices with an initial delivery of a 4.0 fold threshold output with UL "ECT" for even the oldest, most seizure recalcitrant individual, the 100 year old male, whose Multifold Threshold Titration Level Output Intensity (MTTLOI) might then diminish to a 2.0 fold threshold output by the end of a course of "treatment" due to the rise in threshold with "UL 'ECT.'" Weiner's complete statement within the proposed revision tells us:

> While initial seizure thresholds with UL ECT are nearly always below 300mC, they often rise as much as 100% or more over the course of treatments, so that a limit of at least 1200mC is clearly necessary. (International Electrotechnical Commission, 1997, Dec 26, p. 5)

If we accept Weiner's above passage at face value--that UL maximally requires 300mC for an initial (just above) threshold dosage in order to induce an adequate seizure (for the 100 year old male) and that UL ECT requires twice threshold output to be effective (2 x 300mC = <u>600mC</u>) and finally that machines require enough power to accommodate a maximum 100% percent rise in threshold for UL "ECT" over a "treatment course" in order to remain at twice threshold even at the end of the course (2 x 600mC = <u>1200mC</u>)--we can see how Weiner arrives at the alleged 1200mC Charge "necessary" for uniquely "dose sensitive UL 'ECT.'" According to Weiner's logic then, 1200mC of Charge is required for UL "ECT" to remain effective for the oldest recipient, that is, in order to deliver at least a twofold threshold dosage even at the end of a "treatment" course for a 100 year old male (whose Impedance is the highest of all recipients).

Notice, we are now working with Charge only, specific threshold outputs of which are much less familiar. Any discussion of EO in joules has been completely eliminated. Weiner's depiction of UL ECT alone as "dose-sensitive" and that threshold with UL ECT rises "as much as 100% or more over the 'course of treatment'" leaves informees to assume that BL ECT (in 1997) is yet delivered at threshold, even as Weiner implicitly, and later specifically, suggests that threshold output with BL "ECT" also rises 100%. Since UL "ECT" allegedly requires twice the output of BL "ECT" to be effective, but requires only half the electrical output of BL ECT to elicit an adequate seizure, the pre-set machine dosage with UL "ECT" need not differ (nor does it differ) from the pre-set or default electrical "dosage" with BL "ECT" on any modern Brief Pulse device. This means that the same 1200mC "needed" for an initial pre-set 4.0 fold threshold output for the 100 year old male administered UL ECT, resulting in at least a 2.0 fold threshold output even at the end of the treatment course (due to the 100% rise in threshold), should elicit an initial pre-set 2.0 fold threshold output for the same 100 year old male administered BL "ECT" at the beginning of a "course of treatments" and so, (if we assume the same 100% rise in threshold), a just above threshold output with BL ECT even at end of the end of a "treatment" course. In sum, Weiner's own statements attempting to justify his 1997 "standard," infer that as a result of his de facto "standard" allowing up to 1200mC in lieu of the previous 5-600mC, newly enhanced machines under the new standard would newly incorporate a first time Brief Pulse doubling of output with both UL and BL "ECT." In short, according to Weiner, 1200mC is necessary to emit an initial 4.0 and initial 2.0 MTTLOI for UL and BL "ECT" respectively at the beginning of a "treatment" and so a 2.0 MTTLOI and just above threshold output for UL and BL "ECT" respectively even at the end of a "treatment" course. In sum, compared to previous BP devices, the newer machines under the new 1997 Weiner de facto standard would now transition from an initial 2.0 MTTLOI with UL ECT at the beginning of the treatment course to an initial 4.0 MTTLOI with UL ECT at the beginning of the treatment course. In turn, compared to previous BP devices, (due to the 100% rise in threshold) the new machines would transition from a just above threshold titration level output intensity with UL ECT at the end of the treatment course to a 2.0 MTTLOI with UL ECT at the end of the treatment course. For "non-dose sensitive" BL "ECT," the newer machines would transition from an initial just above threshold titration output intensity at the beginning of the treatment course to an initial 2.0 MTTLOI at the beginning of the treatment course, and so from a just below threshold titration level output intensity at the beginning of a treatment course to a just above threshold titration level output intensity at the end of the treatment course. Due to the 100% rise in threshold concern expressed by Weiner then, the new 1200mC ceiling is the newly calculated maximum Charge needed to facilitate changes requiring a new first time "doubling" in output for both UL and BL "ECT" in order for both forms to be effective.

Moreover, Weiner's assertions might have made sense if the first generation 108J MECTA "C" presented to the FDA between 1980-1982, had still been the ECT device used up to 1997 or if the original MECTA "C" had delivered 5-600mC of Charge as Weiner and other manufacturers conspiratorially implied. By 1982, however, some fifteen years before Weiner's 1997 proposal, both MECTA and Somatics, as noted, had already secretly transitioned to second generation BP devices via the "Mectan Transmutation." In fact, second generation MECTA and Somatics BP devices had been emitting initial outputs of about 2.5 fold threshold with BL ECT and 5.0 fold threshold outputs with UL ECT since about 1982 (Beale et al. 1994; Cameron 1994). If threshold indeed rises by a factor of 2.0 over a treatment course and BL "ECT" must remain at least just above threshold at the end of the treatment course to be effective, and if "dose sensitive UL "ECT" must be at least 2.0 fold threshold at the end of the treatment course to be effective, then this "dilemma," as we have discussed, had long ago been addressed and corrected by the manufacturing and marketing of the second generation MECTA and Somatics BP devices introduced many years before 1997, indeed, around 1982. To be sure, an initial 2.5 times threshold with BL "ECT" and an initial 5 times threshold with UL "ECT" means that even if threshold output, that is, Impedance increases by a factor of two by the end a "treatment" series, BL ECT would still be administered at about 1.25 fold threshold, and UL ECT at about 2.5 fold threshold even by the end of a treatment series, more than adequate with "non-dose sensitive" BL ECT (allegedly effective a just above threshold) and more than effective with so-called "dose-sensitive" UL ECT (allegedly effective at two fold threshold). Unfortunately, since manufacturers and their academic affiliates (i.e. Weiner, Abrams, Sackeim, etc.) must have been aware of the covert 1982 Mectan Transmutation ushering in their own second generation BP devices, we have no other choice but to conclude that Weiner and his colleagues conspired to deceive both the public and regulatory agencies in falsely suggesting Weiner's "new" 1997 proviso, a first time doubling of output within the modern Brief Pulse era. We should remember, moreover, that all second generation MECTA and Somatics BP devices contained spurious 100J ceiling readouts, suggestive of first generation BP devices, covering up that what were actually second generation BP devices were, in fact, emitting up to circa 259J—not 100J.

Recollect that in his 1997 explanation of his new 1997 standard, Weiner claimed that ". . . . *initial seizure thresholds with UL ECT are nearly always below 300mC.*" In fact, as noted earlier, with respect to second and even third generation BP machines, both extant at the time of Weiner's 1997 proposal, initial seizure thresholds with UL ECT never required more than 115mC, an assertion proved by Beale in 1994, at which point which Beale identifies initial minimum Charge thresholds with respect to what are actually second generation devices at around 222mC with BL "ECT." By implication, therefore, initial minimum Charge thresholds with UL ECT (which require only half the output of BL "ECT") occur at about 111mC (Beale et al. 1994). As seen above, moreover, threshold outputs for third, fourth, and even fifth generation BP devices generate even lower Charge thresholds.

Weiner should have stated, therefore, that:

> ". . . initial seizure thresholds (in terms of Charge) with **BL ECT**--not UL ECT--are nearly always below "300mC" or that ". . . initial thresholds with **UL ECT** are nearly always below **150mC.**" [144]

In this light, ***1200mC*** is not only enough to double the MTTLOI with BL ECT from just above threshold to 2.0 fold threshold initially and double MTTLOI with UL ECT from 2.0 fold threshold to 4.0 fold threshold initially as Weiner purports,[145] but enough to ***quadruple*** the initial MTTLOI with BL ECT (1200 ÷ 300 = ***4.0***) and thus ***octuple*** the initial MTTLOI with UL ECT (1200 ÷ 150 = ***8.0***) for all age recipients. Indeed, Weiner's new standard is designed to do just that--to “legalize” unreported already augmented third generation MECTA and Somatics BP devices emitting initial MTTLOIs with BL ECT of 4.52 and 4.8 respectively and initial MTTLOIs with UL ECT of 9.04 and 9.6 respectively in all age categories. In brief, Weiner's implication that his 1997 standard allows a first time enhancement, facilitating the doubling of first generation BP devices limited to threshold (with BL ECT) at about 100 maximum joules and twice threshold (with UL ECT) at the same circa 100 maximum joules is disingenuous. Moreover, as previously observed, it is Weiner's, Abrams', and Sackeim's false 5-600mC Charge association with first generation BP devices (ignoring the manufacturing of second generation devices) along with spurious circa 100J machine readouts on all American second generation BP devices which creates this illusion. The maximum 5-600mC Charge, as we have seen, actually pertains to unreported second generation BP devices. Manufacturers' failure to clearly report the first doubling of output and doubling of MTTLOI in 1982 and the misleading 100J readout maximums (on second generation BP devices) unmistakably suppress the existence not only of second generation BP devices but the circa 1995 production of what are actually third generation BP devices. In short, the failure to report what are actually second generation BP devices circa 1982, camouflages the fact that Weiner's 1997 proposition enables not the first, but the second major doubling in power plainly inherent in what are actually third generation Brief Pulse machines, machines which had been illegally manufactured and marketed throughout the world at least two years before the 1989 IEC Standard for ECT was rescinded in 1997 and so at least two years before Weiner's 1997 de facto standard was even presented to the IEC.

More Specifically

The notion that the new 1997 default standard calls for a first time doubling of output, that is, a doubling in power not of second, but of first generation BP devices, is inherent in the false association of circa 100 maximum Joules with 5-600mC of Charge and thus the false sequitur of alleged second generation BP devices (for what were actually third generation devices) "newly" emitting about 200J (in lieu of circa 450J) to then become associated with Weiner's 1997 proposal of 1200mC of Charge. The false association of 5-600mC of Charge with first generation BP devices was fully encouraged, as we have seen, by spurious 100J machine

---

[144] The MECTA “C” emitted a 1.08 MTTLOI at a maximum circa 338mC of Charge with BL ECT, emitting the highest initial threshold of about 313mC. Maximum initial threshold for UL ECT was thus about 157mC (338mC ÷ 1.08 = 313mC ÷ 2 = 157mC). Second and third generation BP devices generate even lower initial maximum thresholds with BL and UL ECT of about 222mC and 111mC respectively. Fourth and fifth generation machines facilitate even lower maximum thresholds.

[145] This had already occurred with second generation devices with less than 600mC maximum Charge.

readout maximums on both MECTA and Somatics second generation BP devices. Indeed, Weiner's suggestion that his 1997 de facto standard was a first time doubling in power was further corroborated by Weiner's implication that his 1200mC proposal would newly allow machines to administer "dose-sensitive" UL "ECT" at an initial 4.0 and thus the "necessary" 2.0 MTTLOI with UL "ECT" at the end of a treatment course. This assertion clearly implies that previous BP devices administered so-called "dose-sensitive" UL ECT at an initial 2.0 MTTLOI, leaving UL ECT at the end of a treatment course "ineffective" at just above threshold output. The same assertion suggests that outputs of alleged "non-dose sensitive" BL ECT were previously administered at just above threshold outputs so that based on Weiner's purported "100% rise in threshold" contention, they would fail to reach threshold at the end of a "treatment" course. Weiner is plainly proposing that his 1997 proviso would allow the doubling of output "for the first time" with newer more powerful "second" generation BP devices so that "non-dose-sensitive" BL ECT could "newly" be administered at 2.0 fold threshold initially and thus just above threshold at the end of a treatment course and that "dose-sensitive" UL ECT could newly be administered at 4.0 fold threshold initially and thus twice threshold at the end of a treatment course (to be effective). In spite of hazy insinuations that both BL and UL "ECT" might be "dose sensitive" then, Weiner could not actually admit that both forms of "ECT" are electro-dependent for fear of challenges to convulsion theory, generally. Moreover, Weiner was fully aware of the numerous studies showing excessive doses of electricity associated with long term memory loss as a result of what was almost certainly brain damage. It is for these reasons that neither Weiner nor the manufacturers could admit to a second doubling in power. In short, manufacturers could not acknowledge that both BL and UL "ECT" depend on adequate amounts of electricity--not adequate convulsion--to be effective. To do so would be to admit that the newest Brief Pulse devices were no longer ECT devices at all, but rather ENR devices, devices deliberately designed to damage the brain via "adequate electrical doses well above that required to induce seizure with either BL or UL electrode placement. Albeit reluctantly then, Weiner continued to suggest BL "ECT" clinically effective at minimal stimulus so that so-called "dose-sensitive" UL "ECT" remained anomalous, that is, that only UL "ECT" is electro-dependent, and that only UL "ECT requires twice threshold output to be effective.

Ultimately, Weiner can only claim that doubling threshold output with BL "ECT" is necessary due to the purported 100% rise in threshold over a treatment course so that "non-dose-sensitive" BL "ECT" is yet able to induce adequate seizures at just above threshold at the end of a "treatment" course. If Weiner were to admit that the doubling in power of second generation BP devices had already used up this rationale, and that Weiner's 1997 proviso was actually necessary to "legalize" already extant third generation BP devices doubling the power of second generation BP devices, Weiner's manufacturers would have been forced to admit that not just one, but, in fact, both forms of "ECT" were electro-dependent, that electro-dependent UL was not an anomaly after all, that it is adequate doses of electricity with both forms of "ECT"--not seizure--that makes the procedure "work." In brief, Weiner and the manufacturers would have been forced to face the critical logic that if efficacy actually depends upon adequate electricity generally and not seizure, efficacy might very well be synonymous with brain damage.

Also used up with second generation BP devices was the rationale that due to the purported 100% rise in threshold over a treatment course, a quadrupling of initial threshold output was necessary for so-called "dose-sensitive" UL "ECT" in order to maintain a 2.0 fold threshold output even at the end of a treatment course. In brief, second generation BP devices had already accomplished this task.

Thus, Weiner's 1997 standard had to appear to facilitate a first time doubling In output of what appeared to be first generation BP devices. That is, Weiner's 1997 proposal had to appear to be a first time doubling of first generation circa 100J BP devices to create "new" second generation BP devices, emitting twice the output of first generation ones, second generation devices newly taking into account the alleged 100% rise in threshold for both "non-dose sensitive" BL "ECT" and "dose-sensitive" UL "ECT." As such, BL "ECT" would supposedly taper off to just above threshold output at the end of a treatment course while UL "ECT" would taper off to the "necessary" 2.0 fold threshold output at the end of a treatment course to assure the "treatment's" efficacy. Such reasoning, of course, totally ignored the existence of the second generation BP devices produced circa 1982.

Fishy Weinerian Logic

According to Weinerian logic above then, the maximum output with BL ECT (for the 100 year old male) previous to his 1997 de facto standard had been just above threshold initially, or a little over 100 maximum Joules. Thus,

Weiner would have us believe that the "new" call for doubling output with BL ECT was not due to the need for more electricity to make the procedure work, but only due to the 100% rise in threshold over a treatment course in which case the increase in electricity was solely needed to induce adequate seizures with BL "ECT" and so that UL "ECT" would remain at a dose-sensitive 2.0 fold threshold even at the end of a "treatment" course. In brief, only "dose-sensitive" UL ECT required excess electricity to make the procedure "work."

By this same logic, as already noted, BP devices just prior to the new 1200mC BP devices Weiner was newly proposing, must have administered BL ECT at just above threshold initially and "dose-sensitive" UL ECT at 2.0 fold threshold initially, similar to the first generation MECTA "C." Previous BP devices, according to Weiner's logic, therefore, must have utilized a circa 100J maximum, i.e. the 108J MECTA "C." Given this and given the premise of a 100% rise in threshold for both "dose-sensitive UL ECT" and "non-dose-sensitive BL ECT" over a "treatment" course, Weiner's 1997 increased output demand for a first time doubling of BP devices appears perfectly justified. "Non-dose-sensitive" BL ECT after all, must be administered just at above threshold even at the end of a treatment course (in order to induce seizure), whereas "dose sensitive" UL ECT must be administered at a 2.0 fold threshold output to be effective even at the end of a "treatment" course initially requiring a 4.0 fold threshold output.

We can now conclude that Weiner's 1997 statement: "recent data have indicated that higher levels of stimulus intensity than previously believed are essential to assure treatment adequacy" refers only to "dose-sensitive UL ECT" so that Weiner is yet indicating "non-dose sensitive BL ECT" remains effective at just above threshold output. Weiner's statement "Present data suggest that with unilateral non-dominant electrode placement, stimulus intensity must be 2-4 times seizure threshold to be optimum from an efficacy standpoint" supposedly justifying the need for the 1997 Weiner proviso, must mean that the newer more powerful machines possible under the 1997 Weiner proviso would administer a 4.0 MTTLOI with UL ECT and thus a 2.0 MTTLOI with UL "ECT," as noted, at the end of a treatment course.[146] Tangentially, as also noted above, newer, more powerful machines newly possible under the same Weiner proviso meant machines would be able to administer a 2.0 MTTLOI with BL "ECT" and thus a just above threshold output with BL "ECT" at the end of a treatment course.

As we have already suspected, however, something smells fishy regarding the Weinerian logic calling for 1200mC of Charge to accomplish these alleged aims. Certainly, the continued implication that BL ECT is effective at just above threshold smells fishy. Indeed, there is a definite fish odor with respect to Weiner's intimation that his proviso represents a first time doubling of Brief Pulse power. Where, after all, did the doubling of output go that occurred around 1982 with what were actually second generation BP devices, some fifteen years prior to Weiner's 1997 call?

Indeed, as we have examined, second generation made-for-America MECTA and Somatics BP devices had been emitting initial circa 5.0 fold threshold outputs with UL ECT, and initial circa 2.5 fold threshold outputs with BL ECT since about 1982. Moreover, as we have seen, these machines did so with maximum Charges of 5-600mC, all patently confirmed by Beale's 1994 study as well as numerous mathematical proofs provided earlier in this manuscript (Beale et al., 1994; see also second generation MECTA and Somatics BP devices in Volume I). Indeed, unlike Weiner's implication, the 1200mC Charge ceiling of Weiner's new 1997 de facto standard, was never designed to legalize already extant second generation BP devices already delivering initial unreported outputs of 5.0 and 2.5 MTTLOIs with UL and BL ECT respectively at maximum Charges of 5-600mC. Rather, Weiner's 1997 proviso, as we have seen, was designed to allow unreported already extant third generation BP devices delivering initial outputs not of at least a 4.0 and 2.0 MTTLOI with UL and BL ECT respectively, but of a circa 10.0 and 5.0 MTTLOI with UL and BL ECT respectively at an already utilized maximum Charge (since 1995) of circa 1200mC. In short, Charge and EO had already circa doubled from about 336mC to circa 5-600mC and from about 100J to about 250 joules via never accurately reported second generation BP devices circa 1982 as we have seen. This means that MTTLOI had already more than doubled from just above threshold to 2.5 MTTLOI with BL "ECT" and from a 2.0 to circa 5.0 MTTLOI with UL "ECT" with the unreported 1982 Mectan Transmutation and the accompanying transition of first generation Brief Pulse devices to what were actually second generation BP devices. Bluntly then, because Weiner, Abrams, Sackeim

[146] If Weiner is proposing 4.0 fold threshold output for UL ECT even at the end of a treatment course, he can "justify" an 8.0 fold threshold output with UL "ECT" at the beginning of a treatment course. However, since default outputs emitted for both UL and BL "ECT" are always the same, BL "ECT" would now have to be administered at 4.0 times threshold which compromises BL's "non-dose-sensitive" status and so an admission that both forms are, in fact, electro-dependent.

and other manufacturer affiliates had participated in the first major power enhancement via the unreported Mectan Transmutation around 1982, they now had to suppress the fact that the Weiner proviso enabled not a first, but a second major enhancement, that is, a second doubling of power and MTTLOI for all age categories. In brief, Weiner's 1997 de facto standard was necessary to permit not unreported second, but unreported third generation BP devices which by 1997, as noted, had already been manufactured, marketed, and utilized in the field since at least 1995 and perhaps earlier. All too clearly then, the 1997 Weiner standard and the numerous attempts to misrepresent its true purpose--legalization of third (fourth and fifth) generation BP devices--is a covert concession to the necessity--not of adequate seizures--but of adequate amounts of electricity in order to make both BL and UL ECT effective. It is a concession that the industry as a whole needed to quell.

To be clear then, second generation BP devices containing the first major enhancement, that is, the doubling in power of first generation BP devices totally expending the industry's "doubling of Impedance" and "dose-sensitive" arguments, continued to remain hidden from view under Weiner's 1997 switch to Charge. In turn, what were actually third generation BP devices, doubling the power of second generation BP devices remained hidden from sight in that what appeared to be a first time doubling of Charge as well as the use of Charge itself in lieu of EO suppressed the "standard's" true significance. Finally, potential fourth and fifth generation BP devices are hidden from view in that Charge outputs, as we have seen, do not appreciably increase from third to fifth generation BP devices while EO increases (in joules) are entirely expunged under the Weiner de facto standard. In a word, the quadrupling of power from first to third generation BP devices, the circa ten-fold increase in power from first to probable fourth generation BP devices and the circa 12 fold increase from first to potential fifth generation BP devices all remain hidden from view under the 1997 Weiner de facto standard.

Plainly, manufacturers deliberately hid these enhancements, in that exposed, Weiner's 1997 de facto standard becomes an overt concession of the necessity of gross electrical outputs for the single purpose of making the procedure effective--not via adequate seizures--but via electrical destruction of neuronal connections within the left prefrontal lobe itself and to and from the left prefrontal lobe and the remaining parts of the brain (Perrin et al., 2012).

SECTION XI: Conformity to Weiner's 1997 de facto Standard

CHAPTER 63

MECTA Second to Third Generation BP Devices: UL vs. BL Outputs

Weiner's 1997 standard doubles the Charge maximum (of what are purportedly "first" generation BP devices) from 5-600mC to 1200mC, allegedly so that UL "ECT" can "newly" be administered at an initial 4.0 fold threshold output (in lieu of an initial 2.0 fold threshold) to accommodate the 2.0 fold threshold output allegedly necessary for efficacy (with UL "ECT") even at the end of a treatment course. Weiner's 1997 standard also doubles the Charge maximum (of what are purportedly "first" generation BP devices) from 5-600mC to 1200mC, allegedly so that BL "ECT" can "newly" be administered at an initial 2.0 fold threshold output (in lieu of an initial 1.0 fold threshold) to accommodate the just above threshold requirement for BL "ECT" administered even at the end of a treatment course. But Weiner's rationale flies directly in the face of the details recounted in Beale's 1994 publication revealing that American BP devices manufactured between 1982 and 1994 [147]--what are actually second generation BP devices--were already emitting pre-set initial doses of 5.0 times threshold with UL ECT (in terms of both charge and EO) and initial doses of 2.5 times threshold (in terms of both Charge and EO) with BL ECT (Beale et al., 1994). In short, acknowledgement of the first major output and MTTLOI enhancement, that is, the first doubling of output which occurred about 1982 for all forms of ECT, is suppressed not only by way of the Mectan Transmutation, the 1989 IEC Standard, and spurious machine readouts, but by way of Weiner's 1997 standard, intentionally designed to cover up the existence of what were actually third generation Brief Pulse machines already marketed at the time of Weiner's 1997 proposal. In their demand for an increase in power, therefore, Weiner and other manufacturer affiliates (i.e. Abrams and Sackeim) conspired to create the Illusion that the 1997 Weiner proviso was the first major Brief Pulse power enhancement since about 1978, deliberately ignoring the initial doubling in power and MTTLOI of second generation BP devices which had occurred circa 1982. In short, Weiner's 1997 statements (in conjunction with Sackeim's and Abrams') together with Weiner's 1997 de facto standard insinuating that UL-"ECT" had up 'til 1997 been clinically administered at an initial 2.0 fold threshold output and so just above threshold at the end of a "treatment series" and that BL-"ECT" had been clinically administered at an initial just above threshold output and so below threshold at the end of a "treatment series," not only omitted, but entirely concealed the first major Brief Pulse enhancement which had taken place some years earlier. Briefly, Weiner's 1997 figures ingenuously call for a "first time" enhancement to accommodate so-called "dose-sensitivity" with UL "ECT" and "doubling of Impedance over a 'treatment course'" with both BL and UL "ECT" already accommodated by clandestine second generation BP devices in use for almost fifteen years at the time of Weiner's 1997 proposal.

---

[147] Beale's published his study in 1994 based upon two years research utilizing MECTA and Somatics devices. Third generation BP devices had not begun to be manufactured until 1994, the year the study published (Beale et al., 1994; Royal College of Psychiatry, 1995).

The truth is, manufacturers were desperate to pass an entirely new standard "legalizing" already extant third generation BP devices altogether illegal under the 1982 APA Standard, illegal even under the Mectan Transmutation, and illegal even under the 1989 IEC European Standard no matter how liberally manufacturers interpreted them. Plainly, Weiner's 1997 proviso standard was meant to legitimize not a first, but a second major Brief Pulse enhancement to accommodate not second, but already existent third generation Brief Pulse devices which had already been manufactured and utilized in the field since at least 1995.

Beginning about 1982, made-for-America second generation BP devices with their never fully reported circa 250 Joule/5-600mC plus ceilings, had come onto the marketplace more than doubling (EO-wise) the circa 108 Joule/336mC maximum output of the archetypal first generation MECTA "C." Indeed, the first generation MECTA "C" presented to the FDA circa 1978, emitted a minimal stimulus output of 108 maximum joules, or a 1.08 MTTLOI, and so just above threshold outputs with BL ECT and thus a pre-set (2 x 1.08 =) 2.16 MTTLOI with so-called "dose-sensitive" UL "ECT" in every age category. Beginning about 1982 then, as noted above, second generation made-for-America, Brief Pulse devices newly incorporating pre-set initial dosages at least 2.5 fold threshold with BL ECT in terms of energy output and pre-set initial dosages of at least 5.0 fold threshold with UL ECT also in terms of energy output (see Beale et al., 1994) were introduced into the marketplace by both MECTA and then Somatics.[148] In doubling energy output, as we have seen, second generation Brief Pulse devices accommodated the so-called "newly discovered need" for a 2.0 MTTLOI with "dose-sensitive" UL ECT even at the end of a "treatment" course as well as the need for an above threshold output with BL ECT (due to the alleged doubling of threshold) at the end of a "treatment" course. Having already accommodated these so-called requirements in 1982, therefore, there should have been no need for a another newer 1997 standard enhancing Charge from 600mC to 1200mC to again accommodate the very same "requirement." In a nutshell, Weiner's 1997 call for an initial 2.0 MTTLOI with BL ECT and an initial 4.0 MTTLOI with UL ECT had already been met by made-for-America second generation BP devices already delivering an initial 2.5 MTTLOI with BL ECT and an initial 5.0 MTTLOI with UL ECT (Beale et al., 1994) since at least 1982 and thus at least a 1.25 MTTLOI with BL ECT and a circa 2.5 MTTLOI with UL ECT even at the end of a "treatment course." (Made for Europe second generation BP devices also met these "requirements.") Plainly, second generation made-for-America and second generation IEC BP devices had already fulfilled Weiner's 1997 doubling demand and, in fact, did so with no more than 500mC maximum Charge--not the 1200mC proposed by Weiner.

Undoubtedly, Weiner's explanation of his 1997 standard calling for a "first time" major energy increase of up to 1200mC Charge in order to administer up to 4 times threshold initially with UL "ECT" and up to 2 times threshold initially with BL "ECT" in keeping with similar assertions made by both Abrams (Somatics) and Sackeim (MECTA) above are not only deceitful, but conspiratorial. The plain truth is, by 1995, manufacturers clearly understood that so-called "ECT" machines worked not by adequate seizure, but by adequate "doses" of electricity alone.

Let us once more scrutinize Weiner's claim that:

> While initial seizure thresholds with UL ECT are nearly always below 300mC, they often rise as much as 100% or more over the course of treatments, so that a limit of at least 1200mC is clearly necessary. (International Electrotechnical Commission, 1997, Dec 26, p. 5)

In order to derive his 1200mC maximum Charge, as noted previously, Weiner claims that the maximum Charge required to elicit an initial adequate seizure with UL ECT is 300mC. That is, a 100 year old recipient may require up to 300mC of initial Charge in order to seize with UL ECT. However, according to Weiner, not only must this minimum 300mC with "dose-sensitive" UL ECT be multiplied by 2.0 to be effective, but due to doubling of threshold over a "treatment" course, must be multiplied by 2.0 again in order to remain effective at the end of a it (2 x 2 x 300mC = 1200mC). In short, according to Weiner, the initial UL ECT dosage of 1200mC for the 100 year old male is a 4.0 fold threshold output of 300mC. By the added supposition of a 100% rise in threshold Impedance at the end of the "treatment" course, then, the alleged 600mC minimum necessary to elicit an initial adequate seizure with "non dose-sensitive" BL ECT for this same 100 year old recipient must also be multiplied by 2.0 (2 x 600mC = 1200mC). To be clear then, according to Weiner, the 1200mC Charge

---

[148] Initial multifold threshold titration level output intensities of circa 2.5 and 5.0 times threshold respectively for BL and UL was not known until ten years after the fact (Beale et al., 1994) and was reported in only the one Beale journal article.

administered to the 100 year old recipient administered UL "ECT," must also be administered to the same 100 year old receiving BL "ECT." In short, the 100 year old recipient must be administered the same 1200mC minimum, whether receiving BL or UL "ECT."

MECTA Second to Third Generation BP Devices Continued: Made-for-America 2nd Generation BP Device to Made-for World 3rd Generation BP Device

So are Weiner's initial threshold output figures with respect to Charge of 300mC with UL ECT and 600mC with BL ECT for the 100 year old recipient a mistake, an exaggeration, or an outright falsehood? Let's again test Weiner's figures with specific MECTA parameters.

Let us begin by examining the maximum Charge emitted by second generation made-for-America MECTA BP devices. Based on Beale's 1994 study, we learned for the first time that the made-for-America JR/SR 2 second generation BP device elicits initial outputs of about 2.5 fold threshold with BL "ECT" from which we can extrapolate that the same made-for-America BP device elicits initial outputs of about (2 x 2.5 =) 5.0 fold threshold with UL "ECT" for all age categories. Specifically, the second generation made-for-America MECTA JR/SR 2 emits a circa unreported 259 maximum Joules at a maximum 576mC Charge for a 100 year old adult. To derive thresholds generally, we simply divide the maximum 576mC by 2.5 and then 5.0 to obtain maximum thresholds in Charge of about (576mC ÷ 2.5 =) 230mC with BL ECT and about (576mC ÷ 5.0 =) 115mC with UL ECT for the 100 year old recipient. However, an even more accurate measure can be derived using EO or Joules. In that 259 Joules (as we have seen previously) represents a 2.59 MTTLOI for all age groups with BL ECT, we can even more accurately divide the maximum Charge not by 2.5, but by 2.59 to deduce an even more accurate BL "ECT" minimum Charge threshold of (576mC ÷ 2.59 =) 222mC for the 100 year old male with BL "ECT. In that UL "ECT: requires half this output to reach threshold for the same 100 year old male, we simply divide 222mC by 2.0 to derive a more accurate UL ECT minimum Charge threshold of (222mC ÷ 2 =) 111mC [149] for the same 100 year old recipient but with UL "ECT," a figure which agrees with Beale's own findings (Beale et al., 1994).

But a 111mC minimum Charge threshold with UL ECT is only about a third of Weiner's asserted 300mC minimum Charge threshold with UL ECT. In fact, applying these figures to Weiner's paradigm, which calls for an initial quadrupling of UL "ECT" threshold output and an initial doubling of BL "ECT" threshold output (for the 100 year old adult), we find that the actual minimum Charge output required is 444mC with both BL and UL "ECT" (2 x 222mC = 444mC; 4 x 111mC = 444mC), not the 1200mC with both BL and UL ECT Weiner purports is needed.

If true, the unreported made-for-America MECTA JR/SR 2 BP device already more than doubles the threshold power with BL "ECT" (576mC ÷ 222mC =) 2.59 (MTTLOI) and more than quintuples the threshold power with UL "ECT" (576mC ÷ 111mC =) 5.18 (MTTLOI) for all age categories. In short, the second generation made-for America BP device, as we have asserted, more than meets Weiner's requirements with but 576mC Charge—not the 1200mC Charge Weiner claims necessary.

Indeed, based on the actual second generation made-for America JR/SR 2 parameters (which maximum outputs, we must remember were never actually reported), Weiner's 1200mC maximum is enough to elicit--***not*** merely an initial 2.0 MTTLOI with BL "ECT" and an initial 4.0 MTTLOI with UL "ECT," but an initial (1200mC ÷ 222mC =) 5.4 MTTLOI with BL "ECT" and an initial (1200mC ÷ 111mC =) 10.8 MTTLOI with UL "ECT." Moreover, Weiner's proposed Charge outputs constitute a doubling--not of the first generation MECTA C BP device which emitted a 1.08 MTTLOI with BL "ECT" for all age categories and a 2.16 MTTLOI with UL "ECT" for all age categories--but a general doubling of unreported second generation made-for-America MECTA BP devices such as the made-for-America MECTA JR/SR 2 which, recall, emits a circa 2.59 MTTLOI with BL ECT and a circa 5.18 MTTLOI with UL "ECT." In short, Weiner's 1997, 1200mC de facto standard limits output to neither an initial 2.0 MTTLOI with BL "ECT" nor an initial 4.0 MTTLOI with UL "ECT," but, in fact, newly allows a circa (1200mC ÷ 222mC =) 5.4 initial MTTLOI with BL "ECT," and an almost (1200mC ÷ 111 = 10.8) 11 MTTLOI with UL "ECT," figures which reflect the hidden MTTLOIs emitted not by what is supposed to be "new" second generation BP devices, but by already extant third generation BP devices, as have seen, for all age categories, suddenly made "legal" (albeit veiled) under Weiner's new unofficial 1997 de facto standard.

---

[149] We could also have multiplied 2.59 x 2.0 = 5.18 fold UL ECT threshold. 576mC ÷ 5.18 = 111mC threshold minimum.

***MECTA** Second to Third Generation BP Devices Continued: Made-for-Europe 2nd Generation BP Device to MECTA 3rd Generation BP Devices*

To be even more thorough, however, let us re-examine the slightly less powerful second generation (made-for-Europe) JR/SR 1 IEC BP device, which emits about 230 Joules (maximum) at a 576mC maximum Charge (for the same 100 year old recipient) and upon which the much more powerful third generation JR/SR 1 is based. For the second generation JR/SR 1 IEC BP device, as already noted, 230 Joules represents an initial 2.3 MTTLOI with BL "ECT" (for all age recipients) and thus an initial 4.6 MTTLOI with UL "ECT" (for all age recipients). Simply dividing the maximum 576mC Charge by 2.3, therefore, we obtain for this particular device, an initial minimum threshold Charge of about (576mC ÷ 2.3 =) 250mC with BL "ECT," slightly higher than the made-for-America MECTA devices which utilize an initial Charge threshold of about 222mC with BL "ECT." In that UL "ECT" requires half this output to reach threshold, we simply divide 250mC by 2.0 (or 576mC by 4.6) to obtain an initial Charge threshold with UL "ECT" on the second generation JR/SR 1 IEC BP device of about (250mC ÷ 2; 576mC ÷ 4.6 =) 125mC for the same 100 year old recipient, again slightly higher than the made-for-America second generation MECTA device which can induce all UL seizures at 111mC minimum.[150] Once again, however, an initial 125mC threshold Charge with UL "ECT" is a distant cry from Weiner's initial minimum Charge threshold claim of 300mC with UL "ECT." Under Weiner's paradigm in which, as we have seen, Weiner calls for a quadrupling of initial threshold output with UL "ECT" and a doubling of initial threshold output with BL "ECT," the second generation made-for-Europe MECTA JR/SR 1 IEC BP device easily satisfies these requirements with just 500mC of its 576mC maximum Charge (2 x 250mC = 500mC; 4 x 125mC = 500mC) with both UL and BL "ECT," in fact, delivering a (576mC ÷ 250mC =) 2.3 MTTLOI with BL "ECT" and a (576mC ÷ 125mC =) 4.6 MTTLOI with UL "ECT" in every age category. Such MTTLOIs do not require the 1200mC maximum Charge Weiner purports them to need. Indeed, Weiner's 1200mC maximum is enough to elicit—not merely the initial 2.3 fold threshold output emitted with BL "ECT" ***or*** the 4.6 fold initial threshold emitted with UL "ECT" with the second generation made-for-Europe MECTA JR/SR 1 IEC BP device, but an initial (1200mC ÷ 250mC =) 4.8 fold threshold output with BL "ECT" and an initial (1200mC ÷ 125mC =) 9.6 fold threshold output with UL "ECT" constituting a doubling--***not*** of ***first*** generation MECTA BP devices--but of ***second*** generation MECTA IEC BP devices, devices encompassing, as we have seen, the unreported third generation BP devices which by 1997 had already been manufactured for circa two complete years.[151] In lieu of an initial 4.0 fold threshold output with UL "ECT" and an initial 2.0 fold threshold output with BL "ECT" as Weiner claims then, Weiner's standard actually facilitates an initial circa 5.0 fold threshold output with BL "ECT," and an initial circa 10 fold threshold output with UL "ECT," figures which reflect the hidden output and MTTLOI not of second, but of then already extant (albeit unreported) third generation BP devices, which Weiner, Abrams, Sackeim and others were desperately attempting to legitimize via Weiner's 1997 de facto standard.[152]

---

[150] Regardless of the slight disparity, both emit BL EO thresholds of a consistent 100 Joules. Charge = EO/Current x Impedance; (Made-for-America JR/SR 2: <u>**100J**</u>/.8A x 562.5Ω = <u>**222mC**</u>; IEC JR/SR 2: <u>**100J**</u>/.8A x 500Ω = <u>**250mC**</u>).

[151] Third generation BP devices actually emit "4.6" and "9.2" MTTLOIs with BL and UL ECT respectively (2.3 x 2 = <u>4.6</u> and 4.6 x 2 = <u>9.2</u>) in that the third generation MECTA JR/SR 1 and 2 BP devices emit 1152mC maximum Charge, almost the full 1200mC allowed by Weiner's 1997 de facto standard (1152mC ÷ 250mC = 4.6; 1152mC ÷ 125mC = 9.2).

[152] The second generation JR/SR 2 IEC BP device may have emitted 240 maximum Joules at 600mC and thus 2.4 and 4.8 Multifold Threshold Titration Level Output Intensities with BL and UL ECT respectively. As such, they emitted the same 125 and 250mC UL and BL threshold Charge outputs (600mC ÷ 4.8 = 125mC; 600mC ÷ 2.4 = 250mC) as the second and third generation JR/SR 1 IEC BP devices.

CHAPTER 64

Somatics Third Generation BP Devices: UL vs. BL Outputs

The second generation made-for America Thymatron DG emits circa 252 Joules maximum at about 504mC maximum Charge for the 100 year old male administered BL "ECT." In that 252 Joules represents an initial 2.52 MTTLOI, we once again, simply divide the maximum Charge by 2.52 to deduce that the Thymatron DG emits an initial (504mC ÷ 2.52 =) 200mC threshold Charge with BL "ECT" for the 100 year old recipient. In that UL "ECT" requires half this output to reach threshold, the same Somatics' second generation Thymatron DG must emit an initial (200mC ÷ 2 =) 100mC threshold Charge (for the 100 year old) with UL ECT, figures which agree with Beale's 1994 findings. (Beale's data utilize Charge.) But a 100mC maximum Charge threshold (for the 100 year old) is once again, a far cry from Weiner's 300mC Charge threshold "required" with UL "ECT." In fact, under Weiner's paradigm, which calls for a quadrupling of initial UL "ECT" threshold output and a doubling of initial BL "ECT" threshold output, we can again see that the second generation Thymatron DG, which emits **504mC** of Charge, more than meets these requirements (2 x 200mC = **400mC**; (4 x 100mC = **400mC**). In short, the maximum Charge required to double the minimum BL "ECT" threshold dosage and quadruple the minimum UL "ECT" threshold dosage is actually only (4 x 100mC =) 400mC, again not the 1200mC Weiner alleges in his 1997 explanation. Based on Charge threshold dosages facilitated by the second generation made-for America Thymatron DG then, Weiner's 1200mC maximum is enough to elicit--***not*** an initial 4.0 MTTLOI with UL "ECT" and an initial 2.0 MTTLOI with BL "ECT" as Weiner contends, but an initial (1200mC ÷ 100mC =) 12 MTTLOI with UL "ECT" and an initial (1200mC ÷ 200mC =) 6.0 MTTLOI with BL "ECT" for all age recipients, figures which again constitute not the doubling of first generation BP devices (which indeed emitted just above threshold dosages with BL "ECT")--but (more than) the doubling of unreported second generation BP devices which, as noted above, emit circa 5.0 and 2.5 initial MTTLOIs with UL and BL "ECT" respectively. In sum, based on the Thymatron DG, Weiner's 1997 1200mC standard facilitates not an initial 4.0 fold threshold output with UL "ECT" and an initial 2.0 fold threshold output with BL "ECT," but an initial 12 fold threshold output with UL "ECT" and an initial 6.0 fold threshold output with BL "ECT," figures which reflect the hidden output and MTTLOIs not only of already then extant third generation BP devices, suddenly to become "legal" (albeit camouflaged) under Weiner's new 1997 de facto standard, but figures which reflect the hidden outputs of probable fourth and even potential fifth generation BP devices.

As we have already gleaned, while Charge thresholds are prone to variance, EO thresholds are prone to constancy.[153] To be thorough, then, we must also examine not only the second generation Thymatron DG, but the initial and final Charge thresholds emitted by Somatics' slightly less powerful second generation made-for-Europe Thymatron DGx IEC BP device (upon which the much more powerful third generation Somatics BP device is actually based). As noted earlier, the made-for-Europe Thymatron DGx emits 226.8 maximum Joules (in lieu of 252J), but at the same 504mC maximum Charge (for the 100 year old recipient) or an initial (227J ÷ 100J =) 2.27 MTTLOI with BL ECT and thus an initial (2 x 2.27 =) 4.54 MTTLOI with UL ECT for all age

[153] EO thresholds may somewhat rise over a course of treatments but compared to Charge thresholds, remain relatively constant. Charge thresholds, on the other hand, vary drastically with changing dynamics such as doubling of Amperage and Voltage, and the reducing of Wave Length by half, possible for fourth and fifth generation BP devices under Weiner's "de facto standard."

recipients. Simply dividing the maximum Charge emitted with the DGx by 2.27, therefore, we obtain the minimum (504mC ÷ 2.27 =) 222mC Charge needed to reach initial threshold with BL ECT via the DGx BP device, slightly more than the second generation made-for-America Somatics DG BP device above which requires an initial minimum output of 200mC to reach threshold with BL "ECT" for the 100 year old recipient. In that UL "ECT" requires half this output to reach threshold, we obtain an initial minimum threshold output with UL "ECT" via the DGx device of (222mC ÷ 2 =) 111mC for the 100 year old recipient, slightly more than the made-for-America DG which can induce an initial UL seizure for the 100 year old with 100mC. Once again, however, an initial Charge threshold of 111mC and 222mC with UL and BL "ECT" respectively for the 100 year old recipient is a far cry from Weiner's purported 300 and 600mC initial Charge minimums with UL and BL "ECT" respectively for the same 100 year old recipient. Under Weiner's paradigm, which calls for four times the initial UL "ECT" threshold output minimum and two times the initial BL "ECT" threshold output minimum, the second generation made-for-Europe Thymatron DGx BP device which emits a 504mC Charge maximum has already exceeded these criteria, criteria fulfilled with but (4 x 111mC =; 2 x 222mC =) 444mC of its 504mC Charge, again not the 1200mC Charge maximum Weiner purports to need.

Based on the threshold outputs of the second generation made-for Europe Thymatron DGx, Weiner's 1200mC maximum is enough to elicit--***not*** merely an initial 4.0 MTTLOI with UL "ECT" and an initial 2.0 MTTLOI with BL "ECT," but an initial (1200mC ÷ 111mC =) 10.8 MTTLOI with UL "ECT" and an initial (1200mC ÷ 222mC =) 5.4 MTTLOI with BL "ECT," figures which once again constitute a doubling--***not*** of implied first generation Brief Pulse devices (which emit just above threshold dosages with BL ECT)--but a doubling of the second generation Thymatron DGx. The second generation DGx already emits, as noted above, an initial 4.54 MTTLOI with UL "ECT" and an initial 2.27 MTTLOI with BL "ECT," once again, more than adequate to accommodate Weiner's alleged requirement of 4.0 times the initial threshold output with UL "ECT" and 2.0 times the initial threshold output with BL "ECT." In lieu of an initial 4.0 MTTLOI with UL "ECT" and an initial 2.0 MTTLOI with BL "ECT," Weiner's de facto standard of up to 1200mC, allowing the 1005mC Charge maximum actually emitted by Somatics third generation "System IV," facilitates an actual (1005mC÷ 111mC =; 452J ÷ 50J =) 9.04 MTTLOI with UL "ECT" and a (1005mC ÷ 222mC =; 452J ÷ 100J =) 4.52 MTTLOI with BL "ECT," once again reflecting the hidden output and MTTLOIs emitted by these already extant third generation BP devices, which by 1997, the year Weiner introduces his "standard," Somatics had been marketing and utilizing for two to three years, a device, as noted above, only "then" to be "newly legalized" under Weiner's 1997 de facto "standard." [154]

[154] The System IV became "legal" world-wide only because the 1989 IEC ECT standard for ECT devices was withdrawn in 1997 so that Weiner's 1997 standard became "de facto," at least in accordance with BP manufacturers. In short, though not official, with the withdrawal of the 1989 IEC standard for ECT in 1997, manufacturers became free to follow whatever "standard" they chose. In effect, the "ECT" device was de-regulated.

CHAPTER 65

Confirmation of Charge Thresholds for 2nd Gen. BP Devices via Conversion to Joules

To confirm the above minimum Charge thresholds for various BP devices, we simply convert minimum Charge thresholds to minimum EO thresholds (Joules). Initial minimum EO threshold, as we have seen and as originally confirmed by Weiner, is actually about 100 Joules with BL ECT and thus about 50 Joules with UL "ECT" for all modern BP devices (for the 100 year old recipient). In 1982, as has been noted, Weiner reported to the FDA:

> Using a pulse device, the [1978 APA] Task Force has determined that only 0.6% of seizure thresholds were greater than 70 [actual] Joules and that none were greater than 100 [actual] Joules. (Department of Health and Human Services, 1982a, p. A53)

For instance, the second generation **made-for-America** MECTA JR/SR 2 uses maximums of .8A and 562Ω. Applying the 222mC threshold minimum with BL "ECT" and 111mC threshold minimum with UL "ECT" derived above for this device, we confirm circa 100 and circa 50J minimums with BL and UL ECT respectively (for all 100 year old recipients).[155]

EO = .222C x .8A x 562.5Ω = **99.99 Joules**.
EO = .111C x .8A x 562.5Ω = **49.95 Joules**.

The second generation **made-for-Europe** MECTA (IEC) JR/SR 2 uses maximums of .8A and a 500Ω. Applying the 250mC initial threshold minimum with BL "ECT" and 125mC initial threshold minimum with UL "ECT" derived above for this device (for all 100 year old recipients), we again confirm 100J and 50J minimums with BL and UL "ECT" respectively (for all 100 year old recipients).

EO = .250C x .8A x 500Ω = **100 Joules**.
EO = .125C x .8A x 500Ω = **50 Joules**.

The (second generation) **made-for-America** Thymatron DG uses maximums of .9A and a 555Ω. Applying the 200mC initial threshold minimum with BL "ECT" and 100mC initial threshold minimum with UL "ECT" derived above for this device (for all 100 year old recipients), we again confirm 100J and 50J minimums with BL and UL "ECT" respectively.

EO = .200C x .9A x 555.5Ω = **99.99 Joules**.

---

[155] The same figures apply to the second generation made-for-America MECTA JR/SR 1 (259J at 576mC; **222mC/111mC** and ***100J/50J*** BL/UL thresholds).

EO = .100C x .9A x 555.5Ω = **49.95 Joules**.

The (second generation) **made-for-Europe** Thymatron DGx uses maximums of .9A and 500Ω. Applying the 222mC initial threshold minimum with BL "ECT" and 111mC initial threshold minimum with UL ECT derived above for this device (seizing all 100 year old recipients), we obtain the same 100 and 50J minimums with BL and UL "ECT" respectively.

EO = .222C x .9A x 500Ω = **99.99 Joules**.
EO = .111C x .9A x 500Ω = **49.95 Joules**.

CHAPTER 66

Minimum Charge Thresholds for Third Generation MECTA BP Devices

In that much more powerful third generation BP devices are based on second generation IEC BP devices, overall Charge and EO double while Charge (and EO) thresholds remain the same (as we would expect). For instance, the third generation MECTA JR/SR 1 emits exactly double the maximum EO and Charge emitted by the second generation made-for-Europe (IEC) MECTA JR/SR 1. In lieu of 230 Joules at 576mC (for the 100 year old adult) then, the third generation MECTA JR/SR 1 elicits 460 Joules at 1152mC. 460 Joules now represents a 4.6 (in lieu of a 2.3) MTTLOI with BL "ECT" (for all age recipients) and thus a 9.2 (in lieu of a 4.6) MTTLOI with UL "ECT" (for all age recipients), twice that of the second generation made-for-Europe (IEC) MECTA JR/SR 1. Simply by dividing the maximum Charge by 4.6 fold (1152mC ÷ 4.6 = 250mC), we can see that the third generation JR/SR 1 MECTA BP device utilizes the same minimum Charge threshold of 250mC (with BL "ECT") as the second generation JR/SR 1 IEC BP device. In that UL "ECT" requires half the output of BL "ECT" to reach seizure threshold, we simply divide the minimum Charge threshold with BL "ECT" by 2.0 to see that the (250mC ÷ 2 =) 125mC minimum that the Charge threshold with UL "ECT" on the third generation JR/SR 1 IEC BP device is precisely that of the minimum Charge threshold for the second generation JR/SR 1 IEC device.[156]

The1152mC maximum Charge elicited by the third generation MECTA JR/SR 1, now "legal" under Weiner's 1997 de facto "standard," as we have seen, is enough to elicit--***not*** merely the initial 4.0 MTTLOI with UL "ECT" and initial 2.0 MTTLOI with BL "ECT" called for by Weiner in his proviso, but an initial 9.2 MTTLOI with UL "ECT" and an initial 4.6 MTTLOI with BL "ECT," figures which constitute, as already noted, a doubling--***not*** of first generation MECTA BP devices (which emitted just above threshold dosages with BL "ECT")--but a doubling of the second generation MECTA JR/SR 1 IEC BP device (which already emitted a 4.6 MTTLOI with UL "ECT" and a 2.3 MTTLOI with BL "ECT"). Weiner, as noted, claims in his 1997 standard, "Present data suggest that with unilateral non-dominant electrode placement, stimulus intensity must be 2-4 times seizure threshold to be optimum from an efficacy standpoint." In lieu of a 4.0 MTTLOI with UL "ECT" at the beginning of a treatment course and a 2.0 MTTLOI at the end of a treatment course with UL "ECT" then, Weiner's 1997 standard actually facilitates and "legalizes" a 9.2 MTTLOI with UL "ECT" at the beginning of the treatment course and a 4.6 MTTLOI with UL "ECT" at the end of a treatment course for what is actually a third generation MECTA JR/SR 1 device which, in fact, by 1997, had already been marketed and utilized for at least two years prior.

To confirm the initial minimum Charge thresholds and the MTTLOI of the third generation MECTA JR/SR 1 above, we again simply convert the minimum Charge thresholds to Joules. If the minimum Charge thresholds are correct, the conversion to Joules should reflect the consistent 100 and 50J threshold minimums with BL and UL ECT respectively for the 100 year old recipient. The third generation MECTA JR/SR 1 again uses maximums of .8A and 500Ω. Using the formula: EO = Charge x Amperage x Impedance, we simply plug in the initial 250mC minimum Charge threshold with BL "ECT" and the initial 125mC minimum Charge threshold with UL ECT to convert to EO in Joules, once again obtaining 100 and 50J minimums respectively.

---

[156] We could also have divided the maximum Charge of 1152mC by 9.2 (fold) = 125mC minimum threshold output with UL ECT.

EO = .250C x .8A x 500Ω = **100 Joules**.
EO = .125C x .8A x 500Ω = **50 Joules**.

Working backwards, we can deduce from both the maximum EO of 460 Joules and the maximum Charge of 1152mC, that the third generation MECTA JR/SR 1 delivers an initial 4.6 MTTLOI with BL "ECT" and an initial 9.2 MTTLOI with UL "ECT" to the 100 year old and thus every other age category.[157]

460J ÷ 100J = 4.6; 1152mC ÷ 250mC = 4.6
460J ÷ 50J = 9.2; 1152mC ÷ 125mC = 9.2

While Charge clearly doubles the power of what are actually second generation BP devices, the quadrupling in Multifold Threshold Titration Level Output Intensity from first generation BP devices via Weiner's 1997 de facto "standard" is difficult to discern. This is plainly due to the elimination of EO in joules (under Weiner's de facto standard) and the fact, as noted above, 5-600mC is erroneously identified with first generation BP devices, making the Weiner enhancement appear to be a first time doubling. In short, the doubling of outputs under the deceptive Mectan Transmutation and the misleading 1989 IEC Standard had been so surreptitious that the conversion from first to second generation BP devices was never publicly acknowledged. Indeed, It was deliberately hidden.

The same principles hold true for the third generation JR/SR 2. The third generation MECTA JR/SR 2 is based on the second generation JR/SR 2 IEC device. In short, the third generation JR/SR 2 exactly doubles the second generation JR/SR 2 both in power and Multifold Threshold Titration Level Output Intensity while threshold outputs in terms of Charge (and of course EO) remain the same (as we would again expect). Thus, the third generation MECTA JR/SR 2 exactly doubles the EO, Charge, and MTTLOI of the second generation made-for-Europe (IEC) MECTA JR/SR 2. For example, in lieu of 240 Joules at 600mC (for the 100 year old recipient) emitted by the second generation made-for-Europe (IEC) MECTA JR/SR 2, the third generation JR/SR 2 device elicits 480 Joules at 1200mC. 480 Joules (and 1200mC) means twice the MTTLOI for every age recipient. Specifically, the third generation device transitions from an initial 2.4 to an initial 4.8 MTTLOI with BL "ECT" (for all "ECT" recipients) and thus from an initial 4.8 to an initial 9.6 MTTLOI with UL "ECT" (for all age recipients). We can simply divide the third generation JR/SR 2 MECTA BP device Charge maximum of 1200mC by 4.8 in order to obtain the same minimum BL threshold output of (1200mC ÷ 4.8 =) 250mC, as the second generation JR/SR 2 IEC BP device (600mC ÷ 2.4 = 250mC). In that UL "ECT" requires half the output of BL "ECT" to reach threshold, we again simply divide the minimum BL threshold Charge of 250mC by 2.0 to derive the same minimum UL threshold output of 125mC (250mC ÷ 2 = 125mC)[158] elicited by the second generation JR/SR 2 IEC device. On the other hand, the new 1200mC maximum (as opposed to 600mC) elicited by the third generation JR/SR 2, now "legal" under Weiner's 1997 de facto standard, elicits--***not*** a 4.8 MTTLOI with UL ECT at the beginning of a treatment course and a 2.4 MTTLOI intensity with UL "ECT" at the end of the treatment course, but a 9.6 MTTLOI with UL "ECT" at the beginning of the treatment course and at least a 4.8 MTTLOI with UL "ECT" at the end of the treatment course, figures which constitute a doubling, as noted -- ***not*** of first generation MECTA BP devices (which emit just above threshold dosages with BL "ECT")--but a doubling of the second generation MECTA JR/SR 2 IEC BP device.

---

[157] To find Charge delivered at every age level, we could use known EO thresholds per age group, multiply by 4.6 and 9.2 respectively to obtain EO in joules and use the above formula to convert to Charge. For example, The EO delivered to the 90 year old on the 3rd generation MECTA JR/SR 1 is 373J. The known threshold output in joules for the 90 year old is about 81J. 373J ÷ 81J = 4.6 fold. The Impedance of the 90 year old is about 450Ω. Thus the EO delivered is 373J and the Charge delivered to the 90 year old is 1036mC. Charge = EO ÷ Amp x Impedance; Charge = 373J ÷ .8A x 450Ω. Charge = 373 ÷ 360. Charge = 1.036C = 1036mC. The seizure threshold for the 90 year old in terms of Charge on the third generation MECTA JR/SR 1 is thus 225mC. (1.036C ÷ 4.6 = .225C = 225mC.) This equates to 373J. 373J ÷ 81J = 4.6. 81J converts to .225C: Charge = 81J ÷ 8A x 450Ω = .225C. 373J converts to 1036mC: .225 x 4.6 = 1036mC. See the 3rd generation MECTA JR/SR 1 chart. Since Charge thresholds change with the device dynamics (see 4th and 5th generation BP devices); whereas, initial EO thresholds remain relatively constant, using Charge thresholds in lieu of EO thresholds is much more circumambulatory and thus vulnerable to manipulation (as we have seen).

[158] We could also have divided 1200mC by 9.6 to obtain 125mC (1200mC ÷ 9.6 = 125mC).

Once again, Weiner's statement in his 1997 "standard," "Present data suggest that with unilateral non-dominant electrode placement, stimulus intensity must be 2-4 times seizure threshold to be optimum from an efficacy standpoint" seems to be suggesting that a 2-4 MTTLOI with UL "ECT" is new (and thus a first time doubling of BP power) so that his 1997 standard accommodates a "first time doubling" (that is, the "2-4 times seizure threshold" with UL "ECT"). Similar to the second generation made-for-Europe JR/SR 1, however, the second generation made-for-Europe JR/SR 2 already emitted a 4.8 MTTLOI with UL "ECT" at the beginning of the treatment course and thus a 2.4 MTTLOI at the end of the treatment course already more than fulfilling Weiner's "criteria." In lieu of the 4.0 fold threshold output with UL "ECT" at the beginning of the treatment course and 2.0 fold threshold output with UL "ECT" at the end of the treatment course, Weiner's 1997 standard actually "legalizes" the third generation MECTA JR/SR 2 which elicits a 9.6 MTTLOI with UL "ECT" at the beginning of the treatment course and at least a 4.8 MTTLOI with UL "ECT" at the end of the treatment course. Weiner's 1997 proposal, in brief, accommodates not a second but a third generation MECTA BP device, moreover, one already manufactured, marketed, and in use at the time of Weiner's 1997 proposal.

To confirm the minimum threshold Charge output and thus MTTLOI for the third generation MECTA JR/SR 2, we can again convert the minimum threshold output to Joules to derive the consistent 100 Joule threshold minimum with BL "ECT" (for the 100 year old recipient) and the consequent 50 Joule threshold minimum with UL "ECT" (for the same 100 year old recipient). In that the (third generation) made-for-Europe MECTA JR/SR 2 uses the same .8A maximum and 500Ω Impedance maximum as the second generation made-for-Europe MECTA JR/SR 2, the same 250mC threshold minimum with BL ECT and 125mC threshold minimum with UL "ECT" emitted by the second generation made-for-Europe MECTA JR/SR 1 is true for the (third generation) made-for-Europe MECTA JR/SR 2, figures which convert to the same 100 and 50 Joule threshold minimum with BL and UL "ECT" respectively as that of the second generation IEC BP device (as expected). (Charge = Current x (hz x 2) x PW x Duration: .8 x 180 x .0014 x 5.96 = 1.200C; 1.200 ÷ 4.8 = **.250C**; 1.200C ÷ 9.6 = **.125C**.)

EO = .250C x .8A x 500Ω = **100 Joules**. 100J x 4.8 = 480J
EO = .125C x .8A x 500Ω = **50 Joules**. 50J x 9.6 = 480J

Working in reverse, we can deduce from both the new EO maximum of 480 Joules and the new Charge maximum of 1200mC that the third generation MECTA JR/SR 2 now delivers an initial 4.8 MTTLOI with BL "ECT" and an initial 9.6 MTTLOI with UL "ECT" at every age level.

480J ÷ 100J = 4.8; 1200mC ÷ 250mC = **4.8**
480J ÷ 50J = 9.6; 1200mC ÷ 125mC = **9.6**

Confirmation of Charge Thresholds for the Third Generation Somatics BP Device

Finally, the same principles hold true for the third generation Somatics System IV. Because the third generation device is based on the second generation made-for-Europe Thymatron DGx, threshold outputs in terms of Charge (and of course EO) remain the same (as we would expect) in spite of the third generation increase in power. On the other hand, the third generation Somatics' System IV doubles the EO and Charge of the second generation made-for-Europe (IEC) Thymatron DGx and thus the MTTLOI. In lieu of 226.8 Joules at 504mC (for the 100 year old recipient), the third generation System IV elicits 453.6 Joules at 1008mC. 454 Joules (as opposed to 226.8J) now represents twice the MTTLOI of the previous Somatics' device, thereby, doubling the power elicited (for all recipients) resulting in a 4.54 (as opposed to 2.26) MTTLOI with BL "ECT" at the beginning of a treatment course and a 9.08 (as opposed to 4.54) MTTLOI with UL "ECT" at the beginning of a treatment course. In administering BL "ECT" with the third generation Somatics IV device, therefore, we can simply divide its maximum 1008mC Charge by 4.54 in order to obtain the same minimum BL threshold output of (1008mC ÷ 4.54 =) 222mC as that of the second generation Thymatron DGx IEC BP device (504mC ÷ 2.268 = 222mC) for the same 100 year old recipient. In that UL "ECT" requires half the output of BL "ECT" to reach threshold, we simply divide the minimum BL threshold dosage of 222mC by 2.0 to obtain the same (222mC ÷ 2 =) 111mC threshold minimum with UL "ECT" as that elicited by the second generation Thymatron DGx IEC device (for the same 100 year old recipient). On the other hand, the 1008mC maximum elicited by the third generation System IV, now legal under Weiner's 1997 standard, as noted, is enough to elicit--***not*** a 4.54 MTTLOI with UL "ECT" at the beginning of a treatment course and thus a 2.27 MTTLOI with UL "ECT" at the end of the treatment course, MTTLOIs already elicited by the second generation DGx, but a 9.08 MTTLOI with UL "ECT" at the beginning of a treatment course and a 4.54 MTTLOI with UL "ECT" at the end of the treatment course (for all recipients). A 9.08 MTTLOI at the beginning and 4.54 MTTLOI at end of a treatment series with UL "ECT" for all recipients constitutes ***not*** a first time doubling of first generation BP devices as Weiner implies--but a second time doubling, that is, a doubling of second generation BP devices; in short, a quadrupling of first generation BP devices. Succinctly, the new MTTLOI constitutes a doubling not of first generation BP devices, but a doubling of the second generation Thymatron DGx IEC BP device. Once again, Weiner's assertion justifying his 1997 enhancement standard, "Present data suggest that with unilateral non-dominant electrode placement, stimulus intensity must be 2-4 times seizure threshold to be optimum from an efficacy standpoint" proves ingenuous. His 1997 enhancement proviso is totally unnecessary to facilitate a 2-4 MTTLOI for UL "ECT" in that, for example, the second generation made-for-Europe Thymatron DGx under the 1989 IEC Standard already emits a default 4.54 MTTLOI with UL "ECT" at the beginning of a treatment course and thus at least a 2.27 MTTLOI with UL "ECT" at the end of the treatment course. In lieu of facilitating the initial 4.0 MTTLOI at the beginning of a treatment course and thus the 2.0 MTTLOI with UL "ECT" at the end of a treatment course, the 1200mC maximum Charge proviso Weiner demands in his 1997 "standard" actually facilitates more than twice the MTTLOI he calls for, in fact, legalizing then already extant third generation BP devices such as the Somatics System IV which, as we have seen, elicits an initial 9.08 MTTLOI with UL "ECT" and at least a 4.54 MTTLOI with UL "ECT" even at the end of a "treatment" course. Clearly, Weiner's 1997 proposal is a desperate bid to "legalize" circa 1200mC third generation BP devices already being manufactured, marketed and utilized since at least 1995 in clear violation of the 1989 IEC Standard for "ECT" (Royal College of Psychiatry, 1995, p. 125).

Confirmation of Charge Thresholds for the Third Generation Somatics BP Device via Conversion to Joules

To confirm the threshold Charge minimum and thus the MTTLOI for Somatics' third generation Somatics' System IV, we can again convert minimum threshold output in Coulombs to minimum threshold output in Joules which should consistently remain at an initial 100 Joules with BL "ECT" (for the 100 year old recipient), and consequently an initial 50 Joules with UL "ECT" (for the same 100 year old recipient). In that the (third generation) System IV uses the same maximums of .9A and 500Ω as the second generation made-for-Europe Thymatron DGx, the same 222mC and 111mC threshold outputs with BL and UL "ECT" respectively apply to both instruments, resulting in the same respective 100 and 50 Joule minimum threshold outputs.

EO = .222C x .9A x 500Ω = **99.99 Joules**.
EO = .111C x .9A x 500Ω = **49.95 Joules**.

Working in reverse, simply by dividing the maximum EO of 454 Joules and the maximum Charge of 1008mC delivered by the third generation System IV with initial circa 100J and 50J or 222mC and 111mC minimum thresholds respectively, we can deduce that the ***third*** generation Somatics BP device, contrary to Weiner's assertion, delivers an initial 4.54 MTTLOI with BL "ECT" and an initial 9.08 MTTLOI with UL "ECT" at every age level.

454J ÷ 99.99J = 4.54; 1008mC ÷ 222mC = 4.54
454J ÷ 49.95J = 9.08; 1008mC ÷ 111mC = 9.08

CHAPTER 67

Confirmation of Charge Thresholds for Fourth Generation BP Devices

Finally, while the same principles hold true of probable fourth generation BP devices, also legal under Weiner's 1997 standard, the total elimination of EO reporting (in Joules), including the elimination of the ER/RRC phrase, cloaks the enhanced power of the device. This is due to an unusual dynamic, as noted earlier, evidently discovered and utilized by Weiner. By doubling Amperage via the doubling of Voltage, and reducing Pulse Width by half, all perfectly legal under the Weiner proviso, seizure thresholds in terms of Charge (but not in terms of EO) are reduced by half. This means that in spite of a doubling of EO in Joules and doubling of MTTLOIs for all age categories, Charge outputs remain unchanged. For instance, simply by doubling Amperage and reducing Pulse Width by half, a fourth generation MECTA JR/SR 2, will double the EO of the third generation JR/SR 2 from a 480J to a 960J maximum output even as maximum Charge remains the same 1200mC as the third generation JR/SR 2. In spite of the fourth generation JR/SR 2 doubling the third generation JR/SR 2 in power and MTTLOI, and in spite of the minimum thresholds in terms of EO with BL and UL "ECT" remaining the same constant (initial) 100 and 50 Joules respectively, the minimum thresholds in terms of Charge with BL and UL "ECT" are reduced by half. As a result, the minimum Charge threshold with BL "ECT" drops from 250mC to 125mC while the minimum Charge threshold with UL "ECT" drops from 125mC to 62.5mC (for the 100 year old recipient). It is due to the drop in Charge thresholds that while the third generation JR/SR 2 emits 480 Joules (for the 100 year old recipient), and the fourth generation JR/SR 2 emits 960 Joules (for the same 100 year old recipient) thereby doubling the MTTLOI, this change takes place with *the same 1200mC Charge maximum emitted by both machines*. In terms of EO, it is quite obvious that the 960 Joules emitted by the fourth generation JR/SR 2 (as opposed to the 480J emitted by the third generation JR/SR 2 device) represents twice the output and MTTLOI. In lieu of an initial (480J ÷ 100 =) 4.8 MTTLOI with BL "ECT" the fourth generation BP device now emits an initial (960J ÷ 100 =) 9.6 MTTLOI with BL "ECT" for all age recipients. In lieu of an initial (480J ÷ 100 = 4.8 x 2 =) 9.6 MTTLOI with UL "ECT," the fourth generation BP device now emits an initial (960J ÷ 100J = 9.6 x 2 =) 19.2 MTTLOI with UL "ECT" for all age recipients. In terms of maximum Charge alone, however, which does not change from third to fourth generation devices, this doubling in both power and MTTLOI remains *invisible*.

In order to obtain the new initial minimum Charge threshold of 125mC with BL "ECT" for the fourth generation JR/SR 2 device, we must divide its maximum 1200mC Charge by its MTTLOI of 9.6, obtained through its 960J EO, impossible to obtain via Weiner's reported parameters, so that we derive (1200mC ÷ 9.6 =) 125mC. 125mC, as we can see, is half the initial BL "ECT" Charge threshold emitted by the third generation JR/SR 2 device (1200mC ÷ 4.8 = 250mC). In that the initial UL "ECT" threshold can be reached with half the output required of BL "ECT," we simply divide the initial BL "ECT" minimum Charge threshold of 125mC (for the fourth generation JR/SR 2) by 2.0 to obtain the new initial minimum Charge threshold with UL "ECT" (for the fourth generation JR/SR 2) of (125mC ÷ 2 =) 62.5mC which applies to the 100 year old recipient. 62.5mC is half the UL "ECT" minimum Charge threshold of the third generation JR/SR 2 IEC BP device (of 125mC) for the same 100 year old recipient. The same 1200mC maximum elicited by the fourth generation JR/SR 2 then, is now enough to elicit--***not*** the third generation JR/SR 2's 9.6 MTTLOI with UL "ECT" at the beginning of the treatment course and at least a 4.8 MTTLOI with UL "ECT" at the end of the treatment course for the same 100 year old recipient, but is now enough to elicit a 19.2 MTTLOI with UL "ECT" at the beginning of the treatment course and at least a 9.6 MTTLOI with UL "ECT" even at the end of the treatment course. These figures constitute a doubling in both power and MTTLOI--***not*** of a first or even second generation BP device--but a doubling of the third generation JR/SR 2 IEC BP device, all "legal" under Weiner's 1997 proviso. In lieu of the initial 4.0 MTTLOI Weiner requires in his 1997 proviso with UL "ECT" at the beginning of a treatment course and at least 2.0 MTTLOI with UL "ECT" at the end of the treatment course, we can now see that Weiner's 1997 standard actually accommodates a fourth generation JR/SR 2 BP device capable of eliciting an initial 19.2 MTTLOI with UL "ECT" at the beginning of a treatment course and at least a 9.6 MTTLOI (in terms of both EO and Charge) with UL "ECT" even at the end of the treatment course in every age category, "legal" under Weiner's de facto standard.

Confirmation of Charge Thresholds for the Fourth Generation MECTA BP Devices Continued via Conversion to Joules

To confirm the minimum Charge threshold and thus MTTLOI for the probable fourth generation MECTA JR/SR 2, we again convert minimum Charge thresholds to minimum EO thresholds from which we again obtain the consistent initial 100 minimum Joules with BL "ECT" (for the 100 year old recipient) and consequently, the consistent initial 50 minimum Joules with UL "ECT." As a result of the fourth generation JR/SR 2 using up to 1.6A, twice that of the third generation JR/SR 2, but with half the Pulse Width of the third generation JR/SR 2, a new reduced minimum Charge threshold of 125mC with BL "ECT" and a new reduced minimum Charge threshold of 62.5mC with UL "ECT" emerge. Converting from minimum Charge thresholds in Coulombs to EO in Joules via the formula: EO = Charge x Current x Impedance, we do indeed obtain the looked for 100 and 50 Joule minimum EO thresholds with BL and UL "ECT" respectively, confirming the Charge Thresholds.

EO = .125C x 1.6A x 500Ω = **100 Joules**.
EO = .0625C x 1.6A x 500Ω = **50 Joules**.

Working in reverse, we can deduce from both the maximum EO of 960 Joules and the maximum Charge of 1200mC, that the fourth generation JR/SR 2 delivers an initial 9.6 MTTLOI output intensity with BL "ECT" and incredibly, an initial 19.2 MTTLOI with UL "ECT" at every age level.

960J ÷ 100J = **9.6**
1200mC ÷ 125.0mC = **9.6**
960J ÷ 50J = **19.2**;
1200mC ÷ 62.5mC = **19.2**

Similarly, a probable fourth generation MECTA JR/SR 1 (as opposed to the probable fourth generation MECTA JR/SR 2) emits a 922J maximum output, doubling the power of the 460J third generation JR/SR 1 even as maximum Charge remains the same 1152mC for both third and fourth generation MECTA JR/SR 1 devices. This is again due to the dynamic of doubling the Amperage (via doubling the Voltage) of the third generation device and reducing the Pulse Width by half, a phenomenon, as noted, which reduces Charge threshold by half and which applies to the probable fourth generation device, “legal” under the Weiner de facto "standard." Once again, minimum Charge threshold with BL "ECT" drops from 250mC to 125mC, while minimum Charge threshold with UL "ECT" drops from 125mC to 62.5mC respectively. In spite of the fourth generation JR/SR 1 doubling both the power and MTTLOI of the third generation JR/SR 1; therefore, once again, maximum Charge output of 1152mC remains unchanged (from the third to the fourth generation MECTA JR/SR 1), making the doubling of power and MTTLOI invisible under Weiner’s 1997 de facto "standard."

It is due to the halving of Charge thresholds (as a result of doubling the current and halving the Pulse Width) that while the third generation JR/SR 1 emits 460 Joules at 1152mC (for the 100 year old recipient), the fourth generation JR/SR 1 emits 922 Joules *at the same 1152mC Charge*. In terms of EO in Joules then, it is easy to see that 922 Joules (as opposed to 460J) represents twice the output and, therefore, twice the MTTLOI of the third generation device, that is, in lieu of an initial (460J ÷ 100J =) 4.6 MTTLOI with BL "ECT," the fourth generation device now emits an initial (922J ÷ 100J =) 9.22 MTTLOI with BL "ECT" for all age recipients. It is also easy to see that in lieu of an initial (460J ÷ 50J =) 9.22 MTTLOI with UL "ECT," the fourth generation BP device now emits an initial (922J ÷ 50J =) 18.44 MTTLOI with UL "ECT" for all age recipients. In terms of Charge alone, however, because maximum Charge remains the same for both third and fourth generation JR/SR 1 devices, the fourth generation doubling of power and MTTLOI remains *invisible.*

In order to obtain the new fourth generation JR/SR 1 device minimum Charge threshold of 125mC with BL "ECT," we must divide the maximum 1152mC Charge by the 9.22 MTTLOI with BL "ECT," only discernable in terms of EO (1152mC ÷ 9.22 = 125mC). The 125mC minimum Charge threshold with BL "ECT" is thus half the minimum Charge threshold of BL "ECT" on the third generation JR/SR 1 device (1152mC ÷ 4.6 = 250mC). In order to obtain the new fourth generation JR/SR 1 device minimum Charge threshold of 62.5mC with UL "ECT," we must divide the initial UL "ECT" maximum Charge of 1152mC by the 18.44 MTTLOI with UL "ECT," again only discernable in terms of EO (1152mC ÷ 18.44 = 62.5mC). 62.5mC is, of course, half the UL "ECT" minimum Charge threshold of the third generation JR/SR 1 IEC BP device (125mC) for the same 100 year old recipient. The same 1152mC maximum elicited by the fourth generation JR/SR 1, therefore, is now enough to elicit--***not*** the third generation JR/SR 1's 9.2 MTTLOI with UL "ECT" at the beginning of the treatment course and 4.6 MTTLOI with UL "ECT" at the end of the treatment course for all age recipients, but enough to elicit an amazing initial 18.44 MTTLOI with UL "ECT" at the beginning of a treatment course and an equally amazing 9.22 MTTLOI with UL "ECT" even at the end of a treatment course for all age recipients. In short, the fourth generation JR/SR 1 MTTLOI doubles the power of the third generation JR/SR 1 BP device. Outputs for the fourth generation JR/SR 1, "legal" under the Weiner proviso, thus constitute a doubling in both power and MTTLOI--***not*** of first or even second generation BP devices--but a doubling of the third generation JR/SR 1 IEC BP device. Thus, in lieu of the 4.0 fold UL "ECT" MTTLOI at the beginning of the treatment course and 2.0 UL "ECT" MTTLOI at the end of the treatment course Weiner claims his 1997 de facto standard accommodates, Weiner's 1997 proviso standard actually accommodates a perhaps already marketed probable fourth generation JR/SR 1 BP device capable of "legally" eliciting an initial 18.44 MTTLOI with UL "ECT" and at least a 9.22 MTTLOI (in terms of both EO and Charge) with UL "ECT" even at the end of a treatment course in every age category. This is more than eight and a half times the power and MTTLOI of the first generation BP device (the MECTA C) presented to the FDA in conformity with the 1982 APA Standard (9.22 ÷ 1.08 = 8.53; 18.44 ÷ 2.16 = 8.53).

To confirm the minimum Charge threshold and thus MTTLOI of the probable fourth generation MECTA JR/SR 1, we once more convert minimum Charge thresholds to Joules to obtain the initial 100J minimum seizure threshold with BL "ECT" (for the 100 year old recipient) and consequently, the initial 50J minimum seizure threshold with UL "ECT" (for the same 100 year old recipient). Because the fourth generation JR/SR 1 may use a 1.6A constant current (possible under Weiner's de facto standard), twice that of the third generation JR/SR 1, the new reduced 125mC minimum Charge threshold with BL ECT and reduced 62.5mC minimum Charge threshold with UL ECT (for the 100 year old recipient) emerge (as derived above). Using a formula (to convert Coulombs to Joules): EO = Charge x Current x Impedance, we, indeed, once again obtain the looked for 100 and 50 Joule minimum threshold outputs respectively with BL and UL "ECT" in terms of Joules, confirming the threshold Charges.

EO = .125C x 1.6A x 500Ω = **100 Joules**.
EO = .0625C x 1.6A x 500Ω = **50 Joules**.

Working in reverse, we can deduce from both the maximum EO of 922 Joules and the maximum Charge of 1152mC, that the fourth generation JR/SR 1 delivers an initial 9.22 MTTLOI with BL "ECT" and an initial 18.44 MTTLOI with UL "ECT" at every age level.

922J ÷ 100J = **9.22**;
1152mC ÷ 125mC = **9.22**
922J ÷ 50J = **18.44**;
1152mC ÷ 62.5mC = **18.44**

As we can see, an 18.44 MTTLOI with UL "ECT" at the beginning of a treatment course and at least a 9.22 MTTLOI with UL "ECT" at the end of a treatment course, "legal" under Weiner's de facto "standard," is now distantly removed from Weiner's enhancement rationale of eliciting an initial 4.0 MTTLOI with UL "ECT" at the beginning of a treatment course in order to elicit a 2.0 MTTLOI with UL "ECT" at the end of a treatment course supposedly necessary for "dose-sensitive UL "ECT" and the alleged doubling of Impedance over a "treatment" course.

The probable fourth generation Somatics System V (under Weiner's de facto standard) emitting a 907.2J maximum output, doubles the power and MTTLOI of the 453.6J third generation System IV even as maximum Charge remains the same 1008mC for both devices. In spite of the doubling in both power and MTTLOI and in spite of the minimum threshold with BL and UL "ECT" remaining a constant 100 and 50 Joules respectively, the minimum threshold in terms of Charge with BL ECT drops from 222mC to 111mC, while minimum Charge threshold with UL ECT drops from 111mC to 55.55mC respectively. Again, the drop is due to the doubling of Amperage and the halving of Pulse Width, both "legal" under Weiner's 1997 de facto standard. It is due to this drop in Charge thresholds, moreover, that while the third generation Somatics IV emits an unreported 453.6 Joules at a reported 1008mC (for the 100 year old recipient), the probable fourth generation Somatics V doubles maximum EO to an unreported 907.2J *at the same reported 1008mC of Charge*. In terms of EO, it is once again easy to see that 907.2 Joules represents twice the power and MTTLOI of the third generation device (at 453.6J). In short, the third generation System IV emits an initial 4.536 MTTLOI with BL "ECT," while the fourth generation "System V" device emits an initial 9.072 MTTLOI with BL "ECT" for all age recipients (907.2J ÷ 100J = 9.07). It is also easy to see that in lieu of an initial 9.072 MTTLOI with UL "ECT" for the third generation BP device, the fourth generation BP device now emits an initial (albeit unreported) 18.144 MTTLOI with UL "ECT" (2 x 9.07 = 18.144; 907.2J ÷ 50J = 18.144) for all age recipients. As in the previous examples, moreover, because maximum Charge remains the same on both devices, the doubling in power is rendered *invisible.*

In order to obtain what might be the new minimum Charge threshold for the fourth generation System V device of 111.5mC with BL "ECT," we must divide the maximum 1008mC Charge by its MTTLOI of 9.072, only discernable in terms of EO to derive (1008mC ÷ 9.072 =) 111mC. We find that the 111mC derived is half the BL minimum Charge threshold of the third generation System IV device of (1008mC ÷ 4.54 =) 222mC and again, this is due to the dynamic of doubling the Amperage (via doubling Voltage) and halving Pulse Width. In that UL "ECT" threshold for any age group requires half the output of BL "ECT" for that same age group, we divide the initial BL minimum Charge threshold of 111mC by 2.0 to obtain the new UL "ECT" minimum Charge threshold of (111mC ÷ 2 =) 55.55mC for the 100 year old recipient on the fourth generation System V. 55.55mC is of course, half the UL minimum Charge threshold of the third generation System IV device (of 111mC) for the same 100 year old recipient. The same 1008mC maximum elicited by the fourth generation System V is now enough to elicit--***not*** the third generation System IV's 9.072 MTTLOI with UL "ECT" at the beginning of a "treatment course" and at least a 4.536 MTTLOI with UL "ECT" at the end of a "treatment course" for the 100 year old recipient, but an 18.144 MTTLOI with UL "ECT" at the beginning of a "treatment course" and at least a 9.072 MTTLOI with UL "ECT" at the end of a "treatment course" (invisibly doubling the MTTLOI of the Somatics third generation BP device at all age levels). These figures constitute a doubling in both power and MTTLOI--***not*** of a first or even second generation BP devices--but a doubling of the third generation System IV BP device. In lieu of the 4.0 MTTLOI with UL "ECT" at the beginning of the "treatment course" and at least 2.0 MTTLOI with UL "ECT" at the end of the "treatment course" for which Weiner claims his 1997 de facto standard is needed, we find that Weiner's 1997 standard actually accommodates a probable, perhaps already marketed fourth generation "System V" BP device now "legally" capable of eliciting, as noted above, an initial 18.144 MTTLOI with UL "ECT" at the beginning of a "treatment course" and at least a 9.072 MTTLOI with UL "ECT" at the end of a "treatment course" in every age category.

To confirm the minimum Charge thresholds and thus the MTTLOI for the potential (and possibly actual) fourth generation Somatics System V (by deriving the 100J and 50J minimum threshold constants with BL and UL ECT), we simply convert minimum Charge thresholds to minimum EO thresholds for which we should obtain an initial 100 minimum Joules with BL "ECT" (for the 100 year old recipient), and consequent initial 50 minimum Joules with UL ECT (for the same 100 year old recipient). In that (under Weiner's standard), the fourth generation "System V" device may use 1.8A ("legal" under Weiner's de facto standard), twice that of the third generation System IV, in conjunction with a halved Pulse Width, as noted above, a new reduced (by half) minimum Charge threshold of 111mC with BL "ECT" and minimum Charge threshold of 55.55mC with UL "ECT" emerge. Converting Charge to Joules through the formula: EO = Charge x Current x Impedance, we indeed obtain the 100 and 50 Joule minimum threshold output constants with BL and UL "ECT" respectively.

EO = .111C x 1.8A x 500Ω = **100 Joules**.
EO = .0555C x 1.8A x 500Ω = **50.0 Joules**.

Working in reverse, we can now confirm from both the maximum EO of 907.2 Joules and the maximum Charge of 1008mC, that the potential or actual fourth generation System V delivers an initial 9.072 MTTLOI with BL "ECT" and an initial 18.14 MTTLOI with UL "ECT" in every age level.

907.2J ÷ 100J = **9.072**
1008mC ÷ 111.1mC = **9.072**
907.2J ÷ 50.0J = **18.14**
1008mC ÷ 55.55mC = **18.14**

CHAPTER 68

Confirmation of Charge Thresholds for Fifth Generation BP Devices

Finally, a potential fifth generation BP device, also legal under Weiner's 1997 standard, emits, as noted above, the maximum 1200 Joules the de facto "standard" allows, exceeding fourth generation BP devices by 200 to 300 Joules. This enhancement occurs even as maximum Charge remains the exact same 1200mC maximum (of the third and fourth generation MECTA JR/SR 2). It is due to the drop in Charge thresholds (in turn due to the further increase in current) that while the third generation MECTA JR/SR 2 emits 480 Joules at 1200mC (for the 100 year old recipient), and the fourth generation MECTA JR/SR 2 emits 960 Joules at 1200mC (for the same 100 year old recipient), that what might be considered a fifth generation JR/SR 2 can potentially emit a full 1200 Joules at the same 1200mC Charge maximum (for the same 100 year old recipient). In terms of EO, it is easy to see that 1200 Joules represents a substantial increase in output and MTTLOI compared to the third and fourth generation BP devices (at 480 and 960J maximums respectively). For example, in lieu of the initial 9.6 MTTLOI with BL "ECT" emitted by the fourth generation JR/SR 2 for all age levels, the potential fifth generation device emits an initial 12.0 MTTLOI with BL "ECT" at all age levels. In lieu of the initial 19.2 MTTLOI with UL "ECT" emitted by the fourth generation JR/SR 2 for all age levels, the fifth generation BP device now emits an initial (2 x 12.0 =) 24.0 MTTLOI with UL "ECT" at all age levels. Because maximum Charge remains the same as third and fourth generation BP devices, however, the gross increases in power alone under Weiner's 1997 de facto standard (sans EO reporting), once again become *invisible.* [159]

In order to obtain the fifth generation JR/SR 2 device's newly reduced minimum Charge threshold with BL "ECT," we must divide the maximum 1200mC Charge by the MTTLOI of 12.0, discernable only in terms of EO. The new reduced minimum Charge threshold of 100mC with BL "ECT" (1200mC ÷ 12.0 = 100mC [160]) has diminished compared to the BL "ECT" minimum Charge threshold of (1200mC ÷ 9.6 =) 125mC emitted by the fourth generation JR/SR 2 device. In that UL "ECT" threshold output is always half that of BL "ECT" threshold output, we divide the initial BL "ECT" minimum Charge threshold of 100mC by 2.0 to obtain the new UL "ECT" minimum Charge threshold of (100mC ÷ 2 =) 50mC for the 100 year old recipient on the fifth generation JR/SR 2. 50mC, of course, has diminished compared to the 62.5mC initial UL "ECT" minimum Charge threshold of the fourth generation JR/SR 2 IEC BP device for the same 100 year old recipient. The same 1200mC maximum elicited by the third and fourth generation JR/SR 2, is now enough to elicit--***not*** the third generation JR/SR 2's 9.6 MTTLOI with UL "ECT" at the beginning of the "treatment course" and at least a 4.8 MTTLOI with UL "ECT" at the end of the "treatment course" for the 100 year old recipient, nor even the fourth generation JR/SR 2's 19.2 MTTLOI with UL "ECT" at the beginning of the "treatment course" and at least a 9.6 MTTLOI with UL "ECT" at the end of the treatment course for the same 100 year old recipient, but is now enough to elicit an

---

[159] One might be tempted to ask, "How do you know EO threshold is the constant? Perhaps it is the reverse; the threshold constant is Charge; EO threshold changes." The answer is right before your eyes. Overall EO increases with each generation; whereas, overall Charge does not increase from third to forth to fifth generation devices. In that the change in EO is manifest, there need be no other reflection. Conversely, in that the change in Charge is not manifest from third to forth to fifth generation devices, the increased power must be reflected internally, i.e. reduced threshold.

[160] The "12.0" fold figure is obtained by dividing 1200 Joules by 100 Joules, maximum machine output by minimum threshold output (100 Joules) for a 100 year old man administered BL ECT. The 100 Joule figure is a relative constant.

unconscionably prodigious 24.0 MTTLOI with UL "ECT" at the beginning of a “treatment course” and at least a 12.0 MTTLOI with UL "ECT" even at the end of a “treatment course” for all age categories. (Weiner, remember, asserts that "dose-sensitive" UL "ECT" must be at least two fold threshold to be effective.) This constitutes an enhancement both in power and MTTLOI--***not*** merely of the first, second, or even third generation MECTA BP device--but an enhancement of the probable fourth generation JR/SR 2 IEC BP device. Thus, in lieu of the 4.0 MTTLOI at the beginning of the “treatment course” with UL "ECT" and a 2.0 MTTLOI at the end of the “treatment course” with UL "ECT" for which Weiner claims his 1997 de facto standard necessary, Weiner's 1997 standard actually accommodates a potential fifth generation JR/SR 2 BP device capable of "legally" eliciting a 24.0 MTTLOI with UL "ECT" at the beginning of a “treatment course” and at least a 12.0 MTTLOI with UL "ECT" even at the end of a “treatment course” at every age level. The MTTLOI legally deliverable under the Weiner de facto standard is now six-fold Weiner's alleged requirement for "dose-sensitive" UL ECT both at the beginning and the end of a “treatment course” (24 ÷ 4 = 6; 12 ÷ 2 = 6). Indeed, the initial 24 MTTLOI for the potential fifth generation BP device is (24 ÷ 2 =) 12 fold that required for alleged UL "ECT' 'dose-sensitivity."

Confirmation of Charge Thresholds for the Fifth Generation MECTA JR/SR 2 BP Device Continued: via Conversion to Joules

To confirm the initial minimum Charge threshold and thus the MTTLOI for the potential fifth generation MECTA JR/SR 2, we can again convert minimum Charge thresholds to Joules for which we should again obtain constants of an initial 100J minimum seizure threshold with BL "ECT" (for the 100 year old recipient) and initial 50J minimum seizure threshold with UL "ECT" (for the same 100 year old recipient). In that the fifth generation JR/SR 2 may use a 2.0A constant current (usable under Weiner's de facto "standard"), even greater than that of the fourth generation JR/SR 2, a newly reduced minimum Charge threshold of 100mC with BL "ECT" and reduced minimum Charge threshold of 50mC with UL "ECT" emerges. Using the conversion formula EO = Charge x Current x Impedance, we indeed obtain the 100 and 50 Joule initial minimum seizure threshold output constants with BL and UL "ECT" respectively in terms of EO.

EO = .100C x 2.0A x 500Ω = **100 Joules**.
EO = .050C x 2.0A x 500Ω = **50 Joules**.

Working in reverse, we can deduce from both the maximum EO of 1200 Joules and the maximum Charge of 1200mC, that the potential fifth generation MECTA JR/SR 2 delivers an initial 12.0 MTTLOI with BL "ECT" and an initial 24.0 MTTLOI with UL "ECT" at every age level.

1200J ÷ **100J** = initial **12.0 MTTLOI with BL "ECT"**
1200mC ÷ **100mC** = initial **12.0 MTTLOI with BL "ECT"**
1200J ÷ **50J** = initial **24.0 MTTLOI with UL "ECT"**
1200mC ÷ **50mC** = initial **24.0 MTTLOI with UL "ECT"**

SECTION XII: Summaries and Charts Pertaining to Weiner's 1997 de facto "Standard"

CHAPTER 69

Summary and Charts 3rd, 4th, and 5th Gen. BP Devices under 1997 de Facto Standard

Note how initial Charge thresholds alter with electrical variations, especially changes in Amperage and Pulse Width; whereas, initial EO thresholds remain constant. For instance, the second generation made-for-America MECTA BP devices utilize initial 222/111mC minimum seizure threshold outputs with BL and UL "ECT" respectively while second and third generation MECTA made-for-Europe BP devices utilize initial 250/125mC minimum seizure threshold outputs with BL and UL "ECT" respectively. The second generation made-for-America Somatics DG device utilizes initial 200/100mC minimum seizure threshold outputs with BL and UL "ECT" respectively while second and third generation Somatics made-for-Europe BP devices utilize initial 222/111mC minimum seizure threshold outputs respectively. The probable (or actual) fourth generation MECTA BP devices may use initial 125/62.5mC minimum seizure threshold outputs with UL and BL "ECT" respectively; whereas, the probable fourth generation Somatics BP device appears to use initial 111/55.5mC minimum seizure threshold outputs with BL and UL "ECT" respectively. Finally the fifth generation MECTA BP device can theoretically use initial 100mC/50mC minimum seizure threshold outputs with BL and UL "ECT" respectively. Note how these threshold outputs do not match Weiner's 1997 assertion that:

> While initial seizure thresholds with UL ECT are nearly always below 300mC, they often rise as much as 100% or more over the course of treatments, so that a limit of at least 1200mC is clearly necessary.

While it is true that seizure thresholds are nearly always below 300mC, much more accurately, they are nearly always below 150mC so that no more than 600mC appears to be necessary to meet Weiner's criteria--not the 1200mC Weiner asserts--and this only if threshold really does double over a "treatment" series and UL "ECT" really is "dose sensitive." In short, like Abrams and Sackeim, Weiner too is actually calling for enough increase in power to a quadruple (and more) the output of first generation BP devices. Moreover, amidst the threshold Charge changes above, initial minimum seizure threshold outputs measured in joules appear to remain a constant 100 and 50 Joules with BL and UL "ECT" respectively, regardless of parameter changes and regardless of increasing power. Indeed, the constancy of threshold outputs in joules can be verified not only formulaically, but by the simple detail that increases in overall maximum EO (in joules) are visible, whereas, in spite of increasing power, overall increases in maximum Charge (in Coulombs), due the reductions in Charge thresholds, can quite deceptively remain the same. Logically, if increasing machine power does not manifest itself externally through increasing Charge, the increased power (always visible via EO) must occur internally and this is exactly what happens via decreasing Charge thresholds. Said differently, if overall Charge does not increase with increasing power, the invariably increasing MTTLOIs (not identified by manufacturers) must occur internally through decreasing seizure thresholds (like we see above). While initial EO seizure thresholds with BL and UL "ECT" remain constant at 100 and 50 Joules successively; therefore, initial Charge thresholds on these devices can vary. Thus, while the reported maximum Charge of about 1200mC for all third, fourth, and fifth generation Brief Pulse devices remain virtually identical, seizure thresholds in Charge decrease by half from third to fourth generation and decrease again from fourth to fifth generation BP devices. Consequently, if only overall Charge maximums are reported, increases in actual power can become invisible. Contrarily, because initial EO seizure thresholds remain constant from third to fourth to fifth generation BP devices, the EO maximums visibly increase from about 500 to about 1000 to 1200 Joules from which we can derive increases from a circa 5.0 , to a circa 10.0 , to a 12.0 MTTLOI in every age category. In short, whereas increases in both power and MTTLOI are consistently and conspicuously visible in terms EO (Joules) maximums, these same increases may well remain invisible if only Charge maximums are reported as is the defect with Weiner's 1997 de fact standard. Without EO reporting, not only do meaningful comparisons of third, fourth, and fifth generation BP devices become indiscernible, but meaningful comparisons to earlier BP devices and even SW devices disappear. Indeed, no meaningful reporting of "ECT" devices has occurred since about 1982. In fact, due to a corrupt series of reporting stratagems and the supplanting of EO with Charge alone, the four increases in power have gone unnoticed. Certainly, only one increase in power appears to have occurred, and this only tangentially reported.

Lists and Succinct Tables of Various Brief Pulse Generations in both Charge and EO:

We can now create lists followed by charts of all modern day Brief Pulse devices. Below are lists containing Overall EO and Charge maximums, minimum Charge Thresholds with BL and UL "ECT" respectively, and minimum EO Thresholds with BL and UL "ECT" respectively. (Note how charge thresholds vary from machine to machine and generation to generation while EO Thresholds Remain Constant.)

Overall EO/Charge Maximums
vs
BL-UL Charge Threshold Minimums
vs
BL-UL EO Threshold Minimums

First generation MECTA C
108J/337.5mC; **312.5mC/156.25mC** and ***100J/50J*** BL/UL thresholds
First generation MECTA D
134J/336.0mC; **250mC/125mC** and ***100/50J*** BL/UL thresholds

Second generation Made-for-America MECTA JR/SR 1
259J/576mC; **222mC/111mC and *100J/50J*** BL/UL thresholds
Second generation Made-for-America MECTA JR/SR 2
259J/576mC; **222mC/111mC and *100J/50J*** BL/UL thresholds
Second generation Made-for-America Somatics Thymatron DG
252J/504mC; **200mC/100mC and *100J/50J*** BL/UL thresholds

Second generation Made-for-Europe MECTA JR/SR 1
230J/576mC; **250mC/125mC and 100J/50J** BL/UL thresholds
Second generation Made-for-Europe MECTA JR/SR 2
240J/600mC; **250mC/125mC and *100J/50J*** BL/UL thresholds
Second generation Made-for-Europe Somatics Thymatron DGx
226.8J/504mC;**222mC/111mC and *100J/50J*** BL/UL thresholds

Third generation MECTA JR/SR 1
460J/1152mC; **250mC/125mC** and ***100J/50J*** BL/UL thresholds
Third generation MECTA JR/SR 2
480J/1200mC; **250mC/125mC** and ***100J/50J*** BL/UL thresholds
Third generation Somatics' System IV
453.6J/1008mC; **222mC/111mC** and ***100J/50J*** BL/UL thresholds

Fourth generation MECTA JR/SR 1
922J/1152mC; **125mC/62.5mC** and ***100J/50J*** BL/UL thresholds
Fourth generation MECTA JR/SR 2
960J/1200mC; **125mC/62.5mC** and ***100J/50J*** BL/UL thresholds
Fourth generation Somatics' System V
907J/1008mC; **111mC/55.5mC** and ***100J/50J*** BL/UL thresholds

Fifth generation generic BP Device
1200J/1200mC; **100mC/50mC** and ***100J/50J*** BL/UL thresholds

Brief List Showing Visible Increases with EO vs Invisible Increases with Charge Alone; 3rd, 4th, 5th Gen Devices use same 1200mC maximum vs Increasing EO

Third generation MECTA JR/SR 2
480J/1200mC; **250mC/125mC** and ***100J/50J*** BL/UL thresholds
Fourth generation MECTA JR/SR 2
960J/1200mC; **125mC/62.5mC** and ***100J/50J*** BL/UL thresholds
Fifth generation generic BP Device
1200J/1200mC; **100mC/50mC** and ***100J/50J*** BL/UL thresholds

Brief Table Again Showing Visible Increases with EO
vs
Invisible Increases with Charge Alone

3rd, 4th, 5th Generation MECTA JR/SR 2

Generation	Min Charge Thresh. BL ECT	Min Charge Thresh. UL ECT	Min EO Thresh. BL ECT	Min EO Thresh. UL ECT	Overall Max Charge	Overall Max EO	MTTLOI BL ECT	MTTLOI UL ECT
3rd	*250mC*	*125mC*	100J	50J	**1200mC**	**480J**	**4.8**	**9.6**
4th	*125mC*	*62.5mC*	100J	50J	**1200mC**	**960J**	**9.6**	**19.2**
5th	*100mC*	*50mC*	100J	50J	**1200mC**	**1200J**	**12**	**24**

Because Charge Thresholds can diminish, dramatic power enhancements via Charge Reporting alone become invisible. Moreover, because the overall maximum Charges are identical, not only are the numbers devoid of meaning, but the machines also appear identical. No manufacturer reports MTTLOI.

Note on the table above how EO maximums (in Joules) and thus MTTLOIs dramatically increase from third to fourth to fifth generation MECTA JR/SR 2 BP devices, while due to decreasing Charge thresholds, Charge maximums remain identical. Manufacturers do not report MTTLOI.

CHAPTER 70

Summation 3rd, 4th, and 5th Gen. BP Devices under Weiner's De Facto Standard Cont'd

While initial threshold minimums in Joules (EO) remain relatively constant at 50J with UL "ECT" and 100J with BL "ECT," initial threshold minimums in terms of Charge may vary dramatically. As a result, power reported as Charge maximums may reflect neither enhancements in power nor increases in MTTLOI. In Weiner's reporting of maximum Charge outputs alone (sans EO in joules); therefore, due to decreases in Charge thresholds, increases in power and thus MTTLOI increases become invisible as is the case with MECTA 3rd, 4th, and 5th generation BP devices (see above). In short, based only on Charge maximums, increasing power outputs per generational device cannot be identified. In short, reports of Charge maximums without accompanying EO maximums in Joules, and even Charge outputs per age group without accompanying EO in Joules, may paint misleading machine profiles as is the case above. On the other hand, in that initial EO thresholds (in Joules) tend to remain constant, increases or decreases in power and thus MTTLOI with respect to each machine generation remain conspicuously visible. One need merely be aware of the 100J rule, that is, the simple trick of dividing a machine's overall maximum EO (in joules) by 100J to obtain the MTTLOI with BL "ECT" administered to all age categories and the overall maximum EO (in joules) by 50J to obtain the MTTLOI with UL "ECT" administered to all age categories with any particular Brief Pulse device. In conclusion, knowledge of the maximum EO (in Joules) divided by 100J, the minimum output needed to reach threshold in even the oldest and most seizure recalcitrant recipient, directly and consistently reflects machine profiles, that is, the increases or decreases in overall power and MTTLOI each particular machine administers to recipients. Charge maximums, on the other hand, may not reflect increases in power, much less MTTLOI. Indeed, Weiner's 1997 de facto standard totally eliminates EO (joules), instead, reporting machine power chiefly in terms of Charge, thereby, failing to reflect increases in power from third to fourth to fifth generation BP devices. As a result, critically dramatic increases regarding MTTLOI or Multifold Threshold Titration Level Output Intensities disappear from view. This is deliberate. Indeed, the simple process of easily identifying the specific BL (and UL) MTTLOI on any BP device for all age categories by dividing maximum overall EO (in Joules) by 100J (and 50J), has never been publicly or journalistically revealed by any manufacturer to date. MTTLOI has never been discussed. In view of the prodigious value and simplicity of such a critically important piece of information, the deliberate deletion of EO reporting under Weiner's 1997 standard suggests that manufacturers have opted to secret generational power increases of Brief Pulse devices. Manufacturers certainly realize that reporting overall maximum Charge and even Charge relative to age category without accompanying EO, fails to identify increases in power, much less MTTLOI regarding each modern Brief Pulse device. Indeed, Charge reporting without EO reporting not only renders power increases invisible; such reporting is entirely misleading. The failure to render overall power (and MTTLOI)--the most important and illuminating characteristics of any "ECT" device--is not just highly negligent, it is highly fraudulent.

In short, Weiner's untenable call for a 1200mC Charge maximum in order to accommodate a 4.0 MTTLOI with UL "ECT" at the beginning of a treatment course and a 2.0 MTTLOI with UL "ECT" at the end of a treatment course (even assuming a 100% rise in threshold) is not only ludicrous, but designedly deceitful. Plainly, reporting Charge alone without taking into account reductions in Charge thresholds is deceptive. Because manufacturers base these machines on constant initial seizure thresholds of 100J and 50J with BL and UL

"ECT" respectively, and because they can only be identified via overall EO maximums and multiples of threshold outputs via relative constants, only the reporting of EO in joules can reliably profile a particular Brief Pulse device. In sum, it is not maximum Charge or even Charge outputs at every age level which provide critical information and so must be reported for every so-called "ECT" device, but each machine's overall EO maximum (in joules) and so the machine's hidden MTTLOI which tells the story, parameters entirely expunged from Weiner's 1997 proviso standard. The author of this manuscript must conclude that via Weiner's stratagem, vitally important information is deliberately concealed from recipients.

SECTION XIII: Weiner's "Dose Sensitive," "Threshold Doubling" Contentions

CHAPTER 71

Questioning Weiner's 1997 Contentions

As already noted, Weiner justifies his 1997 standard thusly:

> While initial seizure thresholds with UL ECT are nearly always below 300mC, they often rise as much as 100% or more over the course of treatments, so that a limit of at least 1200mC is clearly necessary. (International Electrotechnical Commission, 1997, Dec 26, p. 5)

According to Weiner's logic, as indicated above, if UL maximally requires a 300mC initial (just above) threshold dosage to induce adequate seizures, and machines require enough power to accommodate a maximum 100% percent rise in UL threshold over a "treatment course" (2 x 300mC =) 600mC--and at least another 100% enhancement because "uniquely dose sensitive UL" must reach twice threshold even at the end of a treatment course to remain effective (2 x 600mC = 1200mC)--then Weiner's standard for BP devices indeed needs to reach a maximum Charge of (600mC + 600mC =) 1200mC, just as Weiner purports.

The author of this manuscript has, however, already shown that Weiner's 300mC figure for initial UL "ECT" is fallacious, that the initial maximum threshold output for UL ECT is much closer to 100mC than 300mC and, in fact, never exceeds 156mC for even first generation devices, never more than 125mC for second and third generation BP devices, and finally, drops to about 62.5 and 50mC for probable fourth and potential fifth generation BP devices respectively. Moreover, in that Charge thresholds vary, the author has shown that the reporting of Charge outputs alone is not only unreliable, but misleading. That initial threshold ceilings for UL "ECT" rarely rise above circa 100mC (particularly beginning with second generation BP devices), is confirmed by several studies.[161] For example, according to McCall et al. and even Sackeim et al., utilizing modern day BP devices [162] such as the Thymatron DG, just above seizure threshold outputs with UL "ECT" rarely require over about 100mC of Charge even for a 100 year old male (McCall, Reid, Rosenquist, Foreman, and Kiesow-Webb, 1993; Sackeim et al., 1993). Weiner, as has been thoroughly discussed, claims that initial threshold output for UL "ECT" can double by the end of a treatment course and that UL "ECT" requires twice threshold to be effective. Even so, if McCall et al. are correct regarding a 100mC maximum, even by Weiner's Charge quadrupling calculations for UL "ECT" efficacy, and even accommodating Weiner's purported 100% rise in threshold, the maximum Charge with UL "ECT" to remain effective need rarely surpass (2 x 100mC = 200mC; 2 = 200mC =) 400mC even for a 100 year old male--in any case, certainly not the (2 x 300mC = 600mC; 2 x

[161] These studies do not include fourth and fifth generation BP devices, the power potentials of which have never been known prior to this manuscript.

[162] All modern day BP devices are based on stronger bi-directional or alternating current in lieu of the unidirectional or direct current used for early BP devices.

600mC =) 1200mC Weiner alleges in his 1997 de facto standard based on a fallacious initial 300mC maximum Charge threshold with UL "ECT." [163]

Ironically, the less powerful the machine, the higher the initial seizure threshold with UL "ECT" tends to be; conversely, the more powerful the machine, the lower the initial seizure threshold with UL "ECT" tends to be. Moreover, even the least powerful true minimal stimulus MECTA "C" (no longer in use) containing what appears to be the highest initial seizure threshold with UL "ECT" (circa 156mC), under Weiner's 1997 paradigm, would require no more than (2 x 156mC = 312mC x 2 =) 624mC of initial Charge to meet Weiner's requirements, again, nowhere near the 1200mC Weiner purports. Regardless, as machines become even more powerful, the actual Charge threshold required to quadruple the output allegedly needed with UL "ECT" can diminish dramatically. Examining the more powerful clinically applied Brief Pulse devices such as second and third generation MECTA BP devices allowing an occasional 125mC initial minimum Charge threshold with UL "ECT," for instance, we find that in spite of what is actually Weiner's quadrupling paradigm, the overall maximum Charge required with UL (and BL) "ECT" even at the end of a "treatment" course need never exceed (2 x 125mC = 250mC x 2 =) 500mC.[164] This becomes even clearer by measuring EO (in joules). 100J, as has already been noted, is the minimum initial output required to elicit an adequate seizure (for all 100 year old recipients) even at the end of a "treatment" course not with UL, but with BL ECT on any modern day BP device, a fact confirmed by Weiner himself within the 1982 APA Standard (Department of Health and Human Services, 1982a, p. A53). Half this output or 50J is thus the minimum output required to elicit an adequate seizure (for all 100 year olds) even at the end of a "treatment" course with UL ECT on any modern day BP device. According to Weiner's own paradigm then, even doubling the (initial 50J threshold minimum) for so-called "dose sensitive UL "ECT," and then again for the purported threshold doubling of UL "ECT" over a "treatment series, no more than (UL: 4 x 50J =; BL: 2 x 100J =) 200J Joules (with either UL or BL "ECT") should be required to fulfill Weiner's criteria.

By 1997, the year Weiner introduced his new de facto "standard," both European and American-made second generation BP devices, as has been pointed out, had already been eliciting a maximum output of between 227 and 259 unreported joules (via the Mectan Transmutation of the 1982 APA standard) since about 1982. Though typically breached, even the 1989 IEC Standard, as we have seen, "permitted" (an unexplicated and unreported) 217 maximum joules for Brief Pulse machines both in the U.S. and abroad. By Weiner's own 1997 logic, therefore, if, instead of 300mC, the minimum initial seizure threshold needed to elicit an adequate seizure with UL ECT never exceeds 125mC (Beale et al., 1994) with second and even third generation MECTA BP devices, there is absolutely no justification for Weiner's 1997 call for 1200mC Charge. 1200mC Is simply not needed to fulfill Weiner's alleged criteria of doubling threshold output with UL "ECT" at the end of a "treatment" course or maintaining just above threshold with BL "ECT" even at the end of a "treatment" course.[165] In short, second generation BP devices, which by 1997, had been manufactured and utilized for about fifteen years as we have noted, already emitted up to 259 maximum joules (in the U.S.) and did so with never more than 600mC of Charge. Unfortunately, while manufacturers report maximum Charge for second generation BP devices, they do not report maximum EO in joules. (The 259J figure was introduced by the author of this manuscript.) As a result, even up to 1997, instead of the circa 500-600mC/200-260J Charge to EO equivalency second generation BP devices actually emit, manufacturers, had managed to engender a false 500-600mC/100J Charge to EO equivalency indicative not of second, but of first generation BP devices as we have seen (falsely substantiated by circa 100J readout maximums on all MECTA and Somatics second generation BP devices). In brief, as has been noted, the first doubling of power and correspondent doubling of MTTLOI for all age categories with what were actually second generation BP devices beginning as early as 1982, were never reported. In fact, led by Weiner, the 1982 enhancement was entirely suppressed both by numerous spurious reporting and interpretation stratagems and by both major companies depicting circa 100J maximum machine readouts on what were actually their second generation BP devices. Consequently, Weiner's 1997 de facto standard calling for a doubling of Brief Pulse power from between 5-600mC to 1200mC of Charge, as has been observed, was presented as a first time enhancement from what appeared to be circa 100 maximum

[163] A maximum 400mC based on these studies also works for BL "ECT."

[164] The figures are based on MECTA second and third generation IEC BP devices.

[165] Indeed, if Weiner's original promise to the FDA within his 1982 APA Standard is true, that never more than 100J is required with BL "ECT," the same must hold true with UL "ECT," that is, no more than 100J is ever required to double the threshold output with UL "ECT" even at the end of a "treatment" course (Department of Health and Human Services, 1982a, p. A53).

Joules to what would logically seem to be just over 200 Joules (equal to the maximum output of SW).[166] [167] Moreover, in that EO reporting (in joules) was conveniently expunged from Weiner's de facto standard, neither the true power of second generation BP devices nor the quadrupled power of what were actually third generation BP devices, were ever reported at all. In turn, due to near identical Charge maximums, the increasing power of what are actually third, fourth, and fifth generation BP devices has never been reported--until now. In short, both increases and actual outputs from third to potential fifth generation BP devices have never been revealed until now.

Second generation made-for-America and made-for Europe MECTA and Somatics BP devices manufactured between 1982-1994, as we have seen, do, in fact, elicit between 5-600mC of Charge. For example, a maximum 504mC charge is the set dosage for a 100 year old male on the Somatics Thymatron DG, "Just Set To Age and Treat," dial. The correspondent unreported EO as has been seen in this manuscript, is a 252 Joule maximum (reported for the first time by the author), meaning an initial 2.52 MTTLOI with BL "ECT" and thus an initial 5.04 MTTLOI with UL "ECT" at all age levels. This clearly means that with the second generation Thymatron DG Brief Pulse device, the initial minimum Charge threshold with BL "ECT" is (504mC ÷ 2.52 =) 200mC and (the initial minimum Charge threshold with UL "ECT," (504mC ÷ 5.04 =) 100mC--not the 300mC Weiner purports. Similarly, second generation made-for-America MECTA BP devices emit a 576mC Charge maximum (Abrams and Swartz, 1988, back cover; Somatics Incorporated, 1993a; Swartz and Abrams, 1996, back cover; see also Thymatron DG charts in this manuscript), with a correspondent EO maximum of about 259 Joules (reported by the author). This means, as also noted earlier, that the second generation made-for-America MECTA Brief Pulse devices emit an initial 2.59 fold threshold output with BL "ECT" and thus an initial 5.18 fold threshold output with UL "ECT" at all age levels. This, in turn, signifies an initial minimum Charge threshold with BL "ECT" of (576mC ÷ 2.59 =) 222mC and an initial minimum Charge threshold with UL "ECT" of (576mC ÷ 5.18 =) 111mC--again not the 300mC asserted by Weiner. These figures agree with Beale's 1994 findings of what we now know to be second generation made-for-America BP devices, for which he found (what this author has termed) an initial MTTLOI of about 2.5 with BL "ECT" and by extrapolation, an initial MTTLOI of about 5.0 with UL "ECT"-- for every age group--already satisfying Weiner's criteria for increased output.[168] Moreover, this is true not only in terms of Charge (in which Beale et al. reported) as we have seen, but in terms of EO as well.[169] Thus, even conceding Weiner's purported 100% rise in threshold over a "treatment" course, we, once again, find that at the time of Weiner's 1997 call for a 1200mC maximum to deliver a 4.0 MTTLOI with UL "ECT" at the beginning of a "treatment" course and so a 2.0 MTTLOI with UL "ECT" at the end of a "treatment" course, what were actually second generation BP devices had already fulfilled these Weinerian criteria, delivering a circa <u>5.0</u> fold initial threshold output with UL "ECT" and a circa <u>2.5</u> fold threshold output with UL "ECT" (if not more) even at the end of a "treatment" course.[170] Moreover, this was accomplished, which

---

[166] In fact, as we have seen, Weiner's standard allows for up to 1200 maximum Joules.

[167] The Mectan transmutation was never reported while the 1989 IEC standard engendered the ongoing illusion of circa 100 maximum joules. The former reported circa "100J at 220Ω," the latter "100J at 300Ω." Second generation MECTA and Somatics devices actually depicted circa 100 maximum Joules on machine readouts.

[168] The concept of MTTLOI has been coined by the author in order to explain the character of the various BP devices.

[169] The main machine tested was probably the made-for-America MECTA JR/SR 2. For a 100 year old man, the machine emits a [576mC ÷ 111mC (threshold for UL ECT)] = 5.18 fold threshold initially for UL placement and a [576mC ÷ 222mC (for BL ECT initially)] = 2.59 fold threshold initially for BL placement. In terms of EO, the machine's maximum of 259 Joules [÷ 50J (threshold for UL ECT)] = <u>5.18</u> fold threshold initially for UL ECT and [259 Joules ÷ 100J (threshold for BL ECT)] = <u>2.59</u> fold threshold initially for BL ECT. The initial MTTLOI levels are true for all age categories. Thus Beale's indication of 5.0 fold threshold for UL ECT and actual 2.5 fold threshold for BL ECT agree with McCall et al., (1993) and Sackeim et al. (1993).

[170] The Thymatron DG has a 100mC Charge threshold with UL ECT and a 200mC Charge threshold with BL ECT (see above sections), delivering a 504mC Charge maximum. Thus for UL ECT, the DG delivers a (504mC ÷ 100mC =) <u>5.04</u> fold threshold output initially and at least a (5.04 ÷ 2 =) 2.52 fold threshold output even at the end of treatment course. For BL ECT, the DG delivers a (504mC ÷ 200mC =) <u>2.52</u> fold threshold output initially and thus a (2.52 ÷ 2 =) 1.26 fold threshold output with BL ECT even at the end of treatment course. In terms of EO, 100mC is tantamount to a 50J initial minimum threshold output with UL ECT while 200mC is tantamount to a 100J initial minimum threshold output with BL ECT (EO = Charge x Current x Impedance: .100C x .9A x 555.5Ω = <u>50J</u>; .222 x .9 x 555.5 = <u>100J</u>; see Somatics charts) for the 100 year old recipient. Using joules, we obtain the same (252J ÷ 50J =) 5.04 threshold output intensity initially with UL ECT and 2.52 fold threshold output intensity even at the end of treatment course. Using joules with BL ECT, we obtain the same (252J ÷ 100J) = 2.52 fold threshold output intensity initially and 1.26 fold threshold output intensity even at the end of treatment course. MECTA made-for-America second generation devices deliver 575-6mC Charge. Initial minimum thresholds are 111mC with UL initially and 222mC with BL threshold initially which in joules is circa 50J with UL

bears repeating, with never more than 600mC of Charge. Weiner's call for 1200mC to deliver a "new" enhanced 4-2 MTTLOI with UL "ECT" is double the amount needed. Indeed, it is spurious, disingenuous, and fraudulent, the overwhelming evidence of which emphasizes the latter. Plainly, the evidence indicates that what Weiner and the manufacturers were really doing via Weiner's call for a new 1200mC Charge maximum was to both "authorize" and cover up already extant third generation BP devices by this time delivering up to a 9.6 MTTLOI with UL "ECT" at the beginning of a "treatment" course and up to at least at least a 4.8 MTTLOI with UL "ECT" even at the end of a "treatment" course." (The deletion of EO reporting played a major factor in hiding the degree of power these devices utilized.) But why were manufacturers using outputs far beyond that required to induce adequate seizures with BL "ECT, and far beyond that required to double the output with UL "ECT" even at the end of a "treatment" course? Moreover, why did they feel compelled to hide the suprathreshold amounts of electricity already extant third generation Brief Pulse machines actually deliver? Indeed, why have manufacturers hidden the presence and potential existence of third, fourth, and fifth generation BP devices and that they dramatically increase in power with each new Brief Pulse generation?

Weiner's Contentions Concluded Cont'd

In brief, with the possible exception of the first generation MECTA "C" BP device (which may have an initial minimum Charge threshold of 156mC with UL "ECT"), initial minimum seizure threshold with "dose sensitive" ***UL ECT*** never rises above 150mC on any modern day MECTA or Somatics BP device (see minimum machine thresholds above), never the initial 300mC Charge threshold implied in Weiner's explanation of his 1997 de facto standard.[171] Weiner claims, of course, that initial seizure thresholds with UL ECT are nearly always below 300mC. In fact, as the author has shown, initial seizure thresholds with UL ECT are nearly always below circa 150mC. In effect, 156mC has been the greatest initial Charge threshold attained with UL "ECT" amongst all generations of modern BP devices since at least 1978. In sum, even if we accept Weiner's contention that a 2.0 fold threshold output is required with UL "ECT" efficacy and even if we accept an additional 100% rise in threshold over a "treatment course," no modern day Brief Pulse device requires, as we have seen, more than a circa (4 x 150mC =) 600mC Charge to accommodate these Weinerian contingencies, indeed, contingencies met as early as 1982 with all second generation BP devices. Certainly, the (4 x 300mC =) 1200mC maximum Charge output Weiner calls for in his 1997 proviso standard is totally unnecessary to meet the Weinerian contingencies.[172] Tangentially, with the possible exception of the first generation MECTA "C" BP device (which

---

ECT initially (259J ÷ 5.18 = 50J) and 100J with BL ECT initially (259J ÷ 2.59 = 100J). To confirm, we can convert Charge to EO: EO = Charge x Current x Impedance (.111C x .8A x 562.5Ω =) to obtain <u>49.95J</u> with UL ECT and (.222C x .8A x 562.5Ω =) <u>99.99J</u> with BL ECT initially (see MECTA charts); This is a (259J ÷ 50J =) <u>5.189</u> fold threshold output initially with UL ECT and (259J÷ 1000J =) <u>2.59</u> fold threshold output initially with BL ECT which is a 2.59 fold threshold output with UL ECT and 1.295 fold threshold output with BL ECT even at the end of a treatment course. The dynamics of third, fourth, and fifth generation BP devices change via doubling Voltage and Amperage, but halving Pulse Width of the previous BP generation so that threshold outputs are sequentially reduced at which point Threshold output in Joules, though constant, no longer correspond to Threshold output in Charge. Manufacturers apply this formula to hide the dramatic increases in power from third, to fourth, to fifth generation BP devices. Indeed, without EO, the three devices appear comparable.

171 Even the MECTA "C" might not require more than 150mC with UL ECT in that while 100J and 50J are relative constants, these figures may vary slightly. For example, because the MECTA "C" is closer to minimal stimulus, at least with BL placement, the MECTA "C" could contain initial thresholds slightly lower than 50 and 100J for UL and BL ECT respectively. In lieu of 50J and 100J, for example, thresholds might be 45J and 90J, leaving initial Charge thresholds below 150 and 300mC respectively. To illustrate, the MECTA "C" emits 108 maximum joules at a maximum Charge of about 337.5mC and a 400Ω maximum Impedance. This means that instead of a 2.16 and 1.08 initial MTTLOI with UL and BL ECT respectively, the machine might emit a 2.4 and 1.2 initial MTTLOI with UL and BL ECT respectively for all age categories: 108J ÷ 45J = initial <u>2.4 fold threshold with UL ECT</u>; 108J ÷ 90J = initial <u>1.2 fold threshold with BL ECT</u>. In this case, Charge thresholds, just as EO thresholds would decrease accordingly: .3375C ÷ 2.4 = <u>140.6mC for UL ECT</u>; 3375C ÷ 1.2 = <u>281.25mC for BL ECT</u>. To confirm: EO = Charge x Current x Impedance: .1406C x .8A x 400Ω = <u>45J</u>; .28125C x .8 x 400 = <u>90J</u>. In sum, with a slight variation such as an initial 45 and 90J minimum initial thresholds with UL and BL ECT respectively (in lieu of 50 and 100J), at the MECTA C's 108J and 337.5mC machine maximums, instead of 156mC and 312.5mC, initial minimum Charge thresholds could be 140.6mC with UL ECT and 281.25mC with BL ECT. In either case, Weiner's required 1200mC Charge maximum to quadruple the initial UL ECT Charge threshold is wholly spurious (4 x 140.6 = 562.4mC; 4 x 156.25mC = 625mC).

172 Even the MECTA "C" as is would require no more than 625mC (2 x 312.5mC = 625mC); 4 x 156.25mC = 625mC).

may have an initial minimum Charge threshold of 312.5mC with BL "ECT"), initial minimum seizure threshold for "non-dose sensitive" ***BL "ECT"*** never rises above 250mC on any modern-day MECTA or Somatics BP device. (See above.) Indeed, BL "ECT" never requires the 600mC initial Charge threshold Weiner implies in his 1997 de facto "standard." In a nutshell, even if we accept Weiner's 100% rise in threshold and so twice the initial Charge needed in order to remain above threshold at the end of a “treatment course,” no MECTA or Somatics BP device from 1982 forward, ever requires more than a (2 x 250mC =) 500mC Charge maximum to deliver a 2.0 fold threshold output at the beginning of a “treatment course” with ***BL "ECT"*** and thus at least a 1.1 fold threshold output with ***BL "ECT"*** at the end of a “treatment course.” [The same (4 x 125mC =) 500mC maximum is true with UL "ECT."] In no case, then, does an initial 2.0 fold threshold Charge output with BL "ECT" require the 1200mC maximum Charge (2 x 600mC = 1200mC) Weiner purports necessary. In fact, all second generation MECTA and Somatics BP devices emit default outputs greater than an initial 2.0 fold threshold Charge output with BL "ECT" and so greater than an initial 4.0 fold threshold Charge output with UL "ECT." Certainly, Beale showed in 1994, that what were actually second generation made-for-America BP devices deliver circa 2.5 fold initial threshold outputs with ***BL "ECT"*** at the beginning of a “treatment course” (Beale et al. 1994) and so at least a 1.25 fold threshold output with ***BL "ECT"*** even at the end of a "treatment." Moreover, second generation BP devices do so without ever exceeding a 600mC Charge. Even conceding a 100% rise in threshold over a "treatment" course then, the excessive 1200mC Charge output Weiner calls for in his 1997 de facto standard is actually enough to deliver a minimum (1200mC ÷ 250mC =) 4.8 MTTLOI with ***BL "ECT"*** at the beginning of a “treatment" course and so at least a (1200mC ÷ 500mC =) 2.4 MTTLOI with ***BL "ECT"*** even at the end of a "treatment" course. Additionally, these excessive MTTLOIs can be accomplished without the increase in Amperage "useable" under Weiner's 1200mC de facto "standard." Not coincidentally, by 1997, the year Weiner's "standard" becomes the new rogue "benchmark," as we have witnessed, illegal third generation BP devices had already been marketed and utilized since 1995. In effect, the 1008 to 1200mC maximum Charge outputs which third generation BP devices actually deliver, emitting new default MTTLOIs with ***BL "ECT"*** of between 4.52 (see Somatics System IV) and 4.8 (See MECTA's third generation JR/SR 2) at the beginning of a “treatment" course and so a minimum 2.26 to 2.4 MTTLOI with ***BL "ECT"*** even at the end of a “treatment" course for every age recipient, as previously noted, had been in force for at least two years. Amazingly, of course, this means that the same instruments were delivering ***UL "ECT"*** at a 9.04 to 9.6 MTTLOI at the beginning of a “treatment" course and a minimum 4.52 to 4.8 with ***UL "ECT"*** even at the end of a “treatment" course for every age recipient. Weiner must have known that all second generation MECTA and Somatics devices already easily surpassed the 2.0 MTTLOI with ***BL "ECT"*** "required" at the beginning of a “treatment course” and so at least a 1.1 MTTLOI with ***BL "ECT"*** "required at the end of a “treatment course” as well as at least a 4.0 MTTLOI with ***UL "ECT"*** at the beginning of a “treatment course” and so at least a 2.0 MTTLOI with ***UL "ECT"*** at the end of a “treatment course” and had been doing so for many years with no more than 600mC of Charge. Once again, Weiner's chief goal in demanding Brief Pulse machines of up to 1200mC Charge was in order to “authorize” the already extant third generation BP devices emitting default outputs twice the EO Weiner claims Brief Pulse devices needed to meet the Weinerian contingencies. Clearly, Weiner wanted a 1200mC" standard to "legalize" third generation devices already utilizing up to 1200mC of Charge and to make room for even more powerful devices of the future. (See the third generation MECTA JR/SR 2 above.) This could not be known by regulators, however, in that (1) neither manufacturers nor Weiner’s de facto standard any longer reported EO in joules, and in that (2) threshold outputs in terms of Charge deteriorate from third to fourth to fifth generation BP devices. As a result, while machines become more and more powerful, Charge maximums remain almost identical. In terms of Charge reporting alone (in lieu of EO in joules), therefore, neither excesses nor the increasing outputs emitted by third, fourth, and fifth generation BP devices, manifest themselves. In truth, extant third, probable fourth, and hypothetical fifth generation BP devices, as a result of Weiner’s 1997 de facto standard, have remained completely unknown--until this moment.

Conversion to EO in Joules

While it is possible to reveal the character of various Brief Pulse devices through Charge, as we have seen, the process is a complex one, as we have clearly witnessed. In order to make these excesses more easily manifest, as we have heretofore learned, Charge must be converted to Joules, after which, the generationally increasing power of these devices suddenly materializes. As we have noted, a 100J minimum for BL ECT threshold output and a 50J minimum with UL ECT threshold output are relative constants. In short, no MECTA or Somatics BP device requires more than an initial 50 minimum Joules to induce an adequate seizure with ***UL "ECT"*** for even the oldest of recipients and no MECTA or Somatics BP device requires more than an initial 100 minimum Joules to induce an adequate seizure with ***BL "ECT"*** for even the oldest of recipients. In Weiner's own words to the FDA in 1992, before FDA granted permission for the ongoing use of "ECT," Weiner critically asserted:

> Using a pulse device, the [1978 APA] Task Force has determined that only 0.6% of seizure thresholds were greater than 70 [actual] Joules and that none were greater than 100 [actual] Joules. (Department of Health and Human Services, 1982a, p. A53)

Consequently, even conceding Weiner's later 2.0 fold threshold requirement for "dose-sensitive" ***UL "ECT"*** efficacy at the end of a "treatment course" and even conceding Weiner's later alleged 100% rise in threshold over a "treatment course," once again, no more than (4 x 50J =) 200J should ever be required to accommodate these Weinerian "requisites" for even the oldest of recipients using either UL or BL "ECT." Importantly then, all second generation MECTA and Somatics BP devices can generate at least 200J, a fact hidden until this manuscript. Indeed, at the time of Weiner's 1997 demand for 1200mC Charge, as we have seen, some made-for-America second generation BP devices, could deliver unreported outputs of up to 259J, or up to an initial (259J ÷ 50J =) 5.18 MTTLOI for all recipients administered ***UL "ECT"*** and up to an initial (259J ÷ 100J =) 2.59 MTTLOI for all recipients administered ***BL "ECT."*** In short, some second generation BP devices were already delivering at least a (5.18 ÷ 2 =) 2.59 MTTLOI with UL "ECT" at the end of a treatment course and at least a (2.59 ÷ 2 =) 1.3 MTTLOI with BL ECT even at the end a of a "treatment" course, more than accommodating a 100% rise in threshold, thereby already satisfying the 1997 Weinerian criteria.[173] Clearly, Weiner's 1997 proviso demanding 1200mC of Charge to deliver a 4.0 MTTLOI with UL "ECT" at the beginning of a treatment course and a 2.0 MTTLOI with UL "ECT" at the end of a treatment course and a 2 MTTLOI with BL "ECT" at the beginning of a treatment course and a 1.1 MTTLOI with BL "ECT" at the end of a treatment course is excessive. A standard allowing 1200mC only became necessary to "legalize" unknown and undeclared third, fourth, and fifth generation BP devices, all clearly ENR devices, based on adequate electricity for both UL and BL placement.

Three Falsehoods Behind Weiner's 1997 "Standard" for "ECT"

As noted above, then, Weiner's 1997 assertion that 300mC is the initial threshold output minimum required with ***UL "ECT"*** for the 100 year old recipient--is spurious. Such an assertion, moreover, props up the equally false notion that 600mC is the initial threshold output minimum required [for the same 100 year old recipient] with ***BL "ECT."*** Nevertheless, it is these falsehoods in conjunction with Weiner's subsequent assertion that "seizure thresholds rise 100% over a 'treatment' course," that "justify" Weiner's claim of 1200mC needed to make the "ECT" procedure effective (UL: 4 x 300mC = 1200mC; BL: 2 x 600mC = 1200mC).

---

[173] The second generation Thymatron DG delivers a maximum 252J EO and a maximum 504mC Charge for a 100 year old male, which is 2.52 fold threshold in EO and Charge (Beale et al, 1994) for BL ECT (504mC ÷ 2.52 = 200mC threshold). For the 100 year old male, the Thymatron DG must overcome 555.5Ω with .9A constant current (see Thymatron DG chart in "How Manufacturers Figure EO"). Using minimum threshold Charge (200mC) and the formula EO = Charge x Current x Impedance, EO = (.200C x .9A x 555.5Ω =) 100J threshold minimum with BL "ECT" and (100C x .9A x 555.5Ω =) 50J threshold minimum with UL ECT. Since 252J is administered at 504mC on the Thymatron DG, EO is also administered at a 2.52 MTTLOI (252J ÷ 100J = 2.52) with BL "ECT: and 5.04 MTTLOI with UL "ECT" for all age recipients. Second generation MECTA devices deliver 576mC or 259.2J for the 100 year old male, a 2.59 fold threshold in Charge and EO (Joules) with BL ECT and 5.18 fold threshold with UL ECT. Confirmation: BL Threshold: 576mC ÷ 2.59 = 222mC threshold. EO = .222C x .8A x 562.5Ω = **100J**; UL Threshold: 50J for UL ECT; 576mC ÷ 5.18 = 111mC threshold. EO = 111C x .8A x 562.5Ω = **50J**).

There are, in effect, three Weinerian falsehoods regarding UL "ECT." The first is that 1) "the initial minimum threshold required with UL ECT is 300mC." The second is that 2) "UL ECT is 'dose sensitive' requiring twice threshold output to be effective." The third is that 3) "threshold often rises 100% over a treatment course."

Only by combining all three falsehoods can Weiner claim machines must emit up to 1200mC Charge with UL "ECT" to remain "effective" at the end of a "treatment" course.

There are also three falsehoods regarding BL "ECT." The first is that 1) "the initial minimum threshold required with BL 'ECT' for the 100 year old recipient is 600mC." [174] The second is that 2) "BL 'ECT' is 'non-dose sensitive' and so effective at just above threshold." The third is that 3) threshold often rises 100% over a 'treatment' course."

Only by combining all three falsehoods can Weiner claim Brief Pulse machines must emit up to 1200mC of Charge with BL "ECT" to remain "above threshold" at the end of a "treatment" course.

The First Falsehood Behind Weiner's 1997 "Standard" for "ECT"--False Initial Threshold Minimums of 300mC and 600mC with UL and BL "ECT" Respectively

In contrast to Weiner's assertion and as heretofore noted, the minimum initial threshold output required for even the oldest recipient never exceeds 125mC with ***UL "ECT"*** on any second, third, fourth, or fifth generation BP device, just as the minimum initial threshold output required for even the oldest recipient with ***BL "ECT"*** never exceeds 250mC on any second, third, fourth, or fifth generation BP device.[175]

For example, the third generation MECTA JR/SR 2 BP device, which does, in fact, reach Weiner's 1200mC maximum Charge stipulation, utilizes the greatest initial minimum seizure threshold output with ***UL*** and ***BL "ECT"*** (of 125mC and 250mC respectively) of any MECTA or Somatics device reaching 200 or more joules. In short, while the third generation MECTA JR/SR 2 BP device educes the 1200mC Charge Weiner calls for, the initial minimum seizure threshold required with UL "ECT" on this device is still only 125mC and the initial minimum seizure threshold required with BL "ECT" on this device is still only 250mC--not Weiner's declared and implied initial 300mC with UL "ECT" and initial 600mC with BL "ECT." In sum, all three Weiner criteria [176] can be fulfilled with a maximum Charge output of only (4 x 125mC =; 2 x 250mC =) 500mC in lieu of the 1200mC Weiner calls for in his 1997 proviso. Indeed, the maximum 1200mC Charge that the third generation MECTA JR/SR 2 BP actually evinces, delivers a default (1200mC ÷ 125mC =; 480J ÷ 50J =) 9.6 MTTLOI with ***UL "ECT"*** at the beginning of a treatment course and at least a (9.6 ÷ 2 =) 4.8 MTTLOI with ***UL "ECT"*** even at the end of a treatment course for all age recipients even conceding the alleged 100% rise in threshold. Similarly, the same 1200mC maximum Charge delivers a default (1200mC ÷ 250mC =; 480J ÷100J =) 4.8 MTTLOI with ***BL "ECT"*** at the beginning of a treatment course and at least a (4.8 ÷ 2 =) 2.4 MTTLOI with ***BL "ECT"*** even at the end of a treatment course for all age recipients even conceding Weiner's alleged 100% rise in threshold. Moreover, as we have seen, the third generation MECTA JR/SR 2 BP device had been delivering these MTTLOIs since at least 1995, at least two years before Weiner's 1997 de facto standard "newly" calling for the 1200mC Charge maximum the third generation MECTA JR/SR 2 actually evinces. Clearly, Weiner's proposal was not designed to allow a "new" second generation BP device to double the power of first generation BP devices in order to deliver an initial minimum 4.0 MTTLOI with UL "ECT" and an initial minimum 2.0 MTTLOI with BL "ECT" in that the second generation BP device had already been in existence for some fifteen years at the time of Weiner's demand and, in fact, had been more or less "legal" under the 1989 IEC Standard. Rather,

---

[174] Right away, we can see that Weiner has replaced his original claim of a 100J maximum with a less familiar, more indirectly expressed 1200mC maximum to induce an adequate seizure with BL and an effective seizure with UL "ECT" at the end of a "treatment" course. The MECTA "C" used a circa 328mC maximum to induce an adequate seizure in even the oldest most seizure recalcitrant recipient with either BL or UL "ECT" with but a 108J maximum. In short, Weiner has gone from about a 300mC maximum to a 1200mC maximum.

[175] Ironically, minimum initial threshold, that is, initial threshold for the 100 year old recipient on the first generation MECTA "C," possibly surpass, albeit slightly, 125mC and 250mC respectively with UL and BL ECT. This is irrelevant, however, in that the moment the "C" circa doubles in power to reach the status of a "second generation BP device," machine dynamics have altered. Initial minimum threshold no longer exceeds 125 and 250mC respectively.

[176] A) 2 x threshold for "dose-sensitive" UL ECT; B) 2 x threshold for UL ECT to compensate for doubling threshold by the end of a "treatment course;" C) 2 x threshold for "non-dose-sensitive" BL ECT to compensate for doubling threshold by the end of a "treatment course."

Weiner's clear intention, as we have noted, was to legalize unreported already extant third generation BP devices such as the MECTA JR/SR 2 already surreptitiously delivering an initial 9.6 MTTLOI with UL "ECT" and an initial 4.8 MTTLOI with BL "ECT" for all age recipients, more than twice the MTTLOI Weiner claims necessary (4.0 times threshold with initial UL "ECT" and 2.0 times threshold with final UL "ECT"). As had been discussed, by calling for a 1200mC maximum Charge, as has been thoroughly discussed, Weiner is actually attempting to "legalize" already extant clinically applied third generation BP devices already delivering a default MTTLOI quadruple that of first generation BP devices. Moreover, Weiner was attempting to cover up suprathreshold outputs with UL and BL "ECT" both of which require well above threshold outputs to be "effective." In short, Weiner was covering up the supplanting of seizure-dependent devices with electro-dependent devices.

In that MECTA's and Somatics' second generation BP devices already delivered more than 200 Joules of EO at no more than 600mC Charge, that is, in that extant second generation devices already delivered more than an initial 2.0 MTTLOI with ***BL "ECT"*** at the beginning of a treatment course and well over threshold with ***BL "ECT"*** at the end of a treatment course even conceding a 100% rise in threshold, and more than an initial 4.0 MTTLOI with ***UL "ECT"*** at the beginning of a treatment course and well over a 2.0 MTTLOI with ***UL "ECT"*** even at the end of a treatment course even conceding a 100% rise in threshold--and did so with 600mC of Charge or less--Weiner's 1997 de facto standard requiring up to 1200mC of Charge is plainly ***unnecessary*** to fulfill the "standard's" demands. That is, 1200mC is at least twice that necessary to fulfill the Weinerian criteria meted out, as these criteria had already been met, as we have seen, by second generation BP devices years earlier. In short, as already noted, second generation BP devices emitting no more than 600mC maximums were already delivering the 4-2 MTTLOI Weiner calls for in his 1997 proviso. It was, as stated earlier, the false equivalency of 5-600mC with 100 Joules, false machine readouts of circa 100 maximum Joules, and misleading phrases within both the Mectan Transmutation and the 1989 IEC Standard suggesting 100 maximum joules for what were actually second generation MECTA and Somatics BP devices emitting more than 200 unreported joules that covertly "permitted" the manufacturing of second generation BP devices twice the power of first generation BP devices even while suggesting unchanged ceilings of circa 100 maximum joules. In sum, it was the false equivalency of 5-600mC with an illusory 100 maximum Joules together with false machine readouts "substantiating" the notion of circa 100 maximum Joules, and finally misleading American and IEC "standards" that aided in the ongoing illusion that what were actually second generation BP devices were still first generation Brief Pulse devices emitting minimal stimulus outputs at no more than circa 100 joules. Put another way, the veiling of the initial doubling of Brief Pulse device power (which had taken place about 1982) makes Weiner's 1997 proviso appear to be a first time call for doubling Brief Pulse power; whereas, the 1997 proviso was actually a second call to double, that is, to quadruple machine power (relative to first generation BP devices). In lieu of the initial 4.0 MTTLOI with UL "ECT" and initial 2.0 MTTLOI with BL "ECT" at the beginning of a treatment course which Weiner claims to be calling for with his 1997 de facto standard, Weiner's 1997 standard, as should now be clear, was actually an attempt to validate already extant third generation BP devices already emitting more than twice Weiner's called for MTTLOIs. Indeed, Weiner's new 1997 "standard' was actually an effort to sanction an initial circa 10.0 MTTLOI with UL "ECT" (and more) and sanction an initial circa 5.0 MTTLOI (and more) with BL "ECT" at the beginning of a treatment course. Weiner's 1997 call to sanction his "new" 1200mC Charge standard, was essentially a call to quadruple (and more than quadruple) the allowable 110J ceiling for Brief Pulse devices stipulated under the 1982 APA Standard for the purpose of "legalizing" already extant third generation BP devices. Moreover, it was an attempt to legalize ENR devices. Indeed, as we have seen, Weiner's 1997 de facto standard allows so much power, that in effect, it is a covert call for the total deregulation of "ECT" devices generally, making room not only for already extant third generation BP devices as noted, but for probable fourth and even fifth generation BP devices generating even higher EOs and even higher MTTLOIs as has been shown. [177] The 1997 de facto "standard" is, in essence, the covert "legalization" no longer of adequate convulsion "ECT" devices, but, as noted above, electro-dependent ENR devices. Because these devices are entirely disparate from "ECT" devices with an entirely different aim, Weiner and the

---

[177] Regarding raw EO, *third* generation BP devices enhance raw output up to 4.4 fold the EO of first generation BP devices. Future or actual *fourth* generation BP devices emit 8.8 fold the power of first generation BP devices and potential fifth generation BP devices emit more than 11 fold the power of first generation BP devices, all legal under Weiner's new standard. The MECTA JR/SR 2 third generation BP device delivers 480 maximum Joules, a potential or actual fourth generation JR/SR 2 delivers 960 maximum Joules, and a potential fifth generation BP device delivers up to 1200 Joules. 480J ÷ 108J = <u>4.44</u>; 960J ÷ 108J = <u>8.88</u>; 1200J ÷ 108J = <u>11.11</u>. (See charts above and below).

manufacturers must cover up their true power together with the fact that they are well above not only threshold, but well above the output required of the Weinerian contentions of "dose-sensitivity" and "doubling of threshold over a 'treatment' series."

The First Falsehood Behind Weiner's 1997 "Standard" for "ECT—Cont'd

Besides the mathematical proofs in this manuscript together with Beale 's (1994) study showing that what was actually a second generation BP device (manufactured as early as 1982) emitting an initial 2.5 MTTLOI with BL "ECT" and thus an initial 5.0 MTTLOI with UL "ECT," other published studies also confirm the excessive power of second generation BP devices. For example, one such study by Petrides' and Fink's is entitled "Half Age Stimulation Strategy" or "HASS." Indeed, both Max Fink, a well-known "ECT" advocate and author of numerous pro-"ECT" publications and his colleague Georgios Petrides, perhaps inadvertently confirm in their 1996 study "Half Age Stimulation Strategy" (Petrides and Fink, 1997) using the second generation Thymatron DGx, that the machine is set for default outputs of more than twice fold threshold with BL "ECT." The authors claim that, even after reducing the machine's default outputs by half or more, that adequate BL "ECT" seizures could yet be induced 98% of the time. Moreover, in that the study does not differentiate between initial seizures and seizures at the end of a "treatment" course (Petrides and Fink, 1997, p. 48), we must assume that this includes both initial and final "treatments." Succinctly then, these authors verify that the second generation DGx Brief Pulse device delivers more than an initial 2.0 MTTLOI with BL ECT for all age recipients and thus more than an initial 4.0 MTTLOI with UL ECT for all age recipients and that this was confirmed 98% of the time even at the end of a "treatment" course. While the study has been criticized as flawed by a number of Fink's colleagues and may well be so, we can nevertheless clearly conclude from "HAAS Strategy" that second generation BP devices such as the Thymatron DGx are pre-set to administer at least two fold threshold outputs with BL "ECT" for all age recipients. Because UL "ECT" requires only half the dosage of BL "ECT" to induce an adequate seizure, we can also conclude from the HASS Strategy (Petrides and Fink, 1997, p. 48) that second generation BP devices such as the Somatics DGx administer default outputs at least 4.0 times threshold with UL "ECT."

Thus, if between 500mC and 600mC (the maximum output of MECTA and Somatics second generation BP devices) accommodates at least an initial 4.0 MTTLOI with UL "ECT" for all age categories, the logical sequitur is that 1200mC should accommodate at least twice that MTTLOI, in short, at least an initial 8.0 MTTLOI with UL "ECT" and at least an initial 4.0 MTTLOI with BL "ECT" which is precisely what third generation BP devices emitting 1200mC actually do.[178] In essence, Weiner's call for 1200mC of Charge to legalize the already extant third generation BP devices with his 1997 "standard" is actually designed to double the power of never before reported second generation BP devices, that is, to double the 4-5 MTTLOI with UL "ECT" and 2- 2.5 MTTLOI with BL "ECT" already emitted by never fully reported second generation BP devices. Indeed, numerous studies affirm that second generation BP devices already emitted an initial default output of at least a 4.0 MTTLOI with UL "ECT" and an initial default output of at least a 2.0 MTTLOI with BL "ECT" with no more than 600mC overall Charge, and had been doing so for up to fifteen years before Weiner's 1997 call for 1200mC of Charge, "doubling" the power not of first generation BP devices, but of second generation BP devices. Plainly, Weiner's 1997 standard, rather than accommodating what seemed to be a call for "new" second generation BP devices able to emit an initial 4.0 MTTLOI with UL "ECT" for all age recipients and thus an initial 2.0 MTTLOI with BL "ECT" for all age recipients, was actually an attempt to accommodate already extant third generation BP devices, as noted, already using up to 1200mC of Charge to induce an initial 8.0 to 10.0 MTTLOI with UL "ECT" and an initial 4.0 to 5.0 MTTLOI with BL "ECT" for all age recipients, well over seizure threshold. Manufacturer spokesperson Richard Weiner (and consequently BP manufacturers as a whole) were plainly hiding several incriminating facts regarding Brief Pulse "ECT" machines, 1) that "dose-sensitive" as opposed to "non-dose sensitive" "ECT" is a fabrication, 2) that to achieve efficacy, super, suprathreshold electrical dosing is needed with both UL and BL "ECT," and 3) most critically of all, that modern BP machines are not designed to induce adequate seizures at all; rather, they are designed to induce adequate amounts of electricity regardless of which form of electrode placement is used.

---

[178] In fact, with the increased Amperage made usable by the 1997 Weiner standard, 1200mC is enough to double the MTTLOI again for fourth generation BP device, as we have seen.

The Second Falsehood Behind Weiner's 1997 "Standard" for "ECT"--so called "Dose Sensitivity"

The first falsehood within Weiner's 1997 "Standard" is that the minimum thresholds with UL and BL ECT are 300 and 600mC respectively. In fact, they are half that. Subsequently, the second falsehood within Weiner's 1997 Standard for "ECT," is the existence of so-called "dose-sensitivity." For "dose-sensitivity" to be a viable concept, at least one form of "ECT" must be effective at just above threshold. If neither form is effective at just above threshold, that is, effective with adequate seizure alone, "seizure theory" itself is no longer viable. Third generation 1200mC devices elicit initial unreported UL and BL MTTLOIs of at least 8.0 and 4.0 respectively. Thus even conceding a 100% rise in threshold, third generation BP devices elicit at least a 4.0 MTTLOI with UL "ECT" and at least a 2.0 MTTLOI with BL "ECT" not at the beginning, but at the end of a "treatment" course. If such machines emitting this much power for both forms of "ECT" are necessary for efficacy, that is, both require suprathreshold dosages of electricity to be effective, then either both UL and BL "ECT" are "dose-sensitive," or neither is "dose-sensitive." In other words, if both forms of "ECT" require multifold threshold outputs to be effective, that is, if neither form of "ECT" is effective at just above threshold, we can only deduce that so-called "adequate seizure" itself is ineffective. Subsequently, we must conclude that adequate amounts of electricity, not adequate seizure is the working mechanism behind "ECT." Stated another way, if both UL and BL "ECT" require multifold threshold output to be effective, the "ECT" procedure is not really seizure centric at all, but rather electro-centric. Indeed, the necessity of manufacturing third generation BP devices emitting multifold threshold outputs with both BL and UL "ECT" even at the end of a treatment series, indicates that neither "dose-sensitivity theory" nor "seizure theory" is viable. In fact, we are compelled to determine that the ubiquitous manufacturer practice of veiling both the power and thus the MTTLOI of what are actually second and third generation BP devices together with the ubiquitous manufacturer practice of promoting the totally false theory of so-called "dose-sensitivity" is intentionally designed to conceal the failure of "seizure theory" generally by suppressing the wholly electro-centric nature of so-called "ECT" itself. In short, Weiner and manufacturers are covering up the total supplanting of "ECT" with "ENR."

The Third Falsehood Behind Weiner's 1997 "Standard" for "ECT"--100% Rise in Threshold

Thus, the first falsehood within Weiner's 1997 "Standard is that 300mC and 600mC represent minimal threshold outputs for UL and BL "ECT" respectively. The second falsehood is that that "UL ECT" is "dose-sensitive" whereas "BL ECT" is "non-dose-sensitive." The third falsehood within Weiner's 1997 de facto "Standard" for "ECT" is Weiner's assertion of a 100% rise in threshold with UL and BL "ECT" by the end of a "treatment course." Several studies have shown that UL electrode placement rarely--if ever--results in more than a <u>40%</u> increase in threshold over a "treatment course" (Coffey, Lucke, Weiner, Krystal, and Aque,1995, p. 786; Sackeim, Decina, Prohovnik, and Malitz, 1987b, p. 358). This means, for instance, that on the second generation made-for-Europe JR/SR 1 (as well as the third generation JR/SR 1), the initial Charge threshold with UL "ECT" may increase from <u>125mC</u> to <u>175mC</u>, [179] ***not*** the (2 x 125mC =) <u>250mC</u> Weiner suggests based on a purported doubling of Impedance, in any case, certainly not the 300 to 600mC rise Weiner alleges. Thus, without any increase in power, second generation made-for-Europe MECTA BP devices manufactured from about 1984, are not only already pre-set to emit at least 4.6 times threshold initially with UL "ECT" in most instances, but assuming the more likely 40% maximum rise in threshold (denoted above), emit at least a circa (576mC ÷ 175mC =) 3.3 MTTLOI even at the end of a "treatment" course. [180] Consequently, second generation

---

[179] 125mC x .4 = 50mC. 125mC + 50mC = <u>175mC</u>.

[180] A 100 year old is automatically set to receive 504mC charge on Somatics' Thymatron DG dial setting (Abrams and Swartz, 1996, back cover). Beale et al. (1994) discovered that made-for-America second generation Somatics' and MECTA BP devices deliver at least 5.0 times threshold with UL initially, thus initial threshold with UL ECT on the Thymatron DG, for example, is (504mC ÷ 5.04 =) 100mC. Assuming a 40% rise in threshold (140mC), the 504mC is enough power to accommodate a (504mC ÷ 140mC =) 3.6 MTTLOI even at the end of the treatment course. Second generation made-for-America MECTA devices could deliver 576mC and require a 111mC minimum (50 Joules) for initial UL ECT threshold output for the 100 year old male or (576 ÷ 111 =) 5.189 times threshold. A 40% increase = (1.4 x 111 =) 155.4mC or (576mC ÷ 155.4mC) = a 3.7 fold MTTLOI even at the end of treatment course

made-for-Europe BP devices already typically delivered much more than the 2.0 MTTLOI at the end of a "treatment" course Weiner "required" of UL "ECT" in his 1997 de facto standard for "efficacy," machines which at the time of Weiner's call, as once again noted, had already been in existence for close to fifteen years. This means, as also previously noted, that third generation MECTA BP devices, already (albeit illegally) extant at the time of Weiner's suggested proviso, not only emit at least a 9.2 MTTLOI with UL "ECT" at the beginning of a "treatment" course, but most probably, at least a (1152mC ÷ 175mC = 6.82) 6.5 MTTLOI with UL "ECT" even at the end of a treatment course). The probable fourth generation MECTA JR/SR 1 BP device, suddenly "legal" under Weiner's 1997 proviso, emits, if manufactured, an (1152mC ÷ 62.5 =) 18.4 MTTLOI with UL "ECT" at the beginning of a "treatment" course and thus a 13.12 MTTLOI with UL "ECT" even at the end of a "treatment" course, far greater than Weiner's required 4.0 MTTLOI at the beginning of a "treatment" course and 2.0 MTTLOI at the end of a "treatment" course.[181] Potential fifth generation BP devices, also "legal" under Weiner's proviso, would utilize an even higher MTTLOI at the beginning and end of a "treatment" course, none of which has ever been reported.

In fact, if there's any validity to the "HAAS Strategy" (explained above), even after cutting default outputs in half on second generation BP devices and so approaching true threshold outputs, 98% of all BL ECT recipients continued to seize even at the end of a treatment course, again grossly countermanding the alleged 100% rise in threshold Weiner incorporates into his rationale calling for a what was actually a second doubling of Brief Pulse power, generally.

Still other studies suggest that it is BL electrode placement alone--not UL electrode placement--which occasionally results in an approximate 100% rise in threshold over a "treatment" course (Coffey et al.,1995, p. 786; Sackeim et al., 1987b, p. 358) and even when such a rise does occur, the maximum rise in threshold may be closer to 80 than 100%, and this for only a tiny fraction of recipients (Ibid, Ibid).[182] Moreover, the 80% rise appears to pertain only in the oldest age categories. For instance, a study (of which both Weiner and Coffey were a part) found that there was no increase in threshold for 65% of persons 21-39 years of age, no increase for 40% of persons between the ages of 40-49, no increase at all for 30% of persons between the ages of 50-59, no increase for over 40% of persons between the ages of 60-69, and no increase at all for 20% of persons between the ages of 70-89 (Coffey, Lucke, Weiner, Krystal, and Aque, 1995, p 783), findings that Fink's so-called HAAS Strategy seems to confirm. Indeed, there is every reason to believe that 100 Joules is a liberal figure so that even most 100 year old recipients seize at much less than 100J, even at the end of a "treatment" course.

> For pulse stimuli . . . less than 1% of seizure thresholds were greater than 60 Joules. . . .
> (Weiner, Department of Health and Human Services, 1982a, E20)
>
> Using a pulse device, the [APA] Task Force [1978] has determined that only 0.6% of seizure thresholds were greater than 70 Joules and that none were greater than 100 Joules.
> (Weiner, Department of Health and Human Services, 1982a, p. A53)

In sum, the original 108J MECTA "C" most likely seized all age recipients with both BL and UL "ECT" even at the end of a "treatment" series almost 100% of the time. Because adequate seizure alone induced by either BL or UL ECT produces no therapeutic effect, however, manufacturers secretly switched from ECT to ENR, that is, gradually supplanted adequate seizure oriented devices with adequate electricity oriented devices, machines never heretofore described to, submitted to, or condoned by FDA. Certainly, the American public,

---

with UL ECT. Somatics and MECTA third generation BP devices circa double the Multifold Threshold Titration Level Output Intensities of second generation devices at the end of a treatment course.

[181] 62.5 x .4 = 25mC + 62.5 = 87.5mC. 1152mC ÷ 87.5mC = 13.12 fold.

[182] In many instances, no threshold increase occurs at all. There is no increase in threshold for 65% of persons 21-39 years of age, no increase for 40% of persons between the ages of 40-49, no increase at all for 30% of persons between the ages of 50-59, no increase for over 40% of persons between the ages of 60-69 and no increase at all for 20% of persons between the ages of 70-89 (Coffey, Lucke, Weiner, Krystal, and Aque, 1995, p. 783). In accordance with the figures above, it should be pointed out that percentages of increasing threshold over a "treatment course" do increase with increasing stimulus albeit rarely above 69J and never more than 100J. Even so, it is chiefly the practice of suprathreshold dosing itself, paradoxically, which increases Impedance making higher dosing necessary initially.

much less recipients, have never been apprised of what these new devices actually are, how they work, or the injurious effect they have on the brain. Indeed, recipients and physicians alike have been misled into believing that modern day Brief Pulse devices utilize the least amount of electricity possible to induce so-called adequate seizures alone.

Caffeine and Pentylenetetrazol Abandoned

Finally, numerous researchers maintain that both caffeine and pentylenetetrazol have been used effectively to reduce seizure threshold and so maintain threshold consistency throughout the "treatment course" (Abrams, 1992, p. 170; Coffey, Figiel, Weiner, and Saunders, 1990b; Coffey, Weiner, Hinkle, Cress, Daughtry, and Wilson, 1987b). While it might be argued that caffeine can increase the danger of heart palpitations,[183] especially in older persons, according to Somatics owner, psychiatrist Richard Abrams in his book, *Electroconvulsive therapy*, the drug pentylenetetrazol (with no other known medical application other than lowering seizure threshold), is generally recognized as a safe compound, the application of which appears to maintain threshold consistency without side-effects (Abrams, 1992, p. 170). In short, the use of pentylenetetrazol seems to guarantee consistently lower thresholds, eliminating the need for higher outputs to achieve adequate seizure. But pentylenetetrazol has evidently been discontinued due to low demand. So, if the least amount of electricity is truly the goal, why would manufacturers permit pentylenetetrazol to go off the market seemingly without protest and why is there so little demand for it? Certainly, if threshold could be maintained with pentylenetetrazol throughout a treatment course, BL ECT could be delivered at just above threshold without the need for doubling initial output at all, while so-called "dose-sensitive" UL ECT could easily be administered and maintained at the supposedly required 2.0 (rather than 4.0 MTTLOI) at both the beginning and end of a treatment course. Can the lack of interest in pentylenetetrazol be due to the guarded fact that, in truth, convulsion has no relation to efficacy at all, but that efficacy is related to electrical dosing alone? Has the original goal of the most minimal electrical output possible to induce so-called adequate seizures with Brief Pulse totally given way to the now "legal" manufacturing of extraordinarily powerful devices emitting necessarily higher and higher electrical dosages in order to achieve efficacy? Can the lack of interest in pentylenetetrazol be that the much publicized objective of minimal stimulus dosing associated with the Brief Pulse device--is a secretly defunct one? [184]

---

[183] The amount of caffeine required to maintain consistency throughout the "treatment" course is tantamount to only one or two cups of coffee (Coffey, Figiel, Weiner, and Saunders, 1990b; Coffey, Weiner Hinkle, Cress, Daughtry, and Wilson, 1987b).

[184] Though researchers actually developed successful methods of maintaining seizure threshold throughout a "treatment course," it is a moot accomplishment in that minimal stimulus (to induce "adequate" seizures) is hazily known to be ineffective (Sackeim, 1991, p. 233-234). In fact, some researchers see a steep rise in seizure threshold as desirable - a "positive indicator of positive clinical outcome" (Sackeim et al., 1987a, p. 260). Consequently, it is an often used, but misleading argument that increased electrical dosing is necessary solely due to rises in seizure threshold. In short, while rises are preventable, there is no longer any real effort to do so. This is because, in fact, multifold electrical dosing is the necessary factor in achieving efficacy, that is, it is the electricity, not the seizure, which makes the procedure "work." In short, modern BP devices are no longer designed to induce adequate seizures; rather, they are knowingly designed to induce adequate amounts of electricity.

SECTION XIV: Winding Up Weiner

CHAPTER 72

More Proof Machines Already Met 1997 Call for More Power for 2 and 4 x Threshold

But even if we accepted Weiner's so-called "dose-sensitivity" of UL "ECT" and purported 100% rise in threshold over a "treatment course," because initial threshold output with UL "ECT" never exceeds 150mC and initial threshold output with BL "ECT" never exceeds 300mC on any MECTA or Somatics second generation BP device, all second generation MECTA and Somatics BP devices, as we have discussed, had already fulfilled Weiner's 1997 criteria "necessitating" augmentation of power. Indeed, machines based on Weiner's new 1997 power provisions, that is, what are actually third, fourth, and fifth generation devices are completely unneeded to satisfy the Weinerian criteria and this, as we have seen, can be mathematically confirmed. As already noted, Beale, in 1994, found that second generation made-for-America BP devices, capable of delivering maximum Charges of 504 and 576mC respectively, already induced initial (circa) 2.5 fold threshold outputs with BL "ECT" and thus initial circa 5.0 fold threshold outputs with UL "ECT," more than enough to induce adequate seizures with so called "non-dose sensitive BL "ECT" even at the end of a "treatment" series and more than enough to induce the twice threshold output allegedly "required" with so called "dose-sensitive UL "ECT" even at the end of a "treatment" series.[185] To confirm this, even assuming a 100% rise in threshold with both BL and UL "ECT," the **<u>MTTLOIs</u>** at the end of a treatment course with both forms of "ECT" in terms of Charge are provided below for the <u>100 year old recipient</u> on all second generation MECTA and Somatics' Brief Pulse devices. While Charge outputs are only approximate for all ages under 100, there is little doubt of the accuracy of the maximum Charge outputs administered to 100 year old recipients themselves. We can be certain from the evidence below, then, that output surpasses threshold with BL "ECT" and is more than twice threshold for "dose-sensitive" UL "ECT" even at the end of a "treatment" series on all second generation BP devices, the outputs of which have never been accurately reported until now.

<u>MTTLOI at end of a Treatment Course with 2nd Generation BP Devices for the 100 year old Adult</u>

<u>2nd Generation Made-for-America Thymatron DG</u> = (initial minimum Charge threshold with ***<u>UL ECT</u>*** =) **<u>100mC</u>** x 2 (due to 100% increase in threshold) = 200mC needed to seize at end of treatment.[186] Actual Charge emitted = 504mC ÷ 200mC = ***<u>2.52 x threshold</u>*** **<u>even at the end of treatment course with</u> *<u>UL ECT</u>***.

---

[185] Second generation made-for-America Thymatron DG: (504mC ÷ 200mC Charge =) initial <u>2.52 fold</u> with BL ECT and (504mC ÷ 100mC Charge) = initial <u>5.04 fold</u> with UL ECT; second generation made-for-America MECTA JR/SR 1@2: (575mC x 222mC =) initial <u>2.59 fold</u> with BL ECT and (575mC x 111mC =) initial <u>5.18 fold</u> with UL ECT.

[186] We multiply by 2.0 in lieu of 4.0 here to account only for the alleged 100% rise in threshold. Thus the 200mC emitted at the end of the treatment course which was enough to elicit a (504mC ÷ 100mC =) 5.04 fold initial UL ECT titration level is still enough to emit a (504mC ÷ 200mC =) 2.52 fold titration level even at the end of the treatment course.

2nd Generation Made-for-America Thymatron DG = (initial minimum Charge threshold with ***BL ECT*** =) **200mC** x 2.0 (due to 100% increase in threshold) = 400mC needed to seize at end of treatment. Actual Charge emitted = 504mC ÷ 400mC = ***1.26 x threshold* even at the end of treatment course with *BL ECT***.

2nd Generation Made-for-Europe Thymatron DGx = (initial minimum Charge threshold with ***UL ECT*** =) **111mC** x 2 (due to 100% increase in threshold) = 222mC needed to seize at end of treatment. Actual Charge emitted = 504mC ÷ 222mC = ***2.27 x threshold* even at the end of treatment course with *UL ECT***.

2nd Generation Made-for-Europe Thymatron DGx = (initial minimum Charge threshold with ***BL ECT*** =) **222mC** x 2 (due to 100% increase in threshold) = 444mC needed to seize at end of treatment. Actual Charge emitted = 504mC ÷ 444mC = ***1.13 x threshold* even at the end of treatment course with *BL ECT***.

2nd Generation Made-for-America MECTA 1@2 = (initial minimum Charge threshold with ***UL ECT*** =) **111mC** x 2 (due to 100% increase in threshold) = 222mC needed to seize at end of treatment. Actual Charge emitted = 576mC ÷ 222mC = ***2.59 x threshold* even at the end of treatment course with UL ECT**.

2nd Generation Made-for-America MECTA 1@2 = (initial minimum Charge threshold with ***BL ECT*** =) **222mC** x 2 (due to 100% increase in threshold) = 444mC needed to seize at end of treatment. Actual Charge emitted = 576mC ÷ 444mC = ***1.3 x threshold* even at the end of treatment course with *BL ECT***.

2nd Generation Made-for-Europe MECTA JR/SR 1 IEC = (initial minimum Charge threshold with ***UL ECT*** =) **125mC** x 2.0 (due to 100% increase in threshold) = 250mC needed to seize at end of treatment. Actual Charge emitted = 575mC ÷ 250mC = ***2.3 x threshold* even at end of treatment course with *UL ECT***.

2nd Generation Made-for-Europe MECTA JR/SR 1 IEC = (initial minimum Charge threshold with ***BL ECT*** =) **250mC** x 2.0 (due to 100% increase in threshold) = 500mC needed to seize at end of treatment. Actual Charge emitted = 575mC ÷ 500mC = ***1.15 x threshold* even at end treatment course with *BL ECT***.

2nd Generation Made-for-Europe MECTA JR/SR 2 IEC = (initial minimum Charge threshold with ***UL ECT*** =) **125mC** x 2.0 (due to 100% increase in threshold) = 250mC needed to seize at end of treatment. Actual Charge emitted = 600mC ÷ 250mC = ***2.4 x threshold even* at end of treatment course with *UL ECT***.

2nd Generation Made-for-Europe MECTA JR/SR 2 IEC = (initial minimum Charge threshold with ***BL ECT*** =) **250mC** x 2.0 (due to 100% increase in threshold) = 500mC needed to seize at end of treatment. Actual Charge emitted = 600mC ÷ 500mC = ***1.2 x threshold* even at end of treatment course with *BL ECT***.

The MTTLOI at the end of the treatment course for the 100 year old male derived from Charge (in millicoulombs) above, matches the MTTLOI derived from EO (in joules). In short, the same second generation BP devices deliver the same MTTLOI by way of Joules.[187] For example:

2nd Generation Made-for-Europe MECTA JR/SR 1 IEC = (initial minimum **EO** threshold with ***BL ECT*** =) **100J** x 2.0 (due to 100% increase in threshold) = 200J needed to seize at end of treatment. Actual EO emitted = 230J ÷ 200J = ***1.15 x threshold* even at the end of treatment course with *BL ECT***.

2nd Generation Made-for-Europe MECTA JR/SR 1 IEC = (initial minimum **Charge** threshold with ***BL ECT*** =) **250mC** x 2.0 (due to 100% increase in threshold) = 500mC needed to seize at end of treatment. Actual Charge emitted = 575mC ÷ 500mC = ***1.15 x threshold* even at end treatment course with *BL ECT*.**

---

[187] By third generation BP devices, threshold in joules and millicoulombs no longer match due to the increase in Voltage and Amperage and halving of Pulse Width. However, MTTLOI can still be seen via EO in joules which is why EO reporting is eliminated in Weiner's 1997 de facto "standard." We could, of course, create a formula taking into account the doubling of Voltage and thus Amperage as well as the halving of Pulse Width in order to derive accurate MTTLOIs from Charge. However, such derivations are unnecessary in terms of EO or joules.

<u>2nd Generation Made-for-Europe MECTA JR/SR 1 IEC</u> = (initial minimum **EO** threshold with ***<u>UL ECT</u>*** =) **<u>50J</u>** x 2.0 (due to 100% increase in threshold) = 100J needed to seize at end of treatment. Actual EO emitted = 230J ÷ 100J = ***<u>2.3 x threshold</u>*** **<u>even at end of treatment course for *UL ECT*</u>**.

<u>2nd Generation Made-for-Europe MECTA JR/SR 1 IEC</u> = (initial minimum **Charge** threshold for ***<u>UL ECT</u>*** =) **<u>125mC</u>** x 2.0 (due to 100% increase in threshold) = 250mC needed to seize at end of treatment. Actual Charge emitted = 575mC ÷ 250mC = ***<u>2.3 x threshold</u>*** **<u>even at end of treatment course for *UL ECT*</u>**.

CHAPTER 73

All Ages

Finally, MTTLOIs emitted by 2nd Generation BP devices can be derived not only for 100 year old recipients, but for any age category using both Charge and EO. Note the MTTLOIs at the end of a treatment course for, for example, a 40 year old recipient administered default outputs with BL and UL "ECT" administered by the second generation Made-for-Europe MECTA JR/SR 1 IEC Brief Pulse device.

2nd Generation Made-for-Europe MECTA JR/SR 1 IEC Brief Pulse Device for 40 year old Recipient

VOLTAGE	POWER % @ Age	AGE Yrs	Ω Ohms	FREQUENCY (Hz)	DURATION (SECs)	CURRENT mAmps	ENERGY Joules	CHARGE mC
160	40	40	200	60	1.20	800	36.86	230.4

2nd Generation Made-for-Europe MECTA JR/SR 1 IEC = (40 year initial minimum **EO** threshold with ***BL ECT*** =) **16J** x 2.0 (due to 100% increase in threshold) = 32J needed to seize at end of treatment. Actual EO emitted = 36.86J ÷ 32J = ***1.15 fold threshold* even at the end of treatment course with *BL ECT***.

2nd Generation Made-for-Europe MECTA JR/SR 1 IEC = (40 year initial minimum **Charge** threshold with ***BL ECT*** =) **100.17mC** x 2.0 (due to 100% increase in threshold) = 200.34mC needed to seize at end of treatment. Actual Charge emitted = 230.4mC ÷ 200.34mC = ***1.15 x threshold* even at end of treatment course for BL ECT**.

2nd Generation Made-for-Europe MECTA JR/SR 1 IEC = (40 year initial minimum **EO** threshold with ***UL ECT*** =) **8J** x 2.0 (due to 100% increase in threshold) = 16J needed to seize at end of treatment. Actual EO emitted = 36.86J ÷ 16J = ***2.3 fold threshold* even at the end of treatment course with *UL ECT***.

2nd Generation Made-for-Europe MECTA JR/SR 1 IEC = (40year initial minimum **Charge** threshold with ***UL ECT*** =) **50.09mC** x 2.0 (due to 100% increase in threshold) = 100.17mC needed to seize at end of treatment. Actual Charge emitted = 230.4mC ÷ 100.17mC = ***2.3 x threshold* even at end of treatment course with *UL ECT***.

In sum, albeit hidden, all second generation BP devices already emitted more than enough output to induce well over 2.0 fold threshold outputs with so called "dose-sensitive" UL ECT even at the end of a "treatment" course and more than enough to induce an adequate seizure with so called "non-dose sensitive" BL ECT even at the end of a "treatment" course. Thus, the criteria for which Weiner claims the 1997 enhancement is needed is wholly unnecessary in that it has already been met by unreported second generation BP devices marketed in the U.S. and abroad since about 1982 and 1985 respectively.[188] Weiner is actually creating an "anti-standard"

[188] A consistent MTTLOI finding with both EO and Charge can be confirmed via the following method. Based on Beale's 1994 study, we know that BL ECT is approximately 2.5 fold threshold for made-for-America second generation BP devices. We also know from the 1982 APA study that 100 Joules is the minimum output needed to induce a BL ECT threshold for all 100 year old recipients.

with his 1997 de facto proviso designed to "legalize" entirely new electro-dependent ENR devices to completely replace seizure-dependent-ECT devices. Weiner's 1997 de facto "standard" surreptitiously opens the door to electro-dependent outputs and electro-dependent output devices with both BL and UL electrode placement.

Dividing maximum output for Somatics' Thymatron DG by its 252J maximum, we derive an even more accurate 2.52 initial MTTLOI with BL ECT for all age recipients. We can also divide maximum Charge output for the DG (504mC) by 2.52 to derive a circa 200mC just above threshold Charge for a 100 year old man (504mC ÷ 2.52 = 200mC). We can then use the formula: <u>EO = Charge and Current x maximum Impedance</u> formula to covert minimum Charge threshold back to the minimum Joule threshold of 100 Joules for the 100 year old male (.200C x .9A x 555.5Ω = <u>100 Joules</u>). The 2.52 MTTLOI is thus consistent for both Charge and EO for all age groups (on the DG). The second generation MECTA JR 1 (IEC) BP device emits a 575mC maximum Charge and a 230J EO maximum. Dividing 230J by 100J, we obtain an initial 2.3 MTTLOI with BL ECT for all age recipients. Thus, the device uses a (575 ÷ 2.3 =) 250mC minimum Charge threshold and a (230J ÷ 2.3 =) 100J minimum EO threshold for a 100 year old male. For confirmation we can re-convert maximum Charge threshold (.250C) to Joules (EO = Charge x Current x Impedance = .250C x .8A x 500Ω = <u>100J</u>). The same initial 2.3 MTTLOI in terms of Charge and EO is thus consistent for all age groups on the MECTA JR/SR 1 IEC BP device. Thus the MTTLOI can be derived via EO or Charge. Moreover, we can also conclude that the minimum EO threshold for a 100 year old male is a consistent 100J with BL ECT (and 50J with UL ECT) for all modern day BP devices as opposed to minimum Charge thresholds which vary with varying machines for the same 100 year old adult.

CHAPTER 74

The How and the Why of Weiner's 1997 Proviso

To review then, Weiner's purported, but incorrect initial minimum threshold output of 300mC Charge with UL "ECT," as we have observed above, is but Weiner's indirect means of claiming BL "ECT" has a minimum initial threshold output of 600mC, thereby "justifying" his new 1200mC maximum Charge maximum. 1200mC, Weiner would have us believe, allows for a first time accommodation for his alleged "100% rise in threshold" argument as well as his alleged 2.0 fold threshold requirement with UL electrode placement even at the end of a "treatment" course. This falsehood regarding an initial 300mC minimum with so-called "dose-sensitive UL "ECT," an initial 600mC minimum with the putative "non-dose sensitive" BL "ECT," and finally the myth of a 100% rise in threshold to justify Weiner's (2 x 600 = ; 4 x 300mC =) 1200mC call with both is but another means of covering up that both UL and BL electrode placement require suprathreshold dosing to be effective. This manufacturer cover-up, of course, is entirely due to the suppressed detail that it is not adequate seizure, but adequate amounts of electricity that make the procedure "work." In point of fact, UL and BL "ECT" are both "dose-sensitive" in that both depend upon ample amounts of electricity to be effectual. Conversely, neither is "dose-sensitive" in that that "ECT" is a myth. Indeed, we must logically come to the unthinkable conclusion, that what is actually "ENR" works solely by electrically damaging the brain, (for that is what excessive amounts of electricity do), specifically, by drastically reducing neuronal connections chiefly in the left prefrontal lobe, an occurrence supported by the most legitimate and scientific of prospective MRI studies, the 2012 Perrin analysis (Perrin et al. 2012). In short, ENR is the necessary compromise of the left frontal lobe via drastic neuronal reduction as a direct result of adequate amounts of electricity. The systematic research methodically identifying massive reduction of neuronal connectivity in all nine participants following a course of eight BL ECT "treatments" administered with a 2.3 MTTLOI of electricity twice weekly is nothing short of alarming. Following the "ECT" series administered, human brain imagery provided by examination of the recipient study group revealed connectivity within the left frontal lobe and with the rest of the brain reduced by no less than 35% in some participants and up to 100% in others. The figures are especially disturbing when we take into account that the least powerful of the modern ENR devices, the MECTA and Somatics second generation BP instruments titrate BL recipients at an initial 2.3 to 2.5 MTTLOI, while extant third generation BP devices titrate BL recipients with initial default MTTLOIs of 4.6 (third generation JR/SR 1), 4.8 (third generation JR/SR 2), and 4.5 (third generation Somatics System IV), more than double that administered in the Perrin study (Perrin et al. 2012). Disquietingly, probable fourth generation BP devices, also "legal" under the 1997 Weiner proviso, double third generation BP devices, while potential fifth generation BP devices also "legal" under the 1997 Weiner proviso, drastically increase power yet again. At the same time, Weiner's 1997 proviso would have us believe that the "standard" "allows" only enough power to administer a "new" initial 2.0 fold threshold output with BL placement and a "new" initial 4.0 fold threshold output with UL placement. In short, Weiner would convince us that his 1997 standard allows for second generation BP devices and for the first time. In fact, Weiner's proviso actually allows not only third, but quite surreptitiously, fourth and even fifth generation BP devices, doubling, quadrupling, and more than quadrupling the power not of first, but of already extant second generation BP devices emitting a more than 2.0 fold threshold output with BL placement and a more than a 4.0 fold threshold output with UL "ECT" since 1982.

CHAPTER 75

The Easy Way: Back to Joules

Revisiting perhaps the most important passages within the 1982 APA Standard authored by Weiner himself and submitted to the FDA that same year, remind us of the actual maximum EO (in joules) and thus Charge dosage necessary to induce adequate seizures with BL placement via a modern-day Brief Pulse device and why Brief Pulse was introduced to begin with.

> For pulse stimuli . . . less than 1% of seizure thresholds were greater than 60 Joules. . . . (Department of Health and Human Services, 1982a, E20)

> Using a pulse device, the [APA] Task Force [1978] has determined that only 0.6% of seizure thresholds were greater than 70 Joules and that none were greater than 100 Joules. (Department of Health and Human Services, 1982a, p. A53)

Weiner's statement above appears to mean that even the oldest recipient with the highest of seizure thresholds never requires more than 100 joules to seize. Moreover, this 1982 Weiner assertion no doubt refers to BL electrode placement as opposed to UL electrode placement (Abrams, and Swartz, 1996, p. 48) as UL electrode would require much less. Moreover, Weiner's 1982 statement "none were greater than 100 Joules," appears to include outputs even at the end of a "treatment course." [189] UL electrode placement, by implication, never requires more than 50 joules to induce an "adequate" seizure apparently even at the end of a "treatment course." In fact, it is upon the above statement that the original 1982 APA Standard for Brief Pulse devices is based. Indeed, based upon Weiner's assertion, the 1982 APA Standard stipulates an absolute ceiling of 110 Joules (an extra ten to remain above threshold in even the most seizure recalcitrant circumstances), guaranteeing the establishment of minimal stimulus output for all age categories (110J ÷ 100J = 1.1 MTTLOI). This 1.1 MTTLOI ceiling was clearly reflected in the then "new" MECTA "C" Brief Pulse device introduced between 1978-80. In sum, because the minimum output required to induce adequate seizures with UL "ECT" in all Brief Pulse recipients is exactly half that of BL "ECT," Weiner's above statement implies that no adequate UL "ECT" seizure ever requires more than 50 joules, just as no adequate BL seizure ever requires more than 100 joules regardless of age. It was these important assertions that allowed for the "improvement" of ECT via Brief Pulse compared to SW which allegedly uses up to 200J. Indeed, the MECTA "C" was capable of inducing seizures at half the output of SW in almost all age categories, persuading the FDA to approve the continued utilization of "ECT," generally.

---

[189] In that Weiner was communicating directly to the FDA during a precarious period for the ongoing use of "ECT," the author believes Weiner's assertion and implication that no more than 100 joules is ever required to seize an individual with BL ECT, is entirely accurate.

According to the accurately depicted detailed Chart of the second generation made-for America Thymatron DG depicted in this manuscript and according to Weiner's 1982 assertion and implication that no more than 100 Joules is ever required to induce an adequate seizure with BL "ECT" for even the oldest, most seizure recalcitrant recipient even at the end of a "treatment" course, we can conclude that for the Thymatron DG at least, the minimum Charge required to induce an adequate seizure for all recipients is circa 200mC. This figure is determined by plugging the maximum machine Impedance possible (555.5Ω) obtained by the second generation made-for America Thymatron DG into the Charge formula for BP devices along with the DG's constant current of .9A, and the minimum 100J figure (for all recipients) provided by Weiner: (Charge = 100J/.9A x 555.5Ω =) 200mC. [190] Using the same method, we can also determine that the minimum Charge required to induce seizure in all recipients with BL "ECT" on made-for-America MECTA SR 1@ 2 devices is (Charge = 100J/.8A x 562.5Ω =) 222mC. [191] Thus, the minimum initial EO and Charge necessary to induce an adequate seizure for the most seizure recalcitrant recipients with BL "ECT" appears to be 100J correlating with between 200 and 222mC of Charge, depending upon the device, certainly not the 600mC implied by Weiner in his 1997 proviso "justifying" the need for a ridiculous (2 x 600mC =) 1200mC of Charge. Indeed, circa 100J corresponding to between circa 200 and 222mC conform to the conclusions of Beale at al. (1994) whose team measured the output emissions of modern day second generation MECTA and Somatics BP devices such as the MECTA SR 1@2, and the Thymatron DG (for all ages) at about 2.5 fold threshold with BL placement. Maximum output for the DG, as noted, is 251-252 Joules at 504mC of Charge while second generation MECTA devices emit 259.2 Joules at 576mC Charge (see Charts in this manuscript). As noted earlier, then, to derive the minimum threshold output in Joules, we simply divide any of these maximum Charge outputs by the 2.5 fold threshold that Beale found to get a consistent circa 100 minimum Joules to induce seizure in all instances, a figure which once again, agrees with Weiner's 1982 statement regarding a 100J minimum to seize all recipients under any circumstances and around which the 1982 APA Standard stipulating 110 maximum Joules is based (Department of Health and Human Services, 1982a, p. A53).

Thymatron DG = .504 ÷ 2.5 = .2016C; EO = .201C x .9A x 555.5Ω =
<u>100.7 Joules</u>.
JR/SR 1@2 = .576C ÷ 2.5 = .230C; EO = .2304C x .8A x 562.5Ω =
<u>103.68 Joules</u>. [192]

As a shortcut method to obtain the same result, we can simply take maximum EO on any made-for-America second generation device and divide by the 2.5 MTTLOI Beale discovered in order to derive the same consistent 100J figure.

Thymatron DG = 251.7J ÷ 2.5 = **100.7 Joules**
JR/SR 1@2 = 259.2J ÷ 2.5 = **103.68 Joules;** 259.2J ÷ <u>2.59</u> = **100 Joules**

In fact, simply by dividing the maximum machine output (measured in Joules) by the 100 Joule figure Weiner provides above (and which we derive from Beale's findings above), we can derive, as has been noted, the accurate MTTLOI applied to all age groups for any particular Brief Pulse device.

Thymatron DG = 252J ÷ 100J = **2.52 MTTLOI**
JR/SR 1@2 = 259J ÷ 100J = **2.59 MTTLOI**

---

[190] We need only refer to the original APA Standard authored in main by Weiner himself, delineating large charts for the FDA in 1982 clearly stating that minimum seizure threshold to seize all recipients with BP never surpasses 100 Joules compared to SW which never surpasses 200 Joules (Department of Health and Human Services, 1982a,pp. G2-G3, G7). In fact, it was this presentation that appears to have convinced FDA to permit the continuation of "ECT."

[191] Charge = EO/Current x Impedance. Charge = 100J/.8A x 562.5ohms = 222mC. (See JR/SR 2 chart).

[192] The Chart is slightly off here in that Beale approximated 2.5; whereas, the actual MECTA devices emit 2.59 fold threshold outputs. JR/SR 1@2 = .576C ÷ **2.59** = **.222C**; EO = **.222C** x .8A x 562.5Ω = **<u>100 Joules</u>.**

Using the more accurate MTTLOIs, we can then derive the more accurate .200C and .222C minimum Charge thresholds (to seize all recipients) with second generation Somatics and MECTA devices respectively from which we can again derive the same 100J minimum originally asserted by Weiner in his 1982 APA Standard.

Thymatron DG = .504 ÷ 2.52 = .200C; EO = .200C x .9A x 555.5Ω = **100 Joules**.
JR/SR 1@2 = .576C ÷ 2.59 = .222C; EO = .222C x .8A x 562.5Ω = **100 Joules.**

Using this method, we see that the 100J figure originally referred to by Weiner becomes the constant minimum threshold output (with BL ECT) for all modern day BP devices (a figure which applies to the minimum threshold output required to seize even the most seizure resistant 100 year old recipient in any and all circumstances). As such, we can corroborate the consistent 2.52 and 2.59 MTTLOIs respectively on second generation made-for-America Somatics and MECTA BP devices for all age groups with BL "ECT" both in Charge and EO. Moreover, we see that made-for-America second generation BP devices, as Beale noted, were indeed set at multifold threshold levels (with BL ECT) of circa 2.5 fold threshold Charge (and EO) for all ages and thus a circa 5.0 MTTLOI with UL "ECT."

Thymatron DG = 252J ÷ 2.52 = **100J**; 252J ÷ 5.04 = **50J**.

JR/SR 1@2 = 259J ÷ 2.59 = **100J**; 259J ÷ 5.18 = **50J**.

Once again we observe that Charge reporting without EO reporting simply will not do; instead, manufacturers must be made to report maximum EO in joules for every Brief Pulse device as it then becomes a simple matter of dividing by 100J to deduce the overall MTTLOI with BL "ECT" for any Brief Pulse device and by 50J to deduce the overall MTTLOI with UL "ECT" for any Brief Pulse device to obtain the power profile of the specific device. Moreover, just as Weiner seems to purport to the FDA in 1982, there is little reason to think that 100J and 50J is not enough to reach threshold with BL "ECT" and UL "ECT" even at the end of a "treatment" series. Indeed, as we have seen with relative constants, all Brief Pulse devices are secretly centered around the 100J minimum (to seize all recipients) specified by Weiner himself to the FDA in 1982.

Thymatron DG = 252J ÷ 100J = 2.52 MTTLOI; 252J ÷ 50J = 5.04 MTTLOI.

JR/SR 1@2 = 259J ÷ 100J = 2.59 MTTLOI; 259J ÷ 50J = 5.18 MTTLOI.

Initial Charge Thresholds Vary; Initial EO Thresholds are Constant

As already noted then, initial Charge thresholds vary while initial EO thresholds remain constant.[193] For example, the highest initial Charge threshold with BL "ECT" belongs to the second generation made-for-Europe MECTA JR/SR 1 and 2 devices which at their 230J and 240J respective EO maximums and 576mC and 600mC respective Charge maximums, all utilize an initial minimum threshold Charge of 250mC, once again corroborated by the initial minimum EO constant of 100J.

[193] Minimum EO thresholds (in joules) with BL placement remain a constant 100J from one BP machine generation to another, whereas, Charge thresholds may vary. For example, the second generation made-for Europe MECTA JR/SR 2 emits a (.600C ÷ **2.4** =) **.250C** Charge Threshold with BL placement; EO = **.250C** x .8A x 500Ω = **100** Joules, just as the third generation MECTA JR/SR 2 emits the same (1.200C ÷ 4.8 =) **.250C** Charge Threshold with BL placement; EO = **.250C** x .8A x 500Ω = **100 Joules.** However, the fourth generation MECTA JR/SR 2 emits a (1.200C ÷ 9.6 =) **.125C** Charge Threshold with BL placement; EO = **.125C** x 1.6A x 500Ω = **100 Joules.** EO Thresholds (in joules), on the other hand, remain a constant 100J with BL placement for all three devices.

Made-for Europe JR/SR 1 = .576C ÷ 2.3 = .250C; EO = .250C x .8A x 500Ω = **100 Joules.**

Made-for Europe JR/SR 1 = .600C ÷ 2.4 = .250C; EO = .250C x .8A x 500Ω = **100 Joules.**

Let us examine Weiner's 1997 assertion once again:

> While initial seizure thresholds with UL ECT are nearly always below 300mC, they often rise as much as 100% or more over the course of treatments, so that a limit of at least 1200mC is clearly necessary.
> (International Electrotechnical Commission, 1997, Dec 26, p. 5)

and Weiner's subsequent assertion:

> [S]timulus intensity must be 2-4 times seizure threshold . . ..
> (International Electrotechnical Commission, 1997, Dec 26, p. 5)

In light of our above examination, we can now clearly conclude that Weiner's 300mC statement regarding modern day BP devices applies--not to UL ECT as Weiner implies, but to BL ECT, and, in fact, as noted above, initial minimum Charge thresholds with BL ECT never rise above 250mC on any modern-day BP device emitting 200J or more (see lists above). In short, Charge threshold with BL ECT never rises above 250mC on any second, third, fourth, or fifth generation BP device. Moreover, in that UL ECT requires only half the Charge of BL ECT to induce adequate seizures, initial seizure thresholds with UL ECT never rise above 125mC on any second, third, fourth, or fifth generation BP device--certainly not the 300mC Weiner purports. Plainly then, Weiner's statement, " . . . initial seizure thresholds with UL ECT are nearly always below 300mC . . ." applies to BL "ECT." Indeed, Weiner's statement should read: ". . . initial seizure thresholds with UL ECT are nearly always below 150mC while initial seizure thresholds with BL ECT are nearly always below 250mC."

Note too, that while all actual initial minimum Charge thresholds with BL "ECT" vary with varying BP devices, i.e. 201mC, 222mC, and even 250mC,[194] all these devices educe a consistent minimum threshold output with BL placement of 100 Joules, once again demonstrating that while maximum Charge thresholds are inconsistent, "initial" and for the most part "final" minimum EO thresholds (in joules) are constant. Once more then, Charge reporting confuses; EO reporting (in joules) clarifies. Particularly revealing is overall maximum machine output in joules which manufacturers fail to divulge.

Perhaps most importantly, by doubling Amperage and halving Pulse Width, the 1200mC Charge Weiner allowed in his1997 de fact standard can be made to emit 1200J of EO, twelve times that required to induce a seizure with BL placement. Without reporting in joules, however, this output is invisible and hence, has never been reported. Too, because third, fourth, and fifth generation BP devices emit the same approximate maximum Charge, these BP devices, all emitting sequentially greater outputs and sequentially greater MTTLOIs, are impossible to differentiate. In short, their possible presence has never been understood--until now.

Conclusion

The 1982 APA Standard (authored in main by Richard Weiner) asserts that less than 1% of seizure thresholds require more than 60 Joules, only .6% more than 70 Joules, and none more than 100 Joules to induce an adequate seizure with (by paraphrase) what is almost certainly BL ECT in what appears to be even the oldest, most seizure recalcitrant recipient under what appears to be any circumstance on any modern day BP device (Department of Health and Human Services, 1982a, pp. G3-G4).

---

194 The initial minimum Charge thresholds noted above include second and third generation BP devices made by Somatics and MECTA. Fourth and fifth generation BP devices have even lower initial minimum Charge thresholds with BL ECT, while the minimum initial 100J EO threshold remains constant in all generation BP devices.

> For pulse stimuli[,] . . . less than 1% of seizure thresholds were greater than 60 Joules. . . . Using a pulse device, the [APA] Task Force [1978] has determined that only 0.6% of seizure thresholds were greater than 70 Joules and that none were greater than 100 Joules.
> (Weiner, Department of Health and Human Services, 1982a, E20; p. A53)

Weiner's 1982 assertion to the FDA makes no exceptions with respect to either the beginning or the end of a "treatment series." [195] In that a 100J seizure threshold with BL "ECT" can be derived from even the highest initial Charge threshold (250mC) required to induce an adequate seizure on any modern day BP device emitting 200J or more, in short, second, third, fourth, and fifth generation BP devices, Charge thresholds reaching "300mC" with UL "ECT" implied in Weiner's 1997 IEC revision proposal (International Electrotechnical Commission, 1997, Dec 26, p. 5) below, later to become his de facto "standard," (and which should be no more than 125mC), cannot possibly be correct.

> While initial seizure thresholds with UL ECT are nearly always below 300mC, they often rise as much as 100% or more over the course of treatments, so that a limit of at least 1200mC is clearly necessary. (International Electrotechnical Commission, 1997, Dec 26, p. 5)

In sum, the "300mC" initial maximum threshold Weiner referred to can only be with BL "ECT" (Department of Health and Human Services, 1982a, p. A53). In fact, as has been noted, the greatest minimum initial Charge threshold required to induce an adequate seizure with BL "ECT" on any modern day BP device emitting 200J or more, as noted, is 250mC--not even 300mC and again, certainly not the 600mC Weiner implies in his call for BP machine enhancement of up to 1200mC of Charge. Once more, since UL "ECT" requires only half the output of BL "ECT" to induce an adequate seizure, the greatest initial Charge threshold required to induce a seizure with UL ECT on any second, third, fourth, or fifth generation BP device is (half that of BL ECT or 250mC ÷ 2 =) 125mC-- not the 300mC Weiner asserts. If 125mC is truly the initial minimum threshold output needed to induce an adequate seizure with UL "ECT" on any second, third, fourth, or fifth generation BP device, even doubling 125mC due to so-called "dose-sensitivity" and doubling again due to an alleged 100% increase in resistance over a "treatment course," requires no more than (4 x 125mC =) 500mC maximum—not the 1200mC Weiner calls for in his 1997 proviso. The same is true with BL ECT. If 250mC is the minimum threshold output required to induce an adequate seizure with BL ECT on any second, third, fourth, or fifth generation BP device, even doubling that output due to an alleged 100% increase in threshold output over a "treatment course," requires no more than (4 x 250mC =) 500mC maximum—once again not the 1200mC Weiner calls for in his 1997 proviso. In point of fact, 1200mC is enough to administer not a 4.0 fold MTTLOI with UL "ECT," but an initial (1200mC ÷ 125 =) 9.6 MTTLOI with UL "ECT" and at least a 4.8 MTTLOI with UL "ECT," (not a 2.0 MTTLOI) even at the end of a "treatment" course. In turn, 1200mC is enough to administer not an initial 2.0 MTTLOI with BL "ECT," but at least an initial (1200mC ÷ 250 =) 4.8 MTTLOI with BL "ECT" on any second, third, fourth, or fifth generation device for even the most seizure recalcitrant individual and thus at least a 2.4 MTTLOI with BL "ECT" even at the end of a "treatment" course (even assuming a 100% rise in threshold). Weiner has plainly dissembled in order to arrive at 1200mC, a fact clearly recognizable with EO readings in Joules. For example,

> First Generation devices-------108J-134J maximum (1.08 to 1.34 MTTLOI);
> Second Generation devices---227-259J maximum (2.27 to 2.59 MTTLOI);
> Third Generation devices------453-480J maximum (4.53 to 4.80 MTTLOI);
> Fourth Generation devices----907-922J maximum (9.07 to 9.22 MTTLOI);
> Fifth Generation devices-------1200J maximum (12.0 MTTLOI).

If only Charge is used, we get an illusion,

---

[195] In Weiner's 1982 Report to the FDA - inclusive of the APA Standard, Weiner claims, "[N]one were greater than 100 Joules" (Department of Health and Human Services, 1982a, p. A53 - APA Standard). Too, when, in 1982, BP manufacturers wanted to impress FDA with BP's low dosage potential, no rise in threshold over a "treatment course" was mentioned.

1) what appear to be First Generation devices-------336-600mC maximum and
2) what appear to be Second Generation devices---1152mC-1200mC maximum.

In short, using Charge only readings, there appears to be only one major increase in power while third, fourth, and fifth generation BP devices all but disappear.

Using Charge alone, we cannot see the five generations of BP devices with sequentially increasing power. Clearly then, the aim of Weiner's 1997 proviso, as has already been noted above, was to create a new "standard" encompassing and thus "legalizing" unreported third (fourth and fifth) generation BP devices capable of excessive amounts of electricity, illegally marketed at the time of Weiner's demand for increased power while at the same time hiding the existence of third (fourth, and fifth) generation BP devices. Indeed, the unreported "initial" 4.8 and 9.6 fold threshold outputs with UL and BL electrode placement respectively delivered by the MECTA 2 third generation BP device only become possible under Weiner's 1997 revised "standard" allowing 1200mC, and does so even without increased Amperage (newly usable under Weiner's 1997 proviso meaning even greater outputs). What Weiner apparently seeks to cover up is that the unreported 4.8 and 9.6 MTTLOI delivered by what is actually the third generation MECTA 2 is more than ($4.8 \div 1.08 = 4.4$; $9.6 \div 2.16 = 4.4$) quadruple--not double--the power of the original MECTA "C." This, in turn means that BL "ECT" is no longer administered at just above threshold, but well above threshold, just as UL "ECT" is administered at well above threshold even at the end of a "treatment "series, a fact which manufacturers cannot afford to reveal.

Manufacturers and manufacturer affiliated academics such as Weiner, Abrams, and Sackeim are clearly concealing the unfortunate detail that so-called "dose sensitive" UL "ECT" as opposed to "non-dose sensitive" BL "ECT" is pure propaganda. Indeed, neither form works at just above threshold. More plainly, Weiner and manufacturers are secreting the critical fact that suprathreshold electrical dosing is requisite for all forms of "ECT," in order to make the procedure effective. In short, it is the inextricable link between electrical dosing and efficacy that impels manufacturers both to enhance and conceal the true power of their modern era Brief Pulse devices. Quite plainly, manufacturers no longer attempt to induce adequate seizures utilizing the least amount of electricity possible for either form of "ECT." Neither do they attempt to emit just enough electricity to accommodate "dose-sensitive" UL "ECT" or the "doubling of Impedance over a "treatment" course. Rather, manufacturers design modern day BP devices to induce suprathreshold dosages of electricity with both BL and UL electrode placement far exceeding the alleged criteria, all in order to make the procedure operative at the necessary expense of "safety." [196] In short, these machines are clearly electro-oriented in lieu of seizure oriented. Indeed, simultaneous efficacy and safety is not possible at these outputs. In fact, modern day Brief Pulse machines are plainly intended to electrically reduce left prefrontal lobe connectivity both within the lobe itself and, to and from the remaining brain, in some cases disabling left prefrontal lobe circuitry altogether (Perrin et al., 2012). In a word, modern day Brief Pulse devices are intended to emit high enough electrical output to radically diminish neuronal functionality, drastically and effectively reducing communication of the left prefrontal lobe both with itself and other parts of the brain. The modern day "ECT" machine or what Is here deemed the modern day "ENR" (Electro Neurotransmission Reduction) device, is clearly devised to electrically destroy and so drastically reduce left prefrontal lobe connectivity generally, without which the procedure is not "effective." The hidden goal of what is actually ENR, then, is enough electrical damage to left pre-frontal lobe circuitry to achieve gross connective reduction both within and, to and from, the left prefrontal lobe, grossly reducing, if not completely destroying the neuronal connections within and between the left prefrontal lobe and the remaining brain, a procedure which without hyperbole, legitimately compares to an "electrical left prefrontal lobotomy" or an electrical "left prefrontal lobe cingulotomy." Unlike previous era lobotomies, the electrical agent does not destroy gross brain matter. Rather, acting on a nano level, it compromises or destroys electrical circuitry within the brain tissue itself, explicitly targeting, as Perrin et al. discovered, circuitry within and to and from the left prefrontal lobe. Plainly, convulsion is no longer the aim. Indeed, it is only through significant, if not total electrical extirpation of the neuronal connections within and to and from the left prefrontal lobe that

---

[196] BP devices already induced 2.5 times initial threshold for BL placement (Beale, 1994). The new (1997) enhancement thus accommodated increased titration from the second generation 2.5 times initial threshold with BL to more than 4 times initial threshold with BL and so at least to 2 times threshold with BL at the end of the "treatment" course. UL which already emitted 5 times threshold initially with second generation BP devices, increased correspondingly, to about ten times initial threshold output. Clearly, third, fourth, and fifth generation BP devices are electro-dependent ENR devices.

"efficacy" occurs (Perrin et al. 2012). This "efficacy," ironically, can manifest itself as a temporary anti-depressant effect, and may even initially be accompanied by "desirable" changes in behavior. In Perrin et al.'s own words, "This observed decrease in functional connectivity was accompanied by a significant reduction in depressive symptoms" (Perrin et al., 2012). However, this "decrease in functional connectivity" is invariably accompanied by long term memory morbidity which the recipient either never or only begins to discover over time. Indeed, whether connectivity is restored with the subsidence of the anti-depressant effect over a long period of time, or not at all is unknown, but if there is at least partial restoration of neuronal connectors, common sense tells us it takes place over an extended period. In short, whether connectivity is partially restored over months, years, or not at all, is not presently known, though some renewal over time appears plausible.

In sum, what is actually ENR--not "ECT," requires suprathreshold dosages of electricity for both BL and UL placement to "work." We can conclude, moreover, that a procedure which requires adequate amounts of electricity in order to be effective, that is, a procedure which requires electrical outputs far in excess of that required to induce an adequate seizure for both forms of electrode placement, a procedure for which electricity is not merely a catalyst, but the very means by which the procedure works, is no longer "electroconvulsive therapy" at all. Indeed, it is an entirely new procedure, one depending not on adequate convulsion, but on adequate amounts of electricity, specifically, enough electrical output to compromise neuronal connections within a specific area of the brain. Such a disparate procedure requires a new nomination, one the author has deemed "Electro Neurotransmission Reduction" or "**ENR**." The novel goal of the ENR device, in sum, is high enough electrical output to compromise left frontal lobe connectivity, so that communication of the left frontal lobe both with itself and the remaining voxels of the brain is significantly reduced. Logically, each more enhanced machine generation, enhances this reduction.

It should be conceded that until 2012, no one, including manufacturers knew exactly how so-called "ECT," which is actually "ENR"--"works." What manufacturers did know, however, is that contrary to misinformation they themselves have continued to generate, the procedure requires not adequate seizure, but adequate doses of electricity, and that these doses are harmful regarding memory dysfunction without which the procedure fails to "work." It is for this reason that manufacturers have covered up the specific and advancing power of the Brief Pulse machine itself. Indeed, manufacturers have always known that memory dysfunction increases with increasing electrical output, as this problem is the very reason reduced output Brief Pulse was re-introduced to the FDA initially around 1978. Manufacturers are most certainly culpable in knowing that increased power is directly proportional to injury and morbidity, specifically long term memory morbidity. Moreover, manufacturers are wholly culpable in both increasing and hiding the power and rising power of their modern day Brief Pulse devices. Additionally, since the Perrin study of 2012, not only manufacturers, but academics associated with manufacturers, and even administering psychiatrists have or should have suspected reduced connectivity as a result of what is actually "ENR." Quite bluntly, manufacturers, academics, and even administering psychiatrists should have been able to identify long term memory morbidity as brain damage, the specific nature of which appears to be compromise or destruction of the connective circuitry within, to, and from the left prefrontal lobe. Without explaining this "suspicion" to recipients, all administrators, but much more so, manufacturers and manufacturer-associated academics, are at the least guilty of failing to provide Informed Consent. Most culpable, however, are the manufacturers who have avoided informing physicians of the power and thus the dangerousness of their devices.

The rationale following Perrin's 2012 study, of course, is that depressed "patients" have too many connections or a "hyperconnectivity" and the reduction of connectors is necessary to "normalize" an "atypical" condition. But "hyperconnectivity" is pure hypothesis. Moreover, even recipients with ordinary depression are encouraged by manufacturers via physicians (who admittedly are often misinformed) to accept and receive "ECT" as the "standard treatment." What is clear, is that recipients must and should have been informed of the true aim and consequences of ENR, specifically, the gross reduction of neuro-transmissions. Recipients must be lawfully informed that a major study has found that the ENR they are receiving or considering receiving, dramatically reduces brain connectivity, specifically of the left prefrontal lobe both within itself and with other parts of the brain. Moreover, recipients must be lawfully informed that there are no studies regarding the duration of this loss, its possible reversal, or the length of time required for such reversal, and how much, if any reversal is possible. Next, recipients must and should be informed of the debunking of "convulsion theory" and so the power and increasing power of the modern day Brief Pulse device itself. In short, they must be informed that the device works via adequate amounts of electricity—no longer adequate convulsion, that modern day BP devices do not work via minimal outputs of electricity to induce seizure, but rather enough electricity to compromise connectors. In addition, recipients must be informed of the obvious link between the grossly increased electrical power modern day Brief Pulse devices evince and grossly diminished neuro-connectivity. Furthermore, recipients must be informed that while "ECT" was "grandfathered in," "ENR" was not. In a nutshell, recipients must be informed that "ENR" devices have never undergone the FDA approval process, and that they presently operate under a rogue "standard" and so may be operating illegally. Indeed, recipients must be informed that modern day Brief Pulse devices conform to a de facto standard created only by manufacturers, a self-approved "standard" unrecognized by FDA (Food and Drug Administration), and, in fact, overtly rejected by the IEC (International Electrotechnical Commission). Lastly, all recipients must have the right to Perrin-like prospective signal testing, guaranteeing preservation of the precious neuronal connectors within their own pre-frontal lobes.

CHAPTER 76

Tables Delineating Charge vs. EO in Joules

The tables below represent five generations of MECTA JR/SR 1 BP devices, five generations of MECTA JR/SR 2 BP devices, and five generations of Somatics BP devices. Note Weiner's 1997 required, albeit meaningless reporting parameters in the unshaded columns compared to Weiner's expunged albeit meaningful reporting parameters in the gray columns.

Table 1 Five Generations of BP Devices

Device (Generation)	**Year**	**mC/** Phase	**mC/** Sec	**Maximum Duration (Seconds)**	**Total Charge (mC)**	**BL/UL Thres. Min (mC)**	**Total EO Joules**	**BL/UL Threshold Minimum (Joules)**	**ER/RRC**	**MTTLOI (multi-fold dosing) BL/ULECT**
MECTA "C" (American) ***(1st Gen.)***	1976 - 1982	1.2	168	2.0	336	313/ 156	108	100/50	70J@220Ω Conditional	1.08/ 2.16
JR/SR - **1** (American) ***(2nd Gen.)***	1984 - 1994	1.6	288	2.0	576	222/ 111	259	100/50	101J@220Ω Pure	2.59/ 5.18
JR/SR – **1** (IEC) ***(2nd Gen.)***	1989 - 1994	1.6	288	2.0	576	250/ 125	230	100/50	101J@220Ω Pure	2.3/ 4.6
JR/SR - **1** (IEC) ***(3rd Gen.)***	1995 - ?	1.6	288	4.0	1152	250/ 125	460	100/50	202J@220Ω Pure	4.6/ 9.2
JR/SR - **1** (IEC) ***(4th Gen.)***	? - ?	1.6	288	4.0	1152	125/ 62.5	922	100/50	404J@220Ω Pure	9.22/ 18.44
Max under new standard ***(5th Gen.)***	? - ?	2.0	150	4.0	1200	100/ 50	1200	100/50	528J@220Ω Pure	12.0/ 24.0

MECTA "C" (American) ***(1st Gen.)***	1976 - 1982	1.2	168	2.0	336	313/ 156	108	100/50	70J@220Ω Conditional	1.08/ 2.16
JR/SR **- 2** (American) ***(2nd Gen.)***	1984 - 1994	.8	144	4.0	576	222/ 111	259	100/50	101J@220Ω Pure	2.59/ 5.18
JR/SR **- 2** (IEC) ***(2nd Gen.)***	1985 - 1994	1.12	201. 6	2.98	600	250/ 125	240	100/50	105.6J@220Ω Pure	2.4/ 4.8
JR/SR **- 2** (IEC) ***(3rd Gen.)***	1995 - ?	1.12	201. 6	5.96	1200	250/ 125	480	100/50	211.12J@220Ω Pure	4.8/ 9.6
JR/SR **- 2** (IEC) ***(4th Gen.)***	? - ?	1.12	288	5.96	1200	125/ 62.5	960	100/50	422J@220Ω Pure	9.6/ 19.2
Max under new standard ***(5th Gen.)***	? - ?	2.0	150	4.0	1200	100/ 50	1200	100/50	528J@220Ω Pure	12.0/ 24.0
MECTA "C" (American) ***(1st Gen.)***	1976 - 1982	1.2	168	2.0	336	313/ 156	108	100/50	70J@220Ω Conditional	1.08/ 2.16
Thymatron DG (American) ***(2nd Gen.)***	1984 - 1994	.9	126	4.0	504	200/ 100	252	100/50	100J@220Ω Pure	2.5/ 5.0
Thymatron DGx (IEC) ***(2nd Gen.)***	1989 - 1994	.9	126	4.0	504	222/ 111	226	100/50	100J@220Ω Pure	2.26/ 4.52
Thymatron DGx (FDx2) System IV ***(3rd Gen.)***	1995 -?	1.36	190	5.3	1008	222/ 111	452	100/50	200J@220Ω Pure	4.52/ 9.04
Thymatron DGx (FDx2) System V ***(4th Gen.)***	? - ?	1.36	190	5.3	1008	111/ 55.5	904	100/50	398J@220Ω Pure	9.04/ 18.08
Max under new standard ***(5th Gen.)***	? - ?	2.0	150	4.0	1200	100/ 50	1200	100/50	528J@220Ω Pure	12.0/ 24.0

Only by observing the (unreported) shaded columns on the charts above--minimum Charge thresholds, overall maximum Energy Outputs, pure-ER/RRCs, and MTTLOI--for both BL and UL "ECT," do Weiner's 1997 Charge "regulations" (mC/phase; mC/Sec.; total Charge) have any significant meaning.[197] What we can plainly

[197] Neither does Weiner require threshold reporting in terms of Charge.

see from both unreported Charge and EO in the shaded portions of the charts above is that Charge thresholds vary and are thus unreliable, whereas, EO thresholds (in Joules) are constant. In short, 3rd, 4th, and 5th generation BP devices cannot be differentiated under Weiner's 1997 standard reporting in Charge. Moreover, the 2nd generation BP device was reported as a first generation device. In sum, Charge reporting sans EO reporting is abjectly misleading.

For instance, note that the MECTA C, confined to 108 maximum joules, has a greater mC/phase output (1.2mC/phase) than the theoretical 4th generation JR/SR 2 device (1.12mC/phase), which emits (960J ÷ 108J =) 8.8 times the Energy Output and (9.6 ÷ 1.08 =) 8.8 times the MTTLOI with BL ECT as does the MECTA C. Note too, despite gross power increases from 3rd to 4th to 5th generation BP devices, how overall outputs in terms of Charge appear almost identical, creating the impression that these three devices are similar in power. Only by observing the four shaded columns to the right, all of which contain EO readings (in joules), does the alarming increase in and significance of the power enhancements become manifest, particularly with respect to MTTLOI. In addition, only by observing MTTLOI with both BL and UL "ECT," can we see that recipients pf both are administered default outputs at least twice that necessary to accommodate Weiner's UL "dose-sensitivity" and "doubling of Impedance" over a "treatment" course. Only by juxtaposing EO parameters (in joules) then, can we see that later BP devices are no longer based on adequate seizure and so are no longer "ECT" devices at all, but rather ENR devices, based on adequate amounts of electricity.

An Even More Concise Picture

For an even more concise picture, let us focus on the devolving sequence only of the MECTA JR/SR 1 Brief Pulse devices. By using only the MECTA JR/SR 1 sequence, all of which are allowed under the Weiner 1997 proviso, we can even more clearly see the advantages of EO reporting vs. Charge reporting alone. Using Weiner's Charge reporting system of mC/Phase, and mC/Sec. in the unshaded portion on the left, while we do see increases in total Charge output from first to second and second to third generation JR/SR 1 devices, total Charge reporting with respect to third, fourth, and fifth generation devices seem uneventful, making all three devices appear similar in power. Indeed, if we assume first generation devices emit circa 500mC or that second generation devices emit circa 100 maximum joules (as their readouts proclaim), that is, that first and second generation BP devices are both first generation BP devices, there appear only two significant changes, first and second seeming like one device, third, fourth, and fifth seeming like another, in short, only one doubling of output from first to second generation BP devices. Observing the shaded areas on the right, we see there are actually four doublings (the latter an increase of only 25%), five possible generations of BP devices under Weiner's 1997 de facto "standard." Without EO reporting, therefore, even minimum Charge thresholds don't give us much insight. EO reporting alone then, specifically--total EO, pure-ER/RRC with respect to Joules/Impedance, minimum EO thresholds in Joules, and finally the MTTLOI (or titration) with respect to Joules--reveal the pertinent information, revealing dramatically increasing power with each of the five Brief Pulse generations, increases never heretofore reported. See below:

Five Generations of BP JR/SR 1 Devices

Device (Generation)	**Year**	**mC/** Phase	**mC/** Sec	**Duration** (Seconds)	**Total Charge (mC)**	**BL/UL Thres-hold (mC)**	**Total EO Joules**	**BL/UL Threshold (Joules)**	**ER/RRC**	**MTTLOI** (multi-fold dosing) BL/UL ECT
MECTA "C" (American) **(1st Gen.)**	1976 - 1982	1.2	168	2.0	336	313/ 156	108	100/50	70J@220Ω Conditional	1.08/ 2.16
JR/SR **- 1** (IEC) **(2nd Gen.)**	1984 - 1994	1.6	288	2.0	576	222/ 111	230	100/50	101J@220 Ω Pure	2.3/ 4.6

JR/SR - **1** (IEC) **(3rd Gen.)**	1995 - ?	1.6	288	4.0	1152	250/ 125	460	100/50	202J@220 Ω Pure	4.6/ 9.2
JR/SR - **1** (IEC) **(4th Gen.)**	? - ?	1.6	288	4.0	1152	125/ 62.5	922	100/50	404J@220 Ω Pure	9.22/ 18.44
Maximum under new standard **(5th Gen.)**	? - ?	2.0	150	4.0	1200	100/ 50[198]	1200	100/50	528J@220 Ω Pure	12.0/ 24.0

Summary

As noted above, while reports of Charge emissions may be helpful in conjunction with EO emissions, the reporting of even maximum Charge outputs in the absence of maximum EO in joules, minimum EO thresholds, pure-ER/RRCs, and finally default MTTLOIs emitted by each specific machine, is extremely misleading. Note, for instance, that even though the ***third generation* JR/SR 1 BP** device doubles both the maximum Charge and maximum EO of the ***second generation* JR/SR 1**, and the fourth generation doubles the maximum EO of the ***third generation* JR/SR 1**, the second, third, and fourth generation JR/SR 1 BP devices utilize the same 1.6mC/phase and the same 288mC/second Charge. Invisible to the viewer are potential fifth generation BP devices increasing more than (12 fold threshold ÷ 1.08 fold threshold =) 11 fold the MTTLOI of first generation BP devices, fourth generation BP devices increasing more than (9.22 fold threshold ÷ 1.08 fold threshold =) 8.53 fold the MTTLOI of first generation BP devices, third generation BP devices increasing more than (4.6 fold threshold ÷ 1.08 fold threshold =) 4.0 fold the MTTLOI of second generation BP devices and second generation BP devices increasing more than (2.3 fold threshold ÷ 1.08 fold threshold =) 2.0 fold the MTTLOI of first generation devices. These gross increases occur even as the mC/phase and mC/second remain unchanged from second to third to fourth generation BP devices and even as total Charge, as noted, remains virtually unchanged from third to fourth to fifth generation BP devices, veiling the sequential enhancements. Using EO parameters (joules), on the other hand, we can clearly see the increases in power through total EO emitted, the pure-ER/RRC enhancements upon which these devices are based, and most importantly, the sequentially increasing MTTLOI of each succeeding device (never before reported by any manufacturer). This striking clarity in reporting EO in joules is due to the fact that, unlike initial minimum Charge thresholds, minimum EO thresholds are relatively constant.

Again then, we see that without the EO reporting depicted in the shaded columns above, all of which have been dropped under the Weiner proviso, sequential augmentations remain almost wholly obscured.[199] For a more extended example, note above how (for the JR/SR 1 series) the millicoulombs per phase parameters from second to third to fourth to fifth generation BP devices increase only slightly (from 1.16 to 2.0mC/phase) while the millicoulombs per second parameters from second, third, and fourth to the potential fifth generation BP device, actually decrease (from 288mC/sec to 150mC/sec) falsely suggesting a decrease in EO and MTTLOI. Again, note how maximum Charge output from third to fourth to fifth generation BP devices remain almost identical (from 1152mC to 1200mC). The apparent similarity, as has been mentioned, is due to unreported Charge thresholds decreasing by half from third to fourth generation BP devices, invisibly doubling the unreported MTTLOI in every age category. Subsequently, minimum Charge thresholds are invisibly reduced even further from fourth to fifth generation devices making the augmentation appear slight. In terms of EO, however, we can see, for example, that the fourth generation BP device emits an invisible 9.22 MTTLOI with BL "ECT" and an 18.44 MTTLOI with UL "ECT" in every age category while the potential fifth generation BP device emits an invisible 12 MTTLOI with BL "ECT" and an invisible 24 MTTLOI with UL "ECT" in every age category, all invisible under the Weiner proviso.

---

198 1200J ÷ 100J = 100J; 1200mC ÷ 12 = 100mC

199 Conversely, Medcraft's second generation B-25 BP device could emit 840mC of Charge while confined to 100 maximum Joules.

Maximum Charge reporting alone, as heretofore noted, is not only inadequate, but, as we can see, extremely deceptive. In order to identify specific machine emissions and comparative enhancements generally, maximum output in Joules, pure-ER/RRC in joules, and most importantly, MTTLOI (derived from joules) must be reported. In sum, Weiner's mC/phase, mC/second, and maximum Charge "regulations" actually allow gross enhancements of up to 12 fold threshold outputs for all age recipients with BL "ECT" and 24 fold threshold outputs for all age recipients with UL "ECT, while simultaneously veiling these very enhancements.

A Few Last Tables on EO Reporting vs. Charge Reporting

To be redundant, Tables 1 (JR/SR 1) and 3 (JR/SR 2) below represent reported Charge parameters required under the 1997 Weiner standard for what are actually third, fourth, and fifth generation JR/SR 1 and 2 MECTA BP devices. Compare Table 1 (JR/SR 1) containing Charge parameters to Table 2 (JR/SR 1) containing EO parameters and Table 3 (JR/SR 2) containing Charge parameters to Table 4 (JR/SR 2) containing EO reporting for the very same devices. In spite of dramatic power and sequential MTTLOI increases from third to probable fourth, to "allowable" fifth generation MECTA BP devices, the Charge parameters required under the 1997 Weiner proviso, as we can see, depict almost no difference and virtually no augmentation with respect to the sequence of devices.

Table 1-2: Weiner's Required Charge Parameters: 3rd, 4th, 5th Generation MECTA JR/SR 1

Device (3rd, 4th, 5th Generation)	**Year**	**mC/Phase**	**mC/Sec**	**Duration (Seconds)**	**Total Charge (mC)**
JR/SR - **1** (IEC) **(3rd Gen.)**	1995- ?	1.16	288	4.0	1152
JR/SR - **1** (IEC) **(4th Gen.)**	? - ?	1.16	288	4.0	1152
Maximum under 1997 standard **(5th Gen.)**	? - ?	2.0	150	4.0	1200

Under Weiner's 1997 "standard" these devices appear very similar in power.

Table 1-2: Unreported and Excised EO Parameters: 3rd, 4th, 5th Generation MECTA JR/SR 1

Device (3rd, 4th, 5th Generation)	**Year**	**Maximum EO Joules**	**ER/RRC**	**Initial MTTLOI BL ECT**	**Initial MTTLOI UL ECT**
JR/SR - **1** (IEC) **(3rd Gen.)**	1995- ?	460	202J@220Ω Pure	4.6	9.2
JR/SR - **1** (IEC) **(4th Gen.)**	? - ?	922	404J@220Ω Pure	9.22	18.44
Maximum under new standard **(5th Gen.)**	? - ?	1200	528J@220Ω Pure	12.0	24.0

Under requirements within the 1982 APA Standard these devices are exposed as very dissimilar in power.

Table 3-4: Weiner's Required Charge Parameters: 3rd, 4th, 5th Generation MECTA JR/SR 2

Device (3rd, 4th, 5th Generation)	**Year**	**mC/Phase**	**mC/Sec**	**Duration** (Seconds)	**Total Charge (mC)**
JR/SR - **2** (IEC) **(3rd Gen.)**	1995- ?	1.12	201.6	5.96	1200
JR/SR - **2** (IEC) **(4th Gen.)**	? - ?	1.16	201.6	5.96	1200
Maximum under 1997 standard **(5th Gen.)**	? - ?	2.0	150	4.0	1200

Under Weiner's 1997 "standard" these devices appear very similar in power.

Table 3-4: Unreported and Excised EO Parameters: 3rd, 4th, 5th Generation MECTA JR/SR 2

Device (3rd, 4th, 5th Generation)	**Year**	**Maximum EO Joules**	**ER/RRC**	**Initial MTTLOI BL ECT**	**Initial MTTLOI UL ECT**
JR/SR - **2** (IEC) **(3rd Gen.)**	1995- ?	480	211J@220Ω Pure	4.8	9.6
JR/SR - **2** (IEC) **(4th Gen.)**	? - ?	960	422J@220Ω Pure	9.6	19.2
Maximum under new standard **(5th Gen.)**	? - ?	1200	528J@220Ω Pure	12.0	24.0

Under requirements within the 1982 APA Standard, these devices are exposed as very dissimilar in power.

CHAPTER 77

Manufacturer Secret Revealed--Doubling MTTLOI Per Each New BP Generation

Because this simple discovery of how to identify not only the power of various BP devices, but the power emitted per age category is so critical, I shall devote one more short chapter to It. Understanding this derivative, we can never again be deceived by manufacturers with respect to the power of their Brief Pulse machines. We have numerous times understood from Beale's 1994 study that Charge is approximately 2.5 and 5.0 fold threshold with BL and UL "ECT" respectively for every individual recipient administered "ECT" with second generation made-for-America BP devices. Converting to Joules, as we have seen, we find the same 2.5, 5.0 MTTLOI in terms of EO (joules), corroborating the initial constant threshold dosages of 100 and 50 Joules with BL and UL ECT respectively for all 100 year old recipients (250J ÷ 2.5 = 100J; 250J ÷ 5.0 = 50J). Conversely, dividing the default EO administered to the 100 year old age group, that is, the overall maximum EO by 100J and 50J on any BP device, we can determine the MTTLOI delivered with BL (and UL) "ECT" for all age recipients. For example, the Thymatron DG delivers a maximum 252J (to the 100 year old recipient), so that if we divide 252J by 100J and 252J by 50J, we can determine the (252J ÷ 100J =) 2.52 MTTLOI delivered to all age recipients with BL "ECT" and the (252J ÷ 50J =) 5.04 MTTLOI delivered to all recipients with UL "ECT." All manufacturers of Brief Pulse devices secretly use this formula for determining the hidden power of their BP devices with respect to how many times threshold, that is, the MTTLOI for which a machine is set. In fact, if we but divide the maximum default output a machine administers to a particular age category by the MTTLOI of that particular device, we can determine the EO threshold (in joules) of that specific age category. Indeed, the initial threshold output in joules for all age categories is once again listed below in the form of perfect squares. All BP manufacturers use these perfect squares (in joules) as threshold constants so that if a machine is set to deliver a 2.52 MTTLOI for all 40 year old recipients, we simply multiply 16J (the threshold constant used for 40 year old recipients) by 2.52 to determine the (16J x 2.52 =) 40.32J default output delivered to all forty years old recipients on that particular BP device. Conversely, if we know the output delivered to a particular age category, we simply divide by the MTTLOI for that device to deduce the threshold constant. These formulas work with all MECTA and Somatics BP devices and apparently for most, if not all European BP manufactures as well. In short, manufacturers appear to use these threshold constants for all BP devices.

UBIQUITOUS THRESOLD CONSTANTS IN JOULES RELATIVE TO AGE
(Derived from the second generation Thymatron DG)

AGE IN YEARS	OUTPUT AND MTTLOI BASED ON BEALE STUDY AND OUTPUTS OF MADE-FOR-AMERICA THYMATRON DG	INITIAL THRESHOLD CONSTANTS WITH BL ECT in Joules	INITIAL THRESHOLD CONSTANTS WITH UL ECT in Joules
10	2.52J ÷ 2.52 =	**1.00J** (÷ 2 =)	**.5J**
20	10.09J ÷ 2.52 =	**4.00J** (÷ 2 =)	**2.00J**
30	22.68J ÷ 2.52 =	**9.00J** (÷ 2 =)	**4.5J**
40	40.32J ÷ 2.52 =	**16.00J** (÷ 2 =)	**8.0J**
50	63.00J ÷ 2.52 =	**25.00J** (÷ 2 =)	**12.5J**
60	90.72J ÷ 2.52 =	**36.00J** (÷ 2 =)	**18.0J**
65	106.47J ÷ 2.52 =	**42.25J** (÷ 2 =)	**21.13J**
70	123.40J ÷ 2.52 =	**48.97J** (÷ 2 =)	**24.49J**
80	161.28J ÷ 2.52 =	**64.00J** (÷ 2 =)	**32J**
90	204.10J ÷ 2.52 =	**81.00J** (÷ 2 =)	**40.5J**
100	252.00J ÷ 2.52 =	**100.00J** (÷ 2 =)	**50J**

UBIQUITOUS THRESOLD DOSAGES IN JOULES RELATIVE TO AGE
(Derived from the first generation MECTA C)

AGE IN YEARS	OUTPUT AND MTTLOI BASED ON BEALE STUDY AND OUTPUTS OF MADE-FOR-AMERICA THYMATRON DG	INITIAL THRESHOLD CONSTANTS WITH BL ECT in Joules	INITIAL THRESHOLD CONSTANTS WITH UL ECT in Joules
10	1.08J ÷ 1.08 =	**1.00J** (÷ 2 =)	**.5J**
20	4.32J ÷ 1.08 =	**4.00J** (÷ 2 =)	**2.00J**
30	9.72J ÷ 1.08 =	**9.00J** (÷ 2 =)	**4.5J**
40	17.28J ÷ 1.08 =	**16.00J** (÷ 2 =)	**8.0J**
50	27.00J ÷ 1.08 =	**25.00J** (÷ 2 =)	**12.5J**
60	38.88J ÷ 1.08 =	**36.00J** (÷ 2 =)	**18.0J**
65	46.00J ÷ 1.08 =	**42.25J** (÷ 2 =)	**21.13J**
70	52.95J ÷ 1.08 =	**48.97J** (÷ 2 =)	**24.49J**
80	69.12J ÷ 1.08 =	**64.00J** (÷ 2 =)	**32J**
90	87.48J ÷ 1.08 =	**81.00J** (÷ 2 =)	**40.5J**
100	108.00J ÷ 1.08 =	**100.00J** (÷ 2 =)	**50J**

The same threshold constants can be derived from any generation BP device so long as we know the default output administered to that particular age category and the MTTLOI for that particular device.

Because the 100 year old recipient has an initial seizure threshold with BL and UL ECT of exactly 100 and 50 Joules minimum respectively (or because manufacturers assume so) once we learn the maximum EO for any BP device, we need only divide that maximum output by 100 and 50J respectively to determine the MTTLOI (Multifold Threshold Titration Level Output Intensity) administered with BL "ECT" and UL "ECT" to all recipients with that BP device.

For instance, if the maximum output on a particular BP device reaches 922 Joules, we simply divide that maximum by 100J and 50J respectively to obtain the (922J ÷ 100J =) 9.22 and (922J ÷ 50J =) 18.44 MTTLOI with BL and UL "ECT" respectively administered to all age recipients with that device; This method can be confirmed by dividing the default EO administered to any age category by the device's overall MTTLOI from which we can then derive the initial threshold constant (used by manufacturers) for any age category. For example, the Thymatron DG above administers a default output of 40.32J to the 40 year old category (formulaically determined by parameter information provided by Somatics). Dividing this 40.32J by the 2.52

MTTLOI used for this device, we obtain the initial threshold output of 16J with BL "ECT" for the 40 year old and then dividing by 2, the initial threshold output of 8J with UL "ECT" for the same 40 year old recipient. The initial threshold constants for specific age categories remain relatively constant (or manufacturers assume so) regardless of the Brief Pulse device. [200]

Based on the threshold constants directly above, the first, second, and third generation extant BP devices as well as the probable fourth and potential fifth generation BP devices for, for example, the MECTA JR/SR 1 series, all legal under Weiner's 1997 standard, elicit successive circa MTTLOI default increases of 1.08, 2.3, 4.6, 9.22, and 12.0 with BL "ECT," but which, for convenience, we shall round to a 1.25, 2.5, 5.0, 10.0, and 12.0 MLTLOI for the graph below. This also means successive circa MTTLOI default increases with UL "ECT" of 2.5, 5.0, 10.0, 20.0, and 24.0 MTTLOI. Just as raw EO must increase with increasing age/Impedance on any particular BP device, the overall MTTLOI increases with each new, more powerful BP machine generation, consistently doubling the MTTLOI from first through fourth generations in every age category and substantially increasing the MTTLOI for fifth generation device BP devices, all "allowed" (but hidden) under the rogue 1997 Weiner proviso. In addition to the relatively smaller amount of raw output used for the youngest recipient compared to the much larger amount of raw output used for the oldest recipient on each individual BP device, we can once again see from the chart below how the MTTLOI is consistent with respect to all ages for a particular device, but dramatically increases (for all age categories) with each new BP generation, consistently doubling through the fourth generation in every age category, and increasing even further with the potential fifth generation BP device. For instance, while the ten year old is administered at least 1.08J with the first generation MECTA "C" with BL "ECT" and the 100 year old 108J with BL "ECT" by the same device, both the ten year old and the 100 year old receive a consistent 1.08 default MTTLOI delivered by the MECTA "C." Subsequently, while the same ten year old receives at least 12.0 Joules with the potential fifth generation JR/SR 1 BP device and the 100 year old receives at least 1200J with the same fifth generation device, both the ten year old and the 100 year old are administered a consistent 12.0 MTTLOI by the fifth generation JR/SR 1 BP device. Thus, while the EO increases with the advancing age category within each individual machine, the MTTLOI on each device, though increased from the previous device, remains constant on that particular device for all age categories. Because the MTTLOI increases with each new BP generation, however, age related output defaults increase dramatically from one machine generation to the next. Note then, the increasing MTTLOI with BL "ECT" on the graph below for all five MECTA BP device generations. MTTLOI with UL "ECT" doubles that.

[200] MECTA uses a slightly higher threshold assumption for the lowest age category, so that derivations for the ten year old child will be slightly skewed.

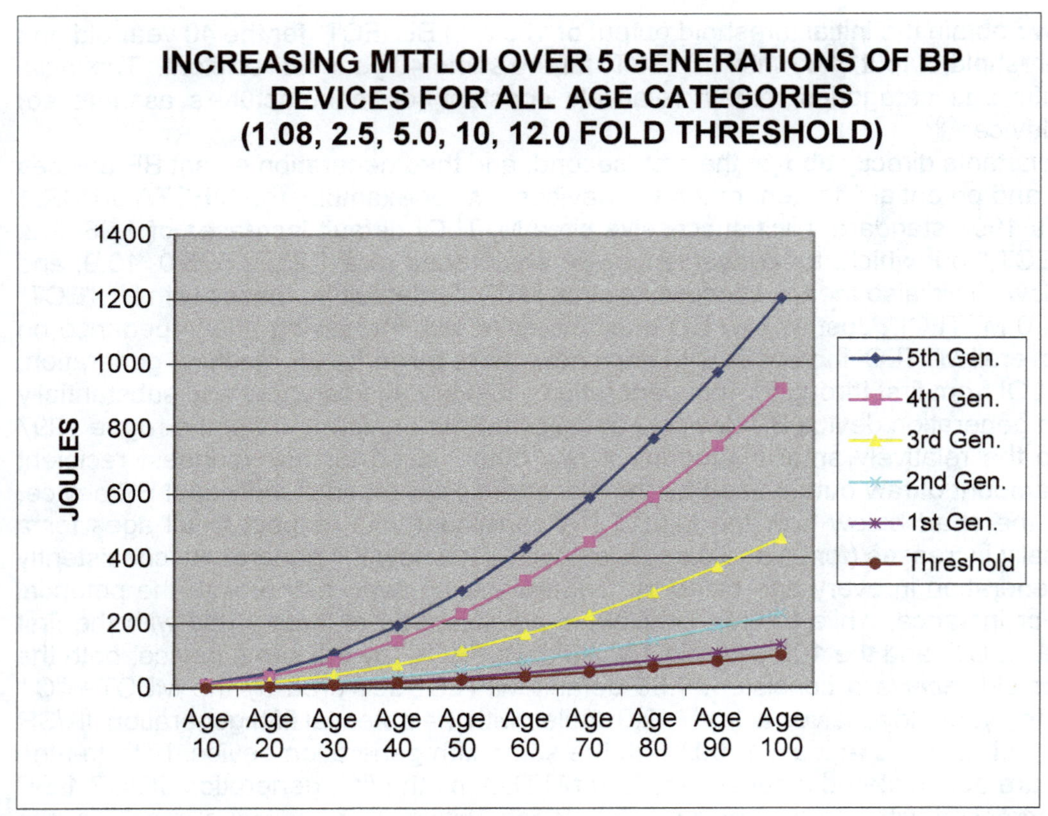
INCREASING MTTLOI OVER 5 GENERATIONS OF BP DEVICES FOR ALL AGE CATEGORIES (1.08, 2.5, 5.0, 10, 12.0 FOLD THRESHOLD)
JOULES
1400
1200
1000
800
600
400
200
0
Age 10
Age 20
Age 30
Age 40
Age 50
Age 60
Age 70
Age 80
Age 90
Age 100
5th Gen.
4th Gen.
3rd Gen.
2nd Gen.
1st Gen.
Threshold

CHAPTER 78

The Dropping of ER/RRC

The 1989 IEC Standard for BP "ECT" devices, in turn a morph of the Mectan Transmutation, in turn a morph of the 1982 APA Standard, all ultimately morph into Weiner's 1997 de facto standard shifting electrical "limiter" reporting from EO to Charge. One dynamic of EO reporting previously present in the 1982 APA Standard and even the 1989 IEC Standard, but utterly discarded in Weiner's newest 1997 de facto proviso, is what the author has deemed ER/RRC or "Equivalent Ratio/Rate Rise Ceiling." Even pure- Equivalent Ratio/Rate Rise Ceiling (as opposed to conditional-ER/RRC) has been discarded in Weiner's 1997 de facto "standard," completing the veiling of increasingly dangerous, extremely high output enhancements regarding each new BP generation. As a result, of course, increasingly hazardous (what this author has deemed) "MTTLOI" (Multifold Threshold Titration Level Output Intensity) enhancements for every age category are veiled.

For instance, under Weiner's 1997 de facto standard, manufacturers are not required to report that, based on the same 500Ω Impedance ceiling, the circa "101J at 220Ω" pure-ER/RRC reported for what were actually second generation MECTA IEC BP devices, increased to a circa (202J/220Ω = 460J/500Ω) "202J at 220Ω" pure-ER/RRC for what are actually third generation IEC BP devices. Had ER/RRC reporting or any other kind of EO reporting (containing joules) remained intact within Weiner's 1997 de facto standard, such a conspicuous increase would almost certainly have attracted attention, figures which meant that what were actually second generation IEC BP devices had transitioned to what are now third generation IEC BP devices via the doubling of EO from circa (<u>101J</u>/220Ω = <u>XJ</u>/500Ω; X =) 230 maximum joules to circa (<u>202J</u>/220Ω = <u>XJ</u>/500Ω; X =) 460 maximum joules.

Moreover, other unreported EO measurements accompanying the doubling of pure-ER/RRC, and thus the doubling of maximum Output in Joules, is the doubling of MTTLOI (indeed, never reported by any manufacturer), and the doubling of Joules per Ohm (J/Ω)—also a parameter never reported by any manufacturer for any BP device (which we will examine in a moment). As has already been noted, MTTLOI administered by a particular BP machine can be derived by dividing maximum machine EO (in joules) by 100J with BL "ECT" and 50J with UL "ECT," in this case revealing that second and third generation BP devices delivering 230 and 460J respectively increase from a (230J ÷100J =) 2.3 MTTLOI to a (460J ÷ 100J =) 4.6 MTTLOI, doubling the power administered to each age category. In addition, we can find a J/Ω default ratio maximum by dividing either the numerator by the denominator of the ER/RRC, that is, ER-EO by the ER-Impedance (i.e. 101J ÷ 220Ω = .46) or by dividing maximum machine output by maximum machine Impedance (i.e. 230J ÷ 500Ω = .46) for any specific BP device. To Illustrate, the <u>2nd generation MECTA IEC JR/SR 1</u> has a pure-ER/RRC of <u>101J at 220Ω</u> and so a (101J ÷ 220Ω =) <u>.46J/Ω</u> default ratio, just as the same <u>2nd generation MECTA IEC JR/SR 1</u> ER/RRC has a maximum EO and maximum Impedance of <u>230J at 500Ω</u> and so the same (230J at 500Ω =) <u>.46J/Ω</u> default ratio. The <u>3rd generation MECTA IEC JR/SR 1</u> has a pure-ER/RRC of 202J at 220Ω and so a much higher (202J ÷ 220Ω =) <u>.92J/Ω</u> default ratio; just as the same <u>3rd generation MECTA IEC JR/SR 1</u> has a maximum EO and maximum impedance of 460J at 500Ω and so the same (460J

÷ 500Ω =) .92J/Ω default ratio. [201] In short, from the J/Ω default ratio maximums, we can see that the .46J/Ω (joules delivered per ohm) default ratio emitted by the second generation MECTA IEC JR/SR 1 BP device transitions to a .92J/Ω default ratio emitted by the third generation MECTA IEC JR/SR 1 BP, thereby doubling overall power.

Had even one of the EO measures--the pure-ER/RRC, the overall maximum EO, the MTTLOI, or the J/Ω ratio--been consistently reported for both the second and third generation JR/SR 1 BP device, the dramatic increase in power, that is, the doubling of output, would have become transparent.[202] Clearly, Weiner influenced manufacturers to drop EO reporting in that the unacceptably high maximum EOs, unacceptably high pure-ER/RRCs, unacceptably high MTTLOIs, and unacceptably high J/Ω ratios allowed under Weiner's 1997 de facto standard would have become visible. Remember, the 1982 APA Standard limited output to a conditional-ER/RRC of "70J at 220Ω" with 110J ceiling while the MECTA "C" was based on a conditional "59J at 220Ω" ER/RRC with 108J ceiling in accordance with the 1982 APA Standard, reflecting minimal stimulus with BL ECT. Had it been known that the overall output allowed under Weiner's 1997 de facto standard had surpassed the unacceptably high 200J maximum output of SW devices, much less to what degree it had surpassed SW, the illusion of the new and improved Brief Pulse device emitting minimal stimulus outputs with much less power than SW would have been annihilated along with the safer than SW Brief Pulse image manufacturers sought to retain. As a result of dropping maximum output reporting, ER/RRC, never reporting the critical MTTLOI, and never reporting J/Ω ratios, power increases from one BP generation to the next become impossible to spot, monitor, compare, or regulate.

In fact, Weiner's 1997 default standard is so permissive that it is, in effect, the deregulation of so-called "ECT" devices. Indeed, it is the approbation of electro-dependent ENR Brief Pulse devices. In fact, by using Charge maximums alone (the tail wagging the dog) based on a now universally accepted 500Ω Impedance maximum, Weiner's 1997 default standard furtively allows an overall "528J at 220Ω" pure-ER/RRC (528J/220Ω = 1200J/500Ω) permitting a potential fifth generation device with a 1200J maximum output capacity, a 12.0 MTTLOI with BL ECT (1200J ÷ 100 = 12.0 fold), a 24.0 MTTLOI with UL ECT and a maximum (528J ÷ 220Ω; 1200J ÷ 500Ω =) 2.4J/Ω ratio--all newly possible under the 1997 Weiner proviso. Based upon the European "300Ω" ER Impedance figure used in the 1989 IEC standard (in lieu of a 220Ω ER-Impedance), a mandatory reporting of ER/RRC would have forced manufacturers to report an increase from a "130J at 300Ω" pure-ER/RRC to a whopping "720J at 300Ω" pure-ER/RRC under the 1997 Weiner de facto standard, from which (using a 500Ω Impedance maximum), we can derive Weiner's frightening 1200 Joule maximum output (720J/300Ω = 528J/220Ω = 1200J/500Ω), allowing a (1200J ÷ 100J =) 12.0 MTTLOI with BL ENR and a (1200J ÷ 50J =) 24.0 MTTLOI with UL ENR as well as the aforementioned (720J ÷ 300Ω =) 2.4J/Ω ratio default maximum. Compare this to the (59J ÷ 220Ω =) .27J/Ω ratio of the MECTA "C" conforming to the 1982 APA Standard—against which Weiner's standard allows a more than (2.4 - .27 = 2.13; 2.13 ÷ .27 = 7.88 =) 789% increase. Under Weiner's 1997 standard, the supplanting of EO (in joules) with Charge parameters alone means regulatory agencies cannot meaningful derive outputs, compare outputs to previous devices, or even see the comparative increases. Specifically, they cannot readily see that seizure-dependent "ECT" devices have now transitioned into electro-dependent ENR Brief Pulse devices.

---

[201] This doubling of the maximum J/Ω ratio reflects the fact that a (230J ÷100J =) 2.3 MTTLOI for a 100 year old recipient has transitioned to a (460J ÷ 100J =) 4.6 MTTLOI, in turn applied to every age category.

[202] Based on the current 500Ω maximum Impedance, the 3rd generation System IV has an unreported ER/RRC of "271.5J at 300Ω" or "200J at 220Ω," the third generation JR/SR 2, "288J at 300Ω" or "211J at 220Ω," and the third generation JR/SR 1, "276J at 300Ω" or "202J at 220Ω," none of which are reported or must be reported under Weiner's 1997 de facto standard.

SECTION XV: To Compare SW with Early and Later BP Devices

CHAPTER 79

J/Ω Ratios

The J/Ω (Joules per Ohm) ratio, as we have just seen, is yet another method of measuring the power profile of any ECT or ENR device. Indeed, once we determine the maximum default J/Ω ratio, that is, the J/Ω ratio delivered to the oldest recipient for a particular BP device, we can then approximate the default J/Ω ratio delivered to any particular age group with any particular BP device. For instance, for a third generation MECTA JR/SR 1 device emitting a 460J maximum at a 500Ω machine maximum based on a 202J at 220Ω pure-ER/RRC (202J/220Ω = 460J/500Ω), we can determine the default J/Ω ratio per age category simply by dividing the default output (delivered) by the general Impedance. For instance, for the twenty year old recipient administered ENR by the third generation MECTA JR/SR 1, we first multiply the machine's MTTLOI by the seizure threshold for any particular age group (i.e. 4J) to derive the default output delivered (4.6 MTTLOI x 4J = 18.4J). We then divide the default output delivered by that age group's approximate Impedance (i.e. 100Ω) to determine the (18.4J ÷ 100Ω =) .184J/Ω ratio delivered. In short, the default J/Ω ratio delivered by the third generation MECTA JR/SR 1 device to the 20 year old age category = .184J/Ω.

We can also determine that the 100 year old on the same MECTA JR/SR 1 third generation BP device receives .918J/Ω. For example, we multiply the 4.6 MTTLOI by the Impedance Threshold (100J) for the 100 year old, then divide by the general Impedance for that age group (500Ω) to derive a (4.6 x 100J = 460J ÷ 500Ω =) .918J/Ω for the 100 year old recipient. Thus, simply by dividing the default outputs of specific age categories by the default Impedances of specific age categories on a particular BP device, we can determine the J/Ω ratios for various age categories. Based on this paradigm, for example, we can derive the following J/Ω ratios for all age categories on the 3rd generation *MECTA JR/SR 1.*

Comparative J/Ω Ratios per Age Category on a 3rd Generation MECTA JR/SR 1

AGE	BP Ω	J/Ω 3rd BP
10	50	.115
20	100	.184
24	120	.221
30	150	.276
40	200	.370
50	250	.460
60	300	.550
65	325	.600
70	350	.645

80	400	.737
90	450	.828
100	500	.920

Some approximation is inevitable due to speculative Impedances. The principle of increasing ratio with increasing age, however, is sound. In any case, the third generation JR/SR 1 delivers 460 maximum joules and thus a 4.6 MTTLOI for all age categories. MECTA assumes an unusual 1.25J threshold output constant for the ten year old child instead of the usual 1.0J. Consequently, MECTA's third generation BP device administers a default (1.25J x 4.6 =) 5.75J output to the ten year old child in lieu of what should actually be a (1.0J x 4.6 =) 4.6J output This means the J/Ω ratio for the ten year old on the third generation MECTA JR/SR 1 is (5.75J ÷ 50Ω =) .115J/Ω instead of the expected (4.6J ÷ 50J) = .092J/Ω ratio which in turn veils the consistent MTTLOI for all other age groups. If, on the other hand, we assume the typical 1.0J threshold and thus a 4.6J output delivered by default to the ten year old child by the third generation JR/SR 1, we see that the ten year old receives a default (4.6J ÷ 50J =) .092J/Ω output ratio just as the 100 year old receives a (460J ÷ 500Ω =) .92J/Ω default output ratio revealing what is actually a consistent pattern. The consistency is such that simply by adding .092 to the .092J/Ω ratio received by the ten year old, we can obtain the .184 J/Ω output ratio administered to the twenty year old (.092 + .092 = .184J/Ω; 18.43J ÷ 100Ω = .184J/Ω). Adding another .092J/Ω, we obtain the default .276J/Ω ratio administered to the 30 year old: (.184J/Ω + .092J/Ω = .276J/Ω; .092J/Ω + 092J/Ω + .092J/Ω = .276J/Ω and so on. We can also, as heretofore noted, obtain the .276J/Ω ratio administered to the thirty year old simply by dividing the default output administered to this age category by the default Impedance for this age category with this particular device (41.47J ÷ 150Ω = .276J/Ω). The chart below contains the approximate default J/Ω ratio delivered to each age category by the 3rd generation *MECTA JR/SR 1 device*. Below is the same chart as that above beginning with .092 in lieu of .115 from which an emerging pattern becomes manifest, the increasing by .092J/Ω of each increasing age category on this specific Brief Pulse device.

Comparative J/Ω Ratios per Age Category Delivered by a 3rd Generation MECTA JR/SR 1 (but with a .0092J/Ω ratio delivered to the ten year old child)[203]

AGE	BP Ω	J/Ω 3rd BP
10	50	.092
20	100	.184
24	120	.221
30	150	.276
40	200	.370
50	250	.460
60	300	.550
65	325	.600
70	350	.645
80	400	.737
90	450	.828
100	500	.920

We can now make some telling comparisons amongst five generations of BP machines. Note how the J/Ω ratio generally doubles from first to second generation, doubles again from second to third generation, doubles again from third to fourth generation and increases once more from fourth to fifth generation BP devices. (The first generation BP device represented here is the MECTA "C" or "D.") In sum, while approximate, the J/Ω ratio doubles in the same age categories with each new BP generation except fifth, which simply increases.

[203] Is MECTA attempting to camouflage a revealing pattern?

J/Ω Ratios For Five generations of BP Devices

BP AGE	BP Imp Ω	J/Ω 1st BP	J/Ω 2nd BP	J/Ω 3rd BP	J/Ω 4th BP	J/Ω 5th BP
10	50	.027	.058	.092	.184	.30
20	100	.050	.092	.184	.369	.48
24	120	.065	.119	.221	.478	.625
30	150	.075	.138	.276	.553	.72
40	200	.101	.185	.370	.735	.96
50	250	.126	.230	.460	.92	1.20
60	300	.151	.276	.550	1.11	1.44
65	325	.164	.299	.600	1.20	1.56
70	350	.177	.323	.645	1.29	1.68
80	400	.202	.370	.737	1.48	1.92
90	450	.255	.413	.828	1.66	2.16
100	500	.268	.460	.920	1.84	2.40

Comparing maximum J/Ω Ratios of Earlier versus Later BP Devices

Simply by utilizing the ER/RRC of each BP generation to determine respective default J/Ω machine maximums (emitted in the 100 year old category), we can in yet another way identify the dramatic rise in power of each new actual, probable, and potential Brief Pulse generation, all "allowable" under the Weiner proviso.

1st generation = 59J at 220Ω = (59J ÷ 220Ω =) .268 J/Ω ratio (maximum)
2nd generation = 100J at 220Ω = (100J ÷ 220Ω =) .455 J/Ω ratio (maximum)
3rd generation = 202J at 220Ω = (202J ÷ 220Ω =) .918 J/Ω ratio (maximum)
4th generation = 404J at 220Ω = (404J ÷ 220Ω =) 1.834 J/Ω ratio (maximum)
5th generation = 528J at 220Ω = (528J ÷ 220Ω =) 2.400 J/Ω ratio (maximum)

We can see that under Weiner's 1997 Standard, the allowable J/Ω ratio is almost (2.4J/Ω ÷ .268J/Ω = 8.95) 9.0 times that of the MECTA "C" or "D," the "C" of which alone conforms to the FDA approved 1982 APA Standard.

Using J/Ω Ratios to Compare BP with SW

With this information, can now make some rather telling comparisons between BP machines and SW devices. For example, the following chart compares J/Ω per age group of a B-24 SW at maximum output with a Third Generation JR/SR 1 Brief Pulse Device. (The data for SW was derived in a previous section on SW devices.)

Default J/Ω Ratios for Five generations of BP Devices
Vs. SW at Maximum Output

AGE	SW Ω	BP Ω	J/Ω SW	J/Ω 1st BP	J/Ω 2nd BP	J/Ω 3rd BP	J/Ω 4th BP	J/Ω 5th BP
10	145	50	1.38	.027	.058	.092	.184	.30
20	195	100	.76	.050	.092	.184	.369	.48
24	215	120	.62	.065	.119	.221	.478	.625
30	245	150	.48	.075	.138	.276	.553	.72
40	295	200	.33	.101	.185	.370	.735	.96
50	345	250	.24	.126	.230	.460	.92	1.20

60	395	300	.185	.151	.276	.550	1.11	1.44
65	420	325	.163	.164	.299	.600	1.20	1.56
70	445	350	.145	.177	.323	.645	1.29	1.68
80	495	400	.118	.202	.370	.737	1.48	1.92
90	545	450	.097	.255	.413	.828	1.66	2.16
100	595	500	.081	.268	.460	.920	1.84	2.40

Note how SW begins with the highest J/Ω ratio in the youngest age group and begins to diminish, emitting the lowest J/Ω ratio in the oldest age group. BP, conversely, appropriately delivers the lowest J/Ω ratio in the youngest age group and the highest in the oldest age group. Moreover, unlike SW, the BP J/Ω ratio consistently increases with each age category. For example, the third generation device begins with a .092 J/Ω ratio in the ten year old age category, and increases .092J/Ω with each succeeding age category. Note too, how the first generation BP device begins to surpass the SW J/Ω ratio only from about age sixty-five and older, while the more powerful second generation BP device begins surpassing SW at about age fifty and older, the more powerful third generation BP device at about age forty and older, the more powerful fourth generation BP device at about age 30 and older, and finally, the fifth generation BP device at about age twenty-four and older. In short, each BP generation surpasses SW in power in an earlier and earlier age category until the default outputs emitted by the fifth generation BP device--except for the ten and twenty year old categories--surpass that of SW even set at maximum output in every other age category.

Output per Impedance (or Joules per Ohm) Cont'd

Once again, because J/Ω ratios are based on speculative Impedances in that (with the exception of some maximum Impedances) manufacturers do not provide age related Impedances, the J/Ω ratios above must be categorized as approximations. Even so, the Impedances are relatively accurate and the principle of ascending and descending ratios sound. Moreover, maximum and increasing Energy Output per single Ohm of Resistance is a rarely discussed parameter which can provide additional insight into the increasing power of modern day BP devices. During the SW era and before the re-introduction of the first generation modern day Brief Pulse device (via the MECTA "C"), SW output allegedly rose so rapidly or so high relative to Impedance that SW companies felt compelled to utilize "glissando" mechanisms to soften the initial electrical impact; (see section on SW). To fully appreciate the earlier and later power of the modern day BP devices as opposed to SW, therefore, we have compared (above) the ascending and successively enhancing J/Ω ratios of five successive generations of BP devices in all the various age categories with SW's deteriorating J/Ω ratios (even at maximum SW settings) in all the same age categories.

Due to the antithetical nature of the SW and BP machines, comparing SW to BP with respect to maximum or default output per single Ohm of Impedance is challenging. SW amperage (current) diminishes with increasing Impedance, in turn diminishing EO, whereas, BP amperage (current) remains constant in spite of increasing Impedance, resulting in increasing EO with increasing age (or Impedance). As a result, output on SW devices is inversely proportional to Impedance. That is, the lower the Impedance the higher the output and the higher the Impedance the lower the output. The output of BP devices on the other hand, is directly proportional to Impedance. That is, the lower the Impedance the lower the output, and the higher the Impedance the higher the output, a demonstrably advantageous dynamic with the earlier BP devices and a demonstrably exploitive dynamic with the later BP devices.[204] To illustrate, with very low Impedance, the B-24 SW can emit up to 200J, while at a higher Impedance, i.e. 400 ohms, due to diminished current, the B-24 SW can emit no more than 72 Joules (see charts below). Because increasing Impedances diminish the current on constant Voltage SW devices, maximum outputs occur at the lowest Impedances (or youngest age groups). This is the opposite of Brief Pulse devices. Maximum outputs on constant current BP devices occur at the highest

[204] The aim of the later constant current BP device is no longer the induction of minimal stimulus convulsions as with first generation BP devices, but maintenance of a consistent Multifold Threshold Titration Level Output Intensity for all age recipients. In short, the early models were based on convulsions induced by minimal amounts of electricity; whereas, later models are based on consistent amounts of electricity over threshold.

Impedances or oldest age categories.[205] SW devices, if we can even say that SW devices contain a RRC (Rate Rise Ceiling), have what might be deemed an inversely proportional RRC (the lower the Impedance, the higher the EO, the higher the Impedance the lower the EO) compared to BP's RRC wherein the lower the Impedance the lower the EO; the higher the Impedance, the higher the EO. On SW devices, in short, the highest J/Ω ratios occur in the youngest age categories, whereas, on BP devices, the highest J/Ω ratios occur in the oldest age categories. To illustrate further, the B-24 SW can reach 200J at a low (for SW) 145Ω, resulting in a J/Ω ratio maximum of (200J ÷ 145Ω) = **1.38J/Ω**. In contrast, the "138J at 300Ω" (or 101J at 220Ω) pure-ER/RRC for the second generation JR/SR 1 IEC BP device readily reveals a maximum output-Impedance ratio of (138J ÷ 300Ω; 101 ÷ 220Ω) = **.46J/Ω**, about a third that of SW maximum. This can be confirmed by dividing the JR/SR 1 IEC BP device's maximum Output of 230 Joules by its maximum Impedance of 500Ω (230J ÷ 500Ω = **.46J/Ω**). [206] From this particular comparison, we can conclude that maximum default output per Impedance for the relatively early second generation JR/SR 1 IEC BP device is yet much lower than the maximum output per Impedance of the B-24 SW device, although in entirely disparate age categories (10 years old compared to 100 years old). On the other hand, the third generation (JR/SR 1 IEC) BP device has a maximum J/Ω ratio of (460J ÷ 500Ω =) **.92J/Ω**, now two thirds the power of SW's maximum J/Ω ratio (**SW: 1.38J/Ω – BP: .92J/Ω = .46J/Ω + .46J/Ω + .46J/Ω = SW: 1.38J/Ω**) though again, in completely disparate age groups (10 years old compared to 100 years old). Tellingly, we can see that the maximum J/Ω ratio for BP devices occurs in the oldest age category (at which maximum BP EO occurs); whereas, the maximum J/Ω ratio for SW occurs in the youngest age category (at which maximum SW EO occurs). While this may appear to be an apples to oranges comparison, we can, in fact, very usefully determine at what point (age-wise) the J/Ω ratios of various BP devices begin to converge and even surpass the J/Ω ratios of SW, that is, in what age categories, the J/Ω ratios of the five successive generations of modern day BP devices equal and then surpass the J/Ω ratios of SW. For example, by the probable fourth generation BP device, the default maximum J/Ω ratio of BP is now one third more powerful than the maximum J/Ω ratio of SW (**922J ÷ 500Ω = BP: 1.84J/Ω - SW: 1.38J/Ω = .46J/Ω** + **.46J/Ω** + **.46J/Ω = SW: 1.38J/Ω)** though once more, in completely disparate age groups (again, 10 years old compared to 100 years old). By the hypothetical, but "allowable" fifth generation BP device, the maximum J/Ω ratio of BP is now 42.5% more powerful than the maximum J/Ω ratio of SW (**1200J ÷ 500Ω = BP: 2.4J/Ω**; **SW: 1.38J/Ω** ÷ **BP: 2.4J/Ω = 57.5%; 100% - 57.5% = 42.5%)** though again, in completely disparate age groups (again, 10 years old compared to 100 years old). In short, BP has completely surpassed SW in power.

Regardless of the inverse association of SW and BP regarding Impedance vs. EO, therefore, valuable comparisons can be made regarding the maximum J/Ω ratios of SW compared to the default J/Ω ratios of the five successive generations of BP devices with respect to the various age categories at which these outputs occur. In this manner, we can trace the converging of J/Ω ratios of SW at various ages with Brief Pulse default outputs via various BP devices. In brief, we can trace the increasing power of BP compared to SW J/Ω ratios in earlier and earlier age categories with each successive BP generation. Identifying the various age categories at which J/Ω ratios converge with SW at maximum settings as BP becomes more and more powerful, allows us to effectively compare not only BP to BP, but BP to SW. Such comparisons provide us with yet another useful variant for comparing the power of successive BP devices not only with one another but with the SW devices of the "past."

Comparing maximum J/Ω Ratios of Earlier versus Later BP Devices

Simply by utilizing the ER/RRC of each BP generation to determine respective default J/Ω machine maximums (emitted by default in the 100 year old category), we can once again identify the dramatic rise in power of each new actual and potential Brief Pulse generation, all "legal" under the Weiner proviso.

1st generation = 59J at 220Ω = .268 J/Ω ratio (100 year old category)
2nd generation = 100J at 220Ω = .455 J/Ω ratio (100 year old category)
3rd generation = 202J at 220Ω = .918 J/Ω ratio (100 year old category)

---

[205] Unlike SW constant Voltage devices, BP devices overcome increasing Impedances with increasing Voltages.

[206] The maximum J/Ω ratio for BP devices can be determined either through its pure-ER/RRC or by dividing simple maximum output by simple maximum Impedance (138J/300Ω = 230J/500Ω; 138J ÷ 300Ω = .46J/Ω; 230J ÷ 500Ω = .46J/Ω).

4th generation = 404J at 220Ω = 1.834 J/Ω ratio (year old category)
5th generation = 528J at 220Ω = 2.400 J/Ω ratio (year old category)

Comparing Typical SW J/Ω Maximums in Every Age Category to Brief Pulse J/Ω Defaults in Every Age Category Emitted by All Five Generations of Brief Pulse

We are now ready to compare SW J/Ω ratios to BP J/Ω ratios in every age category. Maximum outputs for SW, unlike BP, are entirely dependent upon individual Impedances and as such, outputs on SW devices deteriorate in power as age (and thus Impedance) increases. To illustrate, even limited to 1.0A (see 1982 APA), the Medcraft B-24 SW device delivers a 134J maximum output over a one second maximum Duration, but this is only in the 24 year old age category. Limited to 1.0A therefore, 134J is the highest possible output deliverable on the B-24 (see SW devices), moreover, an output emitted in perhaps only 2 to 3 % of all SW emissions (see Weiner's graph below). It is only possible to reach the 200J SW output graphed by Weiner below if the SW device is allowed to surpass the 1.0A APA limit which it does, due to manufacturers' refusal to adopt the 1982 APA Standard. (See Weiner's graph below taken from the 1982 APA Standard.)

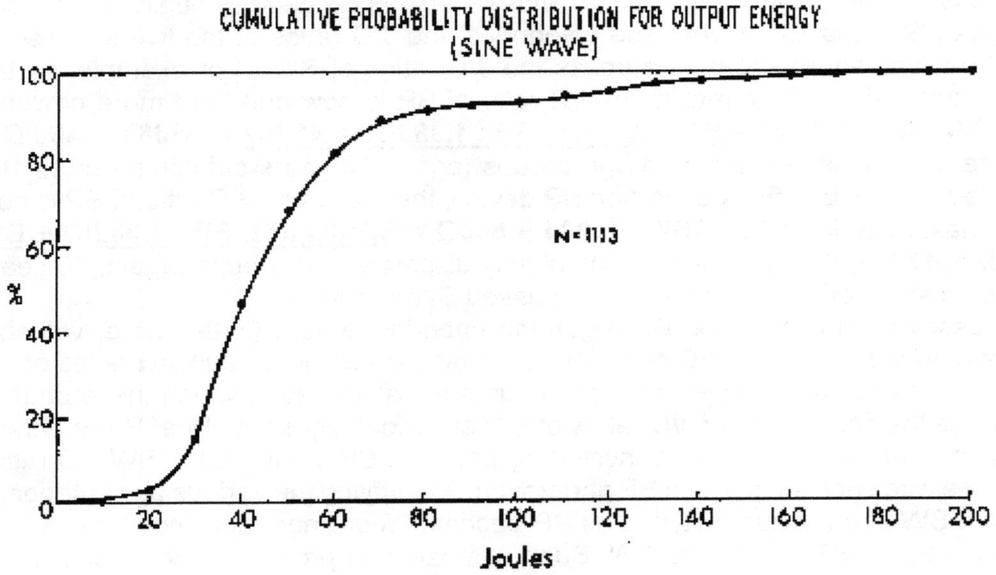

Indeed, Weiner's graph above can be somewhat deceptive in that age is not clearly factored in. For example, the entire graph might represent a ten year old child at various power settings in that Impedance must be abnormally low for the B-24 SW machine to reach 200J. At 100 years of age, for instance, the recipients of whom have the highest Impedances, the SW device may only reach about 50J maximum, very probably not enough power to seize 100 year old recipients. Consequently, the 100 year old recipient may not be represented in the above graph. Nevertheless, the Chart below represents B-24 SW maximums culminating at 200J (as the 1982 APA Standard was never officially adopted). Note that this culmination can only occur in the ten year old category.

J/Ω Ratios for all Age Groups Based on Weiner's SW Depictions Vs. Five Generations of Brief Pulse

AGE	SW Ω	BP Ω	SW EO	BP 1st EO	BP 2nd EO	BP 3rd EO	BP 4th EO	BP 5th EO	SW J/Ω	BP 1st J/Ω	BP 2nd J/Ω	BP 3rd J/Ω	BP 4th J/Ω	BP 5th J/Ω
10	145	50	200	1.33	2.88	5.76	11.5	15	1.38	.027	.058	.115	.23	.30
20	195	100	148	5.04	9.22	18.4	36.9	48	.76	.050	.092	.184	.369	.48
24	215	120	134	7.8	14.3	26.5	57.3	75	.62	.065	.119	.221	.478	.625
30	245	150	118	11.3	20.7	41.5	82.9	108	.48	.075	.138	.276	.553	.72
40	295	200	98.0	20.1	36.9	74.0	147	192	.33	.101	.185	.370	.735	.96
50	345	250	83.8	31.5	57.6	115	230	300	.24	.126	.230	.460	.92	1.20
60	395	300	73.2	45.4	82.9	166	332	432	.185	.151	.276	.550	1.11	1.44
65	420	325	68.6	53.3	97.3	195	389	507	.163	.164	.299	.600	1.20	1.56
70	445	350	64.9	61.8	113	226	452	588	.145	.177	.323	.645	1.29	1.68
80	495	400	58.4	80.6	148	295	590	768	.118	.202	.370	.737	1.48	1.92
90	545	450	53.0	115	186	373	746	972	.097	.255	.413	.828	1.66	2.16
100	595	500	48.6	134	230	460	922	1200	.081	.268	.460	.920	1.84	2.40

The first generation BP device above is based on the MECTA D" which could emit a 134J maximum. (MECTA "C" emitted 108 maximum joules at a circa 400Ω maximum.) Remaining BP devices are represented by the second generation JR/SR 1 IEC device (less powerful than the made-for-America version), the third generation JR/SR 1, the probable fourth generation JR/SR 1, and the potential fifth generation JR/SR 1. To derive J/Ω ratios per age (shaded area), EO for a particular machine at a particular age level is divided by Impedance at that age level. SW here, is set on maximum. Maximum Energy Outputs in joules for SW vs default outputs of BP are identified in the six shaded squares amidst the clear ones (which includes SW in an opposing age category. Maximum or peak J/Ω ratios for SW and BP default J/Ω ratios are identified in the six clear squares amidst the gray ones, including SW in a disparate age category.

Note that it is the 200J maximum for SW occurring only in the ten year old category above which emits the B-24's highest J/Ω ratio (1.38). Note how SW diminishes both in power and J/Ω ratios as age (or Impedance) increases even as BP increases in power and J/Ω ratios as age (or Impedance) increases.

Indeed, if Weiner is attempting to represent all age categories in his above graph and which certainly reflects the surpassing of 1.0A SW, only about 1% of all SW emissions on the graph appear to reach 148 Joules, only about 1/10th of 1% reach 170 Joules, and only about 1/12th of 1% reach the maximum 200J over the same one second maximum Duration. Significantly then, these higher outputs--148 Joules, 170 Joules, and 200 Joules--only correspond to maximum SW settings in the younger, that is, the twenty, sixteen, and ten year old categories respectively (see below). Indeed, these unusually higher outputs (those above 134 Joules) and which can only be reached in the younger age categories, must be emitted at maximum SW settings at Amperages over the APA 1.0A (which is the case).[207] In brief, SW emissions over 134J use a current which surpasses the 1.0A SW ceiling depicted in the 1982 APA Standard (see "Brief Pulse vs Sine Wave . . . ").[208] In that Weiner and the BP manufacturers procrastinated, never officially accepting the 1982 APA Standard, the standard was never officially adopted by the FDA. Consequently, we must assume SW indeed surpasses the 1.0 A limit for SW depicted in the standard. Indeed, both the 1989 IEC Standard and Weiner's 1997 standard "allows" up to 2.0A. But while such SW outputs are both "allowable" and possible in these most vulnerable age categories, note the diminishing power of SW power and so diminishing of J/Ω ratio of SW as age increases--even at maximum output in every age category.

See Appendix A: "Limitation of SW Amperage to 1.0A"

---

207 This is not to underestimate the power of SW in the younger age categories. Indeed, this device should have been banned with the introduction of the MECTA "C" BP device.

208 Limited to 1.0A, as noted above, SW outputs over 134J are not possible (see "Brief Pulse vs Sine Wave . . ." in this manuscript). However, both MECTA and Somatics as well as Medcraft ignore the 1982 APA Standard.

Summary: J/Ω

The Amperages (occurring in the ten and twenty year old age categories) represented in the above table surpass the 1.0A ceiling allowed under the 1982 APA Standard in that the standard was never adopted, Even so, based on Weiner's own graph above, outputs surpassing 134 Joules appear to be atypical, suggesting that in the two younger age categories, such maximum SW settings are only rarely reached. Assuming currents of greater than 1.0A *are* indeed used, however, the corresponding lowest Impedances for these higher outputs are included in the chart above as "148J at 195Ω," occurring in the twenty year old category, "170J at 170Ω" occurring in about the sixteen year old category, and finally "200J at 145Ω," the lowest SW Impedance possible, occurring in the ten year old age group. Thus, the ten year old is the recipient of Weiner's depiction of the highest possible SW output allowing the highest J/Ω ratio possible for the B-24 SW of (200J ÷ 145Ω) = 1.38J/Ω. Indeed, the insidiousness of the SW device is its propensity to deliver the highest outputs in the youngest age categories and its inability to seize in the older age categories--in short, both its dangerousness and inefficacy, in short, its total lack of consistency. (Indeed, Medcraft's priorities regarding the B-24 do not appear to be minimal stimulus or safety, but efficacy alone. In fact, there is ample reason to believe that the B-24 cannot be set for true minimal stimulus even from a SW perspective. But this shall be discussed a little further on). In contrast, all BP devices are pre-set to consistently deliver the specific default outputs portrayed above. The weakness of BP then, is not its lack of consistency, but, rather its consistent delivery of super suprathreshold dosages of electricity to all age categories far above that required to induce seizure, exposing not a weakness in the machine, but in the machine's aim—the delivery of adequate doses of electricity--an aim wholly out of keeping with so-called convulsion theory and thus the minimal stimulus safety notions discussed between 1976 and 1982 before the FDA.

Deriving J/Ω Ratios

All of the above output figures for SW noted in the table above are based on maximum B-24 parameters. In that Output increases on SW devices as Impedance diminishes, output/Impedance ratios can be derived by the inverse proportion formula J = 29000/Ω (see section "Brief Pulse vs. Sine Wave . . ." in this manuscript). [209] Based on SW maximums, and in accordance with speculative, but plausible SW charts created by the author (ibid), the B-24 SW's 200J maximum output (based on inverse proportion as noted above), might be reached at about (200J = 29000/XΩ; X =) 145Ω resulting in a maximum (200J ÷ 145Ω) = 1.38J/Ω (Joule per Ohm) ratio, while a 148J output might be reached at about (148J = 29000/XΩ; X =) 195Ω, resulting in a maximum (148J ÷ 195Ω =) .76J/Ω ratio. The first generation constant current BP device--the MECTA "C"--limited to a "59J at 220Ω" ER/RRC or about a (59J ÷ 220Ω =) .268J/Ω ratio emitting up to circa 108 maximum Joules has a maximum Impedance of about 400Ω (59J/220Ω = 107.5J/XΩ; X = 400Ω) and so a (107.5J ÷ 400Ω =) .268J/Ω ratio which the "C" could deliver over two (in lieu of one) seconds--a greatly reduced output per ohm ratio (compared to SW). A later first generation BP device, the MECTA "D" also limited to a 59J at 220Ω ER/RRC delivered the same maximum .268J/Ω ratio up to 134 Joules and so had a maximum Impedance of 500Ω ("D" = 59J/220Ω = 134J/XΩ; X = 500Ω) and so a 134J ÷ 500Ω =) .268J/Ω maximum. Even so, the maximum J/Ω ratio on first generation BP devices is much lower than SW's 1.38J/Ω maximum (although in disparate age categories). Of course, the SW J/Ω maximum quickly decreases with diminishing current. Nevertheless, neither the "C" nor "D" equaled or surpassed SW's J/Ω ratio in any age group until age 65, at which point the first generation Brief Pulse device emits a .164J/Ω ratio, the same virtual J/Ω ratio as SW (.163J/Ω) in the same age category. Not surprisingly, the lower J/Ω ratios of first generation BP devices reflect their minimal stimulus outputs with BL "ECT" in every age category, manifesting its well-publicized reduced output dynamic over SW. Only in age categories over age sixty-five years do the J/Ω ratios of the first generation BP device begin to surpass the J/Ω ratios of SW, and appropriately so, in that SW devices do not appear capable of inducing

---

[209] 29000 as a constant is derived from the highest output, lowest Impedance combination possible. J = K/Ω. 200J = K/145Ω. K = 29000. Other figures are derived thusly: 200J = 29000/Ω, thus Ω = 145Ω. To confirm: J = 29000/145Ω = 200J; 148J = 29000/XΩ = 195Ω. To confirm: J = 29000/195Ω = 148J. It should be noted that the most enhanced SW outputs, unlike BP devices, are solely dependent upon low Impedances and consequently, cannot be automatically elicited.

adequate seizures in recipients older than sixty-five. Thus, by consistently reducing electrical dosing relative to resistance (compared to SW) for all age groups up to age sixty-five, the "C" device eliminated all outputs over 108 Joules while the "D" eliminated all outputs over 134J. The rarer, higher SW maximums (up to 200J), of course, were entirely eliminated by the first generation "C" and "D" BP devices. Indeed, because the "C" and "D" could induce just above threshold outputs for all age groups (with BL ECT), as well as induce "adequate" seizures in recipients older than sixty-five years of age, first generation BP devices, the MECTA "C" and "D," seemed a legitimately vast improvement over SW regarding safety and assumed efficacy (in that the "C" and "D" produced the same adequate seizures as the B-24), even though the "D" was the first modern day BP device to violate the 110J APA ceiling. [210]

J/Ω Ratios:
First Generation BP
Device vs. SW
at Highest Maximum
Outputs

AGE	J/Ω SW	J/Ω 1st BP
10	1.38	.027
20	.76	.050
24	.62	.065
30	.48	.075
40	.33	.101
50	.24	.126
60	.185	.151
65	.163	.164
70	.145	.177
80	.118	.202
90	.097	.255
100	.081	.268

The J/Ω ratios of first generation BP devices greatly reduced EO from ages 10 to 65, appropriately surpassing that of SW in categories older than 65 in order to induce seizure. The 'C," particularly, appeared to be a vast improvement over SW with respect to reduced EO and what at first appeared to be, efficacy in that first generation BP devices could induce adequate seizures with minimal stimulus output in almost all age categories at generally, half the output of SW.

Made-for-America second generation BP devices utilize a circa "100J at 220Ω" pure-ER/RRC or a maximum delivery of circa (100J ÷ 220Ω = 252J ÷ 555.5Ω =) .45J/Ω, similar to American-made, made-for-Europe second generation BP devices which reach a maximum of (230J ÷ 500Ω =) .46J/Ω, compared to the maximum 1.38J/Ω maximum emitted by the B-24 SW at peak output (200J ÷ 145Ω = 1.38J/Ω). Again, however, these BP and SW maximums occur in totally disparate age categories.[211] More relevantly, the gradually increasing J/Ω ratios for the second generation BP device are greatly reduced compared to that of SW, but only up to age 50 (in lieu of 65), at which point the BP J/Ω ratio converges with that of SW. (While BP J/Ω ratios increase with increasing age, SW J/Ω ratios decrease with increasing age.) Because all second generation J/Ω ratios for second generation BP devices are twice that of first generation BP devices, J/Ω ratios of the second generation BP device equal that of SW at the earlier age of 50 as opposed to 65 on first generation BP devices. Thus, second generation BP devices surpass SW in all age categories older than 50 (as opposed to 65). In sum, while second generation BP devices emit reduced J/Ω ratios in the 10 through 49 year old age categories compared to SW, first generation BP devices emit reduced J/Ω ratios in the 10 to 64 year old categories. In short, the much more powerful second generation BP devices equal the J/Ω ratio of SW fifteen years earlier

---

[210] The MECTA "C" utilized a maximum of about 400Ω resistance; 59J/220Ω = XJ/400Ω = 108J maximum output. At any resistance, however, the "C" was not permitted to surpass 108J maximum. The MECTA "D" may have utilized 500Ω; 59J/220Ω = XJ/500Ω = 134J maximum.

[211] 1.38J/Ω refers to the 10 year old age child category for SW and .45J/Ω refers to the 100 year old adult category on the second generation BP device, generally.

than much less powerful first generation BP devices. Regarding reduced J/Ω ratios then, the increasingly powerful second generation BP device is now an improvement over SW by virtue of reduced EO only from ages 10 to 49; whereas, first generation BP devices are a greater improvement over SW and from ages 10 to 64.

J/Ω Ratios:
Default Output of
Second Generation BP
Device vs. SW
at Highest Maximum
Outputs

AGE	J/Ω SW	J/Ω 2nd BP
10	1.38	.058
20	.76	.092
24	.62	.119
30	.48	.138
40	.33	.185
50	.24	.230
60	.185	.276
65	.163	.299
70	.145	.323
80	.118	.370
90	.097	.413
100	.081	.460

The default J/Ω ratios of second generation BP devices converge with that of SW at age 50, surpassing maximum SW outputs at all ages older than 50.

In sum, second generation BP devices surpass the J/Ω ratios of SW from ages 51 to 100. Both first and second BP generations eliminate the initial electrical wallop of SW, that is, the initial high dosages requiring "glissando." In short, the second generation BP device eliminates the excessively high, but rare maximum SW output of up to 1.38J/Ω occurring in what appears to be about one tenth of 1% of all SW emissions. While first and second generation BP devices do eliminate all of the unpredictably high, but relatively rare output/Impedance ratios of SW then, only the first generation BP device can claim to be a 100% improvement over SW emissions in that all first generation emissions are minimal stimulus or just above seizure threshold by default. Second generation BP devices, in doubling J/Ω ratios in all age categories compared to first generation BP devices, lose almost all publicly proclaimed improvement over SW. Indeed, according to a 1986 study by Squire and Zouzounis (1986) no significant safety gain (over SW) with respect to memory dysfunction remains with the second generation BP device.

The third generation BP device, i.e. the third generation MECTA JR/SR 1 IEC BP device, utilizes a never before reported "202J at 220Ω" pure-ER/RRC or a maximum .91J/Ω output/Impedance ratio at its maximum 460J/500Ω maximum Impedance, and doubles J/Ω ratios compared to second generation BP devices in all age categories. Too, the maximum .91J/Ω of third generation BP devices begins to approach SW's extreme maximum J/Ω ratio of 1.38J/Ω, although third generation BP devices do so in the oldest age category (100 years) as opposed to the ten year old age category with SW. Indeed, only the B-24's mythical and extremely rare 200J output at approximately 145Ω (200J ÷ 145Ω = 1.38J/Ω) emitted in approximately 1/10th of 1% of all SW emissions (at age 10) remains substantially higher than the maximum Output/Impedance ratio delivered by third generation BP devices. Once again, however, and of critical importance, the maximum J/Ω ratio on Brief Pulse devices occur in the oldest age category of 100 at which age Impedance is highest; whereas, the maximum J/Ω ratio on the SW device occurs in the youngest age category at which point Impedance is lowest (revealing the utter treachery of SW in such age categories). Much more relevantly, then, the J/Ω ratios of third generation Brief Pulse devices converge with (and, in fact, slightly surpass) the J/Ω ratios of SW at age 40, more than ten years younger than second generation Brief Pulse devices converge with SW devices. Tellingly, the third generation BP device equals SW, 25 years younger than the age at which first generation Brief Pulse devices converge with SW. In short, the more powerful third generation BP device (compared to first and second generation BP devices) is now an improvement over SW (regarding reduced output) only from ages ten to thirty. Moreover, third generation J/Ω ratios double second generation BP devices, losing even more of the first generation BP advantage over SW. Too, we should remind ourselves that BP increases in J/Ω ratios with increasing age while SW decreases in J/Ω ratios with increasing age. Regarding reduced power, therefore, it Is clear that as BP devices become more and more powerful with each new BP generation, they are less and less advantageous over SW with respect to reduced EO and so safety.

J/Ω Ratios:
Default Output of
Third Generation BP
Devices vs. SW
at Highest Maximum
Outputs

AGE	J/Ω SW	J/Ω 3rd BP
10	1.38	.115
20	.76	.184
24	.62	.221
30	.48	.276
40	.33	.370
50	.24	.460
60	.185	.550
65	.163	.600
70	.145	.645
80	.118	.737
90	.097	.828
100	.081	.920

Note that default J/Ω ratios of third generation BP devices converge at about age 40 with that of SW set for maximum output, surpassing the J/Ω ratio of SW in all categories older than 40. The J/Ω ratio of the third generation BP device now surpasses the J/Ω ratio of SW in the majority of age categories and delivers at least four times that needed to induce a seizure in every age category with BL "ECT."

The probable fourth generation BP device, i.e. the very possibly extant fourth generation JR/SR 1, "legal" under Weiner's 1997 proviso, utilizes an amazing and unrevealed "404J at 220Ω" pure-ER/RRC or (in the 100 year old category) a default maximum output/impedance ratio of 1.84J/Ω at its 922J maximum output and 500Ω maximum Impedance (404J ÷ 220Ω = 922J ÷ 500Ω = 1.84J/Ω). At a maximum 1.84J/Ω (at 922J), the fourth generation BP device surpasses the B-24's highest and rarest 1.38J/Ω output/impedance ratio maximum (at 200J) reached in only one tenth of 1% of all SW emissions. Indeed, the maximum J/Ω maximum of the fourth generation BP device surpasses the 1.38 J/Ω maximum of SW by 1.33 fold (200J ÷ 145Ω = 1.38J/Ω; 1.84J/Ω ÷ 1.38J/Ω = 1.33). Once again, however, the maximum J/Ω ratio for the fourth generation BP device occurs in the oldest age category (100 years), whereas the maximum J/Ω ratio for SW occurs in the youngest age category (ten years old).[212] Even so, the fourth generation BP device now delivers a default ratio of .553J/Ω at age 40, approaching the .62 J/Ω SW maximum occurring at age 30. While the J/Ω ratios delivered by SW at maximum output are yet greater than BP in the ten and 20 year old categories, the J/Ω ratios of fourth generation BP devices now converge with (and, in fact, slightly surpass) the maximum J/Ω ratio deliverable by SW in the 30 year old category, nearly ten years earlier than third generation BP devices, twenty years earlier than second generation BP devices and 35 years earlier than first generation BP devices. In short, the fourth generation BP device only remains an improvement over SW regarding reduced output, from ages ten to about age twenty-seven. In all other age categories, the fourth generation Brief Pulse device, now surpasses both the maximum output and maximum J/Ω ratio delivered by the B-24 SW device (albeit in disparate age

[212] As already noted, the B-24 in rare instances, can emit "200J" at a probable "145Ω" for a peak 1.38J/Ω (200J ÷ 145Ω = 1.38J/Ω). This atypical maximum B-24 output would necessarily have to occur in the ten year old age category whereas the maximum default 1.84J/Ω ratio delivered by the fourth generation BP device is administered to the 100 year old recipient consistently and by default.

categories). Moreover, the J/Ω ratios delivered by the fourth generation BP are now circa nine fold threshold (with BL "ECT") in every age category.

J/Ω Ratios:
Default Output of
Fourth Generation BP
Devices vs. SW
at Highest Maximum
Outputs

AGE	J/Ω SW	J/Ω 4th BP
10	1.38	.23
20	.76	.369
24	.62	.478
30	.48	.553
40	.33	.735
50	.24	.92
60	.185	1.11
65	.163	1.20
70	.145	1.29
80	.118	1.48
90	.097	1.66
100	.081	1.84

Note that the default J/Ω ratios of fourth generation BP devices now converge with (and in fact slightly surpass) the J/Ω ratios of SW by as early as age 30, surpassing the J/Ω ratios of SW in all age categories 30 and older. In brief, the default J/Ω ratios for the fourth generation BP device now surpass that of SW set for maximum output in more than 70% of all age categories.

Finally, theoretical fifth generation BP devices, the "legal" maximum under Weiner's 1997 default standard, could utilize an absurd never before reported "528J at 220Ω" [213] pure-ER/RRC emitting up to a 2.4J/Ω maximum ratio at its maximum 1200J output and maximum 500Ω Impedance (528J ÷ 220Ω = 1200J ÷ 500Ω = 2.4J/Ω), grossly surpassing even the rarest and most dangerous SW output/impedance maximum by 1.74 fold (2.4÷1.38 = 1.74 fold). The B-24's hyperbolic 200J output delivered over one second at about 145Ω, (apparently reached in about one tenth of 1% of all SW emissions) necessarily reaching a peak output to Impedance delivery ratio of (200J ÷ 145Ω =) 1.38J/Ω, now pales in comparison to the 2.4J/Ω output/impedance default maximum of the potential fifth generation BP device. Still, the maximum J/Ω ratio of SW vs. BP occur in totally disparate age categories, SW with the ten year old child, BP with the 100 year old adult. The potential fifth generation BP device now converges with (and in fact, slightly surpasses) the J/Ω ratios of SW at about age 24, nearly six years earlier than fourth generation BP devices, sixteen years earlier than third generation BP devices, twenty-six years earlier than second generation BP devices, and forty-one years earlier than first generation BP devices. In short, regarding J/Ω ratio, the default outputs of the fifth generation BP device are now an improvement over maximum SW outputs regarding reduced output in only the ten and twenty year old categories. The "legally" possible fifth generation BP device now surpasses maximum SW settings both in power and J/Ω ratios in 75% of all age categories. Moreover, the J/Ω ratios of the fifth generation BP device are set by default to emit twelve times that necessary to elicit an adequate seizure in every age category.

---

[213] 528J/220Ω = 1200J/500Ω; 528J ÷ 220Ω = 1200J ÷ 500Ω = 2.4J/Ω.

J/Ω Ratios:
Default Output of
Fifth Generation BP
Devices vs. SW
at Highest Maximum
Outputs

AGE	J/Ω SW	J/Ω 5th BP
10	1.38	.30
20	.76	.48
24	.62	.625
30	.48	.72
40	.33	.96
50	.24	1.20
60	.185	1.44
65	.163	1.56
70	.145	1.68
80	.118	1.92
90	.097	2.16
100	.081	2.40

Note how the J/Ω ratio of the potential fifth generation BP device converges with (and, in fact, surpasses) the J/Ω ratio of SW at age 24, surpassing that of SW (set at maximum output) in all categories older than 24. The default outputs of the fifth generation BP device is now an improvement over SW regarding reduced output in only the two youngest age categories. BP now surpasses even the most extreme J/Ω SW ratio though in an antithetical age category.

The J/Ω Stepladder

With each succeeding BP device generation, all "legal" under Weiner's 1997 de facto standard, BP J/Ω ratios converge with that of SW in earlier and earlier age categories, creating a stepladder effect regarding the increasing power of BP versus SW. [Note the J/Ω ratio of SW in the white box beginning at age 65 (.163 J/Ω) and the parallel white box of the first generation BP (.164 J/Ω) in the same age category. Next see the corresponding 50, 40 30 and 24 year old categories of SW and the parallel J/Ω ratios in the same age categories with each new BP generation]. Indeed, the fifth generation Brief Pulse device now equals SW in the twenty-four year old age category, surpassing the power of SW in all remaining age categories. In a nutshell, the fifth generation BP device is a much more powerful device, generally, than the B-24 SW even when SW is set to maximum output in every age category. Indeed, BP is a much more dangerous device in most age categories. Note too that the potential, but "legal fifth generation BP device, emits circa 12 fold threshold, about ten times the first BP generation J/Ω ratio in every age category.

BP/SW Stepladder of Merging J/Ω Ratios With Each Succeeding Generation of BP

AGE	J/Ω SW	J/Ω 1st BP	J/Ω 2nd BP	J/Ω 3rd BP	J/Ω 4th BP	J/Ω 5th BP
10	1.38	.027	.058	.115	.23	.30
20	.76	.050	.092	.184	.369	.48
24	.62	.065	.119	.221	.478	.625
30	.48	.075	.138	.276	.553	.72
40	.33	.101	.185	.370	.735	.96
50	.24	.126	.230	.460	.92	1.20
60	.185	.151	.276	.550	1.11	1.44
65	.163	.164	.299	.600	1.20	1.56
70	.145	.177	.323	.645	1.29	1.68
80	.118	.202	.370	.737	1.48	1.92
90	.097	.255	.413	.828	1.66	2.16
100	.081	.268	.460	.920	1.84	2.40

Note how by the fifth BP generation, the BP J/Ω ratio equals the SW J/Ω ratio at age 24, surpassing SW J/Ω ratios in all remaining age categories even when SW is set at maximum output. Only in age categories 10 and 20 do SW J/Ω ratios surpass the fifth generation BP device.

Max Fink's Contribution

Psychiatrist Max Fink, a manufacturer-affiliated [214] outspoken advocate of "ECT," developed an especially counterintuitive, if not incriminating technique for administering physicians to determine an end point regarding the number of treatments given to each individual recipient, that is, a tangible method for determining how many individual "treatments" are enough. In lieu of a mere subjective or intuitive measure such as observing the mood, demeanor, behavior, or attitude of the recipient, Fink conceived of the totally concrete method of continuing "treatment" until specific changes in brain wave activity occur, changes scientifically measurable with EEG. In a 1997 article entitled "ECT Update," published in *The Psychiatric Times* (Fink 1997) alluding to Fink's now widely used technique, Fink is quoted as saying:

> Anecdotal case reports argue that the augmentation of clozapine (Clorazil) with ECT is particularly useful (Klapheke).... They conclude that the appearance of an abnormal electroencephalogram (EEG) during a course of clozapine therapy warrants its discontinuation. Such a conclusion may be in error. Psychotropic drugs are effective to the extent that they elicit changes in brain chemistry, which are necessary for the therapeutic efficacy of psychotropic drugs (Fink; Risby). During a course of ECT, patients develop marked changes in the interseizure EEG; mean frequencies slow, amplitudes increase, and prolonged periods of slow wave, spike and slow wave, and spike burst activity appear. These interseizure EEG effects are . . . necessary for a successful treatment course (see Fink and Kahn).[215] This finding has been repeatedly verified. The most recent detailed systematic studies were reported in 1996 [by] (Sackeim and others).

In short, Fink, Kahn, Sackeim [216] and others advocate and have been advocating for many years, the practice of continuing a course of "ECT" treatment until measurably slowed brain wave activity can be maintained as evidenced with EEG monitoring. Psychiatrists are taught to use EEG, then, not to safeguard recipients from prolonged slow brain wave activity (occurring between seizures), as might be expected, but rather to achieve and maintain slow brain wave activity as a determinate goal; EEG, in brief, becomes a measuring mechanism for the purpose of identifying, producing, actively achieving, and maintaining slow brain wave activity. Thus, the very symptoms which neurologists ubiquitously use to identify brain trauma and brain damage become the active goals of ENR--Electro Neurotransmission Reduction.

---

[214] Fink's article, which also appeared on the internet in 1997, is introduced with this warning. "The following article on electroconvulsive therapy is by Dr. Max Fink, one of the nation's leading experts in ECT. However, it should be noted that Dr. Fink also has a financial interest in the manufacturing of ECT devices" (http://www.schizophrenia.com/ami/meds/moreect.html).

[215] The Fink and Kahn study to which Fink is referring is entitled "Relation of EEG delta activity to behavioral response in electroshock: Quantitative serial studies" (Fink and Kahn 1957), the results of which the authors endorse as late as 1997. The study was originally published in 1957 in the Archives of Neurological Psychiatry (Chicago).

[216] Both Fink and Kahn are affiliated with ECT device manufacturers.

PART VII

SECTION XVI: Comparing Sine Wave to Brief Pulse

CHAPTER 80

The Medcraft B-24 SW vs MECTA "C" vs Later BP Devices

It is now time to compare the SW device to the MECTA "C" (as well as the "D") first generation BP device--recognized by the FDA as an improvement over SW by virtue of reduced EO--to later generation BP devices, no longer "improved" over SW in most age categories. To make such comparisons, we must first attempt to identify minimal and maximal B-24 SW outputs.

<u>FORMULAS UTILIZED FOR SW:</u>
EO (for SW) = Current Squared x Impedance x Duration.
EO (for SW) = Volts x Current x Duration.
EO (for SW) = Charge x Current x Impedance
Charge (for SW) = Current x Duration
Ohm's Law: Current = Voltage/Ω; Ω = Voltage/Current; Voltage = Current x Ω

The SW parameters used here are probable albeit speculative as no credible age-to-output or age-to-Multifold Threshold Titration Level Output Intensity (MTTLOI) studies have ever been published regarding SW. It is well known that the BP device can induce adequate convulsions at far less output than SW--the general concession--half. The inefficiency of SW as opposed to BP is in part due to the capacity of BP--through the utilization of briefer wave lengths or pulses--to more precisely emit the required output necessary to induce an adequate seizure relative to age. Moreover, the further inefficiency of the SW device (i.e. the B-24 by Medcraft) is due to its constant Voltage mechanism facilitative of continuously deteriorating current over the B-24's one second maximum Duration resulting in rising Impedances over a single "treatment." This contrasts with the Brief Pulse device's more efficient utilization of automatically rising Voltage to maintain a constant current. Ironically, because the uninterrupted Sine Wave is so abruptly powerful, the device requires a glissando mechanism, that is, a gradual increase in Voltage up to the Voltage set for "treatment" even before the actual treatment begins. Thus, it is the uninterrupted nature of the sine wave itself, deteriorating current, and thus rising Impedance over one second, and finally the glissando or gradual increase in Voltage up to 100V even before "treatment" begins, that results in the much higher energy output required to overcome resistance in the same age category compared to BP. Another factor which may be involved is the high output settings below which SW may not be allowed to "treat." In any case, the initial age related resistance for SW appears to be about 50Ω higher than the initial age-related resistance for BP. Moreover, due to more dramatically rising Impedance over the course of one second, SW appears to require an additional 45Ω for each age category relative to that required for BP.

In that deteriorating amperages in SW devices are both dependent on and inversely proportional to rising Impedances and in that sine waves are much longer in length than BP, micromanaging energy output with SW is neither as practicable nor as attainable as micromanaging energy output with BP.[217] Certainly, it has taken the much more efficient BP device educing adequate seizures at half (or less) the output of SW to begrudgingly reveal that induction of an adequate seizure alone is therapeutically ineffective.[218] In any case, SW's initial age-related Impedances appear to be about 50Ω higher than BP's, and unlike BP, appear to rise an additional 45Ω over the course of a one-second treatment maximum, thereby requiring much greater EO than BP to reach and overcome seizure threshold. In short, the EO required to induce an adequate seizure with SW per each age group, is about twice that needed to induce an adequate seizure with BP for most age categories. Indeed, because both initial and final threshold Impedances are much higher and rise much more dramatically with SW during a single treatment than BP (the initial and final threshold Impedances of which do not rise nearly so dramatically, if at all), SW can require two to three times the output of BP to induce the same adequate seizure. In sum, reduced EO is the touted advantage of BP over SW recognized both by BP manufacturers and the FDA.

Put another way, in that the increasing Voltage and so non-deteriorating current of BP is much more efficient than SW, requiring much less output to induce the same adequate seizure, BP does not require glissando as does SW. Because BP waves are much briefer, moreover, BP's age-related Impedances are more consistent (rising to a much lesser degree if at all), making BP's threshold Energy Outputs more accurate, more predictable, more identifiable, and much lower than SW's. Indeed, based upon Beale's 1994 study, we can accurately identify BP's age related threshold outputs,[219] and even, to a slightly lesser extent, age-related Impedances. Based on the fact that SW requires an average of more than twice the output of BP to reach seizure threshold for the same age-related recipient, we can estimate threshold Impedances required for SW simply by adding 50Ω to the age-related Impedance required for BP and another 45Ω (95Ω in all) for the final threshold Impedance reached by SW after one full second of SW treatment, and so determine both the initial (minimal) outputs required to induce adequate seizures with SW and final (maximal) outputs required to induce adequate seizures with SW. To begin, we speculatively deduce how much EO is required to overcome a given Impedance with SW by identifying to the Output required to overcome those same Impedances on a Brief Pulse device.[220]

For instance, if a ten year old child can be seized by overcoming 50Ω with BP in turn requiring about 1.0J and the same ten year old child must be seized by overcoming not 50Ω, but 100Ω (50Ω + 50Ω = 100Ω) with SW, we can deduce (from BP charts below) that about 4.0J is required to induce the same adequate seizure for the same age recipient with SW as opposed to BP. We deduce this figure by locating the EO required to overcome 100Ω on the BP chart (which happens to be the 20 year old age category for BP).

TYPICAL (THOUGH SPECULATIVE) AGE RELATED THRESHOLD IMPEDANCES AND THRESHOLD OUTPUTS USING MODERN DAY **BRIEF PULSE**

AGE	Impedance Threshold (Ω)	Threshold Output in Joules[221]
10	50	1.06
20	100	4.03

[217] For example, one cannot manually determine or precisely predict threshold output with SW to the same degree as is possible with BP.

[218] It is for this reason that despite the successful induction of adequate seizures at lower outputs than SW, BP manufacturers have been forced to enhance the default outputs administered with each new BP machine generation, altogether losing the safety advantage of BP over SW.

[219] Beale deduced that Charge (and thus EO) for second generation BP devices was set at 2.5 fold threshold, much more than required to induce an adequate seizure. Using the 2.5 fold ratio and charts provided by Somatics, we can deduce EO per age group utilized on second generation BP devices and simply divide by 2.5 to discover threshold dosage. Multiplying by 2.0 for the less efficient SW device, we can discover the approximate electrical dosage for SW to overcome the same Impedance ascribed to various age groups.

[220] While age-related Impedances differ between SW and BP, the output required to overcome a specific Impedance does not.

[221] What we notice regarding the sequence of threshold outputs for Brief Pulse is that the progression increases by 2 with each succeeding output. 4 – 1 = 3; 9 – 4 = 5; 16 – 9 = 7, etc. Thus the second number (4) has increased by 3.0, the third number (9) by 5, the forth number (16) by 7, the fifth number (25) by 9, etc. an increasing progression of 2 (3, 5, 7, 9, etc.). Moreover, each threshold output is a sequence of perfect squares. 1, 4, 9, 16, 25, 36, 49, 64, 81, 100 (1x1, 2x2, 3x3, etc.).

Simply by referring to the Impedance-related threshold output on the Brief Pulse chart then, we can determine the EO (in joules) required for a certain age-group (i.e., the ten year old child) with SW.

TYPICAL (THOUGH SPECULATIVE) AGE RELATED
THRESHOLD IMPEDANCES AND THRESHOLD OUTPUTS
At **MINIMUM SETTINGS** FOR THE B-24 **SINE WAVE**

AGE	Initial Impedance Threshold (Ω)	Threshold Output in Joules
10	100	4.0

Finally, we can speculatively determine the MTTLOI for SW (compared to BP) simply by dividing the EO delivered by SW, by the SW threshold output required for that particular age category.

To illustrate, Seizure Threshold with BP for the ten year old child with a 50Ω Impedance, is about 1.0J. Default EO delivered to the ten year old child by the MECTA "C" Brief Pulse is 1.08J. Thus the MECTA "C" delivers a (1.08J ÷ 1.0J =) 1.08 MTTLOI. On a SW device set for minimal stimulus (if this is possible) for the same ten year old age category, enough EO must be delivered by the B-24 SW to overcome a circa (50Ω + 50Ω =) 100Ω Impedance requiring (via the BP chart) circa 4.0J. Set for minimal stimulus (or about .1 Seconds), we find that SW delivers about 4.9J and so a (4.9J ÷ 4.0J =) 1.23 MTTLOI. While evidence suggests that EO cannot be set for 4.9J or "true minimal stimulus" with SW, for comparative purposes, we shall determine "true minimal stimulus" for SW as if the machine can be adjusted for such.

It should be noted that in spite of similar MTTLOIs with SW, for instance, a 1.23 MTTLOI compared to the MECTA's C's 1.08 MTTLOI, the SW device (set for true minimal stimulus SW) must nevertheless deliver about (4.9 ÷ 1.08 =) 4.5 times the EO delivered by the MECTA C to induce the same adequate seizure in the same ten year old child. The similar MTTLOIs (1.23 v 1.08) are thus misleading in that threshold output for SW (4.0J) is yet much greater than threshold output for BP (1.0J). Despite a similar MTTLOI (1.23 v 1.08) in the ten year old age category then, SW, as expected, even at true minimal stimulus requires much more EO to reach threshold than BP. Such comparisons can be useful. For example, while the default output of the first generation MECTA "C" is superior to SW set for true minimal stimulus (or about .1 Seconds) with respect to much less EO required, the much more powerful third generation MECTA Brief Pulse device in the same ten year old category (as opposed to the First generation MECTA "C"), delivers a default 4.5J, about equal to that of SW set at true minimal stimulus in this same ten year old age category. While using about the same EO, however, the third generation BP device delivers a default 4.5 MTTLOI compared to SW's 1.23 MTTLOI from which we begin to glimpse the inverse exploitation factor of the more efficient, more powerful BP device. In spite of BP's capacity to induce adequate seizures at much less EO than SW then, the more powerful third generation BP device becomes at least as powerful as SW set at true minimal stimulus in this same ten year old age category. The more powerful third generation BP device in short, unlike the MECTA "C," is at least as dangerous as SW set at true minimal stimulus in the ten year old age category. The significance of this fact will be discussed at the end of this Chapter.

In addition to true minimal SW stimulus which can be figured at .1 Seconds, the briefest SW Duration possible, we can also determine SW parameters for maximal stimulus or the output delivered following the 1.0 Second maximum Duration in any age category. As previously mentioned, unlike BP, SW Impedance dramatically increases over a single treatment compared to BP (which may increase slightly, but to a much lesser extent) so that, unlike BP, at the end of 1.0 Seconds, we must add another 45Ω to SW Impedance, requiring even greater EO to overcome threshold. Indeed, the SW device set a maximum output can deliver up to 200J to the same ten year old child at about a 23 MTTLOI, far greater in both EO and MTTLOI than even the exacerbated default power delivered by the third or even fifth generation BP device. In sum, we can generally determine minimal and maximal EO delivered by minimal and maximal SW settings relative to age and compare these figures to first generation as well as second, third, fourth, and fifth generation BP devices. The results are revealing.

CHAPTER 81

The Cameron Paradigm

The chart directly below depicts universal age-related threshold Impedances and outputs for modern day BP. Using our speculative SW paradigm (of adding 50Ω to the BP age-related Impedance for initial SW Impedance (minimal stimulus SW) and another 45Ω for final SW Impedance (at maximal stimulus SW), we can speculatively determine EO thresholds with respect to age for both minimum and maximum SW settings.

This paradigm takes into account the use of "Glissando" before and into the treatment setting, Amperage deterioration due to constant Voltage, relatively dramatic Impedance enhancement over the duration of a single SW treatment, and even the much more modest rise in Impedance with BP devices. Thus, in addition to Amperage deterioration and glissando with SW, we must take into account the critically dramatic Impedance enhancement over the B-24's one Second maximum Duration compared to the much more modest Impedance enhancement over the much more modest duration of BP even over a treatment course.[222] That is, we must take into account initial SW Impedance (for minimum SW settings) and final SW Impedance (for greater than minimum SW settings) to determine the EO required to reach threshold with SW in each specific instance. We can then, compare the cumulative output actually delivered with SW (over the rising Impedance) in each respective circumstance to the single Impedance reading with BP.

To determine the MTTLOI for SW at maximum output for any age category, we simply divide the <u>cumulative output</u> delivered (when set to 1.0 Second maximum Duration) by the <u>threshold output</u> required to induce an adequate seizure at the end of 1.0 second Duration (which takes onto account the additional 45Ω Impedance rise). Once the MTTLOI is determined for SW at various age levels (at minimum or maximum output), we can not only compare the EO delivered by a BP device as opposed to the EO delivered by a SW device for the same age recipient--the most critical comparison--but we can speculatively compare the MTTLOI delivered by a SW device at maximum and improbable minimum outputs to the much more consistent default MTTLOIs delivered by various BP device generations. That is, we now have some means of comparing not only the efficiency of BP and thus the reduced EO of BP compared to SW, but the greater power delivered by later more powerful BP devices compared to SW at both maximum and allegedly minimum outputs. Too, we can compare the later BP devices to the first generation MECTA "C" BP device, the only Brief Pulse device in conformity with the 1982 APA Standard for Brief Pulse approved by the FDA.[223] The first chart below depicts the relatively consistent age-related Threshold Impedances and Threshold Outputs of Brief Pulse at single default outputs, figures which more or less hold, regardless of the BP generation.

---

[222] Rises in Impedance with respect to BP devices appear to occur mainly over a series—only negligibly during a single treatment.

[223] BP devices, regardless of increasing power with each new generation in turn increasing MTTLOI, nevertheless emit consistent MTTLOIs for all recipients with each specific BP device.

TYPICAL (THOUGH SPECULATIVE) AGE RELATED THRESHOLD IMPEDANCES AND THRESHOLD OUTPUTS USING MODERN DAY **BRIEF PULSE**

AGE	Impedance Threshold (Ω)	Threshold Output in Joules[224]
10	50	1.06
20	100	4.03
30	150	9.0
40	200	16.1
50	250	25.2
60	300	36.3
65	325	42.6
70	350	49.4
80	400	64.5
90	450	81.6
100	500	100

Since BP Impedances do not radically rise over Duration, there are no initial and final BP settings; that is, there is only one Impedance and so only one Threshold Output per age category.

A Note about the B-24 at "Minimal Stimulus"

This next section shows us how to calculate minimal stimulus SW outputs. Because the B-24 can supposedly be adjusted with respect to Duration and Voltage, we will pursue Duration settings as little as .1 Seconds, the smallest fraction of time available for the B-24 in order to derive the most theoretically minimal stimulus outputs possible for various age categories with SW. However, evidence suggest that Medcraft does not nor ever has valued minimal stimulus settings. Indeed, Medcraft is the oldest and perhaps the most secretive of all "ECT" manufacturers. Clearly, the device has a history of efficacy at the expense of memory. In truth, it is constructed in a "topsy-turvy" or upside down manner as opposed to Brief Pulse in that the B-24 SW utilizes its greatest output potential in the youngest and most vulnerable age categories while it utilizes its weakest output potential in the oldest least vulnerable age categories. Neither is Medcraft interested in consistency apparently having no misgivings in the machine's capacity to administer a 23 MTTLOI to the 10 year old child as opposed to administering an impotent below threshold output to the 100 year old adult. Because Medcraft appears to be more interested in efficacy than safety, and because of the odd construction of Medcraft's B-25 Brief Pulse device, evidence suggests true minimal stimulus settings are either not recommended to physicians, or more probably, not possible settings on the B-24. To illustrate, the B-25 Brief Pulse device built by Medcraft, avoids true minimal stimulus by circumventing all the potential advantages of Brief Pulse in the younger age categories. Like the B-24, and unlike MECTA and Somatics BP devices, the B-25 emits the highest MTTLOI in the youngest age categories and the lowest MTTLOI in the oldest age categories.

B-25 (Maximum)

MACHINE READOUT	ACTUAL OUTPUT	AGE	ACTUAL MTTLOI
99 J	99 J	10	99
99 J	99 J	20	24.75
99 J	99 J	30	11
99 J	99 J	40	6.18
99 J	99 J	50	3.96

[224] What we notice regarding the sequence of threshold outputs for Brief Pulse is that the progression increases by 2 with each succeeding output. 4 – 1 = 3; 9 – 4 = 5; 16 – 9 = 7, etc. Thus the second number (4) has increased by 3.0, the third number (9) by 5, the forth number (16) by 7, the fifth number (25) by 9, etc, an increasing progression of 2 (3, 5, 7, 9, etc). Moreover, each threshold output is a sequence of perfect squares. 1, 4, 9, 16, 25, 36, 49, 64, 81, 100 (1x1, 2x2, 3x3, etc).

99 J	99 J	60	2.75
99 J	99 J	65	2.34
99 J	99 J	70	2.02
99 J	99 J	80	1.55
99 J	99 J	90	1.22
99 J	99 J	100	1.0

Neither does the machine utilize Brief Pulse to reduce EO to true BP minimal stimulus. Instead, the B-25 at minimal stimulus (discussed in a previous section) may appear something like the following:

B-25 (Minimum)

ACTUAL OUTPUT	AGE	ACTUAL MTTLOI
9 J	10	9
19 J	20	4.7
29 J	30	3.22
39 J	40	2.43
49 J	50	1.96
59 J	60	1.64
64 J	65	1.51
69 J	70	1.41
79 J	80	1.23
89 J	90	1.1
99 J	100	1.0

Medcraft's B-25 BP device, even at its minimal stimulus, apparently facilitates a 9 MTTLOI for the ten year old child, a 4.7 MTTLOI for the 20 year old, a 3.22 MTTLOI for the 30 year old, a 2.4 MTTLOI for the 40 year old, a 2.0 MTTLOI for the 50 year old, a 1.64 MTTLOI for the 60 year old, a 1.5 MTTLOI for the 65 year old, a 1.4 MTTLOI for the 70 year old, a 1.23 MTTLOI for the 8- year old, a 1.1 MTTLOI for the 90 year old, and a 1.0 MTTLOI for the 100 year old. All this, like the B-24, is totally upside down with respect to age. In short, the upside down construction of the B-25 reflects virtually no concern for the safety of its recipients, particularly the young. There can only be one explanation to its unnecessarily upside down construction. The B-25 must be emulating the "popular" (amongst physicians) very "effective" B-24 SW, long known for its memory morbidity. If the B-25 really does emulate the B-24, the B-24 at "probable minimal stimulus" may look something like the following:

B-24 (Possible Minimum)

ACTUAL OUTPUT	AGE	ACTUAL MTTLOI
36 J	10	9
43 J	20	4.7
53 J	30	3.22
63 J	40	2.43
81 J	50	1.96
73 J	60	1.15
69 J	65	.956
65 J	70	.804
58 J	80	.59
53 J	90	.44
49 J	100	.34

Because the archaic construction of both the B-25 and the B-24 reflect little or no concern for actual minimal stimulus and thus little or no concern for recipient safety, both should be immediately banned as ENR devices. Indeed, both, with their suprathreshold outputs in the youngest age categories are clearly brain injurious and deliberately so. Certainly, the destructive B-24 device should have been banned between 1976 and 1982 with the re-introduction of the true minimal stimulus Brief Pulse MECTA "C." It is only because the later Brief Pulse devices, like the B-24 SW of old, were forced to devolve into ENR or adequate electricity devices in order to achieve "efficacy" and so fiscally survive that Weiner could not insist upon the abolition of SW. Indeed, it is for this reason that Weiner, as spokesperson of MECTA, Somatics, and Medcraft to the FDA, ultimately lost his power to demand the demise of the B-24 as he originally implied within the 1982 APA Standard, that SW is yet ongoing. In short, because Weiner could not accept the failure of convulsion theory, Weiner lost his power to do good.

Minimum SW Settings:

Now, let's assume true minimum SW settings are possible relative to age. As such, minimum B-24 outputs might be delivered (over .1 Second minimum) compared to which the necessary output must be emitted to overcome the various age-related SW Thresholds. To find threshold outputs at minimum SW settings, we must refer to the BP chart to find the equivalent age related threshold Impedance with BP. Next, we take into account SW's glissando, deteriorating current, and rising Impedance by adding an additional 50Ω to the BP age-related Impedance, thereby determining the minimum SW Impedance for, for example, the ten year old child (typically at the end of .1 Seconds). Specifically as noted, BP Impedance is circa 50Ω for a 10 year old child. (See BP chart above.) Consequently, we add 50Ω to the 50Ω required for BP at ten years of age to obtain a 100Ω <u>initial threshold Impedance</u> for the 10 year old child administered SW at minimum output, that is, over a .1 Second Duration. To determine age-related <u>initial threshold output</u> for SW at 100Ω, we find the nearest BP Impedance (see 100Ω on the BP chart above which happens to correspond to a 20 year old BP recipient) and identify its corresponding Threshold Output (4J) to determine (if necessary, via ER) the Threshold Output needed for SW at 100Ω for the ten year old child. Since a Threshold Output of 4J is required for a Threshold Impedance of 100Ω, we know that at least 4J is necessary to overcome threshold output for the ten year old child with SW. (Here, no ER derivation is necessary.) Hence, at least 4J is the initial output required for the SW machine to overcome the 100Ω initial Impedance reached after a .1 Second Duration for the ten year old child.[225] Finally, using various SW parameters, we find the least amount of deliverable output necessary to overcome the initial age-related threshold output to determine the MTTLOI (for the ten year old) at minimum SW settings.[226] The chart below contains minimum threshold outputs for SW (determined in this manner) for ages 10-100. (We shall see the complete process later.)

TYPICAL (THOUGH SPECULATIVE) AGE RELATED
THRESHOLD IMPEDANCES AND THRESHOLD OUTPUTS
At <u>**MINIMUM SETTINGS**</u> FOR THE B-24 <u>**SINE WAVE**</u>

AGE	Initial Impedance Threshold (Ω)	Threshold Output in Joules
10	100	4.0
20	150	9.0
30	205	16.4
40	260	26.0
50	320	41.5
60	390	64.2
65	420	72.0
70	445	80.0
80	495	99.0
90	545	120
100	595	143

---

[225] ER derivations here may not be wholly accurate, but suffice as approximations.

[226] We may be able to lower the EO for minimal stimulus through trial and era, for example, using less Voltage and less Amperage as we shall see.

We can note that in all age categories, SW at true minimal stimulus settings per age category, requires more EO than that required for BP to reach threshold. We might also note that as recipient age increases, the SW/BP ratios of required outputs generally decline: Age 10 = 3.78/1; Age 20 = 2.3/1; Age 30 = 1.77/1; Age 40 = 1.56/1; Age 50 = 1.65/1; Age 60 = 1.77/1; Age 65 = 1.7/1; Age 70 = 1.62/1; Age 80 = 1.53/1; Age 90 = 1.47/1; Age 100 = 1.43/1.[227] Thus, the comparative age-related EO ratio required to reach threshold between minimal stimulus SW settings and the minimum EO required for BP at this same age, ranges from circa 4 to 1, to circa 1.4 to 1. Moreover, as we shall soon see, while SW is extremely powerful in the younger age categories, by age 65 and over, SW no longer appears powerful enough to reliably induce seizure with BL "ECT." The average overall SW EO in Joules required to reach threshold at minimal stimulus settings vs BP, specifically the default settings of the first generation MECTA "C" BP device is about 1.87 to 1, approaching twice the EO needed by SW to induce adequate seizure compared to (the first generation MECTA "C") BP (device) even at true minimal stimulus SW settings. 3.78 + 2.3 + 1.77 + 1.56 + 1.65 + 1.77 + 1.7 + 1.62 + 1.53 + 1.47 + 1.43 ÷ 11 = 1.87 Average. In short, even at true minimal stimulus SW settings, with the exception of ages 65 and older at which points, SW may not be powerful enough to induce seizure with BL "ECT," Brief Pulse via the first generation MECTA "C" is superior with respect to reduced EO to reach threshold (and thus reduced morbidity) in every instance compared to SW via the Medcraft B-24. We must remember, however, that this is a comparison of SW versus the First generation Brief Pulse Device, specifically the MECTA "C"--not the more powerful Brief Pulse devices to follow whereupon BP loses the advantage of reduced EO, as we have seen in the previous sections.

Maximum SW Settings:

Next, let's look at maximum SW settings and thus the maximum B-24 outputs possible (over one full second) compared to the output necessary to overcome SW Thresholds in various age categories from which we can then compare age-related SW outputs to the age-related default outputs delivered by various generations of BP devices. For threshold outputs at maximum SW settings, we first use the BP chart to find the equivalent age related threshold Impedance with BP. Next, we take into account SW's glissando, deteriorating current, and rising Impedance by adding (50Ω + 45Ω =) 95Ω to figure the final age-related Impedance for SW at maximum SW settings, in this instance, for the ten year old child at the end of 1.0 Second. For example, for the 10 year old, BP Impedance is circa 50Ω (see BP chart above). Thus we add (50Ω + 45Ω =) 95Ω to the initial 50Ω required for BP to obtain a (50Ω + 50Ω + 45Ω =)145Ω final threshold Impedance for the 10 year old child administered SW at maximum output settings over a maximum 1.0 Second Duration. To determine age-related threshold output for SW at 145Ω, we find the nearest BP Impedance (see 150Ω on the BP chart above which happens to correspond to a 30 year old BP recipient) and identify its corresponding Threshold Output (9J) to determine (via ER) the Threshold Output for SW at 145Ω for the same ten year old child. Since a Threshold Output of 9J is required for a Threshold Impedance of 150Ω for BP, we use 145Ω to set up an ER to determine SW threshold output for the same ten year old child to derive (9J/150Ω = XJ/145Ω; X =) 8.7J. Hence, circa 8.7J is the output required for the ten year old child to overcome the 145Ω maximum Impedance reached after a 1.0 Second maximum Duration.[228] Finally, we divide the output actually delivered by the threshold output required to induce an adequate seizure to determine the age-related MTTLOI for SW at maximum SW settings.

Let us go through the process for determining maximum SW output for a twenty year old. A Threshold Impedance of 100Ω must be overcome with BP to seize the twenty year old recipient. Thus, at maximum output settings for SW, (100Ω + 50Ω + 45Ω =) 195Ω must be overcome (over a 1.0 Second Duration) for the same twenty year old age recipient. Using the 40 year old on a BP device who requires 16.1J to overcome a 200Ω Impedance), we set up an ER determine that (16.1J/200Ω = XJ/195Ω =) 15.7J is needed to overcome 195Ω for SW, that is 15.7J is the speculative threshold output needed to overcome a 195Ω final Impedance for the 20 year old SW recipient at maximum SW settings. (See maximum settings SW Chart below.) All Threshold

---

[227] 4.0/1.06 = 3.78/1; 9.0/4.03 = 2.3/1; 16.0/9 = 1.77/1; 25.0/16.1 = 1.56/1; 41.5/25.2 = 1.65/1; 64.2/36.3 = 1.77/1; 72/42.6 = 1.7/1; 80/49.4 = 1.62/1; 99/64.5 = 1.53/1; 120/81.6 = 1.47/1; 143/100 = 1.43/1.

[228] ER derivations here are not wholly accurate, but suffice as approximations.

Outputs for maximum SW settings on the SW Chart below are deduced in this manner. To determine the MTTLOI for SW at maximum settings, we must determine (via formulas) the EO actually delivered, then divide the maximum output delivered in this twenty year old age category by its final Threshold Output of 15.7J. The chart below identifies Threshold outputs at maximum SW settings for ages 10 to 100.

TYPICAL (THOUGH SPECULATIVE) AGE RELATED
THRESHOLD IMPEDANCES AND THRESHOLD OUTPUTS
At **MAXIMUM SETTINGS** FOR THE B-24 **SINE WAVE**

AGE	Final Impedance Threshold (Ω)	Threshold Output in Joules
10	145	8.7
20	195	15.7
30	245	24.7
40	295	35.7
50	345	48.7
60	395	63.7
65	420	72.0
70	445	80.7
80	495	99.0
90	545	119.9
100	595	142.8

In all age categories, SW at maximum settings requires more EO than the MECTA "C" BP (representing minimal stimulus BP) to reach threshold. Nevertheless, as recipient age progresses, the output SW/BP ratio declines: Age 10 = 8.2/1; Age 20 = 3.9/1; Age 30 = 2.74/1; Age 40 = 2.17/1; Age 50 = 1.93/1; Age 60 = 1.75/1; Age 65 = 1.69/1; Age 70 = 1.63/1; Age 80 = 1.53/1; Age 90 = 1.47/1; Age 100 = 1.43/1.[229] Thus, the age-related EO ratio required to reach threshold between SW and BP ranges from circa 8 to 1, to circa 1.4 to 1. Moreover, as we shall soon see and as reflected in the decreasing ratio, while SW is extremely powerful in the younger age categories, by age 65, SW may no longer be powerful enough to induce seizure at all. The overall average in SW Joules required to reach threshold at maximum settings vs the MECTA "C" Brief Pulse is a little over 2 to 1 or more than twice the EO for SW to induce seizure compared to BP. 8.2 + 2.9 + 2.74 + 2.17 + 1.93 + 1.75 + 1.69 + 1.63 + 1.53 + 1.47 + 1.43 ÷ 11 = 2.5 Average. This is also more or less true for minimal stimulus SW vs minimal stimulus BP as we have seen. In short, compared to the true minimal stimulus BP, i.e. the MECTA "C," Brief Pulse is superior to SW by virtue of reduced EO in every instance. We must again remember, however, that this pertains to SW versus the first generation MECTA "C" Brief Pulse device--not the more powerful Brief Pulse devices following the MECTA "C."

In any case, once we derive maximum and minimum EOs for SW, and also include probable minimal stimulus SW, we can compare these age-related outputs with SW to the default outputs delivered both by the first generation MECTA "C" BP device, and by subsequent BP device generations.

---

229 8.7/1.06 = 8.2/1; 15.7/4.03 = 3.9/1; 24.7/9 = 2.74/1; 35.7/16.1 = 2.17/1; 48.7/25.2 = 1.93/1; 63.7/36.3 = 1.75/1; 72/42.6 = 1.69/1; 80.7/49.4 = 1.63/1; 99/64.5 = 1.53/1; 120/81.6 = 1.47/1; 143/100 = 1.43/1.

CHAPTER 82

Facts about Medcraft's B-24 SW Compared to BP and the Basis of "the Cameron Paradigm"

Weiner implicitly describes Brief Pulse (to the FDA in 1982) as having the capacity to seize any recipient at no more than 100 Joules. Conversely, Weiner describes the B-24 SW by Medcraft (to the FDA in 1982) as having a 200 Joule ceiling and potential peak Current of 1.7 Amperes. This 200J potential is clearly the result of maximum SW output with a maximum 1.7A Current. The following BP graph vs SW graph below are Weiner's, extracted from the 1982 APA Standard for BP devices written in main by Weiner himself.

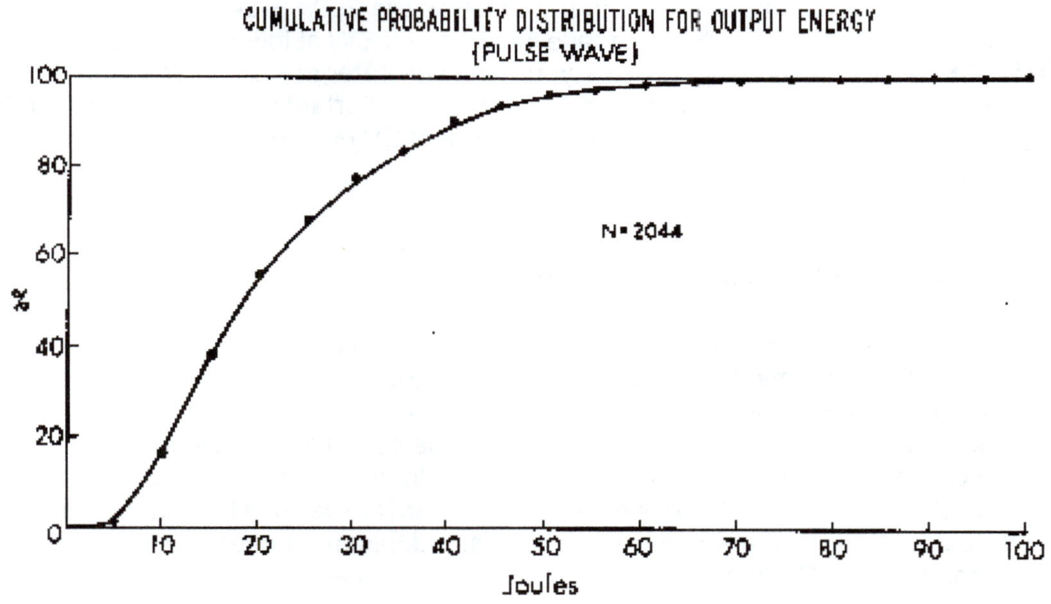

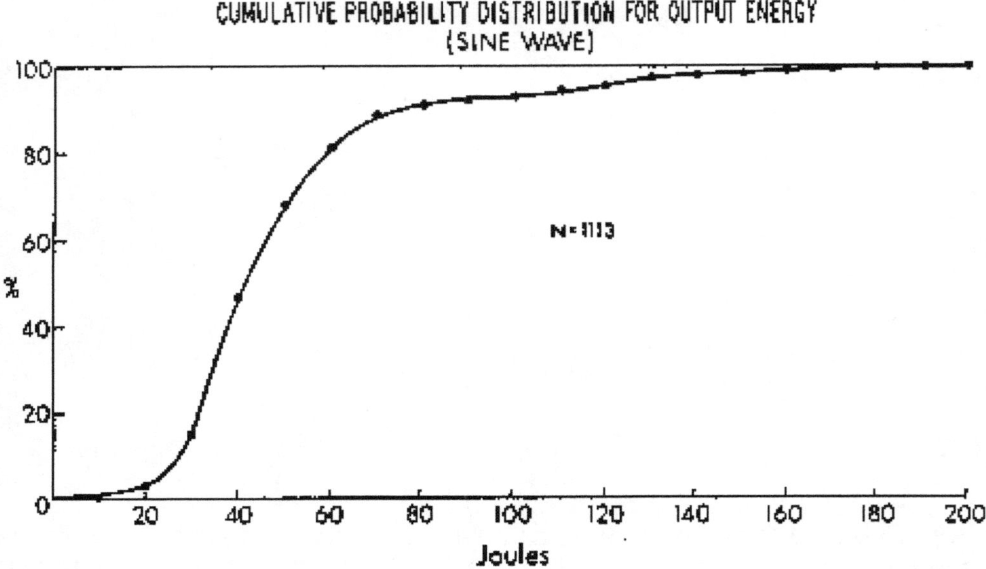

Weiner's charts above comparing BP to SW appear to be based on Weiner's implication that BP can induce a successful or "adequate" seizure in all recipients under any circumstances with no more than 100 Joules. Thus 100 joules is the minimum output with which all recipients can be seized. It is this minimum output upon which the maximum default output of 108J emitted by the First Generation MECTA "C" BP Device and the 110J ceiling of the 1982 APA Standard is based. To this 100J, Weiner compares the 200J B-24 SW apparently at maximum Outputs. The comparison is misleading. It does not take into account SW at lower stimulus settings, it does not reflect that the 200J potential of SW occurs only in the youngest age category, and it does not reflect that the B-24 SW loses power, the older the recipient. Perhaps most importantly, however, Weiner's comparative charts totally neglect the increasing power of the four subsequent BP device generations following the MECTA "C" as we have clearly seen in the previous section.

Supporting the Cameron Paradigm for determining SW Outputs

Let us begin by supporting (what I have deemed) the Cameron Paradigm for determining the age-related threshold outputs for maximum and allegedly minimum SW settings depicted in my maximum and alleged minimum SW Charts above Weiner's. Further explanation of the deduction and depiction of actual maximum and alleged minimum SW outputs delivered at maximum and improbable true minimum SW settings, including the respective MTTLOIs for each of these age-related outputs is to follow. In short, we add 50Ω to the Initial Threshold Impedance (for BP) typically at the end of .1 Seconds and another 45Ω to deduce the Final Threshold Impedance at the end of 1.0 Second for SW. To more completely understand this maneuver, we will construct maximum and minimum output charts for SW for each age category. (See Appendix C: "Summarizing the Cameron Paradigm.")

The Ten Year Old Child

Our first chart is based upon Weiner's assertion of the maximum output possible (200J) for the B-24 SW by Medcraft. Based upon Weiner's information, including Weiner's SW v BP graphs above, the maximum output the B-24 can reach, as noted, is 200J and the maximum Amperage, 1.7A.[230] Medcraft informs us, as we have seen, that maximum Duration for the B-24 SW is 1.0 Seconds and maximum Voltage 170V. Contingent upon the maximum Amperage (1.7A) and the maximum Voltage (170V) reported for the Medcraft B-24 SW device

[230] The APA Standard limits SW to 1.0A, but like BP, SW manufacturers do not honor the standard.

utilized to derive Weiner's maximum 200J parameter above, we can determine that initial maximum Resistance for SW cannot fall below 100Ω (Ohm's Law: Ω = Voltage/Current; 170V/1.7A = 100Ω.), else Amperage rises above the maximum 1.7A assigned to SW. [231] This, at first, seems somewhat problematic in that while 100Ω must be used to derive the 1.7A maximum, a current of 1.7A is too high to derive the maximum SW output of 200 Joules (according to Weiner's assertion). SW Amperage, therefore, as per the Cameron paradigm, must necessarily deteriorate over Duration, specifically, Impedance must rise from 100Ω to 145Ω over one Second.[232] Finally, we must assume that not only does initial SW Impedance rise dramatically over a single treatment, but that by definition, the highest EO of 200J belongs to the individual with the lowest Impedance--the lowest age category—the ten year old child.

EOs relative to Impedance appear to be relative constants, that is, the amount of EO required to overcome any specific Impedance appears to be the same for SW as for BP. On the other hand, SW and BP age-related threshold Resistances are starkly dissimilar, that is, more Impedance must be overcome for the ten year old child with SW than with BP. This is due, as previously noted, to the deterioration of SW current as a result of which Impedance rises dramatically on SW devices even over a single individual "treatment," requiring greater EO to reach threshold compared to BP. In short, age-related Impedance thresholds for SW are higher than age-related Impedance thresholds for BP so that more EO per age category is required to reach threshold with SW as noted, than BP. For example, as has also been noted, on BP devices, a ten year old child has an initial (and final) resistance per individual "treatment" of about 50Ω (see above chart).[233] On the B-24 SW device, we have already discovered that at maximum parameters, according to the necessary Impedance-output relationship, the initial resistance for the same ten year old child must be about 100Ω so that in accordance with our maximum parameter of 200J, SW Impedance can rise over the duration of the individual "treatment" by another 45Ω, that is, over the one Second maximum. This means, as noted above, at maximum SW parameters, that is, at the end of one second, the final Impedance for a ten year old child is about 145Ω and that Current has deteriorated from 1.7A to 1.172A (<u>EO = Voltage x Current x Duration</u>; <u>**200J** = 170V x **1.172A** x 1.0 Seconds</u>. <u>Ω = Voltage/Current</u>; <u>170V/1.172A = **145Ω**</u>.) In short, Impedance has increased <u>from 100Ω to 145Ω</u> and current has deteriorated from <u>1.7A to 1.172A</u> for the ten year old child at maximum SW settings, that is, over one full Second. As we can see, compared to BP, 50Ω has been added to initial Impedance of 50Ω for the ten year old child (50Ω + 50Ω =) <u>**100Ω**</u>, and another 45Ω for final Impedance or (100Ω + 45Ω =) <u>**145Ω**</u>. Adding 50Ω for Initial Impedance and another 45Ω for Final Impedance for SW (compared to BP) becomes the rule; is the paradigm. (These increases in Impedance over a single treatment for SW also take into account the additional glissando output up to and into the actual "treatment" as well as numerous other factors as stated earlier.)

Finding the Constant (K) for the Inverse Relationship Between Impedance and EO for SW

In sum, the alleged maximum 200 Joule SW output (as claimed by Weiner) for the ten year old child necessitates a known deterioration of Current.[234] In short, concomitant to Current deterioration, the already increased Initial Impedance (compared to BP)--in conjunction with Glissando--dramatically increases on SW devices over the course of a single treatment set for the maximum one Second. In that Initial Impedance is 100Ω, and final maximum output for the ten year old child is the 200J alleged by Weiner, final Impedance at that maximum output must necessarily be about 145Ω just as final Current must be about 1.172A (see the first Chart for the ten year old child in the following section below). Obviously, there is a clear inverse relationship between Energy Output and Impedance on a SW device. Indeed, based on the final output/impedance relationship of 200J and 145Ω, we can derive an inverse proportion ratio applicable to SW generally. Using the inverse proportion formula: EO = K/Impedance, we plug in the maximum EO (200J) and Impedance (145Ω) parameters to derive a constant (K) of (<u>200J</u> = K/<u>145Ω</u> =) <u>29000</u>. That is, <u>K = 29000</u>. We can confirm this

---

231 Any Impedance below 100Ω at maximum Voltage increases Amperage over the allowed maximum. For example, using 90Ω, Current = Voltage/Ω. Current = 170V/90Ω = <u>1.88A</u> > Maximum allowed Amperage of 1.7A.

232 EO = Current^2 x Imp. x Duration. 200J = 1.172 x 1.172 x 145Ω x 1.0 Seconds = 200J.

233 Rise in Impedance with BP, particularly over a single treatment, is minimal.

234 Final Current cannot be 1.7A in that with maximum Voltage, EO would be too high. 170V x 1.7A x 1.0 Seconds = 289J. According to Weiner, maximum output with SW is 200J.

inverse relationship of output to Impedance by deriving either the 200J maximum or the 145Ω final Impedance by solving for one or the other with K = 29000: 200J = 29000/XΩ = **145Ω**; XJ = 29000/145Ω = **200J**.

Moreover, if we reverse the process, that is, increase Impedance to 200Ω, EO conversely drops to 145J and vice-versa (XJ = 29000/200Ω = **145J**; 145J = 29000/XΩ = **200Ω**). We can now use this formula containing the constant--29000--to determine and verify other output/impedance relationships with SW where there is an initial and final Impedance, generally, at maximum B-24 SW parameters.

Summary:

Thus, by confining parameters to consistent derivatives between the two SW formulas for discovering Energy Output (Joules = Volts x Current x Duration; Joules = Current squared x Impedance x Duration), and assuming an additional 50Ω is added to the Initial SW Impedance compared to BP plus another 45Ω for Final SW Impedance over 1.0 Second (the Cameron Paradigm), we can determine final outputs relative to age-related thresholds and thus the MTTLOI for both improbable "true" minimal and probable maximal outputs.

To briefly illustrate, 50Ω must be overcome for a ten year old child using BP. Thus, via the Cameron Paradigm, we determine (50Ω + 50Ω =) 100Ω as the initial Impedance for the ten year old child with SW which (consulting the BP chart above) requires about 4J to overcome. We can then determine (through the formulas above as we shall see in more detail) that the actual output is about 4.9J at true minimum output settings for SW (or .1 Seconds) for the ten year old, delivering a MTTLOI of about (4.9J ÷ 4.0J =) 1.23. Adding another 45Ω for a final (100Ω + 45Ω =) 145Ω Impedance, we can determine (using the BP chart above), that the 145Ω final Impedance at the end of 1.0 Second maximum Duration, requires about 8.7J to overcome. Using the formulas above to determine a 200J maximum output at the maximum one second for the ten year old child, we can deduce a (200J ÷ 8.7J =) 23 MTTLOI for the ten year old administered maximum output on the B-24 SW. In sum, by using the Cameron Paradigm, feasible profiles can now be depicted for "minimal" and maximal SW outputs for every age category. In short, using the Cameron paradigm, we can now determine EO and (though inconsistent) MTTLOI for maximum and "minimum" settings in all age categories of SW.

CHAPTER 83

Maximum and "Minimum" SW Settings for All Age Categories

A) Outputs and MTTLOIs for the Ten Year Old Child at Maximum and "Minimum" SW Settings.

Based on the lowest possible initial Impedance of about 100Ω and logically assuming that this Impedance belongs to that of a ten year old child, and a final Impedance of 145Ω at the end of one second of maximum Duration, we can now create metrics, charts, and eventually graphs (see sections below) using Ohm's Law (Voltage = Impedance x Current) and other formulas for, for example, the ten year old child over a .1 Second minimum set at the lowest possible Voltage (70V) and, the same ten year old child over a 1.0 second maximum Duration using the maximum 170 maximum Volts. In addition, we can figure MTTLOI for each setting.

EO (for SW) = Current Squared x Impedance x Duration.
EO (for SW) = Volts x Current x Duration.
EO (for SW) = Charge x Current x Impedance
Charge (for SW) = Current x Duration
Ohm's Law: Current = Voltage/Ω; Ω = Voltage/Current; Voltage = Current x Ω

Minimum Output: For the ten year old child set at "minimal" stimulus with the B-24, that is, using a Resistance of (50Ω + 50Ω =) 100Ω and minimum Voltage of 70V, we can determine an Amperage of (70V ÷ 100Ω =) .7A. Then. using the minimum .1 Second Duration together with the .7A Current, we can determine Charge (.7A x .1Seconds =) .07C. Finally, using the formulas: Voltage x Current x Duration or Charge x Current x Impedance or Current x Current x Impedance x Duration, we can determine the improbable true minimum EO (for SW) deliverable of (70V x .7A x .1Seconds; .07C x .7A x 100Ω; .7A x .7A x 100Ω x .1Seconds =) 4.9J. Because we know that "minimum" Threshold Output for the ten year old child is 4.0J (see above charts for overcoming 100Ω), and that the B-24 set at an improbable true "minimal" stimulus for this age category delivers a circa 4.9J, we can also determine a (4.9J ÷ 4.0J =) 1.23 MTTLOI at "minimal stimulus." Thus:

MINIMUM OUTPUT AT MINIMUM B-24 PARAMETERS (BY MEDCRAFT) (at 10 years of age)

EO	Voltage	Current	Duration	Resistance	Charge
4.9 Joules	70 Volts	.7 Amperes	.1 Seconds	100 Ω	.07 Coulombs

100Ω requires 4J to overcome threshold which we find through trial and error, can be accomplished at 70V, the least amount of Voltage available on the B-24. Also through trial and error, we find the Minimum Output deliverable = 4.9J[235]; Thus, the MTTLOI at Min. Output = (4.9J ÷ 4.0J) = 1.23. However, based on the B-25, there is probable evidence that the B-24 will not deliver less than 36J to the ten year old age category or about a (36J ÷ 4J =) 9 MTTLOI.

---

[235] EO = Volts x Current x Duration; 70V x .7A x .1 Seconds = 4.9J; EO = Current x Current x Ω x Duration = .7A x .7A x 100Ω x .1 Sec. = 4.9J.

Maximum Output: For the ten year old child set at maximum stimulus with the B-24, using the Final Resistance of (50Ω + 50Ω + 45Ω =) 145Ω and maximum Voltage of 170V, we can determine Final Amperage of (170V ÷ 145Ω =) 1.17A. Using maximum Duration of 1.0 Seconds and 1.17A Current then, we determine a Charge of (1.17A x 1.0 Seconds =) 1.172C. Next, using Voltage x Current x Duration or Charge x Current, x Impedance or Current x Current x Impedance x Duration, we can determine the maximum EO delivered of (170V x 1.172A x 1.0 Seconds; 1.172C x 1.172A x 145Ω; 1.17A x 1.17A x 145Ω x 1.0Seconds =) **200J**. Because we know that maximum Threshold Output for the ten year old child is 8.7J (see above charts for 145Ω), and the machine at maximal stimulus for this age category is **200J**, we can deduce a (200J ÷ 8.7J =) **23 MTTLOI**. Using the chart below, we can even determine EO for any Duration between .1 and 1.0 Seconds.

RARE MAXIMUM OUTPUT AT MAXIMUM B-24 PARAMETERS (BY MEDCRAFT) (at 10 years of age)

EO	Voltage	Current	Duration	Resistance	Charge
28.9 Joules	170 Volts	1.7 A	.1 Seconds	100 Ω	.170 Coulombs
55.07	170	1.62	.2	105	.324
79.05	170	1.55	.3	110	.464
100.6	170	1.48	.4	115	.591
120.7	170	1.42	.5	120	.708
138.7	170	1.36	.6	125	.816
155.9	170	1.31	.7	130	.915
171.3	170	1.26	.8	135	1.007
185	170	1.21	.9	140	1.093
200 J	**170**	**1.172**	**1.0**	**145**	**1.172**

The 200J output above might only occur at the maximum 170 Volts applied to a young child of ten for the maximum 1.0 Seconds. Note the dwindling current. Note also the Charge output of almost 1200mC tantamount to third, fourth, and even fifth generation BP devices. (Maximum Output) 200J [236] ÷ 8.7J (Threshold Output) = 23 MTTLOI.

Indeed, for Sine Wave devices, the excessively high 200J output indicated by Weiner, can only be emitted with naturally occurring low Resistances (over which the machine has no control) and thus high Amperage, i.e. the initial 1.7A deteriorating to 1.172A together with maximum Voltage (170V) and maximum Duration (1.0 Seconds).[237] [238] The highest possible SW emission such as that depicted in the chart above requires the lowest possible Impedance, one typically seen in young children. Judging from the alleged rarity of the (200J) extremely high output--about one twelfth of one percent of all B-24 SW emissions (according to a literal interpretation of Weiner's charts)--we can assume that either Impedances normally tend to be much higher suggesting recipients typically older, or much more likely--that the machine is only rarely set for maximum settings for very young recipients (perhaps only experimentally). Conversely, the higher the recipient Impedance (i.e. the older the recipient), the lower the resulting Amperage on SW-constant Voltage devices, and consequently the lower the EO emitted even at maximum settings, as we shall see.

Outputs and MTTLOIs for the Ten Year Old Child at Maximum and Minimum SW Settings Continued

Threshold EO (the least amount of EO required to induce adequate seizure) in direct accordance with specific Impedances, as noted, appear to be relatively constant, applying to both BP and SW. Because age-related SW Impedances are higher than age-related BP Impedances and because we can identify initial and final

[236] EO = Volts x Current x Duration; 170V x 1.172A x 1.0 Seconds = 200J; EO = Current x Current x Ω x Duration = 1.172A x 1.172A x 145Ω x 1.0 Sec. = 200J.

[237] SW devices, as constant Voltage devices, have no means of maintaining current, thus as Impedance increases, the current dwindles. On the other hand, the lower the Impedance, the higher the Amperage, and thus the higher the EO. The excessively high outputs above require naturally occurring low Impedances such as might be exhibited by a small child.

[238] It goes without saying that adequate seizures can be elicited in all recipients with much less current, specifically with BP devices. Liberson did so in 1953 with BP devices emitting extremely low Amperages.

Impedances for SW for the ten year old child, we can also identify the Threshold Outputs for SW for the same ten year old child. (See SW charts depicted at the beginning of this section made for all age categories.) Indeed, we can simply use the SW charts at the beginning of this section to correlate initial and final SW Impedances with minimum and maximum threshold EOs for any particular age.

Notably, the SW charts depicted above are created from BP Charts as has been noted. For example, because we know that a ten year old child has a 100Ω initial Impedance (at "minimum" settings) with SW and a 145Ω final Impedance (at maximum settings) with SW, we can simply refer to the age-related BP chart to see that at 150Ω, threshold output is about 9J. Via ER, therefore, we can determine that at 145Ω or maximum SW output for the ten year old age category, threshold output is about 8.7 Joules (150Ω/9J = 145Ω/8.7J). Similarly, at 100Ω or "minimum" SW output, we find (by checking the same 100Ω Impedance on the BP chart) that threshold output set for "minimal stimulus" for the same 10 year old child (at 100Ω with SW) is about 4.0J.

Finally, we can simply consult the Age-Related/Threshold Output SW Charts above to deduce the MTTLOI of maximum and "minimum" outputs with SW. For example, once we have deduced that the final output delivered to the ten year old recipient with SW at 145Ω at the maximum 1.0 Second Duration is 200J, we simply divide the 200J output by the minimum SW threshold output of 8.7J to determine the age-related MTTLOI at full SW power, in this case, an unconscionable (200J ÷ 8.7J =) 23 fold threshold or 23 MTTLOI. Similarly, we can derive the MTTLOI for the same ten year old child set for "minimum" SW stimulus. Since it takes it takes at least 4J to overcome the initial Impedance of 100Ω (see BP chart or SW Chart for Minimal Stimulus) and we can deduce a 4.9J "minimum" stimulus output (based on 70V, the least amount of Voltage available on the B-24 in conjunction with .1 Seconds Duration), we can determine a true minimum MTTLOI (for SW) of about (4.9J ÷ 4.0J =) 1.23 for the same ten year old child set for true "minimal" stimulus. However, there is evidence that no less than 36J can be delivered to the 10 year old child for a MTTLOI of about a (36J ÷ 4.0J =) 9 MTTLOI.

For comparative purposes, we should remember that while threshold output for "minimal" stimulus requires about 4.0J for the ten year old on SW, threshold output on a modern day BP device for the same ten year old child (based on Beale's 1994 study), can be as low as 1.0 Joule, one fourth the power of "minimal stimulus" SW. (See BP chart above for EO required to overcome 50Ω.) This is mainly due to the difference in Impedances as noted, 50Ω vs 100Ω for the same ten year old child, the former—BP--requiring 1.0J, the latter--SW--requiring 4.0J (set for true "minimal stimulus"). However, the delivery of just over 1.0J with BP (for the ten year old child) only applies to the First generation MECTA "C" BP device—not to any other subsequent BP device, as we shall soon observe in more detail.

Indeed, later generation BP devices have greatly surpassed SW in raw output over the years in most age categories. On the other hand, the surpassing power of BP falls predominantly in the older age categories, while--due to their low Resistances--the surpassing power of SW falls predominantly in the youngest age categories. As we have observed in a previous chapter—"Third Generation BP Devices"--the default MTTLOI for BP depends upon the device, in all cases increasing with each subsequent generation.

In sum, the maximum power and maximum MTTLOI for SW devices is far greater than BP default outputs in the younger age categories; whereas, the default power and default MTTLOI for BP devices is far greater than SW in the older age categories. For instance, maximum SW power for those who are 10 years of age or younger, is more than (200J ÷ 4.6J = 43.5) 43 times the power of the third generation BP device in this same age category and more than (23 ÷ 5 = 4.6) four times the circa 5.0 MTTLOI of the third generation BP. In addition, maximum SW power for those who are 10 years of age or younger is more than (200J ÷ 9.2J = 21.7) 21 times the power of the fourth generation BP device in this same age category and more than (23 ÷ 10 = 2.3) two times the circa 10.0 MTTLOI delivered by the fourth generation BP device in the same ten year old age category.

On the other hand, as discussed, the default power and default MTTLOI for later generation BP devices is far greater than SW in the older age categories. To illustrate, the default power of the third generation BP device in the 100 year old age category is more than (460J ÷ 49J = 9.38) nine times the maximum power of SW in this same age category and more than (5.0 ÷ .34 = 14.7) 14 times the circa .34 MTTLOI of SW in this same 100 year old age category. In addition, the default power of the potential fourth generation BP device in the 100 year old age category is more than (922J ÷ 49J =) 18 times the power of SW in this same age category and more than (10 ÷.34 = 29.4) 29 times the circa .34 MTTLOI of SW in this same 100 year old age category, as we shall see.

On the other hand again, by reducing Voltage to 70V on the B-24 SW device, we can create a 1.23 MTTLOI (at true minimal stimulus for SW) even for the ten year old child, comparable to the 1.08 MTTLOI of the first generation MECTA "C." However, the 4.9J EO delivered to the ten year old child by SW at true minimal stimulus (for SW) is (4.9J ÷ 1.08J =) 4.54 times the power delivered by the First Generation MECTA "C" in this same age category. But while the MECTA "C" BP device is superior to the B-24 SW in terms of Energy Output reduction even at "true minimal stimulus" for SW, the "C" is an anomaly amongst modern-day BP devices. For example, because extant third generation BP devices educe a consistent (circa) 5.0 MTTLOI for the ten year old child, third generation BP devices deliver circa 4.6J to the ten year old child, about the same EO as true minimal stimulus SW in this same age category. The point is, the third (and even second) generation BP device has lost its reduced EO advantage over SW. Indeed, third generation BP devices emit a circa 5.0 MTTLOI for all age categories, emitting about 460 Joules (in the oldest age category as we have observed), much higher than the most extreme SW output (200J), albeit in a totally opposing age category (i.e. the 100 year old as opposed to the ten year old) as noted. Noteworthy, the fourth generation BP device emits about 960 maximum Joules, almost (960J ÷ 200J = 4.9) five times the overall maximum output of SW though again, in an entirely disparate age category (i.e. 100 year old as opposed to ten years old). In fact, unlike SW, the fourth generation BP device is capable of emitting a consistent (circa) 10.0 MTTLOI not merely to 10 year old recipients, but to every age recipient, as we have seen. Finally, there is the added complication that true minimal stimulus (for SW) may not be allowed on the B-24 for efficacy reasons. Indeed, probable evidence exists (based on the B-25 Brief Pulse device also by Medcraft), that no less than 36J is allowed in the 10 year old age category or a (36J ÷ 4J =) 9 MTTLOI.

The importance of comparisons between maximal, true minimal, and probable minimal SW outputs to all five BP device generations shall become clearer as we identify SW outputs in every age category.

Results

The results of comparing SW to Brief Pulse, as we shall see, are mixed. For example, in some areas, all generations of BP emit less EO than SW. The default outputs of all generations of BP devices, for instance, utilize far less EO in the ten year old age category than SW set at maximum output in the ten year old category. Third generation BP devices, to illustrate, use only about 4.6J Joules to deliver their circa 5.0 MTTLOI to ten year old recipients, a fraction of the 200J EO delivered by SW set at maximum output in the same ten year old category. SW, on the other hand, need not be set at maximum for this age class and, in fact, is almost certainly not set at maximum in the great majority of cases. On the other hand again, convincing evidence suggests that SW can only be set for a 9 MTTLOI minimum in this age category. Thus, while only about one twelfth of one percent of all B-24 SW emissions reach the alleged 200 Joule maximum according to a literal interpretation of Weiner's graphs viewed at the beginning of this section, neither is SW typically set at true minimal stimulus in the ten year old age category. Indeed, the B-24 SW may not be allowed to deliver below a 36J minimum in the ten year old age category.

In any case, it is of paramount significance that only the First Generation MECTA "C" BP device emits less EO (generally half) than SW set to true minimal stimulus (for SW) in all age categories for which an "adequate" seizure can be induced. Conversely, second, third, fourth, and fifth generation BP devices are powerful enough at their default settings to elicit a circa 2.5, 5, 10, and 12 MTTLOI respectively for every age category consistently, an impossible feat for SW, even at maximum Energy Output.[239] Critically then, only the first generation MECTA "C," utilizes much less power than SW, generally at both true "minimum" and maximum SW settings.

B) Output and MTTLOI for the Twenty Year Old at Maximum and Minimum SW Settings

Threshold Impedance for BP in the twenty year old age category is 100Ω, which means--according to the Cameron paradigm--initial threshold Impedance for the twenty year old age recipient with SW is about (100Ω + 50Ω =) 150Ω with a final SW Impedance at maximum output (at the end of one maximum Second) of about (150Ω + 45Ω =) 195Ω. In short, we have an even higher initial SW Resistance for the twenty year old of about

---

[239] SW can deliver a 23 MTTLOI to the ten year old child, but cannot maintain this power for other age categories.

150Ω (compared to the 100Ω initial Resistance for the ten year old) as well as a higher final Impedance for the twenty year old of about 195Ω (compared to 145Ω for the ten year old). Maximum SW Voltage is 170V and maximum Duration is 1.0 Seconds.

EO (for SW) = Volts x Current x Duration.
Current = Voltage/Ω
Charge (for SW) = Current x Duration

Voltage (120) and Duration (.1 Sec.) is the true SW minimum for the 20 year old.

MINIMUM OUTPUT FOR B-24 SW by MEDCRAFT (for 20 years of age)

EO	Voltage	Current	Duration	Resistance	Charge
9.6 Joules	120 Volts	.8 Amperes	.1 Seconds	150 Ω	.113 Coulombs

The 20 year old profile directly above is derived from minimum B-24 settings. Using the BP chart at the beginning of this section, we find that at least 9J is required to overcome 150Ω. Thus, through trial and error, we find that the least amount of Voltage required to equal or surpass 9J is about 120V. Based on Initial Resistance of 150Ω, via Ohm's Law, we find that Current is (120V ÷ 150Ω =) .8A. True Minimum EO delivered = Volts x Current x Duration = 9.6J; MTTLOI = 9.6J ÷ 9J (Threshold output) = 1.06 MTTLOI. There is probable evidence, however, that that the B-24 will not allow output below 43J or about a (43J ÷ 9J =) 4.8 MTTLOI for the 20 year old recipient.

For maximum output in this age category, we use maximum Voltage (170) which remains constant, and maximum Duration of 1.0 Sec. (See below). 150Ω is the initial Impedance which increases to 195Ω over 1.0 Seconds. Based on Ohm's Law, we find an initial Amperage of 1.13A (at 170V) which deteriorates to .872A at final Impedance. We find this final Amperage via Ohm's Law (Current = Voltage/Ω). Charge (for SW) = Current x Duration. EO (for SW) = Current x Current x Impedance x Duration; Volts x Current x Duration; or EO = Charge x Current x Impedance. By assuming Impedance increases in equal increments of 5Ω per .1 Second, we can fill in all other parameters. Charge (for SW) = Current x Duration.

FAIRLY RARE 148J MAXIMUM FOR B-24 SW by MEDCRAFT (for 20 years of age)

EO	Voltage	Current	Duration	Resistance	Charge
19.26 J	170 Volts	1.13 A	.1 Seconds	150 Ω	.113 Coulombs
37.29	170	1.097	.2	155	.219
54.19	170	1.062	.3	160	.3186
70	170	1.03	.4	165	.412
85	170	1.0	.5	170	.500
99	170	.971	.6	175	.583
112.38	170	.944	.7	180	.661
125	170	.919	.8	185	.735
136.9	170	.895	.9	190	.805
148.2 J	**170**	**.872**	**1.0**	**195**	**.872**

The 20 year old profile above is derived from maximum B-24 settings. Note the 148J delivered. Maximum Output = 148.2J; Threshold Output = 15.7J. Maximum MTTLOI = 148.2J ÷ 15.7J = 9.44

Using maximum SW parameters, then, Amperage naturally deteriorates as Impedance once again rises 45Ω from a 150Ω initial Impedance to 195Ω final Impedance over the one second maximum Duration. Using the maximum 170 Volts, and the higher 150Ω initial Resistance results in a lower initial Amperage of about 1.13A, reasonably deteriorating over one second to .872A. Overall maximum EO settings for the 20 year old category is thus reduced (compared to the ten year old profile) to about 148J (in lieu of 200J), still unusually high.[240]

[240] The outcome of other various combinations suggests that the above graph is more or less correct. For example, let us allow the Impedance to increase up to a very unlikely 500Ω with a .62A final current and a final EO of 192J. In this case, we would have to use

Though speculative, we can approximate our hypothetical final output/impedance relationship with the inverse proportion formula: EO = 29000/Impedance. XJ = 29000/195Ω = circa 148J; 148J = 29000/XΩ = circa 195Ω.) According to a literal reading of Weiner's graph, such a (148J) scenario is again rare for SW, occurring in only one to two percent of all B-24 SW emissions.[241] At the final 195Ω Impedance, threshold output required for SW devices has risen to about 15.7 Joules (that of about 40 years old for BP). Based on the 148.2J cumulative emission at the end of one second, we obtain a Multifold Threshold Titration Level Output Intensity for the 20 year old at maximum SW settings of about (148.2J ÷ 15.7 =) 9.44 fold threshold. Once again we see that administering SW to younger people (in this case, 20 years of age), that is, those with lower Impedances, results in potentially higher MTTLOIs and thus the greatest potential electrical intensities (148J), particularly at maximum settings. The MTTLOI at maximum SW parameters for 20 year olds is thus about 10.0 fold threshold, tantamount to the MTTLOI consistently delivered by potential **fourth generation BP devices**, as we have seen.

Here, we can conclude that second generation BP devices, in spite of their circa 230-250J maximum outputs, and ubiquitous 2.3-2.5 MTTLOI for all age categories, utilize only about 10 Joules for the 20 year old category. Consequently, default settings for the dangerous second generation BP devices appear safer than maximum SW settings for the 20 year old age category.[242]

Third generation BP devices, educe a dangerous circa 5.0 MTTLOI at about 20 Joules for the twenty year old category which is yet safer than SW in this age category set for maximum output.

Dangerous fourth generation BP devices elicit about the same MTTLOI as that elicited by SW at maximum SW settings for the 20 year old age group (9-10 fold), but at about 40 Joules or about 27% the cumulative energy output of SW (148J) at maximum SW settings. In that both the fourth generation BP device at default settings and the SW device at maximum settings educe an approximate 10.0 MTTLOI for this age category, though extremely dangerous, fourth generation BP devices yet appear safer than maximum SW settings in the 20 year old age category.

Theoretical but "legal" and extremely dangerous Fifth generation BP devices elicit a greater MTTLOI than that elicited by SW at maximum SW settings for the 20 year old age group (circa 12 fold), but at about 48 Joules or about 32% the cumulative energy output of SW (148J) at maximum SW settings. Even though the fifth generation BP device at default settings elicits a 12.0 MTTLOI and the SW device at maximum settings educes an approximate 10.0 MTTLOI for this age category, even fifth generation BP devices appear "safer" than maximum SW settings in the 20 year old age category set for maximum output.

While the fourth and fifth generation BP devices are superior (by virtue of less EO) to maximum SW settings in the twenty year old category in that their circa 10.0 and 12.0 fold threshold titration levels can be delivered with about a quarter of the EO of SW at maximum settings, we must nevertheless ask the question: "If the body's Impedance threshold is the body's final line of defense beyond which harm begins to occur, just because BP devices are "safer" than a 10.0 fold threshold level of SW at an unconscionable 148J, is a 10.0 or 12.0 fold threshold level of BP at 40J and 48J respectively, "safe"? The answer, of course, is "No."

Too, we must consider that the maximum 148J B-24 SW emission discussed here may be elicited in only one to two percent of all B-24 SW emissions suggesting that most SW emissions in this age category are not set to maximum parameters. BP devices, on the other hand, are set at defaults and though the raw EO is less than that of SW set for maximum in this age category, third, fourth, and fifth generation BP devices elicit consistent circa 5.0 , 10, and 12 fold threshold outputs respectively virtually 100% of the time.[243]

---

about 310 Volts, impossible in that maximum Voltage is 170V (EO = Voltage x Current x Duration; 310V x .62A x 1.0Sec = 192J). What if we increase the final Amperage to .82A but use a 500Ω final Impedance? Using the 500Ω final Impedance we would derive a 336J output, non-existent on the B-24 (.82A x .82A x 500Ω x 1.0 Seconds = 336 Joules). What, then, if we lower the final Impedance to the more acceptable 195Ω maximum? In this instance, we yet use a final Current of .872A from which we derive about 148J. This indeed is plausible.

[241] If true, either much older individuals receive the majority of ECT and consequently recipients with much higher Impedances or much more likely, the device is not typically operated at maximum settings (maximum Voltage and/or Duration) in this age category.

[242] Most clinicians in the field no doubt use BP default settings. However, it should be noted that just as there is no actual statute preventing SW administrators from using any SW setting for any age recipient, neither is there any statute preventing BP clinicians from deviating from turning the dial to an age category higher or lower than the recipient's actual age.

[243] Almost all physicians follow the default instructions of the BP manufacturer, that is, physicians typically adhere to the chart or dial instructions corresponding to age and gender.

C) Output and MTTLOI for the Twenty-four Year Old at Maximum and Minimum SW Setting

Following our same paradigm, let us now proceed to a twenty-four year old age category. Threshold Impedance for BP in this age category is 120Ω, thus SW's initial threshold Impedance for the twenty-four year old is (120Ω + 50Ω =) 170Ω while Final Impedance in this age category is (170Ω + 45Ω =) 215Ω. In short, we have an even higher initial SW Resistance for the twenty-four year old (compared to the twenty year old) of about 170Ω (compared to the 150Ω initial Resistance for the twenty year old) as well as a higher final Impedance of about 215Ω for the twenty-four year old (compared to 195Ω for the twenty year old). Maximum and Minimum Amperage, in turn, drop, as does EO. Maximum Voltage is 170V and maximum Duration is 1.0 Seconds. True Minimum Voltage is 160V and true minimum Duration .1 Seconds for the 24 year old.

EO (for SW) = Volts x Current x Duration.
Current = Voltage/Ω
Charge (for SW) = Current x Duration

MINIMUM OUTPUT FOR B-24 SW by MEDCRAFT (24 years of age)

EO	Voltage	Current	Duration	Resistance	Charge
15.06J	160 Volts	.94A	.1 Seconds	170 Ω	.1 Coulombs

The 24 year old profile above is derived from improbable true minimum B-24 settings. From an ER based on the BP chart, we find that at least (200Ω/16J = 170Ω/XJ =) [244] 13.6J is required to overcome 170Ω. Thus the least amount of Voltage required is about 160V from which we derive a (Ohm's law: 160V ÷ 170Ω =) .94A current. True Minimum EO is (160V x .94A x .1Sec. =) 15.06J; Threshold Output = 13.6J. True Minimum MTTLOI is (15.06 ÷ 13.6J =) 1.11. Once again, however, there is probable evidence that the B-24 will not allow less than about 48J or a (48J ÷ 12.1J =) 3.96 MTTLOI in the 24 year old category.

TYPICAL MAXIMUM OUTPUT FOR B-24 SW by MEDCRAFT (24 years of age)

EO	Voltage	Current	Duration	Resistance	Charge
17 Joules	170 Volts	1.0 A	.1 Seconds	170 Ω	.1 Coulombs
33.03	170	.871	.2	175	.174
48.17	170	.944	.3	180	.283
62.5	170	.919	.4	185	.368
76.05	170	.895	.5	190	.447
88.92	170	.872	.6	195	.52
101.15	170	.85	.7	200	.595
112.78	170	.829	.8	205	.663
123.86	170	.810	.9	210	.729
134.42	**170**	**.791**	**1.0**	**215**	**.791**

The 24 year old profile above is derived from maximum B-24 settings. Note the 134.42J delivered. Maximum Output = 134.42J; Threshold Output = 19J. Maximum MTTLOI is (134.42J ÷ 19J =) 7.08

For all practical purposes, and according to a literal reading of Weiner's graph depicted at the beginning of this section, 170 to 200J maximums rarely occur on the B-24. Moreover, according to a literal interpretation of Weiner's graph, a 148J maximum output only appears in about 1% of all SW emissions while even a 134J maximum output occurs circa 2-3% of the time. In fact, according to Weiner's SW graph, zeniths of 100J may occur in only 4% of all SW emissions or stated differently, the majority of all SW emissions may never surpass 100J. In 1982, as a safeguard, Weiner appropriately suggested (to the FDA) limiting Amperage for SW devices to one Ampere (Department of Health and Human Services, 1982a, A46),

---

[244] We can see from the BP chart at the very beginning of this section that at least 16J is required to overcome 200Ω. Thus, via ER, 170Ω requires about 13.6J to overcome seizure threshold.

following which, Weiner's suggestion became part of the 1982 APA Standard for SW (Ibid). Indeed, by 1989, the IEC Standard for ECT Devices identified as "potentially hazardous," any ceiling of more than one Ampere regarding any "ECT" device (International Electrotechnical Commission, 1989, p. AA29). In fact, even at maximum settings, beginning at about 24 years of age, the B-24 SW device self-limits current to about 1.0 maximum Ampere--due to increased Impedance. Even for ten and twenty year old recipients, if limited to a 1.0 Ampere maximum current, even when using the maximum 170V and the 1.0 second maximum duration for SW, we obtain a maximum output--not of 200J or even 148J, but of <u>134J</u> occurring at a 215Ω Impedance.[245] Indeed, limited to 1.0A, 134J is the maximum output possible on the B-24 (as can be seen above; see Appendix A: Limitation of SW Amperage to 1.0A). Unfortunately, in that Weiner's 1982 APA Standard was never officially adopted, there remains no 1.0A ceiling for SW and so we must assume, that the B-24 SW can at times emit the 200J maximum it is touted to elicit. However, based on the rarity of output potentials as high as 200J, we can assume that maximum B-24 settings are not typically utilized in the younger age categories (except experimentally and so unconscionably). In any case, it is at about age 24 that even at the B-24's maximum 170 Volts and maximum 1.0 Second Duration, the machine self-limits to about 1.0 Ampere. Here, the maximum EO for the B-24 SW appears to be about the **<u>134J</u>** depicted on the Chart above, an output which may only occur about 2-3% of all SW emissions.[246]

In sum then, Final Threshold output with SW for the 24 year old recipient above is circa 19J (based on 215Ω—see BP and SW charts at the beginning of this Section [247]). Thus, at maximum SW settings, the 24 year old is administered a maximum EO of 134J and a MTTLOI of (134.42J ÷ 19J =) 7.08, greater than the 2.5 MTTLOI elicited by a second generation BP device at 14.5J, greater than the circa 5.0 MTTLOI elicited by a third generation BP device at 30J, but no longer greater than the circa 10.0 MTTLOI elicited by a Fourth generation BP device at 60J, and no longer greater than the circa 12.0 MTTLOI elicited by a theoretical Fifth generation BP device at 78J.

Thus, while SW at maximum output is yet more dangerous than BP in this age range, a pattern begins to emerge suggesting that as recipients increase in age, SW, even set for maximum output, becomes less and less powerful compared to BP and BP more and more powerful compared to SW. Moreover, this relationship of SW to BP intensifies with each new BP generation. In fact, with increasing age and each new BP generation, SW becomes less and less powerful compared to the default settings of BP until BP eventually supersedes the power of SW altogether, as we shall see.

On the other hand, only the First generation BP device at a 1.08 MTTLOI elicits less EO than true minimal stimulus SW (by half) wherein SW is capable of inducing seizure. Too, at probable minimal stimulus, fourth and fifth generation BP devices surpass the EO of SW, while at the same probable minimal stimulus, third, fourth, and fifth generation BP devices surpass SW's MTTLOI in this age category.

D) Output and MTTLOI for the Thirty Year Old at Maximum and Minimum SW Settings

Following our same paradigm, let us now proceed to the thirty year old age category at maximum SW settings. Threshold Impedance for BP in this age category is 150Ω, thus initial threshold Impedance for SW for the thirty year old is (150Ω + 50Ω =) <u>200Ω</u>. To account for rising Impedance, we add another 45Ω for the final SW Impedance to obtain (200Ω + 45Ω =) <u>245Ω</u> for the thirty year old. Consequently, we now have higher initial and final Resistances of 200Ω and 245Ω respectively (compared to the previous age category) and thus even lower Amperage. For true minimum settings, we begin with .1 Seconds and 200Ω, but soon realize 70V is too small. In fact, we begin with a maximum Voltage of 170V at .1 Seconds which gives us 14.45J—still not enough. (We need at least 16J). We then proceed to .2 Seconds, which is a probability.

---

245 Ohm's Law: Current = Voltage/Resistance. 170 Volts/215Ω = .791 Amperes. Then, EO = Voltage x Current x Duration. 170 Volts x .791 x 1 Second = <u>134 Joules</u> maximum at 215 Ohms.

246 Again, we can verify the output/impedance relationship above with our inverse proportion formula: EO = 29000/Impedance. XJ = 29000/215Ω = circa 134J; 134J = 29000/XΩ = circa 215Ω.

247 From 200 to 250Ω, threshold output increases 9 Joules (25 – 16J = 9J) in a sequential progression. 215Ω is almost one third way between 200 and 250Ω and thus we add the approximation of 3J to 16J (= 19J) to derive the threshold output for 215Ω. Other threshold outputs are close enough to Impedances within the BP chart depicting threshold outputs to simply use Equivalent Ratio.

EO (for SW) = Volts x Current x Duration.
Current = Voltage/Ω
Charge (for SW) = Current x Duration

REDUCED OUTPUT FOR B-24 SW by MEDCRAFT FOR 30 YEAR OLD RECIPIENT

EO	Voltage	Current	Duration	Resistance	Charge
14.45J	170 Volts	.85A	.1 Seconds	200 Ω	.085 Coulombs
28.2	170	.829	.2	205	.166

Referring to our BP charts, we find that 200Ω requires at least 16J to overcome seizure threshold. Because we can only get 14.45J at .1 Seconds, we must go to .2 Seconds, where at 170Ω, we find we can overcome the 205Ω Impedance at this Duration with 26.2J, so that 28.2J is more than enough to reach threshold. Since it takes about 16J to overcome 200Ω, via ER, we determine that it requires about (200Ω/16J = 205Ω/XJ =) 16.4J to overcome 205Ω. We get (170V ÷ 205Ω = .829A; 170V x .829A x .2 Seconds =) 28.2J at .2 Seconds and 170V from which we get a (28.2J ÷ 16.4J =) 1.72 MTTLOI for minimal stimulus output. But, through trial and error, we find we can use even less Voltage of circa 140V and thus less Amperage (circa .68A) to reduce output even further to 19J (see below), yet more than the 16.4J we need to overcome 205Ω (See below).

MINIMUM OUTPUT FOR B-24 SW by MEDCRAFT FOR 30 YEAR OLD RECIPIENT

EO	Voltage	Current	Duration	Resistance	Charge
9.8 Joules	140 Volts	.7 Amperes	.1 Seconds	200 Ω	.085 Coulombs
19.0	140	.68	.2	205	.166

140V ÷ 205Ω = .682A; 140V x .682A x .2 Seconds = 19.0J = Minimum EO; 19J ÷ 16.4J = 1.15 MTTLOI.[248]

Of course, there is probable reason to believe (based on the B-25 Brief Pulse device), that the B-24 SW will not allow less than 53J for the 30 year old recipient so not less than a (53J ÷ 16.5J =) 3.22 MTTLOI.

For maximum Output, we begin with a maximum 170V and maximum Duration of 1.0 Seconds.

MAXIMUM OUTPUT FOR B-24 SW by MEDCRAFT FOR 30 YEAR OLD RECIPIENT

EO	Voltage	Current	Duration	Resistance	Charge
14.45J	170 Volts	.85A	.1 Seconds	200 Ω	.085 Coulombs
28.2	170	.829	.2	205	.166
41.29	170	.810	.3	210	.243
53.77	170	.791	.4	215	.316
65.68	170	.773	.5	220	.387
77.01	170	.756	.6	225	.454
88.0	170	.739	.7	230	.517
98.38	170	.723	.8	235	.578
108.37	170	.708	.9	240	.637
118	**170**	**.694**	**1.0**	**245**	**.694**

Ohm's Law: 170V ÷ 245Ω = .694A. 170V x .694A x 1.0 Seconds = 118J; Maximum Output for the 30 year old with SW is thus circa 118J; Through ER, we find it takes about 24.7J to overcome 245Ω at the end of 1.0 Seconds (see above). Thus, MTTLOI at Maximum Output is about (118J ÷ 24.7 =) 4.78.

Even using maximum SW parameters in this age category, Amperage naturally deteriorates as Impedance once again rises (45Ω) over the one second Duration. Using the maximum 170 (constant) Volts, the higher 200Ω initial Resistance now results in an even lower initial Amperage of perhaps .85A deteriorating over one

---

[248] Interestingly, the MECTA C and only the MECTA "C" uses 9.72J for the 30 year old recipient at a consistent 1.08 MTTLOI, only about half the EO of minimal stimulus SW.

second to a final Amperage of about .694A. Overall maximum EO is again reduced compared to the 24 year old, this time to about 118J (compared to circa 134J for the 24 year old). Weiner's graph above, if read literally, suggests that a 118J emission occurs in only about four percent of all B-24 SW emissions.

We can once again verify the relationship of final Impedance and EO with our inverse proportion formula using the constant: 29000: EO = 29000/Impedance. XJ = 29000/245Ω = circa 118J; 118J = 29000/XΩ = circa 245Ω. At the final 245Ω Impedance, threshold output required for SW devices has risen to about 24.7J (based on 245Ω—see BP chart) that of about a 49 year old on a BP device. Based on the 118J cumulative emission at the end of one second, we thus obtain a MTTLOI for the 30 year old at maximum settings of about (118J ÷ 24.7J =) 4.78 fold. The MTTLOI at maximum SW parameters for 30 year olds is thus about 5.0 fold threshold, tantamount to the MTTLOI consistently delivered by **third generation BP devices**. Interestingly, the MTTLOI drops so precipitously with increasing age on SW, that the 30 year old at maximum SW settings receives half the MTTLOI of the 20 year old at the same maximum SW settings (4.78 vs 9.44). At the thirty year old age level, SW delivering 118J set at maximum settings is yet more dangerous than that of second generation BP devices, which deliver their ubiquitous 2.3-2.5 MTTLOI in this age range at about 20 Joules, and even third generation BP devices which use about 40 Joules (compared to 118J) to deliver the same circa 5.0 fold threshold MTTLOI. On the other hand, potential and legal fourth generation BP devices elicit twice the MTTLOI (circa 10 fold threshold) as that elicited by SW (circa 5 fold threshold) for the same 30 year old age group although the fourth generation BP device delivers its 10 fold threshold BP at about 80 Joules as opposed to SW's 118J, about (80J ÷ 118J =) 68% the output of SW in this, the thirty year old age category The potential Fifth generation BP device delivers a circa 12.0 MTTLOI at about 108J, slightly less than SW at maximum output settings, or about (108J ÷ 118J =) 91% of SW set for maximum output in the thirty year old age category.

Critically, only the First generation BP device at a 1.08 MTTLOI delivering 9.72J elicits less EO than true minimal stimulus SW which delivers 19J to the thirty year old recipient, about (19J ÷ 9.72 = 1.95) twice that of the MECTA "C." The second generation BP device delivers 21J, more than (21J ÷ 9.72J = 2.16) twice that of the "C" and slightly more than SW at minimal stimulus (21J vs 19J). The third generation BP device delivers 41J, more than (41J ÷ 9.72J = 4.2) four times the "C" and more than (41J ÷ 19J = 2.15) twice true minimal stimulus SW. The fourth generation BP device delivers 83J, more than (83J ÷ 9.72J =) 8.5 times the "C" and more than (41J ÷ 19J = 2.16) twice SW at true minimal stimulus. Finally, the theoretical fifth generation BP device delivers 108J in this age category, more than (108J ÷ 9.72J = 11.1) eleven times the "C" and more than (108J ÷ 19J = 5.7) five times true minimal stimulus SW. On the other hand, as mentioned above, based on the B-25 Brief Pulse device, the B-24 SW may not allow less than 53J for the 30 year old recipient so not less than a (53J ÷ 16.5J =) 3.22 MTTLOI. In this case, only the fourth and fifth generation BP devices surpass SW EO at probable minimal stimulus in the thirty year old age category while third, fourth, and fifth generation BP devices surpass SW MTTLOI at probable minimal stimulus in this age category.

In any case, as heretofore noted, while both machines are dangerous, a pattern has emerged suggesting that as recipients increase in age, SW becomes less and less dangerous compared to BP and BP more and more dangerous compared to SW, a dynamic which becomes sharper with each new BP device generation. In short, with both increasing age and later BP device generations, the disparity in raw power between SW and BP begins to diminish until the default outputs of BP surpass SW altogether. Clearly, by age 30, based on output delivered and MTTLOI, except for the MECTA "C," all subsequent generational BP devices have lost their reduced EO advantage over SW, generally.

E) Output and MTTLOI for the Forty Year Old at Maximum and Minimum SW Settings

Following our same paradigm, let us now proceed to the forty year old age category at maximum SW settings. For maximum settings at this age, we again use a maximum Voltage of 170 and maximum Duration of 1.0 Seconds. Threshold Impedance for BP in this age category is 200Ω, thus (according to our paradigm) initial threshold Impedance for SW for the forty year old category is (200Ω + 50Ω =) 250Ω, followed by a final Threshold Impedance of (250Ω + 45Ω =) 295Ω. Once again, we have higher initial and final Resistances (than the previous age group) now of 250Ω and 295Ω respectively (and thus even lower Amperage) compared to 200Ω and 245Ω respectively in the previous age category. For minimum settings, we begin with .1 Seconds and 250Ω.

EO (for SW) = Volts x Current x Duration.
Ohm's Law: Current = Voltage/Ω; Ω = Voltage/Current; Voltage = Current x Ω
Charge (for SW) = Current x Duration

MINIMUM OUTPUT FOR B-24 SW by MEDCRAFT FOR 40 YEAR OLD RECIPIENT

EO	Voltage	Current	Duration	Resistance	Charge
11.56J	170 Volts	.68A	.1 Seconds	250 Ω	.068 Coulombs
22.67	170	.667	.2	255	.133
33.35	170	.654	.3	260	.196

It takes about 25J to overcome 250Ω so that the SW machine must emit at least .3 Seconds as a result of which It must now overcome a 260Ω Impedance (see above) at minimal stimulus which requires about (250Ω/25J = 260Ω/X =) 26J. (See SW and charts at beginning of this section.) Through trial and error, we find we can use 150V to obtain a (Current = 150V ÷ 260Ω =) .576A Current to obtain a (150V x .576A x .3Sec. =) 26J EO, barely enough to overcome 260Ω or a [26J (EO delivered) ÷ 26J (EO threshold)] = 1.0 MTTLOI. To be certain of seizure, we discard this output and admit the necessity of 170V and .654A to reach (170V ÷ 260Ω = .654A; 170V x .654A x .3 Seconds =) 33.35J for minimal stimulus and thus a (Output delivered ÷ Threshold Output = MTTLOI; 33.35J ÷ 26J =) 1.28 MTTLOI for the 40 year old recipient at true minimal stimulus. Of course, based on the B-25, there is probable evidence that the B-24 may not allow less than 63J for the forty year old category, and so a (63J ÷ 26J =) 2.43 MTTLOI.

MAXIMUM OUTPUT FOR B-24 SW by MEDCRAFT FOR 40 YEAR OLD RECIPIENT [249]

EO	Voltage	Current	Duration	Resistance	Charge
11.56J	170 Volts	.68A	.1 Seconds	250 Ω	.068 Coulombs
22.67	170	.667	.2	255	.133
33.35	170	.654	.3	260	.196
43.62	170	.642	.4	265	.257
53.52	170	.63	.5	270	.315
63.05	170	.618	.6	275	.371
72.25	170	.607	.7	280	.425
81.12	170	.596	.8	285	.477
89.69	170	.586	.9	290	.527
97.97	**170**	**.576**	**1.0**	**295**	**.576**

Using the BP chart and ER, we find that it takes about 35.7J to overcome 295Ω of Resistance. Current = 170V ÷ 295Ω = .576A. EO = 170V x .576A x 1.0Sec. = 97.97J. 97.97J (EO delivered) ÷ 35.7J (EO threshold) = 2.74 MTTLOI for the 40 year old recipient at maximum settings.

Still using maximum SW parameters, Amperage naturally deteriorates once again as Impedance once again rises (45Ω) over the one second Duration. Using the maximum 170 (constant) Volts, the higher 250Ω initial Resistance now results in an even lower initial Amperage of .68A deteriorating over one second to .576A. Overall maximum EO is thus reduced to about 100J. (Note how maximum output decreases with advancing age on SW.) Once again referring to a literal reading of Weiner's SW graphs above, a 100J output with SW occurs only about ***7% of the time***. Accordingly, 93% of all SW emissions may be 100J or less.

---

[249] To review, we set up the above chart by using initial Impedance (which we have derived from BP and SW charts at the beginning of this section). Next we have determined Amperage for initial Impedance by Ohm's Law: Current = Voltage/Ω, initial EO by Volts x Current x Duration and initial Charge by Current x Duration. We can determine final Impedance in the same way (derived from BP and SW charts at the beginning of this section), final EO by Volts x Current x Duration and final Charge by Current x Duration. We then fill in the remaining figures gradationally. For example, 295Ω - 250Ω = 45Ω ÷ 9 (steps) = 5Ω per step. 250Ω + 5Ω = 255Ω. 255Ω + 5Ω = 260Ω, etc. Once we have determined cumulative output, we can divide Cumulative Output (97.97J) by Threshold output (35.7J--see SW Chart at beginning of Section) to determine the MTTLOI at maximum settings for, for example the 40 year old recipient. 97.97J + 35.7J = 2.74 MTTLOI.

Once more, we can verify the relationship of final Impedance and EO required with our inverse proportion formula using the constant: 29000: (EO = 29000/Impedance. XJ = 29000/295Ω = circa 97.97J; 97.97J = 29000/XΩ = circa 295Ω.) At the final 295Ω Impedance, threshold output required for SW devices has risen to about 35.7J (based on 295Ω—see BP chart), that required of about a 59 year old recipient on a BP device. Based on the 97.97J cumulative emission at the end of one second of SW, we obtain a (98 ÷ 35.7J =) 2.75. MTTLOI for the 40 year old at maximum SW settings.

The MTTLOI for the 40 year old at maximum SW parameters is thus about 2.75 (fold threshold), slightly surpassing the 2.3-2.5 MTTLOI consistently delivered by **second generation BP devices** for all age categories. Interestingly, titration levels drop so precipitously with increasing age on SW, that the 40 year old at maximum SW settings now receives a little more than half the 4.78 MTTLOI of the 30 year old at maximum SW settings. At the 40 year old age level, SW set at maximum settings delivering almost 100J is yet more dangerous than that of second generation BP devices which deliver about 40 Joules in this age category, and even third generation BP devices which emit about 80 Joules (compared to SW's 100J). On the other hand, due to inversion, that is, the exploitation of BP's greater efficiency and power, potential and legal fourth generation BP devices at circa 10 MTTLOI approach almost (10 ÷ 2.75 = 3.6) four times the MTTLOI as the 2.75 MTTLOI elicited by SW for the same 40 year old age group. The fourth generation BP device, moreover, at about 150 Joules, delivers (150J - 100J = 50J ÷ 100J =) 50% more EO than SW 's 100J delivery in this age category. This decidedly makes the fourth generation BP device more dangerous than SW in terms of both the MTTLOI (circa 10.0 fold vs. 2.75 fold) and raw EO emitted (150J vs. 100J) even at maximum SW settings. Finally, the Fifth generation BP device delivers a circa 12.0 MTTLOI at about 192J, almost twice the EO of SW set at maximum SW parameters in the 40 year old category, in short, almost (192J – 100J = 92 ÷ 100J = .92) 100% more power than SW even at maximum SW settings.

On the other hand, only the First generation MECTA "C" BP device at a 1.08 MTTLOI delivering 17.28J elicits less EO than SW set for true minimal stimulus (SW) which delivers 33.35J to the forty year old recipient or about (33.35J ÷ 17.28J = 1.92) twice the EO of the MECTA "C." The second generation BP device delivers a default 40J surpassing SW at true minimal stimulus as does the third generation BP device at a default 80J, the fourth generation BP device at a default 150J and the fifth generation BP device at a default 192J, all much higher than true minimal stimulus SW in the forty year old category. However, there is ample reason to believe that the B-24 does not allow less than 63J or a 2.43 MTTLOI in this age category. In this case, both the first and second generation BP devices deliver less EO than (probable) minimal stimulus SW while third, fourth, and fifth generation BP devices yet surpass SW. Moreover, the second generation BP device, more or less equals the MTTLOI of probable minimal stimulus SW; whereas, the MTTLOI of third, fourth, and fifth generation BP devices all surpass the MTTLOI of probable minimal stimulus SW in this age category. In any case, in this age category, with the exception of the MECTA "C," all subsequent BP devices have lost their BP advantage over SW generally, with respect to reduced EO and MTTLOI.

Indeed, as previously noted, a pattern has materialized revealing that as recipients increase in age, SW at both minimum and maximum power, becomes less and less dangerous compared to BP and BP more and more dangerous compared to SW, a relationship which enhances with each new BP generation. Indeed, with increasing age, the disparity in power between the default outputs of later generation BP devices and maximum SW output diminishes, until eventually, BP completely surpasses even maximum SW output with respect to EO delivered, as we shall see.

F) Output and MTTLOI for the Fifty Year Old at Maximum and Minimum SW Settings

Following our paradigm, let us now proceed to the fifty year old age category at maximum SW settings. Threshold Impedance for BP in this (fifty year old) age category is 250Ω, thus initial threshold Impedance for SW for this same fifty year old is 300Ω (250Ω + 50Ω = 300Ω) while final Impedance is (300Ω + 45Ω =) 345Ω. Consequently, we have even higher initial and final Resistances of 300Ω and 345Ω respectively (than the previous age category of 250 and 295Ω) reducing maximum Amperage even further on SW. SW Voltage (170) and SW Duration (1.0 Sec.) remain at maximum. For minimum settings, through trial and error, we begin with .5 Seconds and 320Ω.

EO (for SW) = Volts x Current x Duration.

Charge (for SW) = Current x Duration
Ohm's Law: Current = Voltage/Ω; Ω = Voltage/Current; Voltage = Current x Ω

MINIMUM OUTPUT FOR B-24 SW by MEDCRAFT FOR 50 YEAR OLD RECIPIENT

EO	Voltage	Current	Duration	Resistance	Charge
9.63 Joules	170 Volts	.567A	.1 Seconds	300 Ω	.057 Coulombs
18.95	170	.557	.2	305	.113
27.97	170	.548	.3	310	.164
36.70	170	.54	.4	315	.219
45.16	170	.531	.5	320	.266

It takes about 36J to overcome 300Ω so that we cannot begin to overcome seizure until at least .4 Seconds. In fact, we should begin at about .5 Second to insure adequate seizure. Through trial and error, we find we must use the maximum Voltage (170V) limited to .5 Seconds to obtain a .531A Current to obtain a 45J EO, enough to overcome 320Ω, the Threshold Output of which is about 41.5J. (See Threshold Outputs on the charts for Minimal stimulus SW at the beginning of this section.) Current = 170V ÷ 320Ω = .531A. 170V x .531A x .5Sec. = 45J delivered. 45J (EO delivered) ÷ 41.5J (EO threshold) = 1.08 MTTLOI for SW true minimal stimulus settings in this age category. On the other hand, based on the B-25 BP device, there is reason to suspect the B-24 does not allow less than 81J, or a (81J ÷ 41.5J) = 1.95 MTTLOI, about the same as SW at maximum output in this age category. Practically speaking, probable minimal stimulus (81J) and maximal stimulus (83.7J) have merged.

MAXIMUM OUTPUT FOR B-24 SW by MEDCRAFT FOR 50 YEAR OLD RECIPIENT

EO	Voltage	Current	Duration	Resistance	Charge
9.63 Joules	170 Volts	.567A	.1 Seconds	300 Ω	.057 Coulombs
18.95	170	.557	.2	305	.113
27.97	170	.548	.3	310	.164
36.70	170	.54	.4	315	.219
45.16	170	.531	.5	320	.266
53.35	170	.523	.6	325	.314
61.30	170	.515	.7	330	.361
69.02	170	.508	.8	335	.406
76.50	170	.500	.9	340	.450
83.77	**170**	**.493**	**1.0**	**345**	**.493**

Using the BP chart and ER, we find that it takes about 48.7J to overcome 345Ω of Resistance (See SW chart for Maximum Threshold Outputs at the beginning of this section.). Current = 170V ÷ 345Ω = .493A. 170V x .493A x 1.0Sec. = 83.77J. 83.77J (EO delivered) ÷ 48.7J (EO threshold) = 1.72 MTTLOI for maximum settings in the 60 year old age category.

Still using maximum SW parameters, Amperage naturally deteriorates as Impedance once again rises (45Ω) over the one second Duration. Using the maximum 170 (constant) Volts, the higher 300Ω initial Resistance now results in an even lower initial Amperage of .567A deteriorating over one second to an even lower final Amperage of .493A. Overall, maximum EO is thus reduced to about 84J (similar to probable minimal stimulus) while true minimum EO rises to about 45.16J. According to a literal reading of Weiner's SW graph at the beginning of this section, an 84J output occurs about ***9% of the time***. Stated differently, according to a literal reading of Weiner's graph, 91% of all SW emissions are 84J or less.

We can once again verify the relationship of final Impedance and EO with our inverse proportion formula using the constant: (29000: EO = 29000/Impedance. XJ = 29000/345Ω = circa 83.77J; 83.77J = 29000/XΩ = circa 345Ω.) At the final 345Ω Impedance for maximum output, threshold output required for SW devices has risen to about 48.7J (based on 345Ω—see BP chart at beginning of this Section--that required of about a 69 year old recipient on a BP device). Based on the maximum 83.77J cumulative output emission at the end of one second of SW, as seen above, we now obtain a MTTLOI for the 50 year old at maximum SW settings of about (83.77 ÷ 48.7J =) 1.72. The MTTLOI at maximum SW parameters for 50 year olds is thus about 1.72 (fold threshold), slightly surpassing the MTTLOI consistently delivered at default by **first generation BP**

devices (of 1.08). Titration levels (or MTTLOI) on the SW device even at maximum settings have now dropped so precipitously with increasing age (and Impedance), that the MTTLOI for the 50 year old at maximum SW output is but (1.72 ÷ 2.75 =) 62.5% the MTTLOI delivered to the 40 year old. For the 50 year old age level, therefore, maximum SW settings are as expected, more dangerous than the first generation MECTA "C" BP device which delivers its ubiquitous circa 1.08 MTTLOI in this age range at about 27 Joules compared to SW's 1.72 MTTLOI at 83.77J (27J ÷ 83.77J =.322), 32% the power of SW. But compared to **second generation BP devices** which use about 60 Joules to deliver a 2.3-2.5 MTTLOI, BP now shows only a slight advantage over SW even at maximum SW output in this age category delivering (60J ÷ 83.77J =) 71.6% the output delivered by SW. Compared to **third generation BP devices** which use about 115 Joules (in lieu of SW's 83.77J) to deliver a circa 5.0 MTTLOI (in lieu of SW's 1.72 MTTLOI), due to inversion exploitation (see below) is now about (115J - 83.77J = 31.23J ÷ 83.77J =) 37.2% more dangerous than SW even at maximum SW settings in this age category. Potential and already legal **fourth generation BP devices** which elicit a circa 10 MTTLOI, or about (10 ÷ 1.72 = 5.81) 5.5 times the MTTLOI of that elicited by SW delivering about 230 Joules in lieu of SW's circa 83.77J, circa (230J - 83.77J = 146.23 ÷ 83.77 =) 174% more power than SW even set at maximum output in this age category. Finally, **Fifth Generation BP devices** BP are decidedly more dangerous than SW even set at maximum SW output in this age category, both in the MTTLOI delivered (circa 12 fold ÷ 1.72 fold = 6.98) about 7 times that of SW and in the raw 300J EO delivered (300J - 83.77J = 216.23 ÷ 83.77) 258% more dangerous than SW.

Regarding minimal stimulus SW settings, once again, only the First generation MECTA "C" BP device at a 1.08 MTTLOI delivering 27J elicits less EO than SW set for true minimal stimulus which may deliver 45.16J to the fifty year old recipient at about twice the EO of the MECTA "C." The second generation BP device surpasses SW at true minimal stimulus delivering a default 58J compared to SW's 45.16J, the third generation BP device a default 115J compared to SW's 45.16J, the fourth generation BP device a default 230J compared to SW's 45.16J, and the fifth generation BP device a default 300J compared to SW's 45.16J, all in the 50 year old age category. On the other hand, there is reason to believe the B-24 does not allow less than 81J delivered to the 50 year old recipient, in which case, probable minimal stimulus with SW more or less merges with maximum SW stimulus. Indeed, as previously noted, a pattern has emerged revealing that as recipients increase in age, SW at both minimum, probable minimum, and maximum output becomes less and less dangerous compared to BP and BP more and more dangerous compared to SW with respect to each subsequent BP generation. In short, with increasing age, the disparity in power between the default outputs of later generation BP devices and the power delivered at even maximum SW output diminishes, until BP completely overtakes SW with respect to greater output delivered. Only the MECTA "C" retains its reduced EO advantage over SW's true minimal stimulus and probable minimal stimulus output in this age category.

G) Output and MTTLOI for the Sixty Year Old at Maximum and Minimum SW Settings

Following the Cameron paradigm, let us now proceed to the sixty year old age category at maximum SW settings. Threshold Impedance for BP in this age category is 300Ω, thus initial threshold Impedance for SW for the same sixty year old category is (300Ω + 50Ω =) <u>350Ω</u>. Final SW Impedance is (350Ω + 45Ω =) <u>395Ω</u>. Consequently, we have the progressively higher initial and final Resistances of 350Ω and 395Ω respectively compared to 300Ω and 345Ω (of the previous age category) reducing maximum Amperage even further on SW. Voltage (170) and Duration (1.0 Sec.) remain at maximum for maximum SW settings. For true minimum settings, through trial and error, we arrive at .9 Seconds and 390Ω.

EO (for SW) = Volts x Current x Duration.
Charge (for SW) = Current x Duration
Ohm's Law: Current = Voltage/Ω; Ω = Voltage/Current; Voltage = Current x Ω

MINIMUM OUTPUT FOR B-24 SW by MEDCRAFT FOR 60 YEAR OLD RECIPIENT

EO	Voltage	Current	Duration	Resistance	Charge
8.26 Joules	170 Volts	.486 A	.1 Seconds	350 Ω	.049 Coulombs
16.28	170	.479	.2	355	.096
24.08	170	.472	.3	360	.142
31.67	170	.466	.4	365	.186
35.05	170	.459	.5	370	.230
46.24	170	.453	.6	375	.272
53.24	170	.447	.7	380	.313
60.05	170	.442	.8	385	.354
66.70	170	.436	.9	390	.392

It takes about 49J to overcome 350Ω so that we cannot begin to overcome seizure until at least .9 Seconds at which point we must overcome 390Ω which requires about 62.4J (See SW Charts for Minimum Settings at the beginning of this section). Thus, the 66.7J at .9 Seconds looks just about right. We find we can use 170V to obtain a (170V ÷ 390Ω =) .436A current to obtain the (EO = 170V x .436A x .9Sec. =) 66.7J EO, enough to overcome the 390Ω of Resistance at this Duration. 66.7J (EO delivered) ÷ 62.4J (EO threshold) = 1.07 MTTLOI for true minimal stimulus in the 60 year old age category. On the other hand, based on the B-25, there is reason to suspect the B-24 does not allow less than 73J in this age category which merges with maximum SW output below.

MAXIMUM OUTPUT FOR B-24 SW by MEDCRAFT FOR 60 YEAR OLD RECIPIENT

EO	Voltage	Current	Duration	Resistance	Charge
8.26 Joules	170 Volts	.486A	.1 Seconds	350 Ω	.049 Coulombs
16.28	170	.479	.2	355	.096
24.08	170	.472	.3	360	.142
31.67	170	.466	.4	365	.186
35.05	170	.459	.5	370	.230
46.24	170	.453	.6	375	.272
53.24	170	.447	.7	380	.313
60.05	170	.442	.8	385	.354
66.70	170	.436	.9	390	.392
73.16	**170**	**.430**	**1.0**	**395**	**.430**

Using the BP chart and ER recorded in the SW Maximum Settings Chart at the beginning of this section, we find that it takes about 63.7J to overcome 395Ω of Resistance (See SW chart for Maximum Threshold Outputs at the beginning of this section) while the machine at maximum settings delivers about (Current = 170V ÷ 395Ω = .430A. EO = 170V x .430A x 1.0Sec. =) 73.16J. MTTLOI = 73.16J (EO delivered) ÷ 63.7J (EO threshold) = 1.15 MTTLOI at maximum output.

At maximum SW parameters, Amperage naturally deteriorates as Impedance once again rises (45Ω) over the one second Duration. Using the maximum 170 (constant) Volts, the higher 350Ω initial Resistance now results in an even lower initial Amperage of .486A deteriorating over one second to an even lower .430A. Overall, maximum EO is thus reduced to about 73.16J. According to a literal reading of Weiner's SW graph at the beginning of this section, a 73J output occurs about ***12% of the time*** using SW. Thus, 88% of all SW emissions appear to be 73J or less.

We can once again verify the relationship of final Impedance and EO with our inverse proportion formula using the constant: 29000: (EO = 29000/Impedance. XJ = 29000/395Ω = circa 73.16J; 73.16J = 29000/XΩ = circa 395Ω.) At the final 395Ω Impedance, Threshold Output required for SW devices in this age category has risen to about 63.7J (based on 395Ω—see BP chart), that required of about a 79 year old recipient on a BP device. Based on the 73.16J Cumulative Output at the end of one second of SW, we obtain a maximum MTTLOI for the 60 year old at SW maximum settings of about (73.16 ÷ 63.7J =) 1.15. The MTTLOI at maximum SW parameters for 60 year old recipients is now only slightly above the MTTLOI consistently delivered by the **first generation MECTA "C BP device** of a 1.08 MTTLOI. Titration levels on the SW device, even at maximum settings, have now dropped so precipitously with increasing age (and Impedance), that at maximum SW settings for the sixty year old, MTTLOI has dropped another 33% compared to the MTTLOI of the 50 year old (1.72 fold) at maximum SW settings (1.15 ÷ 1.72 = 67%; 100% - 67% = 33%). The 1.15 MTTLOI for the 60 year old at maximum SW settings is now tantamount to the **first generation MECTA "C" BP device** which delivers a similar but ubiquitous circa 1.08 MTTLOI, but at about 45 Joules compared to SW's 73J in the same age category or 1.62 times the power of the "C" (73J ÷ 45J = 1.62). Compared to **second generation BP devices** which use about 83 Joules to deliver a 2.3-2.5 MTTLOI, the SW device even at maximum power has now become less powerful and so less dangerous in this age category than BP. **Third generation BP devices** which use about 166 Joules (in lieu of SW's 73.16J) in this age category to deliver a circa 5.0 MTTLOI (in lieu of SW's 1.15 fold threshold), due to inversion (see below), are now much more dangerous than SW in this age category, delivering more than four times the MTTLOI (5.0 ÷ 1.15 = 4.34) and about 2.27 fold the raw EO of SW (166J ÷ 73.16J = 2.27) even at maximum SW settings. The circa 10 MTTLOI delivered by the potential but "legal" **fourth generation BP devices** deliver more than 8.0 times the MTTLOI of that elicited by SW even at maximum settings for this same 60 year old age group (10.0 ÷ 1.15 = 8.69) and at circa 330 Joules or about 4.5 times the power of SW (330J ÷ 73.16J = 4.5) even at maximum SW settings. Finally, the default output delivered by theoretical, but "legal" **Fifth Generation BP devices** delivering seven times the MTTLOI (circa 12 ÷ 1.72 fold = 7) and more than five times the raw power of SW (432J ÷ 83.77J = 5.16) are many more times as dangerous as SW even at maximum SW settings in this age category. Indeed the theoretical Fifth Generation BP device is about (432J - 83.77J = 348.2J ÷ 83.77J =) 417% more powerful than SW even at maximum power in the sixty year old age category.

Regarding true minimal stimulus SW settings, once again, only the **First generation BP device** at a 1.08 MTTLOI delivering 39J elicits less EO than SW which delivers 66.7J to the sixty year old recipient, approaching twice the EO of the MECTA "C" (66.7J ÷ 39J = 1.71). However, **the second generation BP device** surpasses SW set for true minimal stimulus in this age category, delivering a default 82J compared to SW's 66.7J, the **third generation BP device** delivers a default 167J compared to SW's 66.7J at true minimal stimulus, 2.5 time the power of true minimal stimulus SW (167J ÷ 66.7J = 2.5), the **fourth generation BP device** a default 332J compared to SW's 66.7J, five times the power of SW at true minimal stimulus (332J ÷ 66.7 = 4.98) , and the **fifth generation BP device** a default 432J compared to SW's 66.7J, six and a half time the power of SW (432J ÷ 66.7 = 6.48) set at minimal stimulus output in the 60 year old age category. Of course, there is strong evidence that the B-24 does not allow less than 73J in this age category so that probable minimum and maximum SW output completely merge by this age category. Even at probable minimal stimulus, however, as with maximum SW settings in the sixty year old age category, second, third, fourth, and fifth generation BP devices surpass the output delivered by SW.

Indeed, as previously noted, a pattern has emerged revealing that as recipients increase in age, SW becomes less and less dangerous compared to BP and BP more and more dangerous compared to SW and with respect to each subsequent BP generation. In short, with increasing age, the disparity in power between the default outputs of later generation BP devices and the power delivered at minimum, probable minimum, and maximum SW settings diminish, until BP completely overtakes SW with respect to the greater EO delivered. Note too, how maximum and even true minimum output on the SW device has begun to merge. Finally, and of chief import, as we have seen, only the first generation MECTA "C" continues to remain an improvement over SW set at true minimal stimulus in every seizure inducible age category.

H) Output and MTTLOI for the Sixty-five Year Old at Maximum and Minimum SW Settings

Again, following our paradigm, let us now proceed to the sixty-five year old age category at minimum and maximum SW settings. Threshold Impedance for BP in this age category is 325Ω, thus initial threshold Impedance for SW for the same sixty-five year old is (325Ω + 50Ω =) <u>375Ω</u>. Final Impedance in this age category is (375Ω + 45Ω =) <u>420Ω</u>. Consequently, we again have the progressively higher initial and final Resistances of 375Ω and 420Ω respectively (compared to 350 and 395Ω) reducing maximum Amperage even further compared to the previous age category. Voltage (170) and Duration (1.0 Sec.) remain for maximum settings, while we start at .9 Seconds and 415Ω for minimal stimulus with SW, only to find that the maximum 1.0 Seconds and 420Ω works even better. In essence, both minimum and maximum SW settings merge at about age 65.

EO (for SW) = Volts x Current x Duration.
Charge (for SW) = Current x Duration
Ohm's Law: Current = Voltage/Ω; Ω = Voltage/Current; Voltage = Current x Ω

It takes about 56.5J to overcome 375Ω so that we cannot begin to overcome seizure until at least 1.0 Second where we must actually overcome a 420Ω Impedance which requires about 72J (See BP and SW charts at the beginning of this section). We can use the maximum 170V to obtain a (Current = 170V ÷ 420Ω =) .405A Current to obtain a (170V x .405A x 1.0Sec. =) 68.81J EO, not quite enough to overcome 420Ω (which requires 72J). [68.85J (EO delivered) ÷ 72J (EO threshold)] = .956 MTTLOI. (See below.) No probable minimum output is needed here in that maximum and minimum have merged.

MINIMUM & MAXIMUM OUTPUT FOR MEDCRAFT B-24 SW FOR 65 YEAR OLD RECIPIENT

EO	Voltage	Current	Duration	Resistance	Charge
7.71 Joules	170 Volts	.453A	.1 Seconds	375 Ω	.045 Coulombs
15.21	170	.477	.2	380	.095
22.52	170	.442	.3	385	.133
29.64	170	.436	.4	390	.174
36.58	170	.430	.5	395	.215
43.35	170	.425	.6	400	.255
50.00	170	.420	.7	405	.294
56.39	170	.415	.8	410	.332
62.68	170	.410	.9	415	.369
68.81	**170**	**.405**	**1.0**	**420**	**.405**

Using maximum SW parameters above, Amperage naturally deteriorates as Impedance once again rises (45Ω) over the one second Duration. Using the maximum 170 (constant) Volts, the higher 375Ω Initial Resistance now results in an even lower initial Amperage of .453A deteriorating to an even lower final Impedance over one second of .405A. Overall maximum EO is thus reduced to about 68.81J. According to a literal reading of Weiner's SW graph at the beginning of this section, a circa 70J output occurs about ***15%*** of the time with SW. Thus, 85% of all SW emissions appear to be 70J or less. We need no minimal output table here as maximum and minimum outputs have merged.

We can once again verify the relationship of final Impedance and EO with our inverse proportion formula using the constant: 29000: (EO = 29000/Impedance. XJ = 29000/420Ω = circa 68.85J; 68.85J = 29000/XΩ = circa 420Ω.) At the final 420Ω Impedance, Threshold Output required for SW devices in this age category has risen to about 72J (based on 420Ω—see BP and SW charts), that required of about an 84 year old recipient on a BP device. Based on the 68.85J Cumulative Output at the end of one second of SW, we obtain a MTTLOI for the 65 year old at maximum SW settings of about (68.85 ÷ 72J =) .956, not quite threshold. The MTTLOI at maximum/minimum SW parameters for 65 year olds is thus just about or just under threshold even at maximum settings, now less than the 1.08 MTTLOI consistently delivered by **first generation BP devices** in this same age category. Titration levels (MTTLOI) on the SW device even at maximum settings have now dropped another (.956 ÷ 1.15 = 83%. 100% - 83% =) 17% compared to the MTTLOI of the previous age category, the 60 year old (1.15 fold) at maximum SW settings. For the 65 year old age group then, and for the first time, the .956 MTTLOI at maximum SW settings is now less than the first generation MECTA "C" BP device which delivers its ubiquitous circa 1.08 MTTLOI in the 65 year old age range at about 50 Joules compared to SW which nevertheless delivers its .956 MTTLOI at about 69J. Thus, even though SW may not have enough power to reach threshold for all recipients in this age category, the first generation BP device yet delivers less EO than SW. Second generation BP devices which use about 100 default Joules to deliver a 2.3-2.5 MTTLOI to 65 year olds, are decidedly more powerful and thus more dangerous than SW at both maximum and minimum SW settings, which now delivers a common 69J output. Due to inversion (see below), Third generation BP devices which use about 195 Joules (in lieu of SW's 69J) to deliver a circa 5.0 MTTLOI (in lieu of SW's .956 MTTLOI), are now many times more powerful and many times more dangerous than SW in this age category set for either maximum or minimum SW output. Potential and already legal Fourth generation BP devices which theoretically elicit a circa 10 MTTLOI or more than 10.0 times the MTTLOI elicited by SW even at maximum settings for this same 65 year old age group, elicit about 390 Joules in lieu of SW's circa 69J maximum (and minimum), now exponentially more powerful and more dangerous than SW both in their MTTLOI delivered (circa 10 fold vs. .956 fold) and the raw EO delivered about (390J ÷ 69J =) 5.65 times that delivered by SW. Finally the **fifth generation BP device** delivers a default 507J compared to SW's 69J at both maximum and minimum stimulus settings in the 65 year old age category, about (507J ÷ 69J =) 7.3 times the raw power of SW.

Indeed, as previously noted, SW has become less and less dangerous the older the recipient compared to BP which has become more and more dangerous. In fact, SW in this age category is actually ineffective compared to BP and BP more and more dangerous with respect to the default outputs delivered by each subsequent BP generation compared to SW. In short, as age increases, BP devices increase in power compared to SW and with each subsequent BP generation, until BP completely overtakes SW with respect to the EO delivered. Indeed, SW verges on inefficacy by the 65 year old age category where maximum and minimum settings have merged. Of paramount importance, in terms of reduced EO, only the first generation MECTA "C" continues to remain an improvement over SW in this age category.

l) Output and MTTLOI for the Seventy Year Old at Maximum and Minimum SW Settings

Following our paradigm, let us now proceed to the seventy year old age category at maximum SW settings. Threshold Impedance for BP in this age category is 350Ω, thus Initial Threshold Impedance for SW for the same seventy year old recipient is (350Ω + 50Ω =) 400Ω while Final Impedance is (400Ω + 45Ω =) 445Ω. Consequently, we again have the progressively higher initial and final Resistances of 400Ω and 445Ω respectively (compared to 375 and 420Ω in the previous age category), reducing maximum SW Amperage even further. Voltage (170) and Duration (1.0 Sec.) remain maximum settings, while we utilize the same Voltage (170) and Duration (1.0 Sec.) for minimum settings and thus the same final 445Ω for both maximal and minimal SW settings. In that both minimum and maximum SW settings have merged by age 70, probable minimum is the same as true minimum.

EO (for SW) = Volts x Current x Duration.
Charge (for SW) = Current x Duration
Ohm's Law: Current = Voltage/Ω; Ω = Voltage/Current; Voltage = Current x Ω

It takes about 64J to overcome 400Ω so that we cannot overcome seizure threshold even at the end of 1.0 Second in that at this Duration, SW requires us to overcome a 445Ω Impedance which requires about 80J. Here again, minimum and maximum EO meet as the machine does not appear powerful enough even at maximum settings to overcome any of the chart's Impedances. In short, the B-24 does not appear powerful enough to overcome threshold for most 70 year old recipients using BL "ECT." Even though we use the maximum 170V and maximum 1.0 Seconds, we can only attain a (Current = 170V ÷ 445Ω =) .382A Current and a (170V x .382A x 1.0Sec. =) 65J EO maximum and thus only a (65J ÷ 80J =) .81 MTTLOI or 81% of the EO necessary to reach threshold using BL-"ECT."

MINIMUM & MAXIMUM OUTPUT FOR MEDCRAFT B-24 SW FOR 70 YEAR OLD RECIPIENT

EO	Voltage	Current	Duration	Resistance	Charge
7.23 Joules	170 Volts	.425A	.1 Seconds	400 Ω	.043 Coulombs
14.27	170	.420	.2	405	.095
21.15	170	.415	.3	410	.125
27.86	170	.410	.4	415	.164
34.40	170	.405	.5	420	.203
40.80	170	.400	.6	425	.240
47.01	170	.395	.7	430	.277
53.15	170	.391	.8	435	.313
59.11	170	.386	.9	440	.347
64.94	**170**	**.382**	**1.0**	**445**	**.382**

Still using maximum SW parameters, Amperage naturally deteriorates as Impedance once again rises (45Ω) over the one second Duration. Using the maximum 170 (constant) Volts, the higher 400Ω Initial Resistance now results in an even lower initial Amperage of .425A, deteriorating over one second to .382A. Overall maximum EO is thus reduced to about 64.94J. According to a literal reading of Weiner's SW graph at the beginning of this section, a circa 65J output occurs about ***18%*** of the time on SW. Conversely, 82% of all SW emissions appear to be 65J or less.

We can once again verify the relationship of final Impedance and EO with our inverse proportion formula using the constant: 29000: (EO = 29000/Impedance. XJ = 29000/445Ω = circa 64.94J; 64.94J = 29000/XΩ = circa 445Ω.) At the final 445Ω Impedance, Threshold Output required for SW devices has risen to about 80.7J (based on 445Ω—see BP chart), that required of about an 89 year old recipient on a BP device. Based on the 64.94J Cumulative Output at the end of one second of SW in this age category, we obtain a MTTLOI for the 70 year old at maximum SW settings of about (64.94 ÷ 80.7J =) .804, well below threshold and thus probably not enough to induce seizure for most 70 year old recipients with BL "ECT." The MTTLOI at maximum SW parameters for the 70 year old recipient, in short, is well under threshold, even less even than the MTTLOI (1.08) consistently delivered by the **first generation MECTA "C" BP device**. The MTTLOI for the 70 year old (.804) on the SW device even at maximum settings has now dropped another 16% compared to the MTTLOI of the 65 year old (.956 fold) at maximum SW settings (.804 ÷ .956 = 84%. 100% - 84% = 16%).

For the 70 year old age level then, maximum SW settings now emit a weaker MTTLOI than the **first generation MECTA "C" BP device** which delivers its ubiquitous circa 1.08 fold threshold output in this age range at about 53 Joules, still less than maximum or minimum SW settings in this age category which delivers about 65J. **Second generation BP devices** which use about 113 Joules to deliver a 2.3-2.5 MTTLOI for 70 year old recipients, are thus decidedly more powerful and more dangerous than SW (at 65J) in this age category even at maximum SW settings. **Third generation BP devices** which use a circa 5.0 MTTLOI (as opposed to a .8 MTTLOI) at about 225 Joules (in lieu of SW's 65J), due to inversion exploitation (see below), are now (225J ÷. 65J =) 3.46 times more powerful and thus 3.46 times more dangerous than SW in this age category even at maximum SW settings. Potential and already legal **fourth generation BP devices** which theoretically elicit a circa 10 MTTLOI, more than (10 ÷ .8 =) 12.5 times the MTTLOI elicited by SW even at maximum settings for the 70 year old age category, and which emit a default 450J in lieu of SW's circa 65J maximum at this age level, are now about (450J ÷ 65J =) 6.9 times more powerful than SW, making fourth generation BP devices exponentially more powerful and exponentially more dangerous than SW in this age category even at maximum SW settings. Finally the theoretical **fifth generation BP device** at a circa 12.0 MTTLOI compared to SW's .8 MTTLOI, delivers a default 588J compared to SW's 65J at both maximum and minimum stimulus settings in the 70 year old age category, or about (588J ÷ 65J =) 9.05 times the raw power of SW even at maximum SW settings.

Here again, as previously noted, SW has become less and less dangerous, indeed, ineffective compared to BP and BP more and more dangerous compared to SW with respect increasing age and each subsequent BP generation. In short, with increasing age, the default outputs of the later generation BP devices continue to increase in power compared to maximum SW outputs which continue to decrease in power, until BP completely overtakes SW with respect to the greater EO delivered. Also of chief importance is that in spite of SW's inefficacy at this point, only the first generation MECTA "C" delivering 53J in this age category, continues to deliver less EO than SW, that is, only the MECTA "C" continues to remain an improvement over SW (at 65J) in terms of reduced EO.

J) Output and MTTLOI for the Eighty Year Old at Minimum and Maximum SW Settings

EO (for SW) = Volts x Current x Duration.
Charge (for SW) = Current x Duration
Ohm's Law: Current = Voltage/Ω; Ω = Voltage/Current; Voltage = Current x Ω

It takes about 81J to overcome the initial Impedance of 450Ω so that we cannot reach seizure threshold even at the end of 1.0 Second in that this Duration requires us to overcome a 495Ω Impedance which requires about 99J. (See BP and

SW charts at the beginning of this section.) Here again, minimum and maximum EO meet as the SW machine is not powerful enough to overcome the minimum 495Ω required even at maximum SW output. While we can create a table then, the B-24 does not appear powerful enough to overcome threshold for the 80 year old, at least with BL "ECT." 58.31J (EO delivered) ÷ 99J (Threshold EO required) = a .59 MTTLOI or about 59% of that required to reach threshold.

MINIMUM & MAXIMUM OUTPUT FOR MEDCRAFT B-24 SW FOR 80 YEAR OLD RECIPIENT

EO	Voltage	Current	Duration	Resistance	Charge
6.41 Joules	170 Volts	.377A	.1 Seconds	450 Ω	.038 Coulombs
12.72	170	.374	.2	455	.075
18.87	170	.370	.3	460	.111
24.89	170	.366	.4	465	.146
30.69	170	.361	.5	470	.181
36.52	170	.358	.6	475	.215
42.13	170	.354	.7	480	.248
47.74	170	.351	.8	485	.281
53.10	170	.347	.9	490	.312
58.31	**170**	**.343**	**1.0**	**495**	**.343**

Using maximum SW parameters, Amperage naturally deteriorates as Impedance once again rises (45Ω) over the one second Duration. Using the maximum 170 (constant) Volts, the higher 450Ω Initial Resistance now results in an even lower initial Amperage of .377A deteriorating over one second to .343A. Overall maximum EO is thus reduced to about 58.31J. According to a literal reading of Weiner's SW graph at the beginning of this section, a circa 58J output occurs about ***21%*** of the time on SW. Conversely, 79% of all SW emissions appear to be 58J or less.

We can once again verify the relationship of final Impedance and EO with our inverse proportion formula using the constant: 29000: (EO = 29000/Impedance. XJ = 29000/495Ω = circa 58.59J; 29000/58.59J = XΩ = circa 495Ω.) At the final 495Ω Impedance, Threshold Output required for SW devices in this age category has risen to about 99J (based on 495Ω—see BP chart), that required of about a 99 year old recipient on a BP device. Based on the 58.31J Cumulative Output at the end of one second of SW in this age category, we obtain a MTTLOI for the 80 year old at maximum (and minimum) SW settings of about (58.31 ÷ 99J =) .59, well below threshold and thus not enough to induce seizure with BL "ECT." The MTTLOI at maximum SW parameters for the 80 year old recipient, in short, is well under threshold, even less than the MTTLOI (1.08) consistently delivered by **first generation MECTA "C" BP device**. The MTTLOI for the 80 year old (.59) on the SW device even at maximum settings has now dropped another (.59 ÷ .81 = 72%. 100% - 72% =) 28% compared to the .81 MTTLOI of the previous 70 year old age category even at maximum SW settings.

For the 80 year old age level then, maximum SW settings are now weaker in both raw EO and MTTLOI than the **first generation MECTA "C" BP device** which delivers its ubiquitous circa 1.08 fold threshold output in the 80 year old age range at about 69 Joules, for the first time, surpassing that of SW which, though ineffective, yet delivers about 58J. **Second generation BP devices** which use about 147 Joules to deliver a 2.3-2.5 MTTLOI for 80 year old recipients, are, of course, decidedly more powerful and more dangerous than SW (delivering 58J) in this age category delivering (147J ÷ 58J = 2.53) 2.5 times the power of SW even at maximum SW settings. **Third generation BP devices** which use a circa 5.0 MTTLOI (as opposed to a .59 MTTLOI) at about 295 Joules (in lieu of SW's 58J), due to inversion exploitation (see below) are now (295J ÷ 58J =) 5.09 times more powerful and thus 5.09 times more dangerous than SW even at maximum SW settings in this age category. Potential and already legal **fourth generation BP devices** which theoretically elicit a circa 10 MTTLOI, more than (10 ÷ .59 =) 17 times the MTTLOI elicited by SW even at maximum SW settings for the 80 year old age category (see Inverse exploitation), delivers 590J in lieu of SW's circa 58J maximum at this age level, now about (590J ÷ 58J =) 10 times as powerful as SW. In short, fourth generation BP devices are now exponentially more powerful and exponentially more dangerous than SW in this particular age category. Finally the **fifth generation BP device** at a circa 12.0 MTTLOI is (12 ÷ .59 =) 20 times greater than SW in this age category, delivering a default 768J compared to SW's 59J even at maximum SW stimulus or about (768J ÷ 58J =) 13 times the raw power of SW. There is no probable minimal stimulus as maximum and minimum SW output have merged.

Here again, in accordance with the emerging pattern, SW has become less and less dangerous, indeed, ineffective and BP more and more dangerous compared to SW with respect to increasing age and each subsequent BP device generation. In short, we once again see that with increasing age and BP generation, the default outputs of the later generation BP devices increase exponentially compared to maximum SW settings, until BP has completely overtaken SW with respect to the greater EO delivered and so the greater morbidity. Indeed, due to deteriorating Current and increasing Impedance, maximum and minimum SW settings merge beginning at about 65 years of age becoming, in fact, incapable of inducing adequate seizures with BL-ECT. Importantly too, even as SW has become more and more inefficient, only here, at age 80 does the first generation MECTA "C" delivering 69J (compared to SW's 58J) surpass SW in terms of EO. Even so, the MECTA "C" maintains its 1.08 MTTLOI, minimal stimulus status, and can deliver adequate seizures, thus legitimately maintaining its status as an "ECT" device; whereas. SW fails completely. While the MECTA "C" is a true "ECT" device, capable of inducing adequate seizures with the least amount of EO possible with "BL-ECT," however, this is not to say that the MECTA "C," that is, that "ECT" is effective as a therapeutic. Indeed, the evidence shows that it is not effective, but only because so-called "convulsive therapy," that is, the so-called "therapeutic" induction of the "adequate seizure" is mythological. Conversely, while second, third, fourth, and fifth generation BP devices are in a manner, "effective," with respect to a short term anti-depressant effect and even behavioral modification, neither are they "ECT" devices in that the principle behind these later devices is no longer adequate seizure, but rather, adequate amounts of electricity. As such, all but first generation BP devices, i.e. the MECTA "C," are ENR devices inextricably married to morbidity.

K) Output and MTTLOI for the Ninety Year Old at Minimum and Maximum SW Settings

EO (for SW) = Volts x Current x Duration.
Charge (for SW) = Current x Duration
Ohm's Law: Current = Voltage/Ω; Ω = Voltage/Current; Voltage = Current x Ω

It takes about 100J to overcome 500Ω so that we cannot overcome seizure threshold even at the end of 1.0 Second with BL "ECT" in that this Duration requires us to overcome a 545Ω Impedance which requires about 120J. Indeed, the B-24 SW device, in this ninety year old age category, can only muster 53.04J at maximum (and minimum) output. Here again, minimum and maximum EO meet as the machine is not powerful enough to overcome even the minimum 500Ω, much less the maximum 545Ω, even at maximum SW settings. While we can again create a table, the B-24 does not appear powerful enough to overcome threshold for the 90 year old with BL "ECT" and perhaps not even with UL "ECT." At ninety years of age, the B-24 delivers a [53.04 (SW EO delivered) ÷ 119.9J (SW Threshold EO required)] = .44 MTTLOI or about 44% of that required to reach threshold.

MINIMUM & MAXIMUM OUTPUT FOR MEDCRAFT B-24 SW FOR 90 YEAR OLD RECIPIENT

EO	Voltage	Current	Duration	Resistance	Charge
5.78 Joules	170 Volts	.34 Amperes	.1 Seconds	500 Ω	.034 Coulombs
11.46	170	.337	.2	505	.067
17.00	170	.333	.3	510	.099
22.44	170	.330	.4	515	.132
27.80	170	.327	.5	520	.164
33.01	170	.324	.6	525	.194
38.20	170	.321	.7	530	.225
43.25	170	.318	.8	535	.254
48.20	170	.315	.9	540	.284
53.04	**170**	**.312**	**1.0**	**545**	**.312**

Using maximum SW parameters of 1.0 Seconds and 170V, Amperage naturally deteriorates as Impedance once again rises (by 45Ω) over the one second Duration. Using the maximum 170 (constant) Volts then, the higher 500Ω Initial Resistance now results in an even lower initial Amperage of .34A deteriorating over one second to .312A. Overall maximum EO is thus reduced to about 53.04J. According to a literal reading of

Weiner's SW graph at the beginning of this section, a circa 53J output occurs about **23%** of the time on SW. Conversely, 77% of all SW emissions appear to be 53J or less. There is no probable minimal stimulus as true minimum and maximum outputs have merged.

We can once again verify the relationship of final Impedance and EO with our inverse proportion formula using the constant: 29000: (EO = 29000/Impedance. XJ = 29000/545Ω = circa 53.21J; 29000/53.21J = XΩ = circa 545Ω.) At the final 545Ω Impedance, Threshold Output required for SW devices has risen to about 119.9J (based on 545Ω—see BP chart), that required of about a 109 year old recipient on a BP device, if the BP device allowed it. Based on the 53.04J Cumulative Output at the end of one second of SW in this age category, we obtain a MTTLOI for the 90 year old at maximum SW settings of about (53.04 ÷ 119.9J =) .44, well below threshold and thus not enough to induce seizure with BL "ECT." The MTTLOI at maximum SW parameters for the 90 year old recipient, in short, is well under threshold, even less than the 1.08 MTTLOI consistently delivered by the **first generation MECTA "C" BP device**. The MTTLOI for the 90 year old (.44) on the SW device even at maximum settings has now dropped another (.44 ÷ .59 = 74%; 100% - 74% =) 26% compared to the MTTLOI of the 80 year old (at .59 fold) even at maximum SW settings.

For the 90 year old age level then, maximum SW settings are now even weaker in both raw EO (53J) and MTTLOI (.44) than the **first generation MECTA "C" BP device** which delivers its ubiquitous circa 1.08 fold threshold output in this age range at about 87.5 Joules, compared to SW's .44 MTTLOI delivering only about 53J maximum. Of course, SW here, completely fails to induce seizure. **Second generation BP devices** which use about 187.5 Joules to deliver a 2.3-2.5 MTTLOI for 90 year old recipients, are about (187.5J ÷ 53J =) 3.5 times more powerful and thus more dangerous than SW in this age category even at maximum SW settings. **Third generation BP devices** which use a circa 5.0 MTTLOI as opposed to a .44 MTTLOI and about 373 Joules (in lieu of SW's 53J), due to inversion exploitation (see below) are now (373J ÷ 53J =) 7.04 times more powerful and thus 7.04 times more dangerous than SW even at maximum SW settings in this age category. Potential and already legal **fourth generation BP devices** which theoretically elicit a circa 10 MTTLOI, more than (10 ÷ .44 =) 22.7 times the MTTLOI elicited by SW even at maximum settings for the 90 year old age category deliver about 746J in lieu of SW's circa 53J maximum at this age level, now about (746J ÷ 53J =) 14 times as powerful as SW, making fourth generation BP devices exponentially more powerful and exponentially more dangerous than SW in this age category. Finally the **fifth generation BP device** at a circa 12.0 MTTLOI compared to SW's .44 MTTLOI, (12 ÷ .44 =) 27.3 times the MTTLOI elicited by SW even at maximum SW settings, delivering a default 972J compared to SW's 53J at both maximum and minimum stimulus settings in the 90 year old age category, is about (972J ÷ 53J =) 18 times more powerful than SW in this age category.

Here again, as previously noted, SW has become less and less dangerous, indeed, ineffective and BP more and more dangerous compared to SW with respect to increasing age and subsequent BP machine generation. In short, once again we see that with increasing age and BP device generation, the default outputs increase exponentially even compared to maximum SW settings, until BP completely overtakes SW with respect to the greater EO delivered and so danger and morbidity. Indeed, due to deteriorating Current and increasing Impedance, maximum and minimum SW settings merge from at least 65 years of age and older, becoming more and more ineffective with respect to inducing an "adequate seizure." Importantly too, as SW becomes more inefficient with age, even the first generation MECTA "C," which delivers 87.5J in the 90 year old age category, now surpasses SW in terms of EO by an even greater margin than the previous age category. Even so, the MECTA "C" maintains its 1.08 MTTLOI minimal stimulus status, and thus standing as an "ECT" device in that it delivers output at just above threshold; whereas, SW cannot deliver at all. While the MECTA "C" is a true "ECT" device, capable of inducing adequate seizures with the least amount of EO possible with "BL-ECT"; however, this is not to say that the MECTA "C," that is, that co-called Electro Convulsive Therapy is effective as a therapeutic. Indeed, as we have seen, the evidence shows that the MECTA "C," despite its capacity to induce adequate seizures in all age categories, is not effective. In short, the necessity of more powerful BP devices prove that the induction of the adequate seizure by and unto itself, is inadequate--indeed--mythological. Conversely, while second, third, fourth, and fifth generation BP devices are--in a manner--"effective" with respect to a short term anti-depressant effect and even temporary behavioral modification, they are by no means "ECT" devices. In brief, the principle behind the later BP devices is no longer the adequate seizure at all, but, as has been clearly proven here--adequate doses of electricity. In short, the later BP devices, just as is SW [250] (where it can induce seizure), are no longer ECT devices at all, but ENR devices. As such both SW and the later BP devices are inextricably married to morbidity.

L) Output and MTTLOI for the One Hundred Year Old at Minimum and Maximum SW Settings

EO (for SW) = Volts x Current x Duration.
Charge (for SW) = Current x Duration
Ohm's Law: Current = Voltage/Ω; Ω = Voltage/Current; Voltage = Current x Ω

It takes about 121J to overcome 550Ω so that we cannot overcome seizure threshold even at the end of 1.0 Second in that this Duration requires the B-24 to overcome a 595Ω Impedance which requires about 143J, whereas, the B-24 in this one hundred year old age category can only muster 48.62J at maximum (and minimum) output. Here again, minimum and maximum EO have merged as the machine is not powerful enough to overcome the initial 550Ω, much less the Final 595Ω, even at maximum SW settings. While we can once again create a table then, the B-24 does not appear powerful enough to overcome threshold for the 100 year old recipient with BL "ECT" and perhaps not even with UL "ECT." 48.62 (EO delivered) ÷ 143J (Threshold EO required) = .34 MTTLOI or about 34% of that required to reach threshold.

MINIMUM & MAXIMUM OUTPUT FOR MEDCRAFT B-24 SW FOR 100 YEAR OLD RECIPIENT

EO	Voltage	Current	Duration	Resistance	Charge
5.25 Joules	170 Volts	.309A	.1 Seconds	550 Ω	.031 Coulombs
10.40	170	.306	.2	555	.061
15.50	170	.304	.3	560	.091
20.46	170	.301	.4	565	.120
25.33	170	.298	.5	570	.149
30.19	170	.296	.6	575	.177
34.87	170	.293	.7	580	.205
39.58	170	.291	.8	585	.233
44.06	170	.288	.9	590	.259
48.62	**170**	**.286**	**1.0**	**595**	**.286**

Using maximum SW parameters of 1.0 Seconds and 170V, Amperage naturally deteriorates as Impedance once again rises (by 45Ω) over the one second Duration. Using the maximum 170 (constant) Volts, the higher 550Ω Initial Resistance now results in an even lower initial Amperage of .309A deteriorating over one second to an even lower .286A (compared to the 90 year old category). Overall maximum EO is thus reduced to about 48.62J. According to a literal reading of Weiner's SW graph above, a circa 49J output (or above) occurs about ***30%*** of the time on SW. Conversely, 70% of all SW emissions appear to be 49J or less.

We can once again verify the relationship of final Impedance and EO with our inverse proportion formula using the constant: 29000: (EO = 29000/Impedance. XJ = 29000/595Ω = circa 48.62J; 29000/48.62J = XΩ = circa 595Ω.) At the final 595Ω Impedance, Threshold Output required for SW devices has risen to about 142.8J (based on 595Ω—see SW chart), that required of about a 119 year old recipient on a BP device, if the BP device allowed for it. Based on the 48.62J Cumulative Output at the end of one second of SW in this age category, we obtain a (48.62 ÷ 142.8J =) .34 MTTLOI for the 100 year old at maximum SW settings, well below threshold and thus not enough to induce seizure with BL "ECT." The MTTLOI at maximum SW parameters for the 100 year old recipient, in short, is well under threshold, even below the 1.08 MTTLOI consistently delivered by the **first generation MECTA "C" BP device**. The MTTLOI (of .34) for the 100 year old on the SW device even at maximum settings has now dropped another (.34 ÷ .44 = 77%; 100% - 77% =) 23% compared to the (.44) MTTLOI of the 90 year old at maximum SW settings.

For the 100 year old age level then, maximum SW settings are now even weaker in both raw EO and MTTLOI than the **first generation MECTA "C" BP device** forming an even greater BP-SW disparity between

[250] SW is actually an ENR device by virtue of it inducing seizures even at minimum stimulus at outputs at least twice that necessary to do so. This was revealed by the MECTA "C" and even earlier by early BP devices.

the now .34 MTTLOI of SW at circa 49J and the 1.08 MTTLOI of the MECTA "C" at 108J. On the other hand, SW cannot induce adequate seizures at these low outputs. Without doubt, then, **Second generation BP devices** which use about 230 Joules to deliver a 2.3-2.5 MTTLOI for 100 year old recipients, are about (230J ÷ 49J =) 4.7 times more powerful and more dangerous than SW in this age category even at maximum SW settings. **Third generation BP devices** which use a circa 5.0 MTTLOI as opposed to SW's .34 MTTLOI and which emit about 460 Joules in lieu of SW's 49 Joules, due to inversion exploitation (see below), are now (460J ÷ 49J =) circa 9.4 times more powerful and thus 9.4 times more dangerous than SW in this age category even at maximum SW settings. Potential and already legal **fourth generation BP devices** which theoretically elicit a circa 10 MTTLOI, more than (10 ÷ .34 =) 29 times the MTTLOI elicited by SW even at maximum SW settings for the 100 year old age category as well as 922J in lieu of SW's circa 49J maximum, are now about (922J ÷ 49J =) 18.8 times more powerful than SW at this age level, making fourth generation BP devices exponentially more powerful and exponentially more dangerous than SW. Finally the hypothetical but "legal" **fifth generation BP device** at a circa 12.0 MTTLOI compared to SW's .34 MTTLOI delivers (12 ÷ .34 =) 35.3 times the MTTLOI of SW, while the default 1200J output these theoretical fifth generation BP machines deliver in the 100 year old age category, is circa (1200J ÷ 49J =) 24.5 times the raw power of SW.

Here again, as previously noted, with increasing age and increasing BP power with each subsequent machine generation, SW becomes less and less dangerous, indeed, ineffective compared to BP and BP more and more dangerous, indeed, perilous compared to SW. In short, once again we see that with increasing age, the default outputs of the later generation BP devices become exponentially more powerful than SW, until BP completely overtakes SW with respect to greater and greater EO delivered. Indeed, due to deteriorating Current and increasing Impedance, maximum and minimum SW settings merge from about age 65 and older, becoming more and more impotent until even the first generation MECTA "C" at 108 maximum Joules exceeds SW in terms of EO which at age 100, delivers an ineffective 49J maximum. While SW loses its capacity to even induce seizure, however, the MECTA "C" maintains its 1.08 MTTLOI, minimal stimulus status, and thus legitimate standing as an "ECT" device in even the oldest age category. While the MECTA "C" is a true "ECT" device, capable of inducing adequate seizures with the least amount of EO possible with "BL-ECT;" however, this is not to say, as previously noted, that the MECTA "C," that is, that Electro Convulsive Therapy in and of itself, is effective as a therapeutic. Indeed, the necessity of more and more powerful BP devices shows not only that the MECTA "C" is ineffective, but that the therapeutic effect of the adequate seizure alone is mythological. Conversely, while second, third, fourth, and fifth generation BP devices are--in a manner--"effective" with respect to a short term anti-depressant effect and even behavioral modification, they are by no means "ECT" devices in that the principle behind all later model BP devices (and even SW where it can induce seizure) is not adequate seizure at all, but adequate doses of electricity. As such, as we have heretofore noted, both SW and the second, third, fourth, and fifth generation BP devices are inextricably married to morbidity even as morbidity is inextricably married to "efficacy."

Overall Conclusion of SW vs BP

While BP can use less power than SW in all age brackets at either minimum or maximum output settings to deliver adequate seizures with consistent MTTLOIs--except for the MECTA "C"—extremely powerful modern day BP machines only do so in the younger age brackets. In fact, BP devices subsequent to the MECTA "C" equal and then surpass SW both in power and MTTLOI as age and thus Impedance levels increase and with each subsequent BP generation. More specifically, at maximum settings, SW is initially more powerful than BP generally, but becomes progressively weaker and more ineffective as age increases until at about age 65 and older, SW becomes altogether ineffectual even at maximum settings. Too, with each new BP generation, BP surpasses maximum SW settings in earlier and earlier age categories. Indeed, by maintaining a consistent MTTLOI through automatically increasing Voltages, later BP devices deliver frighteningly higher and higher outputs with each increasing age category even through year 100, power that is exacerbated with each new BP device generation. SW, on the other hand, though frighteningly powerful in the younger age categories, at about age 65 and older, actually becomes impotent even at maximum settings with respect to the induction of so-called adequate seizures with BL "ECT." Moreover, evidence suggests that true minimal stimulus for SW is not allowed either by the machine or some sort of age to output chart which Medcraft secrets from the public. Evidence suggests that a modicum of reduced output settings are possible between about age ten and forty years of age, after which maximum SW outputs merge with probable "minimum" SW outputs. Indeed, true minimal stimulus even for SW does not appear possible with the B-24 SW. Certainly, this agrees with Medcraft's longstanding albeit secret policy of efficacy over safety in all age categories. Alarmingly, in all cases, unlike Brief Pulse, the greatest outputs appear to be administered to the most vulnerable populations. Due to the machine's design, those with the least resistance to electricity are administered the highest outputs, in short, the most damaging and brain-injurious doses. Indeed, both SW and Brief Pulse are ENR devices based on adequate amounts of electricity. The idea of safety by means of minimal stimulus has long ago faded into the past.

To summarize: The SW device and the BP device operate on inverse principles, SW on diminishing Amperage due to constant Voltage, BP on constant Amperage due to rising Voltage. Thus, in order to compare the two, a SW paradigm has been created in order to identify the Impedance-Age/Output relationship of SW in light of its diminishing current compared to the Impedance- Age/Output relationship of BP in light of its constant current. In sum, we find that the B-24 SW, even using maximum parameters, does not appear to have the capacity to surpass threshold for recipients from about 65 years of age and older (with BL "ECT) while all BP devices emit consistent MTTLOIs for all recipients up to 100 years of age requiring inordinately never before soaring outputs up to 1200 Joules--six times the 200J maximum output of SW, in itself only possible with extraordinarily low SW Impedances. On the other hand, SW Output can and does dangerously surpass all Brief Pulse machines in the younger age categories, at both maximum and probable minimal stimulus settings.

Of paramount importance, only the First Generation MECTA "C" is superior to SW with respect to reduced EO in all seizure inducible age categories at both true minimal and maximal SW settings. Certainly, through inverse exploitation of power, second, third, fourth, and fifth generation BP devices have lost their reduced EO advantage over SW generally. This is crucial in that only the first generation MECTA "C" conforms to the 1982 APA Standard in turn approved by the Utah Biological Test Laboratory and thus the FDA, a standard which, had it been officially adopted, would have facilitated the upgrade for the Brief Pulse device generally, from Class III [251] to Class I, [252] which both manufacturers and the APA Committee on ECT had for so long sought. Instead, manufacturers avoided condonation and adoption of the 1982 APA Standard, opting instead for more powerful Brief Pulse devices, surpassing that of SW in both power and MTTLOI in most age categories, as we have seen. Indeed, both SW and the later modern day Brief Pulse devices are ENR devices long since abandoning the idea of minimal stimulus. Both kinds of manufacturers know full well that their devices are brain injurious and only work via brain injury due to excessive doses of electricity. Both have gone to great lengths to hide this information from the public.

---

[251] Medical devices for which no standard can or has been written or approved)

[252] Medical devices with approved FDA standards considered safe with respect to benefit vs risk

CHAPTER 84

Summation of Max/Min SW Settings in Terms of Dangerousness vs Current BP Devices [253]

100 Year Old Recipients:

In this age category, SW does not appear to have enough power to seize any recipient 100 years old or older, even with UL ECT. For 100 year old SW recipients, Threshold Output for SW is about 143J while the B-24 SW device even at maximum power can only emit about 48.6 Joules of Cumulative Output. In short, in the 100 year old age category, SW at maximum power (which is also minimum power) delivers a (49J ÷ 143J =) .34 MTTLOI or about 34% of that required to reach Threshold--not even enough to induce seizure using UL "ECT." Compare this to modern day BP devices below. In sum: the 100 year old age category for both SW and BP is as follows:

The B-24 SW Device (at max) delivers a .34 MTTLOI at 49J:

The B-24 SW Device (at prob min) delivers a .34 MTTLOI at 49J

The B-24 SW Device (at true min) delivers a .34 MTTLOI at 49J

First Generation BP Devices: deliver a circa: 1.08 MTTLOI at about 108J.

Second Generation BP Devices deliver a: 2.3-2.5 MTTLOI at about 230J.

Third Generation BP Devices deliver a circa: 5.0 MTTLOI at about 460J.

Fourth generation BP Devices deliver a circa: 10.0 MTTLOI at about 922J

Fifth generation BP Devices deliver a circa : 12.0 MTTLOI at about 1200J

In the 100 year old category, even at maximum SW power, SW cannot reach threshold with either BL or UL ECT. In fact, SW in this age category, even at maximum output, delivers less EO (49J) than the First generation BP device (108). Nevertheless, the First Generation BP Device stands as an improvement over SW in that it can induce adequate seizures by minimally surpassing threshold with the same consistent 1.08 MTTLOI it emits for all other age categories. Needless to say that while the SW device cannot reach threshold in this age category with either BL or UL ECT, the Second, Third, Fourth, and Fifth generation BP devices,

[253] While it is not known whether or not it has been manufactured, the theoretically possible Fifth Generation BP device, legal under the Weiner Standard as we have seen, has been included here.

none of which are minimal stimulus devices, all deliver a much greater MTTLOI (2.4, 5.0, 10.0, 12.0) respectively than SW (.34 MTTLOI) in this age category, but also at much greater, indeed, excessive outputs of 230J, 460J, 922J, and 1200J respectively compared to the inadequate EO delivered by SW of 49J. Not surprisingly, Second, Third, Fourth, and Fifth generation BP devices deliver much greater outputs than necessary to induce seizure. It is the First Generation BP Device alone which can induce adequate seizures in this age category at minimal stimulus output (108J) with BL ECT. Indeed, it is the First Generation BP device alone which can induce the same adequate seizures as its more powerful successors, but at less than (230 ÷ 108J = 2.13; 108J ÷ 230J = 47%) half the output of the Second Generation BP Device less than (108J ÷ 460J = 23.5%) 25% the output of the Third Generation BP Device, less than (108J ÷ 922J = 11.7%) 12% the output of the Fourth Generation BP Device and less than (108J ÷ 1200J =) 9% the output of the Fifth Generation BP Device. Although the "C" is an improvement over SW in this age category by virtue of having the capacity to reach threshold at minimal stimulus, all four BP successors of the MECTA "C" unnecessarily surpass threshold multifold times with respect to inducing an adequate seizure. It Is the First generation MECTA "C" BP Device alone which delivers just above seizure threshold output in all age categories with BL placement. In short, all four successors of the MECTA "C" are conspicuously more dangerous not only than SW in this age category, but also more dangerous than the MECTA "C" BP Device which can successfully induce the same adequate seizure at much lower EOs. In sum, only the first generation BP Device is an improvement over SW with respect to inducing adequate seizure with less EO than SW in all seizure inducible age categories. Moreover, it is only the MECTA "C" BP device which induces adequate seizures with minimal stimulus output with BL ECT in accordance with the 1982 APA Standard.

90 Year Old Recipients:

SW does not appear to have enough power to seize any recipient 90 years old or older with BL ECT. For 90 year old SW recipients, Threshold Output is about 120J while the B-24 SW device even at maximum power emits only about 53.04 Joules of Cumulative Output. In short, in the 90 year old age category, SW at maximum power (which is also minimum and probable minimum power in this age category) delivers a (53J ÷ 120J =) .44 MTTLOI or about 44% of that required to reach Threshold--not enough to induce seizure with BL ECT and barely enough to induce seizure with UL ECT if at all. Compare this to modern day BP devices. In sum: the 90 year old age category for both SW and BP is as follows:

The B-24 SW Device (at max) delivers a .44 MTTLOI at 53J:

The B-24 SW Device (at prob. min) delivers a .44 MTTLOI at 53J

The B-24 SW Device (at true min) delivers a .44 MTTLOI at 53J

First Generation BP Devices: deliver a circa: 1.08 MTTLOI at about 87.5J.

Second Generation BP Devices deliver a: 2.3-2.5 MTTLOI at about 187J.

Third Generation BP Devices deliver a circa: 5.0 MTTLOI at about 373J.

Fourth generation BP Devices deliver a circa : 10.0 MTTLOI at about 746J

Fifth generation BP Devices deliver a circa : 12.0 MTTLOI at about 972J

In the 90 year old category, even at maximum SW power, SW cannot reach threshold, at least with BL ECT and just barely with UL ECT, if at all. In fact, SW delivers less EO (53J) than the First generation BP device (87.5J) in this age category. Nevertheless, the First Generation BP Device is an improvement over SW because it minimally surpasses threshold with the same consistent 1.08 MTTLOI as all other age categories; whereas the SW device fails to reach threshold altogether, perhaps, as noted above, even with UL ECT. Needless to say that while the SW device cannot reach threshold in this age category with BL ECT, the Second, Third, Fourth, and Fifth generation BP devices, none of which are minimal stimulus devices, all deliver a much greater MTTLOI at (2.4, 5.0, 10.0, 12.0) respectively than SW (at a .44 MTTLOI), but also at much greater, in fact, excessive outputs of 187J, 373J, 746J, and 972J respectively compared to the inadequate EO of SW at 53J. Not surprisingly, then, Second, Third, Fourth, and Fifth generation BP devices deliver much greater outputs than necessary to induce seizure. Regardless of its surpassing threshold, whereas, SW does not, it is the First Generation BP Device alone which can induce adequate seizures in this age category at minimal stimulus output (of 87.5J) with BL ECT. Indeed, it is the First Generation BP device alone which can induce the same adequate seizures as its more powerful BP successors, but at less than (87.5J ÷ 187 = 47%) 50% the output of the Second Generation BP Device, less than (87.5J ÷ 373 = 24%) 25% the output of the Third Generation BP Device, less than (87.5J ÷ 746J = 11.7%) 12% the output of the Fourth Generation BP Device and about (87.5J ÷ 972J =) 9% the output of the theoretical, but "legal" Fifth Generation BP Device. Only an improvement over SW in this age category by virtue of having the capacity to reach threshold, all four BP generation successors (to the "C") unnecessarily surpass threshold multifold times as opposed to the First generation MECTA "C" BP Device which alone delivers just above seizure threshold in all age categories. In short, all four successors of the MECTA "C" are conspicuously more dangerous not only than SW in this age category, but also more dangerous than the MECTA "C" BP Device which can successfully induce the same adequate seizures at a much lower EO. Only the first generation MECTA "C" BP Device is an improvement over SW with respect to inducing adequate seizure with the least amount of EO possible with BL ECT.

80 Year Old Recipients:

SW does not appear to have enough power to seize any recipient 80 years old or older, at least not with BL ECT. For 80 year old SW recipients, Threshold Output is about 99J to overcome 495Ω while the B-24 SW device, even at maximum power, emits only about 58.31 Joules of Cumulative Output at the end of one second. In short, in the 80 year old age category, SW at maximum power (which is also minimum and probable minimum in this age category) delivers a (58.31J ÷ 99J =) .59 MTTLOI or about 59% that required to reach Threshold--not enough to induce seizure with BL ECT. Compare this to modern day BP devices below. In sum: the 80 year old age category for both SW and BP is as follows:

The B-24 SW Device (at max) delivers a .59 MTTLOI at 58J:

The B-24 SW Device (at prob min) delivers a .59 MTTLOI at 58J

The B-24 SW Device (at true min) delivers a .59 MTTLOI at 58J

First Generation BP Devices: deliver a circa: 1.08 MTTLOI at about 69J.

Second Generation BP Devices deliver a: 2.3-2.5 MTTLOI at about 147J.

Third Generation BP Devices deliver a circa: 5.0 MTTLOI at about 295J.

Fourth generation BP Devices deliver a circa : 10.0 MTTLOI at about 590J

Fifth generation BP Devices deliver a circa : 12.0 MTTLOI at about 768J

In the 80 year old category, even at maximum SW power, SW cannot reach threshold, at least with BL ECT, and, in fact, for the first time delivers less EO (58J) than the First generation MECTA "C" BP device (which delivers 69J). Nevertheless, the First Generation BP Device is an improvement over SW in that it minimally surpasses threshold with a 1.08 MTTLOI; whereas, the SW device fails to reach threshold in this age category altogether, at least with BL ECT. Needless to say that while the SW device cannot reach threshold in this age category with BL ECT, the Second, Third, Fourth, and Fifth generation BP devices, none of which are minimal stimulus devices, all deliver a much greater MTTLOI at (2.4, 5.0, 10.0, 12.0) respectively than SW (at its .59 MTTLOI), but also much greater outputs at (147J, 295J, 590J, and 768J respectively) than SW (at 58J). On the other hand, the Second, Third, Fourth, and Fifth generation BP devices deliver much greater outputs than necessary to induce "adequate" seizure. Regardless of their capacity to surpass threshold, whereas, SW does not, then, it is the First Generation BP Device alone which can induce adequate seizures in the 80 year old age category at minimal stimulus output with BL ECT, in short, a 1.08 MTTLOI at 69J, barely above that unsuccessfully generated by SW (at 59J). Indeed, it is the First Generation BP device alone which can induce the same adequate seizures as its more powerful BP successors, but at less than (69J ÷ 147J = 46.9%) 50% the output of the Second Generation BP Device, less than (69J ÷ 295J = 23.4%) 25% the output of the output of the Third Generation BP Device less than (69J ÷ 590J = 11.7%) 12% the output of the Fourth Generation BP Device and about (69J ÷ 768J =) 9% the output of the Fifth Generation BP Device. Although an improvement over SW in this age category by virtue of having the capacity to reach threshold, all four BP successors of the MECTA "C" consistently and unnecessarily surpass threshold multifold times as opposed to the First generation MECTA "C" BP Device which alone delivers just above seizure threshold in all age categories. In short, all four successors of the MECTA "C" are conspicuously more dangerous not only than SW in this age category, but conspicuously more dangerous than the MECTA "C" BP Device which can successfully induce the same adequate seizure as its successors, but at much lower EO. Once again, only the first generation BP Device is an improvement over SW in this age category with respect to both inducing adequate seizures and inducing adequate seizures with the least amount of EO possible with BL ECT.

70 Year Old Recipients:

SW does not appear to have enough power to seize any recipient 70 years old or older with BL "ECT." For 70 year old SW recipients, Threshold Output is about 80.7J while the B-24 SW device even at maximum power emits only about 64.94 Joules of Cumulative Output. In short, in the 70 year old age category, SW at maximum power (which is also minimum and probable minimum power in this age category) delivers an (64.94J ÷ 80.7J =) .804 MTTLOI or about 80% of that required to reach Threshold--not enough to induce seizure with BL "ECT." Compare this to modern day BP devices below. In sum: the 70 year old age category for both SW and BP is as follows:

The B-24 SW Device (at max) delivers a .804 MTTLOI at 65J:

The B-24 SW Device (at prob min) delivers a .804 MTTLOI at 65J

The B-24 SW Device (at true min) delivers a .804 MTTLOI at 65J

First Generation BP Devices: deliver a circa: 1.08 MTTLOI at about 53J.

Second Generation BP Devices deliver a: 2.3-2.5 MTTLOI at about 113J.

Third Generation BP Devices deliver a circa: 5.0 MTTLOI at about 225J.

Fourth generation BP Devices deliver a circa : 10.0 MTTLOI at about 450J

Fifth generation BP Devices deliver a circa : 12.0 MTTLOI at about 588J

In the 70 year old category, even at maximum SW power, SW cannot reach threshold as noted, at least with BL ECT, even while delivering slightly more EO than the First generation MECTA "C" BP device. Not only is the MECTA "C" BP Device an improvement over SW in that it delivers less power than minimal stimulus SW in this age category at the same approximate MTTLOI, but the First Generation MECTA "C" BP Device is superior to SW in that it surpasses threshold; whereas, the SW device cannot seize most 70 year old recipients in this age category with BL "ECT." Needless to say that while the SW device does not reach threshold in this age category with BL ECT, the Second, Third, Fourth, and Fifth generation BP devices, none of which are minimal stimulus devices, do, all delivering a much greater MTTLOI at (2.4, 5.0, 10.0, 12.0) respectively than SW (at .804) and a much greater output at (113J, 225J, 450J, and 588J) respectively) than SW (at 65J) even at maximum SW output. Critically, at 53J, the First Generation MECTA "C" BP Device can induce the same adequate seizures as all four successive BP devices in this age category at much lower EO. Thus, while all four later BP devices dramatically surpass SW in power even at maximum SW settings, the First Generation MECTA "C" BP device can induce the same adequate seizures at less than (53J ÷ 113 = 47%) half the output of the Second Generation BP Device, less than (53J ÷ 225J = 23.5%) 25% the output of the Third Generation BP Device, less than (53J ÷ 450J = 11.8%) 12% the output of the Fourth Generation BP Device, and less than (53J ÷ 588J =) 9% the output of the Fifth Generation BP Device. Only an improvement over SW in this age category by virtue of having the capacity to reach threshold, all four later generation BP devices unnecessarily surpass threshold multifold times as opposed to the First generation MECTA "C" BP Device. As such, all four later generation BP devices are conspicuously more dangerous than SW in this age category, but also more dangerous than the MECTA "C" BP Device which can induce the same adequate seizures in this age category at far less EO. In sum, only the first generation MECTA "C" BP Device in conformity with the 1982 APA Standard is an improvement over both SW and all other successive BP devices with respect to induction of adequate seizures with less EO as well as the least amount of EO possible with BL-ECT.

65 Year Old Recipients:

SW may or may or may not have enough power to seize a 65 year old recipient with BL-ECT. For 65 year old SW recipients, <u>Threshold Output</u> is about 72J while the B-24 SW device even at maximum power can emit only about 68.85 Joules of <u>Cumulative Output</u>. In short, in the 65 year old age category, SW at <u>maximum and minimum power</u> delivers a (68.85J ÷ 72J =) .956 MTTLOI or about 96% of that required to reach Threshold--perhaps enough to induce seizure with BL ECT in this age category at the beginning of a series. Compare this to modern day BP devices below. In sum: the 65 year old age category for both SW and BP is as follows:

<u>The B-24 SW Device</u> (at max) delivers a <u>.956 MTTLOI at about 69J</u>:

<u>The B-24 SW Device</u> (at prob min) delivers a <u>.956 MTTLOI at about 69J</u>

<u>The B-24 SW Device</u> (at true min) delivers a <u>.956 MTTLOI at about 69J</u>

<u>First Generation BP Devices</u>: deliver a circa: <u>1.08 MTTLOI at about 46J</u>.

<u>Second Generation BP Devices</u> deliver a: <u>2.3-2.5 MTTLOI at about 97J</u>.

<u>Third Generation BP Devices</u> deliver a circa: <u>5.0 MTTLOI at about 195J</u>.

<u>Fourth generation BP Devices</u> deliver a circa : <u>10.0 MTTLOI at about 390J</u>

<u>Fifth generation BP Devices</u> deliver a circa : <u>12.0 MTTLOI at about 507J</u>

In the 65 year old category, SW even at maximum (and minimum) SW power of 69J, can barely reach Threshold with BL-ECT, if at all. Indeed, as Impedance rises with increasing age, SW Amperage becomes weaker and weaker until at about age 65 and older, threshold with BL ECT, may not be reachable at all. But let us suppose that SW can reach threshold at least sometimes in this age category. Even so, we will not find it surprising that although MTTLOIs are comparable (BP-1.08 vs SW-.956), only the First generation MECTA "C"

BP device at 46J, delivers less output than SW at 69J in this age category. Specifically, SW, delivers (69J ÷ 46J =) 1.5 fold the output of the First Generation MECTA "C" BP device in this age category, so that compared to all other subsequent BP generations, only the First generation MECTA "C" BP device is an improvement over SW in this age category by virtue of reduced EO.[254] In short, the MECTA "C" alone delivers (46J ÷ 69J =) 67% the output of SW in this age category. Conversely, while admittedly inducing adequate seizures, the Second, Third, Fourth, and Fifth generation BP devices deliver far greater MTTLOIs as well as much more power than SW in this age category even at maximum SW settings. Compared to the circa 1.0 MTTLOI and circa 69J output of SW in this age category for both minimum and maximum output settings, the default output of the Second Generation BP device delivers a 2.4 MTTLOI at 97J, (97J ÷ 69J =) 1.4 times the EO of SW. The Third Generation BP device delivering a circa 5.0 MTTLOI at 195J is (195J ÷ 69J =) 2.8 times the EO of SW, the Fourth Generation BP Device delivering a circa 10.0 MTTLOI at 390J is (390J ÷ 69J =) 5.7 times the EO of SW and the Fifth Generation BP Device delivering a circa 12.0 MTTLOI at 507J is (507J ÷ 69J =) 7.3 times the EO of SW. In short, Second, Third, Fourth, and Fifth generation BP devices cannot be deemed improvements over SW in the 65 year old category by virtue of reduced EO, but are, in fact, categorically more dangerous than SW at both maximum and minimum SW output in this age range. The First generation MECTA "C" BP device alone is an improvement over SW by virtue of induction of an adequate seizure with reduced output compared to SW at both minimum and maximum SW settings (which have merged). All four later generation BP devices which are not "ECT" devices at all, unnecessarily surpass threshold multifold times as opposed to the First generation MECTA "C" BP Device. As such, all four later generation BP devices are conspicuously more dangerous than the MECTA "C" BP Device which can induce the same adequate seizures in this age category at minimal stimulus with BL placement. Specifically, the MECTA "C" induces adequate seizures at (46J ÷ 97J =) 47% the EO of second generation BP devices, (46J ÷ 195J =) 24% the EO of third generation BP devices, (46J ÷ 390J) = 11.8% the EO of fourth generation BP devices, and (46J ÷ 507J =) 9% the EO of theoretical but legal fifth generation BP devices. In short, only the first generation MECTA "C" BP Device is an improvement over SW with respect to induction of adequate seizures with less EO than SW in this age category and only the MECTA "C" induces adequate seizure with the least amount of EO possible with BL-ECT in accordance with the 1982 APA Standard. As such, only the First generation MECTA "C" BP device Is an "ECT" device. Indeed, Second, Third, Fourth, and Fifth generation BP devices are no longer "ECT" devices, having lost the Brief Pulse reduced EO advantage over SW including this, the 65 year old age category.

60 Year Old Recipients:

SW begins to have enough power to consistently surpass threshold and so seize recipients at about 60 years of age. For 60 year old SW recipients, maximum Threshold Output is circa 63.7J while the B-24 SW device at maximum power emits only about 73.16 Joules of Cumulative Output, just above threshold. In short, in the 60 year old age category, SW at maximum power and probable minimum power delivers a (73.16J ÷ 63.7J =) 1.15 MTTLOI or about 115% of that required to reach Threshold--which is enough to induce seizure with BL ECT. At true minimum stimulus in this same age category (if such settings are possible), the SW device emits about 66.7J; whereas, true Minimum Threshold output is about 64.2J so that at true minimum stimulus, the SW machine emits a circa 1.07 MTTLOI at about 66.7J. Compare maximum and probable minimum to modern day BP devices. In sum: the 60 year old age category for both SW and BP is as follows:

The B-24 SW Device (at max) delivers circa: 1.15 MTTLOI at about 73.16J:

The B-24 SW Device (at prob min) delivers circa: 1.15 MTTLOI at about 73.16J

The B-24 SW Device (at true min) delivers circa: 1.04 MTTLOI at about 66.7J

254 Only the First Generation BP device, the MECTA "C," delivers less EO than SW by about half at age 65 and younger, even when SW is set to true minimal stimulus. It is for this reason that only the MECTA "C" was approved by Utah Biological Test Laboratory employed by the FDA to do an independent study of "ECT" about 1978 and so by proxy, approved by the FDA. Not surprisingly, only the MECTA "C" conforms to the 1982 APA Standard never pushed for approval by Weiner and the APA ECT Committees who, in fact, wrote the 1982 APA Standard.

<u>First Generation BP Devices</u>: deliver a circa: <u>1.08 MTTLOI at about 39J</u>.

<u>Second Generation BP Devices</u> deliver a: <u>2.3-2.5 MTTLOI at about 83J</u>.

<u>Third Generation BP Devices</u> deliver a circa: <u>5.0 MTTLOI at about 167J</u>.

<u>Fourth generation BP Devices</u> deliver a circa : <u>10.0 MTTLOI at about 332J</u>

<u>Fifth generation BP Devices</u> deliver a circa : <u>12.0 MTTLOI at about 432J</u>

Not surprisingly, in the 60 year old category at maximum and probable minimum SW power, the First generation MECTA "C" BP device delivering a consistent at 1.08 MTTLOI at a default 39J is not only far less dangerous than SW set at maximum and probable minimum output (which have merged) delivering a 1.15 MTTLOI at 73.16J, but also less dangerous than SW at true minimum stimulus settings of about a 1.04 MTTLOI at 66.7J of power in this age category. Indeed, though it can induce seizure, SW at true minimal stimulus settings yet delivers about (66.7 ÷ 39J =) 1.7 fold more power than that of the of the First Generation MECTA "C" BP device in this same age category. At maximum and probable minimum (which have merged), SW yet delivers (73.16 ÷ 39J =) 1.88 fold more power than that of the MECTA "C." On the other hand, Second, Third, Fourth, and Fifth generation BP devices deliver more power at a greater MTTLOI than SW at minimum, probable minimum, and maximum settings in this, the 60 year old age category, and so are all more dangerous than SW in this age group. Specifically, compared to maximum and probable minimum SW settings of a 1.15 MTTLOI at 73.16J and true minimum of a 1.04 MTTLOI at 66.7J respectively, Second Generation BP devices deliver a default output of a circa 2.4 MTTLOI at 83J, (83J ÷ 73J =) 1.13 times the EO of SW at maximum stimulus and (83J ÷ 67J =) 1.2 times the EO of SW at true minimum stimulus. Third Generation BP devices deliver a default output of a circa 5.0 MTTLOI at 167J. (167J ÷ 73J =) 2.28 times the EO of SW at maximum and probable minimum stimulus, and (167J ÷ 67J =) 2.49 times the EO of SW at true minimum stimulus. Fourth Generation BP devices deliver a default output of a circa 10.0 MTTLOI at 332J, (332J ÷ 73J =) 4.54 times the EO of SW at maximum stimulus and (332J ÷ 67J =) 4.95 times the EO of SW at true minimum stimulus. Finally, Fifth Generation BP devices deliver a circa 12.0 MTTLOI at 432J, (432J ÷ 73J =) 5.91 times the EO of SW at maximum and probable minimum stimulus and (432J ÷ 67J =) 6.45 times the EO of SW at true minimum stimulus in this same age category. Thus, while the Second Generation BP device is more powerful and more dangerous than SW at minimum, probable minimum, and maximum SW settings in this age category, third, fourth, and fifth generation BP devices are exceedingly more dangerous than SW in this age category at maximum, probable minimum, and minimum SW settings. Once again, only the First generation MECTA "C" BP device is an improvement over SW set at minimal, probable minimal, and maximal stimulus settings. Finally, while all BP devices induce adequate seizure, the MECTA "C" does so at (39J ÷ 83J =) 47% the EO of second generation BP devices, (39J ÷ 167J =) 23% the EO of third generation BP devices, (39J ÷ 332J =) 11.7% the EO of fourth generation BP devices, and (39J ÷ 442J =) 8.8% the EO of theoretical, but "legal" fifth generation BP devices. Not surprisingly, as we have noted, Second, Third, Fourth, and Fifth generation BP devices are no longer "ECT" devices at all, and so have lost their Brief Pulse advantage over SW. Only the First Generation MECTA "C" BP device delivers adequate seizures at a reduced EO compared to SW at minimal, probable minimal, and maximum SW settings so only the First Generation MECTA "C" BP Device is an improvement over SW by virtue of reduced EO in this age category. Finally, only the MECTA "C" induces adequate seizures in every age category at minimal stimulus output with BL ECT in accordance with the 1982 APA Standard.

50 Year Old Recipients:

SW easily has enough power at maximum settings to surpass threshold and so seize recipients at 50 years of age. For 50 year old SW recipients, maximum <u>Threshold Output</u> for SW is about 48.7J, while the B-24 SW device at maximum power can emit about 83.77 Joules, approaching twice threshold. In short, in the 50 year old age category, SW at <u>maximum power</u> (which is also the probable minimal stimulus for SW), delivers a

(83.77J ÷ 48.7J =) 1.72 MTTLOI or about 172% of that required to reach Threshold--easily enough to induce seizure with BL ECT. Set for true minimal stimulus (if possible), SW may be able to deliver about 45J with respect to a 41.5J Minimum Threshold Output, that is, a (45J ÷ 41.5J =) 1.08 MTTLOI. On the other hand, In that Medcraft appears to value efficacy over safety, it is highly unlikely that the B-24 emits true minimal stimulus even for SW. Compare these outputs to modern day BP devices. In sum: the 50 year old age category for both SW and BP is as follows:

The B-24 SW Device (at max) delivers a 1.72 MTTLOI at about 83.77J:

The B-24 SW Device (at prob min) delivers a 1.72 MTTLOI at about 83.77J [255]

The B-24 SW Device (at true min) delivers a 1.08 MTTLOI at about 45.0J

First Generation BP Devices: deliver a circa: 1.08 MTTLOI at about 27J.

Second Generation BP Devices deliver circa: 2.3-2.5 MTTLOI at about 58J.

Third Generation BP Devices deliver a circa: 5.0 MTTLOI at about 115J.

Fourth generation BP Devices deliver a circa : 10.0 MTTLOI at about 230J

Fifth generation BP Devices deliver a circa : 12.0 MTTLOI at about 300J

In the 50 year old category at maximum and probable minimum SW power (which merge), the First generation MECTA "C" BP device delivering a consistent at 1.08 MTTLOI at a default 27J is not only far less dangerous than SW set at maximum (and probable minimum) output delivering a 1.72 MTTLOI at 83.77J, but the MECTA "C" also induces less EO than SW even at true minimum stimulus settings (if such a setting is even possible) of about a 1.08 MTTLOI or 45J in this age category. In short, unlike four generations of successive BP devices, only the First Generation MECTA "C" BP device delivers a similar 1.08 MTTLOI, but at a reduced 27 joules even compared to true minimal stimulus SW settings which may deliver 45J in this age category. Indeed, SW, even at true minimal stimulus settings, yet delivers about (45J ÷ 27J =) 1.67 times the power of the of the First Generation MECTA "C" BP device in this same age category while at maximum (and probable minimum) SW settings (which have merged), SW delivers (83.77J ÷ 27J =) 3.1 times the power of the MECTA "C" in this same age category. Of the second, third, fourth and fifth generation BP devices, only the Second generation BP device delivers less power than SW at maximum (and probable minimum) stimulus, while the remaining Third, Fourth, and Fifth generation BP devices all deliver more power and at a greater MTTLOI than SW at minimum, probable minimum, and maximum SW settings in this, the 50 year old age category. In short, only the First generation MECTA "C" BP device is an improvement over SW set for true minimal stimulus in this age category and only the First and Second generation BP devices are less dangerous than SW set at maximum (and probable minimum) SW settings.

Specifically, compared to the maximum and probable minimum SW setting of a 1.72 MTTLOI at 83.77J and true minimum SW settings of a 1.08 MTTLOI at 45J in the fifty year old age category, SW at maximum (and probable minimal) stimulus delivers (83.77J ÷ 58J =) 1.44 times the EO emitted by the second generation BP device, while the second generation BP device delivers (58J ÷ 45J =) 1.3 times the EO emitted by SW set for true minimum stimulus (if such settings are possible) in this same age category. Third Generation BP devices deliver a default circa 5.0 MTTLOI at 115J or (115J ÷ 84J =) 1.36 times the EO of SW set for maximum (and probable minimum) stimulus in this age category, and (115J ÷ 45J =) 2.56 times the EO of SW set for true minimum stimulus (if such settings are possible) in this age category. Fourth Generation BP devices deliver a default 10.0 MTTLOI at 230J or (230J ÷ 84J =) 2.74 times the EO of SW set for maximum (and probable minimal) stimulus and (230J ÷ 45J =) 5.11 times the EO of SW set for true minimal stimulus (if such settings

[255] Here, we must accept maximum output as the default output for "probable minimum stimulus." In essence, minimum and maximum have merged.

are possible) in this age category. Finally, hypothetical, but "legal Fifth Generation BP devices deliver a circa 12.0 MTTLOI at 300J or (300J ÷ 84 =) 3.57 times the EO of SW set at maximum (and probable minimum) stimulus and (300J ÷ 45J =) 6.67 times the EO of SW set at true minimum stimulus (if such settings are possible) in this same age category.

Thus, while the Second Generation BP device is slightly less powerful and thus slightly less dangerous than SW at maximum (and probable minimum) SW settings in the 50 year old age category, the Second Generation BP device is yet more dangerous than SW set for true minimal stimulus (if such settings are possible) in the 50 year old age category. Third, Fourth, and Fifth generation BP devices are more powerful and thus more dangerous than SW at maximum, probable minimum, and true minimum SW settings in this age category. In sum, only the first and second generation BP devices emit less power than SW at maximum and probable minimum) SW settings, while only the First Generation BP device delivers reduced EO compared to both true minimal, probable minimal, and maximal SW settings.

Once again, while all BP devices can induce seizure in this age category, the MECTA "C" induces adequate seizure at (27J ÷ 58J =) 47% the EO of second generation BP devices, (27J ÷ 115J =) 23.5% the EO of third generation BP devices, (27J ÷ 230J =) 11.7% the EO of fourth generation BP devices, and (27J ÷ 300J =) 9% the EO of theoretical, but "legal" fifth generation BP devices.

Not surprisingly, as we have noted, Second, Third, Fourth, and Fifth generation BP devices are no longer "ECT" devices at all, and so have generally lost their Brief Pulse advantage over SW in this and most other age categories. Only the First Generation MECTA "C" BP Device is an improvement over SW by virtue of reduced EO at maximum, probable minimum, and minimum SW settings in this age category. Unsurprisingly then, only the MECTA "C" adheres to the 1982 APA Standard approved by the Utah Biomedical Test Laboratory originally condoned by the FDA around 1982. In sum, it is only the First generation MECTA "C" BP device which can be deemed a true ECT device and thus an overall improvement over SW in the 50 year old age category by virtue of its capacity to induce adequate grand mal seizures with reduced minimal stimulus EO compared to SW.

40 Year Old Recipients:

As we regress in age, SW becomes more and more powerful, as we have seen. Thus, SW easily has enough power to surpass threshold and so seize recipients at 40 years of age. For 40 year old SW recipients, Threshold Output is about 35.7J while the B-24 SW device at maximum power can emit a maximum of about 98 Joules of Cumulative Output, or 2.75 fold threshold. In short, in the 40 year old age category, SW at maximum power delivers a (98J ÷ 35.7J =) 2.75 MTTLOI or about 275% of that required to reach Threshold--easily enough to induce seizure with BL "ECT." Set for minimal stimulus, SW might be made to deliver about 33J with respect to a 26J Minimum Threshold Output, that is, a (33.35J ÷ 26J =) 1.28 MTTLOI at about 33.35J. This is unlikely however, in that Medcraft appears to be more interested in efficacy than safety (with respect to minimal stimulus outputs). Indeed, there is reason to believe, based on the Medcraft B-25, that the B-24 cannot emit less than 63J in this age category at a 2.43 MTTLOI. Compare this to modern day BP devices. In sum: the 40 year old age category for both SW and BP is as follows:

The B-24 SW Device (at max) delivers a 2.75 MTTLOI at about 98J:

The B-24 SW Device (at prob min) delivers a 2.43 MTTLOI at about 63.0J

The B-24 SW Device (at true min) delivers a 1.28 MTTLOI at about 33.35J

First Generation BP Devices: deliver a circa: 1.08 MTTLOI at about 17.28J.

Second Generation BP Devices deliver a: 2.3-2.5 MTTLOI at about 37J.

Third Generation BP Devices deliver a circa: 5.0 MTTLOI at about 74J.

Fourth generation BP Devices deliver a circa : 10.0 MTTLOI at about 147J

Fifth generation BP Devices deliver a circa : 12.0 MTTLOI at about 192J

In the 40 year old category, at maximum SW power, the First Generation MECTA "C" BP device, as expected, again uses far less power to deliver a consistent 1.08 just above threshold MTTLOI compared to SW at maximum output which can deliver an almost 3.0 MTTLOI at about (98J ÷ 17.28J =) 5.5 times the EO of the MECTA "C" BP device. Indeed, counterintuitively, SW power and MTTLOI increases with decreasing age on SW devices.[256] But even at true SW minimal stimulus (if possible), the B-24 uses almost (33.35J ÷ 17.28J = 1.93) twice the EO of the First generation MECTA "C" BP device. Without doubt, the First Generation BP device (the MECTA "C") is a vast improvement over SW even at true minimal stimulus SW settings (if this setting is possible for the B-24) in this age category. Moreover, the MECTA "C" is certainly an improvement over probable minimum stimulus output with SW in this age category by a factor of (63J ÷ 17.28J =) 3.65.

The default output of Second generation BP devices is also an improvement over SW at maximum output settings in the 40 year old age category, emitting a slightly lower MTTLOI (BP-2.4 vs SW-2.75) but at a much lower EO (BP 37J vs SW-98J) than maximum output SW. Indeed the SW device at maximum output emits (98J ÷ 37J =) 2.65 times the EO of the second generation BP device. On the other hand, at true minimal stimulus SW settings, both the MTTLOI (BP-2.4 vs SW-1.28) and the default output (BP-37J vs SW-33.35J) of Second Generation BP devices are higher in this age category and thus no longer advantageous to SW (set at minimal stimulus). Only the MECTA "C" is an improvement. Finally, compared to probable minimum SW in this age category of a 2.43 MTTLOI at 63J, the second generation BP device emits a similar 2.3 to 2.5 MTTLOI at about 37J or about (37J ÷ 63J =) 59% the power of SW.

The Third Generation BP devices almost double the MTTLOI of SW even at maximum SW output in this age category (BP-5.0 vs SW-2.75), but now even the Third Generation BP device delivers a lower default 74J output as opposed to 98J delivered by SW at maximum SW settings. Indeed SW at maximum output in this age category delivers about (98J ÷ 78J =) 1.26 times the EO of Third generation BP devices. Set for probable minimal stimulus of a 2.43 MTTLOI at 63J, however, SW is less powerful than third generation BP devices at a 5.0 MTTLOI at 74J. On the other hand, SW set for true minimal stimulus (if this is possible) in this age category, the Third generation BP device delivers a default output roughly 4.0 times the MTTLOI of SW (BP-5.0 ÷ SW- 1.28 = 3.9) and more than twice (BP-74J ÷ SW-33.35J = 2.21) the EO of SW. In any case, the Third generation BP device has lost its reduced EO advantage over SW generally, in this age category.

The default output of the Fourth Generation BP device emits a MTTLOI more than (BP-10-MTTLOI ÷ SW-2.75-MTTLOI =) 3.5 times that of SW even at maximum SW output as well as a default EO (147J ÷ 98J =) 1.5 times the maximum EO of SW in this, the 40 year old age category. At probable minimal stimulus, SW delivers a 2.43 MTTLOI at 63J compared to a 10 MTTLOI at 147J for the super powerful Fourth generation BP device, making the Fourth generation BP device (10 ÷ 2.43 =) 4.1 times as powerful with respect to MTTLOI and (147J ÷ 63J =) 2.3 times as powerful as SW with respect to EO in this age category. Not surprisingly, at true minimum SW settings (if this is possible) in this age category, the Fourth generation BP device delivers a default output roughly (BP-10.0 ÷ SW- 1.28 = 7.8) 8.0 times the MTTLOI of SW (BP-10.0 ÷ SW- 1.28 = 7.8) and almost (BP-147J ÷ SW-33.35J =) 4.4 times the EO of SW. Plainly, the fourth generation BP device has lost Its reduced EO advantage over SW in the 40 year old category.

Finally, even at maximum SW settings, the Fifth Generation BP Device more than (BP-12.0 ÷ SW-2.75 = 4.36) quadruples the MTTLOI of SW in this age category at almost (192J ÷ 98J = 1.96) twice the EO even at maximum SW settings. Not surprisingly, at true minimal stimulus SW settings (if this is possible), the Fifth generation BP device delivers a default output more than (BP--12.0 ÷ SW--1.28 = 10.72) 10 times the MTTLOI of SW and almost (192J ÷ 33.35J = 5.75) six times the EO of SW. At the more probable minimal stimulus for SW in this age category, the super powerful fifth generation BP device emits almost (12 ÷ 2.43 = 4.9) five times the MTTLOI of SW and more than (192J ÷ 63J =) 3 times the EO of SW in this age category.

In sum, because SW becomes more and more powerful the younger the recipient, now only the Fourth and Fifth generation BP devices are more powerful and more dangerous than SW set for maximum SW settings in this, the forty year old age category while at probable minimal stimulus, the third, fourth, and fifth generation

---

[256] Because Threshold for SW is higher than Threshold for BP, in comparing SW to BP, the important figure is actually raw EO, not MTTLOI.

BP devices are more powerful. In short, because SW becomes potentially more and more dangerous the younger the recipient, not only the first, but even the powerful second, and third generation BP devices emit less default power than SW at maximum SW settings. On the other hand, the Second, Third, Fourth, and Fifth generation BP devices deliver more EO and are thus more dangerous than SW set at either true minimal stimulus (if this is possible) or probable minimal stimulus output in this age category. No longer "ECT" devices at all, the later BP devices have lost their Brief Pulse advantage over SW generally, in this and most other age categories.

It is only the First Generation MECTA "C" BP device which can be said to be an improvement over SW at both minimum, probable minimum, and maximum SW settings delivering reduced EO compared to both minimal and maximal SW settings in this age category. Unsurprisingly, it is the MECTA "C" alone which adheres to the 1982 APA Standard approved by the Utah Biomedical Test Laboratory condoned by the FDA and so the MECTA "C" alone which remains an overall improvement over SW in the 40 year old age category by virtue of reduced EO. Moreover, the MECTA "C" induces adequate seizures at much lower EO than all four subsequent BP devices at (17.28J ÷ 37J =) 47% the EO of second generation BP devices, (17.28J ÷ 74J =) 23% the EO of third generation BP devices, (17.28J ÷ 147J =) 11.8% the EO of fourth generation BP devices, and (17.28J ÷ 192J =) 9% the EO of theoretical fifth generation BP devices. Unfortunately, as is evidenced by more and more powerful BP device generations, simple induction of the adequate seizure does not equal efficacy.

30 Year Old Recipients:

In this even younger age category, SW easily has enough power to surpass threshold and so seize recipients at 30 years of age. For 30 year old B-24 SW recipients, Maximum Threshold Output is about 24.7J while the B-24 SW device at maximum power can emit about 118 Joules, about 4.78 fold threshold (MTTLOI). In short, in the 30 year old age category, SW at maximum power delivers a (118J ÷ 24.7J =) 4.78 MTTLOI or about 478% of that required to reach Threshold--much more than enough to induce seizure using BL ECT. Set for probable minimal stimulus, the B-24 emits a 3.22 MTTLOI at about 53J in this age category. Set for (an unlikely) true minimal stimulus, SW can theoretically deliver about 19J with respect to a 16.4J Minimum Threshold Output, that is, a circa (19J ÷ 16.4J =) 1.15 MTTLOI at about 19J. Compare this to modern day BP devices. In sum: the 30 year old age category for both SW and BP is as follows:

The B-24 SW Device (at max) delivers a 4.78 MTTLOI at about 118J:

The B-24 SW Device (at prob min) delivers a 3.22 MTTLOI at about 53.0J

The B-24 SW Device (at true min) delivers a 1.15 MTTLOI at about 19.0J

First Generation BP Devices: deliver a circa: 1.08 MTTLOI at about 9.72J.

Second Generation BP Devices deliver a: 2.3-2.5 MTTLOI at about 21J.

Third Generation BP Devices deliver a circa: 5.0 MTTLOI at about 41J.

Fourth generation BP Devices deliver a circa : 10.0 MTTLOI at about 83J

Fifth generation BP Devices deliver a circa : 12.0 MTTLOI at about 108J

In the 30 year old category, at maximum SW power, the First Generation MECTA "C" BP device, as expected, once again uses far less power (9.72J) to deliver a consistent 1.08 just above threshold MTTLOI compared to SW which can deliver a 4.78 MTTLOI at 118J, about (118J ÷ 9.72 =) 12 times the EO of the MECTA "C" in this age category. Even when we theoretically set the SW device for an unlikely true minimal stimulus with SW at 19J in this age category, the default 9.72J output emitted by the First generation MECTA

"C" yet delivers (9.72J ÷ 19J = 51%) half the output of the SW device. In short, while the MTTLOI of SW theoretically set at true minimal stimulus is similar to the MTTLOI of the MECTA "C" (BP-1.08; SW-1.15), the MECTA "C" yet induces adequate seizure at half the EO of SW and so is yet a vast improvement over SW with respect to reduced EO. At the more probable SW minimal stimulus of 53J at a 3.22 MTTLOI, SW delivers almost (3.22 ÷ 1.08 = 2.98) three times the MTTLOI and almost (53J ÷ 9.72J = 5.45) six times the EO of the MECTA "C." In the thirty year old age category, then, the MECTA "C" is a great improvement over SW with respect to reduced power at maximum, probable minimum, and even true minimal stimulus output for SW.

Due to the increasing power of SW in the younger age categories, even powerful Second generation BP devices are an improvement over SW set at maximum output in this age category. Second generation BP devices emit a lower more consistent MTTLOI (of 2.3 to 2.5) compared to SW's 4.78 MTTLOI at a much lower 21J EO compared to SW's 118J. However, when SW is theoretically set at true minimum output for SW (if this is possible), the Second Generation BP Device fails to remain an improvement over SW regarding either MTTLOI (SW-MTTLOI-1.15 vs BP-MTTLOI-2.4) or reduced EO (SW-19J vs BP-21J) delivering just slightly more EO than SW. At the more probable minimal stimulus SW settings, however, the second generation BP device at a 2.4 MTTLOI emitting 21J in this age category is yet less dangerous than SW at a 3.22 MTTLOI and a 53J EO. Indeed SW is so powerful in this age category that even probable minimal stimulus SW surpasses the MTTLOI of the second generation BP device by (3.22 ÷ 2.4 =) 1.43 fold and the EO of the second generation BP device in this age category by (53J ÷ 21J =) 2.5 fold.

Powerful Third Generation BP devices emit a similar 5.0 MTTLOI compared to the 4.78 MTTLOI of SW even set at maximum output in this age category, but because SW becomes more powerful the younger the recipient, SW set at maximum output is so powerful in this age category, it delivers about (118J ÷ 41J =) 2.87 times the EO of even the Third Generation BP device. On the other hand, set at an improbable true minimal stimulus, SW theoretically delivers less than a (1.15 ÷ 5 = 23%) quarter the MTTLOI and less than (19J ÷ 41J = 46%) half the EO of the Third Generation BP device in this same thirty year old age category. At the more probable SW minimal stimulus, however, while the B-24 emits a lower 3.22 MTTLOI compared to the circa 5.0 MTTLOI of the Third generation BP device, the powerful B-24 emits 53J compared to 41J emitted by even the third generation BP device.

Although the powerful Fourth Generation BP device emits a default circa 10 MTTLOI, more than (10 ÷ 4.78 = 2.09), twice that of SW at a 4.78 MTTLOI, SW is so powerful in the thirty year old age category that even the Fourth Generation BP device at 83J delivers only about (83J ÷ 118J =) 70% the 118J delivered by SW set for maximum output in this age category. On the other hand, when SW is set to a theoretical true minimal stimulus output, the default output of the powerful Fourth Generation BP device emits almost (10 ÷ 1.15 = 8.7) 9.0 fold the MTTLOI of SW and more than (83J ÷ 19J = 4.37) 4.0 fold the EO of SW. Even set to the more probable SW minimal stimulus, the super powerful Fourth generation BP device emits a MTTLOI more than (10 ÷ 3.22 = 3.1) threefold that of SW, and an EO more than (83J ÷ 53J = 1.56) one and half times that of SW. While SW at maximum output is more dangerous than even the Fourth generation BP device in this age category, then, the powerful Fourth generation BP device is somewhat more dangerous than SW set for probable minimal stimulus. While SW at maximum output surpasses even the powerful Fourth generation BP device in this age category, it is fair to say both SW and BP are dangerous ENR devices in this age category. Certainly, the Fourth generation BP device has lost its reduced EO advantage generally, in this and all other age categories.

Finally, while the Fifth Generation BP Device emits a default 12 MTTLOI, about (12 ÷ 4.78 =) 2.5 fold the 4.78 MTTLOI of SW even at maximum SW settings, the extremely powerful SW device in this age category delivers a 118J EO, slightly higher than the 108 joules delivered by the extremely powerful Fifth Generation BP Device in this same age category. On the other hand, if SW could be set to a hypothetical minimal stimulus for SW, the default output of the Fifth Generation BP device would emit more than (12.0 ÷ 1.15 = 10.04) 10.0 fold the MTTLOI of SW and more than (108J ÷ 19J = 5.6) 5.0 fold the EO of SW in this age category. Even set for the higher, much more probable minimal stimulus settings with SW in this age category, the powerful Fifth generation BP device yet emits (12 ÷ 3.22 =) 3.73 fold the MTTLOI of SW and more than (108J ÷ 53J = 2.03) twice the EO of SW. Needless to say, that although SW is a powerful and dangerous ENR device in this age category, particularly at maximum output, the Fifth generation BP device is also a powerful and dangerous ENR device in this age category. Without question, the Fifth generation BP device has totally lost its reduced output advantage.

In sum, while we might conclude that all five Brief Pulse Device Generations are "safer" than SW set at maximum output in this, the thirty year old age category, this is due to the unacceptably high output potential of SW in the younger age categories. Certainly, we cannot call the Fifth generation BP device “safe” in this or any other age category. In fact, compared to both improbable and probable minimal stimulus settings with SW, the default outputs of the Second, Third, Fourth, and Fifth Generation BP devices are clearly more dangerous than SW even in this 30 year old age category. This is because just like SW, the Second, Third, Fourth, and Fifth Generation BP devices are no longer "ECT" devices at all, that is, no longer minimal stimulus instruments, all clearly having lost their BP advantage generally with respect to the induction of adequate seizures with reduced or minimal stimulus output.

Indeed, only the First generation BP Device, i.e. the MECTA "C" remains superior to SW with respect to safety by virtue of its capacity to induce adequate seizures at reduced EO compared to SW set for improbable or probable minimal stimulus output in this age category. Thus, only the First Generation MECTA "C" Brief Pulse device remains an improvement over SW with respect to reduced EO at both minimal and maximal SW settings. Moreover, while all five generation of BP can induce adequate seizures in this age category, the MECTA C does so at (9.72J ÷ 21J =) 46% the EO delivered by second generation BP devices, (9.72J ÷ 41J =) 24% the EO delivered by third generation BP devices, (9.72J ÷ 83J =) 11.7% the EO delivered by fourth generation BP devices, and (9.72J ÷ 108J =) 9% the EO delivered by theoretical fifth generation BP devices. It is no mystery why only the MECTA "C" conforms to the 1982 APA Standard condoned by the FDA. Unfortunately, as is substantiated by subsequent BP generations of adequate electricity devices, the MECTA "C" adequate convulsion or true ECT device, does not reflect efficacy.

24 Year Old Recipients:

Because SW becomes more and more powerful the younger the recipient, SW easily has enough power to surpass threshold and so seize recipients at 24 years of age. For 24 year old SW recipients, Threshold Output is about 19J while the B-24 SW device at maximum power can emit 134.42 Joules in this age category, about 7.07 fold threshold. In short, in the 24 year old age category, SW at maximum power delivers a (134.42J ÷ 19J =) 7.07 MTTLOI or about 707% that required to reach Threshold--much more than enough to induce seizure with BL placement. Set for an improbable minimal stimulus, SW may be able to deliver about 15J with respect to a 13.56J minimum Threshold Output, that is, a 1.11 MTTLOI (15.06J ÷13.56J = 1.11) at about 15.06J. On the other hand, set for the higher, more probable minimal stimulus settings for SW in this age category, the B-24 may deliver a minimum 3.96 MTTLOI and a minimum 48J in this age category. Compare this to modern day BP devices. In sum: the 24 year old age category for both SW and BP is as follows:

The B-24 SW Device (at max) delivers a 7.07 MTTLOI at about 134.42J:

The B-24 SW Device (at prob min) delivers a 3.96 MTTLOI at about 48.0J

The B-24 SW Device (at true min) delivers a 1.11 MTTLOI at about 15.06J

First Generation BP Devices: deliver a circa: 1.08 MTTLOI at about 7J.

Second Generation BP Devices deliver a: 2.3-2.5 MTTLOI at about 14.5J.

Third Generation BP Devices deliver a circa: 5.0 MTTLOI at about 30J.

Fourth generation BP Devices deliver a circa : 10.0 MTTLOI at about 60J

Fifth generation BP Devices deliver a circa : 12.0 MTTLOI at about 78J

In the 24 year old category, the First Generation MECTA "C" BP device delivers a consistent just above threshold 1.08 MTTLOI at 7J compared to SW at maximum output which can deliver a more than 7.0 MTTLOI at 134J, almost (134J ÷ 7J = 19.14) twenty times the EO of the First Generation MECTA "C" BP device in this specific age category. Even if SW could be set for an improbable minimal stimulus of a 1.11 MTTLOI at circa 15J, the MECTA "C" Brief Pulse device still proves superior in delivering about the same MTTLOI (1.08 compared to 1.11), but at about 7J, less than half (7.0J ÷ 15.06J = 46%) the EO of SW. At the more probable 3.96 MTTLOI and 48J minimal stimulus settings for SW in this age category, SW yet delivers (3.96 ÷ 1.08 =) 3.66 fold the MTTLOI and (48J ÷ 7J =) 6.86 fold the EO delivered by the MECTA "C." The First Generation MECTA "C" BP device, therefore, is certainly a great improvement over SW by virtue of reduced EO in this age category, even when SW is set for both improbable "true minimal stimulus output" and the much more probable higher minimal stimulus in this age category.

Due to the great power of SW in the younger age categories, not surprisingly, second generation BP devices are also an improvement over SW set for maximum output in this age category, emitting a relatively lower and much more consistent circa 2.4 MTTLOI compared to SW's 7.07 MTTLOI, almost (7.07 ÷ 2.5 = 2.8) three times that of the second generation BP device. Moreover, SW at maximum output is so powerful in this age category, that at 134J, SW delivers more than (134J ÷ 14.5J = 9.24) nine times the EO of the second generation Brief Pulse device. Even if SW could be set to an improbable true SW minimal stimulus in this age category, SW at 15J compared to the Second Generation BP device at 14.6J would yet be about equally dangerous in this age category in spite of the second generation BP device evincing (2.1 ÷ 1.1 = 1.9) twice the MTTLOI as SW. Regarding much more probable minimal stimulus SW settings, SW is so powerful in this age category that it yet emits a 3.96 MTTLOI as opposed to a 2.4 MTTLOI or about (3.96 ÷ 2.4 =) 1.65 fold the MTTLOI of the second generation BP device. Moreover, the much more probable minimal stimulus settings of SW yet emit about (48J ÷ 14.5J =) 3.3 times the default output of the second generation BP device in the 24 year old age category. Clearly, the SW device in this age category emits inordinate power both at maximum and probable minimal stimulus compared to even the second generation BP device. Even so, neither the SW device nor the Second generation BP device is any longer an ECT device in this age category. Plainly, both are powerful ENR devices depending upon electricity in lieu of adequate convulsion.

Even Third Generation BP devices in the 24 year old age category emitting 30J at a default circa 5.0 MTTLOI are weaker than the inordinate 134J at a 7.07 MTTLOI emitted by SW at maximum output. As powerful as the third generation BP device is, it emits only about (30J ÷ 134J =) 22% the EO emitted by SW at maximum output in this age category. On the other hand, compared to an improbable true minimal stimulus SW output in this same age category, the Third Generation BP device would yet deliver almost (5 ÷ 1.1 = 4.5) 5.0 times the MTTLOI and almost (30J ÷ 15.06J = circa 2.0) twice the EO of SW. But this is almost certainly not allowed by Medcraft. Compared to the most probable minimal stimulus SW settings of 48J at a 3.96 MTTLOI, SW is so powerful in this age category that even the third generation BP device delivers a lower circa 30J output although at a circa 5.0 MTTLOI, dangerous, but less dangerous than SW in this age category. There is no question that neither the SW device nor the third generation BP device can be deemed ECT devices in this age category. Both are clearly ENR devices, neither of which is any longer convulsion dependent, but clearly electro-dependent mechanisms.

The Fourth Generation BP device emits a default circa 10.0 MTTLOI compared to a 7.07 MTTLOI of SW set at maximum output in this age category, about one and a half times greater than SW (10 ÷ 7.07 = 1.41). On the other hand, due to the increasing power of SW as age decreases and so the awesome power of SW in this age category, even the 60J delivered by the Fourth generation BP device is less than (60J ÷ 134J = 44.7%) half the 134J Energy Output delivered by SW set for maximum output in this age class. If SW could be set to true minimal stimulus for SW in this same age category, of course, the powerful Fourth Generation BP device at a circa 10 MTTLOI compared to the very improbable 1.11 MTTLOI of SW, would deliver a default MTTLOI 9 times that (10 ÷ 1.11 = 9 MTTLOI) of SW and about (60J ÷ 15.06J = 3.98) four times the EO of SW. Even set for the much more probable minimal stimulus most likely allowed by Medcraft, moreover, the powerful fourth generation BP device at a circa 10 MTTLOI and 60J EO in this age category surpasses the power of SW at a 3.96 MTTLOI by a factor of (10 ÷ 3.96 =) 2.52 due to inverse exploitation. SW, in this age category, on the other hand, is so powerful in this age category, that the even the powerful Fourth generation BP device only surpasses the 48J EO delivered by SW at probable minimal stimulus by a factor of (60J ÷48J =) 1.25. Thus, while the Fourth generation BP device may be less dangerous than the awesome power of SW set for maximum output in this age category, the Fourth Generation BP device is only slightly more dangerous than SW set for probable minimal stimulus. In short, due to the enhanced power of both SW and Brief Pulse in this age category and the adequate electricity premise, both the SW and the Fourth generation BP device have lost all semblance of minimal stimulus or safety. Clearly, both are dangerous and injurious ENR devices striving to make their devices "effective" at the expense of safety in the 24 year old age category.

Finally, the unimaginably powerful Fifth Generation BP device emits a default 12.0 MTTLOI, about (12 ÷ 7.07 = 1.69) one and a half times the super-powerful 7.07 MTTLOI of SW even set at maximum SW output in this age category. But again, due to the increasingly dangerous power of SW as age decreases, even the 78J emitted by the Fifth generation BP device in this age group, is only about (78J ÷ 134J = 58.2%) 60% the 134J Energy Output emitted by SW at maximum output. Not surprisingly, on the other hand, compared to a highly improbable true minimal stimulus output for SW in this same 24 year old age category, the incorrigibly powerful circa 12 MTTLOI, 78J default output of the Fifth Generation BP device in this age category would deliver almost (12 ÷ 1.11 = 10.8) eleven times the 1.11 MTTLOI and (78J ÷ 15.06J = 5.12) five times the 15.06J delivered by SW. Of course, true minimal stimulus even for SW is almost certainly not allowed by Medcraft in this age category. Most probably, SW minimal stimulus in this age category (based on the B-25 by Medcraft) delivers a much higher 3.96 MTTLOI at about 48J compared to which the supra powerful Fifth generation BP device yet delivers a 12.0 MTTLOI at 78J in this age category, (12 ÷ 3.96 =) 3.03 times the MTTLOI of SW but only (78J ÷ 48J =) 1.6 times the EO of SW at probable minimal stimulus. Not surprisingly, then, while the Fifth generation BP device has obviously lost its BP reduced EO advantage over SW in this age category, both the powerful B-24 SW and the fifth generation BP device are clearly ENR devices, relying on injurious doses of electricity to make their procedures "work."

In sum, due to SW's astoundingly unregulated power in the younger age categories, all five BP device generations are an improvement over SW set at maximum output in the 24 year old age category. When SW is set to an improbable true minimal stimulus for SW in this same age category, however, the Second Generation BP device fails to be an improvement over SW with respect to reduced EO while the third, fourth, and fifth generation BP devices are decidedly more dangerous than SW. When SW is set to probable minimal stimulus for SW in this same age category, moreover, SW remains more powerful than the default outputs emitted by First, Second and third Generation BP devices, while only the fourth and fifth generation BP devices remain decidedly more dangerous than SW. Once again, only the first generation MECTA "C" BP device, the single device in accordance with by the 1982 APA Standard, is a vast improvement over SW in all categories of maximum, minimum, and probable minimum stimulus. Indeed, while all five BP generations induce adequate convulsions in all age categories, the MECTA "C" does so at (7J ÷ 14.5J =) 48% the EO delivered by the second generation BP device in this age category, (7J ÷ 30J =) 23% the EO delivered by the Third Generation BP device in this age category, (7J ÷ 60J =) 11.7% the EO delivered by the Fourth Generation BP device in this age category, and (7J ÷ 78J =) 9% the EO delivered by the theoretical Fifth Generation BP device in this same age category.

Plainly, neither the B-24 SW, nor the Second, Third, Fourth, and Fifth generation BP devices in this age category are any longer "ECT" devices at all, but adequate electricity devices, all of which have lost the advantage of the First Generation MECTA "C" BP Device with respect to the induction of adequate seizures at reduced output. In sum, only the First generation MECTA "C" BP Device remains superior to SW by virtue of inducing adequate seizures with reduced EO in all seizure inducible age categories. Once again, however, as evidenced by the existence of second, third, fourth and fifth generation ENR BP devices as well as the continued existence of the ENR B-24 SW device, adequate seizure does not equal efficacy. Instead, efficacy, whether achieved through Sine Wave or Brief Pulse, requires adequate doses of electricity- outputs inextricably associated in all instances with deliberate brain injury and long term memory morbidity.

20 Year Old Recipients:

SW has more than enough power to surpass threshold and so seize recipients at 20 years of age. For 20 year old SW recipients, Maximum Threshold Output is about 15.7J while the B-24 SW device can emit a maximum output of about 148.2 Joules of Cumulative Output in this age range or about a 9.5 MTTLOI. In short, in the 20 year old age category, SW at maximum power delivers a (148.2 ÷ 15.7J =) 9.44 MTTLOI or about 944% of that required to reach Threshold--again, much more than enough to induce seizure using BL "ECT." Set for a highly improbable true minimal stimulus for SW, SW might be able to deliver about 9.6J with respect to a 9J Minimum Threshold Output, that is, a (9.6J ÷ 9.0J =) 1.06 MTTLOI at about 9.6J. On the other hand, set for the much more probable SW minimal stimulus Medcraft allows, SW emits a 4.7 MTTLOI at about 43J in this age category. Compare this to modern day BP devices. In sum: the 20 year old age category for both SW and BP is as follows:

The B-24 SW Device (at max) delivers a 9.44 MTTLOI at about 148.2:

The B-24 SW Device (at prob min) delivers a 4.7 MTTLOI at about 43.0J

The B-24 SW Device (at true min) delivers a 1.06 MTTLOI at about 9.6J

First Generation BP Devices: deliver a circa: 1.08 MTTLOI at about 4.32J.

Second Generation BP Devices deliver a: 2.3-2.5 MTTLOI at about 9.2J.

Third Generation BP Devices deliver a circa: 5.0 MTTLOI at about 18.5J.

Fourth generation BP Devices deliver a circa : 10.0 MTTLOI at about 37J

Fifth generation BP Devices deliver a circa : 12.0 MTTLOI at about 48J

In the 20 year old category even at a highly unlikely true minimum SW output in this age category, the First Generation MECTA "C" BP device, as expected, uses far less power to deliver a consistent just above threshold 1.08 MTTLOI at 4.2J compared to SW which may be able to deliver a 1.06 MTTLOI at 9.6J, more than (9.6J ÷ 4.32J = 2.22) twice the output of the MECTA "C." Compared to the MECTA C's 1.08 MTTLOI at a default 4.32J, SW at maximum output delivers a 9.5 MTTLOI at 148.2J, almost (9.5 ÷ 1.08 = 8.8) nine times the MTTLOI, and almost (148.2J ÷ 4.32J = 34.3) thirty-five times the EO of the First Generation MECTA "C" BP device in this age category. At the much more probable higher minimal SW output in this age category of a 4.7 MTTLOI at 43J, SW emits more than (4.7 ÷1.08 = 4.35) four fold the MTTLOI and (43J ÷ 4.3J =) 10 times the EO of the First generation MECTA "C." The First Generation BP device is thus a vast improvement over SW at maximum, probable minimum, and even an improbable true minimum SW in this age category with respect to inducing adequate seizures at greatly reduced EO.

Due to the great power of SW in the youngest age categories, even the default outputs of Second generation BP devices are a vast improvement over SW (at maximum output) in this age category, emitting a lower more consistent 2.4 MTTLOI at a much lower EO of about 9.2J compared to the 9.44 MTTLOI and 148.2J maximum EO emitted by the B-24 SW. In short SW at maximum Output in this age category is so powerful that it delivers almost (9.44 ÷ 2.5 = 3.8) four times the MTTLOI and more than (148.2J ÷ 9.2J = 16.1) sixteen times the EO of even second generation BP devices. This is actually not surprising in that SW becomes more and more powerful as age decreases. Even compared to SW set for an improbable true minimum stimulus SW output in this age category, while Second generation BP devices deliver a higher circa 2.4 MTTLOI, they do so at a slightly lower 9.2J compared to SW's 1.06 MTTLOI at 9.6J. Thus, the SW device is so powerful in this age category, that even at a true minimal stimulus SW output, the Second generation BP device emits a slightly lower EO. Moreover, the much more probable minimal stimulus below which the B-24 may not be allowed to go, the SW device may well emit a 4.7 MTTLOI at 43J, circa (4.7 ÷ 2.4 = 1.95) twice the MTTLOI and almost (43J ÷ 9.2J = 4.6) five times the EO of the second generation BP device. Thus, while the Second Generation BP Device is unnecessarily suprathreshold (with respect to induction of the "adequate" seizure), SW has become so powerful in the twenty year old age category that at both maximum and probable minimum, SW elicits more than 16 fold and 4.6 fold respectively the output of the second generation Brief Pulse device.

So powerful is SW at maximum output due to the increasing power of SW with respect to decreasing recipient age, SW at maximum output in the twenty year old age category delivers a 9.44 MTTLOI at 148.2J, almost (9.44 ÷ 5.0 = 1.8) twice the MTTLOI and (148.2 ÷ 18.5 =) 8 times the EO of even third generation BP devices. On the other hand, if SW could be set for an improbable true minimum stimulus for SW in this age category, the powerful Third Generation BP device would deliver its circa 5.0 MTTLOI and 18.5J at (5.0 ÷ 1.06 = 4.71) 5.0 times the MTTLOI of SW and almost (18.5J ÷ 9.6J = 1.92) twice the EO of SW in this age category. However, at the much higher, much more probable minimal stimulus output for SW in this age category of a

4.7 MTTLOI at 43J, the third generation BP device emits about the same 5.0 MTTLOI as SW at a 4.7 MTTLOI but at less than (18.5J ÷ 43 = 43%) half the EO of SW. Thus, SW is so powerful in the twenty year old age category, that even the very powerful Third Generation BP device is less dangerous than SW set for either maximum output or probable minimal stimulus. In short, while the Third generation BP device has clearly lost its reduced EO advantage generally, both SW and the third generation Brief Pulse in this age category are dangerous electro-dependent ENR devices in lieu of convulsion-dependent ECT devices all in order to make the procedure "work."

Again due to the increasing power of SW with respect to decreasing recipient age, SW at maximum output in the twenty year old age category, as we have seen, delivers a 9.44 MTTLOI at 148.2J compared to the circa 10.0 MTTLOI at 37J of even the extremely powerful Fourth Generation BP devices in this age category. In short, while the 9.44 MTTLOI of SW at maximum output in this age category appears equivalent to the circa 10.00 MTTLOI of the Fourth generation BP device, the SW device delivers four times (148.2 ÷ 37J = 4) the EO of even the Fourth generation BP device. This is not surprising given the greater output of SW relative to equivalent MTTLOI, but also to the increasing power of SW, the younger the recipient. Only when SW is set at an improbable true minimal stimulus does the circa 10 MTTLOI of the Fourth Generation BP device surpass the 1.06 MTTLOI of SW by almost (10 ÷ 1.06 = 9.4) 10 fold and the 37J emitted by BP surpass the 9.6J emitted by SW almost (37J ÷ 9.6J = 3.9) four fold in this age category. On the other hand, even at the much more probable minimal stimulus allowed for SW in this age category below which Medcraft may not allow the B-24 to operate, the extremely powerful SW device at a 4.7 MTTLOI, roughly (4.7 ÷ 10 = 47%) half the circa 10.0 MTTLOI of the extremely powerful Fourth generation BP device, yet delivers 43J compared to the 37J delivered by the fourth generation BP device. In short, not only is maximum output via SW in this age category much more dangerous than even the super powerful fourth generation BP device in this same age category, but even at probable minimal stimulus settings, SW delivers more power than the super powerful fourth generation BP device. In sum, the SW device set at maximum output is four times as dangerous as the default output delivered by the Fourth Generation BP Device (148J ÷ 37J = 4.0) in this age category, and SW even at probable minimal stimulus, is slightly more powerful than the Fourth Generation Brief Pulse device. Even so, due to its suprathreshold nature, the Fourth generation BP device has lost its reduced EO advantage generally. Indeed, both SW and BP are dangerous ENR devices in the twenty year old age category.

Once more, due to the increasing power of SW with respect to decreasing recipient age, while the Fifth Generation BP device emits a default circa 12.0 MTTLOI, (12 ÷ 9.44 =) 1.27 times greater than the 9.44 MTTLOI of SW even set for maximum output in this age category, the Fifth generation BP Device delivers its 12.0 MTTLOI at about 48J, or circa (148.2J ÷ 48J = 3.08) one third the 148.2J of SW set for maximum output in this, the twenty year old age category. This is not surprising given the superordinate power of SW in the younger age categories. Only when SW is set at an improbable true minimal stimulus does the super powerful Fifth Generation BP device at a 12.0 MTTLOI deliver more than (12 ÷ 1.06 = 11.3) eleven times the 1.06 MTTLOI of SW at 48J, circa (48J ÷ 9.6J = 5.0) five times the 9.6J EO of SW at true SW minimal stimulus. On the other hand, at the much more probable higher minimal stimulus below which Medcraft may not allow the machine to operate, SW delivers a 4.7 MTTLOI at 43J, compared to the 12.0 fold MTTLOI delivered by the fifth generation BP device at a similar, only slightly higher 48J. Thus, even the Fifth Generation BP Device (at 48J) is less dangerous by a factor of (148J ÷ 48J = 3.08) 3.0 than SW set for maximum output. So powerful is SW in this age category that even SW set for a probable minimal stimulus output of 43J below which Medcraft may not allow the machine to operate, is almost as powerful as the super powerful fifth generation BP device which delivers 48J in this age category. While the suprathreshold nature of the Fifth Generation BP device has clearly lost its reduced output advantage generally, then, both BP and SW in this age category are extremely dangerous ENR devices designed to inflict much deliberate harm (via the reduction of many neuronal connectors). In sum, SW set at maximum output in the twenty year old age category is so powerful that it is three times more dangerous than the default output of even the supra powerful Fifth Generation BP device in the same twenty year old category. Even at probable minimal stimulus settings for SW, moreover, the B-24 remains almost as dangerous the Fifth Generation BP device.

In sum, the MECTA "C" is yet the only true ECT device in the modern era. Unlike SW, while all five BP generations can induce adequate seizures in all age recipients, the MECTA "C" does so at (4.32J ÷ 9.2J =) 47% the EO of the second generation BP device, (4.32 ÷ 18.5J =) 23% the EO of the third generation BP device, (4.32 ÷ 37J =) 11.7% the EO of the fourth generation BP device, and (4.32 ÷ 48J =) 9% the EO of the theoretical fifth generation BP device. Importantly then, neither SW nor the Second, Third, Fourth, and Fifth generation BP devices are "ECT" devices at all. These devices are but dangerous ENR devices designed for "efficacy" alone via adequate doses of electricity. Only the first generation MECTA "C" BP device delivers the minimal stimulus or the just above threshold outputs required under the 1982 APA Standard. Only the MECTA "C" conforms to the 1982 APA Standard approved by the Utah Biomedical Test Laboratory and in turn, FDA. In short, only the MECTA "C" BP device can be labeled ECT. Neither the B-24 SW nor Second, Third, Fourth, and Fifth generation BP devices are ECT devices. Rather they are adequate electricity devices, entirely different in kind and aim. As such, neither the B-24 SW nor Second, Third, Fourth, and Fifth generation BP devices were legally grandfathered in, in that adequate electricity or ENR devices have never been described in the literature, much less submitted for FDA approval.

10 Year Old Recipients:

In this, the youngest age category, SW has more than enough power to surpass threshold and so seize 10 year old recipients. Indeed, it is in this youngest age category that SW is the most potentially powerful and thus the most potentially destructive. For 10 year old SW recipients, Maximum Threshold Output is about 8.7J while the B-24 SW device can emit about 200 Joules at maximum output in this age category, a circa potential (200J ÷ 8.7J =) 23 fold threshold output or 23 MTTLOI. In short, in the youngest age category, SW at maximum power has the capacity to deliver an unconscionable 2300% of that required to reach Threshold--far in excess of that needed to induce seizure using BL "ECT." Ironically, Resistance to electricity diminishes with diminishing age until the ten year old child has almost no Resistance at all to electric current. Set for an improbable true minimal stimulus with SW, SW might be made to deliver about 4.9J with respect to a 4J Minimum Threshold Output, that is, a (4.9J ÷ 4.0J =) 1.23 MTTLOI at about 4.9J. At the much more probable minimum output below which the Medcraft may not allow the machine to operate, however, the B-24 may elicit a more likely 9.0 MTTLOI at about 36J. Compare this to modern day BP devices. In sum: the 10 year old age category for both SW and BP is as follows:

The B-24 SW Device (at max) delivers a 23.00 MTTLOI at about 200J:

The B-24 SW Device (at prob min) delivers a 9.0 MTTLOI at about 36J

The B-24 SW Device (at true min) delivers a 1.23 MTTLOI at about 4.9J

First Generation BP Devices: deliver a circa: 1.08 MTTLOI at about 1.08J.

Second Generation BP Devices deliver a: 2.3-2.5 MTTLOI at about 2.3J.

Third Generation BP Devices deliver a circa: 5.0 MTTLOI at about 4.6J.

Fourth generation BP Devices deliver a circa : 10.0 MTTLOI at about 9.2J

Fifth generation BP Devices deliver a circa : 12.0 MTTLOI at about 15J

In the 10 year old category, the First Generation MECTA "C" BP device uses far less power to deliver a consistent just above threshold 1.08 MTTLOI than SW at maximum power which emits a 23 MTTLOI at 200J, more than (23 ÷1.08 = 21.3) twenty one times the MTTLOI and more than (200J ÷ 1.08J =) 185 times the default EO of the MECTA "C." Even if SW could be set for an improbable true SW minimal stimulus of a 1.23 MTTLOI at 4.9J, the First Generation MECTA "C" BP device yet uses only (1.08 ÷ 4.9J =) 22% the EO emitted by true minimal stimulus SW to induce the same adequate seizure in this age category. Of course, at the much more probable higher minimal stimulus SW output of a 9.0 MTTLOI at 36J, SW delivers a MTTLOI (9.0 ÷1.08 =) 8.33 times the that of the MECTA "C" and (36J ÷ 1.08J =) 33.33 times the EO of the MECTA "C making the

MECTA "C" a vast improvement over SW at maximum, probable minimum, and even an improbable true minimum SW output.

So powerful is SW at maximum output in the ten year old category, delivering a possible 200J output at a possible 23 MTTLOI, that even the Second generation BP device delivering a circa 2.4 MTTLOI and a 2.4J output is far superior to SW in this age category. Indeed, maximum SW output in this age category delivers (23 ÷ 2.4 = 9.5) ten times the MTTLOI and (200J ÷ 2.4J =) 83 fold the EO delivered by the second generation BP device. Set for a probable minimal stimulus output for SW in this age category, SW yet delivers more than (36J ÷ 2.4J =) 15 times the EO and (9 ÷ 2.4 =) 3.75 times the MTTLOI delivered by the powerful second generation BP device. Even set for an improbable 4.9J true minimal stimulus, SW delivers (4.9J ÷ 2.4J = 2.04) twice the EO delivered by the Second generation BP device in this age category.

So potentially powerful is SW in the ten year old category at maximum output delivering a 200J output at a 23 MTTLOI that even Third generation BP devices delivering circa 4.6J at a circa 5.0 MTTLOI are easily less dangerous than SW at this age. Indeed, the powerful Third Generation BP device emits only about (4.6J ÷ 200J =) 2.3% the power of SW set at maximum output in the ten year old age category. Stated differently, the 200J EO potentially delivered by SW at maximum output in the ten year old category is almost 44 times the power (200J ÷ 4.6J = 43.5) and at least (23 ÷ 5 =) 4.6 times the MTTLOI emitted by the Third Generation BP Device in this age category. Even if SW could be set for an improbable true minimal stimulus SW output in the ten year old age category, while the Third Generation BP Device might emit (4.6 ÷ 1.23 =) 3.75 times the MTTLOI, the third generation BP device at 4.6J would deliver slightly less EO than SW at 4.9J. Indeed, at the much more probable minimal stimulus output under which Medcraft may not allow the B-24 in this age category, SW still delivers almost (9.0 ÷ 5.0 = 1.8) twice the MTTLOI and almost (36J ÷ 4.6J = 7.82) eight times the EO of the super powerful third generation BP device in this age category. While the third generation BP device emits about 5.0 times threshold in every age category, SW is so powerful in this age category that BP pales by comparison. Even so, both SW and the second generation BP device are dangerous ENR devices in this age category, SW inordinately so in the ten year old age category.

So potentially powerful is SW in the ten year old category set for maximum output delivering a 200J output at a 23 MTTLOI that even Fourth generation BP devices delivering circa 9.2J at a circa 10.0 MTTLOI are conspicuously less dangerous than SW in this age category. In fact, even the super powerful Fourth Generation emits only about (9.2J ÷ 200J =) 4.6% the power of SW and less than (10 ÷ 23 = 43%) half the MTTLOI of SW set at maximum output in the ten year old age category. In short, the 200J EO delivered by SW at maximum output in the ten year old category is about 22 times the default power (200J ÷ 9.2J = 21.7) of even the super powerful Fourth Generation BP Device. Only if SW could be set at a very improbable true minimal stimulus in this age category, would the Fourth generation BP device deliver (10 ÷ 1.23 =) 8 times the MTTLOI of SW and roughly (9.2J ÷ 4.9J = 1.9) twice the output of SW in this, the ten year old age category. However, at the much more probable minimal stimulus for SW of a 9.0 MTTLOI and a 36J output below which the machine may not be allowed to operate in this age category, SW is yet so powerful that even the supra powerful Fourth generation BP device while emitting about the same MTTLOI (10 vs 9), emits only (9.2 ÷ 36J = 25.5%) one quarter the power of SW in this age category. Plainly, SW is more powerful than even the supra powerful fourth generation BP device in this age category. Nevertheless, both devices are dangerous as both have devolved into brain stultifying electro-dependent ENR devices.

Finally, so potentially powerful is SW in the ten year old category set for maximum output delivering a 200J output at a 23 MTTLOI that even the unconscionably powerful Fifth generation BP devices delivering circa 15J at a circa 12.0 MTTLOI in this age category is much less powerful and so, amazingly enough, much less dangerous than SW. In brief, even the extremely powerful Fifth Generation BP device emits only about (12 ÷ 23 =) 52% the MTTLOI of SW and only about (15J ÷ 200J =) 7.5% the power of SW set at maximum output in the ten year old age category. Indeed, the 200J EO delivered by SW at maximum output in the ten year old category can deliver more than 13 times the default power (200J ÷ 15J = 13.3) of the Fifth Generation BP Device in the ten year old age category. The tremendous power of SW in this age category, as noted, is due to the increasing power of SW in conjunction with decreasing age and Impedance. Only if the SW device could be set for a very improbable true minimal stimulus for SW in this age category could the Fifth generation BP device at a 12 MTTLOI deliver about 10 times (12 ÷ 1.23 = 9.7) the 1.23 MTTLOI and about (15J ÷ 4.9J =) 3.06 times the 4.9J delivered by SW in this age category. On the other hand, based on a very probable 9 MTTLOI at a 36J minimal stimulus output below which Medcraft may not allow the B-24 to operate, SW is so powerful in this age category, that although the fifth generation BP device emits a 12.0 MTLOI compared SW's 9.0

MTTLOI, the SW device nevertheless emits (36J ÷ 15J =) 2.4 times the power of even the supra powerful fifth generation BP device in this age category. Thus, while the Fifth generation BP device, like the second, third, and fourth generation BP devices, has wholly lost its reduced EO advantage generally, it yet pales in comparison to the power of SW in the ten year old age category. In sum, we can say without hesitation that the prodigious power of SW set for maximum output in the ten year old age category is at least (200J ÷ 15J =) 13 times more dangerous than even the Fifth Generation BP device in this same age category while SW set for probable minimal stimulus for SW is yet 2.4 times more dangerous than the prodigious power of the fifth generation BP device. Even so, both SW and Brief Pulse are clearly brain injurious ENR devices in this age category.

What we can conclude from this pattern is that at maximum output, the SW device becomes more and more dangerous, the younger the recipient, indeed, more dangerous in the youngest age category than the most powerful BP device in even the last successive BP device generation. In addition, because neither Brief Pulse nor SW is any longer based on convulsion and so the least amount of electricity possible but rather, both are clearly adequate electricity devices, both BP and SW manufacturers must be aware their machines do injury to the brain in order to make the procedure "effective." Finally, both SW and BP manufacturers have gone to great lengths to keep this paramount truth a secret. Indeed, only the First generation MECTA "C" BP device can induce adequate seizures at half (1.08 ÷2.3J = 47%) the EO of the second generation BP device, a quarter (1.08 ÷ 4.6J = 24%) the EO of the third generation BP device, (1.08 ÷ 9.2J =) 11.7% the EO of the fourth generation BP device, (1.08 ÷15J =) 7.2% the EO of the theoretical fifth generation BP device, as well as half the EO of SW even set for true SW minimal stimulus output in this age category.

Importantly, both SW and Second, Third, Fourth, and Fifth generation BP devices are falsely labeled "ECT" devices. Only the first generation MECTA "C" BP device delivers minimal stimulus or the just above threshold outputs required under the 1982 APA Standard and only the MECTA "C" BP device delivers less EO than SW set for true minimal stimulus in all age categories wherein adequate seizure is inducible. Not surprisingly, as has been noted, only the first generation MECTA "C" amidst other first generation BP devices and certainly amongst all other successive BP generations, conforms to the 1982 APA Standard approved by the Utah Biomedical Test Laboratory and so, the FDA. Clearly, only the MECTA "C" BP device can be deemed an "ECT" device. Conversely, both the B-24 SW and second, third, fourth, and fifth generation BP devices are not ECT, but ENR devices. Clearly, ENR devices are entirely different both in kind and aim than ECT devices. Thus, while the MECTA "C" ECT device was legitimately grandfathered in, in 1976, SW and the 2nd, 3rd, 4th, and 5th generation BP devices were not, in that they are not "ECT" devices. Indeed, no such devices have ever been publicly acknowledged, constructed, or described, much less submitted to FDA for approval. The B-24, in short, was falsely described as an "ECT" device before 1976; whereas, current Brief Pulse devices have all devolved into ENR devices. Not surprisingly, only the MECTA "C" BP device is capable of inducing "adequate seizures" at true minimal stimulus output with BL ECT, and so the only device based on adequate seizure, a fact recognized both by Utah and the FDA in their condonation of the 1982 APA Standard. Quite disappointingly, on the other hand, adequate seizure based devices, that is, ECT devices, clearly do not work.

Extrapolation:

Even though we can see that SW set at maximum parameters is remarkably dangerous for children, adolescents, and recipients between twenty and about forty-five years of age, and even though the most powerful BP devices represent dramatic improvements over maximum SW settings in the younger age population, we cannot say that second, third, fourth, and fifth generation BP devices are safer than SW. Indeed, second, third, fourth, and fifth generation BP devices surpass SW in EO generally, indeed, exponentially in the older age categories. Moreover, second, third, fourth, and fifth generation BP devices are all suprathreshold instruments clearly based on adequate doses of electricity in order to be effective. Only the First Generation MECTA "C" BP device emits lower EO than SW in every age category in which BL seizure is possible. Indeed, only the MECTA "C" emits circa half the output of SW even set for an improbable true minimal stimulus for SW. Indeed, the "C" only surpasses SW set for an improbable minimal stimulus when SW is no longer powerful enough to induce adequate seizures with BL "ECT" (about age 68 and older). We must conclude, as did Utah in 1978, therefore, that only the First generation MECTA "C emitting just above threshold outputs in every age category is capable of reduced Energy Output in every relevant age category compared to SW so that only the

MECTA "C" is an overall improvement over SW by virtue of reduced EO. Not surprisingly, as has been heretofore acknowledged, it is the MECTA "C" BP alone that conforms to the 1982 APA Standard originally recommended by both Utah and the FDA. Critically, any Brief Pulse device conforming to the APA Standard must emit reduced EO compared to SW at all seizure inducible minimal stimulus SW settings and only the MECTA "C" does so. Unfortunately, as noted, this does not mean the MECTA "C" BP device is effective and this is evidenced by the manufacturing of much more powerful, adequate electricity or ENR BP devices to follow, a fact generally unknown by both the FDA and Utah, indeed, never revealed by manufacturers at large. Clearly, second, third, fourth, and fifth generation BP devices have lost their Brief Pulse advantage over SW, generally.[257] Both SW and modern day BP are based on adequate doses of electricity. Thus, both are ENR devices deliberately designed and calibrated to electrically destroy and so diminish neural connectors, particularly in the left prefrontal cortex. While BP is more dangerous than SW in the older age categories, SW is more dangerous than BP in the younger age categories. Revealingly, Weiner's misleading graphs comparing SW to Brief Pulse represents the destructive 200 joules emitted by SW in the ten year old age category at maximum output compared to the circa 100J necessary to induce adequate seizure with Brief Pulse in every age category, criteria to which only the MECTA "C" conforms. Clearly, the much more powerful and so much more destructive second, third, fourth, and fifth generation BP devices are not represented in Weiner's graphs.

---

[257] **"Class I includes devices with the lowest risk and Class III includes those with the greatest risk."** Manufacturers could have had Brief Pulse moved to Class II and even Class I had they abided by the 1982 APA Standard under which only the MECTA "C" conforms. Tellingly, neither Weiner nor manufacturers applied to codify the 1982 APA Standard, soon abandoning the MECTA "C" for much more powerful BP devices.

CHAPTER 85

SW Charts of True Min., Probable Min. and Max. Outputs for All Age Categories

Thanks to the Cameron Paradigm, we can now make SW Charts Containing Maximum Outputs, True Minimum Outputs, and Probable Minimum Outputs with MTTLOIs for all three Categories.

B-24 **SINE WAVE** at **MAXIMUM** SETTINGS for **MAXIMUM** OUTPUTS and **MAXIMUM** MTTLOIs with AGE RELATED THRESHOLD IMPEDANCES and JUST ABOVE THRESHOLD OUTPUTS

AGE	Final Impedance Threshold (Ω)	Threshold Output in Joules	Maximum Output in Joules	MTTLOI
10	145	8.7	200	23
20	195	15.7	148.2	9.44
30	245	24.7	118.0	4.78
40	295	35.7	98.0	2.75
50	345	48.7	83.77	1.72
60	395	63.7	73.16	1.15
65	420	72.0	69.0	.956
70	445	80.7	65.0	.804
80	495	99.0	58.0	.59
90	545	119.9	53	.44
100	595	142.8	49	.34

B-24 **SINE WAVE** at **TRUE MINIMUM** SETTINGS for **TRUE MINIMUM** OUTPUTS and **TRUE MINIMUM** MTTLOIs with AGE RELATED THRESHOLD IMPEDANCES and JUST ABOVE THRESHOLD OUTPUTS

AGE	Initial Impedance Threshold (Ω)	Threshold Output in Joules	Minimum Output in Joules	MTTLOI
10	100	4.0	4.9	1.23
20	150	9.0	9.6	1.06
30	205	16.4	19.0	1.15
40	260	26.0	33.35	1.28
50	320	41.5	45.0	1.08
60	390	64.2	66.7	1.04
65	420	72.0	69.0	.956
70	445	80.0	65.0	.804
80	495	99.0	58.0	.59
90	545	120	53	.44
100	595	143	49	.34

B-24 **SINE WAVE** at **PROBABLE MINIMUM** SETTINGS for **PROBABLE MINIMUM** SW OUTPUTS and **PROBABLE MINIMUM** SW MTTLOIs

AGE	Threshold Output in Joules	Prob Minimum Output in Joules	MTTLOI
10	4.0	36.0	9
20	9.0	43	4.7
30	16.4	53	3.22
40	26.0	63	2.43
50	48.7	83.7	1.72
60	63.7	73.16	1.15
65	72.0	69.0	.956
70	80.0	65.0	.804
80	99.0	58.0	.59
90	120	53	.44
100	143	49	.34

The above figures represent probable minimal stimulus outputs as opposed to improbable true minimal stimulus outputs for SW. It is the author's opinion that, except where it can't be avoided, Medcraft calibrates its B-24 SW device to avoid true minimal stimulus outputs, instead, creating higher "minimums below which the B-24 device cannot go. This speculation is based both on the strange construction of the Medcraft's B-25 Brief Pulse which seems to be made in the image of the B-24, and because Medcraft, like Brief Pulse manufacturers Somatics and MECTA most likely found true minimal stimulus, even with SW, ineffective.

Line Graphs:

From the three SW charts above, it is now possible to create line graphs of age-related true minimum, probable minimum, and maximum B-24 SW settings. The chart below graphs maximum SW output against an improbable true minimum SW output.

Maximum and True Minimum EO for SW Settings with respect to Age

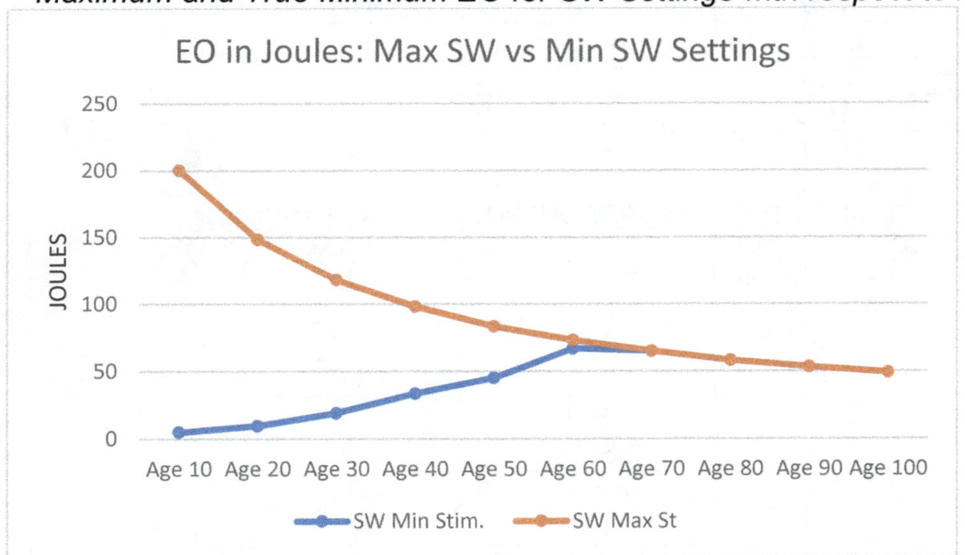

As expected, minimum and maximum SW outputs are starkly contrasting in the younger age categories. Note, however, how minimum and maximum settings merge at about age 65 so that past age 65, there is no output difference at all. This merging is due to dwindling current as a result of increasing impedances with increasing age. In short, while maximum SW is inordinately powerful from about ten to forty years of age, "maximum" settings become weaker and weaker as age, increases, eventually merging with true minimal stimulus.

Below is the same chart with SW Seizure Thresholds:

Maximum and True Minimum EO for SW Settings with Seizure Thresholds

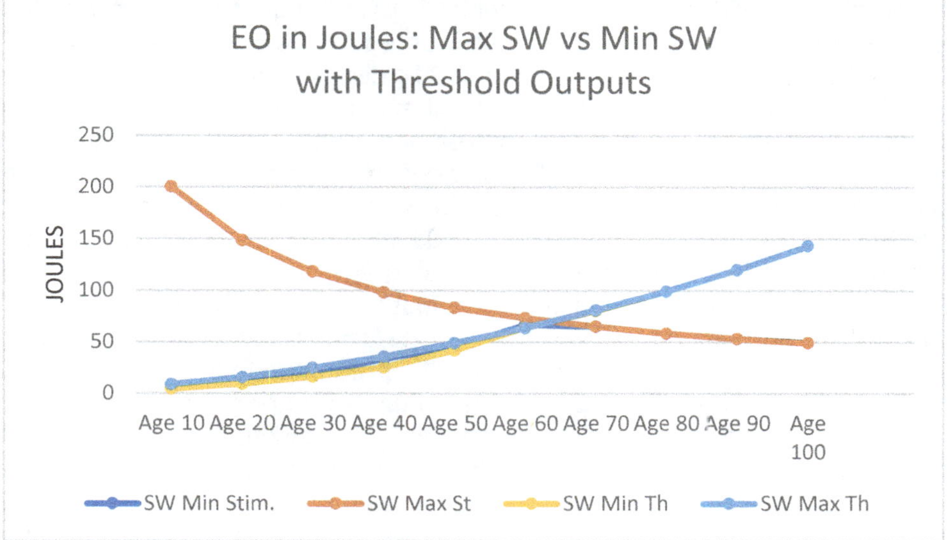

Note how maximum SW settings are inordinately powerful in the younger age categories, emitting up to 200J at age ten, but begin to dwindle as age increases until true maximum and true minimum merge. Indeed, note how SW becomes so weak past the age of about 65, it can no longer reach threshold. In short, while maximum SW is dangerously destructive from about age 10 to 45, the machine may not even induce seizure with BL "ECT" past the age of about 65.

Maximum, Probable Minimum, and True Minimum EO for SW Settings

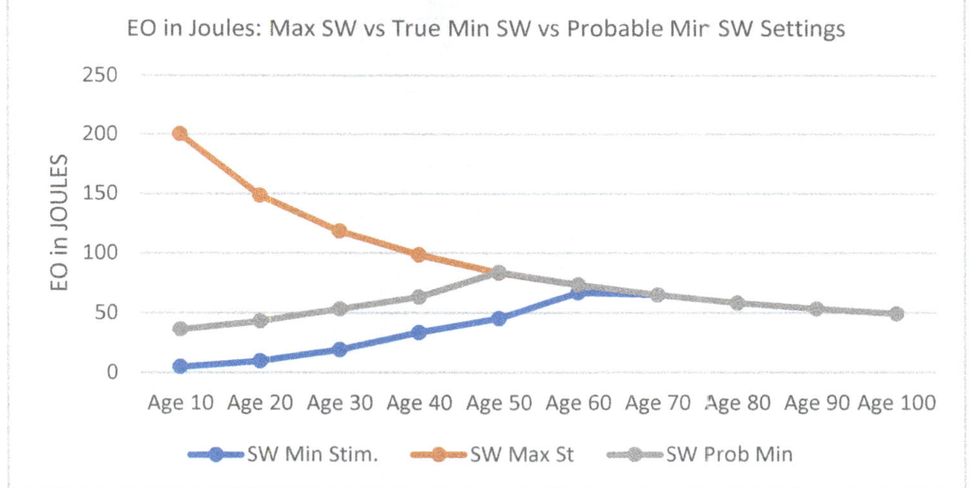

Note that Medcraft's B-24 SW device most likely cannot be set to true "SW minimal stimulus," but only between maximum and probable minimums below which the Medcraft may not allow the machine to operate due to "inefficacy." Even so, we must not lose sight of the inordinately destructive power of SW in the younger age categories between ages 10 to about 40 or 45.

Before we go any further, let us revisit parameters of the MECTA "C," the single BP device approved by the Utah Biomedical Test Laboratory (Grahn) also approved by the FDA. In short, it is the single modern day BP device to wholly conform to the 1982 APA Standard and so the single modern Brief Pulse device properly labeled "ECT."

First Generation MECTA "C" and "D" BP Devices

The MECTA "C" is the only true modern day ECT device in that it is the single device capable of inducing so-called adequate seizures at just above threshold in every age category with BL-ECT in full accordance with the 1982 APA Standard. Indeed, it is the only device approved by the Utah Biomedical Test Laboratory around which a legitimate standard for ECT was written (Grahn). Indeed, its circa 108J ceiling makes it the only modern day BP device based on just above threshold output with respect to the 100J minimum required to adequately seize all recipients up to 100 years of age, a concept clearly depicted in Weiner's 1982 BP vs SW comparative charts (an official part of the 1982 APA Standard). The 108J MECTA "C," in brief, conforms to the APA Standard which permits a buffer of up to ten joules above the universal BP threshold of 100J and so allows up to 110 maximum Joules. (Too, the "C" is limited to gradational outputs by a 70J at 220Ω ER/RRC (Equivalent Ratio/Rate Rise Ceiling), meaning all outputs have to decrease with decreasing age according to age-related seizure thresholds.[258]) Thus, the MECTA "C" is designed to limit output to just above threshold with BL ECT for every recipient in every age category, slightly surpassing the "electrical doses" required to induce grand mal seizures with BL-ECT in all age categories. Because the archetypal MECTA "C" presented to the FDA between 1978-80 is the only true ECT Brief Pulse device designed for BL ECT manufactured during the modern Brief Pulse Era in full accordance with the 1982 APA Standard, we will compare the "C" to all other modern day BP devices and to the B-24 SW device. For accuracy then, let us reintroduce the basic parameters of the MECTA "C."

MECTA "C" (CONDITIONAL ER/RRC) limited to 108 maximum Joules and thus 1.08 fold threshold in every age category

AGE	Threshold Output in Joules	MECTA "C" EO (Joules)	Multifold Thresh. Titration Level
10	1.0	1.08	1.08
20	4.0	4.32	1.08
30	9.0	9.72	1.08
40	16.0	17.28	1.08
50	25.0	27	1.08
60	36.0	38.88	1.08
65	42.6	46	1.08
70	49.0	52.95	1.08
80	64.	69.12	1.08
90	81.	87.48	1.08
100	100	108	1.08

See Graph of the MECTA "C" below:

[258] C: 59J/220Ω = 108J/402Ω or 80J/300Ω = 108J/402Ω

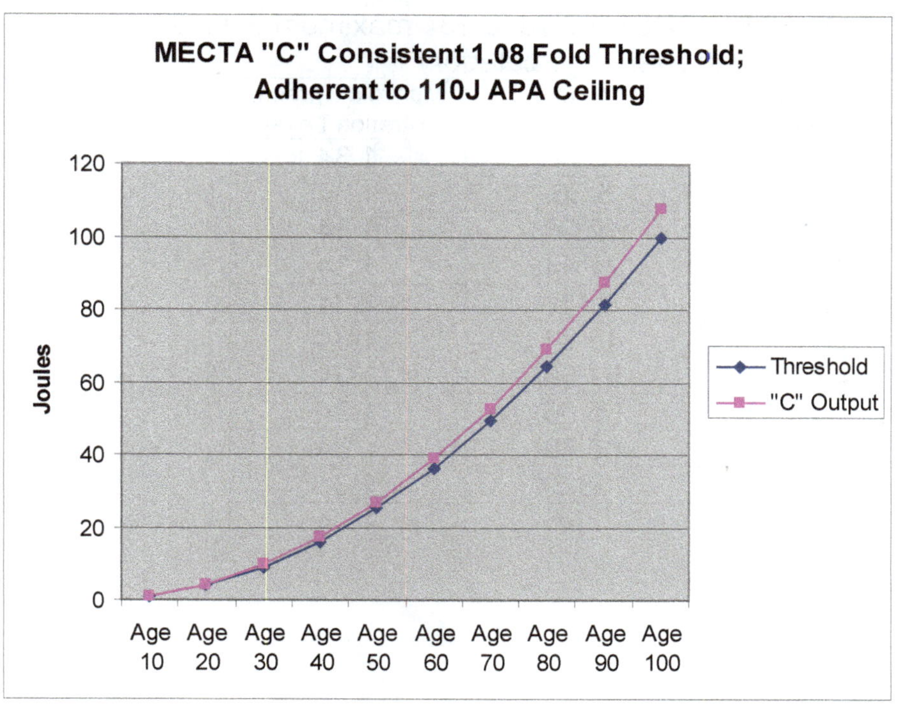

The MECTA "C" above is the prototypical true Brief Pulse Electroconvulsive Therapy Device introduced to the FDA between 1976 and 1982. Note how all outputs are just above seizure threshold. This device alone represents the improvement over SW by virtue of reduced output (compared to SW) that FDA and allegedly APA sought with Brief Pulse in order to sanction the continuation of "ECT" into the latter part of the twentieth century and beyond. The MECTA "C" device alone, as noted, conforms to 1982 APA Standard for Brief Pulse, approximating the 100J minimum for Brief Pulse depicted in Weiner's Brief Pulse graph at the beginning of this section juxtaposed with Weiner's SW graph approximating 200J or twice the output of Brief Pulse to induce adequate seizures.

The MECTA "D" device is also a first generation BP device with respect to the new BP Era, in that it too, is technically a "just above threshold BP device" though more powerful than the MECTA "C" in every age category. Like the "C," the "D" is a first generation BP device in that, unlike second generation BP devices, it does not double or more than double the output depicted within the 1982 APA Standard nor does it violate the 1982 APA Equivalent Ratio/Rate Rise Ceiling Standard of "70J at 220Ω" (discussed in previous sections).[259] However, It is the first to violate the 1982 APA ceiling Standard of 110J. Supposedly, the slightly more powerful "D" was needed to overcome rarer, higher Impedances which the "C" couldn't overcome. But this is questionable. Very probably, the "D" was merely manufacturers' first BP attempt to breach the 110J APA ceiling. What is certain is that once the ceiling was breached and FDA did not respond, BP manufacturers began increasing Voltage with each new BP generation until all subsequent Brief Pulse machines began breaching both the 1982 APA ER/RRC and the 1982 APA Energy Output ceiling, a trend covered up by the Brief Pulse industry. In short, the "D," though only slightly more powerful than the MECTA "C," (108J vs 134J) was the first BP device within the modern BP era to breach the 1982 APA Standard which it did by surpassing the 110J ceiling. All BP devices subsequent to the "D," as noted, breach both the ER/RRC and the Energy Output ceiling depicted within the 1982 APA Standard. Critically then, only the MECTA "C" conforms to the 1982 APA Standard; therefore, only the MECTA "C" meets the full criteria of the APA Standard recommended by both the Utah Biomedical Test Laboratory and the FDA. Importantly, the "C" could induce adequate seizures in every age category very nearly 100% of the time.

---

[259] XJ/220Ω = 134.4J/500Ω = <u>59J at 220Ω</u>; XJ/300Ω = 134.4/500Ω = <u>80.6J at 300Ω</u>. "59J at 220Ω" is below the ceiling of "70J at 220Ω" depicted within the 1982 APA Standard. For further elaboration, see First Generation BP Devices in this manuscript.

The MECTA "D" (CONDITIONAL ER/RRC) limited to 134 maximum Joules and thus 1.34 fold in every age category

AGE	Threshold Output in Joules	MECTA "D" EO (Joules)	Multifold Thresh. Titration Level
10	1.0	1.34	1.34
20	4.0	5.36	1.34
30	9.0	12.06	1.34
40	16.0	21.44	1.34
50	25.0	33.5	1.34
60	36.0	48.24	1.34
65	42.6	57.08	1.34
70	49.0	65.66	1.34
80	64.0	85,76	1.34
90	81.0	108.64	1.34
100	100	134	1.34

See Graph of the MECTA "D" below:

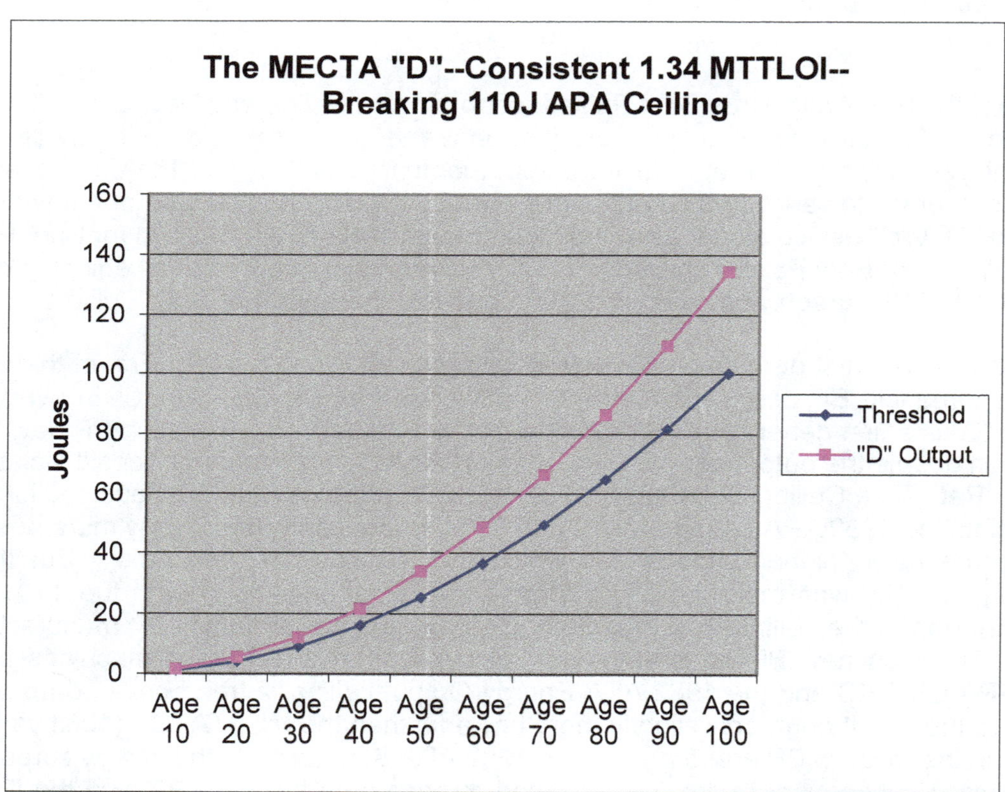

First generation "D," first to breach the 110J ceiling of the 1982 APA Standard.

Comparing Brief Pulse Devices with Sine Wave

Based on information gleaned from the Cameron Paradigm for SW and BP Charts created in the previous section, we can now create visual graphs comparing the B-24 SW to Modern Day Brief Pulse devices. First let depict SW set for Maximum versus True Minimum. Next, let us add Probable Minimum SW Settings. Finally let us compare SW to all Five Generations of Modern Day BP Devices. Keep in mind that Brief Pulse was supposed to be an improvement over SW by virtue of reduced EO and that only the First Generation MECTA "C" achieved this goal.

***Maximum* v *True Minimum* SW EOs**

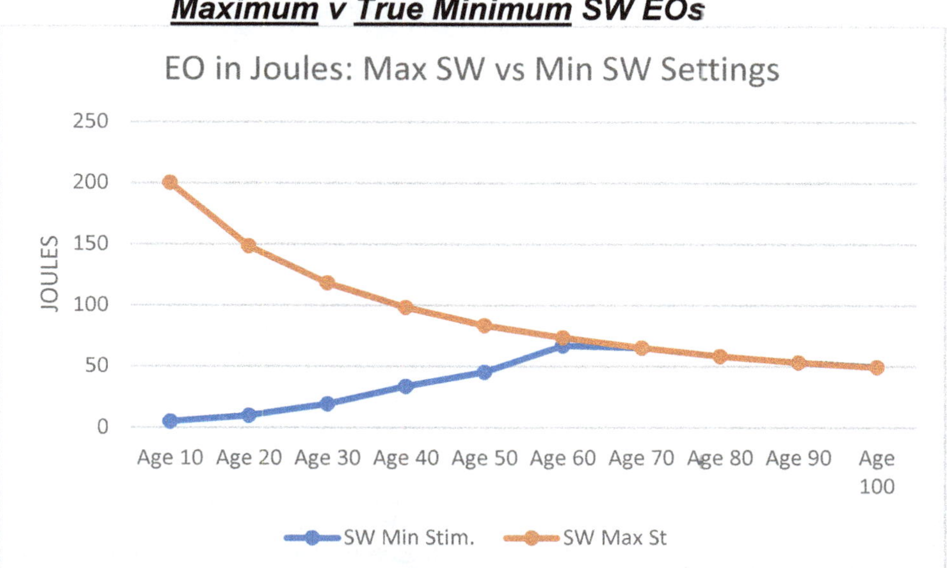

Note how maximum output begins to dwindle with increasing age until maximum and minimum merge at about 65 years.

***Maximum*, *Probable Minimum*, and *True Minimum SW* EOs**

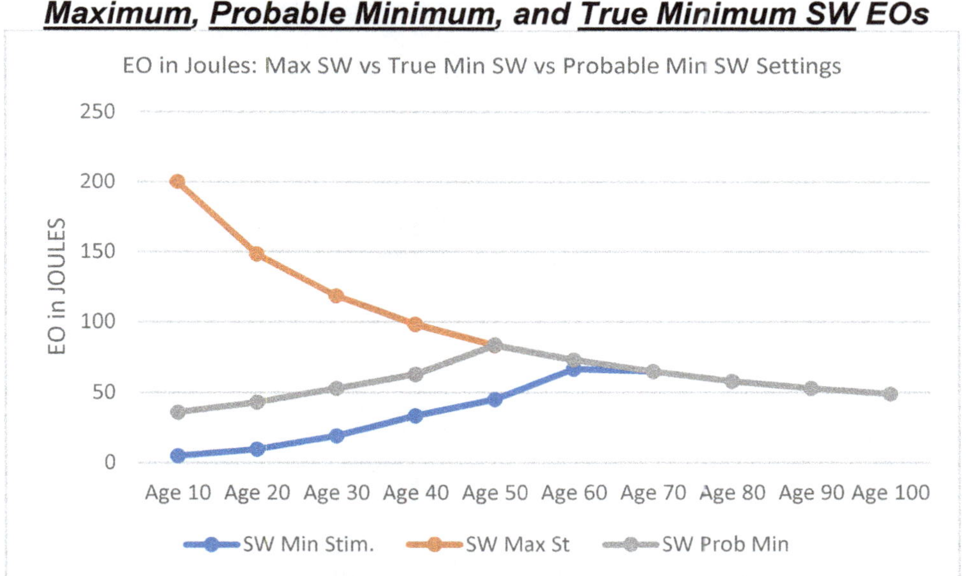

The author suspects that the B-24 SW either cannot be adjusted to true minimal stimulus for SW or that Medcraft discourages true minimal stimulus settings with SW due to its quest for electrical efficacy. Indeed, there is reason to suspect the B-24 SW device cannot be set for less than 36J in the 10 year old age category, 43J in the 20 year old age category, 53J in the thirty year old age category, 63J in the forty year old age category, 83.27J in the 50 year old age category, and 73J in the 60 year old age category. All categories older than about 60 may not reach threshold with SW. Probable minimal stimulus outputs are designed to achieve a minimum 9 MTTLOI in the 10 year old age category, a minimum 4.7 MTTLOI in the 20 year old age category, a minimum 3.22 MTTLOI in the 30 year old age category, a minimum 2.43 MTTLOI in the 40 year old age category, a minimum 1.72 MTTLOI in the 50 year old age category, and a minimum 1.15 MTTLOI in the 60 year old age category. These probable minimal outputs may be designed to assure efficacy at the expense of safety. In short, true minimal stimulus even with SW appears to be avoided, in spite of long term memory morbidity. It is no exaggeration to say that Medcraft has been in the business of injuring brains for more than 75 years.

EO of MECTA "C" v Max SW v Probable Min SW v True Min SW

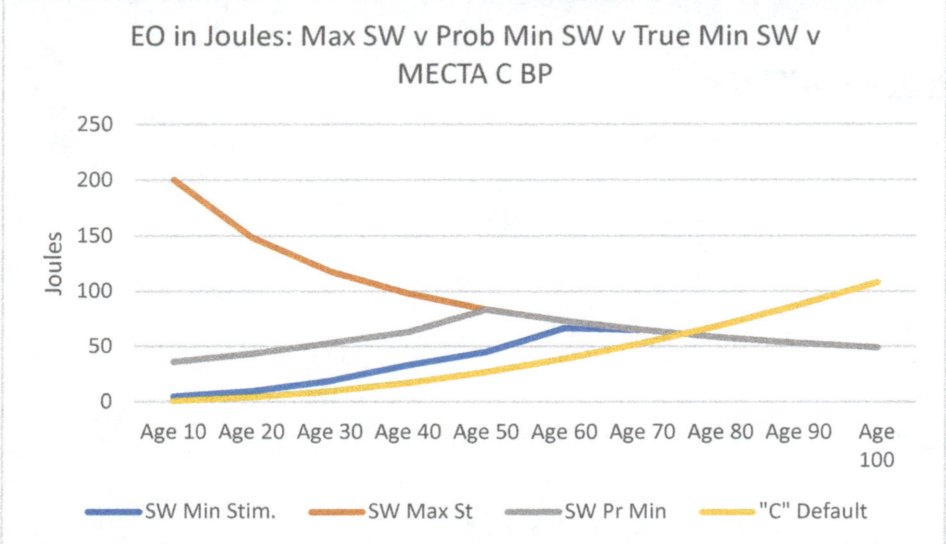

With respect to reduced EO, note how the First Generation MECTA "C" BP device is superior to SW even at true minimum stimulus. The "C," of course, is also superior to probable minimum, and maximum SW settings, successfully using less Energy Output than SW until about Age 80. The "C" surpasses SW at this point only due to the necessity of inducing so-called "adequate" seizures with BL-ECT, which SW fails to do from about Age 65 and older. Of critical importance, then, the MECTA "C" is the only modern day BP device which conforms to the 1982 APA Standard designed to induce adequate seizures with reduced EO compared to SW, even at true minimal stimulus SW settings.

EO of MECTA "C" v Maximum SW v True Minimum SW v Probable Minimum SW v 2nd Gen. BP Device

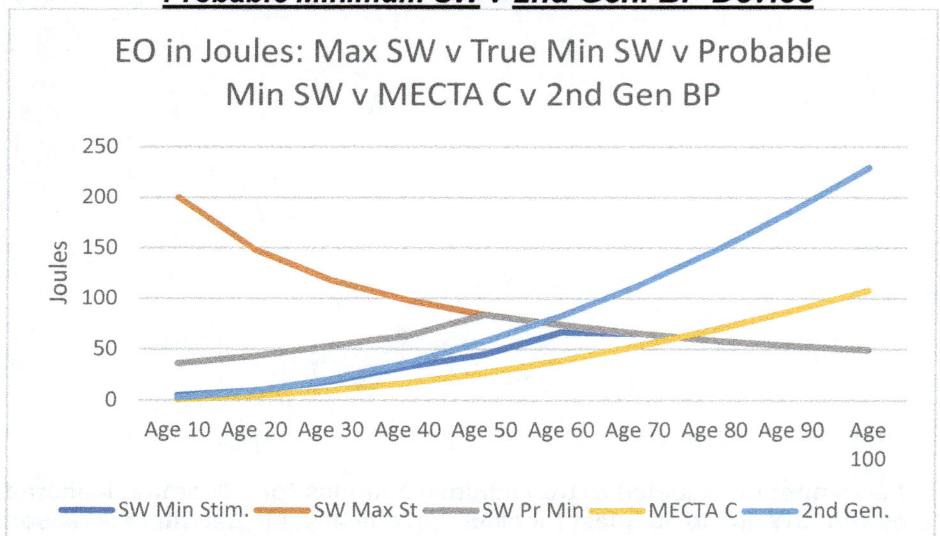

Note the second BP device in light blue. Compared to SW set for true minimum stimulus (dark blue) in every age category, the 2nd generation BP device utilizes less EO than SW only up to age 30, after which it surpasses SW (at true Minimal stimulus) in every other age category. Compared to SW sat maximum output (orange) and probable minimal stimulus (gray), the 2nd generation BP device yet utilizes less EO than SW up to about age 55, after which BP surpasses SW in every other age category. Unlike SW, both the 1st and the 2nd generation BP devices can induce adequate seizures in every age category with a consistent MTTLOI, although the 1st generation MECTA "C" BP device does so at less than half the EO of the 2nd Generation BP device. In short, the 2nd generation BP device uses twice the EO necessary to induce so-called "adequate" seizures with BP. Moreover, we must not lose sight of the awesome power of SW at both maximum and probable minimum in the younger age categories for which it chiefly appears to be used. For example, nothing prevents physicians from administering 200J at a 23 MTTLOI with SW in the ten year old age category.

EO of MECTA "C" v Maximum SW v True Minimum SW v Probable Minimum SW v 3rd Gen. BP Device

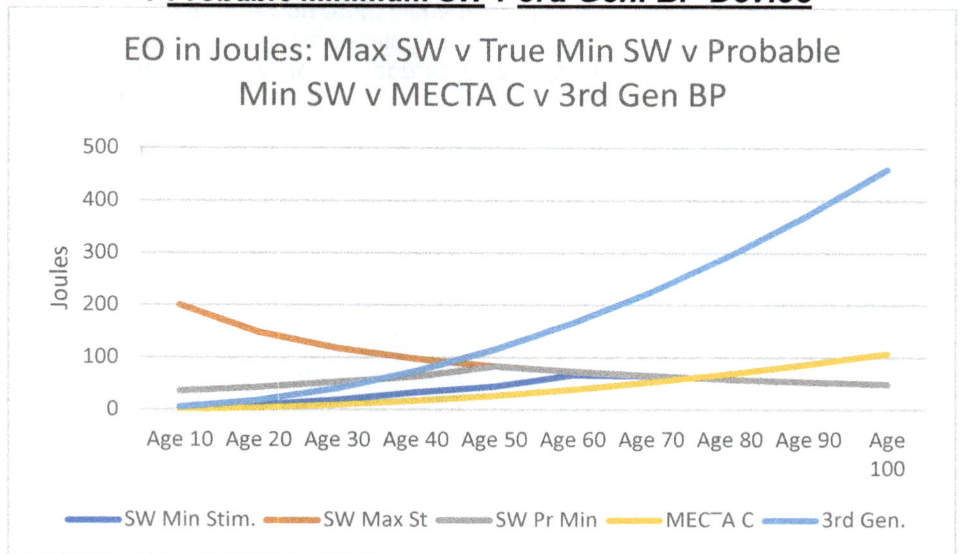

Compared to SW set for an improbable true minimum stimulus (dark blue) in every age category, the extant 3rd generation BP device (light blue) utilizes less EO than SW only up to age 10, after which it surpasses SW in every other age category. Compared to SW set at maximum output (orange) in every age category, the 3rd generation BP device now utilizes less EO than SW only up to age 40, after which it surpasses SW in every other age category. Compared to probable minimal stimulus settings (gray), the 3rd generation BP device uses less EO than SW only up to age 32, after which it surpasses SW in every other age category. Unlike SW, both the 1st and the 3rd generation. BP devices can induce adequate seizures in every age category with a consistent MTTLOI, although the first generation MECTA "C" BP device now does so at less than a quarter the default EO of the 3rd Generation Brief Pulse. While the third generation BP device does surpass SW at much earlier age than the second generation BP device, SW yet emits more power than even the third generation BP device from ages 10 to about 30 or 40 even at probable minimal stimulus. While BP dramatically increases in power, therefore, we must not forget that SW yet remains a devastating suprathreshold device in the younger age categories.

EO of MECTA "C" v Maximum SW v True Minimum SW v Probable Minimum SW v 4th Gen. BP Device

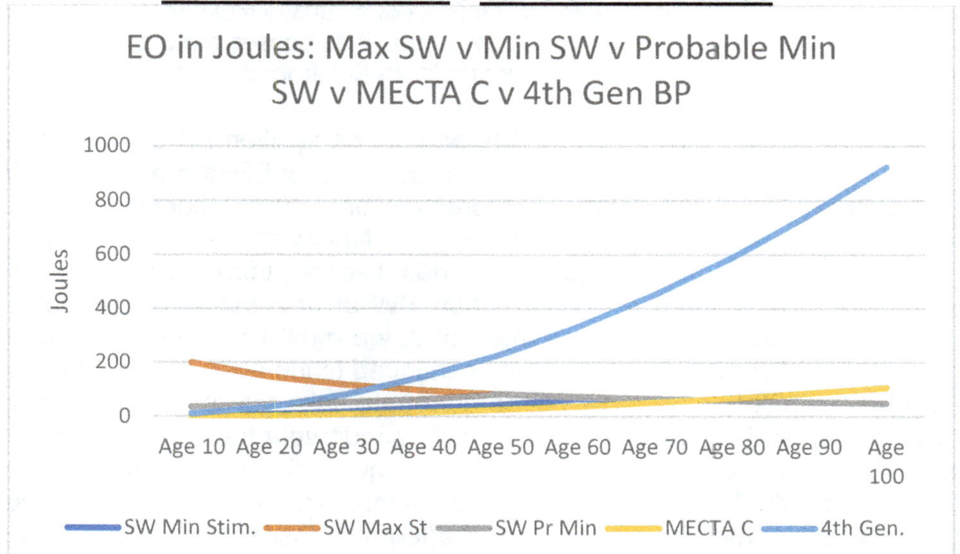

Compared to SW set for maximum output (orange), the 4th generation BP device now utilizes less EO than SW only up to age 33, after which it surpasses SW in every age category. Compared to SW set for an improbable true minimum stimulus, the theoretical but "legal" (under Weiner's de facto "standard") 4th generation BP device (light blue) now emits more EO than SW in every age category. Compared to high y probably minimal stimulus SW settings (gray), the powerful 4th generation BP device now surpasses SW in every age category past the age of about 22. Unlike SW, both 1st (orange) and 4th Gen. BP devices induce adequate seizures with BL-ECT in every age group with a consistent MTTLOI, although the 1st generation MECTA "C" does so at about <u>one nineth</u> the EO of the 4th Gen. Brief Pulse device. While the fourth generation BP device does surpass SW at an even earlier age than the third generation BP device and is more powerful than even maximum SW output in most age categories, SW at maximum output yet emits more power than even the supra powerful fourth generation BP device from about age 10 to 33. While BP has once again increased in power, therefore, we must not forget that SW yet remains a devastating force in the younger age categories for whom it appears to be primarily used. Moreover, no regulation prevents facilitators from so doing.

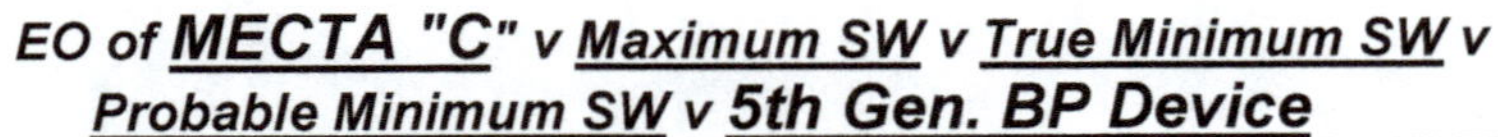

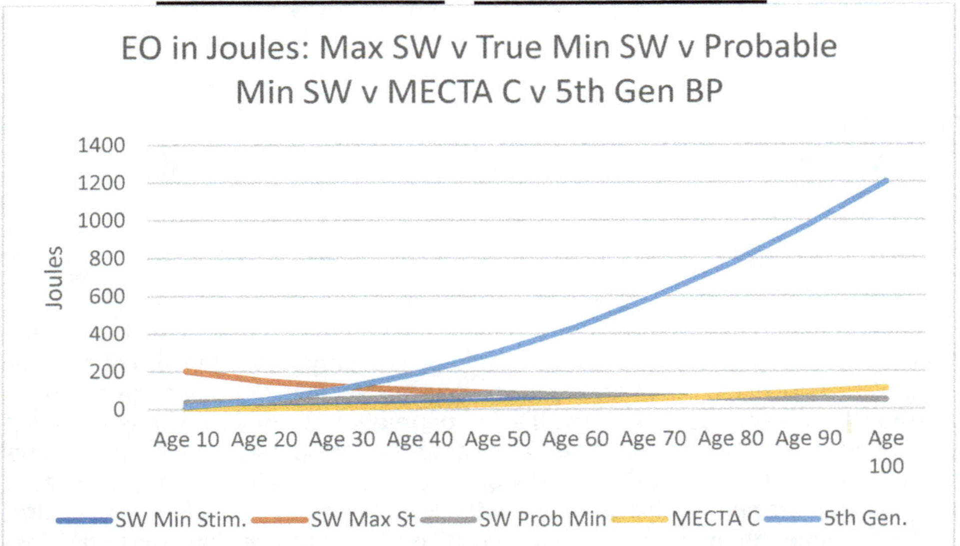

Compared to SW set for maximum output (orange) in every age category, the 5th generation BP device (light blue) now utilizes less EO than SW only up to age 30, surpassing SW in every other age category. Compared to SW set for true minimum stimulus (dark blue) in every age category, the theoretical but "legal" (under Weiner's "standard") 5th generation BP device emits more EO than SW in every age category. Compared to SW set for probable minimal stimulus (gray) in every age category, the 5th generation BP device now utilizes less EO than SW only up to about age 20 , surpassing SW in every other age category. Unlike SW, both 1st and 5th generation BP devices can induce adequate seizures in every age category with BL-ECT with a consistent MTTLOI, although the 1st generation MECTA "C" does so at about one eleventh the EO. However, while the fifth generation BP device is concerningly supra powerful, we must not lose sight of the awesome power of SW in the very youngest categories wherein at maximum output, it surpasses the output of even the fifth generation BP device up to about age 30. Too, no regulation prevents administrators from doing so.

In sum, the MECTA "C" alone compared to SW and all 2nd, 3rd, 4th, and 5th generation BP devices, can be deemed an "ECT" device in that the "C" alone takes advantage of the reduced EO of BP compared to SW to induce adequate minimal stimulus seizures in every age category. Moreover, only the "C" conforms to the 1982 APA Standard approved by Utah Biomedical Test Laboratory and the FDA. Not even the first generation MECTA "D" conforms. With the exception of the very youngest age categories, second, third, fourth, and fifth generation BP devices are more powerful and thus more dangerous than SW at true minimum, probable minimum, and maximum settings in most age categories. On the other hand, we must not ignore the great power of SW in the younger age categories. That BP manufacturers have continued to increase the EO in each succeeding BP generation despite the MECTA "C's" capacity to induce adequate seizures at far less output than SW in all seizure inducible age categories, and that even SW appears to circumvent the least amount of electricity possible, indicates that manufacturers of both kinds of devices long ago realized adequate seizure alone has little or no "therapeutic" effect. In short, the history of both SW and the modern day Brief Pulse device shows that efficacy is clearly the result--not of adequate convulsions--but of adequate doses of electricity. Such devices, cannot be deemed Electro Convulsive Therapy devices and so were never legally "grandfathered" in. Moreover, while SW devices were mislabeled “ECT” devices before 1976, second, third, fourth, and fifth generation BP devices only appeared following the grandfathering in of the MECTA “C.”

For even greater clarity, let us first exclude maximum SW output, only comparing EO Delivered at True Minimal and Probable Minimal Stimulus SW Settings to all five generations of Brief Pulse

The B-24 at TRUE MINIMAL STIMULUS and PROBABLE MINIMAL STIMULUS vs the FIRST GENERATION MECTA "C"

While we can get important information from comparing maximum settings of the B-24 to the default outputs of various BP device generations, we can get also get vital information from true and probable minimal SW settings versus the default settings of various BP device generations. After all, if BP cannot emit less EO than SW at true minimal or probable minimal SW settings, what is the point of Brief Pulse at all?

First, let us attempt to graph the B-24 at Minimal and Probable Minimal Stimulus outputs alone (without maximum) at various age groups compared to the default settings of the MECTA "C" at various age groups. The MECTA "C," as we have seen, is the single BP device with which there is a legitimate improvement over SW regarding reduced EO compared to both theoretical true minimal stimulus SW and probable minimal stimulus SW, as we have seen. We derive true minimal stimulus for SW by dividing the SW Threshold Output for a specific age group by the least amount of EO required to induce an adequate seizure. (Probable Minimal stimulus is based on the minimal MTTLOIs allowed by the B-25.) Since the B-24 SW can only be broken down into one tenth of a Second increments and into Voltages between 70 to 170, but mainly due to a deteriorating and therefore inconsistent current, there is no consistent MTTLOI for SW. Nor does the Minimal Stimulus Threshold rise consistently with SW. Indeed, the only two elements over which the operator has control on the B-24, are increments of Duration from .1 to 1.0 Seconds and the eleven increments of Voltage from 70 to 170V. From these, the operator can only indirectly control Amperage, and only to a limited extent. For example, at one tenth of a second (.1 Seconds), we can theoretically set the B-24 SW to deliver 4.9J to the ten year old child who, at this setting, requires 4.0J to seize. The minimal MTTLOI in this age group, as we have seen earlier, is thus a (4.9J ÷ 4.0J =) 1.23 MTTLOI. While this seems comparable to the MTTLOI of the MECTA "C" (which is a 1.08 MTTLOI), because SW threshold is higher than BP threshold, SW yet requires 4J in this age category as opposed to the 1.08J emitted by the MECTA "C." Thus, despite the appearance of a comparable MTTLOI, because SW threshold outputs are higher than BP Threshold outputs, SW actually requires much more EO to reach threshold and seize a particular age category.[260]

In any case, we derive theoretical true minimal stimulus outputs for SW by setting the machine as close to just above threshold as possible. Another example might be at a .3 Second setting, the B-24 SW can theoretically be made to deliver about 33.35J to the forty year old recipient who requires 26J to seize. The minimal MTTLOI in this age group is thus about a (33.35J ÷ 26J =) 1.28 MTTLOI and again, while this appears comparable to the MECTA "C" (at a 1.08 MTTLOI), SW requires 33.35J to overcome threshold for the forty year old, whereas, the First generation MECTA "C" requires only about 17.8J in this same age category to overcome seizure threshold, about half the output of SW. Note too, SW's MTTLOI inconsistency (10 yrs.-1.23, 20 yrs.-1.06, 30 yrs.-1.15; 40 yrs.-1.28; 50 yrs.-1.08; 60 yrs.-1.07; 65 yrs.-.956; 70 yrs.-.804; 80 yrs.-.59; 90 yrs.-.44; 100 yrs.-.34) compared to the consistent 1.08 MTTLOI of the MECTA "C" in all age categories. Finally, note that at about 65 years of age, SW is no longer very effective at inducing seizures with BL ECT, that is, it is either unreliable with respect to inducing "adequate" seizures (with BL "ECT") or altogether unable to do so. Conversely, the MECTA "C" can induce adequate seizures with less EO than SW in every age category at which the SW device is capable of inducing seizure.

Though true minimal stimulus SW is theoretically possible, there is doubt whether or not the B-24 can be adjusted for true minimal stimulus. This doubt is mainly due to the extremely odd construction of Medcraft's B-25 Brief Pulse device which appears to be an attempt to imitate the B-24 SW device using Brief Pulse. (Medcraft, at one point assumed it would have to replace the "popular" B-24 SW device with Brief Pulse and the B-25 was to be its replacement response.) The fact that the B-25 does not appear to be able to deliver outputs below a certain MTTLOI suggests that neither does the B-24 deliver outputs below specific MTTLOIs,

---

260 This does not mean that either SW or BP is effective at minimal stimulus. Thus, SW facilitators don't necessarily set their machines for minimal stimulus. In fact, they may be unable to do so. Moreover, this does not mean that later BP devices, that is, those succeeding the MECTA "C" are not set for multifold threshold outputs, despite BP's capacity to induce adequate seizure at much less EO. Manufacturers of both kind of devices have to set their devices for multifold threshold outputs in order to make the procedure "work."

perhaps MTTLOIs very similar to that of the B-25. Consequently, if, like the B-25, the B-24 does not allow true minimal stimulus in the younger age categories, probable minimal stimulus may be based on the following MTTLOIs (similar to those used by the B-25): (10 yrs.-9.0; 20 yrs.-4.7; 30 yrs.-3.22; 40 yrs.-2.43; 50 yrs.-1.72; 60 yrs.-1.15; 65 yrs.-.956; 70 yrs.-.804; 80 Yrs.-.59; 90 yrs.-.44; 100 yrs.-.34). In any case, at age 65, maximum and minimum B-24 MTTLOIs merge so that the device cannot reliably overcome threshold at age 65 and older.

EO Delivered at True Minimal Stimulus SW and Probable Minimal Stimulus SW v SW Thresholds

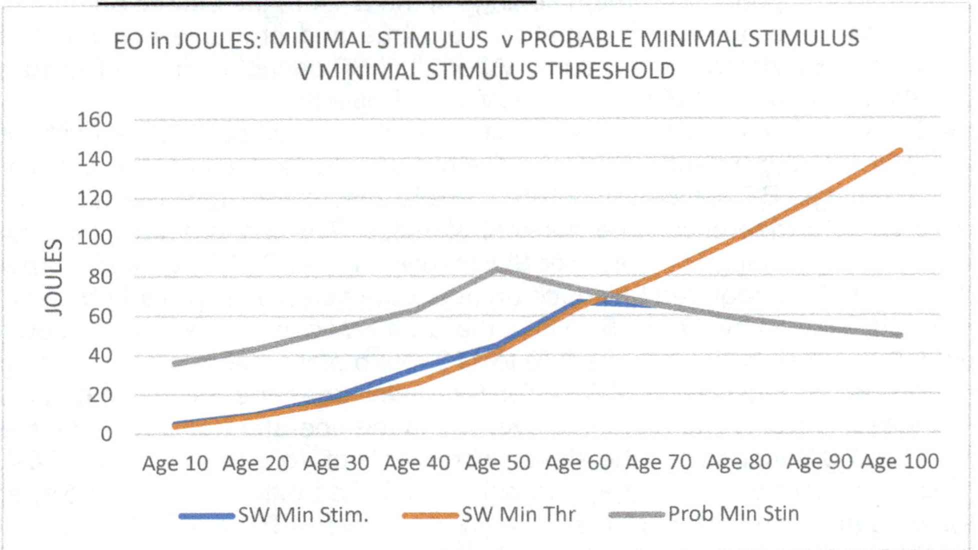

Note inconsistency in true minimal stimulus, probable minimal stimulus, and threshold outputs with SW. Note also the much higher probable minimal outputs compared to theoretical true minimal outputs for SW.

EO Delivered by the MECTA "C" BP with BP Threshold v True Minimal Stimulus SW v Probable Minimal Stimulus SW with SW Thresholds

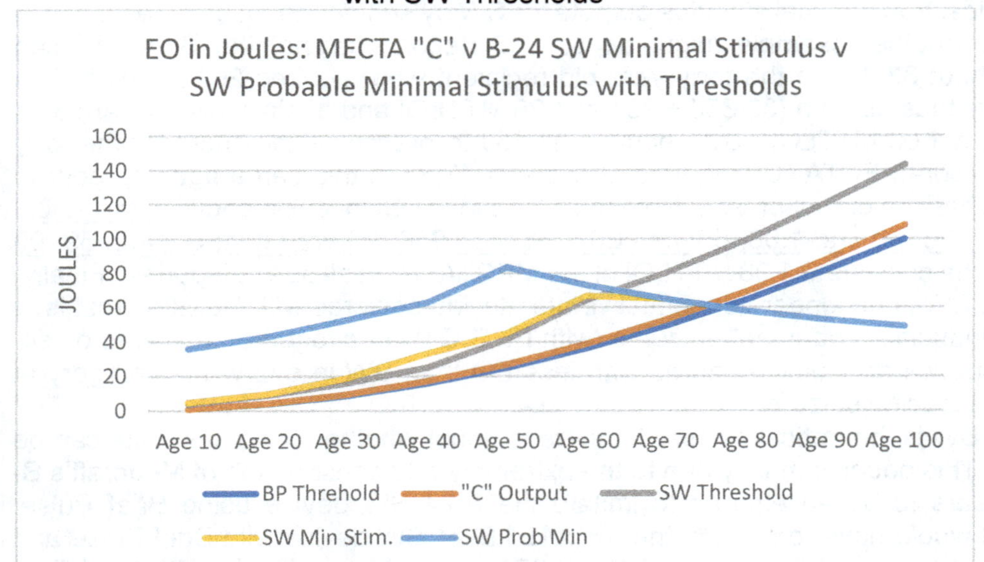

Note how both BP Threshold Outputs (dark blue) and actual EO delivered by the MECTA "C" BP (orange) are lower by about half than SW thresholds (gray) and even SW set at true minimal stimulus (yellow). Indeed, observe how the MECTA "C" ECT device delivers dramatically reduced outputs compared to both true minimal stimulus SW and Probable Minimal Stimulus SW delivered by the B-24.

Note SW's inconsistency with true minimal stimulus outputs, probable minimal stimulus outputs, and Minimal Stimulus Thresholds compared to the MECTA "C." We can conclude that the MECTA "C" is a vast improvement over even true minimal stimulus SW with respect to reduced EO, and certainly compared to probable minimal stimulus outputs delivered by the B-24. Without doubt, the MECTA "C," successfully reduced morbidity with the BP advantage of reduced output, delivering a consistent MTTLOI to all age categories and inducing adequate seizures at just above seizure threshold with Brief Pulse. In short, the MECTA "C" Brief Pulse could induce adequate seizures in every age category at which the B-24 is capable of inducing seizure but at much lower EOs. Moreover, unlike the B-24, the "C" could induce adequate seizures at age 65 and older.

It is easy to see why the FDA approved the 1982 APA Standard calling for parameters met by the MECTA "C," begging the question, "Why did manufacturers abandon the MECTA "C" for far more powerful BP devices no longer superior to SW with respect to reduced output and thus greatly reduced memory morbidity? Moreover, with the introduction of the far superior MECTA "C," why didn't the APA together with MECTA and Somatics fight to get the B-24 SW device permanently banned in America? Below is the same graph comparing the MECTA "C" to SW at both true and probable minimal stimulus outputs, but without thresholds.

EO Delivered by the MECTA "C" BP v True Minimal Stimulus SW
v Probable Minimal Stimulus SW without Thresholds

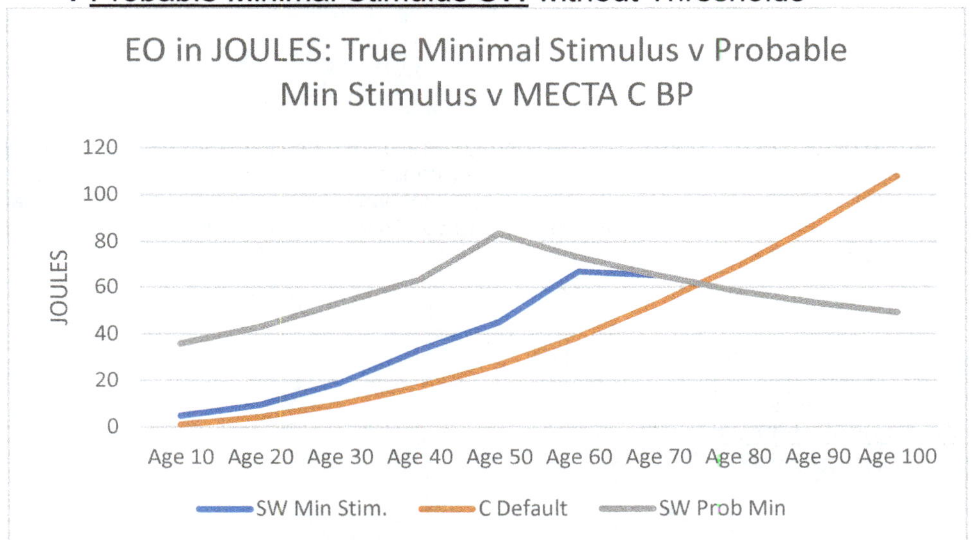

EO of True Minimal Stimulus SW (blue) vs Probable Minimal Stimulus SW (gray) vs Default Output of MECTA "C" BP (orange) all without Thresholds. Note the superiority of the MECTA "C" regarding reduced EO, only surpassing SW in recipients older than 75 or 80 in order to induce seizure, whereas, SW altogether fails to induce seizure from about 65 years and up with BL-ECT. Only the MECTA "C" emits half the EO of SW at true minimal stimulus. In fact, Medcraft may not allow true minimal stimulus, instead resorting to probable minimal stimulus to make the procedure "effective."

EO Delivered by the MECTA "C" BP v
EO Delivered by True Minimal Stimulus SW v
EO Delivered by Probable Minimal Stimulus SW v
EO Delivered by the 2nd Generation BP Device

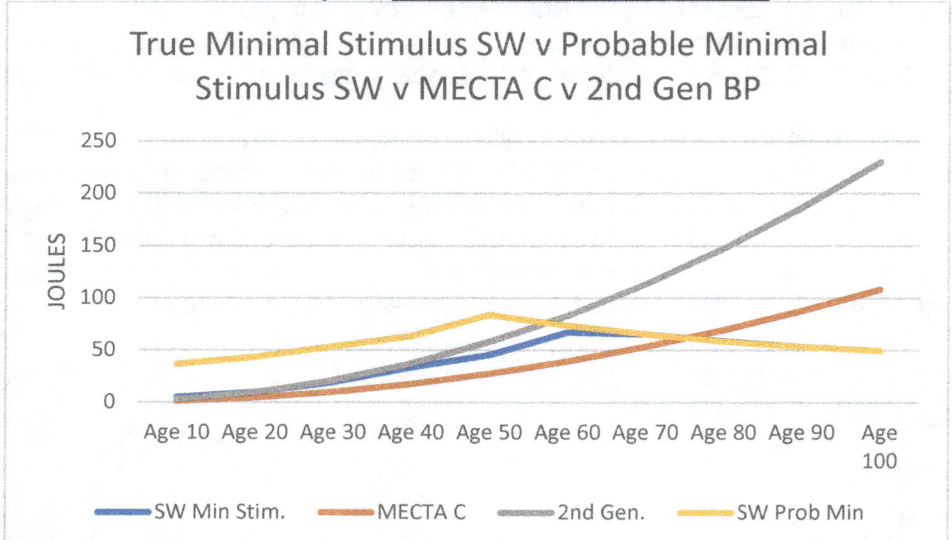

Second Generation BP (gray): We can see that the default outputs emitted by second generation BP devices surpass true minimal stimulus SW outputs (blue) at the age of about 40 and older. Thus, only the MECTA "C" (orange) induces less EO than SW at true minimal stimulus in every inducible age category. We can also see that SW is so powerful in the younger age categories that even at probable minimal stimulus it continues to surpass the second generation BP device until age 55. Only the "C" is an overall improvement over SW by virtue of reduced EO in every inducible age category.

EO Delivered by the MECTA "C" BP v
EO Delivered at True Minimal Stimulus SW v
EO Delivered at Probable Minimal stimulus SW
EO Delivered by the 3rd Generation BP Device

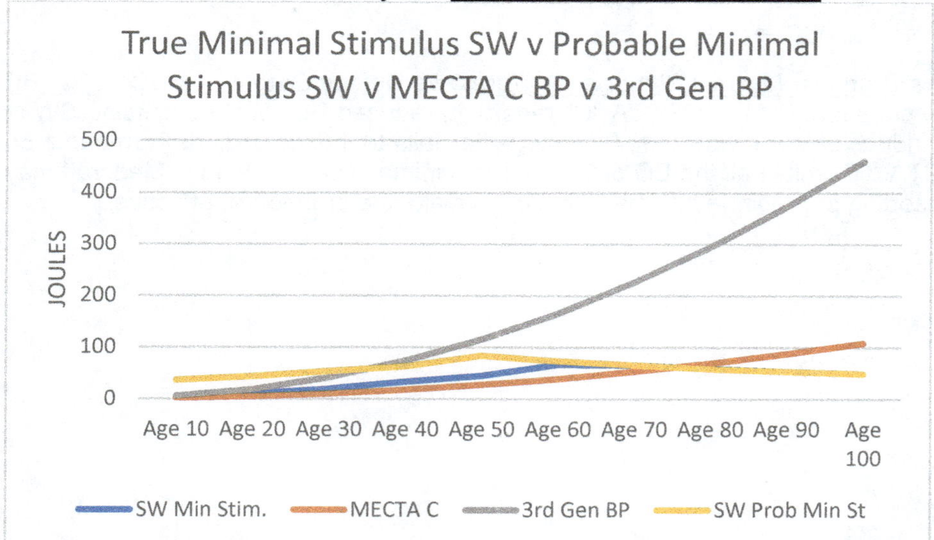

Third Generation BP (gray): We can see that the default outputs emitted by third generation BP devices are no longer advantageous compared to either true minimal stimulus SW (blue) past the age of about 15 or probable Minimal stimulus SW (yellow) past the age of about 33. On the other hand, we must not lose sight of SW's awesome power in the younger age categories at which point even probable minimal stimulus SW surpasses the powerful third generation BP device form age 10 to about age 33.

EO Delivered by the MECTA "C" BP v
EO Delivered by True Minimal Stimulus SW v
EO Delivered by Probable Minimal Stimulus v
EO Delivered by the 4th Generation BP Device

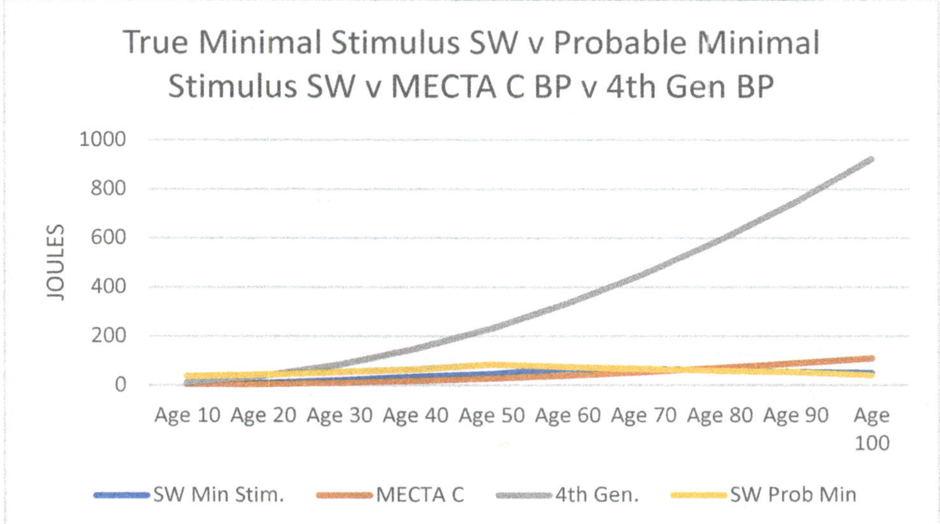

Fourth Generation BP (gray): We can see that the default outputs emitted with fourth generation BP devices are no longer advantageous to true minimal stimulus SW (blue) in any age group. Neither is the 4th generation superior to probable Minimal Stimulus SW (yellow) past the age of about 25. On the other hand again, we must not lose sight of the great power of SW in the younger age categories which even at probable minimal stimulus surpasses the powerful fourth generation BP device between the ages of about 10 and 30. In these younger age categories, SW is more dangerous than even the prodigiously powerful Fourth Generation BP device.

EO Delivered by the MECTA "C" BP v
EO Delivered at True Minimal Stimulus SW v
EO Delivered at Probable Minimal Stimulus SW v
EO Delivered by the 5th Generation BP Device

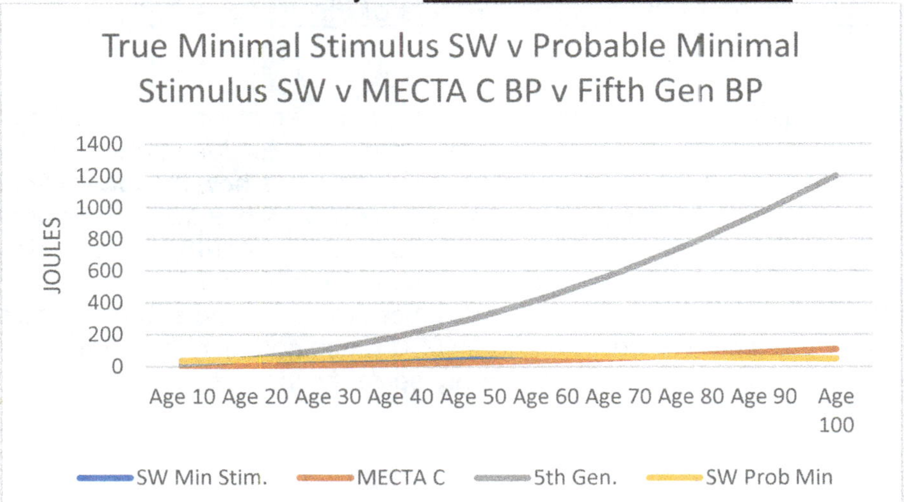

Fifth Generation BP (gray): We can see that the default outputs emitted by 5th generation BP devices are no longer advantageous to true minimal stimulus (blue) SW in any age category and no longer advantageous to Probable Minimal Stimulus (yellow) past the age of about 15. In essence, the BP device surpasses SW by greater and greater margins as age and BP generation increases. Even so, SW yet delivers even more power than the prodigious power of the Fifth generation BP devices in the youngest age categories.

EO DELIVERED BY ALL FIVE BP GENERATIONS v
EO DELIVERED AT TRUE AND PROBABLE MIMIMAL STIMULUS SW

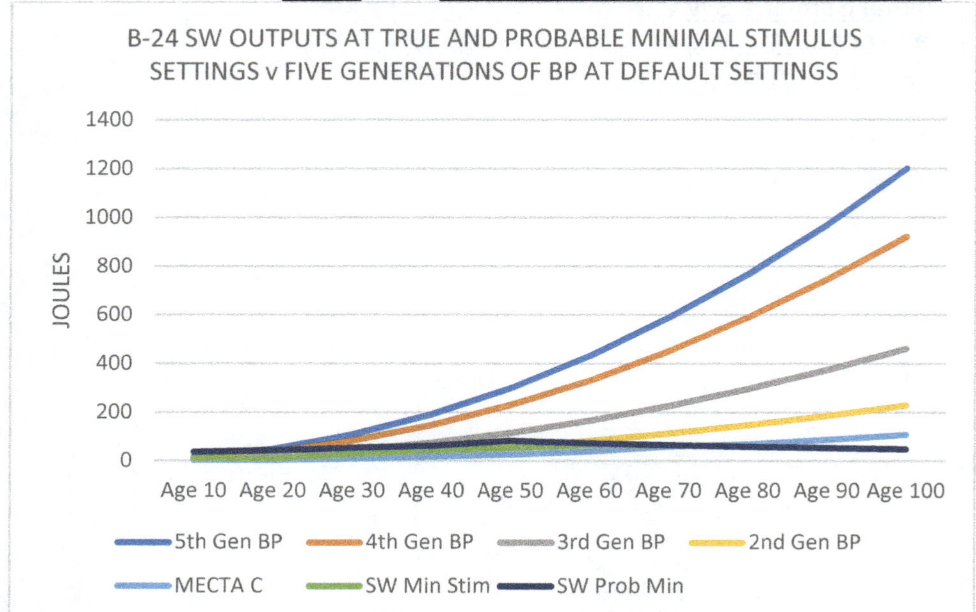

Only the first generation MECTA "C" BP device (light blue) reduces output in every inducible age category compared to SW set for minimal (green) and probable minimum stimulus (black) with BL-ECT in all age categories.[261] In spite of the induction of adequate seizures up to age 65 with SW and up to age 100 with BP, however, neither true minimal stimulus SW nor true minimal stimulus BP appear effective. This is because "therapeutic seizure" is a myth. Both SW and BP must rely on adequate (brain damaging) doses of electricity to be "effective." It is for this reason that SW is either rarely or never set for true minimal stimulus and that both SW and Brief Pulse manufacturers rejected the 1982 APA Standard. Rejecting the MECTA "C," BP manufacturers instead created a new standard for BP allowing for much more power and upon which all later generation BP devices are based. Medcraft, maker of the B-24, remains content with its continued existence.

Now let us Compare Only Maximum SW Settings to the Default Outputs of the Various BP Generations.

The Table below depicts the B-24 SW's initial (top half) and final (bottom half) Impedances at maximum settings along with corresponding EOs and ages. This evolution during a single "treatment" is due, unlike BP, to deteriorating current and thus rising Impedance over one second maximum duration. Note how the lowest final Impedance (the ten year old child at 145Ω) results in the highest maximum output (200J) while the highest final Impedance (the one hundred year old adult at 595Ω) results in the lowest maximum output of (48.6J), reflecting the upside down nature of SW. (See footnote below for SW's inverse proportion verifications in relation to Impedance.[262]) Finally, while SW's maximum 200J output at ten years old is both extreme and extremely rare (1/12th of 1%); neither can the machine easily overcome more than about 400Ω (culminating in the 60-65 year old categories) and thus does not appear to be powerful enough to reliably seize individuals (using BL ECT) from about 65 years and older.

---

[261] This does not include the 65 years and older categories which requires more power than that emitted by SW to induce seizure, but which the MECTA "C" yet delivers at just above threshold.

[262] XJ = 29000/145Ω = circa 200J; XJ = 29000/195Ω = circa 149J; XJ = 29000/215Ω = circa 134J; XJ = 29000/245Ω = circa 118J; XJ = 29000/295Ω = circa 98J; XJ = 29000/345Ω = circa 84J; XJ = 29000/395Ω = circa 73J; XJ = 29000/420Ω = circa 69J; XJ = 29000/445Ω = circa 65J; XJ = 29000/495Ω = circa 58J; XJ = 29000/545Ω = circa 53J; XJ = 29000/595Ω = circa 49J.

EO Maximums of Initial (top half) and Final Impedances (bottom half) of the B-24 SW Deteriorating Current Device at Maximum Settings for All Age Categories [263]

AGE	EO	Voltage	Current	Duration	Resistance	Charge
10 Yrs	28.9 J	170	1.7 Amp	.1 Sec	100 Ω	.17 Coul.
20	19.6 J	170	1.13 A	.1 Sec.	150 Ω	.113 C
24	17 J	170	1.0 A	.1 Sec	170 Ω	.100 C
30	14.25 J	170	.85 A	.1 Sec	200 Ω	.085 C
40	11.56 J	170	.68 A	.1 Sec	250 Ω	.068 C
50	9.63 J	170	.567 A	.1 Sec	300 Ω	.057 C
60	8.26 J	170	.486 A	.1 Sec	350 Ω	.049 C
65	7.71 J	170	.453 A	.1 Sec	375 Ω	.045 C
70	7.23 J	170	.425 A	.1 Sec	400 Ω	.043 C
80	6.42 J	170	.378 A	.1 Sec	450 Ω	.038 C
90	5.78 J	170	.34 A	.1 Sec	500 Ω	.034 C
100	5.26 J	170	. 309 A	.1 Sec	550 Ω	.031 C
		170		.2 Sec		
		170		.3 Sec		
		170		.4 Sec		
		170		.5 Sec		
		170		.6 Sec		
		170		.7 Sec		
		170		.8 Sec		
		170		.9 Sec		
10 Yr	200 J	170	1.172 A	1.0 Sec	145 Ω	1.172 C
20	148.2 J	170	.872 A	1.0 Sec	195 Ω	.872 C
24	134.42 J	170	.791 A	1.0 Sec	215 Ω	.791 C
30	118 J	170	.694 A	1.0 Sec	245 Ω	.694 C
40	97.97 J	170	.576 A	1.0 Sec	295 Ω	.576 C
50	83.77 J	170	.493 A	1.0 Sec	345 Ω	.493 C
60	73.16 J	170	.430 A	1.0 Sec	395 Ω	.430 C
65	68.81 J	170	.405 A	1.0 Sec	420 Ω	.405 C
70	64.94 J	170	.382 A	1.0 Sec	445 Ω	.382 C
80	58.4 J	170	.343 A	1.0 Sec	495 Ω	.343 C
90	53 J	170	.312 A	1.0 Sec	545 Ω	.312 C
100	48.6 J	170	.286 A	1.0 Sec	595 Ω	.286 C

Note the simultaneous increase in Impedance and deterioration of Current characteristic of constant Voltage SW devices. At maximum settings, the final maximum SW outputs above emit the following MTTLOIs per age category: 10 Yrs: 23 fold at 200J; 20 Yrs: 9.44 fold at 148J; 24 Yrs: 7.08 fold at 134 J; 30 Yrs: 4.8 fold at 118J maximum; 40 Yrs: 2.75 fold at 98J maximum; 50 Yrs: 1.72 fold at 84J; 60 Yrs: 1.75 fold at 73J; 65 Yrs: .95 fold--barely threshold at 69J; 70 Yrs: no seizure at 65J; 80 Yrs: no seizure at 58J; 90 Yrs: no seizure at 53J; 100 Yrs: no seizure at 49J. It is assumed that while Impedance may moderately rise over a course (or series) of BP, unlike SW, BP Impedances do not significantly rise within a single BP procedure. Thus, initial and final Impedance for BP within a single "treatment" are more or less synonymous; whereas, initial and final Impedances for SW are discrepant. This factor makes BP more effective and consequently much more powerful in the older age groups, and, in fact, more powerful, generally. Compare maximum SW EO (200J) to modern day second (circa 230-250J) and third generation (circa 500J) BP devices (though in disparate age categories). Note how maximum SW Charge of 1.172C at maximum SW output is comparable to maximum Charge of modern-day third, fourth

[263] To confirm inverse relationship between EO and Impedance at .1 Seconds, we must create a new constant using the formula: EO = K/Ω. From the first row in the above chart, 28.9J = K/170Ω = **2890**; Thus 2890/100Ω = 28.9J; 2890/150Ω = circa 19J; 2890/170Ω = 17J, etc.

and fifth generation BP devices (1.0-1.2 C) though again in disparate age categories. Maximum B-24 settings are potentially extremely destructive in the younger age categories. Conversely, MTTLOI with SW diminishes with increasing age until by age 65, threshold, and so seizure, is not readily achievable.

The following table depicts a simpler version of SW at maximum settings, respective MTTLOIs, and maximum EOs relative to age.

EO Maximums B-24 SW Deteriorating Current Device at Maximum Settings--All Age Levels [264]

AGE	EO	Voltage	Current	Duration	Resistance	Charge
10 Yr	200 J	170	1.172 A	1.0 Sec	145 Ω	1.172 C
20	148.2 J	170	.872 A	1.0 Sec	195 Ω	.872 C
24	134.42 J	170	.791 A	1.0 Sec	215 Ω	.791 C
30	118 J	170	.694 A	1.0 Sec	245 Ω	.694 C
40	97.97 J	170	.576 A	1.0 Sec	295 Ω	.576 C
50	83.77 J	170	.493 A	1.0 Sec	345 Ω	.493 C
60	73.16 J	170	.430 A	1.0 Sec	395 Ω	.430 C
65	68.81 J	170	.405 A	1.0 Sec	420 Ω	.405 C
70	64.94 J	170	.382 A	1.0 Sec	445 Ω	.382 C
80	58.4 J	170	.343 A	1.0 Sec	495 Ω	.343 C
90	53 J	170	.312 A	1.0 Sec	545 Ω	.312 C
100	48.6 J	170	.286 A	1.0 Sec	595 Ω	.286 C

Below, more Simply Still are Three Critical Readings at Max. SW Settings for All Age Categories

AGE	EO	MTTLOI
10	200 J	23
20	148.2 J	9.44
24	134.42 J	7.07
30	118 J	4.78
40	97.97 J	2.75
50	83.77 J	1.72
60	73.16 J	1.15
65	68.81 J	.956
70	64.94 J	.804
80	58.4 J	.59
90	53 J	.49
100	48.6 J	.41

Using our SW paradigm (based on Weiner's initial figures for the ten year old child), we can create the following table comparing maximum B-24 SW output settings for all age categories to, for instance, extant third generation BP devices for the same age categories.

---

[264] To confirm inverse relationship between EO and Impedance at .1 Seconds, we must create a new constant using the formula: EO = K/Ω. From the first row in the above chart, 28.9J = K/170Ω = **2890**; Thus 2890/100Ω = 28.9J; 2890/150Ω = circa 19J; 2890/170Ω = 17J, etc.

B-24 SW at Maximum Settings for all Age Groups v Consistent Emissions of 3rd Generation JR/SR 1 IEC BP Device in the Same Age Categories

Yr	SW	BP	SW	BP	SW	BP	SW	BP	SW	BP	SW	BP	SW	BP
	Imp	Imp	Volt	Volt	Amp	Amp	Sec	Sec	Chg	Chg	*MTTLOI*	*MTTLOI*	Joule	Joule
10	145	50	170	40	1.17	.8	1.0	.5	1.17	.14	***23.0***	**5.0**	200	5.76
20	195	100	170	80	.870	.8	1.0	.8	.872	.23	***9.44***	**5.0**	148	18.4
24	215	120	170	96	.791	.8	1.0	.96	.791	.28	***7.08***	**5.0**	134	26.5
30	245	150	170	120	.694	.8	1.0	1.2	.694	.35	***4.80***	**5.0**	118	41.5
40	295	200	170	160	.576	.8	1.0	1.6	.576	.46	***2.75***	**5.0**	98.0	74
50	345	250	170	200	.493	.8	1.0	2.0	.493	.58	***1.72***	**5.0**	83.8	115
60	395	300	170	240	.430	.8	1.0	2.4	.430	.69	***1.15***	**5.0**	73.2	166
65	420	325	170	260	.405	.8	1.0	2.6	.405	.75	***.95***	**5.0**	68.6	195
70	445	350	170	280	.38	.8	1.0	2.8	.38	.81	***.80***	**5.0**	64.9	226
80	495	400	170	320	.343	.8	1.0	3.2	.343	.92	***.59***	**5.0**	58.4	295
90	545	450	170	360	.312	.8	1.0	3.6	.312	1.04	***.44***	**5.0**	53	373
100	595	500	170	400	.286	.8	1.0	4.0	.286	1.15	***.34***	**5.0**	48.6	460

Note above that B-24 SW at maximum settings is super powerful in the younger age categories, but ineffective at ages 65 and older. The machine cannot generally overcome more than 400Ω and may not be able to seize individuals 65 and over (shaded areas on bottom rows above) with BL-ECT. Note too, how MTTLOI emitted by the Third Generation BP device equals and then surpasses SW at about age 30 and up, Note to, how the 3rd generation BP delivers Energy Outputs in joules equaling and then surpassing maximum B-24 SW settings from about age 45 and up. Also note, however, the surpassing power of SW from ages 10 to 40.

Simplifying the above chart, we can compare SW EO and MTTLOI alone to Third Generation BP EO and MTTLOI alone with respect to age:

Critical Readings at Maximum SW Settings vs 3rd Generation BP Device for All Age Categories

Age	SW	BP	SW	BP
	Joule	*Joule*	*MTTLOI*	*MTTLOI*
10	200	5.76	***23.0***	**5.0**
20	148	18.4	***9.44***	**5.0**
24	134	26.5	***7.08***	**5.0**
30	118	41.5	***4.80***	**5.0**
40	98.0	74	***2.75***	**5.0**
50	83.8	115	***1.72***	**5.0**
60	73.2	166	***1.15***	**5.0**
65	68.6	195	***.95***	**5.0**
70	64.9	226	***.80***	**5.0**
80	58.4	295	***.59***	**5.0**
90	53	373	***.44***	**5.0**
100	48.6	460	***.34***	**5.0**

We can, of course, expand the chart to include all five BP generations:

Critical Readings at Maximum SW Settings vs All Five BP Generations for All Age Categories

Age	SW Joule	BP 1st Joule	BP 2nd Joule	BP 3rd Joule	BP 4th Joule	BP 5th Joule	SW MTTLOI	BP 1st MTTLOI	BP 2nd MTTLOI	BP 3rd MTTLOI	BP 4th MTTLOI	BP 5th MTTLOI
10	**200**	1.08	2.40	5.76	11.52	15	***23.0***	*1.08*	2.4	**5.0**	*10.0*	*12.0*
20	**148**	4.32	9.60	18.43	36.86	48	***9.44***	*1.08*	2.4	**5.0**	*10.0*	*12.0*
30	**118**	9.72	21.6	41.47	82.94	108	***4.80***	*1.08*	2.4	**5.0**	*10.0*	*12.0*
40	**98.0**	17.28	38.4	73.73	147.46	192	***2.75***	*1.08*	2.4	**5.0**	*10.0*	*12.0*
50	**83.8**	27	60.0	115.2	230.4	300	***1.72***	*1.08*	2.4	**5.0**	*10.0*	*12.0*
60	**73.2**	38.88	86.4	165.88	331.76	432	***1.15***	*1.08*	2.4	**5.0**	*10.0*	*12.0*
65	**68.6**	46	101.4	194.68	389.36	507	***.95***	*1.08*	2.4	**5.0**	*10.0*	*12.0*
70	**64.9**	52.95	117.5	225.8	451.6	588	***.80***	*1.08*	2.4	**5.0**	*10.0*	*12.0*
80	**58.4**	69.12	153.6	295	590	768	***.59***	*1.08*	2.4	**5.0**	*10.0*	*12.0*
90	**53J**	87.48	194.4	373	746	972	***.44***	*1.08*	2.4	**5.0**	*10.0*	*12.0*
100	**48.6J**	108	240J	460J	922J	1200J	***.34***	*1.08*	2.4	**5.0**	*10.0*	*12.0*

Based on these configurations, we can create the graphs below comparing extant default outputs of all five BP generations to maximum SW settings.

We can Now Use Graphs to Compare EO Delivered at Maximum SW Settings Alone to the Default Energy Outputs Delivered by the Various Modern BP Device Generations.[265]

Based on tables above deduced from the Cameron paradigm, the B-24 SW at Maximum EO Settings vs SW Maximum Threshold Outputs looks something like the graph below.

EO at Maximum SW Settings v Maximum SW Thresholds

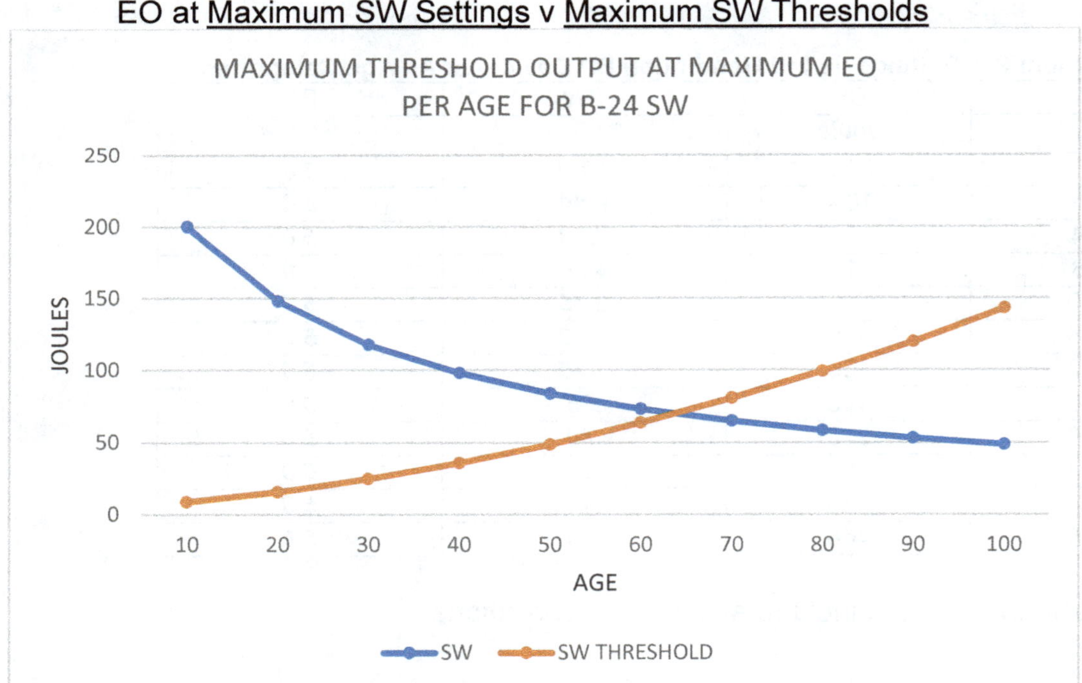

Here we can see the upside down construction of SW, the most powerful outputs delivered to the youngest age categories with the least resistance to electricity, the least powerful outputs delivered to the oldest age categories with the highest resistance to electricity.

[265] For More Details of the B-24 in Chart Form--See Appendix II.

Now let us compare SW at Maximum to the Default EO Delivered by All 5 BP Generations individually:

EO DELIVERED by FIRST GENERATION MECTA C BP DEVICE v
EO DELIVERED BY B-24 SW DEVICE AT MAXIMUM SETTINGS

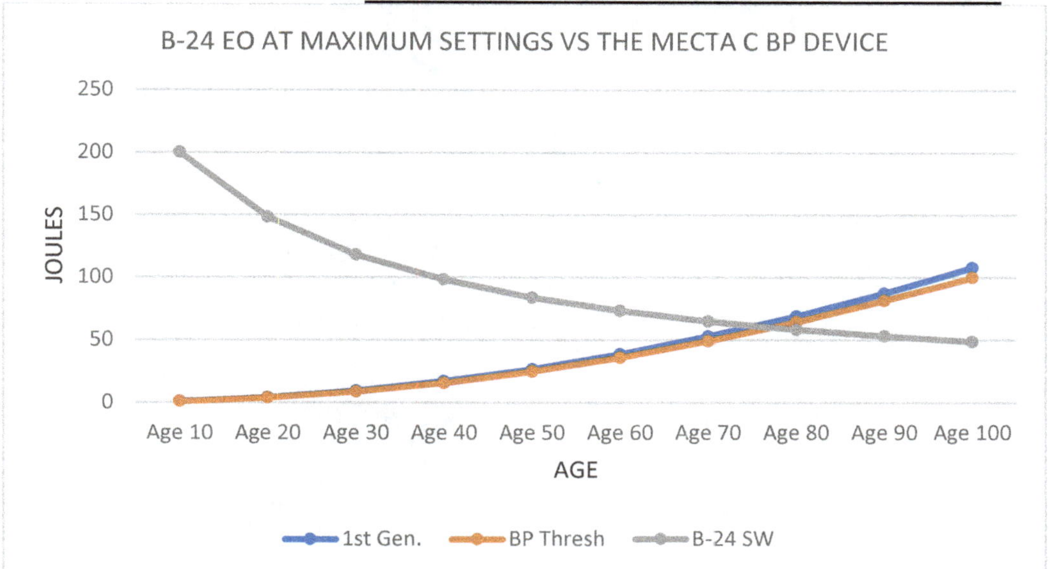

Note the MECTA C (blue) gradually climbs in power in accordance with increasing age and so higher and higher Resistance to electricity as opposed to the upside down paradigm of SW (gray). Note the "C" emits output just above threshold in all age categories culminating at 108J maximum, quite the opposite of SW which administers the highest outputs in those age categories with the least Resistance to electricity culminating at 200J in the youngest age category.

EO DELIVERED by SECOND BP GENERATION DEVICE v
EO DELIVERED BY B-24 SW DEVICE AT MAXIMUM SETTINGS

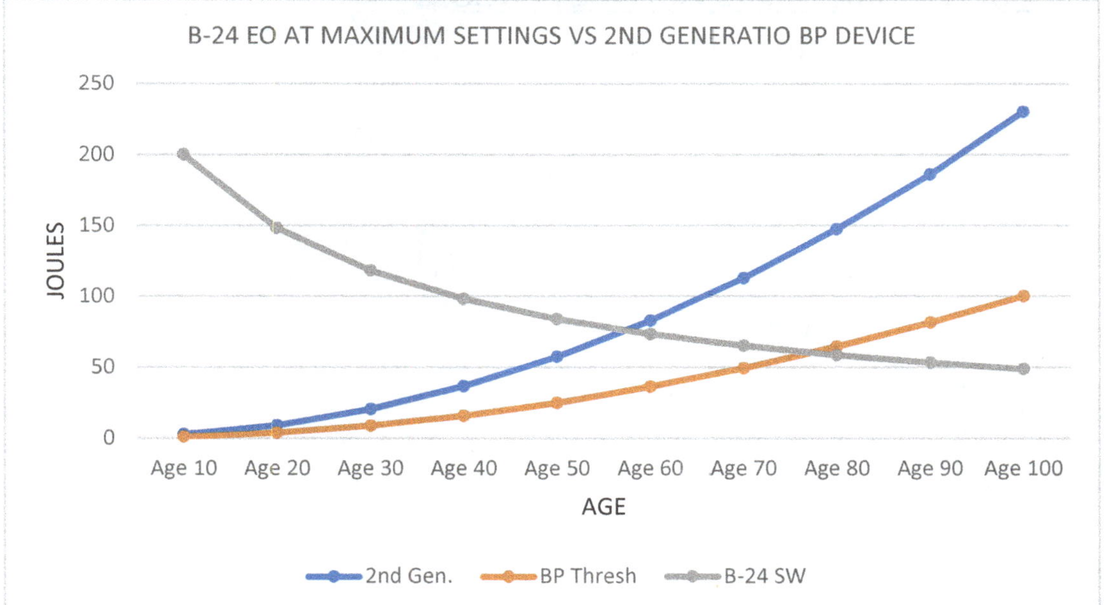

Note how the second generation BP device (blue) increases its distance from threshold as it more than doubles the power of the MECTA "C" in all age categories. Nevertheless, BP power properly increases with increased Resistance, the opposite of SW which increases in power with decreasing Resistance, creating the highest MTTLOI in the youngest age categories. Note how the second generation BP device surpasses SW at maximum settings by about age 55. Note too BP's 240J maximum output surpassing the 200J output of SW although in disparate age categories.

EO DELIVERED by THIRD GENERATION BP DEVICE v EO DELIVERED BY B-24 SW DEVICE AT MAXIMUM SETTINGS

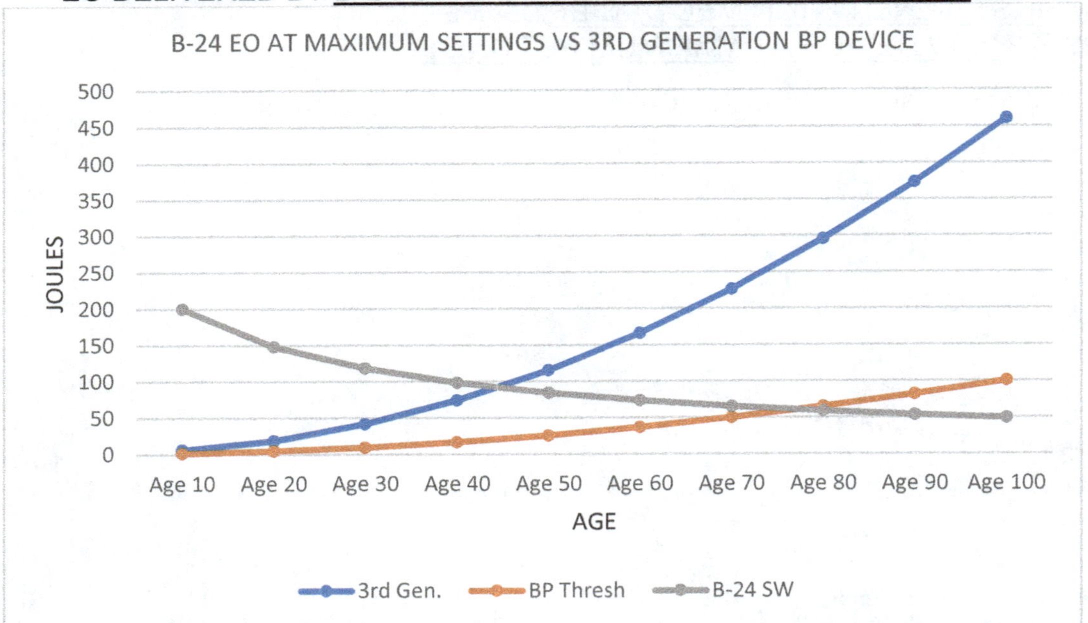

The third generation BP device (blue) doubles the power of the second generation BP device in every age category, Note how by about age 42, the third generation BP device becomes exponentially more powerful than SW even at maximum SW Settings, emitting 460 to 480J compared to the 200J output of SW albeit in disparate age categories. Note too, on the other hand, the upside down power paradigm of Sine Wave, decreasing in power, the older the recipient, increasing in power the younger the recipient, incredibly destructive in the younger age categories.

EO DELIVERED by FOURTH GENERATION BP DEVICE v EO DELIVERED BY B-24 SW DEVICE AT MAXIMUM SETTINGS

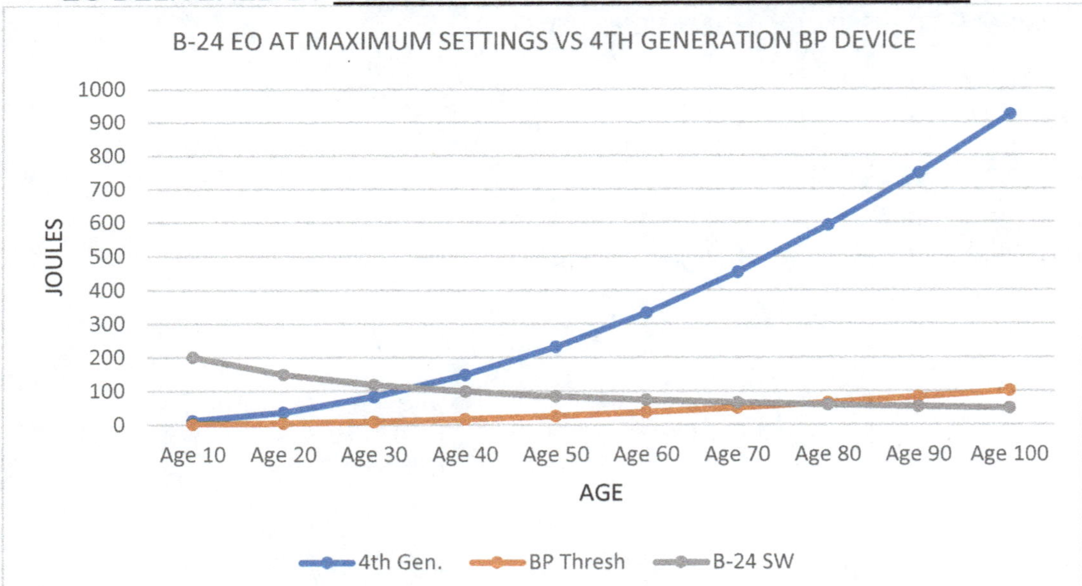

The fourth generation BP device (blue) doubles the power of the third generation BP device so that by age 32 or 33, BP becomes exponentially more powerful than SW (gray) even at maximum SW output in all but the youngest age categories. Note the 922J output of BP compared to the 200J output of SW, albeit in opposing age categories. Note too, however, the upside down nature of SW, emitting its 200J maximum in the ten year old age category, those with the least resistance to electricity, but becoming impotent in the 65 and older categories, those with the greatest resistance to electricity.

EO DELIVERED by FIFTH BP GENERATION DEVICE v
EO DELIVERED BY B-24 SW DEVICE AT MAXIMUM SETTINGS

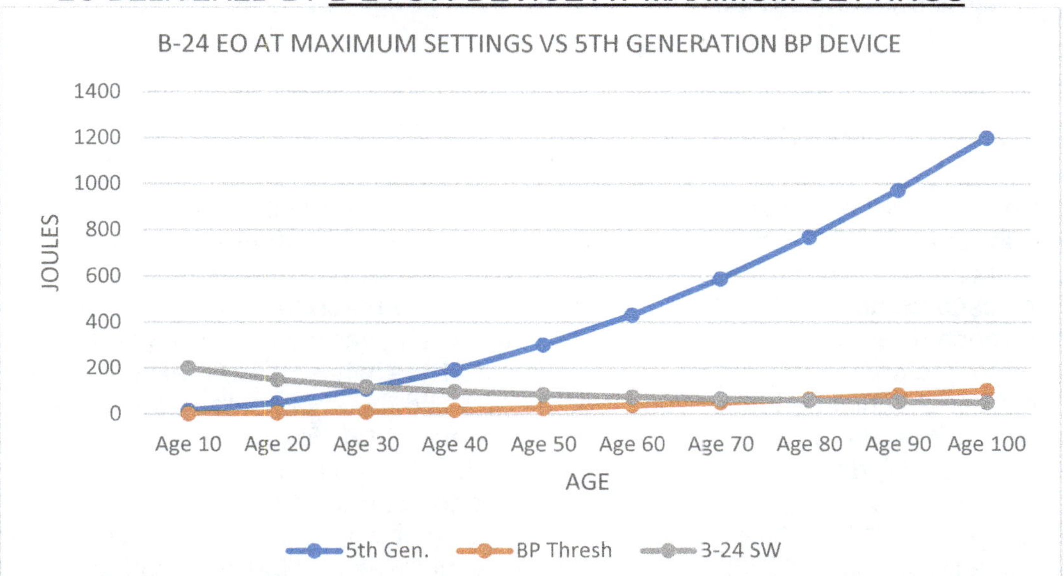

The hypothetical but "legal" fifth generation BP device (blue) increases in power relative to the fourth generation BP device in all age categories so that by age 29 or 30 and older, BP becomes greater in power than SW (gray) in all subsequent age categories. Note the 1200J emitted by the fifth generation BP device, dwarfing the 200J SW device in cumulative power. On the other hand, note how SW is prodigiously more powerful than even the super powerful Fifth generation BP device from ages 10 to about 30, reflecting the upside down nature of the B-24 SW device, emitting its greatest power in the youngest age categories, dwindling in power in the older age categories, those with the greatest resistance to electricity.

EO DELIVERED BY ALL FIVE BP GENERATIONS Vs
EO DELIVERED BY B-24 SW DEVICE AT MAXIMUM SETTINGS

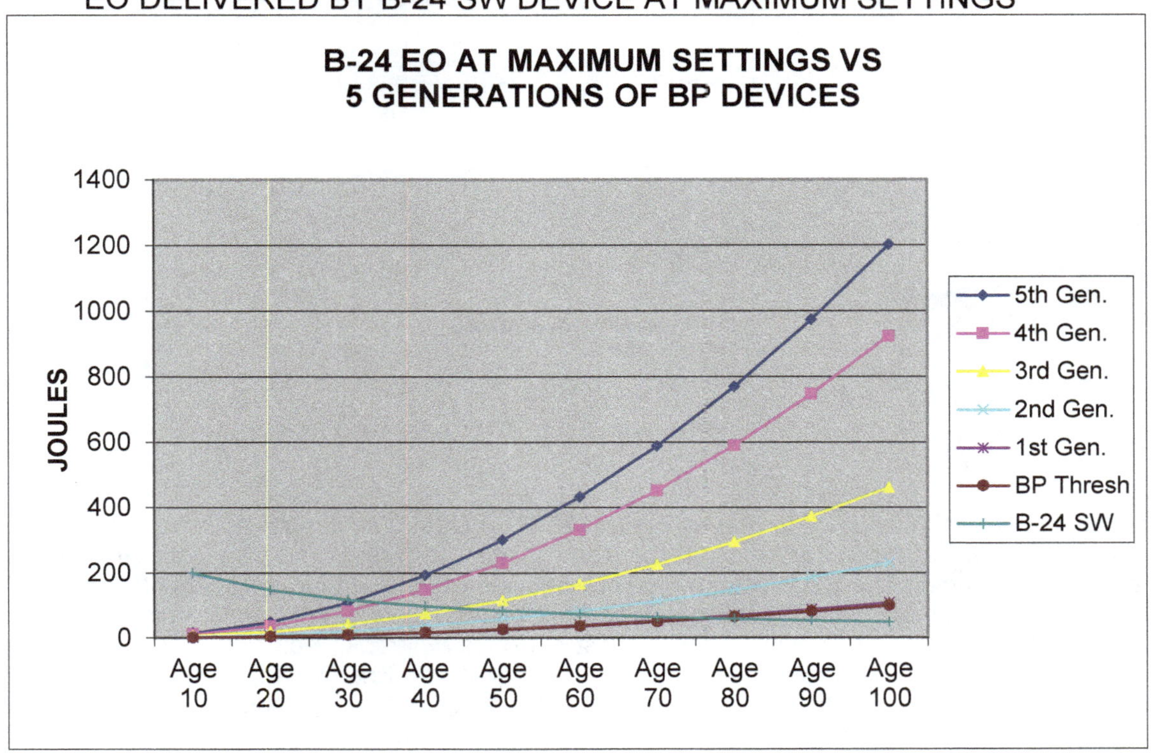

It is easy to see that Brief Pulse has become more and more powerful with each BP generation until BP surpasses SW (dark green) in most age categories even at maximum SW settings. Even so, we must take note that the B-24 surpasses even the power of the most powerful Brief Pulse device in the 10 to 30 year old age categories. Moreover, this would remain true even at probable minimal stimulus SW and SW limited to 1.0A. Frighteningly, SW is predominantly used in the younger age categories.

MTTLOI OF BP v MTTLOI OF SW AT MAXIMUM SETTINGS

MTTLOI or Multifold Threshold Titration Level Output Intensity is the multifold threshold output a machine delivers in all age categories. In short, MTTLOI is the default multiple of threshold output BP machines are designed to deliver to all recipients and the SW device delivers to individual recipients. Comparing SW MTTLOI to BP MTTLOI is not totally correspondent in that SW requires more energy to reach threshold than BP. For example, it takes 8.7 joules to reach threshold at maximum output for the ten year old child on a SW device and 1.0 joule to reach threshold for the same ten year old on a BP device. Thus, while SW at maximum output can emit 200 joules for the ten year old child and so a (200J ÷ 8.7J =) 23 fold threshold output, the same ten year old child on a first generation BP device BP device might be administered 1.08J for a (1.08J ÷1.0J =) 1.08 MTTLOI, 2.5J on a second generation BP device for a (2.5J ÷1.0J =) 2.5 MTTLOI, 5J on a third generation BP device for a (5J ÷ 1.0J =) 5 MTTLOI, 10J on a fourth generation BP device for a (10J ÷ 1.0J =) 10 MTTLOI, and 12J on a fifth generation BP device for a (12 ÷ 1.0J =) 12 MTTLOI. Put another way, the BP device could emit a 23 fold threshold output for the ten year old with only 23 joules, whereas, it takes 200 joules to emit a 23 fold threshold output with a SW device. Nevertheless, the comparison can be useful, particularly compared to BP devices manufactured after the MECTA "C" based on specifically increasing Multifold Threshold Titration Level Output Intensities. As such, the defining characteristic of modern day BP devices is its specific MTTLOI.

Let us first graph the MTTLOI for SW at maximum settings v SW Threshold. Note SW's precipitous MTTLOI decline due to declining Current.

MTTLOI at <u>MAXIMUM SW SETTINGS</u> v SW THRESHOLD

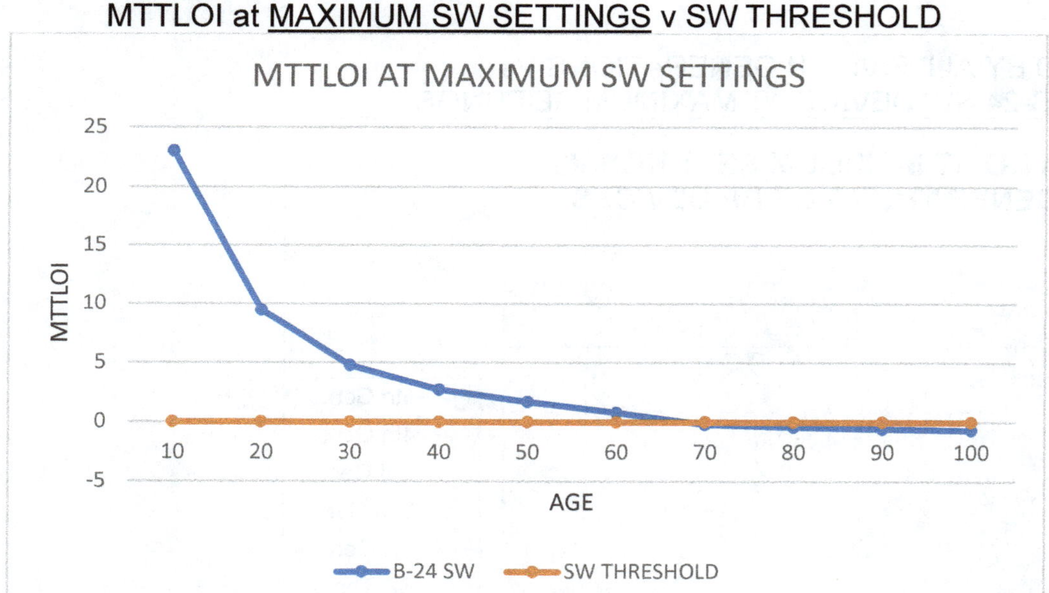

Note that at maximum output, the B-24 SW appears to deliver about a 23 MTTLOI at 200J for the ten year old year old recipient who, of course, has the lowest Resistance, whereas, at about age 65, the B-24 machine is barely efficient enough to induce seizure even at maximum output. The SW machine may not induce seizure at all for recipients older than 65 years of age, at least with BL "ECT." At maximum SW settings, recipients with the lowest Resistance, that is, the very youngest, receive the highest raw Energy Output and so the highest MTTLOI; whereas, recipients with the highest Resistance, that is, the very oldest, even at maximum settings, receive the lowest raw Energy Output and so the lowest MTTLOI. It must be concluded that the B-24 SW machine at maximum settings is both incredibly dangerous and incredibly inefficient. Compare the B-24's inconsistent MTTLOI to the MECTA "C" depicted below.

<u>MTTLOI</u> of B-24 <u>SW at MAXIMUM</u> SETTINGS v
<u>MTTLOI</u> of <u>FIRST GENERATION MECTA C BP DEVICE</u>

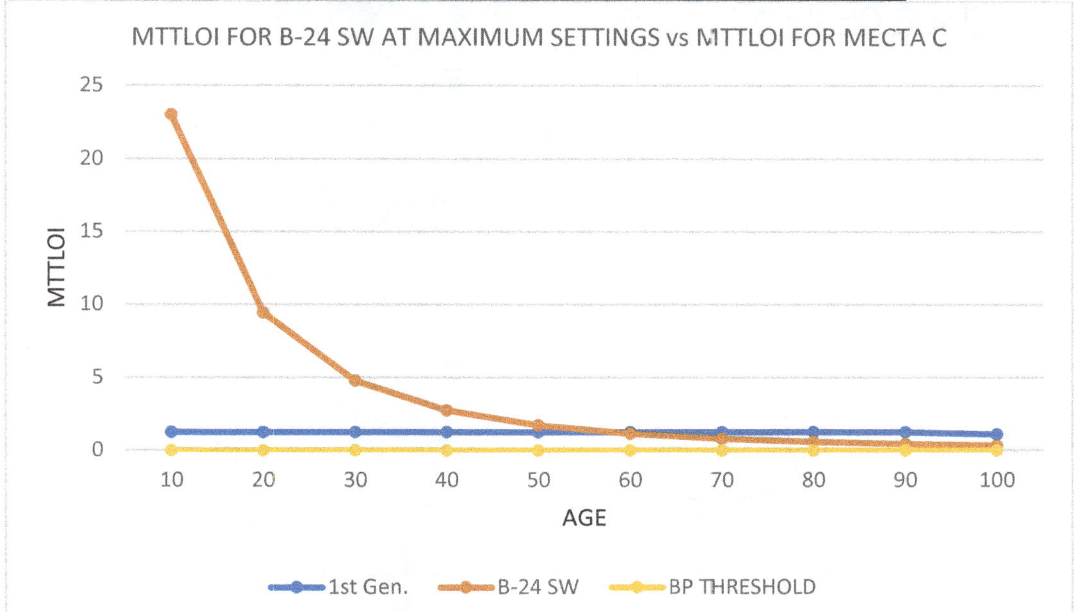

SW (orange) at maximum output, begins with an extremely high MTTLOI, then dramatically declines. The MECTA "C" (blue) on the other hand, designed to induce seizure at just above threshold output with BL ECT, has a consistent 1.08 MTTLOI in all age categories, only surpassing SW at about age 60 in order to induce seizure. <u>Defining characteristic of "C"--1.08 MTTLOI</u>.

<u>MTTLOI</u> of <u>B-24 SW at MAXIMUM SETTINGS</u> v
<u>MTTLOI</u> of <u>SECOND GENERATION BP DEVICE</u>

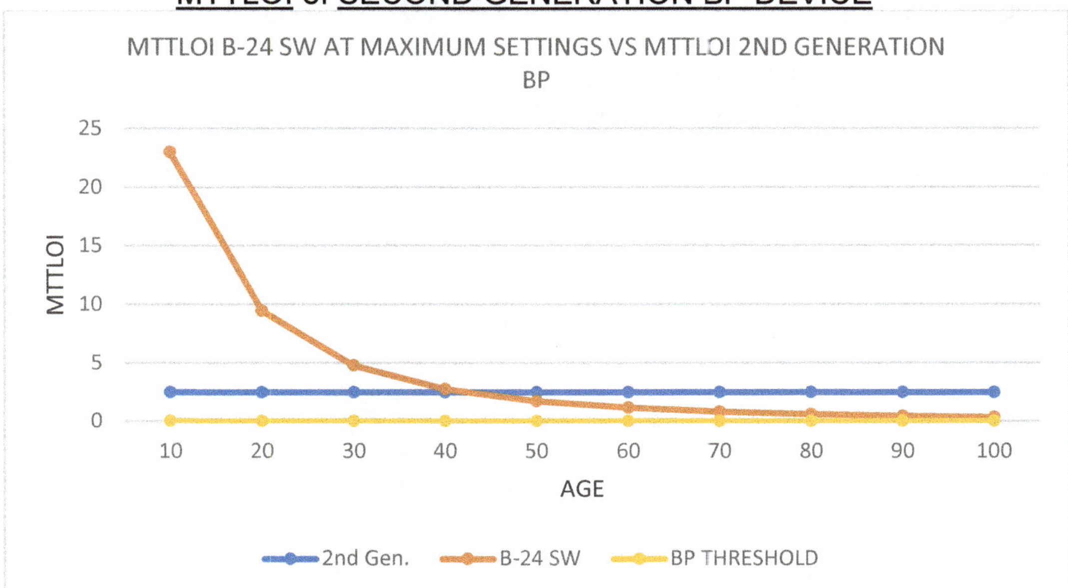

SW (orange) at maximum output, as we have seen, begins with an extremely high MTTLOI, then drops dramatically. 2nd Generation BP Devices (blue), on the other hand, have a consistent albeit high 2.3-2.5 MTTLOI in all age groups, more than twice that of the MECTA "C." Note how the consistent MTTLOI of the 2nd generation BP device now surpasses the declining MTTLOI of SW after the earlier age of about 40. Note too, that SW at maximum output dramatically surpasses the MTTLOI of the second generation BP device in the younger age categories between ages 10 and 40. <u>Defining 2nd Gen. BP characteristic--2.3-2.5 MTTLOI</u>.

MTTLOI of B-24 SW at MAXIMUM SETTINGS v MTTLOI of THIRD GENERATION BP

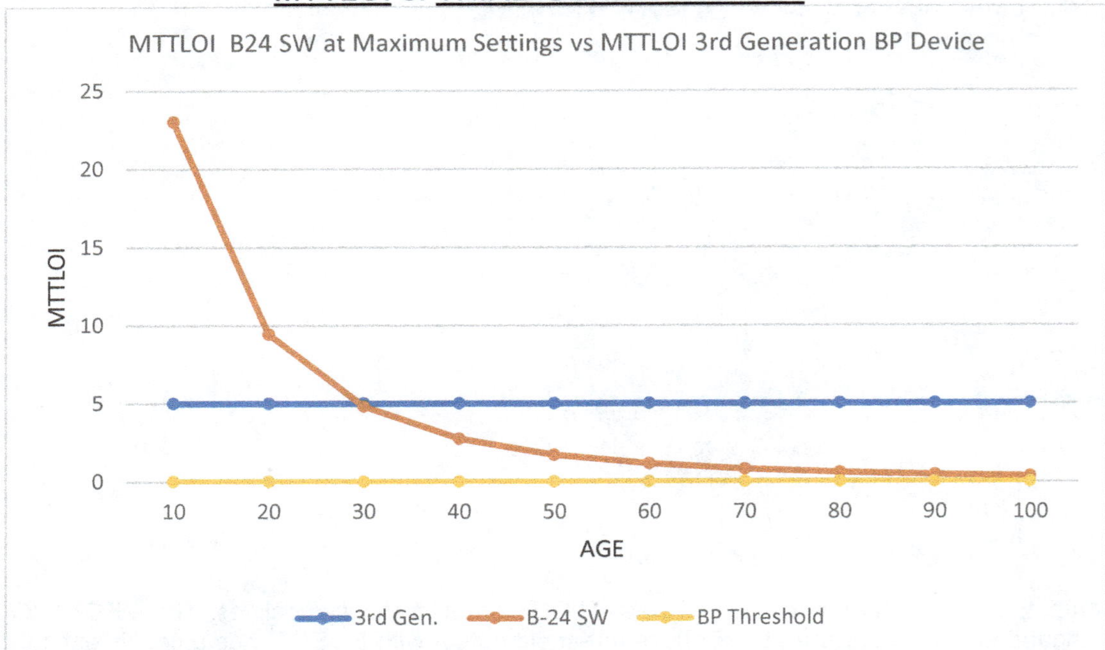

SW (orange) at maximum output, as we have seen, begins with a high MTTLOI, then drops dramatically. 3rd Generation BP Devices (blue), on the other hand, twice as powerful as second generation BP devices, have a consistent albeit extremely high circa 5.0 MTTLOI in all age groups. Note how the MTTLOI of the BP 3rd generation BP device surpasses the maximum MTTLOI of SW after the earlier age of about 30. Note too, however, that in the confined age range between about 10 and 30 years, the MTTLOI of SW surpasses even the MTTLOI of the 3rd generation BP device.
Defining 3rd Gen. BP characteristic--4.6 MTTLOI.

MTTLOI OF B-24 SW at MAXIMUM SETTINGS v MTTLOI OF FOURTH GENERATION BP DEVICE

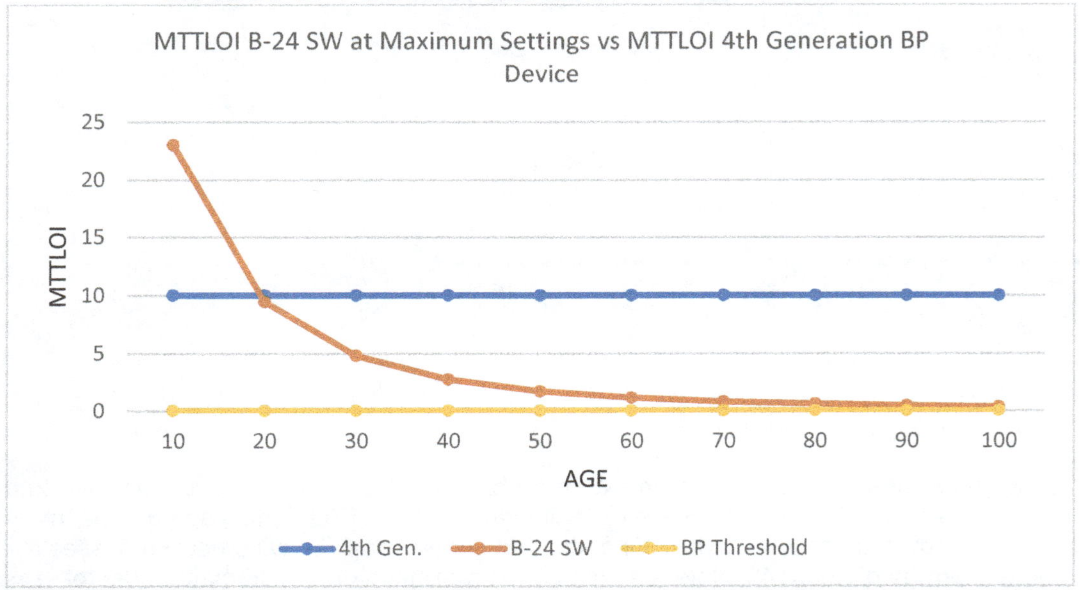

SW (orange) at maximum output settings begins with dramatically high MTTLOI, dropping exponentially. 4th Generation BP Devices (blue), twice as powerful as third generation BP devices, have consistent albeit extremely high circa 10.0 MTTLOI in all age groups.

Note how the MTTLOI of 4th generation BP surpasses maximum MTTLOI of SW after the even earlier age of 20. Note confined range between 10-20 yrs. during which SW surpasses the MTTLOI of even the 4th generation BP device. 4th Gen. characteristic--9.2 MTTLOI.

MTTLOI OF B-24 SW at MAXIMUM SETTINGS v MTTLOI OF FIFTH GENERATION BP DEVICE

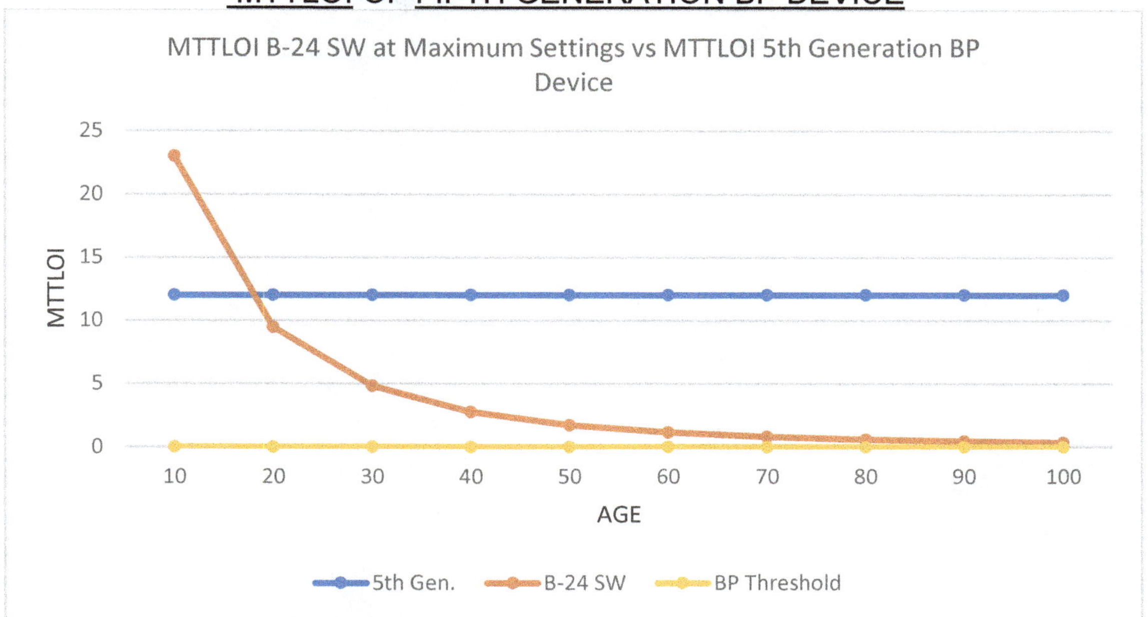

SW (orange) at maximum settings begins with dramatically high MTTLOI, dropping exponentially. 5th Generation BP Devices (blue), much more powerful than 4th generation BP devices, unlike SW, have a consistent albeit extremely high circa 12.0 MTTLOI at all ages. Note how the MTTLOI of 5th generation BP surpasses MTTLOI of maximum SW settings after the even earlier age of about 17. Note the small range from 10 to 17 at which SW surpasses MTTLOI of 5th generation BP devices. Main trait--12.0 MTTLOI.

MTTLOI OF B-24 SW at MAXIMUM SETTINGS v MTTLOI OF ALL FIVE BP GENERATIONS

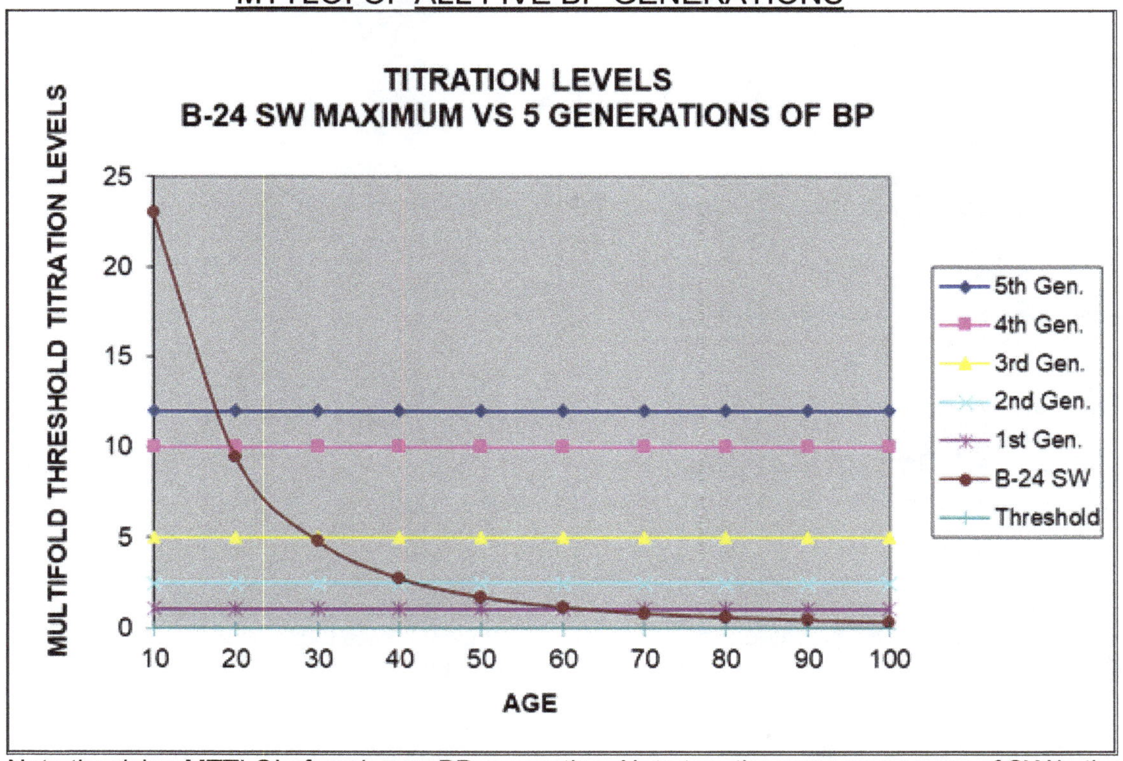

Note the rising MTTLOI of each new BP generation. Note too, the awesome power of SW in the youngest age categories.

MTTLOI OF B-24 SW at MAXIMUM SETTINGS v MTTLOI of B-24 SW AT PROBABLE MINIMAL STIMULUS SETTINGS v DEFAULT MTTLOI OF ALL FIVE BP GENERATIONS

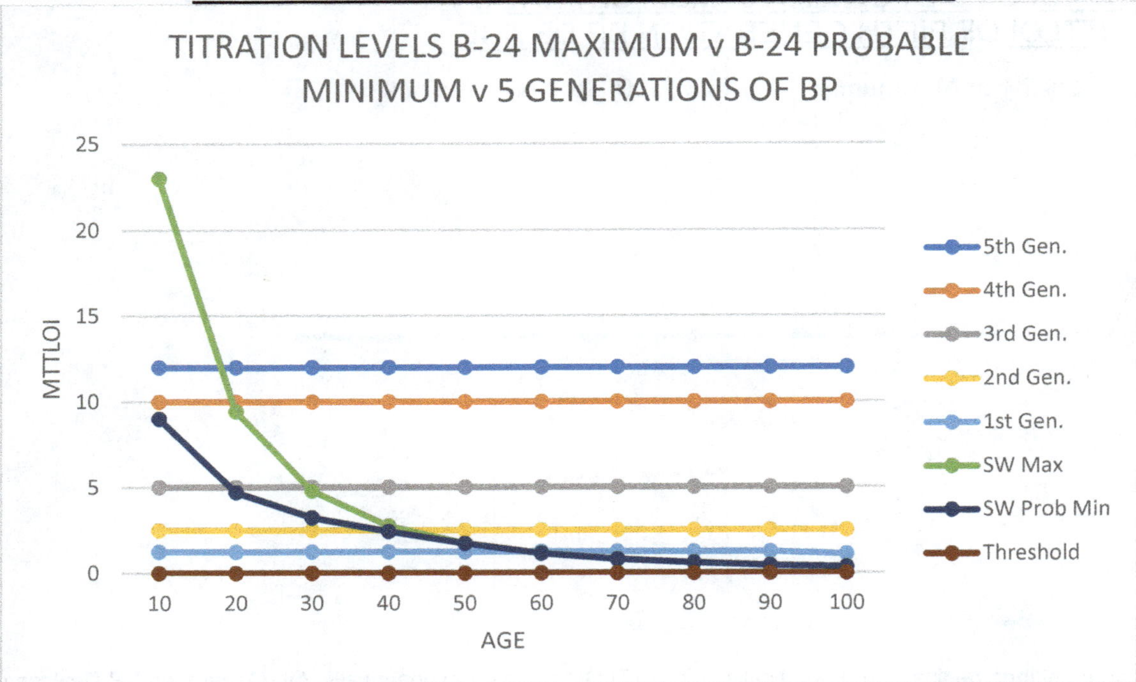

Note that even set for probable minimal stimulus SW (black), the lowest probable outputs for which the SW device can be set, true minimal stimulus settings appear circumvented in order to assure "efficacy." Note too, that even at probable minimal stimulus, the SW device is almost as powerful as the fourth generation BP device (orange) in the ten year old age category.

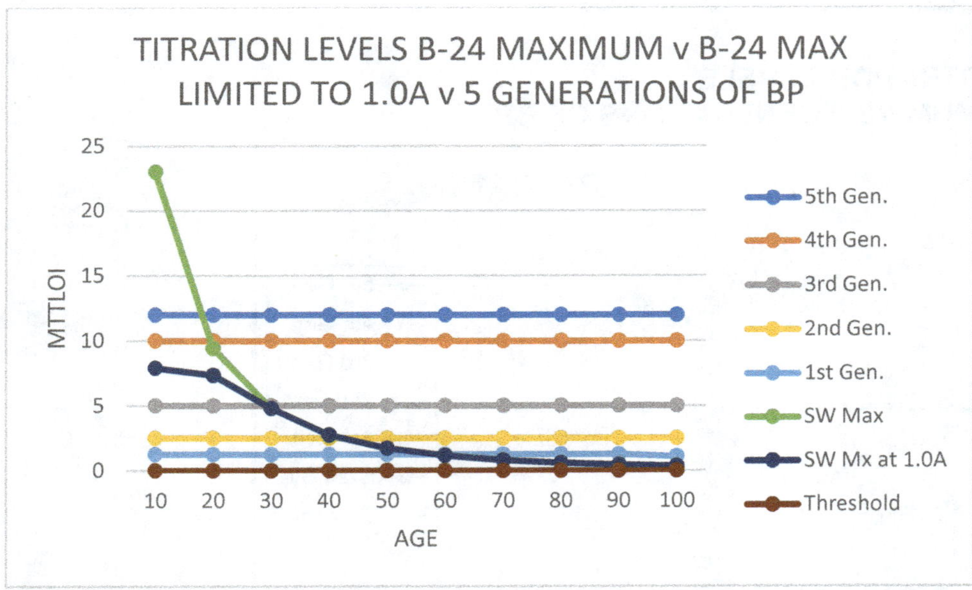

Note that even set for maximum output limited to 1.0A, another possibility for "minimal stimulus" SW (black) settings, true minimal stimulus settings again appear circumvented in order to assure "efficacy." Note too, that at maximum settings limited to 1.0A minimal stimulus, the SW device is yet more powerful than the 3rd generation BP device (gray) in age categories 10 through 30.

We can see from the above graphs that SW devices are remarkably inefficient and inconsistent; ranging from incredibly dangerous and unmanageable multifold threshold doses of electricity for younger recipients to barely minimal stimulus and below minimal stimulus for older recipients even set for maximum output. The initial BP device introduced at the beginning of the BP era in 1976, the MECTA "C" which delivered a consistent 1.08 fold threshold output for all age recipients, never surpassing 108 maximum Joules, appears to have represented a remarkable improvement in safety, efficiency, and consistency regarding induction of the adequate seizure compared to SW. Even set for true minimal stimulus settings, the MECTA "C" could induce adequate seizures at half the EO of SW. Moreover, SW, even at maximum SW settings cannot be relied upon to reach threshold (with BL ECT) for recipients sixty-five years of age and older. For recipients about sixty years of age, even maximum SW settings emit a 1.15 fold threshold, about that of first generation BP devices; about 1.72 fold threshold for fifty year old recipients, more than that of first generation BP devices, but less than that of second generation BP devices, and about a 2.75 MTTLOI, for forty year old recipients, slightly more than second generation BP devices, but only half that of third generation BP devices. For thirty year olds, maximum SW settings elicit about a 4.8 MTTLOI, about that of third generation BP devices and for twenty year olds, maximum SW settings elicit a 9.44 MTTLOI, about that of potential fourth generation BP devices. Finally, for ten year old recipients, maximum SW settings elicit an unconscionable 23 MTTLOI, about twice that of potential but legal super powerful fifth generation BP devices. Administering SW to younger people at maximum output is much more dangerous than administering maximum SW to older individuals whose Impedances are much higher and who are thereby much less affected by it. On the other hand, the default outputs of later generation BP devices are now much more powerful and thus much more dangerous than SW for older people even at maximum SW output in that later generation BP devices elicit consistent circa 2.5, 5.0, 10.0, and 12.0 fold threshold dosages in accordance with the MTTLOI designated to Second, Third, Fourth, and Fifth generation BP devices respectively for all age recipients. BP's tremendously high outputs for older age categories are due to its automatically enhancing Voltages necessary to overcome very high Impedances to maintain consistent Multifold Threshold Titration Level Output Intensities per specific BP generational devices. While there are instances in which SW may deliver a greater MTTLOI and greater cumulative EO than BP (within the younger age categories), particularly at maximum output, default electrical dosages of BP are generally much higher than the highest SW outputs in all the later age categories. While Medcraft claims that outputs on the B-24 can be adjusted down via Voltage and Duration, it is the author's opinion, based on the unusual varying of MTTLOI assigned to each age category via Medcraft's B-25 Brief Pulse device and which appears to be patterned after the B-24 SW device, that the B-24 cannot be set for true minimal stimulus (for SW). It is the author's opinion that the B-24 cannot elicit below about 36J or a 9 MTTLOI in the 10 year old age category, 43J or a 4.7 MTTLOI in the 20 year old category, 53J or a 3.22 MTTLOI in the 30 year old category, and 63J or a 2.43 MTTLOI in the 40 year old age category, all MTTLOIs under which the B-25 is not allowed in these same age categories.[266] A second possibility is that via Voltage and Duration, the B-24 at "minimal stimulus" must be set to maximum outputs limited to 1.0 Ampere, again, so that true minimal stimulus even with SW is not possible in the younger age categories. (Weiner, in the 1982 APA Standard suggests SW remain limited to 1.0A.) In this case, the B-24 (based on maximum thresholds) cannot elicit below 68.9J or a 7.9 MTTLOI in the 10 year old category, 115J or a 7.35 MTTLOI in the twenty year old age category, 118J or a 4.8 MTTLOI in the thirty year old age category, 98J or a 2.75 MTTLOI in the forty year old age category, 83.8J or a 1.72 MTTLOI in the 50 year old age category, and 73J or a 1.15 MTTLOI in the 60 year old age category.[267] Due to deteriorating current, the remaining age categories, even set for maximum output may not reach threshold at all. (See probable minimal stimulus MTTLOI in the graph above.) In short, while SW inherently requires more power to induce seizure than BP, overwhelming evidence suggests that both the later Brief Pulse devices and the B-24 SW device circumvent true minimal stimulus outputs in that neither is adequate convulsion based. Rather, both are adequate electricity based. In short, neither the later modern day Brief Pulse device nor the B-24 SW device is an ECT apparatus. Both are ENR devices.

While the BP device can, of course, be hand-titrated to minimal stimulus output for all recipients at greatly reduced and more efficient outputs than SW (see the MECTA "C"; see also safety studies), this almost never occurs in the field. (Safety studies meant for publication, particularly with BP typically exploit hand-titrated

[266] These outputs are speculatively based on probable minimum MTTLOIs of the B-25.

[267] These outputs are speculatively based on maximum outputs limited to 1.0A and below using maximum SW thresholds. For example, at 1.0A, 68.9J ÷ 8.7J = a 7.9 MTTLOI in the 10 year old category.

minimal stimulus outputs.) It is far easier and indeed, common practice for physicians to set or dial the instrument to the recipients age and simply trust the machine to deliver the "correct" amount of electricity. Physicians typically have no idea of the increasing MTTLOI per each new BP device generation, resulting in modern day BP devices of much greater power than SW, generally. For instance, third generation BP devices are made to emit a circa 5.0 MTTLOI for all age recipients while the fourth generation device emits a circa 10.0 MTTLOI for all age recipients which then become the defining (albeit unpublished) characteristics of third and fourth generation BP devices. In both instances, the physician simply dials the "patient's" age and presses a button. The administrator does not see or experience drastically enhanced electrical dosing from machine to another and may genuinely believe a convulsion was induced with but a "tiny, relatively harmless amount of electricity." In fact, while the MECTA "C" can and does deliver outputs half as powerful as SW even set for true SW minimal stimulus, evidence shows that neither subsequent BP devices nor SW is designed to deliver minimal stimulus; rather, both are deliberately designed to deliver Multifold Threshold Titration Level Output Intensities, generally. Clearly, the so-called therapeutic effect of the adequate convulsion is mythology so that both kinds of devices must be made to emit Multifold Threshold Titration Level Output Intensities of electricity in order to achieve the looked for effect—reasonably long periods of mood and behavior change and so greater tractability, generally. Not surprisingly then, SW is primarily "effective" in the 10 to 40 year old age categories to whom it can deliver supra powerful does of electricity; whereas, the suprathreshold doses of electricity delivered by modern day Brief Pulse devices are "effective" in all age categories, including the oldest. It should be said that the upside down construction of the SW device results in suprathreshold doses of electricity delivered in a somewhat rag-tag manner. The later BP devices, on the other hand, though far in excess of minimal stimulus, deliver consistent MTTLOIs to recipients of every age bracket. In short, Brief Pulse devices are more precisely calculated than SW. In both cases, however, suprathreshold brain injurious electrical doses of electricity are delivered without which, the procedure is clearly "ineffective"

In comparing the devices to one another, what we generally see is that BP manufacturers have enhanced BP devices following the MECTA "C" so that they emit the same high MTTLOI as SW except that the later BP devices have been designed to deliver these MTTLOIs more efficiently and so more consistently, indeed, beyond age 30 or 40. While even later BP devices are superior to maximum SW settings in the younger age categories regarding reduced output, later BP devices nevertheless emit suprathreshold dosages of electricity in both older and younger age categories. In short, the later BP devices far surpass SW devices in power, generally, far surpassing SW the older age categories even compared to maximum SW settings. In fact, SW appears to be almost inapplicable for older age recipients with respect to the induction of adequate seizure; whereas, the later generation BP devices have reclaimed the elder market. In any case, while both SW and modern day Brief Pulse are clearly adequate electricity or ENR devices, BP devices are more consistent and more consistently powerful than SW, generally. Of course, none of the subsequent modern day BP devices are designed to emit minimal stimulus outputs any more than SW; consequently, none conform to the 1982 APA Standard. In sum, none are ECT devices.

While SW at maximum settings yet delivers much more raw power than BP in the younger age categories, the later BP devices have surpassed SW in the emission of raw energy output generally—indeed--many times over. For example, while SW, in rare instances, can deliver an unthinkable 23 MTTLOI, it can do so only in the youngest age category; whereas, fourth and theoretical, but "legal" fifth generation BP devices can deliver supra powerful a circa 10 and circa 12 MTTLOI respectively at every age level consistently, including the eldest. It must be admitted that BP, with its briefer pulses and greater power, is more manageable and more predictable with respect to titration and output per individual age group compared to SW which is crude, and hit and miss by comparison. It must also be admitted that SW set for maximum output in the younger age categories exceeds even the most powerful fifth generation BP device. On the other hand, it must also be acknowledged that the clinical and consistent administering of powerful pre-set multifold threshold doses of electricity via extremely powerful later model BP devices now surpass SW even at maximum SW settings in most age categories. Clearly, both BP and SW are designed to deliver supra powerful brain injurious doses of electricity. Moreover, in both instances, the amount of power as well as the means by which they work, are designedly hidden from view. Indeed, if we compare SW settings to the default outputs of all five generations of modern BP devices, we see the dangerously inconsistent nature of SW in the younger age categories; whereas, we see the intentionally increasing, deliberately calibrated nature of Brief Pulse devices, with their augmenting MTTLOI profiles with each new BP generation.

Conclusion of Comparing Maximum and Probable Minimum SW Settings to all Five Modern Day BP Devices

Defying common sense, at maximum SW settings, the youngest individuals receive the greatest MTTLOI and greatest EO; conversely, the oldest individuals receive the lowest MTTLOI and the lowest EO. BP, on the other hand emits consistent MTTLOI for all recipients with gradational outputs in accordance with age and Impedance. Unfortunately, and contrary to original intent, MTTLOI began to rise with each succeeding BP machine generation becoming the defining characteristic of each new BP machine. It is true that BP manufacturers, unlike SW manufacturers, utilize gradational output, that is, the younger the individual, the lower the EO emitted, the older the individual, the higher the EO and that the MTTLOI is consistently applied to all recipients according to each specific BP machine generation. Although more consistent and more efficient than SW, however, the stark rise in MTTLOI and thus the stark rise in EO per each individual age category with respect to each new BP device generation, totally undermines induction of "adequate seizure" with the least amount of electricity possible. In fact, the increasing and unconscionably high MTTLOI completely contradicts "adequate seizure theory" altogether. With the exception of the MECTA "C," then, modern day BP devices have become so powerful that current devices have actually surpassed the EO of SW in most age categories. This unfortunate fact altogether defeats the original advantage of Brief Pulse-- that of inducing so-called "adequate seizures" with much less EO than SW. Indeed, the pattern, once again like SW, bespeaks of adequate electricity in lieu of adequate seizure--an entirely different concept, an entirely different aim, and so an entirely different procedure than "ECT." No longer convulsive therapy mechanisms, these new medical devices are based on an entirely different concept. Like SW devices of the past, current Brief Pulse devices are actually Electro Neurotransmission Reduction devices based on adequate amounts of electricity for the specific purpose of eliminating tens of thousands of neurotransmitters in the brain.

Extrapolation Concluded:

Certainly, with the exception of maximal settings in the younger age categories where SW can theoretically reach 200J, we can categorically declare that the 2.5, 5.0, 10.0, and 12 fold threshold outputs delivered by later Brief Pulse devices are more dangerous than SW generally, but that SW is more dangerous than even the powerful fifth generation BP device in the younger age categories. In short, due to the extremely low thresholds of younger age recipients who are uniquely susceptible to long-term brain injury from the intense electrical emissions by which both SW and later BP devices actually work, SW is more inherently dangerous than BP. On the other hand, due to BP's consistent Amperage BP is more inherently dangerous than SW in the older age categories, as well as inherently dangerous, generally. Deductively, seizure threshold is the brain's final defense, beyond which protection begins to collapse and neuronal injury commences. Even the so-called minimal stimulus MECTA "C" device delivering outputs just beyond threshold whereupon seizure occurs is no doubt injurious, although much less so than either SW or the later more powerful BP devices. There is little doubt that advanced prospective Perrin-like techniques counting neuronal connections before and after ECT will reveal as much albeit to a much smaller degree than either SW or second, third, fourth, and fifth generation BP devices. In this same vein, the degree of neuronal reduction no doubt increases with each new Brief Pulse generation just as Brief Pulse manufacturers have calculated. Finally, while it is theoretically possible--although not likely--to set SW to so-called "minimal stimulus," even minimal stimulus SW outputs twice the minimal stimulus outputs delivered by the MECTA "C," are injurious. But even if minimal stimulus SW settings are possible, like minimal stimulus BP outputs, they are in all probability, rarely, if ever, utilized. Indeed, there is no prohibitory dynamic preventing administrators from using full force SW even in the youngest age categories. Indeed, Medcraft (which makes the B-24) is extremely guarded regarding its recommended settings relative to age and Impedance. Almost certainly, actual SW setting recommendations, just as default settings via the later model Brief Pulse devices, are suprathreshold wherever possible. In fact, the suprathreshold construction of Medcraft's B-25 BP device seems to be based on suprathreshold settings delivered by Medcraft's B-24 SW device. Tellingly, as we have seen, the safest of modern day devices, the MECTA "C" Brief Pulse, was abandoned soon after the FDA hearings, and supplanted by much more powerful Brief Pulse devices set by default at multifold threshold titration level outputs of electricity in all age categories.

Mechanism at Work

Even though surpassing seizure threshold is required in every instance, common sense tells us that multifold threshold electrical outputs from either SW or second, third, fourth, and fifth generation Brief Pulse devices are more harmful than the minimum amount of electricity required to induce adequate seizures such as delivered by the MECTA "C." The clear aim of the MECTA "C" is to induce adequate convulsions with the least amount of electricity possible and so, the least amount of harm. Thus, if seizure itself does induce injury, the MECTA "C" induces the least amount of injury as it emits the least amount of electricity. Studies are clear that the chief factor in morbidity is excessive electricity, the principal inspiration for the MECTA “C” Brief Pulse. Indeed, both with SW and the with the circa 2.5. 5.0, 10.0, and 12.0 MTTLOI emitted with later model BP devices as opposed to the just above threshold outputs of the MECTA "C," serious injury is not only inevitable, but calculated. In fact, while SW clearly causes more injury than the MECTA "C," BP devices subsequent to the MECTA "C"--due to their overall greater power in almost all age categories--appear to cause as much or more injury than SW, generally. Such injury occurs not in spite of BP's superior efficiency with respect to SW, but because of BP's superior efficiency wherein more excessive power than SW (generally) can be emitted in most age categories. Restated, we can by no means assume the utilization of circa 2.5, 5, 10, and 12 times the output required to induce an adequate seizure with BP reduces morbidity compared to SW merely because the more mechanically efficient BP device has the theoretical capacity to overcome threshold at half the EO of SW. In short, if the reduced EO advantage is not utilized and, in fact, exploited, BP has no advantage at all. In fact, if inversely exploited, the more efficient BP device may produce even more power and thus even more morbidity than SW, generally.

Of paramount importance then, only the MECTA "C" (and other First Generation BP devices), can be regarded as an improvement over SW by virtue of inducing adequate seizures with less EO than SW, a point corroborated by the Utah Biomedical Test Laboratory originally employed by the FDA. Moreover, we should keep in mind that, as suggested by Weiner's graphs (as seen in the next section), maximum SW output can only be delivered in the youngest age categories; whereas, default Brief Pulse multifold threshold settings are predetermined for all age categories consistently, thereby both uniform and non-deteriorating. In short, the later BP devices following the 1976-1982 FDA hearings on "ECT" which quickly replaced the MECTA "C" have not only dwarfed the MECTA “C” in electrical output, but have surpassed SW in power and MTTLOI in all but the youngest age categories. Indeed, the only BP device which was capable of inducing adequate seizures at half the EO of SW in almost all age categories--the MECTA "C"-- is now defunct. The single plausible conclusion for both the continuation of SW in conjunction with the invention of enhanced BP devices is inefficacy of the adequate seizure, that is, that adequate seizure itself has little to no "therapeutic" value. It is for this reason that both SW and the later generation BP devices no longer depend upon the adequate convulsion for “efficacy,” but rather adequate amounts of electricity. In short, machines in the field today improperly deemed "ECT" devices actually do not “work” via adequate convulsion, but by the application of enough electricity to eliminate in a more or less controlled manner, and to a more or less specific extent, neurotransmitters and thus a more or less specific percentage of neuronal pathways specifically within the left prefrontal lobe (Perrin et al., 2012). In brief, the second generation BP device with its 2.3-2.5 MTTLOI destroys 2.3 to 2.5 fold more neuronal pathways than the MECTA "C" in all age categories, whereas, the third generation BP device with its 4.6 MTTLOI destroys twice as many neuronal pathways as the second generation BP device in all age categories and so on. That this is intentional is proved by manufacturers’ numerous strategies for hiding the degree of power their machines emit.

CHAPTER 86

Weiner's 1982 APA Criteria Charts for Writing the 1982 APA Standard

Reviewing Weiner's 1982 APA charts comparing BP to SW suggesting that SW emits up to 200J as opposed to BP which requires no more than 100 Joules to induce an adequate seizure in all recipients including the oldest age category, we can now see that Weiner excludes the later 2nd, 3rd, 4th, and 5th generation BP devices soon following the 1976-1982 FDA hearings. Only the 108J MECTA "C" BP device introduced to the FDA during the hearings is reflective of the 100J minimum required to induce seizures in all age categories depicted in Weiner's comparative charts of SW v BP. Moreover, while the B-24 SW can emit 200 Joules at maximum settings at 1.7A, it can only do so in the ten year old age category where Resistance is almost non-existent. While it is accurate to say that BP can induce EO at half that of SW generally as Weiner purports in his comparative charts, only the MECTA "C" BP device does so. In brief, only the MECTA "C" is or was an improvement over SW with respect to reduced EO. Indeed, no BP device succeeding first generation BP devices reduces output generally compared to SW. By using the probable percentage of recipients receiving various outputs with SW and BP, Weiner's charts are misleading in that they do not reflect SW's 200J output in the youngest age category alone, nor do they reflect the Brief Pulse adequate electricity instruments used in field soon following the FDA hearings. In brief, the charts do not reflect the decreasing power of SW over increasing age nor do they reflect the increasing power of Brief Pulse emitted by subsequent Brief Pulse generations. If we were to juxtapose for the FDA, modern day 1st, 2nd, and 3rd BP generations as well as "legally" potential 4th and 5th generation BP devices with SW in the same manner Weiner juxtaposed the 200J maximum output potential of SW with the 100J needed with BP circa 1982, current SW v BP graphs would look something like those below.[268]

[268] Since Weiner depicts probability with the 100J maximum he himself claims is required of BP to induce adequate seizures in all recipients and he then divides this 100J "maximum" into 10J increments, we simply multiply the MTTLOI of the C, the 2nd, the 3rd, the 4th, and the 5th generation BP devices respectively by each respective 10J increment to obtain comparable figures.

WEINER'S DEPICTION OF MAXIMUM OUTPUT POTENTIAL WITH **SINE WAVE** USING BL-ECT—**200J MAXIMUM**. See the **B-24.**

SW-200J (maximum potential with BL-ECT)

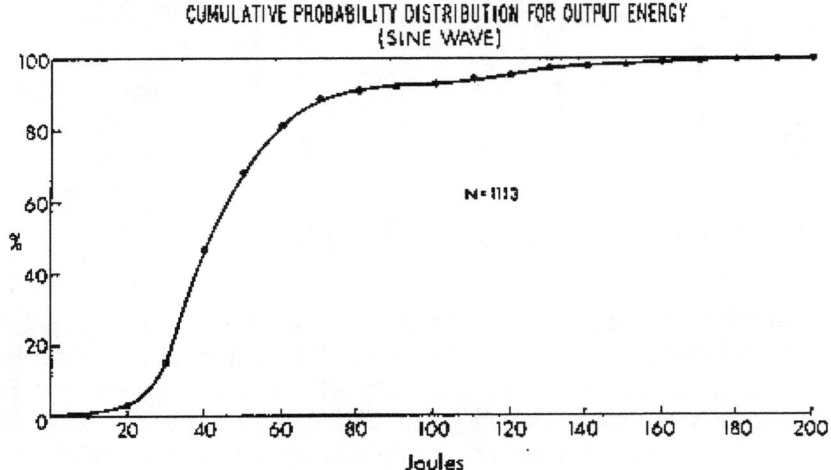

WEINER'S DEPICTION OF MAXIMUM OUTPUT POTENTIAL WITH **BRIEF PULSE** USING BL-ECT—**100J MAXIMUM** See the **MECTA "C"**

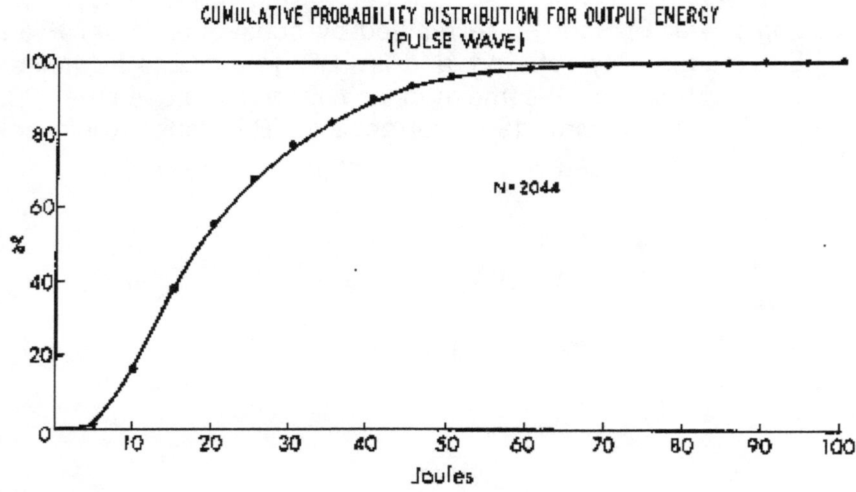

Let us now include the four BP device generations following the MECTA “C”:

EXTANT **SECOND GENERATION BP DEVICE-230J-250J** (2.3 X 100J)

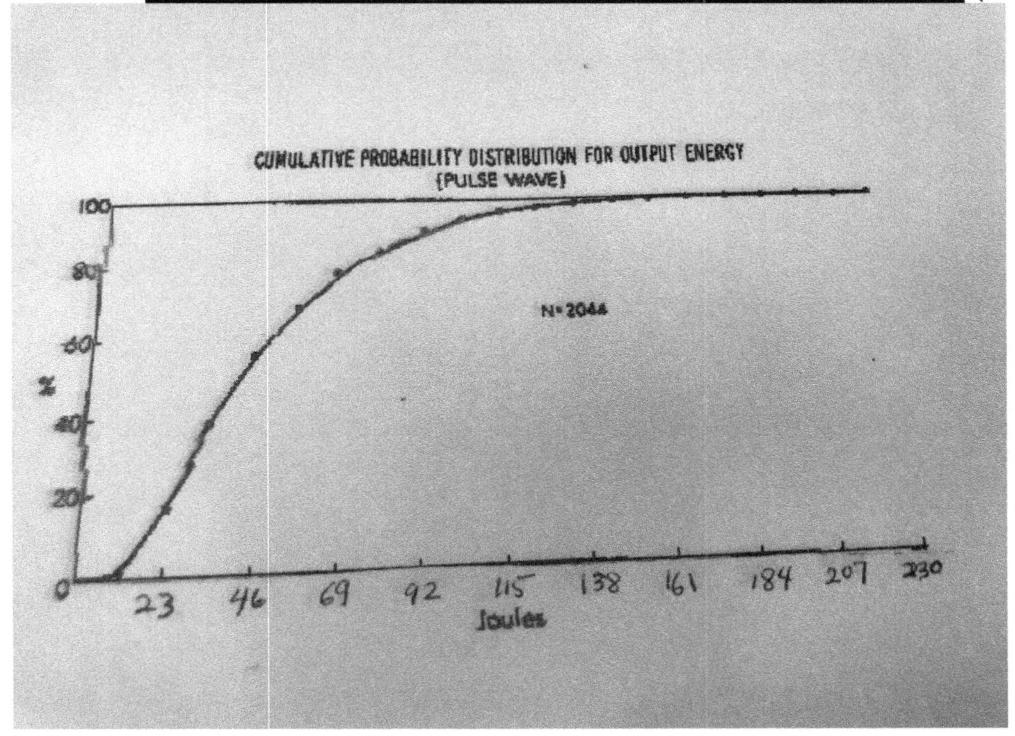

EXTANT **THIRD GENERATION BP DEVICE-460J** (4.6 X 100J)

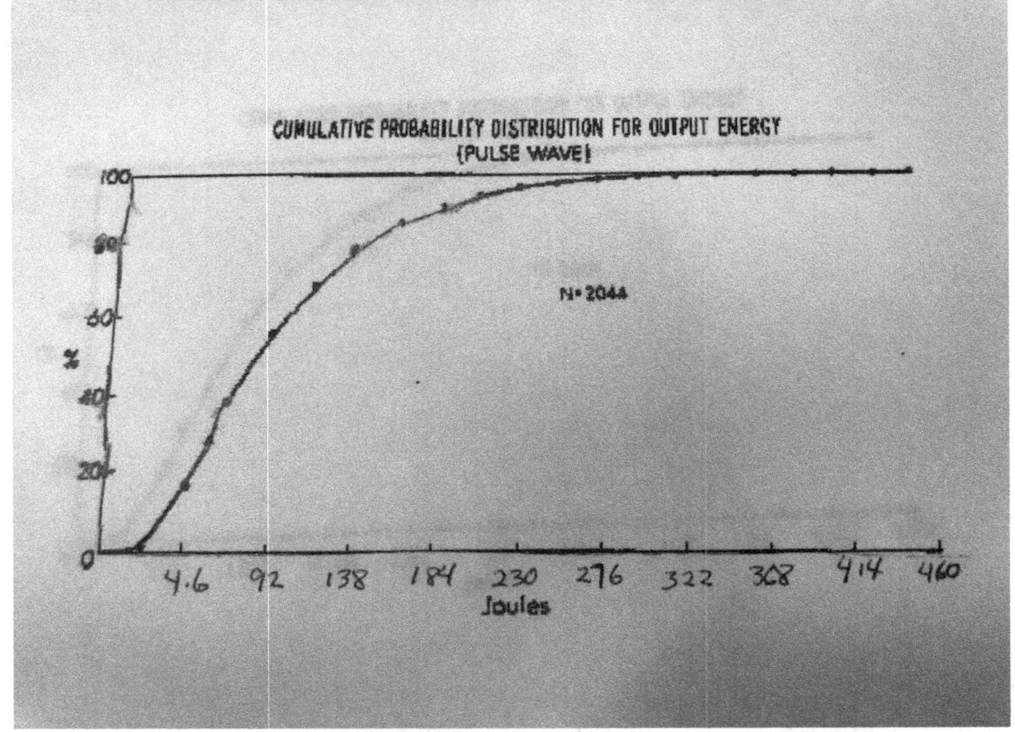

PROBABLE **FOURTH GENERATION BP DEVICE-922J** (9.2 X 100J)

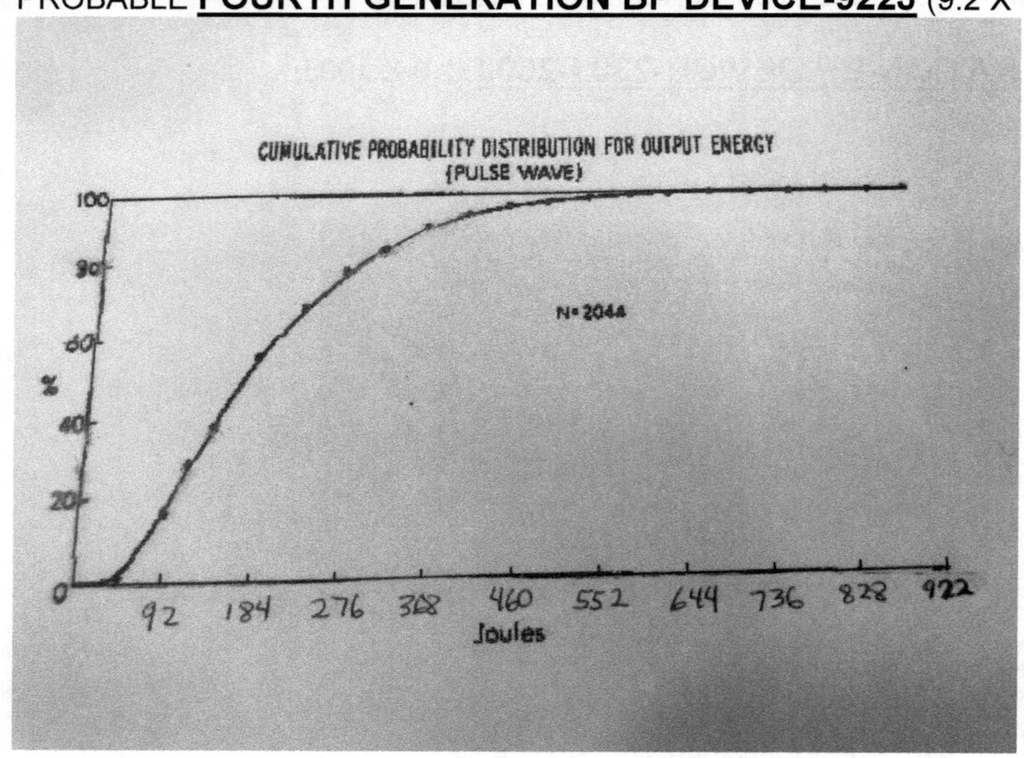

"LEGAL" **FIFTH GENERATION BP DEVICE-1200J** (12 X 100J)

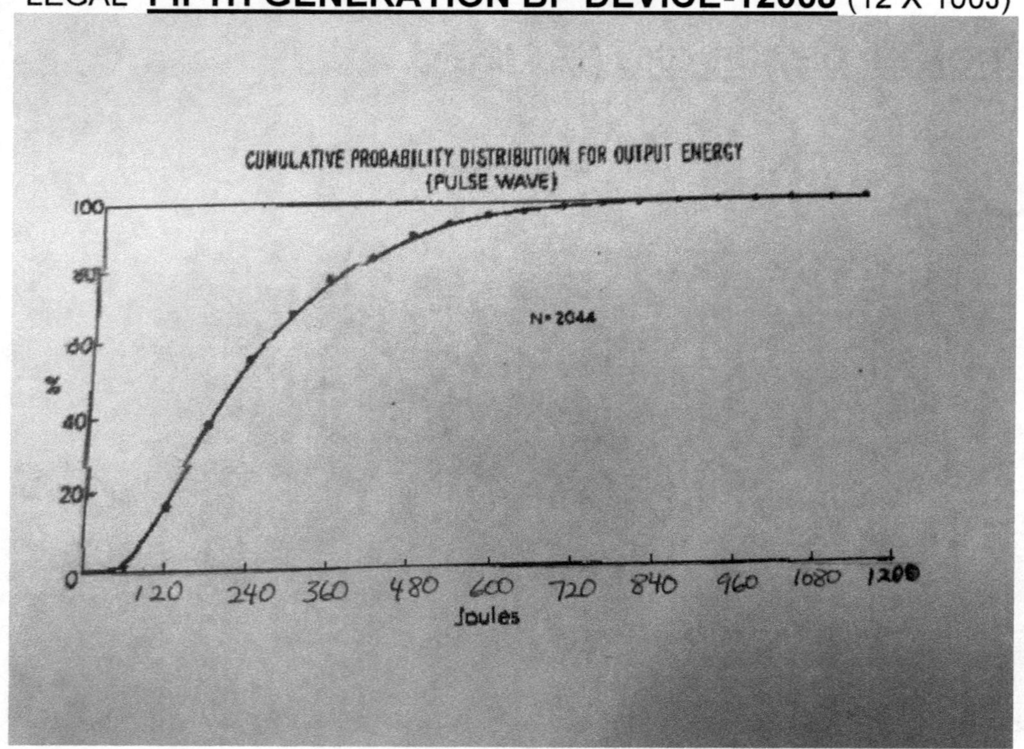

In short, THE MODERN DAY Brief Pulse DEVICE has grossly surpassed SW in cumulative output in all but the younger age categories.

CHAPTER 87

Early BP

In order to understand the comparative relevance of the MECTA "C," touted to emit adequate seizures at greatly reduced EOs compared to the B-24 SW by Medcraft, it is helpful to compare the 1976-1982 American MECTA "C" BP device to the original, much earlier BP devices utilized by the American Brief Pulse inventor, W.T. Liberson during the SW Era between 1938-1976 (Liberson, 1948). While difficult to pinpoint exact electrical parameters for Liberson's earliest device, early estimations of Liberson's first BP apparatus appear to be very similar to those depicted in the chart below:

1946--FIRST LIBERSON-OFFNER DC CONSTANT CURRENT BRIEF PULSE DEVICE TRUE ECT DEVICE

EO	Voltage	Current	Duration	Resistance	Charge
.21 Joules	20 Volts	.350 Amps	.5 Seconds	57 Ω	.011 Coulombs
.36	28	.350	.6	80	.013
.53	36	.350	.7	103	.015
.74	44	.350	.8	126	.017
.99	52	.350	.9	149	.019
1.26 J	**60 Volts**	**.350 Amps**	**1.0 Sec.**	**171 Ω**	**.021 C**

Liberson's first BP machine was unidirectional in lieu of bi-directional, utilized up to 120 unidirectional Pulses, and used a .2-.5 millisecond pulse width. Maximum parameters above are based on calculations derived from maximum Amperage (.350), maximum Pulse Width (.5 msec) and maximum Duration (1.0 Sec) provided by Alexander (1953, p. 63).[269] EO and Impedance are derived from constant Amperage and estimated Voltage. Characteristic of BP, Voltage must automatically rise in order to maintain constant current.

Unfortunately, Alexander (1953) neglected to provide Voltage and thus Impedance and EO. While Amperage, Duration, and Charge are actual then, Voltage is estimated [270] and corresponding Impedance and EO derived subsequently. Even so, we can observe that with the invention of Constant Current BP (as Liberson invented both constant current and BP), only 1.26 Joules is alleged to overcome Impedances of up to 171Ω. But how could this particular device reach seizure threshold at such low EO? In applying the 1946-Offner Brief Pulse device, three and perhaps four aspects of the early procedure may have entirely changed the machine dynamics even relative to modern day BP devices. First, the BP device above, unlike modern day BP, is based on DC current in lieu of

[269] From constant Amperage and maximum Voltage provided, maximum Impedance is derived utilizing Ohm's Law. Utilizing 120 pulses and maximum wave length of .5 milliseconds provided, Charge is derived utilizing the formula: Charge = Current x Pulses x Wave length x Duration. EO is then derived from: EO = Charge x Current x Impedance.

[270] The 60 Volt estimated maximum for Liberson's first BP device is probably a liberal estimate. There is reason to believe the original Voltage was somewhat lower, perhaps 40 Volts.

alternating current (half as powerful as AC) requiring lower EO, and second, the unidirectional pulses (.2-.5 milliseconds or .0002-.0005 seconds) are no more than half the width of modern day BP devices (1.0 and 2.0 millisecond widths or .001 and .002 seconds). Third, the Duration is one half to one quarter the Duration of modern day BP devices. Finally, producers of the machine almost certainly measured output in terms of UL ECT (another early discovery) in lieu of BL ECT. In short, the procedure and makers of the device used every possible strategy to induce adequate seizures with the least amount of electricity possible--the clear goal of BP then, in 1946, and later, in 1978. But if these outputs are faithful, the later MECTA "C" BP introduced into the modern day BP Era about 1978 as the Brief Pulse prototype, was already (108J ÷ 1.25J =) 86 times as powerful with respect to cumulative output as the prototype Liberson introduced in 1946 (Alexander, 1953, p. 63). The maximum output of the MECTA "D" introduced about 1981, would have emitted about (134J ÷ 1.25J =) 107 times the maximum output of the 1946 LIBERSON-OFFNER apparatus above. Modern day second generation BP devices manufactured from 1983 to 1994 are conservatively 200 times as powerful as Liberson's first constant current BP device, and modern day third generation BP devices manufactured from 1994 to the present, are 400 times as powerful as Liberson's prototypical BP device.[271] Most importantly then, if credible, threshold could be reached using a fraction of the output of even modern first generation BP devices (such as the MECTA "C").

Perhaps because the machine didn't always induce convulsion, and almost certainly because it was not effective even when convulsion was reached, and ultimately therefore, did not sell, a more powerful 105 to 125 Volt BP device was subsequently manufactured by Liberson and Offner (Liberson's electrical engineer). If we apply Liberson's final ultimate 105-125 Volts to the original BP device above, we generate the Chart below.

1946 LIBERSON-OFFNER BRIEF DC CURRENT PULSE DEVICE BASED ON A LIBERAL 125 VOLT MAXIMUM

EO	Voltage	Current	Duration	Resistanc e	Charge
1.1 Joules	105 Volts	.350 Amps	.5 Seconds	300 Ω	.011 Coulombs
1.42	109	.350	.6	311	.013
1.70	113	.350	.7	323	.015
1.99	117	.350	.8	334	.017
.99	121	.350	.9	346	.019
2.30 J	**125 Volts**	**.350 Amps**	**1.0 Sec.**	**357 Ω**	**.021 C**

The BP device above utilizes 120 pulses of unidirectional current with maximum .5 millisecond pulse widths, and a constant current of .350 Amperes. The maximum Voltage, however, more than doubled.

Even if Liberson's original BP device was made to more than double the Voltage of the earlier model, utilizing up to 125 Volts (in lieu of 60V), nevertheless, as a result of a) very low unidirectional current, b) very brief pulses, c) a 1.0 second maximum Duration, and because it was d) based exclusively on UL ECT, the early Liberson device continued to emit incredibly low Charge and EO maximums of 21 millicoulombs and 2.3 Joules respectively. Note that with constant current, Liberson could now allegedly overcome resistances of up to 357Ω at an incredibly low 2.3 Joules.[272] If the machine above (emitting a 2.3J maximum) really could overcome 357Ω of resistance, this early BP procedure would have been efficient enough to induce seizures in 95% of all ECT recipients (Abrams, 1996, p. 703; Abrams, 1988, p. 114; Department of Health and Human Services, 1982a,

---

[271] MECTA "C": 108J ÷ 1.26J = 86 fold. MECTA "D": 134J ÷ 1.26 = 106. Thymatron DG: 250J ÷ 1.26J = 198 fold. Thymatron DGx-FDx2: 500J ÷ 1.26 = 396.

[272] This was the original idea behind BP Constant Current--to utilize the least amount of EO, Charge and Current to induce adequate seizures. Later BP devices, just as later utilization of UL electrode placement (Cameron, 1994, p. 194, footnote 17), appeared to exploit the original concept by inducing the greatest rather than the least EO possible, completely undermining the advantage of BP as well as totally distorting Liberson's original intent.

pp. 7, A46, G7). Even using a 125 Voltage maximum for Liberson's 1946 constant current BP prototype therefore, the 1976 MECTA "C" prototype of the modern day BP Era was yet circa (108 ÷ 2.3 =) 47 times as powerful as this early Liberson prototype. The later, first generation MECTA "D" was about 60 times as powerful, modern day second generation BP Devices over 100 times as powerful, and modern day third generation BP devices, between 200 to 260 times as powerful as Liberson's .350A constant current BP device depicted here.[273]

One of the last, perhaps the most powerful BP device manufactured by Liberson and Offner continued to utilize the above Voltages--105V-125V--but with greatly expanded Duration and Pulse Width compared to Liberson's 1946 prototype. By 1953, in spite of Liberson's alleged attainment of adequate seizures with much less powerful prototypes, in an effort to make his failing (market-wise) constant current BP device commercially viable,[274] Liberson and Offner dramatically increased Voltage, Duration, Charge, and Pulse Width yet again. Moreover, they switched from DC to AC current. Early researchers were beginning to understand that adequate seizure had little or no "therapeutic effect" and that electricity played at least some part in efficacy, a critical factor suppressed even by today's so-called "ECT" manufacturers. Based upon known parameters, the Chart below depicts skeletal characteristics of Liberson's final and most powerful BP device, the 735-B.

1953 - Model 735-B - CONSTANT CURRENT BP DEVICE
LIBERSON-OFFNER - (AC)

EO	Voltage	Current	Duration	Resistance	Charge
	105 Volts	.300 Amps			Coulombs
		.300			
		.300			
		.300			
		.300			
22.5 J	**125 Volts**	**.300 Amps**	**5.0 Sec.**	**416.6 Ω**	**.180 C**

The above BP machine, deemed the 735-B, is based upon an AC current of 60 Hz maximum (120 pulses), a maximum Duration of five seconds (increased from one second previously), a 300mA constant Current (decreased from 350mA), a maximum 1.0 millisecond Pulse width (increased from .5 milliseconds previously) and a maximum 125 Volts (dramatically increased from Liberson's original BP device of 60V). Note the resulting 22.5J maximum output.

The 735-B as depicted above may have been Liberson's final and most powerful BP Constant Current apparatus.[275] Similar to modern-day BP devices, as noted above, Liberson and Offner had dramatically enhanced the pulse width from .0005 to .001 seconds, Duration from 1.0 to 5.0 Seconds, Voltage from 60 to 125 maximum Volts, and finally, Liberson and Offner had switched to Alternating Current, twice as powerful as Direct Current, all similar to modern day BP devices (except that later modern day BP devices are exponentially more powerful). Even with enhanced parameters, however, maximum voltage (125V) was relatively low compared to modern day BP devices, i.e. second and third generation BP devices (emitting about a 400V maximum). In short, the 735-B Amperage, though utilizing constant current, was yet much lower (at .3A) compared to that of modern BP devices (at .8A to .9A), generating about three times the Amperage of the 735-B. Charge on the 735-B, reaching .18C, while enhanced 8 fold from Liberson's earlier device, is nevertheless low compared to, for example, modern day third generation BP devices (which can now reach 1.2C), more than (1.2C ÷ .18C =) 6.6 fold Liberson's most powerful BP device. The number of pulses per second, which remained at 120, were slightly less than that of modern BP devices containing between 140 and 180 pulses per second, even equaling that of some second and third generation BP devices. Though utilizing much lower Current and EO, Liberson's final 735-B Constant Current BP device, was nevertheless able to overcome Resistances of up

---

[273] 108J ("C") ÷2.3J = 47. 135J ("D") ÷2.3J = 59. 250J (Thymatron DG) ÷2.3J = 108.6. 500J (Thymatron DGx(FDx2) ÷2.3 = 217. 1200J (new Standard) ÷2.3J = 521

[274] Liberson's BP devices failed in efficacy (with respect to desired results, mostly from the perspective of administering physicians) and thus marketability--not in inducing adequate seizures.

[275] Liberson was unsuccessful at marketing even his most powerful BP device in that clinicians deemed it ineffective not at inducing adequate seizures, but regarding desired patient results compared to the much more powerful SW (Cameron, 1994). Early BP devices were thus eventually discarded (Ibid).

to 416.6Ω, similar to the probable Resistance ceiling of the MECTA "C" (400Ω), but at only 22.5 maximum Joules compared to the 108 maximum Joules emitted by the 1978 MECTA "C."[276] Liberson's last BP device, the 735-B then, appears to have been able to reach threshold with even less EO than the first generation BP devices in the modern BP era. This, however may not be the case. Although Liberson's device depended more upon Duration (5.0 Seconds) than Amperage[277] in that the dynamics of his final BP device were similar in almost all respects to modern BP devices, reaching threshold at lower EOs than modern day BP devices seems unlikely. Certainly, the lack of anesthesia may have reduced threshold output somewhat, but this cannot account for the dramatic decrease in output Liberson claims to have attained (relative to, for example, the MECTA "C"). Rather, because Liberson was seeking the lowest electrical output possible, he almost certainly utilized UL ECT in lieu of BL ECT. Thus, while the maximum output emitted was about 25 Joules for a circa 400Ω recipient (or about a 70 year old male), if we double this dosage for BL ECT (to about 50J), the output becomes comparable to that emitted by the MECTA "C" for the same 70 year old man (60J). In fact, if we divide the C's output by 2.0 for UL ECT, we derive the same threshold output of about 25 Joules for the same 70 year old recipient. Liberson's final BP device then, was more or less comparable to the MECTA "C." The difference appears to have been that the 735B was exclusively designed to elicit UL ECT seizures at just above threshold, and only up to about 70 or 75 years of age. In short, Liberson had succeeded in inventing a method of consistently eliciting adequate seizures at about a quarter the output of the B-24 SW (when using UL ECT) up to about age 70 or 75, similar to the MECTA "C" (which can elicit seizures up to 100 year of age).[278] Liberson's earlier direct current brief pulse device, on the other hand, the dynamics of which were dramatically different from modern day BP devices, could purportedly elicit seizures at what must be deemed true minimal stimulus threshold outputs.[279] Historically, in fact, we can trace Liberson's BP devices as more and more powerful with each succeeding generation, in spite of the capacity of earlier models to successfully induce so-called adequate grand mal seizures with UL "ECT," up until his BP device began approaching the power of the modern day MECTA "C."

The MECTA "C" and the Modern BP Era

In accordance with the 1982 APA Standard, The MECTA "C" prototypical BP device at 108 Joules maximum with enhanced Voltage (as opposed to Liberson's early but final 735-B Brief Pulse device) and which announced the modern BP Era about 1978, was designed with BL ECT in mind for all age categories up to 100 years of age, thereby incorporating almost 5.0 times the raw power of Liberson's early 1953 735B Brief Pulse (at 22.5 Joules) apparently, as previously noted, designed for up to age 70. In spite of Liberson's machine being exclusively designed for UL ECT and the MECTA "C" for BL ECT, therefore, Liberson's device and the MECTA "C" appear equivalent regarding age related threshold dosages of electricity.[280] From 1978 forward, moreover, although Brief Pulse threshold output remains constant, modern day BP devices, just as Liberson's series of BP devices of the previous BP era, increase in raw power and MTTLOI with each new BP generation. For example. the 1980 MECTA "D" (134J) incorporated 6.0 times the raw power of Liberson's 735-B, while second generation BP devices of the modern BP Era (following the MECTA "C" and "D") are approximately 10.0 times as powerful as Liberson's 735-B with respect to raw energy output. Indeed, modern day third

---

[276] Liberson's device utilized about one-third the Amperage of the MECTA "C."

[277] Without anesthesia, waiting for the electrical build-up to reach seizure was "problematic" for Liberson's recipients and no doubt contributed to its ultimate failure.

[278] 134J ÷ 22.5 = 5.96.

[279] That Liberson's machines were never commercially viable and that manufacturers favored much more powerful devices, including the SW devices of old, appears to have been due to the fact that adequate seizures are simply not "effective" compared to adequate dosages of electricity and this was understood very early on (see Cameron 1994 (ECT: Sham Statistics, the Myth of Convulsive Therapy, and the Case for Consumer Misinformation").

[280] On modern day BP devices, a 70 year old man seizes with BL ECT at about 49J (see MECTA "C" chart above); whereas, the 1953 735B could emit a maximum of 22.5J, about that required to induce an adequate seizure with UL ECT for a 70 year old man (49 ÷ 2 – ***24.5J***). Indeed, the MECTA "C" appears to have emitted a default of about 53 Joules for the 70 year old man, slightly more than enough to induce an adequate seizure using BL ECT (at a 1.08 MTTLOI). Thus the early 735B Brief Pulse at 22.5J and the MECTA "C" at 26.5J (53J ÷ 2 = 26.5J), though the former was exclusively utilized for UL ECT and the latter for BL ECT, were based on about the same electrical dosing to evince so-called "adequate seizures."

generation BP devices are approximately 18 to 20 times more powerful than Liberson's 1953 BP apparatus. In short, compared to Liberson's final most powerful BP model, the MTTLOI emitted by modern day BP devices, has, once again, risen exponentially with each new BP generation.[281] Importantly then, due to UL ECT, an extremely early discovery, DC (Direct Current), greatly reduced wave lengths, and age categories up to 70 in lieu of 100, the earliest of the Liberson BP devices (all of which commercially failed) could purportedly elicit adequate seizures at much reduced threshold outputs than even that of the MECTA "C." The last Liberson-Offner AC device, the 735B, though designed for UL ECT alone and thus less powerful than the MECTA "C" was nevertheless, as noted, comparable to the MECTA "C" in threshold output so that the MECTA "C," one of the first modern day BP devices emerging around 1978, seemed to begin where Liberson and Offner left off. Indeed, though Liberson's 735-B Brief Pulse was designed for UL ECT alone and the MECTA "C" for BL ECT, both were "minimal stimulus" AC devices and thus true ECT apparatuses. (The "C" too, can induce adequate seizures in all age categories with half its 108J maximum output using UL ECT [282].) Critically, although modern BP devices have become progressively more and more powerful with higher and higher MTTLOIs, Liberson's 735B Brief Pulse is comparable both to the MECTA "C" and all other modern day (AC) BP devices regarding the age related EO required to reach threshold with Brief Pulse.

We can conclude, therefore, that the 735-B, Liberson's final and most powerful BP apparatus, based on the same age-related threshold outputs as the MECTA "C" (and all other modern day [AC] BP devices), could, by using minimal stimulus UL-ECT induce adequate seizures for most recipients with half the output used by the "C" for BL-ECT (Abrams, 1996, p. 703; Department of Health and Human Services, 1982a, pp. 7, A46, G7; Royal College of Psychiatry, 1995). Certainly, by utilizing UL ECT alone then, Liberson's 735B BP device could induce adequate seizures with half the output of the "C," a third of the Current, and half the Charge.[283] From this early history of Brief Pulse, in re-introducing BP via the prototypical MECTA "C" around 1980, the only modern BP device to conform to the 1982 APA Standard, modern day BP manufacturers must have suspected the inefficacy not only of minimal stimulus induced UL ECT, but minimal stimulus induced BL ECT in that the 735-B was well known to have failed on the market-place. That is, from the early history of Brief Pulse, modern Brief Pulse manufacturers at the time of the FDA hearing must have suspected the inadequacy of so-called "adequate convulsions" alone. Indeed, it might be argued that the modern day MECTA "C" was simply a convenient ploy to persuade FDA that a safer, "new and improved" reduced EO method of administering "ECT" (compared to SW) had only recently been discovered, that the "C" was a necessary lie to stay the impending death knell of so-called "ECT" itself, when, in fact, manufacturers even at the time of the "C"'s introduction about 1980, already understood of its impending failure. Indeed, even as the "C" was being introduced as the prototype with the solemn promise of a standard comprehensively designed to protect all future recipients, manufacturers appear to have been secretly planning the construction of much more powerful Brief Pulse devices with much higher MTTLOIs in order to make the procedure "work." That is, the evidence suggests that manufacturers were already planning the production and implementation of BP devices much more potent than the MECTA "C," that manufacturers were simply waiting for FDA agreement to the continuation of "ECT," based on newly promised reduced output devices like the MECTA "C" guaranteed by the promised APA standard, and the hearing safely behind them.[284] In short, unbeknownst to regulators, manufacturers must have known

---

281 108J ("C") ÷ 22.5J (735B) = 4.8. 135J ("D) ÷ 22.5J = 6.0. 236J (Thymatron DG) ÷ 22.5J = 10.5. 480J [Thymatron DGx (FDx2)] ÷ 22.5J = 21.3. 1200J (new IEC Standard) ÷ 22.5J = 53.33

282 Manufacturers eventually invent the myth that UL ECT requires two fold minimal stimulus while BL ECT "remains effective" at minimal stimulus.

283 Modern day BP devices average .9 Amperes (Medcraft B-25 = 1 Ampere; Thymatron DG = .9 Amperes; MECTA = .8 Amperes) compared to Liberson's .3 Ampere (735B) constant current BP device. Thus, modern day BP manufacturers initiated their BP machines in the modern BP Era (1976) with three times the Amperage of Liberson's most powerful BP device (1946-1953). The higher Amperage created by modern day BP manufacturers is accomplished with phenomenally higher Voltages, approximately four times that of Liberson's 735B [500V(Thymatron DG) ÷ 125V(735B) = 4.0 fold], as well as generally longer "brief" pulses.

284 Modern day BP manufacturers in all probability were aware of the failure Liberson experienced with early BP devices--not in inducing adequate seizures, but in making the procedure effective--that is--obtaining a so-called "therapeutic effect." In fact, the Liberson experiments, along with other early reduced power experiments by Wilcox, Friedman, and others, clearly showed the failure of convulsion theory when adequate seizures were accomplished at low electrical dosages but without the desired efficacy, a phenomenon manifested through their failure on the marketplace and subsequent abandonment (Cameron, 1994). Clearly, the electric current, the main identifiable culprit behind the undesirable "side-effects" with respect to memory dysfunction, cognitive dysfunction, and brain damage, is necessary to make the "ECT" device work and is the obvious reason behind progressively more and more powerful BP devices generally. All manufacturers, beginning with SW manufacturers, have hidden this unsavory fact from the public

that even the so-called "minimal stimulus" MECTA "C" based on AC current in lieu of DC current, and BL ECT in lieu of UL ECT (requiring twice the EO of previous BP devices to induce adequate seizures), was already, in effect, a suprathreshold instrument requiring twice the necessary output needed to induce adequate seizures with UL "ECT." In short, manufacturers must have understood, that like SW, which depended upon adequate doses of electricity to work, more powerful BP devices would be needed to make the procedure "effective." In sum, history suggests that manufacturers already knew that adequate seizure alone is ineffective, that so-called "ECT" is mythological, and that what was actually required to make the procedure "effective," was not adequate seizure at all, but adequate doses of electricity--the precise dynamic which made the SW device so dangerous, much more risky than beneficial, and that the chance of causing harm with even newer more powerful devices was 100%. Indeed, given the history of Brief Pulse as described in this book and the history of Sine Wave, we should not be too surprised to find modern day second, third, fourth, and fifth generation BP devices surpassing SW both in raw power and MTTLOI, generally. Neither should we be too stunned at manufacturers' calculated suppression of this unequivocally essential fact.

---

for well over fifty years, falsely claiming their devices are "convulsive therapy devices" utilizing minimal electrical stimulus for the sole purpose of inducing "adequate convulsions" with the least amount electricity possible. The premise, of course, is false.

CHAPTER 88

Inversion Exploitation of Brief Pulse

Clearly, electrical waves with intervals in the current, otherwise known as "Brief Pulses," were originally devised to reduce EO compared to SW (Liberson 1948; Alexander, 1953; Grahn et al. 1977) and so reduce morbidity. On the other hand, maintenance of the current, that is the Constant Current feature of BP devices, (unlike the Deteriorating Current feature of SW), can emit much longer duration trains, usually four, but sometimes six seconds or more compared to usually one second of SW, all while maintaining a consistent Amperage. The intervals in the current, and even the constant current dynamic, of course, can dramatically reduce both output and intensity, generating seizures with much greater efficiency and significantly reduced outputs as well as both consistent and reduced MTTLOIs, altogether enhancing the safety of "ECT." This decrease in threshold and thus electrical output in general compared to SW, can greatly reduce brain dysfunction and brain damage which for years has manifested itself via recipient complaints of long term memory dysfunction. It is ironic, then, that the constant current feature of so-called Brief Pulse devices, the effect of automatically increasing Voltages to overcome deteriorating current (in lieu of constant Voltage which permits current deterioration), can enhance rather than reduce both the EO emitted as well as the MTTLOI relative to both SW and minimal stimulus BP devices such as the MECTA "C." Paradoxically, in fact, and contrary to its' stated purpose, the modern Brief Pulse, increasing voltage, constant current device, with few exceptions, has actually become more consistently powerful and more consistently intense generally, than the constant voltage, deteriorating current, SW device it was allegedly supposed to supplant as an improvement by virtue of reduced EO. Just as UL (unilateral) "ECT" was originally devised to utilize the lowest EO possible to induce adequate seizures (Wilcox 1946), but is presently exploited to justify incredibly high EOs [285] (Swartz and Abrams 1996), the constant current feature of modern-day BP devices has now been exploited to emit higher (rather than lower) EOs with both BL and UL ECT as well as higher (rather than lower) MTTLOIs than SW instruments in most age categories--an exploited inversion of the original, intended use of BP. This exploitation of the BP device is almost unknown to both layman and professional alike. The inversion or exploitation of constant current in order to administer incredibly dangerous, destructive MTTLOIs of electricity, of course, is necessary both to make the procedure "effective" and relatively "long-lasting" with respect to the actual goal of "improved" mood and behavior modification. Unfortunately, the little known, little understood phenomenon of inverting the constant current feature to enhance rather than reduce EO for the purpose of delivering not only consistent, but increasingly augmented Multifold Threshold Titration Level Output Intensities of electricity not only negates the alleged safety aspect of BP but ipso facto, actually guarantees injury. This fact is not only unknown generally, but has actually been veiled by the false impression that BP is safer than SW by virtue of "reduced EO" to induce "adequate seizures," in short, the false notion that modern day BP devices induce adequate seizures with the least amount of

---

[285] UL "ECT," though capable of inducing so-called adequate seizures at half the output of BL"ECT," has been proclaimed "dose-sensitive," allegedly requiring twice threshold EO to be as effective as BL "ECT" justifying massive increases in Multifold Threshold Titration Level Output Intensities of the later BP devices.

electricity possible.[286] [287] Rather than the "gentler, kinder" apparatus the Brief Pulse device is purported to be; however, default outputs generated by modern day Brief Pulse devices have actually become more dangerous and more destructive than SW in most age categories.

Inversion Exploitation of Brief Pulse Continued

Well known is the fact that due to intermittent briefer or intermittent pulses compared to continuous unbroken Sine Waves,[288] and due to constant current [289] in lieu of deteriorating current, BP can induce seizures more efficiently, and at lower Charge and lower EO than SW, generally.[290] It is also the Constant Current (due to increasing Voltage), however, which enables the utilization of much longer BP duration trains than SW in that there is no current deterioration. In short, no current decline occurs even in the face of the very highest Impedances. It is the Constant Current feature, ironically, which makes later model BP devices much more powerful and much more dangerous than SW in most age categories, capable, in fact, of emitting much higher cumulative EO than SW generally at much higher Impedances. While BP can emit both lower EO and lower Charge than SW (as exemplified by the MECTA "C"), we can observe the inversion process in the equalizing and then surpassing of BP Charge compared to SW Charge. For instance, when conveying approximately 100 Joules of energy, early modern day BP devices such as the first generation MECTA "C" as well as the second generation Thymatron DG and second generation MECTA SR 1 and 2 devices--at 100J--emit circa .300 to .325 Coulombs of Charge (see detailed charts). The B-24 SW by Medcraft, on the other hand, at maximum Voltage, typically requires .500-.600 Coulombs of Charge to emit the same circa 100 Joules. Thus, the B-24 SW requires approximately twice the Charge of first and even second generation BP devices to emit the same EO.[291] Inverting this process (as BP devices become more and more powerful), however, we see that at equal Charge emissions (in lieu of equal EO emissions of BP vs SW), modern day BP devices can be made to emit much higher EO than SW. For instance, at .576 Coulombs Charge,[292] second generation MECTA SR 1 and 2 devices emit approximately 256 Joules of EO while at .504 Coulombs Charge, the second generation Thymatron DG emits 252 Joules of EO (Cameron, 1994), surpassing the overall EO emitted by SW. Comparatively, the B-24 SW at the same .500-.600 Coulomb Charge only emits 85 to 100 Joules EO (see numerous SW Charts above). In short, although BP devices utilize about half the cumulative electricity (Charge) of SW devices to produce equal EOs (making BP potentially safer), inverting this process--that is--making BP utilize the same cumulative amount of electricity (Charge) as SW, BP devices more than double the EO (or power) of SW, making BP more powerful and thus more dangerous than SW, generally.[293]

To state the principle differently, an emission of .504C Charge does not limit BP to 100 Joules as it does SW. Instead, at .504C Charge, second generation BP devices, for example, deliver about 250 Joules. In fact, because of their efficiency, Constant Current Brief Pulse devices can emit much more energy, and thus, much more power from .504C of electricity than can the same amount of electricity (Charge) delivered by a SW

[286] The respective features of BP—brief pulse and constant current--have been used to emphasize safety and efficacy in safety and efficacy brain and memory studies as we have seen, resulting in perhaps the greatest instance of fraud in medical history.

[287] While the MECTA "C" and "D" incorporated improvements in consistency and ubiquitous minimal stimulus (BL) ECT over SW, early second generation BP devices are actually equivalent in raw power to the exceptionally powerful B-24 SW though in disparate age categories. While the "C" and "D" were indeed advantageous to SW with respect to safety and efficacy, BP devices developed since the MECTA "C" and "D" have become much more powerful than the B-24 generally and thus generally more destructive.

[288] In fact, even SW is not actually continuous, but like BP, is actually intermittent. Though the interval is much smaller than that which exists in BP, the disparity between BP and SW gaps has closed considerably. In short, compared to early BP devices, brief pulses in later BP devices have become progressively less and less brief.

[289] Constant current allows for a lower threshold generally than SW which allows rising Impedances over single "treatments,' due to deteriorating current. Only if administered at minimal stimulus, however, is BP advantageous to SW regarding lower EO.

[290] Not extremely well known publicly--grand mal seizures, once they are induced, require no supportive or additional electricity to occur "adequately." Indeed, it was this early discovery that permitted Wilcox and Liberson to successfully experiment with reduced energy devices only powerful enough to stimulate adequate seizures. While successful in inducing adequate seizures, however, not well known is the fact that adequate seizures alone do not produce so-called therapeutic effects (Cameron, 1994).

[291] The MECTA "C" emitted a maximum of 108 Joules at about .336 Coulombs.

[292] The first generation BP devices, the "C" and "D" did not reach .576C of Charge.

[293] The enhanced power of BP devices at equal Charges compared to SW may well be the reason modern day BP manufacturers prefer to report Charge alone rather than EO, thereby concealing accompanying EO as we shall examine further in the last Section.

device. In brief, due to BP's greater efficiency, second generation BP devices deliver two and a half times the EO of SW at the same Charge emission. The two graphs below do not display seizure threshold and thus do not show the reduced EO potential of BP compared to SW in inducing seizures, an advantage, however, which becomes moot as later generation BP devices begin delivering greater and greater MTTLOIs rather than minimal stimulus. Indeed, the charts below display the incredible efficiency of BP compared to the inefficiency of SW and thus the superior power of BP at equal Charge emissions. The graphs below display how much more powerful ***second*** generation BP devices are than SW. (***Third generation*** BP devices are even more exponentially powerful, etc.). The graphs below, then, display equal EOs at disparate Charges (which could depict the MECTA "C" compared to SW) followed by equal Charges at disparate EOs (which accurately depict second generation BP devices). In short, the first graph first reveals the reduced power potential of BP compared to SW, the second, the inverted or enhanced power potential of later model BP devices compared to SW.

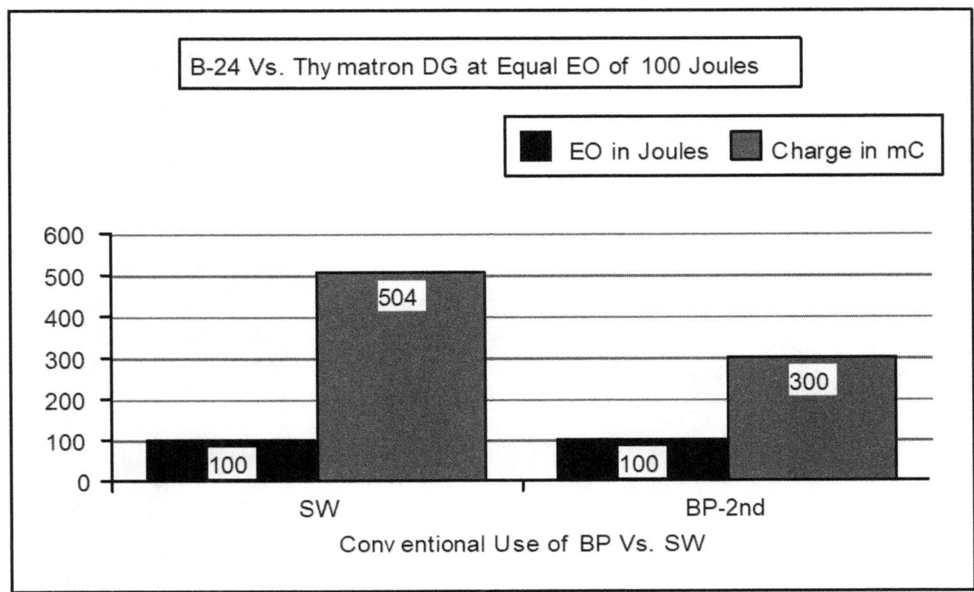

Usually, BP is seen as a reduced EO device compared to SW. The above chart shows the approximate Charge required for SW at 100J v Charge required for BP at 100 Joules comparable to the maximum output emitted by the MECTA "C." When comparing equal EOs, the reduced Charge potential and thus overall advantage of BP is self-evident, indicating BP can induce seizures at much less EO than SW making BP advantageous at minimal stimulus.

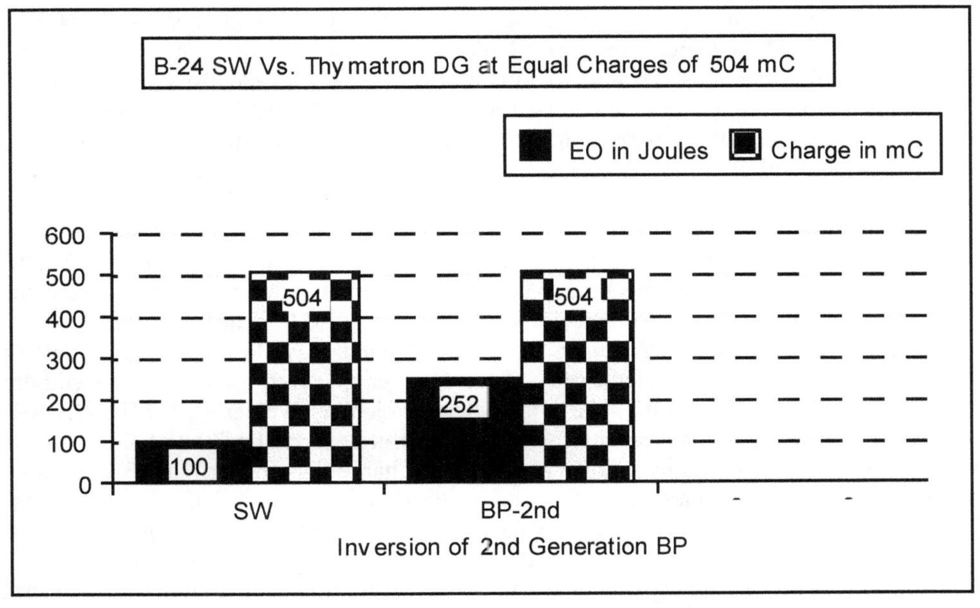

When comparing EO at equal Charges in lieu of equal EO, an inversion process becomes visible. At equal Charges, modern day BP devices actually enhance rather than reduce EO compared to SW. Much more energy efficient BP devices such as the second generation BP device depicted above, emit much more energy output than SW at the same Charge. In short, due to constant current as a result of increasing Voltage and thus the enhancement of MTTLOI, the second generation BP device has now become more than twice as powerful as SW at the same Charge, emitting more than twice the EO of SW. [294] [295] [296] [297]

Another example is as follows. It takes circa 1200 millicoulombs of Charge to emit 200J on technically illegal SW devices; whereas, the third generation JR/SR 2 BP device, for example, can emit the same 200J at about 770 millicoulombs (or less) of Charge. Conversely, while SW can emit an illegal 200J maximum at 1200 millicoulombs Charge, (see the SW device charts above), the third generation (MECTA) JR/SR 2 BP device at the same 1200 millicoulombs of Charge, delivers 480 maximum Joules, well over twice the EO of SW. [298] [299]

See graphs below:

[294] It is for this reason that as cumulative electricity (Charge) has increased in BP devices, BP manufacturers have stopped reporting EO maximums altogether. It is also for this reason that BP manufacturers prefer Charge ceilings rather than EO ceilings which would limit the power of their devices.

[295] While the B-24 SW by Medcraft can of course surpass both 100 Joules (typically 134J maximum) and 504 millicoulombs of Charge, if theoretically limited to .504C the B-24 could not surpass 100 Joules whereas BP devices, at this same .504C Charge, can.

[296] While limiting SW devices to .504C and thus 100 Joules would appear logical, it would also appear logical to limit BP devices to about .300C Charge (100 Joules) or to simply forbid any device from surpassing 100 Joules altogether. Indeed this appears to have been the intent of the 1982 FDA approved APA Standard for BP as well as the intent of both general and specific 1989 IEC Standards applying to both BP and SW. In fact, both BP (and SW) manufacturers have fought this regulation and both continue to be in violation of the original regulatory intent.

[297] That relatively safe minimal stimulus dosages of 100 Joules and under are not effective if distributed according to age and that injurious dosages--both invariably suprathreshold and often exceeding 100J *are* effective--is a strong indication that "ECT" works as a result of electrical injury to the brain, specifically neuronal connections. The impossibility of simultaneous safety and efficacy--the main FDA criterion for approval of medical devices--is precisely why so-called "ECT" should be banned.

[298] Use of these third generation BP devices were illegal under the 1989 IEC Standard while Weiner's 1997 default standard "legalized" these supra-inversed BP devices world-wide, as we have seen. Though never approved by the IEC, the withdrawal of the 1989 IEC Standard on ECT devices accomplished the same end—the default "legalization" of Weiner's 1997 IEC-proposed standard now used by manufacturers generally, as we have seen in the previous section. (See third generation BP devices.)

[299] Liberson's BP devices could allegedly emit many times less EO and Charge than modern day BP devices. First generation BP devices in the modern BP Era were limited to around 100 Joules, utilized half the Charge of SW, to emit its 109J EO maximum. Second generation modern day BP devices, now inverse exploitation devices, are capable of emitting between 226-250 (hidden) Joules in lieu of SW's 100J at the same .500 Coulombs. (For later BP devices, only the Coulombs have been reported.) SW devices emitting up to 1.200 C of Charge (technically illegal) are capable of eliciting a rare 200 Joules of output in the youngest age category. But at the same 1.200 Coulombs Charge, once illegal third generation BP devices can now emit up to circa 500 Joules of EO, consistently.

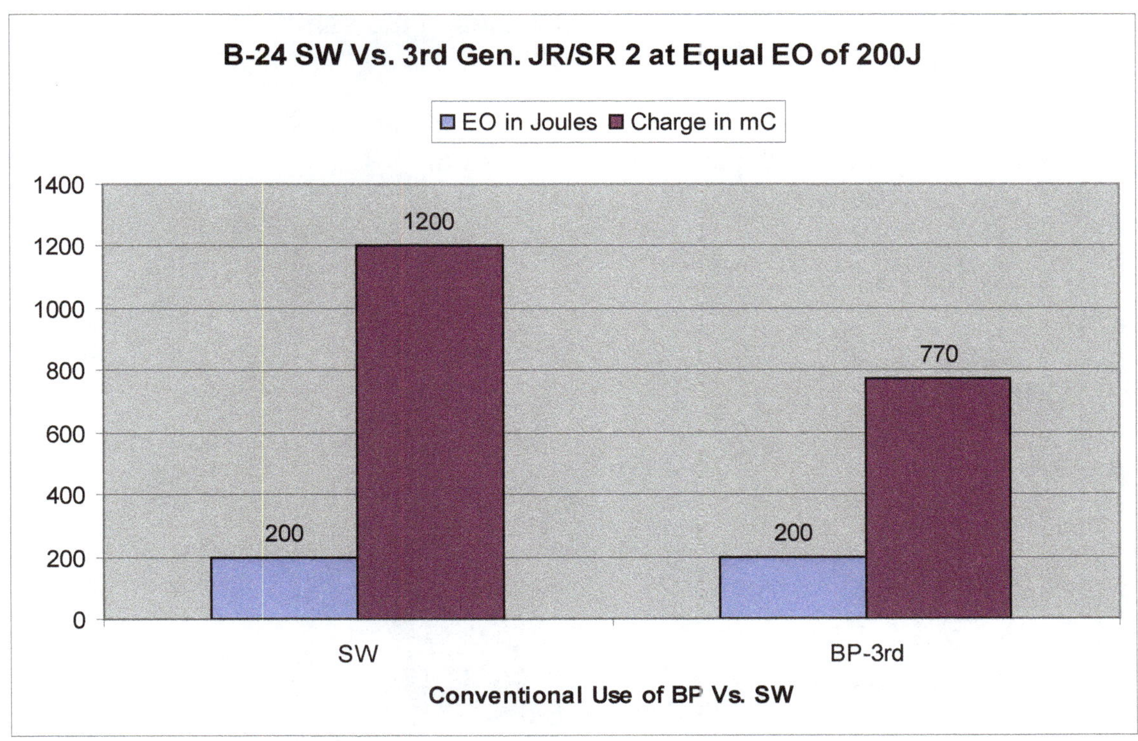
B-24 SW Vs. 3rd Gen. JR/SR 2 at Equal EO of 200J
EO in Joules
Charge in mC
1400
1200
1000
800
600
400
200
0
1200
770
200
200
SW
BP-3rd
Conventional Use of BP Vs. SW

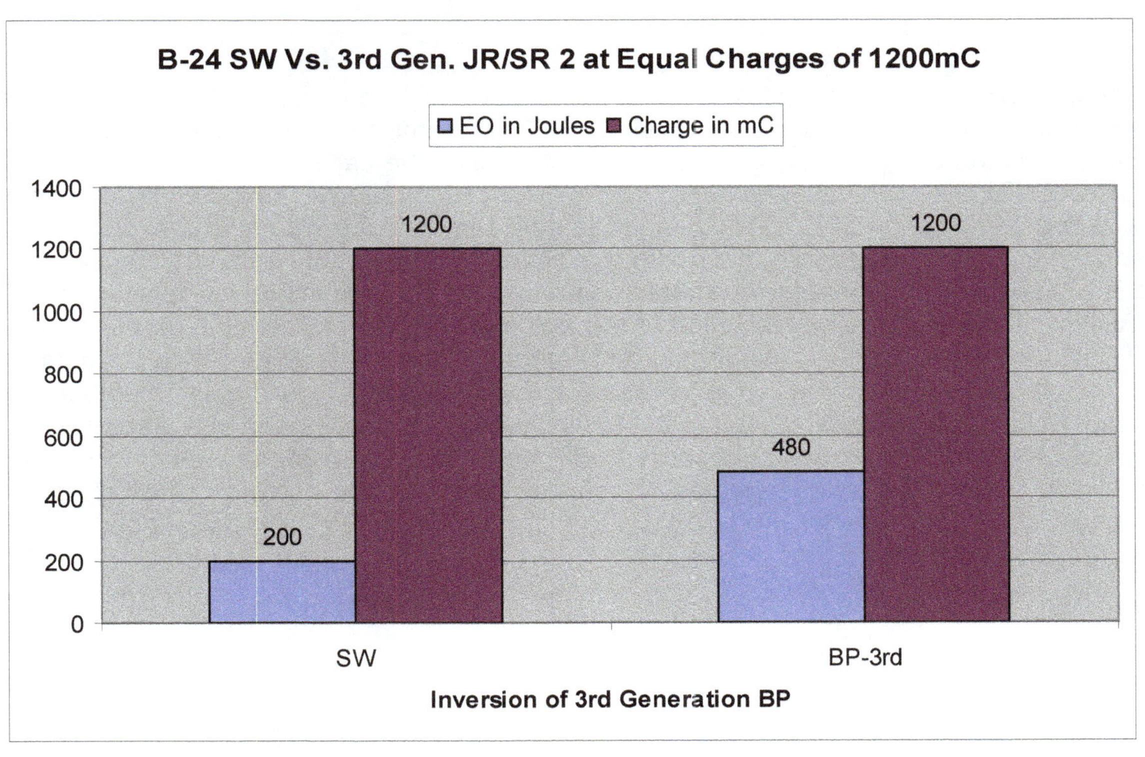
B-24 SW Vs. 3rd Gen. JR/SR 2 at Equal Charges of 1200mC
EO in Joules
Charge in mC
1400
1200
1000
800
600
400
200
0
1200
1200
480
200
SW
BP-3rd
Inversion of 3rd Generation BP

Probable fourth generation BP devices can emit almost 1000 Joules at the same 1200mC of Charge it takes to emit 200J of SW.

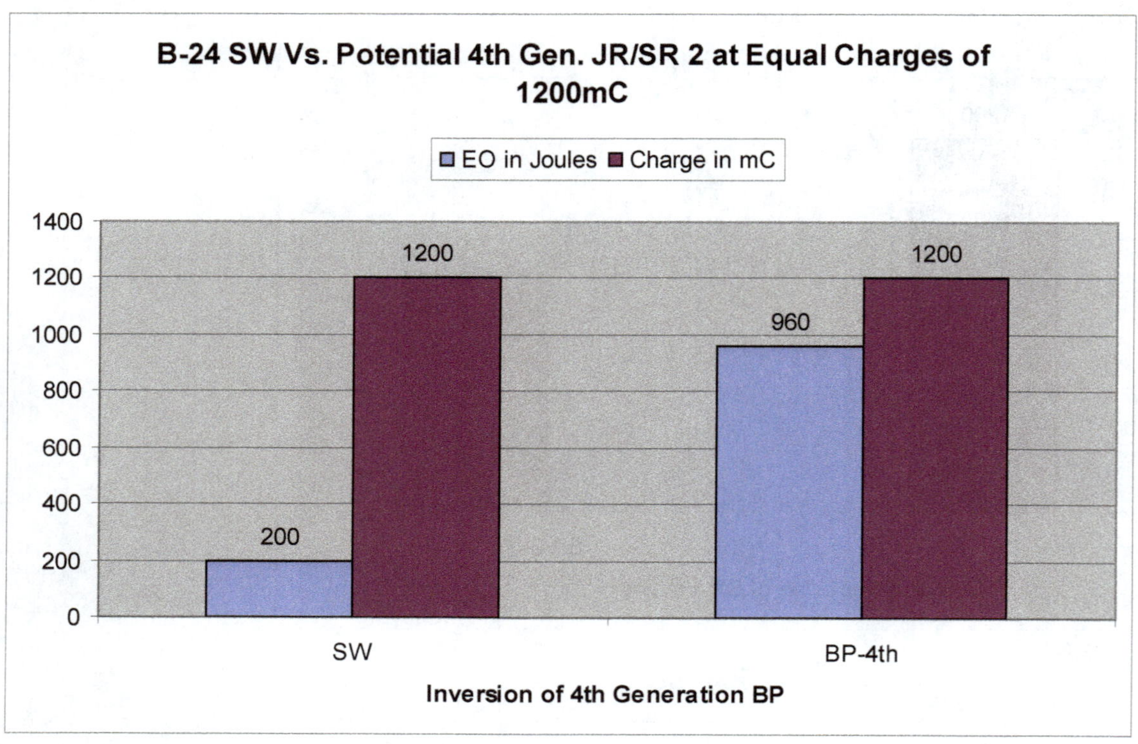

The surpassing power of BP (at equal Charges) is due to the higher and automatically increasing Voltage of BP (further increasing with each generation's increasing MTTLOI), emitting non-deteriorating current regardless of Resistance. This feature gives BP Constant Current devices the capacity to deliver consistent and increasingly enhanced MTTLOIs of EO at even very high Resistances for all age groups even at the end of long duration trains. It is a combination of Brief Pulse and the efficiency of constant current, which enable BP devices to emit reduced EO and Charge with respect to the induction of adequate seizures compared to SW. It is this reduced EO capacity which manufacturers have emphasized with respect to the depiction of BP as safer than SW. However, it is the inverse exploitation of the automatically ascending Voltage aspect and thus the incredible efficiency of Brief Pulse's Constant Current feature, [300] which enables BP to become an enhanced EO device compared to SW in most age categories. Consequently, it is the augmentation of consistent MTTLOIs through higher and higher Voltages both in individual BP devices and with each new BP generation which facilitates the exploited inversion capacity of BP, generally. The hidden result of increasing MTTLOIs is augmented and augmenting output (in lieu of minimal stimulus), the outcome of which is the antithesis of manufacturers' stated purpose for replacing the SW apparatus of "old" with the alleged "safer" reduced EO Brief Pulse device of the "future." [301]

[300] Constant Current is overlooked in the sense that it can make BP an enhanced EO device as opposed to a reduced EO device.

[301] This feature, exploited by all BP Manufacturers, is important to device manufacturers in that, in fact, efficacy depends upon electrical dosage and MTTLOI--not adequate seizure (induced by minimal stimulus). It is for this same reason that BP manufacturers have kept the ubiquitous clinical application of inverse exploitation a secret from the general public, advertising BP's reduced output potential (compared to SW) for PR purposes alone.

Spurious Referencing

Royal College of Psychiatry makes several references to an alleged .504 Coulomb ceiling within the 1989 IEC Standard 60601-1 (safety requirements for medical electrical equipment in general) [International Electrotechnical Commission, 1977, 1988; Royal College of Psychiatry, 1995, pp. 126 (footnote 7), 134 (footnote 9), 140 (footnote 11), 146]. In fact, no such ceiling within the now defunct 1989 IEC Standard exists.[302] The .504 C ceiling was merely reported by manufacturer, Somatics, for its 1989 IEC second generation BP devices (Abrams, and Swartz, 1988, back cover; Swartz and Abrams, 1996, back cover) in lieu of its actual (never reported) EO of up to 252J (Cameron, 1994).[303] [304] Certainly, the invention and utilization of BP was never intended to permit the unreported emission of up to 252J at, for instance, Somatics' reported .504C ceiling for its second generation Thymatron DG and DGx, thus circumventing the 1982 APA Standard even while continuing to suggest 100 absolute Joules. Nor is it acceptable that a Charge ceiling, i.e. the alleged .504C output ceiling (and now a 1200mC ceiling as we have seen) should permit an inversion exploitation of BP, that is, enhanced EO in lieu of reduced EO compared to SW (both in the U.S. and abroad) and thus high MTTLOIs in lieu of minimal stimulus. Rather, the logical assumption is that both the 1982 APA Standard and the 1989 IEC Standard, as per the illusion, should have limited all Brief Pulse "ECT" devices to no more than 110 absolute Joules and so minimal stimulus for all age groups, as promoted.[305] In that BP, an alleged reduced EO device, was specifically advertised and allegedly produced to enhance safety by its capacity to induce adequate seizures at far less EO and Charge than SW, a Charge ceiling enabling BP devices to surpass SW in overall output and MTTLOI (in most age categories) is to stand on its head the proposed purpose of BP, a fact which has been altogether missed by FDA, ERA, and perhaps even IEC regulatory officials. The purported purpose of BP is clearly seen through the original and unambiguous 1982 APA ceiling Standard of 110 maximum joules (as well as the "70J at 220Ω" ER/RRC) proposed to the FDA in 1982 by Weiner himself in accordance with the Utah Biomedical Test Laboratory's final report (Grahn et al. 1977). The purported purpose of Brief Pulse as a reduced EO device (compared to SW) is even suggested through the single and specific 100 Joule allusion within the 1989 IEC Standard (albeit falsely) suggestive in this case, of a circa 100J ceiling.[306] SW, of course, already too powerful at 200J, should have been instantly banned. The fact that BP at .504C can emit 252 Joules, and BP at 1200mC can emit circa 1200 Joules—never reported energy output parameters--

---

[302] That no .504C ceiling exists within the IEC Standard 60601-1 was confirmed in a private conversation with Charles Sidebottom, Coordinator of the IEC 62A Committee overseeing 60601-1. The author could find so such Standard within a manual search of IEC 60601-1; whereas Sidebottom searched a CD Rom of 60601-1 with the same result.

[303] Charge x Current x Impedance = EO. In the U.S., for Somatics' devices, .504C is tantamount to 252J. .504C x .9A x 555.5Ω = 252J, but never reported in Joules. IEC permits up to one Ampere but limits Impedance to 500Ω. 504C x 1.0A x 500Ω = 252J. Apparently manufacturers reported to Royal College of Psychiatry a non-existent .504C ceiling rather than reveal actual EO for their BP devices.

[304] The juxtaposition of a seeming 100J ceiling with an actual .504C output is reinforced by the 1989 IEC single featured allusion to 100 Joules and to readouts on second generation MECTA and Somatics' BP devices. (See Somatics under How Manufacturers Figure . . . in this manuscript.)

[305] Safety through use of minimal stimulus based upon convulsion theory, the hypothesis upon which these devices are allegedly based would indicate that all BP and SW devices should be limited to circa 100 absolute Joules as well as minimal stimulus—the seeming original intent of both APA and IEC Standards. It is with this respect to the standards--safety and purported convulsion theory--that an EO ceiling (of 100 Joules), minimal stimulus at all age levels, and EO reporting in general should never have been abandoned. A Charge ceiling of .504 C not only provides no public safeguard from SW manufacturers allowing multifold levels of titration but also BP manufacturers practicing inversion exploitation and so allowing their devices, for example, two and one half times (and more) the originally intended 110 Joule ceiling. Moreover, BP manufacturers recommended IEC ceilings of 1.200 Coulombs (see Weiner's default standard in "Third Generation BP Devices") and indeed, now permit the use of third generation BP devices capable of emitting five to six times the original 100 Joule ceiling--more powerful than any SW device generally--all without reporting EO, as we have seen.

[306] The newest and final Standard proposed by Weiner et al. but denied by the IEC, is now used by default in that all IEC standards for "ECT were removed at Weiner's request. The so-called default "standard" increases the .504 C Charge ceiling to 1.2 Coulombs. This is the opposite of what Utah suggested to the FDA to assure benefit outweighs risk (Grahn et al. 1977). Rather, the Charge ceiling for BP should have been limited to about .336 C with corresponding Impedance, Voltage, Duration, and Frequency ceilings to prevent BP from ever surpassing 110 Joules. Because the alleged "therapeutic effect" of "adequate seizure" is a myth, however, and because the procedure really "works" by damaging neuronal pathways through adequate amounts of electricity," manufacturers, led by Weiner, had to abandon the 110J ceiling for a never before reported 1200J ceiling, six times the power of SW.

far surpassing the EO of SW generally, as well as surpass the MTTLOI of SW in most age categories--has gone unseen both by FDA and IEC regulatory bodies. The result of this oversight has been the inverted exploitation model of the modern day BP device with augmented rather than reduced electrical dosing, and thus rising MTTLOI devices in lieu of the minimal stimulus device that BP is touted to be.

Double Standard

The BP device, therefore, while capable of inducing seizures at half or even much less than half the EO of SW, is currently utilized to emit much higher power generally, much more constantly than SW, and has been, in fact, increasingly augmented for the purpose of emitting consistently high MTTLOIs of electricity at every age level. This latter, little known and unreported feature--the inversion exploitation of BP-- is exactly how modern day BP devices are purposely designed, clinically utilized, and applied in today's medical market place. Succinctly, the Brief Pulse device can perform two very disparate functions--it can reduce output required to induce the "adequate seizure" for the purpose of administering the least amount of electricity for all age groups (used in most so-called "safety studies") or it can elicit consistent very high Multifold Threshold Titration Level Output Intensities of electricity at all age levels (used in clinical practice) much more reliably and at much higher outputs than SW generally, for the specific purpose of destroying and so reducing neural pathways. The first function of Brief Pulse works on adequate seizure constituting an ECT (Electro Convulsive Therapy) device, the second function on adequate electricity constituting an ENR (Electro Neurotransmission Reduction) device. Insidiously, then, it is the reduced EO potential of BP for ECT which has been utilized in safety studies, that is, where adequate seizure (in lieu of adequate electricity) is required for safety as opposed to the enhanced EO potential of BP for ENR which is utilized in actual clinical practice, that is, where adequate electrical dosage (in lieu of adequate seizure) is utilized to make the procedure “work.”

The reduced stimulus function of BP used in most safety studies, of course, and the enhanced function of BP used to achieve "efficacy" are starkly discrepant. Thus, it is BP's minimizing capacity to induce reduced output minimal stimulus seizures compared to SW and BP’s equal capacity to deliver Multifold Threshold Titration Level output intensities of electricity more powerful than SW generally, which makes the confusing double standard possible. In sum, it is the superimposition of BP's minimizing capacity to induce seizures at just above threshold outputs, upon its equal capacity to induce amplified Multifold Threshold Titration Level Output Intensities of electricity, which has made it possible for manufacturers to dramatically increase the power of their BP devices while at the same time maintaining its image as a "new and improved” mechanism by virtue of “reduced output." In short, it is this unusual double capacity of BP and thus the subtle superimposition of one function upon the other which has enabled BP manufacturers, despite BP's advancing power, to successfully maintain the deceptive notion of improved safety over SW via greatly reduced output. The notion of reduced EO devices though an entirely false depiction, has been wholly consumed both by the medical community and the lay public at large. Indeed, it is this anomalous superimposition of the one feature (minimal stimulus) upon the other (inverse exploitation) which has been behind the mass confusion and thus the ongoing struggle between Advocates and Opponents of “ECT” for almost fifty years (1976-2022) beginning with the re-introduction of Brief Pulse via the MECTA "C." It is the superimposition of BP's inherent double potential, then, the one function upon the other that lies behind the greatest ongoing hoax in modern medical history--a hoax played not only upon the lay public at large, but generations of professionals--indeed upon lay, regulatory, and medical spheres concurrently. So powerful is the illusion created by this confusing superimposition, that it is but the direct complaints of recipients themselves which continue to call into question both the "ECT" of the past (See Frank 1978), and the so-called "kinder, gentler, new and improved 'ECT'" of the present (see Andre 2009).

CHAPTER 89

Conclusion

Under the false guise of "convulsive therapy," manufacturers have currently granted themselves unregulated freedom to produce brain diminishing devices for "effectively" educing temporary reduction of depression and behavioral modification, the same cause and effect rationale once used for various forms of "psychosurgery." In that out and out brain damage is no longer acceptable as "therapy" either to control behavior or temporarily diminish depression, manufacturers have suppressed all evidence of the enormous electrical enhancements inherent in BP devices produced since 1982. Instead manufacturers have propagated the myth that BP has greatly improved "convulsive therapy" by virtue of diminished output compared to SW, thereby diminishing the potential for electrical brain injury manifested through the universal complaint of long-term memory dysfunction. Manufacturers concede that some electrical enhancement has been necessary for "dose sensitive" UL ECT and in order to compensate for a rise in threshold over a treatment series with both BL and UL "ECT," but somehow, in spite of this concession, yet claim to use much less electricity than SW. Moreover, manufacturers suggest that, whereas, some "necessary" electrical enhancements have been made for the purported contingencies of “dose-sensitive UL ECT” and the alleged doubling of threshold (with both BL and UL ‘ECT’) by the end of a treatment series,” and even for “stronger seizures,” that the Brief Pulse wave by and unto itself is "less harmful" than SW. There is no evidence for such a claim. One machine is less harmful than another only by virtue of reduced electrical output and where this reduction does not exist, the Brief Pulse advantage disappears (Squire and Zouzounis, 1986). Following the deceptive reporting of what appears to be around 100 maximum Joules for second generation BP devices, therefore, while manufacturers acknowledge some vague notion of electrical increase, the practice of deceptive and deliberately inconsistent reporting stratagems leaves the degree of BP electrical augmentation "fuzzy" at best. Indeed, the false inference that the "new and improved" BP device emits greatly reduced outputs compared to SW is yet highly prevalent in both lay and academic literature alike.

American "ECT" devices were grandfathered in under the Medical Device Act of 1976, but following a review of the literature by Utah Biomedical Test Laboratory (Grahn 1976; 1977) at the behest of the FDA, all ECT devices should have been made to conform to the FDA inspired 1982 APA Standard, favoring the use of reduced output BP over SW. This 1982 standard limited parameters constitutive of the MECTA "C," the prototypical Brief Pulse device presented to the FDA between 1976 and 1982 as the "new and improved ECT device" of the future by virtue of its capacity in induce adequate seizures in all age categories via its true 108J ceiling. Indeed, the 1982 APA Standard limiting all BP output to just above threshold or minimal stimulus for all age categories with BL ECT (reducing electrical output by half compared to SW even set for minimal stimulus SW), identified the minimum output needed to induce all age recipients with BP as 100 absolute joules. “Improvement” with BP logically seemed to point in the direction of less and less electrical output to induce the same adequate seizures previously induced with the 200J SW device.

“ECT” in 1976 was clearly “grandfathered in” as "convulsive therapy," in turn founded on "convulsion theory." Based on this definition of ECT, it was assumed that all American “ECT” devices would adhere to the FDA condoned 1982 APA Standard limiting maximum output to 110 maximum Joules (as well as a “70J at 220Ω” ER/RRC) from circa 1982 forward. By implication then, and by direct description, an “ECT device” is one that emits the least amount of electricity possible to induce “adequate convulsions” in turn defined as 25 or more seconds in length. In effect, any device surpassing the electrical parameters identified within the 1982

APA Standard, that is, any device surpassing the amount of electricity required to induce "adequate convulsions" with the least amount of electricity possible in all age categories is not a device based on "adequate convulsion," and so cannot be defined as an "ECT" device. Indeed, any device surpassing 110 joules is more accurately described as an electro-dependent "ENR" device. Sine Wave, by this same reasoning, was soon to be eliminated. In short, devices not based on adequate convulsion, but adequate doses of electricity could not and cannot be labeled "ECT" devices as they do not work via adequate convulsion or adequate convulsion alone, but rather adequate amounts of electricity. To that end, this manuscript has re-nominated adequate electricity based devices ENR or "Electro Neurotransmission Reduction" devices in that reduced brain connections is not only the direct consequence of applying more electricity than that required to induce an adequate seizure alone, but is the actual aim of the ENR device. That the reduction of neural transmitters and so reduction of transmissions is the deliberate aim of an ENR or adequate electricity device is convincingly supported by 1) the 2012 Perrin study (Perrin et al. 2012), 2) numerous studies directly associating the degree of electricity administered with the degree of brain damage suffered and so memory morbidity endured, and 3) proof in this manuscript of enhanced machine power with each new modern BP generation. Indeed, the information revealed in this present document clearly exposes "convulsive therapy" as myth. In short, the actions of the manufacturers themselves have shown us that convulsion in and of itself has very little if any "therapeutic" value. That is, manufacturers themselves have begrudgingly debunked convulsion theory via the clear necessity of Brief Pulse devices capable of emitting higher and higher outputs of electricity with each new Brief Pulse generation in order to make the device "work." Certainly, the entire history of the modern day Brief Pulse device from 1976 to the present, as we have now seen, during which machines have become more and more powerful, emitting greater and greater Multifold Threshold Titration Level Output Intensities to make the procedure "effective" is a direct admission of the inefficacy of the adequate seizure. At the same time, manufacturers have been forced to suppress this information in order to keep the "convulsion theory" myth alive in that all present devices are licit or legal only as "ECT" devices. In a nutshell, only "Electro Convulsive Therapy" devices were grandfathered in, in 1976. Additionally, the deliberate destruction of neuronal brain circuitry or gross diminishment of connectivity as a result of deliberately high electrical outputs far greater than that necessary to induce convulsion, or more bluntly, deliberate brain damage, is to a more informed society, unacceptable as a mental health "treatment." In short, intentional brain damage is unpalpable and insupportable to the present-day public, just as lobotomy is no longer acceptable to modern-day society.

As shown in this manuscript, even the 2.3 to 2.6 MTTLOI emitted by second generation BP devices is more than enough power to absorb both the 100% rise in threshold with BL "ECT" and the more than 2.0 fold threshold output with UL ECT even at the end of a "treatment" course proclaimed necessary by manufacturers. In fact, because second generation BP devices fulfilled this dynamic around 1982, manufacturers were forced to secret third generation BP devices emitting default outputs of at least 4.5 fold threshold with BL "ECT" and 9.0 fold threshold with UL "ECT" in all age categories. Indeed, Weiner's 1997 standard, allowing for not only third, but much more powerful fourth and even fifth generation BP devices up to 12.0 fold threshold with BL "ECT" and 24 fold threshold with UL "ECT" cannot by any stretch of the imagination be justified as "convulsive therapy" or "ECT." The reason for manufacturer obfuscation is clear. Manufacturers are fully aware that efficacy does not depend upon adequate convulsion, but rather adequate doses of electricity. Because the Brief Pulse advantage over SW (regarding long term memory damage) was lost even with the advent of second generation BP devices (Squire and Zouzounis 1986), that is, lost as soon as Brief Pulse devices began emitting more than the minimal electrical output needed to elicit so-called "adequate grand mal seizures," manufacturers were forced to mislabel second and certainly third generation BP machines as "ECT devices." A procedure based on adequate doses of electricity, that is, adequate MTTLOIs of electricity in order to make the procedure "work" as opposed to the induction of "adequate convulsions" with the least amount of electricity possible as depicted within 1982 APA Standard, is not an "Electro Convulsive Therapy" device and cannot be labeled as such. A machine such as the second generation BP device (see Perrin et al. 2012) designed to emit adequate amounts of electricity for the single purpose of reducing connectivity not possible with convulsion alone is clearly not "convulsive therapy." This becomes even clearer, as noted, with the introduction of the third generation BP device, in that the simple induction of adequate convulsions can no longer be mistaken as the aim or purpose of such a device. With adequate convulsion clearly no longer the goal of second and certainly third generation BP devices, the incidental occurrence of convulsion can only be seen as "unavoidable" if not a "convenient" side-effect easily exploited for camouflaging the machines' true character and purpose through mislabeling.

Based both on the original description of "ECT" as early as 1938 and the 1976-1982 Weiner-manufacturer promise to the FDA via the 1982 APA Standard to emit the least amount of electricity possible to induce adequate convulsions, modern day Brief Pulse devices no longer qualify as the "ECT" "grandfathered in," in 1976. Rather, they are new devices deliberately designed to electrically diminish neuronal connections through electricity, devices which have clearly devolved into entirely different machines properly labeled Electro Neurotransmission Reduction devices. Such devices, in brief, are unquestionably based on adequate doses of electricity as are the SW devices they were supposed to replace. In that the adequate electrical dosing required of the modern ENR device is patently not the required adequate convulsion around which "ECT" was conceived, labeled, and defined, ENR is plainly not the procedure "grandfathered in," in 1976. Indeed, there has never been an accurate description submitted to the FDA either before or after 1976 of the modern day ENR device with its specific aim of reducing connectivity. Neither has there been FDA safety testing performed on such devices. No machine designed to generate enough electricity to diminish enough neural connections within the left prefrontal lobe to positively affect mood and behavior has ever been submitted to the FDA either prior to or following the congressionally mandated FDA assignation in 1976, nor has such a device ever been evaluated in terms of risk versus benefit. SW, moreover, both because it is inherently suprathreshold, and because evidence suggests SW too is set for suprathreshold MTTLOIs both inherently and deliberately, specifically in the younger age categories, is also fraudulently labeled as "ECT." They too are ENR devices based not on adequate convulsion, but adequate doses of electricity.

If manufacturers argue that the "ECT" device has simply "evolved" over the years, manufacturers must admit that with respect to reduced EO or electricity, modern day "ECT" has not "evolved," but devolved. Indeed, the ENR device is not based on the convulsion function at all, much less the aim of adequate convulsion alone. ENR, it must be admitted, is based on an entirely different function—electricity--with an entirely different aim—reduction of a large percentage of neural connections--neither of which has ever been described, submitted, examined, or evaluated by FDA at any time as a mental health treatment. No description of such a device can be found during the 1976--1982 official investigation of "ECT"--nor in any previous or subsequent period. Indeed, almost all FDA evaluations of the so-called "ECT" device, just as almost all safety studies, have been based on the least amount of electrical stimulus possible to induce a so-called adequate convulsion, clearly identified within the 1982 APA Standard as the sole therapeutic agent in ECT. It follows that the concerted use of adequate electrical dosage upon which the ENR device is based should by law effective FDA policy, be instantly prohibited, until, like any new procedure implemented by any new medical device, both the machine and the effect have undergone standard FDA evaluation and approval. All new medical device procedures must first meet FDA criteria of safety and efficacy, specifically, risk versus benefit analysis before being marketed. Certainly, recipients must not be administered or continue to be administered a procedure from any new medical device without its first undergoing FDA assessment and meeting safety standards. Nor must any new procedure occur without full disclosure of both of the actual process and the actual aim. Certainly, a new procedure cannot be falsely labeled as some other medical procedure merely to qualify for "grandfathering" thereby circumventing FDA criteria. In conclusion, this completely new and unapprised adequate electrical dosage or ENR device must by law mandated FDA policy be halted and recalled until FDA assessment and final safety evaluations have been performed. This, as noted, applies to BP and SW, both of which depend upon suprathreshold doses of electricity to be effective. SW naturally requires more EO than BP to reach threshold and so is inherently suprathreshold, whereas modern day BP is artificially suprathreshold. In short, neither the more archaic SW nor the modern day BP is a an ECT device.

Finally, following Perrin et al., accurate safety testing should consist of prospective MRI-signal testing identifying before and after connectivity like that used in the Perrin study (2012). Of course, such machines must be tested at the default MTTLOI and EO administered by each ENR apparatus in the field—not the hand-titrated minimal stimulus outputs previously used to evaluate safety. Indeed, other than the Perrin study, no so-called "ECT" studies, specifically prospective MRI studies, have ever been performed with the outputs administered by modern day ENR devices, all of which emit much higher electrical outputs in the field than those used in previous so-called safety studies. Bluntly then, ENR devices are not Electro Convulsive Therapy devices any more than evaluative studies of Electro Convulsive Therapy devices are evaluative studies of ENR devices. Certainly, safety testing at true minimal stimulus with either SW or BP does not constitute safety testing with modern ENR devices based on "adequate electrical outputs." In fact, the conspiratorial manufacturer concealment of machine enhancements covering up an entirely new procedure administered with an entirely unrelated device with an entirely different aim, even if mislabeled for one hundred years previously, warrants immediate recall and immediate re-evaluation via FDA once mislabeling has been discovered. Certainly, the deliberate passing off of ENR as ECT constitutes a clear case of fraud. [307]

It is perhaps due to the greed of a few, but also to the industry's frustration as a whole at the very difficult prospect of effectively controlling mood and managing unwanted behavior, that manufacturers have felt compelled to hide behind the myth of "convulsive therapy" and thus the myth of the reduced output BP device compared to SW even as the actual goal of ENR is the reduction of a specified percentage of neurotransmissions through high doses of electricity, neither the aim nor the means of which has ever been acknowledged by any manufacturer. ENR, in point of fact, has never been scrutinized, much less condoned by FDA, ERA, IEC or any other modern day regulatory body. All that can be said is, the machines grossly exceed every FDA, ERA, or IEC standard. Indeed, Weiner's 1997 de facto standard was out and out rejected by the International Electrotechnical Commission in Switzerland in 1997 as a result of which the then IEC "ECT" standard had to be dropped from the IEC Standard as a whole. Indeed, the ENR device, designed with the aim of electrically diminishing or eliminating neural connections within the left prefrontal cortex, might never enjoy FDA, ERA, or IEC approval, or, if it does, will no doubt be subject to a very different set of rules, including extremely discriminative use, together with an extremely comprehensive informed consent. Certainly, with comprehensive informed consent, the appeal of ENR will be greatly condensed if not totally abandoned. Forced procedures should be entirely discontinued.

Below is the FDA ruling regarding banning medical devices.

- The FDA has the authority to ban a medical device intended for human use if it finds, on the basis of all available data and information, that the device presents a substantial deception to patients or users about the benefits of the device, or an unreasonable and substantial risk of illness or injury, which cannot be corrected by a change in the labeling. (see Section 516 (a) of the Federal Food, Drug and Cosmetic Act; 21 CFR 895.20)

In addition:

[Code of Federal Regulations]
[Title 21, Volume 8]
[CITE: 21CFR895.20]

TITLE 21--FOOD AND DRUGS
CHAPTER I--FOOD AND DRUG ADMINISTRATION
DEPARTMENT OF HEALTH AND HUMAN SERVICES
SUBCHAPTER H - MEDICAL DEVICES

PART 895 -- BANNED DEVICES

Subpart A - General Provisions

Sec. 895.20 General.

The Commissioner may initiate a proceeding to make a device a banned device whenever the Commissioner finds, on the basis of all available data and information, that the device presents substantial deception or an unreasonable and

[307] Even the MECTA "C" should be re-tested using the Perrin method for prospective connectivity. Even if loss of connectivity is discovered, however, this does not mean the device is an ENR device as the goal of minimum stimulus is adequate convulsion. On the other hand, we may learn that even true ECT devices cause damage albeit the least amount of damage compared to ENR devices.

substantial risk of illness or injury that the Commissioner determines cannot be, or has not been, corrected or eliminated by labeling or by a change in labeling, or by a change in advertising if the device is a restricted device.

[44 FR 29221, May 18, 1979, as amended at 57 FR 58405, Dec. 10, 1992]

Evidence in this manuscript clearly shows the description and aim of current devices spurious, and that other than first generation BP devices, all modern day Brief Pulse and SW devices are wrongly labeled, a substantial deception. Moreover, the "error" cannot be corrected by a simple change in labeling in that the machines' efficacy is fully dependent upon adequate amounts of electricity, the aim of which is neurotransmission reduction, or more bluntly, neuronal destruction. While the MECTA "C" alone does conform to the 1982 APA (safety) Standard, the MECTA "C" is not effective in that the "adequate seizure" is not effective for which reason manufacturers abandoned it. In sum, all current SW and BP medical devices are fraudulently labeled and so must be immediately discontinued and, indeed, banned, in accordance with Code of Federal Regulations, Part 895, Subpart A, Section 895.20, Title 21, Volume 8 (21CFR895.20). [44 FR 29221, May 18, 1979, as amended at 57 FR 58405, Dec. 10. 1992].

Appendix A

Limitation of SW amperage to 1.0A

The 1982 APA Standard calls for limiting SW to 1.0A. However, American manufacturers never petitioned to adopt the standard so the standard is moot. But even if it had been adopted, a 1.0A ceiling affects only the first few age categories, as we shall see in this section.

According to Weiner's 1982 graphs at the beginning of this section, 93% of (B-24) SW procedures utilize 100J or less, which in most instances translates into a current of 1.0A or below. Instances in which outputs surpass 1.0 Amperes can result in unconscionably high and thus excessively destructive multiplicities of MTTLOI, all of which occur exclusively in the younger age categories (from ages 10-24).[308] For example, the inordinately high SW output of "200J" (though far less raw power than the 500J maximum emitted by third generation BP devices) only occurs at the highest possible SW current of 1.7A, only achievable at the lowest possible initial SW Impedance (of 100Ω). In short, the highest possible SW Amperage can only occur at maximum SW settings applied to very young children.[309] As a result, not only the MTTLOI, but the potential raw power of SW administered to these young recipients can be relatively enormous. In 1982, as a safeguard, Weiner properly suggested to the FDA limiting Amperage for SW devices to one Ampere (Department of Health and Human Services, 1982a, A46), following which, Weiner's suggestion became part of the 1982 APA Standard for SW (Ibid). In 1989, the IEC Standard for ECT Devices, in effect, also identified a ceiling of more than one Ampere (for all 'ECT') devices as "potentially hazardous" (International Electrotechnical Commission, 1989, p. AA29). Maximum SW settings at 1.0A do reduce maximum outputs in age categories 10, 20, and 24, but only somewhat. At first glance, simply by plugging in all maximum B-24 SW parameters with 1.0A (170V x 1.0A x 1.0 Seconds = 170J or $1.0A^2$ x 170Ω x 1.0 Seconds = 170J), the new reduced maximum output appears to be 170J in lieu of 200J. This oversimplified conclusion represented below, however, does not take into account the Amperage deterioration and Impedance enhancement characteristic of SW.

Unrealistic **170J EO Maximum for Medcraft's B-24 SW at Maximum Settings based on Non-deteriorating Current**

EO	Voltage	Current	Duration	Resistance	Charge
17 Joules	170 Volts	1.0 A	.1 Seconds	170 Ω	.100 Coulombs
34	170	1.0	.2	170	.200
51	170	1.0	.3	170	.300
68	170	1.0	.4	170	.400
85	170	1.0	.5	170	.500
102	170	1.0	.6	170	.600

[308] Density of the skin, though perhaps fallaciously, is often cited as the rationale for the higher resistances in older recipients.

[309] Children have thinner and smaller skull casings and thus extremely low resistances to electricity.

119	170	1.0	.7	170	.700
136	170	1.0	.8	170	.800
153	170	1.0	.9	170	.900
170 Joules	**170 Volts**	**1.0 Amps**	**1.0 Secs**	**170 Ω**	**1.00 C**

For the above 170J maximum to occur, no deterioration in the current and no increase in resistance can occur, an unrealistic scenario for Constant Voltage SW devices.

In short, both the maximum legal Current (of 1.0 Ampere) and the lowest legal Impedance permitted at the maximum 170V is 170Ω. Otherwise, Current exceeds 1.0A; (170V/170Ω = 1.0A). But the current and the Impedance would have to remain constant throughout the entire one second maximum emission for the machine to emit 170J, as seen above. [310] This scenario is not feasible in that a SW device, by definition, is not a Constant Current apparatus, but rather a Constant Voltage, deteriorating current machine.[311] Limited to 1.0A, therefore, the B-24 would not mechanically be able to emit its mathematical potential of 170J.

According to our SW paradigm in which current deteriorates and Impedance rises 45Ω over the one second maximum Duration at the maximum 170V, limited to 1.0A, while initial Impedance cannot descend below 170Ω final Impedance most probably ascends to about 215Ω, gradually deteriorating the 1.0A maximum current to about .791A. Limited to a 1.0 Ampere current, therefore, maximum possible emission on the B-24 is not 170J, but circa 134 maximum Joules. This familiar profile belongs to our twenty-four year old recipient (see age-related resistances for BP).

TYPICAL and REALISTIC MAXIMUM OUTPUT FOR B-24 SW by MEDCRAFT (24 year OLD)

EO	Voltage	Current	Duration	Resistance	Charge
17 Joules	170 Volts	1.0 Ampere	.1 Seconds	170 Ω	.1 Coulombs
33.03	170	.871	.2	175	.174
48.17	170	.944	.3	180	.283
62.5	170	.919	.4	185	.368
76.05	170	.895	.5	190	.447
88.92	170	.872	.6	195	.52
101.15	170	.85	.7	200	.595
112.78	170	.829	.8	205	.663
123.86	170	.810	.9	210	.729
134.42	**170**	**.791**	**1.0**	**215**	**.791**

A 134J output may only occur in only 2-3% of all SW emissions (see Weiner's SW graph at the beginning of this Section).

Again limited to a 1.0A ceiling, should we set the constant B-24 Voltage at a lower setting, i.e. 140V, we see that Impedance must not fall below 140Ω. (Otherwise, Amperage surpasses 1.0A; 140V/140Ω = 1.0A). As Impedance descends, conversely, Voltage cannot rise above the numerical value of the lowest possible Impedance (i.e. 140Ω, otherwise the current rises above 1.0A). In short, a 140Ω minimum Resistance demands a maximum Voltage of no more than 140V (140V/140Ω = 1.0A). Even with Voltage limited to 140, however, by simply plugging in the maximum Voltage, maximum Duration and minimum Impedance allowed (140V, 1.0 seconds, 140Ω), we again reach the oversimplified conclusion that maximum output at this setting is (140V x 1.0A x 1.0 Seconds = 140J; 1.0A² x 140Ω x 1.0 Seconds =) 140J. If we again create a Table depicting such a profile, we once again see that in order to achieve the theoretical maximum output (of 140J in this instance), current cannot deteriorate nor can Impedance rise. Both the lowest legal Impedance[312] permitted at 140V (140Ω) and the maximum legal Current (1.0 Ampere) would, therefore, have to remain constant throughout the

[310] SW devices rarely utilize more than 1 full second in that, due to increasing Resistance, the dwindling Current might spontaneously abate.

[311] The increasing Voltage of Constant Current (BP) devices, unlike SW devices, maintain the Current throughout.

[312] With respect to SW, the lower the Impedance, the higher the Current.

entire one second emission--totally uncharacteristic of SW constant Voltage devices. This thoroughly implausible paradigm is depicted in the Table below.

Unrealistic **140J (Legal) EO Maximum of the B-24 SW at a Constant 140V setting Based on Non-Deteriorating Current (18 yr. old)**

EO	Voltage	Current	Duration	Resistance	Charge
14 Joules	140 Volts	1.0 Ampere	.1 Seconds	140 Ω	.100 Coulombs
28	140	1.0	.2	140	.200
42	140	1.0	.3	140	.300
56	140	1.0	.4	140	.400
70	140	1.0	.5	140	.500
84	140	1.0	.6	140	.600
98	140	1.0	.7	140	.700
112	140	1.0	.8	140	.800
126	140	1.0	.9	140	.900
140 Joules	**140 Volts**	**1.0 Amps**	**1.0 Secs**	**140 Ω**	**1.00 C**

For the above 140J maximum to occur at a 140V setting, no deterioration in the current and no increase in resistance can occur, not possible for Constant Voltage SW devices.

Limited to 1.0A, therefore, the B-24 SW set at 140V would not be able to emit the 140J mathematical potential output depicted above. To account for rise in Impedance and deterioration of Current then, we must once again use our SW paradigm by adding 45Ω over the maximum one second Duration now reflected in the table below.

Realistic **140J (Legal) EO Maximum of the B-24 SW at a Constant 140V setting (18 yr old)**

EO	Voltage	Current	Duration	Resistance	Charge
14 Joules	140 Volts	1.0 Ampere	.1 Seconds	140 Ω	.100 Coulombs
27.03	140	.966	.2	145	.193
39.20	140	.933	.3	150	.28
50.58	140	.903	.4	155	.361
61.25	140	.875	.5	160	.438
71.27	140	.849	.6	165	.509
80.71	140	.824	.7	170	.577
89.60	140	.800	.8	175	.640
97.99	140	.778	.9	180	.700
105.95 J	**140 Volts**	**.757 Amps**	**1.0 Secs**	**185 Ω**	**.757 C**

The above profile, belonging to an 18 year old recipient,[313] is now limited (via the 1.0A ceiling), not to 140J, but to a circa 106J maximum. Moreover, we begin to see that limited to 1.0A, the maximum B-24 output possible is the 134J maximum of the 24 year old recipient above. Limited to 1.0A, in that his/her Impedance is circa 170Ω, the 24 year old profile represents the lowest Impedance at which the B-24's maximum 170V can first be utilized (170V/170Ω = 1.0A). Limited to 1.0A, therefore, maximum Voltage (170V) can no longer be administered to individuals under the age of 24 years

To illustrate further, let us once again examine the youngest probable recipient who concomitantly has lowest possible Impedance, allowing for the infamous 200J maximum depicted in Weiner's graph at the

[313] We simply take the initial Impedance, 140Ω and according to our paradigm, subtract 50Ω to find the age category on the BP chart at the beginning of this section.

beginning of this section (administered an initial 1.7A current). Excluding the 1.0A ceiling limit, in order for 200 Joules of EO to occur, an initial Impedance floor [314] of 100Ω at the 170V maximum setting is needed. In this instance, the initial 100Ω Impedance must rise at the end of the one second maximum duration to a 145Ω final Impedance (see chart for the ten year old age category with 1.7A) causing the initial and maximum 1.7A initial Amps to deteriorate to a 1.17A final Amperage at the end of one second, thereby emitting the 200J ceiling.[315] Extreme correspondences such as these in which, for example, the 170 maximum Volts is applied to the 100Ω minimum Impedance become technically prohibited, as noted, under both FDA (1982 APA) and (1989) IEC Standards (Ibid) which limit SW devices to a 1.0 Ampere current. In fact, even before the 1.0A ceiling, utilization of maximum SW settings on a small ten (or under) year old child, for instance, to derive Weiner's 200J maximum is even by Weiner's chart, extremely rare (perhaps one twelfth of one per cent of all SW emissions). On the other hand, no present standard prohibits it. (The APA Standard, remember, was never officially adopted.)

Limited to 1.0A, our ten year old with a Resistance of 100Ω for instance, can no longer be administered the B-24's 170V maximum, but rather a maximum of 100V. (Otherwise current will surpass 1.0A; 100V/100Ω = 1.0A). The new maximum SW output for ten year old children (limited to 1.0A) is now limited to about 69 maximum Joules at one full second, reflected in the table below.

OUTPUT BASED ON MEDCRAFT'S MAXIMUM B-24 PARAMETERS LIMITED TO THE 1.0A CEILING FOR 10 YEAR OLD CHILD

EO	Voltage	Current	Duration	Resistance	Charge
10 Joules	100 Volts	1.0 Ampere	.1 Seconds	100 Ω	.1 Coulombs
19.05	100	.95	.2	105	.191
27.27	100	.909	.3	110	.273
34.78	100	.87	.4	115	.348
41.67	100	.833	.5	120	.417
48.0	100	.80	.6	125	.480
53.85	100	.769	.7	130	.539
59.26	100	.741	.8	135	.593
71.43	100	.21	.9	140	.714
68.9 J	**100**	**.69**	**1.0**	**145**	**.69**

While much improved, the ten year old child at the new reduced maximum output (from 200J to 69J maximum) receives a disconcerting (68.9J ÷ 8.7J =) 7.9 MTTLOI in lieu of the terrifying 23 MTTLOI possible before limiting Amperage to 1.0A. Theoretically, Duration can be further limited to .3 Seconds in which case the child receives a total of 27.27 Joules or a (27.27 ÷ 8.7J =) 3.14 MTTLOI. Voltage can also be theoretically reduced, etc. On the other hand, there is evidence to suggest that outputs at minimal stimulus for this device cannot fall below circa 36J or a 9 MTTLOI (using minimal threshold outputs, i.e. 36J ÷ 4J = 9 MTTLOI) or that minimal outputs are limited to a maximum output of 1.0A maximum and so cannot fall below 68.9J or the 7.9 MTTLOI in this age category.

In turn, (based on a 1.0A maximum) maximum output for the twenty year old is no longer 148J but 115.39J. In that initial Impedance is still 150Ω, maximum Voltage is now limited to 150V. (Otherwise, Amperage will surpass 1.0A; i.e. Current = V/Ω = 155V/150Ω = 1.03A; 150V/150Ω = 1.0A). The new 115.4J maximum for twenty year old recipients is reflected in the Table below.

[314] For SW, the lower the Impedance, the higher the current, therefore instead having an Impedance ceiling, we have an Impedance floor.

[315] 170 Volts/145Ω = 1.17 Amperes (final Amperage). 1.17A x 170V x 1.0 Sec. = circa 200J. Currents surpassing one Ampere could have been avoided (and apparently often were) simply by reducing Voltage to the numerical value of the initial Impedance (100V/100Ω = 1.0A)

OUTPUT BASED ON MEDCRAFT'S MAXIMUM B-24 PARAMETERS LIMITED TO THE 1.0A CEILING FOR 20 YEAR OLD RECIPIENT

EO	Voltage	Current	Duration	Resistance	Charge
15 Joules	150 Volts	1.0 Amperes	.1 Seconds	150 Ω	.1 Coulombs
29	150	.968	.2	155	.194
42.19	150	.938	.3	160	.281
54.55	150	.909	.4	165	.364
66.18	150	.882	.5	170	.441
77.14	150	.857	.6	175	.514
87.50	150	.833	.7	180	.583
97.30	150	.811	.8	185	.649
106.58	150	.790	.9	190	.711
115.39 J	**150**	**.769**	**1.0**	**195**	**.769**

The twenty year old at the new maximum settings (limited to 1.0A) receives a somewhat improved maximum though yet still disconcerting (115.39J ÷ 15.7 =) 7.35 MTTLOI in lieu of the even more disconcerting 9.44 MTTLOI prior to the 1.0A limit. Of course, other much lower settings are theoretically possible. For instance, Duration can be theoretically limited to 0.5 Seconds in which case the twenty year old receives circa 85 Joules or a (85J ÷ 15.7 =) 5.41 MTTLOI. Voltage too, can theoretically be reduced. On the other hand, there is evidence suggesting that the B-24 cannot be set lower than 43J for the 20 year old, which is a 4.7 MTTLOI using minimal stimulus thresholds or that the machine cannot emit lower than maximum output limited to 1.0A or 115.4J at a 7.35 MTTLOI (using maximum threshold outputs).

By 24 years of age, as seen above, the B-24, even at the maximum 170V and 1.0 Second maximum Duration, self-limits to 1.0A in any case. Maximum output possible for the B-24 within a 1.0A limit is thus circa 134 Joules, the same output elicited at maximum settings for a probable 24 year old male even when higher than 1.0 Amperages are allowed.

TYPICAL MAXIMUM OUTPUT FOR B-24 SW by MEDCRAFT (24 years of age)

EO	Voltage	Current	Duration	Resistance	Charge
17 Joules	**170 Volts**	**1.0 Amps**	**.1 Sec.**	**170 Ω**	**.100 Coul.**
33.03	170	.871	.2	175	.174
48.17	170	.944	.3	180	.283
62.5	170	.919	.4	185	.368
76.05	170	.895	.5	190	.447
88.92	170	.872	.6	195	.52
101.15	170	.85	.7	200	.595
112.78	170	.829	.8	205	.663
123.86	170	.810	.9	210	.729
134.42	**170**	**.791**	**1.0**	**215**	**.791**

In sum, limiting maximum Amperage from 1.7 to 1.0A affects only the first two age categories, the ten year old child and the twenty year old young man or woman.

The 1.0A limit was never officially authorized in that American manufacturers avoided adopting either the 1982 APA Standard or the 1989 IEC standard. However, based on the rarity of the 200J output and even 150J outputs, it stands to reason that practitioners typically reduce parameters in the younger age categories. For both these reasons then, the unofficial 1.0A ceiling stipulation as well as evidence pointing toward reduced settings for individuals 10 to 24 years of age, the typical maximum output and even the technically legal maximum output for the B-24 SW may not, in fact, be 200J, but rather 134 Joules, about that of one of the later, first generation BP devices, the MECTA "D" (though very importantly, <u>in totally opposing age groups</u>). Maximum MTTLOI (limited to a 1.0A ceiling) on the other hand, yet delivers to the 10 year old age category a 7.9 fold

MTTLOI at circa 69J, excessive by any standards. By the twenty year old age category, maximum MTTLOI (based on the same 1.0A current maximum) drops to 7.35 fold and finally, for the 24 year old, maximum MTTLOI drops to (134.42J ÷ 19J =) 7.08, the same maximum emitted without the 1.0A limit. The maximum MTTLOI (for the B-24 limited to 1.0A) is thus 7.9 fold threshold (in the ten year old age category), greater than third generation BP devices at 5.0 fold (for this same age category), but less than probable fourth generation BP devices at a circa 10 MTTLOI. The potential 200J, 23 MTTLOI, therefore, though horrifyingly possible, is by no means a typical maximum for the B-24. On the other hand, nothing prohibits administrators from using maximum output in the ten year old age category. Moreover, there is reason to suspect that the machine cannot emit lower than maximum output with 1.0A in every age category in which case, even set for "minimum SW settings," the machine could yet deliver 134.42J or a 7.08 MTTLOI in the 24 year old age category, extraordinarily high in this age class.

While never enforced, then, in that manufacturers never officially adopted either the 1982 APA Standard or the 1989 IEC standard for ECT devices, both the 1982 APA Standard and 1989 IEC Standard at least encouraged limiting overall current to one Ampere, a ceiling never required, however, and so never officially limiting the B-24 SW by Medcraft to a 134 Joule final maximum ceiling and or a 7.9 MTTLOI [316] (Department of Health and Human Services, 1982a, p. A46; International Electrotechnical Commission, 1989, p. AA29). [317] Even adhering to a one Ampere ceiling, moreover, while Medcraft's B-24 SW output at its maximum 170V and 1.0 Second Duration setting no longer emits a 200J maximum and 23 fold threshold titration level output intensity, it yet can emit a circa **134J** maximum output and a 7.9 MTTLOI, still extremely high for this specific age category.[318]

Thus, respecting the one Ampere ceiling, Weiner's graph, representing Medcraft's B-24 SW as a 200 Joule output device (Department of Health and Human Services, 1982a, G3-G4; H12-H13) becomes moot. With Weiner's recommended one Ampere ceiling in place via FDA/IEC Standards, Weiner's B-24 SW Chart used for comparing SW to BP would have to be modified to represent a maximum EO for the B-24 SW, not of 200 Joules, but of 134 maximum Joules. It must be noted, of course, that the 134J maximum occurs in the younger age category where it is most inappropriately administered, whereas, while BP emits much higher outputs, it does so in much older age categories. BP never reaches these SW potentials in the youngest age categories. On the other hand, BP far surpasses SW in the older age categories with extremely powerful BP devices, all allowable under Weiner's 1997 de facto standard.

Importantly, only age categories 10-20 are affected by the 1.0A ceiling. Indeed, higher Resistance levels of individuals from about age 24 years and up automatically inhibit Current from rising above 1.0A. In short, the machine is physically limited to 1.0A for recipients twenty-four years of age and older, thus restricting the B-24 SW to a 134J maximum overall, past the age of about twenty or twenty-two. On the other hand, SW does emit its greatest power in the younger age categories, whereas, BP emits its greatest power in the older age categories.[319]

The modified Table below depicts the B-24 SW by Medcraft at modified initial and final Impedances limited to 1.0 maximum Amperes at otherwise maximum settings, i.e., the B-24's one second maximum Duration and 170V maximum, along with modified corresponding maximum EOs. (Compare this to the same Table surpassing the 1.0A ceiling in a previous section and in the chart below the following chart). In short, then, how

---

[316] In that Amperage deteriorates with SW, the highest Amperage occurs initially. A one amp ceiling, therefore, confines the 170V maximum setting to an initial 170Ω floor (A = 170V/170Ω = 1.0A). Based on our paradigm, 170Ω (Initial Impedance) + 45Ω = 215Ω (final Impedance). 170V/215Ω = .791A (Final Current). EO = 170V x .791A x 1.0 Seconds = 134.41J maximum).

[317] The B-24 emit can emit lower Voltages and thus lower initial Impedances, but all of which will be lower than 134J. For example, at 150V, a 150Ω initial Impedance is allowed but which will culminate at one second in a 195Ω or 115J maximum. (150V/195Ω = .77A x 150V x 1.0 Seconds = 115J).

[318] In limiting current to 1.0A, where Impedances fall below an initial 170Ω, the maximum 170V can no longer be used. In fact, Voltage can never rise above the numerical value of the initial Impedance. For example, at an initial 100Ω, Voltage cannot rise above 100V (100V/100Ω = 1.0A). 110V, for instance cannot be used with a 100Ω initial Impedance in that initial Amperage surpasses 1.0A (110V/100Ω = 1.1A).

[319] Weiner's suggestion of SW/BP two to one EO correspondence is somewhat skewed. While generally true compared to, for example, the MECTA "C, the inverse ratio, that is, SW's propensity to emit more EO for younger age groups as opposed to BP's propensity to emit higher EOs for older groups is a more complex relationship than we are given to believe from Weiner's BP Vs SW graphs.

only the 10 and 20 year old age groups are affected (via the1.0A ceiling). Based on the extreme rarity of the B-24's alleged 200J potential, most practitioners appear to limit the B-24 to the 1.0A recommended by Weiner, affecting the first two younger age categories (10-20). However, this is by no means mandatory and exceptions do occur. (See Ted Chabasinski, 2022.) Since enough power to induce seizures only becomes problematic for older age categories (with SW), maximum B-24 settings must be used for recipients 60 or under. Only in the 10-20 age category, can the machine surpass 1.0A. As noted, due to higher resistances the machine is automatically circumscribed to a 1.0 Ampere maximum current (and often below 1.0A). In short, past the age of twenty, the B-24 SW is not physically capable of surpassing the 1.0A ceiling. Consequently, while the machine can reach 200J, a more typical maximum output for the B-24 appears to be about 134 Joules. On the other hand, such outputs in the younger age categories are exceptionally devastating, reflecting the upside down construction of the B-24. The figures below depicting maximum settings limited to 1.0A reflect the more typical maximum B-24 outputs.[320]

Typical EO Maximums of the B-24 SW Deteriorating Current Device at Various Typical Max Impedances at Maximum Settings Limited to 1.0A. (See Initial and Final Impedances.)

AGE	EO	Voltage	Current	Duration	Resistance	Charge
10 Yrs	10 J	100	1.0 A	.1 Sec	100 Ω	.1 Coul.
20	15 J	150	1.0 A	.1 Sec.	150 Ω	.1 C
24	17 J	170	1.0 A	.1 Sec	170 Ω	.1 C
30	14.25 J	170	.85 A	.1 Sec	200 Ω	.085 C
40	11.56 J	170	.68 A	.1 Sec	250 Ω	.068 C
50	9.63 J	170	.567 A	.1 Sec	300 Ω	.057 C
60	8.26 J	170	.486 A	.1 Sec	350 Ω	.049 C
65	7.71 J	170	.453 A	.1 Sec	375 Ω	.045 C
70	7.23 J	170	.425 A	.1 Sec	400 Ω	.043 C
80	6.42 J	170	.378 A	.1 Sec	450 Ω	.038 C
90	5.78 J	170	.340 A	.1 Sec	500 Ω	.034 C
100	5.26 J	170	.309 A	.1 Sec	550 Ω	.031 C
				.2		
				.3		
				.4		
				.5		
				.6		
				.7		
				.8		
				.9		
10 Yr	68.9J	100V	.690 A	1.0 Sec	145 Ω	.690 C
20	115.39J	150V	.769 A	1.0 Sec	195 Ω	.769 C
24	134.42 J	170 V	.791 A	1.0 Sec	215 Ω	.791 C
30	118 J	170 V	.694 A	1.0 Sec	245 Ω	.694 C
40	97.97 J	170 V	.576 A	1.0 Sec	295 Ω	.576 C
50	83.77 J	170 V	.493 A	1.0 Sec	345 Ω	.493 C
60	73.16 J	170 V	.430 A	1.0 Sec	395 Ω	.430 C
65	68.81 J	170 V	.405 A	1.0 Sec	420 Ω	.405 C
70	64.94 J	170 V	.382 A	1.0 Sec	445 Ω	.382 C
80	58.4 J	170 V	.343 A	1.0 Sec	495 Ω	.343 C

[320] This is not to say that outputs limited to 1.0A in the younger age categories are not devastating in that such outputs yet means excessively high Multifold Threshold Titration Level Output Intensities.

90	**53 J**	**170 V**	**.312 A**	**1.0 Sec**	**545 Ω**	**.312 C**
100	**48.6**	**170 V**	**.286 A**	**1.0 Sec**	**595 Ω**	**.286 C**

As mentioned above, note below how limiting Amperage to 1.0A only affects the first two age categories.

Max Stimulus Limited to 1.0A v Max Stim Limited to 1.7A

AGE	**EO**	***MTTLOI***	**EO**	***MTTLOI***
10 yr	68.9J	***7.9***	200	***23.0***
20	115.39J	***7.35***	148	***9.44***
24	134 J	***7.08***	134	***7.08***
30	118 J	***4.8***	118	***4.8***
40	98.0 J	***2.75***	98.0	***2.75***
50	83.8 J	***1.72***	83.8	***1.72***
60	73.2 J	***1.15***	73.2	***1.15***
65	68.6 J	***.95***	68.6	***.95***
70	64.9 J	***.81***	64.9	***.80***
80	58.4 J	***.59***	58.4	***.59***
90	53 J	***.44***	53	***.44***
100	48.6	***.34***	48.6	***.34***

In sum, Maximum SW Output limited to 1.0A compared to maximum output limited to 1.7A above affects only two age categories, ten and twenty year olds. In the ten year old age category, maximum output drops from a 200J maximum potential to a circa 70J maximum output potential and so from a 23 MTTLOI to a circa 8 MTTLOI. In the twenty year old age category, maximum output drops from a 148J maximum output potential to a 115J maximum output potential and so from a 9.44 MTTLOI to a 7.9 MTTLOI. While somewhat "safer," the outputs administered to ten and twenty year olds limited to maximum output at 1.0A is yet devastating. Indeed, there is a possibility that the B-24 does not allow settings below maximum output limited to 1.0A in any age category. In either case, limited to 1.0A or 1.7A, the highest outputs are yet delivered to the younger recipients. Moreover. the machine is mainly used between the ages of ten to about 50, chiefly targeting children, adolescents, and young men and women for whom the machine is particularly "effective" albeit particularly devastating. Indeed, from about age 65 to 100, those with the highest resistances to electricity, the B-24 is more or less impotent with respect to inducing seizure.

Unlike SW, the recipient of today's modern day BP devices may just as likely be mature.[321] Indeed, more than half of all present "ECT" recipients may be 65 years or older (Texas and California Reporting System, CMHS).

---

[321] Older people (whose resistances are higher) are a major target population of ECT today, particularly with Brief Pulse. Children, on the other hand, except where prohobited by law (Texas Health and Safety Code, Title 7, Subtitle C, Chapter 578, Section 578.001) may be targeted by SW. In that Amperage decreases with increasing Impedance in SW and increased Impedances are overcome with increased Voltage in BP, today's BP is much more devastating to older people than SW devices of the past. On the other hand, in that current increases with decreased resistance in SW, SW is still more devastating to children, adolescents, and young men and women, (whose resistances are lower) than even the most powerful of today's BP devices.

Appendix B

More Details of B-24 in Chart Form Limited and Not Limited to 1.0A Compared to BP

If we compare the second, but particularly the extant third generation BP device to SW, we clearly see that by the third generation BP apparatus, there is no longer any clear superiority of BP over SW with respect to safety. In fact, as Impedance increases, the third generation BP device clearly becomes more powerful and more dangerous both with respect to raw power and multifold threshold titration level output intensities in most age categories. Importantly, both the SW and BP device elicit multifold threshold titration level output intensities of electricity; however, SW cannot compare to the third generation BP's power and efficiency in delivering consistent 5.0 fold threshold dosages at all age levels. While it is true that SW is particularly dangerous and still more powerful than BP for younger age categories and that SW appears almost completely ineffective past age 65, the extant third generation BP device, in delivering its consistent circa 5.0 fold threshold titration level to all recipients up to age 100, is certainly not a minimal stimulus device any more than SW and can no longer be considered a convulsive therapy device.

Since even at maximum settings, the B-24 for the 25 to 100 year old age categories is automatically limited (via higher Impedances) to 1.0A and below, the surpassing of the 1.0A SW ceiling aids only the 10-20 year old age categories. The table below represents maximum SW output (limited to 1.0A) of about 134 Joules. In fact, there is some evidence supporting the hypothesis that "minimal stimulus" for the current B-24 SW device is maximum output in all age categories limited to 1.0A. If so, there is very little room for adjustment on the B-24 SW as only the categories below are affected by the 1.0A ceiling.

The Chart Below Compares Maximum EO Delivered by the B-24 SW Limited to 1.0A in 10-24 Age Category Compared to Consistent Emissions of 3rd Generation JR/SR 1 IEC BP Device

Yr	SW	BP	SW	BP	SW	BP	SW	BP	SW	BP	SW	BP	SW	BP
	Ω	Ω	Volt	Volt	Amp	Amp	Sec	Sec	Chg	Chg	***MTTLOI***	***MTTLOI***	Joule	Joule
10	145	50	100	40	.690	.8	1.0	.5	.690	.14	***7.90***	***5.0***	68.9	5.76
20	195	100	150	80	.769	.8	1.0	.8	.769	.23	***7.35***	***5.0***	115	18.4

According to Medcraft, the B-24 SW is adjustable from .1 to 1.0 Seconds and from 70-170 Volts. On the other hand, there is evidence that the B-24 does not have great flexibility and cannot be set to "true minimal stimulus" SW settings. Even limited to 1.0A, moreover, the maximum SW settings in the 10-20 year old categories are yet high enough to deliver between a circa 8 and 7 multifold threshold titration level output intensity respectively, somewhere between the power of third and potential fourth generation BP devices in these age categories. Indeed, third and fourth generation BP devices, deliver their circa 5 to 10 fold threshold outputs in these particular age categories with much less EO and Charge than SW.

Let us compare the Third Generation BP Device first to the table below representing maximum SW output at all age levels ***without*** the 1.0A ceiling and then to maximum SW output at all age levels ***with*** the 1.0A ceiling. It is assumed that while Impedance may rise over the complete course (or series) of BP "treatments," BP

Impedances, unlike SW, do not significantly rise within a single BP procedure. Thus initial and final Impedances for BP within a single "treatment" are constant, whereas, initial and final Impedances for SW are discrepant. (The table below contains final SW Impedances.)

B-24 SW at Maximum Settings for all Age Groups *Sans* 1.0A Ceiling
Vs.
Consistent Emissions of
3rd Generation JR/SR 1 IEC BP Device in Same Age Groups

Yr	SW	BP	SW	BP	SW	BP	SW	BP	SW	BP	SW	BP	SW	BP
	Ω	Ω	Volt	Volt	Amp	Amp	Sec	Sec	Chg	Chg	*MTTLOI*	*MTTLOI*	Joule	Joule
10	145	50	170	40	1.17	.8	1.0	.5	1.17	.14	**23.0**	**5.0**	200	5.76
20	195	100	170	80	.870	.8	1.0	.8	.872	.23	**9.44**	**5.0**	148	18.4
24	215	120	170	96	.791	.8	1.0	.96	.791	.28	**7.08**	**5.0**	134	26.5
30	245	150	170	120	.694	.8	1.0	1.2	.694	.35	**4.80**	**5.0**	118	41.5
40	295	200	170	160	.576	.8	1.0	1.6	.576	.46	**2.75**	**5.0**	98.0	74
50	345	250	170	200	.493	.8	1.0	2.0	.493	.58	**1.72**	**5.0**	83.8	115
60	395	300	170	240	.430	.8	1.0	2.4	.430	.69	**1.15**	**5.0**	73.2	166
65	420	325	170	260	.405	.8	1.0	2.6	.405	.75	**.95**	**5.0**	68.6	195
70	445	350	170	280	.38	.8	1.0	2.8	.38	.81	**.80**	**5.0**	64.9	226
80	495	400	170	320	.343	.8	1.0	3.2	.343	.92	**.59**	**5.0**	58.4	295
90	545	450	170	360	.312	.8	1.0	3.6	.312	1.04	**.44**	**5.0**	53	373
100	595	500	170	400	.286	.8	1.0	4.0	.286	1.15	**.34**	**5.0**	48.6	460

Note above that B-24 SW at maximum settings without the 1.0A ceiling is super powerful for younger age categories, but ineffective at ages 65 and older. The B-24 machine cannot generally overcome more than 400Ω consistently and may not be able to reliably seize individuals 65 and over (darkest areas on bottom rows with SW), at least not with BL ECT. Note too, how SW surpasses the third generation BP device in power from ages 10 to 40 while the third generation BP device surpasses SW in power from ages 50 to 100. Regarding MTTLOI, note how SW surpasses the third generation BP device from ages 10 to 24 and how the third generation BP device equals and then surpasses SW from age 30 and above. Clearly SW is super dangerous in the younger age categories while the 3rd generation BP device loses its advantage over SW from age 50 and older even when SW is set to maximum output. Probable fourth generation BP devices and hypothetical fifth generation BP devices lose their advantage over SW (even at maximum output) in earlier and earlier age categories.

B-24 SW at maximum Settings for all Age Groups *Limited* to 1.0A
Vs.
Consistent Emissions of
3rd Generation JR/SR 1 IEC BP Device at Same Age Groups

Yr	SW	BP	SW	BP	SW	BP	SW	BP	SW	BP	SW	BP	SW	BP
	Ω	Ω	Volt	Volt	Amp	Amp	Sec	Sec	Chg	Chg	*MTTLOI*	*MTTLOI*	Joule	Joule
10	145	50	100	40	.690	.8	1.0	.5	.690	.14	**7.90**	**5.0**	68.9	5.76
20	195	100	150	80	.769	.8	1.0	.8	.769	.23	**7.35**	**5.0**	115	18.4
24	215	120	170	96	.791	.8	1.0	.96	.791	.28	**7.08**	**5.0**	134	26.5
30	245	150	170	120	.694	.8	1.0	1.2	.694	.35	**4.80**	**5.0**	118	41.5
40	295	200	170	160	.576	.8	1.0	1.6	.576	.46	**2.75**	**5.0**	98.0	74
50	345	250	170	200	.493	.8	1.0	2.0	.493	.58	**1.72**	**5.0**	83.8	115
60	395	300	170	240	.430	.8	1.0	2.4	.430	.69	**1.15**	**5.0**	73.2	166
65	420	325	170	260	.405	.8	1.0	2.6	.405	.75	**.95**	**5.0**	68.6	195
70	445	350	170	280	.38	.8	1.0	2.8	.38	.81	**.80**	**5.0**	64.9	226
80	495	400	170	320	.343	.8	1.0	3.2	.343	.92	**.59**	**5.0**	58.4	295
90	545	450	170	360	.312	.8	1.0	3.6	.312	1.04	**.44**	**5.0**	53	373
100	595	500	170	400	.286	.8	1.0	4.0	.286	1.15	**.34**	**5.0**	48.6	460

Note that maximum B-24 settings limited to 1.0A affects only the 10 and 20 year old age categories. All other categories are unaffected. Though yet unconscionably powerful from age 10 to about age 40, output and MTTLOI are now spectacularly reduced in the ten year old age category, going from a maximum 23 fold to a 7.9 fold maximum and from a 200J maximum to a 69J maximum. The 20 year old age category is only somewhat affected, going from a 9.44 maximum MTTLOI to a 7.35 maximum MTTLOI and from a 148J maximum output to a 115J maximum output. All other age categories at maximum SW output remain unaffected by the 1.0A ceiling limit. Note too, that in either case, extant third generation BP devices consistently equal and then surpass SW regarding MTTLOI from ages 30 and older while equaling and then surpassing SW regarding raw Energy Output from about ages 45 and older. From ages 65 and older, SW begins to be completely ineffective while the third generation BP now elicits outputs in the same 65-100 year old age categories ranging from about 200J to 460J, surpassing SW in cumulative power with much more output than needed to elicit an adequate seizure.

While much improved with the 1.0A ceiling, then, the ten year old child at the new reduced maximum output (from 200J to 69J maximum) receives a much amended though yet disconcerting (68.9J ÷ 8.7J =) 7.9 MTTLOI in lieu of the terrifying 23 MTTLOI. Supposedly, much lower settings are possible. For instance, in theory, Duration can be limited to .3 Seconds in which case the child will receive a total of 27.27 Joules or a (27.27 ÷ 8.7J =) 3.14 MTTLOI, still devastatingly high. Voltage can also be reduced. On the other hand, evidence suggests that the current B-24 cannot emit lower than 36J or a 9 MTTLOI in the ten year old age category (using minimal stimulus thresholds) or maximum settings limited to 1.0A. In any case, no standard prohibits maximum output in the younger age categories.

Though limited to 1.0A, the above chart is still based on the paradigm: initial Impedance = BP initial Impedance + 50Ω, which then rises 45Ω over the individual "treatment." For example, based on a ceiling of 1.0A, a 10 year old child has initial Impedance threshold of 100Ω on a SW device--(50Ω on a BP device--plus 50Ω for SW = 100Ω). The maximum Voltage possible, however, drops from 170V to 100V in order to remain at or under the new 1.0A ceiling (100V/100Ω = 1.0A) which is also initial Amperage. Impedance then rises 45Ω to the same final 145Ω to derive a new <u>68.9J</u> maximum (as opposed to the previous 200J maximum). At the same 145Ω, the ten year old child continues to have the same threshold output as a 19 year old (8.7J) on a BP device. Thus, at the new 68.9J maximum output emitted at the new 1.0A ceiling, the ten year old now experiences a new (68.9J ÷ 8.7 =) <u>7.9</u> MTTLOI maximum as opposed to the previous 200J at a 23 MTTLOI, yet unconscionably high.

Based on the new 1.0A ceiling, a 20 year old recipient has an initial Impedance threshold of 150Ω (100Ω on a BP device--plus another 50Ω for SW = 150Ω). The maximum Voltage possible, however, drops from 170V to 150V in order to remain at the new 1.0A ceiling (150V/150Ω = 1.0A). Impedance then rises the paradigmatic 45Ω to the same 195Ω to derive a new <u>115J</u> maximum (Current = V/Ω = 150V/195Ω = .769A. EO = Voltage x Current x Duration = 150V x .769A x 1.0Sec = <u>115.4J</u>) as opposed to the previous 148J maximum based on Amperage greater than 1.0A. At the same 145Ω, the twenty year old recipient continues to have the same 15.7J Threshold Output (based on 195Ω—see BP chart). Thus, at the new 115J maximum output emitted at the new 1.0A ceiling, the twenty year old now experiences a new (115.4J ÷ 15.7 =) <u>7.35</u> **MTTLOI** maximum as opposed to the previous 148J at a 9.44 MTTLOI, still destructively high. Moreover, evidence exists suggesting the current B-24, not limited to 1.0A cannot be set for lower than 43J or a 4.7 MTTLOI (using minimal stimulus thresholds) or a minimum output based on maximum outputs limited to 1.0A.

Based on the new 1.0A ceiling at otherwise maximum SW settings, and using the same SW paradigm, a **twenty-four year old man** has an initial Impedance threshold of (120Ω + 50Ω =) 170Ω. As a result, the maximum 170V need not be reduced in that the B-24's maximum 170V will not surpass 1.0A (170V/170Ω = 1.0A). Impedance now rises to the same final Impedance of 215Ω. At the maximum 1.0 seconds, the B-24 limited to 1.0A at otherwise maximum settings emits the same (Current = V/Ω = 170V/215Ω = .791A. EO = Voltage x Current x Duration = 170V x .791A x 1.0Sec =) 134J to the 24 year old man as the machine not limited to 1.0A. His threshold output is the same circa 19J (based on 215Ω—see BP chart [322]), and thus **at**

[322] From 200 to 250Ω, threshold output increases 9 Joules (25 – 16J = 9J) in a sequential progression. 215Ω is almost one-third way between 200 and 250Ω and thus we add the approximation of 3J to the initial 16J to derive the 19J threshold output for 215Ω. Other threshold outputs are close enough to Impedances within the BP chart depicting threshold outputs to simply use equivalent ratio.

maximum SW settings, the 24 year old experiences the same (134.41J ÷ 19J =) **7.08 MTTLOI** as before. In that Impedances of 170Ω and above automatically limit Amperage to 1.0A or below, all recipients 24 years of age and older are thus unaffected by the 1.0A ceiling. However, evidence exists suggesting that the current B-24 not limited to 1.0A cannot be set under circa 47J in the 24 year old age category, or about a 4.0 MTTLOI based minimal threshold outputs or maximum outputs limited to 1.0A. Another possibility is that the machine can only be adjusted down to 1.0A maximum at otherwise maximum settings.

Third generation BP devices may soon be or already have been replaced with "legal" fourth generation BP devices doubling yet again both in output and MTTLOI (see Section entitled: "Fourth Generation BP Devices"). In comparing SW to extant third generation (and even second generation) BP devices, we can see clearly that BP can no longer be deemed a "reduced EO" or "ECT" device nor does BP any longer deliver minimal stimulus or just above threshold dosages of electricity. By about age 45, the third generation BP device has more than visibly lost its advantage over SW in most age categories surpassing SW in every subsequent age category. Moreover, the advantage diminishes even further as the BP machines grow more and more powerful. Even now, at every age level, modern day BP devices are plainly no longer convulsive therapy devices (any more than SW devices), but, like SW, have devolved into electrical dosage or ENR devices emitting in the case of third generation BP devices, as noted above, consistent circa 5.0 MTTLOIs, far beyond that necessary to induce so-called "adequate convulsions" in every age category. Moreover, the 5.0 MTTLOI which the third generation BP device delivers refers to BL ECT. Using UL ECT, third generation BP devices deliver a circa 10.0 MTTLOI.

Appendix C

Summarizing the Cameron Paradigm

We now have the following paradigm for discovering age-related outputs for SW at both maximum and (albeit improbable) true minimum (for SW) outputs. The paradigm is as follows:

For SW true minimal stimulus for a specific age, 1) First, we identify the specific age-related threshold Impedance for Brief Pulse 2) Next we add 50Ω to discover the initial age-related Impedance for SW. 3) Next, we look up the EO required to overcome the initial age-related Impedance for SW.

We then 4) use the lowest possible Voltage (i.e. 70V) and lowest possible Duration (i.e. .1 Second), to deduce through trial and error the lowest possible Current required (Current = Voltage/Ω) for the lowest possible EO (EO = Volts x Current x Duration) needed to deliver an EO just greater than initial threshold output for the age administered. 5) To figure the MTTLOI, we divide Output delivered by Initial Threshold Output, that is, Output delivered by Output required to overcome Initial Impedance (Output Delivered ÷ Initial Threshold Output = MTTLOI). For example, (4.9J ÷ 4.0J =) 1.23 MTTLOI for the ten year old child at minimal stimulus. It should be noted, however, except in the older age categories where it cannot be avoided due to deteriorating Current, evidence suggests that the B-24 cannot be set below a probable 36J or a 9.0 MTTLOI in the 10 year old age category, a probable 43J or a 4.7 MTTLOI in the twenty year old age category, a probable 53J or a 3.22 MTTLOI in the thirty year old age category, a probable 63J or a 2.43 MTTLOI in the forty year old age category, a probable 84J or a 1.72 MTTLOI in the fifty old age category, and a probable 73J or a 1.15 MTTLOI in the sixty year old age category. We obtain the MTTLOI by dividing Output Delivered by minimal threshold outputs. These MTTLOIs are speculative, based upon minimal stimulus MTTLOIs of the B-25, seemingly based on the B-24. (For age groups 65 and older, the B-24 may not reach threshold due to deteriorating current.) Other possible outputs below which the B-24 may not be allowed are based on maximum outputs limited to 1.0A (using maximum threshold outputs) in which case, very little flexibility is possible. This too is speculative.

For SW maximal output for a specific age, 1) First, we identify the specific age-related threshold Impedance for Brief Pulse. 2) Next we add 50Ω to discover the Initial age-related Impedance for SW which is the same Impedance used for minimal stimulus). 3) Next, we add an additional 45Ω to discover the Final Age-related Impedance for SW (used at the end of the chart). 3) Subsequently, we look up the EO required to overcome the Final age-related Impedance for SW.

We then 1) use the highest possible Voltage (i.e. 170V) and highest possible Duration (i.e. 1.0 Second), to deduce the highest possible Current (Current = Voltage/Ω) for the highest possible EO (EO = Volts x Current x Duration). 5) To figure the MTTLOI, we divide Output delivered by Final Threshold Output (Output Delivered ÷ Final Threshold Output = MTTLOI). For example, (200J ÷ 8.7J =) 23 MTTLOI for the ten year old child at maximal stimulus.

Appendix D

J/Ω Limited to 1.0A

The table below represents outputs limited to 1.0A. In short, we can now compare the maximum EO and J/Ω ratios for SW limited to the "legal" 1.0A against the default outputs of the same five generations of BP devices--all legal under Weiner's 1997 de facto standard. Only the first two age categories in the SW columns are affected by the 1.0A limit, that is, only the outputs and J/Ω ratios in the ten and twenty year old categories vary from the table allowing more than 1.0A. In short, limited to 1.0A, the highest SW output (134J) and highest J/Ω maximum (.62J/Ω) is now in the 24 year old category in lieu of the ten and twenty year old categories and maximum output is no longer 200J, but 134J.

J/Ω Ratios for all Age Groups Based on Typical SW Maximums (Limited to 1.0A) Vs. Five Generations of Brief Pulse

AGE	SW Ω	BP Ω	SW EO	BP 1st EO	BP 2nd EO	BP 3rd EO	BP 4th EO	BP 5th EO	SW J/Ω	BP 1st J/Ω	BP 2nd J/Ω	BP 3rd J/Ω	BP 4th J/Ω	BP 5th J/Ω
10	145	50	68.9	1.33	2.88	5.76	11.5	15	.48	.027	.058	.115	.23	.30
20	195	100	115	5.04	9.22	18.4	36.9	48	.58	.050	.092	.184	.369	.48
24	215	120	134	7.8	14.3	26.5	57.3	75	.62	.065	.119	.221	.478	.625
30	245	150	118	11.3	20.7	41.5	82.9	108	.48	.075	.138	.276	.553	.72
40	295	200	98.0	20.1	36.9	74.0	147	192	.33	.101	.185	.370	.735	.96
50	345	250	83.8	31.5	57.6	115	230	300	.24	.126	.230	.460	.92	1.20
60	395	300	73.2	45.4	82.9	166	332	432	.185	.151	.276	.550	1.11	1.44
65	420	325	68.6	53.3	97.3	195	389	507	.163	.164	.299	.600	1.20	1.56
70	445	350	64.9	61.8	113	226	452	588	.145	.177	.323	.645	1.29	1.68
80	495	400	58.4	80.6	148	295	590	768	.118	.202	.370	.737	1.48	1.92
90	545	450	53.0	115	186	373	746	972	.097	.255	.413	.828	1.66	2.16
100	595	500	48.6	134	230	460	922	1200	.081	.268	.460	.920	1.84	2.40

The first generation BP device above is based on the MECTA "C" or "D." Remaining BP devices are represented by the second generation JR/SR 1 IEC device (less powerful than the made-for-America version), the third generation JR/SR 1, the probable fourth generation JR/SR 1, and the potential fifth generation JR/SR 1. To derive J/Ω output per age (shaded areas), EO for a particular machine at a particular age level is divided by Impedance at that age level. Except for the 10 and 20 year old age categories (which are held to a 1.0A "legal" maximum above), SW is set on maximum. Maximum or peak J/Ωs for SW and default J/Ωs for BP are identified in the six clear squares amidst the gray ones. Let us now turn the information above into graphs.

GRAPHS COMPARING DEFAULT OUTPUTS of the 3rd GENERATION BP Device Vs SW at MAXIMUM OUTPUT LIMITED to 1.0A

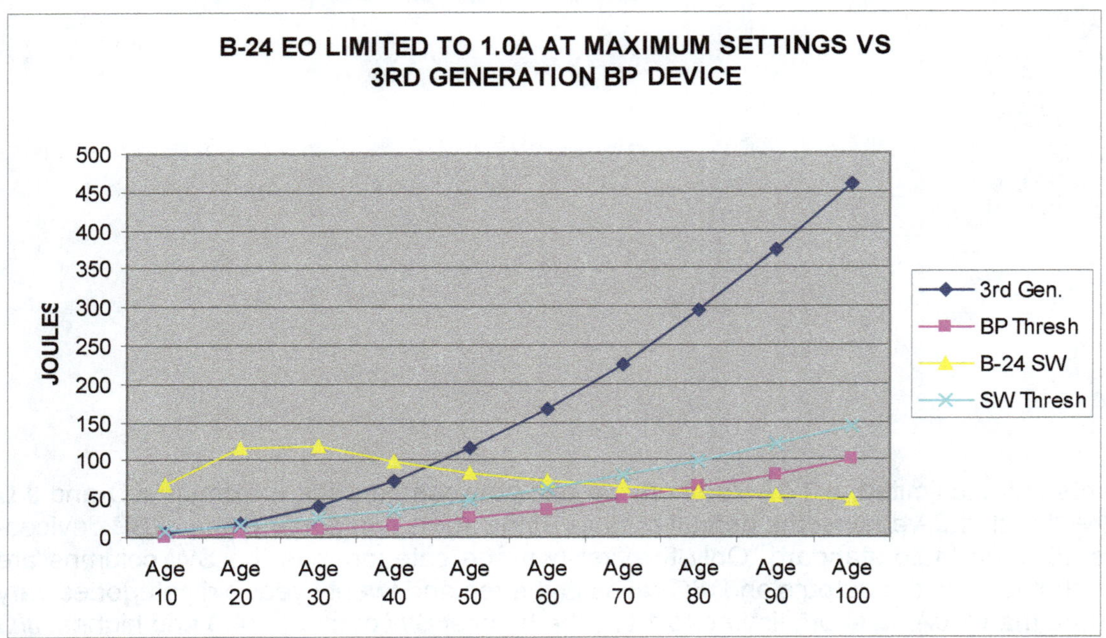

Note how the Third Generation BP Device exceeds SW in raw EO from about age 45 and older even at maximum SW output. Note SW EO in the 10 and 20 year old age categories. While reduced to circa 70 and 115J due to the 1.0A ceiling, SW output is yet greater and more dangerous than even the powerful third generation BP device in these age categories.

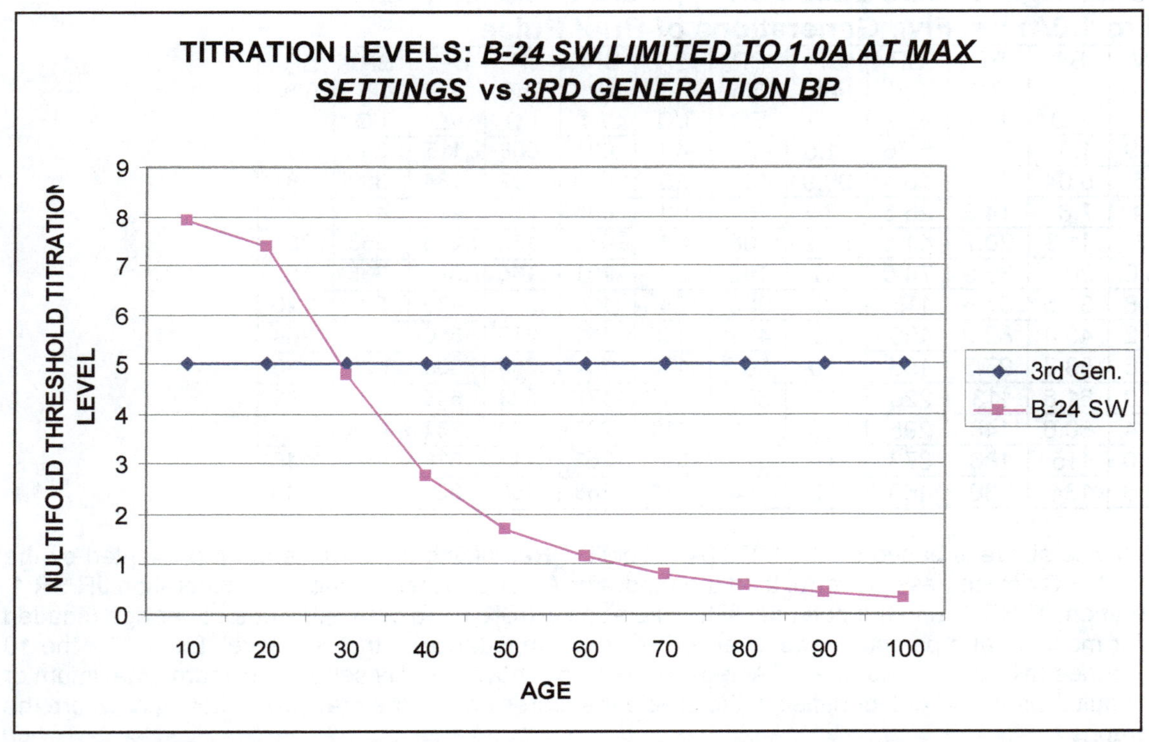

Note how SW surpasses the consistent 5.0 MTTLOI of the Third Generation BP Device from age 10 to about 30 in all age categories even when SW is limited to 1.0A. On the other hand, note how the 5.0 MTTLOI of the third generation BP device surpasses SW from about age 30 and older,

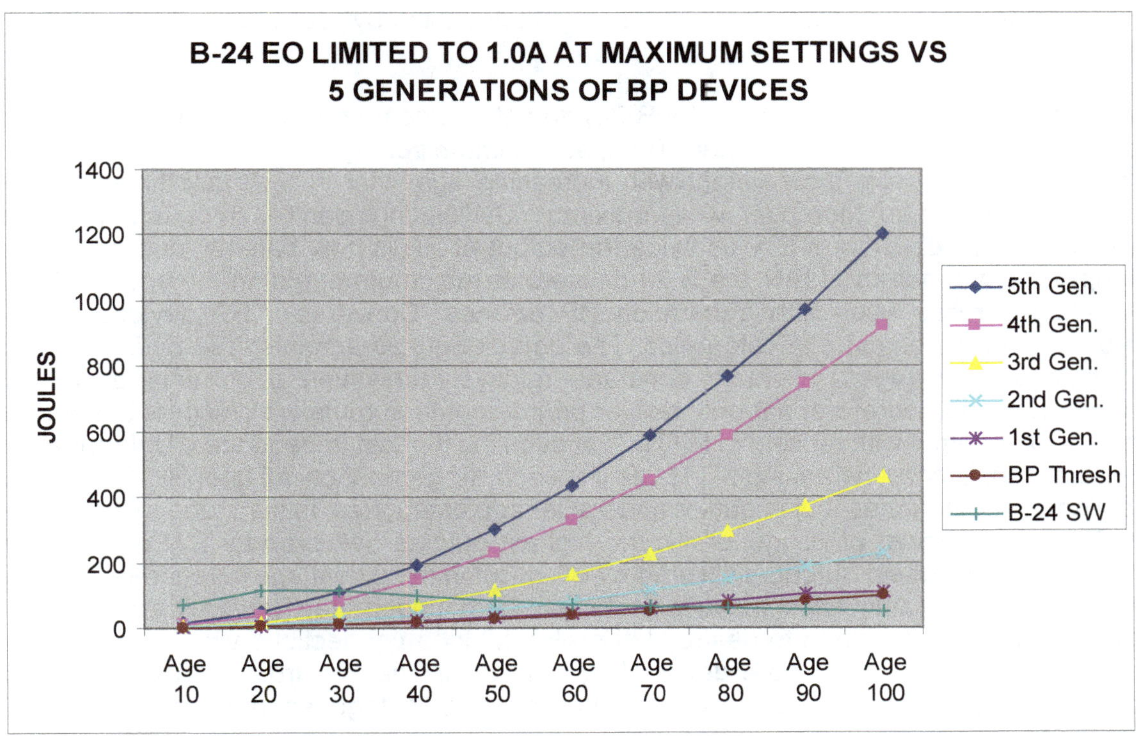

Note how only the First Generation BP device emits just abcve threshold outputs for all age categories. Note how the 5th Generation BP Device surpasses SW in raw power even at maximum output in every instance from about age 30 and older. Note too, how BP raw EO surpasses SW in earlier and earlier age category with each new BP generation even at maximum SW output. But also note how SW is yet more powerful than all five BP generations in the 10-24 year old age categories even when SW is limited to 1.0A. There is the possibility that maximum SW Output limited to 1.0A represent the lowest EOs allowed on the B-24.

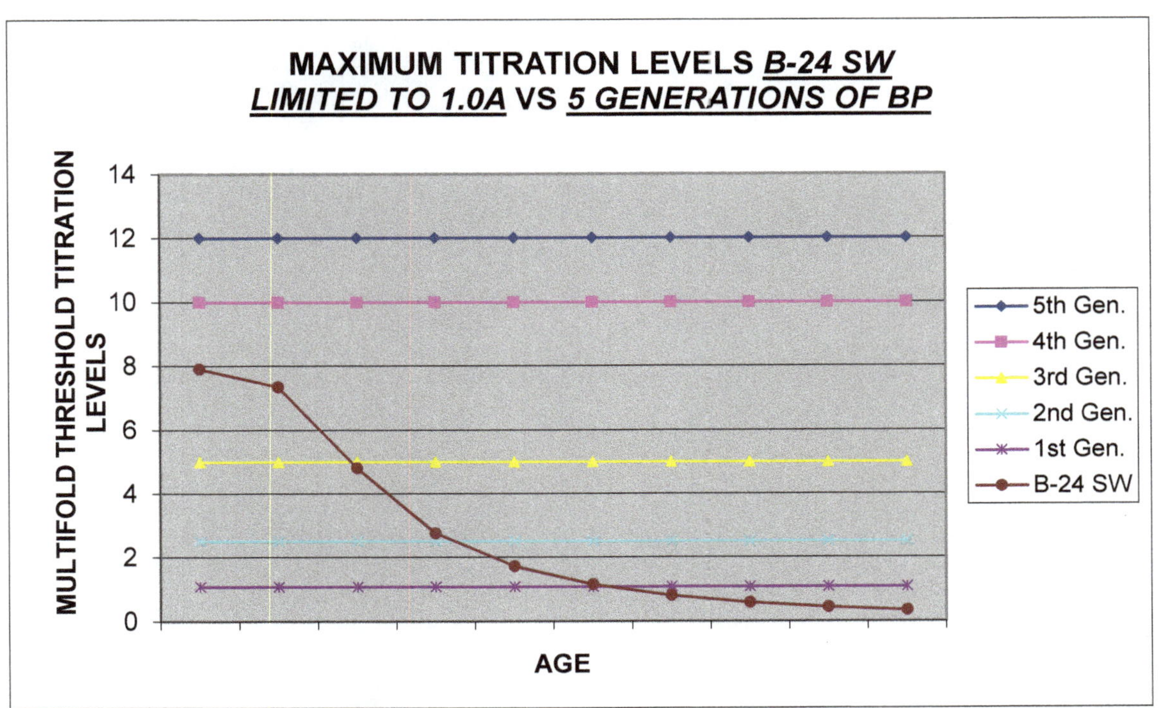

Note how each new BP generation increases the MTTLOI so that Fourth and Fifth Generation BP devices surpass SW in all age categories including the youngest even at maximum SW output. Note too how each new generation of BP surpasses the MTTLOI of SW in earlier and earlier age categories even at maximum SW output until it surpasses SW MTTLOI in all age categories.

Unlike BP, constant Voltage SW devices (such as the B-24) do not overcome resistances and particularly higher resistances in a consistent or predictable manner. Thus, at maximum settings, due to dwindling current, the output administered by SW is grossly inconsistent with increasing age, that is, SW fails to administer proportionate outputs with respect to age. Moreover, while maximum SW settings can reach up to 200J in the younger age categories, Weiner's depiction of SW as twice the output of BP is now patently untrue. On the other hand, due to the upside down nature of SW, the B-24 delivers its maximum output in the youngest age categories at outputs which surpass even fifth generation BP devices. Conversely, BP devices deliver surpassing maximum outputs in the oldest age categories. The default outputs administered by BP devices through automatically increasing Voltages, maintain constant, relatively unwavering currents even with increasing age and Impedance, and, therefore, not only deliver proportionate outputs with respect to age, but a predictable maximum machine output with respect to MTTLOI at even the highest Impedances. Unfortunately, because Brief Pulse delivers consistently increasing MTTLOIs per each BP generation, all later BP devices not only surpass SW in the older age categories, but in earlier and earlier age categories. In sum, due to the upside down nature of SW and the great power of BP generally, the highest outputs delivered by SW occur in the youngest age categories, while the highest outputs delivered by BP occur in the oldest age categories. Limiting SW Amperage to 1.0A does not significantly affect these facts. Finally, both modern day Brief Pulse and archaic SW devices are clearly ENR devices designed to destroy left prefrontal lobe connections via excessive non-minimal stimulus outputs of electricity, SW is more devastating than BP in the 10 through 45 year old age categories, BP more devastating than SW in the 35 to 45 to 100 year old age categories, depending on the BP generation.

Appendix E

"ECT" Compared to Tasers and Defibrillators

"ECT" is sometimes compared to tasers and defibrillators with the rationale that that the latter two have extremely high Voltages compared to "ECT." This is sometimes offered as a rationale for the comparative safety of "ECT" as both tasers and defibrillators pass electric current directly through the heart apparently with no permanent injury. For example some tasers use Voltages of between 7000 and 10000 Volts, whereas ECT uses up to 500V. This simple logic comes into question, however, in light of the relatively well known fact that "ECT" passing through the heart, results in injury or death. So why is the high Voltage taser or defibrillator safer than "ECT"?

Electricity is basically the passage of electrons though some medium. Impedance is the measure of resistance various objects offer, some more and some less than others. Voltage is the power or potential power, and Current, measured in Amperes or milli-Amperes is the rate of electron flow. The relationship among these three factors—Voltage, Impedance, and Current, constitutes Ohm's Law. That is, the greater the Voltage, the faster or higher the current, modified in turn by the resistance of the medium. But there is another factor with respect to machines like defibrillators, tasers, and ECT devices that is critical, and that is, Duration-- how long the current is allowed to flow and thus how much electricity or how many electrons are actually allowed to pass through the medium. This is known as Charge. We can measure the amount of electricity or electrons which have been allowed to flow through an object, from point A to point B, through coulombs, which is simply a fixed bundle of electrons. (1 coulomb is about 6.2 x 10 to the 18 electrons.) Thus, increasing or decreasing Duration is one form of controlling the amount of electricity allowed to flow from point A to point B and thus the Charge delivered regardless of Voltage or Current and this is the critical difference between tasers, defibrillators, and the so-called "ECT" device.

For example, while a taser may use up to 10,000 Volts and thus a very high Current, the Duration is actually measured in microseconds, which may be one, one millionth of a second. At maximum, then, the taser may deliver a pulse lasting between 32 to 60µs, and usually much briefer, that is, between 32 and 60 millionths of a second. Consequently, the Charge delivered, that is, the overall amount of electrons or electricity delivered, is miniscule compared to an ECT device which delivers electrons in terms of actual seconds or even parts of a second. For example, the Charge delivered by a taser is measured in microcoulombs and may be between 70 to 120µC compared to the Charge delivered by an "ECT" device measured in Coulombs or millicoulombs. A microcoulomb is one, one millionth of a Coulomb and one, one thousandth of a millicoulomb. The Charge delivered by an "ECT" device, in effect, is much greater than that of a taser, despite Voltage or Amperage.

Defibrillators, judging from a hodgepodge of information on the internet, appear to use Sine Wave and may be either AC or DC. The first closed chest defibrillators (mid-1950s) used about 1000V, but only delivered their current for a Duration of from 100 to 150 milliseconds (100/1000th to 150/1000th of a Second). This is .1 to .15 seconds, that is, ten, one-hundredths to fifteen one-hundredths of a second. Even modern day defibrillators using between 200 to 100 Volts only deliver current for a maximum Duration of about 12 milliseconds or twelve one thousandths of a second. Other sites claim the device can use up to 3000V, or about 16 to 17A of current for .001 Seconds. But even delivering between 16 and 17A for a Duration of up to one one-thousandth of a second (.001Seconds), equals to a total Charge of about sixteen millicoulombs or (16A x .001Sec.) = .016

Coulombs compared to Brief Pulse devices which deliver a maximum of between .336C to about 1.2C, (.336C ÷.016C =) twenty-one to (1.2C ÷ .016C =) seventy-five times greater Charge than a defibrillator, very possibly fatal if passed through the heart. In sum, the difference between both tasers and defibrillators is greatly reduced Charge or total electricity delivered due to extremely brief Durations compared to "ECT," so that regardless of high Voltage or Amperage,[323] the amount of electricity delivered by either the taser or the defibrillator is much less than that delivered by even the most minimal stimulus "ECT" device.

[323] The idea behind tasers and defibrillators is the administering of a jolt for which high Voltage, but extremely brief Durations are appropriate.

Works Cited

Abrams, R. (1996). ECT stimulus parameters as determinants of seizure quality. *Psychiatric Annals,* 26(11), 701-704.

Abrams, R. (1988). *Electroconvulsive therapy*. Oxford, New York: Oxford University Press.

Abrams, R. (1992). *Electroconvulsive therapy*. Oxford, New York: Oxford University Press.

Abrams, R., and Swartz, C. (1988). *ECT instruction manual.* Lake Bluff, Illinois: Somatics, Inc.

Abrams, R., and Swartz, C. (1985). *Thymatron instruction manual.* Lake Bluff, Illinois: Somatics, Inc.

Abrams, R., Taylor, M.A., Faber, R., Tso, T.O.T., Williams, R.A., and Almy, G. (1983). Bilateral vs. unilateral electroconvulsive therapy: Efficacy in meloncholia. *American Journal of Psychiatry*, 140, 463-465.

Alexander, L., (1953). *Treatment of mental disorder.* Philadelphia: W.B. Saunders.

Alexander, L., and Lowenbach, H. (1944). Experimental studies on electro-shock treatment. *Journal of Neuropathology and Experimental Neurology, 3,* 139-171.

American Psychiatric Association. (1979, July 9). Letter to Acting Commissioner Sherwin Gardner from Medical Director of American Psychiatric Association Melvin Sabshin, M.D. *Department of Health and Human Services*, Hearing Clerk's Office, 5600 Fishers Lane, Rockville, Maryland 20857, Rm 4-65, HFA-305; 78N; C00010/ANS, HFK-1, K-571, 7902883.

American Psychiatric Association. (1990). *The practice of electroconvulsive therapy: Recommendations for treatment, training, and privileging. Task Force on ECT.* Washington, D.C.: American Psychiatric Association.

American Psychiatric Association. (1992). *American Psychiatric Association fact sheet: Electroconvulsive therapy (ECT)* [three page flyer]. Washington, D.C.: American Psychiatric Association.

American Psychiatric Association - Draft (1999). *The practice of electroconvulsive therapy: Recommendations for treatment, training, and privileging. Second Edition (Completely Revised) A Task Force Report of the American Psychiatric Association.* Washington, D.C.: American Psychiatric Association.

American Psychiatric Association Task Force on ECT (1978). *Electroconvulsive therapy: Task force report 14.* Washington D.C.: American Psychiatric Association.

Andre, L., (2009) *Doctors of Deception—What They Don't Want You to Know about Shock Treatment.* New Brunswick: Rutgers University Press.

Andre, L., (1991). *Electroshock as head injury.* Unpublished manuscript, Committee For Truth In Psychiatry, 13 St. Marks (7-F), New York, New York 10003.

Andre versus Somatics et al. (1987). New York State Supreme Court, New York, New York, File Number 9220-87.

Andreasen, N.C., Ernhardt, J.C., Swayze, V.W., Alliger, R.J., Yuh, W.T.C., Cohen, G., and Ziebell, S. (1990). Magnetic resonance imaging of the brain in schizophrenia. *Archives of general Psychiatry*, 47, 35-44.

Appel, K.E., Meyers, J., and Sheflin, A. (1953). Prognosis in psychiatry. *Archives of Neurological Psychiatry*, 70, 459-468.

Association for the Advancement of Medical Instrumentation. (1998). *"8th Annual International Standards Conference on Medical Devices."* [six page information flyer]. Arlington, Virginia: Association for the Advancement of Medical Instrumentation.

Association for the Advancement of Medical Instrumentation. (1998, February 4). Letter from Nick Tongston to members of the IEC/SC 62D and IEC/SC 62D/WG 2 committee. Subject: Vote on review of IEC 60601-2-14, Ed.1, Medical electrical equipment - Part 2: Particular requirements for the safety of electroconvulsive therapy equipment. Ballot Deadline: 25 March 1998.

Bayles, S.; Busse, E.W., and Ebaugh, F.G. (1950). "Square waves (BST) versus sine waves in electroconvulsive therapy." *American Journal of Psychiatry,* 107, n.p.

Beale, M.D., Kellner, C.H., Pritchett, J.T., Bernstein, H.J., Burns, C.M., and Knapp, R. (1994). Stimulus dose-titration in ECT: A 2-year clinical experience. *Convulsive Therapy* , 10(2), 171-176.

Bergsholm, P., Larsen, J.L., Rosendahl, K., and Holsten, F. (1989). Electroconvulsive therapy and cerebral computed tomography: A prospective study. *Acta Psychiatria Scandanavia*, 80, 566-572.

Blachley, P. (1976a). New developments in electroconvulsive therapy. *Diseases of the Nervous System*, 37, 356-358.

Blachley, P. H., (1976b). (Ed.) *Convulsive Therapy Bulletin.,* 1(3), City not known: Publisher not known.

Blachley, P., Denney, D., and Fling, J.L. (1974). A new stimulus generator and recorder for electroconvulsive therapy. *Unpublished Manuscript*. (Cited in Grahan, A.R., Jerhrich, J.L., Couvillon, L.A., and Moench, L.G., 1977, p. 98).

Blachley, P., Denney, D., and Fling, J.L. (1976?). Engineering and electrical considerations necessary for safe apparatus for electroconvulsive therapy. *Unpublished Manuscript.* (Cited in Grahn et al, 1977, p. 33).

Blachley, P., and Gowing, D. (1966). Multiple monitored electroconvulsive treatments. *Comprehensive Psychiatry*, 7, 100-109.

Bolwig, T.G., Westergaard, E. (1977a). Acute hypertension causing blood-brain barrier breakdown during epileptic seizures. *Acta Neurologica Scandinavia,* 56, 335-342.

Bolwig, T.G., Hertz, M.M., Paulson, O.B., Spotoft, H. and Rafaelsen, O.J. (1977b). The permeability of the blood-brain barrier during electrically induced seizures in man. *European Journal of Clinical Investigations,* 7, 87-93.

Bradley, W.G., Waluch, V., Brandt-Zawadzki, M., Yardley, R.A., and Wyckoff, R.R. (1984). Patchy perventricular white matter lesions in the elderly: A common observation during NMR imaging. *Noninvas Imaging*, 1, 35-41.

Braffman, B.H., Grossman, R.I., McCallister, T., Price, T.P.R., Gyulai, L., Atlas, S.W., Hackney, D.B., Goldberg, H.I., Bilaniuk, L.T., and Zimmerman, R.A. (1988). MR imaging prior to and following electroconvulsive therapy in patients with major affective disorders. *American Journal of Neuroradiology (Abstracts)* , 9, 1933.

Breggin, P.R. (1979). *Electroshock: Its brain disabling effects.* New York: Springer Publishing Company.

Breggin, P.R. (1991). *Toxic Psychiatry.* New York. St. Martin's Press.

Breggin, P.R. (1998). Electroshock: Scientific, ethical, and political issues. *International Journal of Risk & Safety in Medicine,* 11, 5-40.

Breggin, P.R. (2007). Brain disabling treatments in psychiatry: Drugs, Electroshock, and the psychopharmaceutical complex. New York: Springer Publishing Company.

Breggin, P.R. (2007). ECT damages the brain: Disturbing news for patients and shock doctors alike. *Ethical Human Psychology and Psychiatry,* 9(2), 83-86.

Calloway, S.P., Dolan, R.J., Jacoby, R.J., and Levy, R. (1981). ECT and cerebral atrophy: a computed tomographic study. *Acta Psychiatric Scandanavia,* 64, 442-445.

Cameron, D.G. (1979). *How to survive being committed to a mental hospital.* New York: Vantage Press.

Cameron, D.G. (1994). ECT: Sham statistics, the myth of convulsive therapy, and the case for consumer misinformation. *Journal of Mind and Behavior,* 15, 177-198.

Cameron, D.G. (1997). *Horror Stories from the mental health system: ECT: 200 cases of permanent memory loss, volumes 1 and 2.* unpublished manuscripts.

Cameron, D.G. (1998). *EST: Morbidity and Mortality with Suprathreshold Dosing.* unpublished article.

Canadian Psychiatric Association, (1981), Quote - march 20, *Psychiatric News,*16(6), 7, 15.

Carney, M.W.P., and Sheffield, B.F. (1974). The effects of pulse ECT in neurotic and endogenous depression. *British Journal of Psychiatry,* 125, 91-94.

Cerletti, U. and Bini, L. (1938). Un nuevo motodo di shockterapie "l'elettro-shock." *Boll. Acad. Med. Roma,* 64, 136-138.

Chabasinski, Ted. (2022, October 24). Mad in america. *Science, Psychiatry, and Social Justice.*

Chamberlin, J. (1977). *On our own: Patient controlled alternatives to the mental health system.* New York: Hawthorne.

Coffey, C.E., Hinkle, P.E. Weiner, R.D., Nemeroff, C.B., Krishnan, K.R.R., Varia, I. and Sullivan, D.C. (1987a). Electroconvulsive therapy of depression in patients with white matter hyperintensity. *Biological Psychiatry,* 22, 629-636.

Coffey, C.E., Weiner, R.D., Hinkle, P.E., Cress, M., Daughtry, G., and Wilson, W.H. (1987b). Augmentation of ECT seizures with caffeine. *Biological Psychiatry,* 22, 637-649.

Coffey, C.E., Figiel, G.S., Djang, W.T., Sullivan, D.C., Herfkens, R.J., and Weiner, R.D. (1988a). Effects of ECT on brain structure: A pilot prospective magnetic resonance imaging study. *American Journal of Psychiatry,* 145, 701-706.

Coffey, C.E., Figiel, G.S., Djang, W.T., Cress, M., Saunders, W.B., and Weiner, R.D. (1988b). Leukoencephalopathy in elderly depressed patients for ECT. *Biological Psychiatry,* 24, 143-161.

Coffey, C.E. and Weiner, R.D. (1989). Subcortical white matter hyperintensity on magnetic resonance imaging: Clinical and neuroanatomic correlates in the depressed elderly. *Journal of Neuropsychiatry and Clinical Neurosciences,* 1, 135-145.

Coffey, C.E., Figiel, G.S., Djang, W.T., Weiner, R.D. (1990a). Subcortical hyperintensity on magnetic resonance imaging: a comparison of normal and depressed elderly subjects. *American Journal of Psychiatry,* 147, 187-189.

Coffey, C.E., Figiel, G.S., Weiner, R.D., and Saunders, W.B. (1990b). Caffeine augmentation of ECT. *American Journal of Psychiatry, 147,* 579-85.

Coffey, C.E., and Weiner, R.D. (1990c). Electroconvulsive therapy: An update. *Hospital and Community Psychiatry, 41(5),* 515-520.

Coffey, C.E. (1991a). Structural brain abnormalities in the depressed elderly. In: P. Hauser (Ed.), *Brain imaging in affective disorders* (pp. 89-111). Washington, D.C.: American Psychiatric Press.

Coffey, C.E., Weiner, R.D., Djang, W.T., Figiel, G.S., Soady, S.A.R., Patterson, L.J., Holt, P.D., Spritzer, C.E., Wilkinson, W.E. (1991b). *Brain anatomic effects of electroconvulsive therapy: A prospective magnetic resonance imaging study.* Archives of General Psychiatry, 48, 1013-1021.

Coffey, C.E., Wilkinson, W.E., Weiner, R.D., Parashos, I.A., Djang, W.T., Webb, M.C., Figiel, G.S., and Spritzer, C.E. (1993). Quantitative cerebral anatomy in depression: A controlled magnetic resonance imaging study. *Archives of General Psychiatry,* 50, 7-16.

Coffey, C.E., Lucke, J., Weiner, R.D., Krystal, A.D., and Aque, M. (1995). Seizure threshold in electroconvulsive therapy (ECT) II: The anticonvulsant effect of ECT. Biological Psychiatry, 37, 777-778.

Cole, M.W., Yarconi. T., Repovs, G., Anticevic, & A., Braver, T. (2012). Global Connectivity of prefrontal cortex predicts cognitive control and intelligence. *Journal of Neuroscience, Jun 27, 32*(26): 8988-8999.

Coleman, L. (1984). *The reign of error.* Boston: Beacon Press.

Cook, L.C. (1940). Has fear any therapeutic significance in convulsion? *Journal of Mental Science, 40,* 414.

Council of the European Communities (June 14, 1993). Council, directive 93/42/EEC of 14 June 1993 concerning medical devices . *Official Journal of the European Communities. 12(7),* L169/2-L169/43.

Cronholm, B., and Ottosson, J.O. (1963). Ultrabrief stimulus techniques in ECT. II. Comparative studies of therapeutic effects and memory disturbances in treatment of endogenous depression with the Elther ES apparatus and Siemens Konvulsator III. *Journal of Nervous and Mental Diseases, 137,* 268-276.

Daniel, W.F., Weiner, R.D., and Crovitz, H.F. (1983). Autobiographical amnesia with ECT: An analysis of the roles of stimulus wave form, electrode placement, stimulus energy, and seizure length. *Biological Psychiatry*, 18(1), 121-126.

Davies, R.K., Detre, T.P., Egger, M.D., Tucker, G.J., and Wyman, R.J. (1971). Electroconvulsive therapy Instruments - should they be reevaluated?. *Archives of General Psychiatry*, 25, 97-99.

d'Elia, G. (1970). Unilateral electroconvulsive therapy. *Acta Psychiatria Scandanavia (Supplement),* 215.

d'Elia, G., Ottosen, J.-O., and Stronmerg L.S. (1983). Present practice of electroconvulsive therapy in scandinavia. *Archives of General Psychiatry*, 40, 577-581.

d'Elia, G., and Raotma, H. (1975). Is unilateral ECT less effective than bilateral ECT? *British Journal of Psychiatry*, 126, 83-89.

Delmas-Marsalet, P.L. (1942). L'electro-choc par courant continu. *Comptes rendus des Seances. Societe de Biologie et de ses Filiales et Associees (Paris),* 136, 551-553.

Department of Health and Human Services, (1982a). *Petition to reclassify.* Silver Spring, Maryland: Food and Drug Administration.

Department of Health and Human Services, (1982b). *Summary minutes, seventh meeting, neurological section, respiratory and nervous system device panel.* Silver Spring, Maryland: Food and Drug Administration.

Department of Health and Human Services, (1982c). *Open public hearing regarding reclassification of ECT.* Silver Spring, Maryland: Food and Drug Administration.

Devanand, D.P., Dwork, A.J., Hutchinson, M.S.E., Bolwig, T.G., and Sackheim, H.A. (1994). Does ECT alter brain structure? *American Journal of Psychiatry*, 151, 957-970.

Dolan, R.J., Calloway, S.P., Thacker, P.F., and Mann, A.H. (1986). The cerebral cortical appearance in depressed subjects. *Psychological Medicine,* 16, 775-779.

Dunn, A., Giuditta, A., Wilson, J.E., and Glassman, E. (1974). The effect of electroshock on brain RNA and protein synthesis and its possible relationship to behavioral effects. In M. Fink, S. Kety, and J. McGaugh (Eds.), *Psychobiology of convulsive therapy* (pp. 185-197). New York: Wiley.

Dupont, R.M., Jernigan, T.L., Butters, N., Delis, D., Hesselink, J.R., Heindel, W., and Gillin, J.C. (1990). Subcortical abnormalities detected in bipolar affective disorders using magnetic resonance imaging: clinical and neuropsychological significance. *Archives of General Psychiatry,* 47, 55-59.

Dwork, A.J., Arango, V., Underwood, M., Ilievski, B., Rosoklija, G., Sackeim, H. A., and Lisanby, S. H. (2004). Absence of histological lesions in primate models of ECT and magnetic seizure therapy. *The American Journal of Psychiatry,* 161(3): 576-78.

Dwork, A.J., Arango, V., Underwood, M., Ilievski, B., Rosoklija, G., Sackeim, H. A., and Lisanby, S. H. (2005). Dr. Dwork and colleagues reply. *The American Journal of Psychiatry,* 162: 196.

Echlin, F.A. (1942). Vasospasm and forced cerebral ischemia. *Archives of Neurological Psychiatry, 47,* 77-96.

Elcot Incorporated. (1993). Microprocessor-Controlled, MULTI-FUNCTION ECT Units[flyer]. New York, New York: Elcot Incorporated.

Essman, W.B. (1968). Electroshock-induced retrograde amnesia in seizure-protracted mice. *Psychobiological Reports, 22,* 929-935.

Farmer, F. (1973). *Will there really be a morning?* New York: Putnam.

Field, E. (1964). *The white shirts.* Los Angeles: Tasmania Press.

Fink, M., and Kahn, R.L. (1957). Relation of EEG delta activity to behavioral response in electroshock. *Archives of Neurological Psychiatry,* 78, 516-525.

Fink, M. (1957). *A unified theory of the action of physiodynamic therapies.* Journal of Hillside Hospital, 6, 197-206.

Fink, M. (1978). Efficacy and safety of induced seizures (EST) in man. *Comprehensive Psychiatry*, 19(1), 1-18.

Fink, M. (1979). Convulsive therapy: Theory and practice. New York: Raven Press.

Fink, M. (1997). ECT update. *(Internet).* http://www.mhsource.com/edu/psytimes/p970439.html.

Fink, M., Kahn, R.L., and Green, M. (1958). Experimental process of the electroshock process. *Diseases of the Nervous System*, 19, pp. 113-118.

Fodero, L. (1993, July 19). With reforms in treatment, shock therapy loses shock. *New York Times,* p. A1, A16.

Food and Drug Administration. (1978, November 28). *Federal Register,* pp. 55729-30.

Food and Drug Administration. (1979, May 29). Neurological section: Respiratory and nervous systems devices panel (public meeting). Department of Health, Education, and Welfare.

Food and Drug Administration. (1979, September 4). Neurological devices: Classification of electroconvulsive therapy devices. *Federal Register*, Volume 44, Number 172, 21 CFR Part 882, Docket Number 78N-1103.

Food and Drug Administration. (1984). Electroconvulsive Therapy Devices - 510K. *Somatics Incorporated Premarket Notification Submission: Reference K843923. Product: Electroconvulsive Therapy Device, Thymatron.* Center for Devices and Radiological Health. Food and Drug Administration, Rockville MD 20857.

Food and Drug Administration. (1985). Electroconvulsive Therapy Devices - 510K. *MECTA Corporation Premarket Notification Submission: Reference K852069. Product: Electroconvulsive Therapy Device, MECTA D; JR/SR1; JR/SR2.* Center for Devices and Radiological Health. Food and Drug Administration, Rockville MD 20857.

Food and Drug Administration. (1986A). Electroconvulsive Therapy Devices - 510K. *Medcraft Corporation Premarket Notification Submission: Reference K860467. Product: Electroconvulsive Therapy Device, B-24; B-25.* Center for Devices and Radiological Health. Food and Drug Administration, Rockville MD 20857.

Food and Drug Administration. (1986B). Electroconvulsive Therapy Devices - 510K. *Elcot Incorporated Premarket Notification Submission: Reference K863815. Product: Electroconvulsive Therapy Device, Model MF-1000.* Center for Devices and Radiological Health. Food and Drug Administration, Rockville MD 20857.

Food and Drug Administration. (1990, September 5). Neurological devices: Proposed rule to reclassify the electroconvulsive therapy device intended for use in treating severe depression. *Federal Register*, Volume 55, Number 172, 21 CFR Part 882, Docket Number 82P-0316, pp. 36578-36590.

Food and Drug Administration. (1995, August 14). Order for Certain Class II Devices; Submission and Effectiveness Information; Notices. *Federal Register*, Volume 60, No. 156, Part III, Docket Number 94N-0417, pp. 41986-41989.

Food and Drug Administration. (1995, October 26). (Substantially Equivalent Letters For Some 510(k)'s). *Somatics, Incorporated Premarket Notification Submission: Reference K945120. Product: Electroconvulsive System, Model: Thymatron 2000. Product Code: GXC.* Center for Devices and Radiological Health. Food and Drug Administration, Rockville MD 20857.

Food and Drug Administration. (1996, September 18). (Substantially Equivalent Letters For Some 510(k)'s). *MECTA Corporation Premarket Notification Submission: Reference K960754. Product: Spectrum 5000Q, 5000M, 4000Q, 4000M. Product Code: 84GXC* . Center for Devices and Radiological Health. Food and Drug Administration, Rockville MD 20857.

Food and Drug Administration. (1997, March 6). (Substantially Equivalent Letters For Some 510(k)'s). *MECTA Corporation Premarket Notification Submission: Reference K965070. Trade Name: SpECTrum 5000 and 4000 ECT Devices. Product Code: 84GXC* . Center for Devices and Radiological Health. Food and Drug Administration, Rockville MD 20857.

Frank, L.R. (1978). (Ed.) *The history of shock treatment.* San Francisco: Frank.

Freeman, C.P.L. and Kendell, R.E. (1980). (Interviews with patients in Scotland from one to two years after routine ECT in 1976): Part 1, ECT: Patients' experiences and attitudes. *British Journal of Psychiatry,* 137, 8-16.

Friedberg, J. (1976). *Shock treatment is not good for your brain.* San Francisco: Glide Publications.

Friedberg, J. (1977). Shock treatment, brain damage, and memory loss: A neurological perspective. *American Journal of Psychiatry,* 134(9), 1010-1014.

Friedberg, J. (2005). Dr. Friedberg retorts. *The American Journal of Psychiatry,* 162: 196.

Friedman, E. (1942). Unidirectional electrostimulated convulsive therapy. *American Journal of Psychiatry,* 99, 218-223.

Friedman, E., Wilcox, P.H., and Reiter, R.M. (1942). Electrostimulated convulsive doses in intact humans by means of unidirectional currents. *Journal of Nervous and Mental Disease,* 96, 56-63.Gangadhar, B.N., Janakiramaiah, N., Dutt, D.N., and Motreja, S. (1997). Strength symmetry index: A measure of seizure adequacy in ECT. *Convulsive Therapy,* 13(1), 18-24.

Glen, M., and Weiner, R. (1983). *Electroconvulsive therapy: A programmed text.* Washington, D.C.: American Psychiatric Press.

Glueck, B.C., Reiss, H., and Bernard, L.E. (1957). Regressive electric shock therapy. *Psychiatric Quarterly*, 31, 117-135.

Gordon, D. (1982). Electroconvulsive therapy with minimal hazard. *British Journal of Psychiatry, 141,* 12-18.

Gotkin, J. and Gotkin, P. (1974). *Too much anger, too many tears: A personal triumph over psychiatry.* New York: Quadrangle.

Gould, E., Reeves, A.J., Fallah, M., Tanapat, P., Gross, C.G., & Fuchs, E. (1999). Hippocampus neurogenesis in adult Old World primates. *Proceedings National Academy of Science, USA (96)*9, 5263-5267.

Grahn, A.R. (1976, October 15). *Summary of presentation to FDA Neurology Panel: Study of Electroconvulsive Therapy device: Safety and Efficacy,* FDA Docket Number 78N-1103, Contract 223-74-5253, Task Order Number 22, Utah Biomedical Test Laboratory. Utah: University of Utah Research Institute, 520 Wakara Way, Salt Lake City, Utah, 84108.

Grahn, A.R., Jerhrich, J.L., Couvillon, L.A., and Moench, L.G. (1977). *Final Report (Revision A): A Study of Safety and Performance for ECT Devices*, TR 226-001, December 15, Utah Biomedical Test Lab. Utah: University of Utah Research Institute, 520 Wakara Way, Salt Lake City, Utah, 84108.

Greenblatt, M. (1977). Efficacy of electroconvulsive therapy in affective and schizophrenic illness. *American Journal of Psychiatry,* 134, 1001-1005.

Greenblatt, M., Freeman, H., and Meshorer, E. (1966). Comparative efficacy of anti-depressant drugs and placebo in relation to electric shock treatment. In: M. Rinkel (Ed.), *Biological treatment of mental Illness*, (574-594) New York: L.C. Page.

Greenblatt, M., Grosser, G.H., and Wechsler, H. (1964). Differential response of hospitalized depressed patients to somatic therapy. *American Journal of Psychiatry*, 120, 935-943.

Hauser, P., Altshuler, L.L., Berrittini, W., Dauphinais, Gelernter, J., and Pos, R.M. (1989). Temporal lobe measurement in primary affective disorder by magnetic resonance imaging. *Journal of Neuropsychiatry and Clinical Neuroscience,* 1, 128-134.

Hickie, I., Scott, E., Mitchell, P., Wilhelm, K., Austin, M-P. and Bennett, B. (1995). Subcortical hyperintensities on magnetic resonance imaging: Clinical correlates and prognostic significance in patients with severe depression. *Biological Psychiatry,* 27, 151-160.

Hordern, A., Burt, C.G., and Holt, N.F. (1965). *Depressive states.* Springfield, IL: Charles C. Thomas.

Hotchner, A.E. (1966). *Papa Hemmingway.* New York: Random House, pp. 291-335.

Imlah, N.W., Ryan, E., and Harrington, J.A. (1965). The influence of antidepressant drugs on the response to electroconvulsive therapy and on subsequent relapse rates. *Neuropsychopharmacology,* 4, 438-42.

Impastato, D. (1957). Prevention of fatalities in electroshock therapy. *Diseases of the Nervous System*, 18, 34-75.

Impastato, D., Berg, S., and Gabriel, A.R. (1957). The Molac-II - an alternating current electroshock therapy machine incorporating a new principle. *Journal of Nervous and Mental Disease*, 125, 380-384.

International Electrotechnical Commission. (1977, 1988). *International Standard: Medical electrical equipment: Part 1: General requirements for safety: IEC 601-1*. Bureau de la Commission Electrotechnique Internationale, 3, rue de Varambe, Geneve, Suisse.

International Electrotechnical Commission. (1989). *Medical electrical equipment. Part 2: Particular requirements for the safety of electroconvulsive therapy equipment. CEI/IEC International Standard, 601-2-14.* Bureau de la Commission Electrotechnique Internationale, 3, rue de Varambe, Geneve, Suisse.

International Electrotechnical Commission. (1991). *International Standard: Medical electrical equipment: Amendment 1 (to 1988), Part 1: General requirements for safety: IEC 601-1*. Bureau de la Commission Electrotechnique Internationale, 3, rue de Varambe, Geneve, Suisse.

International Electrotechnical Commission. (1997, Dec 26). Document Dispatch Advice Note. Subcommittee 62D. Vote on Review of IEC 60601-2-14. Review of International Standard. Comments on 62D/201/CD from the United States National Committee. Revision of IEC 60601-2-14, Ed.2, Part 2-14: Particular requirements for the safety of electroconvulsive therapy equipment. *International Electrotechnical Commission*, 1211 Geneva 20, Switzerland.

Isenberg, K.E., Dinwiddle, S.H., Heath, A.C. (1996). Effect of stimulus parameters on seizure threshold and duration. *Convulsive Therapy,* 12, 68. Abstract.

Janis, I. (1950). Psychologic effects of electric convulsive treatments (I, II, III, post treatment amnesia). *The Journal of Nervous and Mental Disease*, 3, 360-397; 469-489.

Johnstone, L. (1992). Is the use of ECT a non-issue for psychologists? *Clinical Psychology Forum*, 30-31.

Kay, D.W., Fahy, T., and Garside, R.F., (1970). A seven-month double-blind trial of amitriptyline and diazepam in ECT-treated depressed patients. *British Journal of Psychiatry,* 150, 112-114.

Kellner, C.H. (1994, February 2). *Electroshock with Susan Spencer* [television interview]. In C. Lasiewicz [Producer], 48 Hours. New York: CBS.

Kellner, C.H., Rubinow, D.R., Gold, P.W., and Post, R.M. (1983). Relationship to cortisol hypersecretion to brain CT scan alterations in depressed patients. *Psychiatry Residence*, 8, 191-197.

Kesey, K. (1962). *One flew over the cuckoo's nest.* New York: Viking.

Kolbeinson H., Arnaldson, O.S., Peturrson, H. and Skulason, S. (1986). Computer Tomographic Scans in ECT-patients. *Acta Psychiatrica Scandinavica,* 73, 28-32.

Krystal, A.D., Weiner, R.D., and Coffey, C.E. (1995). The ictal EEG as a marker of adequate stimulus intensity with unilateral ECT. *Journal of Neuropsychiatry,* 7, 295-303.

Krystal, A.D., Weiner, R.D., and Gasseert, D. (1996). The relative ability of three ictal EEG frequency bands to differentiate ECT seizures on the basis of electrode placement, stimulus intensity, and therapeutic response. *Convulsive Therapy,* 12, 13-14.

Krystal, A.D., Weiner, R.D., and McCall, W.V. (1993). The effects of ECT stimulus dose and electrode placement on the ictal electroencephalogram: An intra-individual cross-over study. *Biological Psychiatry,* 34, 759-767.

Laing, R. D. (1967). *The politics of experience and the bird of paradise.* United Kingdom. Penguin Press.

Lambourn, J., and Gill, D.A. (1978). A controlled comparison of simulated and real ECT in depressive illness. *British Journal of Psychiatry*, 133, 514-519.

Lapon, L. (1986). *Mass murderers in while coats.* Springfield, Massachusetts: Psychiatric Genocide Research Institute.

Leiknes, Keri Ann at al. (2012) *Contemporary use and practice of electroconvulsive therapy worldwide.* Brain and Behavior, 2(3), 283-344.

Lewis, S. (1922) *Babbitt.* United States: Harcourt, Brace and Company.

Liberson, W.T. (1945a). Study of word association processes, part II: Reactions to "average emotional" and "average neutral" words in normal and abnormal populations. Effects of electric convulsive therapy. *Digest of Neurology and Psychiatry, 13,* pages unknown.

Liberson, W.T. (1945b). Time factors in electric convulsive therapy. *Yale Journal of Biological Medicine*, 17, 571-578.

Liberson, W.T. (1946). Physiological basis of electric convulsive therapy. *Connecticut State Medical Journal,* 10, 754-756.

Liberson, W.T. (1948). Brief stimulus therapy. *American Journal of Psychiatry* , 105, 28-39.

Liberson, W.T. (1949). Review of psychiatric progress. 1948. Electroencephalography. *American Journal of Psychiatry, 105,* 503-505.

MacQueen, G. et al. (2007). The long term impact of treatment with electroconvulsive therapy on discrete memory systems in patients with bipolar disorder. *Journal of Psychiatry and Neuroscience,* 32(4), 241-249.

Malitz, S., Sackeim, H.A., Decina, P. (1979). ECT in the clinical treatment of major affective disorders: Clinical and basic research issues. *Psychiatric Journal of the University of Ottawa, 7,* 126-134.

Malitz, S., Sackeim, H.A., Decina, P., Kanzler, M., and Kerr, B. (1986). The efficacy of electroconvulsive therapy: dose response interactions with modality. *Annals of the New York Academy of Sciences*, 462, 56-64.

Mander, A.J., Whitfield, D.M.K., Smith, M.A., Douglas, R.H.B., and Kendell, R.E. (1987). Cerebral and brain stem changes after ECT revealed by nuclear magnetic resonance imaging. *British Journal of Psychiatry*, 151, 69-71.

Mangaoang, M.A. and Lacey, J.V. (2007). Cognitive rehabilitation assessment and treatment of persistent memory impairments following ECT. *Advances in Psychiatry,* 13, 90-100.

Marks, J. (1979). *The Search For The Manchurian Candidate. The CIA and Mind Control.* New York: New York Times Books.

Masson, J.M. (1984). *The Assault On Truth* . New York: Farrar, Straus, and Giroux; Toronto: Collins Publishers.

McCall, W.V., Reid, S., Rosenquist, P., Foreman, A., and Kiesow-Webb, N. (1993). A reappraisal of the role of caffeine in ECT. *American Journal of Psychiatry,* 150, 1543-1545.

McGaugh, J.L. and Alpern, H.P. (1966). Effects of electroshock on memory: Amnesia without convulsions. *Science, 152,* 665-666.

MECTA Corporation. (1987). *Health information network for hospitals and professionals* [video]. Lake Oswego, Oregon: MECTA Corporation.

Medcraft Corporation. (1984). *Medcraft B24III, Electroconvulsive Therapy Instrument* [flyer]. Darien, Connecticut: Medcraft Corporation.

Medcraft Corporation. (1986a). *Medcraft B25 Electroconvulsive Therapy Instrument* [flyer]. Darien, Connecticut: Medcraft Corporation.

Medcraft Corporation. (1986b). *Operation/Maintenance Manual B-25: Electroconvulsive Therapy Device.* Darien, CT: Medcraft Corporation.

Mellish, R.G. (1998). E-mail communication. Medical Devices Agency, Elephant and Castle, London, SE1 6TQ.

Mindham, R.H., Howland, C., and Shepherd, M. (1973). An evaluation of continuation therapy with tricyclic antidepressants in depressive illness. *Psychological Medicine,* 3, 5-17.

Nasrallah, H.A., Coffman, J.A., and Olson, S.C. (1989). Structural brain-imaging findings in affective disorders: an overview. *Journal of Neuropsychiatry Clinical Neuroscience,* 1, 21-26.

National Institutes of Mental Health and Center for Mental Health Services. (1994). Treatment methods: Biomedical therapies: Electroconvulsive treatment (ECT). *Decade of the Brain: A Consumer's Guide to Mental Health Services,* NIH Publication No. 94-3585, pp. 15-16.

Nobler, M.S., Sackeim, H.A., and Solomou, M. (1993). EEG manifestations during ECT: Effects of electrode placement and stimulus intensity. *Biological Psychiatry,* 34, 321-330.

Offner, F. (1946). Stimulation with minimum power. *Journal of Neurophysiology*, 9, 387-390.

Ottosson, J.O. (1960). Experimental studies on the mode of action of electroconvulsive therapy. *Acta Psychiatrica Scandanavia* (Supplement 145), 30, 1-141.

Pande, A.C., Grunhaus, L.J., Aisen, A.,M., and Haskett, R.F. (1990). A preliminary magnetic resonance imaging study of ECT-treated depressed patients. *Biological Psychiatry*, 27, 102-104.

Perrin et al. (2012). Electroconvulsive therapy reduces frontal cortical connectivity in severe depression disorder. *PNAS* , 109(14), 5464-8.

Perry, P., and Tsuang, M.T. (1979). Treatment of unipolar depression following electroconvulsive therapy. Relapse rate comparisons between lithium and tricyclic therapies following ECT. *Journal of Affective Disorders,* 1, 123-129.

Petrides, G., and Fink, M. (1996). The "half-age" stimulation strategy for ECT dosing. *Convulsive Therapy*, 12(3), 138-136.

Petrides, G., and Fink, M. (1997). Clinical common sense versus theoretical correctness. *Convulsive Therapy*, 13(1), 41-43.

Philpot, M., Collins, C., Trivedi, P., Treloar, A., Gallacher, S., and Rose, D. (2004). Eliciting users' views of ECT in two mental health trusts with a user-designed questionaire. *Journal of Mental Health,* 13(4), 403-413.

Plath. S. (1971). New York: Harper and Roe.

Press, G.A., Amaral, D.G., and Squire, L.R. (1989). Hippocampal abnormalities in amnesic patients revealed by high-resolution magnetic resonance imaging. Hippocampal abnormalities in amnesic patients revealed by high-resolution magnetic resonance imaging. *Nature*, 341, 54-57.

Proctor, L.D., and Goodwin, B.A. (1943). Comparative electroencephalo-graphic observations following electroshock therapy using raw 60 cycle alternating and unidirectional fluctuating current EEG. *American Journal of Psychiatry, 99,* 525-530.

Rabins, P.V., Pearlson, G.D., Aylward, E., Kumar, A.J., and Dowell, K. (1991). Cortical magnetic resonance imaging changes in elderly inpatients with major depression. *American Journal of Psychiatry*, 148, 617-620.

Read, John, and Bentall, Richard. (2010). The effectiveness of electroconvulsive therapy: A literature review. *Epidemiologia e Psichiatria,* 19(3), 333-347.

Reed, K. (1988). Electroconvulsive therapy: A clinical discussion. *Psychiatric Medicine, 6,* 29.

Rice, M. (1982). *Testimony of Marilyn Rice concerning the American Psychiatric Association's petition to reclassify ECT devices from class III to class II for presentation at hearings of neurological panel, FDA, on Nov 4-5, 1982.* In: Department of Health and Human Services, Silver Spring, Maryland: Food and Drug Administration. (pp. 82P-0316-TS003).

Robin, A., and De Tissera, S. (1982). A double blind controlled comparison of the therapeutic effects of low and high energy electroconvulsive therapies. *British Journal of Psychiatry*, 141, 357-366.

Rose, D. et al. (2003). Patient perspective on electroconvulsive therapy: Systematic review. *British Medical Journal,* 326, 1363-1365.

Royal College of Psychiatry. (1977). Memorandum on the use of ECT. *British Journal of Psychiatry*, 131, 261-272.

Royal College of Psychiatry. (1995). *The ECT handbook: Second report of the Royal College of Psychiatrists' Special Committee on ECT. Council report 39.* London: Royal College of Psychiatrists.

Sackeim, H.A. (1991). Are ECT devices underpowered? *Convulsive Therapy,* 7, pp. 233-6.

Sackeim, H.A. (1997) Comments on the "half-age" method of stimulus dosing. *Convulsive Therapy*, 13(1), 37-40.

Sackeim, H.A., Decina, P., Portnoy, P., Neeley, P., and Malitz, S. (1987a). Studies of dosage, seizure threshold, and seizure duration in ECT. *Biological Psychiatry*, 22, 249-268.

Sackeim, H.A., Decina, P., Prohovnik, I., and Malitz, S. (1987b). Seizure threshold in electroconvulsive therapy: Effects of sex, age, electrode placement, and number of treatments. *Archives of General Psychiatry*, 44, 355-360.

Sackeim, H.A., Debanand, D.P., and Prudic, J. (1991). Stimulus intensity,seizure threhold, and seizure duration: Impact on the efficacy and safety of electroconvulsive therapy. *Psychiatric Clinic North America,* 14, 803-843.

Sackeim, H.A., Luber, B., Katzman, G.P. (1996). The effects of electroconvulsive therapy on quantitative electroencephalograms. Relationship to clinical outcomes. *Archives of General Psychiatry,* 53(9), 814-824.

Sackeim, H.D., and Malitz, S. (1987c). Seizure threshold in electroconvulsive therapy: Effects of sex, age, electrode placement, and number of treatments. *Archives of General Psychiatry*, 44, 355-360.

Sackeim, H.A., Portnoy, S., Neeley, P., Steif, B.L., Decina, P., and Malitz, S. (1986). Cognitive consequences of low-dosage electroconvulsive therapy. *Annals New York Academy of Sciences,* 462, 326- 340.

Sackeim, H.A., Prohovnik, I., Moeller, J.R., Brown, R.P., Apter, S., Prudic, J., Devanand, D.P., and Mukherjee, S. (1990). Regional cerebral blood flow in mood disorders. *Archives of General Psychiatry,* 47, 60-70.

Sackeim, H.A., Prudic, J., Devanand, D.P., Kiersky, J., Fitzsimmons, L., Moody, B.J., McElhiney, M.C., Coleman, E.A., and Settembrino, B.A. (1993). Effects of stimulus intensity and electrode placement on the efficacy and cognitive effects of electroconvulsive therapy. *Journal of the American Medical Association,* 328(12), 839-846.

Sackeim, H.A., and Weiner, R.D. (1993). *MECTA Instruction Manual, SR and JR Models.* Lake Oswego, Oregon: MECTA Corporation.

Sament, S. (1983). In favor of wider ECT ban. *Clinical Psychiatry News,* 11.

Satcher, David (August 16,1999). Adults and Mental Health. *Surgeon General's Report - Draft, p 4-45.*

Scott, A.I.F., Douglas, R.H.B., Whitfield, A., and Kendell, R.E. (1990). Time course of cerebral magnetic resonance changes after electroconvulsive therapy. *British Journal of Psychiatry,* 156, 551-553.

Scott, A.I.F., Rodger, C.R., Stocks, R.H., and Shering, P.A. (1992). Is old-fashioned electroconvulsive therapy more efficacious?: A randomized comparative study of bilateral brief-pulse and bilateral sine-wave treatments. *British Journal of Psychiatry,* 160, 360-364.

Seager, C.P., and Bird, R.L., (1962). Imipramine with electrical treatment in depression - a controlled trial. *Journal of Mental Science,* 108, 704-707.

Sheline, Yvette I., Price, Joseph L., Yan, Zhizi, and Mintun, Mark A. (2010). Resting-state functional MRI in depression unmasks increased connectivity between networks via the dorsal nexus. *PNAS,* 107 (24) 11020-11025.

Shelton, R.C., and Weinberger, D.R. (1986). X-ray computerized tomography studies in schizophrenia; A review and synthesis. In: H.A. Nasrallah and D.R. Weinberger (Eds.), *The neurology of schizophrenia. Handbook of schizophrenia* (1, 207-250). Amsterdam, the Netherlands: Elsevier Science Publishers.

Small, J.G., and Small, I.F. (1981). Electroconvulsive therapy update. *Psychopharmocology Bulletin*, 17, 29-42.

Somatics Incorporated. (1993a). *"Just Set To Patient's Age and Treat."* [two page information flyer]. Lake Bluff, Illinois: Somatics Incorporated.

Somatics Incorporated. (1993b). *The Only ECT Instrument that Determines Seizure Length.* [eight page information flyer]. Lake Bluff, Illinois: Somatics Incorporated.

Somatics Incorporated. (1997a). *Setting The ECT Stimulus By Age* [flyer], Lake Bluff Illinois: Somatics Incorporated.

Somatics Incorporated. (1997b). *Somatics, Inc.: Makers of the Thymatron: Distributors.* http://www.thymatron.com/distribu.htm Internet: Lake Bluff Illinois: Somatics, Inc.

Somatics Incorporated. (1998). "Upgrade To The Only Integrated ECT System: Thymatron DGx by Somatics." [eight page information flyer]. Lake Bluff, Illinois: Somatics Incorporated.

Somatics Incorporated. (1999). "Advanced ECT: Just Became a Lot Easier to Give: Thymatron IV™ by Somatics." [eight page information flyer]. Lake Bluff, Illinois: Somatics Incorporated.

Squire, L. (1986). Memory functions as affected by electroconvulsive therapy. *Annals of the New York Academy of Sciences*, 462, 307-313.

Squire, L.R., and Chace, P.M., (1975). Memory functions six to nine months after electroconvulsive therapy. *Archives of General Psychiatry,* 32, 1557-1564.

Squire, L., and Slater, P.C. (1983). Electroconvulsive therapy and complaints of memory dysfunction: A prospective three-year follow-up study. *The British Journal of Psychiatry*, 142, 1-8.

Squire, L., Slater, P.C., and Miller, P.L. (1981). Retrograde amnesia and bilateral electroconvulsive therapy: Long-term follow-up. *Archives of General Psychiatry*, 38, 89-95.

Squire, L., and Zouzounis, J.A. (1986). ECT and memory: Brief pulse versus sine wave. *American Journal of Psychiatry,* 143(1), 596-601.

Sterling, Peter. (2000). ECT damage Is easy to find If you look for it. *Nature*, 403, 242.

Stone. G. (1994, November 14). When prozac fails . . . electroshock works. *New York* (Magazine), 55-59.

Sulzbach, W., Tillotson, K.J., Guillemin, V., and Sutherland, G.F. (1943). A consideration of some experiences with electric shock treatment in mental diseases, with special regard to various psychosomatic phenomena and to certain electrotechnical factors. *American Journal of Psychiatry,* 99, 519-524.

Susko, M. (1991). *Cry of the invisible.* Baltimore, Montreal: Conservatory Press.

Swartz, C.M., and Abrams, R. (1996). *ECT instruction manual.* Lake Bluff, Illinois: Somatics, Inc.

Swayze, V.W., Andreasen, N.C., Alliger, R.J., Ehrhardt, J.C., and Yuh, W.T.C. (1990). Structural brain abnormalities in bipolar affective disorder: Ventricular enlargement and local hyperintensities. *Archives of General Psychiatry*, 47, 1054-1059.

Szasz, T. (1974). *The myth of mental illness.* New York: Harper and Row.

Texas Department of Mental Health and Mental Retardation. (2001). *ECT Equipment Registration History.* Austin, Texas: Texas Department of Mental Health and Mental Retardation.

Tresise and Stenhouse, (1968). ECT phases with and without anaesthesia: a preliminary statistical study. *British Journal of Psychiatry*, 114, 1383-1386.

Ulett, G.A., Smith, K., and Gleser, G.C. (1956). Evaluation of convulsive and subconvulsive shock therapies utilizing a control group. *American Journal of psychiatry*, 112, 795-802.

Underwriters Laboratories, Incorporated. (1997). *UL Services For Medical Devices Manufacturers: Worldwide Conformity Assessment For the Medical Equipment Industry.* [eight page brochure]. New York, New York: Underwriters Laboratories, Incorporated.

United States v Karl Brandt (1946-1949). Nuremberg Code: Permissible medical experiments: Trials of war criminals before the Nuremberg military tribunals under control council law 10, Volume 2, 181-182. Washington: U.S. Printing Office.

Valentine, M., Keddie, K.M.G., and Dunne, D. (1968). A comparison of techniques in electroconvulsive therapy. *British Journal of Psychiatry,* 114, 989-996 .

von Meduna, L. (1938). General discussion of cardiazol therapy. *American Journal of Psychiatry,* 94, 46.

Weaver, L.A., Ives, J.O., Williams, R., and Nies, A. (1977). A comparison of standard alternating current and low-energy brief pulse electrotherapy. *Biological Psychiatry*, 12, 525-543.

Weaver, L.A., Ravaris, C.L., Rush, S., and Paananen, R. (1970; 1971). Final report: Sequential and other parameters of electroshock treatment. *Department of Psychiatry, Department of E.E. Instrument and Model Facility.* University of Vermont. (Unpublished).

Weinberger, D.R., Torrey, E.F., Neophytides, A.N., and Wyatt, R.J. (1979a). Lateral cerebral ventricular enlargement in chronic schizophrenia. *Archives of General Psychiatry*, 36, 735-739.

Weinberger, D.R., Torrey, E.F., Neophytides, A.N., and Wyatt, R.J. (1979b). Structural abnormalities in cerebral cortex of chronic schizophrenic patients. *Archives of General Psychiatry*, 36, 935-939.

Weiner, R.D. (1979). The psychiatric use of electrically induced seizures. *American Journal of Psychiatry*, 136, 1507-1517.

Weiner, R.D. (1980), ECT and seizure threshold: Effects of stimulus waveform and electrode placement. *Biological Psychiatry*, 15, 225-241.

Weiner, R.D. (1988). The first ECT devices. In M. Fink (Ed.), *Convulsive therapy* (pp. 50-61). New York: Raven Press, Ltd.

Weiner, R.D. (1997). Stimulus dosing with ECT: To titrate or not to titrate - that is the question. *Convulsive therapy,* 13(1), 7-9.

Weiner, R.D., Rogers, H.J., Davidson, J.R.T., and Kahn, E.M. (1986a). Effects of electroconvulsive therapy upon brain electrical activity. *Annals New York Academy of Sciences*, 462, 271-281.

Weiner, R.D., Rogers, H.J., Davidson, M.B., and Miller, R.D. (1982). Evaluation of the central nervous system risks of ECT. *Psychopharmacology Bulletin*, 18(1), 29-31.

Weiner, R.D., Rogers, H.J., Davidson, J.R.T., and Squire, L.R. (1986b). Effects of stimulus parameters on cognitive side effects, in electroconvulsive therapy. *Annals New York Academy of Sciences*, 462, 315-325.

Welch, C.A. Weiner, R.D., Weir, D., Cahill, J.F., Rogers, H.J., Davidson, M.B., Miller, R.D., and Mandel, M.R. (1982). Efficacy of ECT in the treatment of depression: Wave form and electrode placement considerations. *Psychopharmocology Bulletin*, 18(1), 31-34.

Wilcox, P.H. (1946). Brain facilitation, not brain destruction, the aim in electroshock therapy. *Diseases of the Nervous System*, 7, 201-204.

Wilson, I.C., Vernon, J.T., Guin, T., Sandifer, M.G. (1963). A controlled study of treatments of depression. *Journal of Neuropsychiatry,* 4, 331-337.

www.ingramcontent.com/pod-product-compliance
Lightning Source LLC
Chambersburg PA
CBHW051750200326
41597CB00025B/4503

* 9 7 9 8 9 8 8 1 2 8 0 1 4 *